SPECIAL EDITION

USING

Adobe®

Photoshop® 7

Peter Bauer

Jeff Foster

201 W. 103rd Street
Indianapolis, Indiana 46290

SPECIAL EDITION USING ADOBE PHOTOSHOP 7

International Standard Book Number: 0-7897-2760-9

Library of Congress Catalog Card Number: 2002105212

Printed in the United States of America

First Printing:

05   04   03   02   4   3   2   1

Trademarks

Warning and Disclaimer

Executive Editor
Candace Hall

Acquisitions Editors
Lloyd Black
Loretta Yates

Development Editors
Laura Norman
Sean Dixon

Managing Editor
Thomas Hayes

Project Editor
Carol Bowers

Production Editor
Lisa M. Lord

Indexer
Heather McNeill

Proofreader
Cindy Long

Technical Editors
Richard Romano
Kate Binder

Team Coordinator
Cindy Teeters

Interior Designer
Anne Jones

Cover Designer
Anne Jones

Page Layout
Cheryl Lynch

Contents at a Glance

CONTENTS

II Critical Concepts

6 Pixels, Vectors, and Resolution   155

7 Color Theory and Practice   173

ABOUT THE AUTHORS

Peter Bauer is the help desk director for the National Association of Photoshop Professionals (NAPP), the largest graphics association of its kind. He is an Adobe Certified Expert in both Adobe Photoshop and Adobe Illustrator. A computer graphics consultant, he writes a weekly column for the graphics portal PlanetPhotoshop.com and is a contributing editor for *Photoshop User* and *Mac Design* magazines. He is also a member of the instructor "Dream Team" for Photoshop World.

Pete is the author of *Special Edition Using Adobe Illustrator 10*, *Sams Teach Yourself Adobe Illustrator 10 in 24 Hours* (with Mordy Golding), *Special Edition Using Adobe Illustrator 9*, and a contributing author for *Photoshop 6 Web Magic*. He has also served as technical editor on a number of computer graphics books. Pete writes software documentation and does software testing for a variety of Photoshop- and Illustrator-related products.

Pete and his wife, Professor Mary Ellen O'Connell of the Ohio State University Moritz College of Law, live in the historic German Village area of Columbus, Ohio.

Jeff Foster is an artist/musician of 30 years, and is currently working out of his Fullerton, California studio. His production studio has been a beta site for such companies as Apple Computer, Adobe Systems, Inc., Ultimatte, Pixar, and MetaCreations, and has played an integral part in their product developments over the years.

Jeff has been in the forefront of illustrative art and computer graphic design, creating images and animations for clients such as Sanyo, McDonnell Douglas, FOX Television, Universal Studios, and Disney. He has also co-developed multimedia programs for the California Department of Labor and the Grand Central Art Center in Santa Ana, CA. He has taught, lectured, and developed computer graphics and multimedia programs at several Southern California colleges. Jeff appears regularly as a member of the instructor "Dream Team" at Photoshop World and has also been a featured speaker at Macworld.

Jeff's publications include *Animation Magazine* and *Publish* magazine, and *Photoshop Web Magic 2* and *Photoshop 6 Web Magic*. In addition, he was a contributing author for *Photoshop Filter Finesse* by Bill Niffenegger and *Special Edition Using Photoshop 3*.

DEDICATION

Special Edition Using Adobe Photoshop 7 is dedicated to our families and the families of our team at Que. Their patience and understanding during the late nights and long weeks is matched only by our love for them.

ACKNOWLEDGMENTS

First, Jeff wishes to thank his wife, Cheryl, and daughters Jillian, Brittany, and Chelsea, and Pete thanks his wife, Mary Ellen, for their patience and support during the production of this book.

At the top of our acknowledgement list must certainly be the entire team at Que. Laura Norman's dedication to this project was unmatched—rumor has it she was trying to finish editing a chapter on her way to the delivery room. Sean Dixon and Loretta Yates had to play catch-up after being assigned to a half-completed project, and never missed a step. Lisa Lord did an excellent job of making sure that the information within these covers is presented in the clearest, most understandable manner possible. (Lisa, was that redundancy okay?) Carol Bowers shepherded the project through the home stretch. Richard Romano wore two large hats for this project. In addition to serving as technical editor, he's a contributing author, lending his print expertise for several chapters and an appendix.

We'd also like to thank those individuals and companies that supplied the "goodies" you'll find on the CD: Stephanie Robey of PhotoSpin, Ed Sanchez at nik Multimedia, Al Ward of ActionFX, Ethan Dunham of FontHead.com, and AlienSkin. Thanks, too, to our colleagues at the National Association of Photoshop Professionals (especially Scott and Jeff Kelby and Dave Moser) and to the good folks at Adobe and all the enthusiastic professionals involved in testing Photoshop prior to its release. Their willingness to share their experience and expertise helped make this a richer, more complete product for you.

We'd certainly be remiss if we didn't acknowledge Jeff Schultz whose confidence and faith in us got this project rolling.

And a special thanks to Gracie Marie Norman, for waiting to be born long enough for Laura to get us going. Welcome!

TELL US WHAT YOU THINK!

As the reader of this book, *you* are our most important critic and commentator. We value your opinion and want to know what we're doing right, what we could do better, what areas you'd like to see us publish in, and any other words of wisdom you're willing to pass our way.

As an executive editor for Que, I welcome your comments. You can e-mail or write me directly to let me know what you did or didn't like about this book—as well as what we can do to make our books better.

Please note that I cannot help you with technical problems related to the topic of this book. We do have a User Services group, however, where I will forward specific technical questions related to the book.

When you write, please be sure to include this book's title and author as well as your name and phone or fax number. I will carefully review your comments and share them with the author and editors who worked on the book.

E-mail: feedback@quepublishing.com

Mail: Candace Hall
Executive Editor
Que
201 West 103rd Street
Indianapolis, IN 46290 USA

For more information about this book or another Que title, visit our Web site at www.quepublishing.com. Type the ISBN (excluding hyphens) or the title of a book in the Search field to find the page you're looking for.

INTRODUCTION

WHO SHOULD READ THIS BOOK?

In keeping with the goals of this series, *Special Edition Using Adobe Photoshop 7* is an intermediate-to-expert reference book. However, even advanced beginners with a working knowledge of the program will find this to be an extraordinarily useful volume. Everything is presented clearly and concisely, with an eye toward readability. We want it to be as easy as possible for you, the reader, to understand what is being explained.

As with other *Special Edition Using* titles, this book is factual, nononsense, and practical. It's designed for the individual or group who works with Photoshop, professionally or as a serious hobbyist. It's for those who have deadlines to meet, goals to achieve, images to perfect, visions to capture. It is for you, the Photoshop user.

Special Edition Using Adobe Photoshop 7 is aimed at the high-level user as well as those striving for that status. Most readers will be experienced Photoshop users, either transitioning to Photoshop 7 or expanding their knowledge of the program. They come to this book for answers. No single volume can cover every aspect of this incredibly complex program and all the applicable techniques, but this book goes beyond the basics and explains what you need to know to make things happen the way you want them to happen.

Even after years of working with Adobe Photoshop in various versions, there's always more to learn. New releases bring new features. New assignments demand different techniques. Changing technology (and jobs) require new skills. There may be some capabilities of Photoshop that are perfect for one person's workflow, yet remain unknown because of the program's complexity. Often there are several ways to produce the same result, and the best way is often situational. This book helps explain the differences among similar techniques and procedures.

Reaching new levels of efficiency and capability within the bounds of your normal work is possible. Gaining a better understanding of Photoshop's capabilities, and the theories behind them, is a good place to start. Even if you work with the same tools, in the same way, day after day, there's likely something more to learn. That something is likely between these book covers.

Similarly, few individuals know Photoshop from top to bottom, from left to right, from front to back. Most are well versed in the aspects of the program with which they work regularly. Some create Web graphics, some work in prepress, some are artists, some specialize in photo retouching—there are many examples. When a Web specialist is asked to prepare the company's brochure ("Well, you're the Photoshop guy, aren't you?"), or the digital video expert is tasked with creating Web site navigation bars ("They're *just* graphics!"), answers are needed. Photoshop professionals who need to work outside their particular fields don't want a beginner book. They know what the Move tool does. They're familiar with cropping. Instead, they require a reference that fills in the gaps, that answers the questions. In that spirit, we perhaps could have written a series of books titled *Photoshop for the Web Guy Forced to Do Prepress* and *Photoshop for Digital Photographers Trying to Create Their Own Web Sites*, and so on. Rather, we've put together a single book that covers all those bases. How? By being thorough. Just as a Web specialist may learn something new about ImageReady or Save for Web, so too will that digital photographer learn what he or she needs to know to get that Web site started.

Readers who use Photoshop on a daily basis can reach for this book to check specific details, to understand the application of a new technique, or simply to see if there's a better way to accomplish a certain task. If you work with Photoshop less frequently, you'll find this book of even more value. You can discover what a particular feature does, how a particular command works, what options there are for a particular tool.

If you're brand new to Photoshop, in all honesty, this should not be your first book. Get a copy of *Sams Teach Yourself Adobe Photoshop 7 in 24 Hours* by Carla Rose. When you've learned the basics, make this your *second* book. After you've got a handle on how Photoshop works and what it does, you'll be better prepared for this more advanced look at the program.

WHY YOU SHOULD USE ADOBE PHOTOSHOP 7

If you work with digital images, there's no program more powerful than Photoshop. It is the industry standard for a reason—it allows you to do what needs to be done.

Prepress Power

Many of the things you can do with Photoshop 7 can be done with Photoshop Elements or the older Photoshop LE. Prepress is not on that list—the "light" versions of Photoshop don't support the CMYK color mode. (Photoshop 7 adds native support for Pantone metallic colors, too.)

Photoshop offers sophisticated (yet ever easier to use) color management, along with strong soft-proofing tools. View out-of-gamut colors onscreen, view proofs of individual plates as well as composites, and convert images to or apply specific color profiles, each in just a click or two.

Photoshop 7's Print with Preview dialog box (see Figure 1) offers the opportunity to add registration and crop marks, as well as captions and labels, to your printed work. You can also print for specific separations, choosing emulsion up or down, and positive or negative.

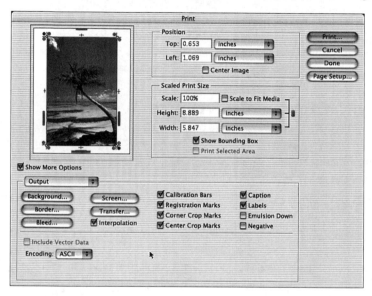

Figure 1
Print with Preview allows you to scale and position the image on the page—for any image, whether it's CMYK for process printing or RGB for inkjets.

Web Graphics and More

ImageReady. Need we say more? No other raster image editing program offers the incredible power of ImageReady. A dedicated, standalone Web graphics creation tool, ImageReady is packaged with and tied to Photoshop 7. ImageReady 7's new features include dithering for variable transparency (make an image fade into any background, even patterns and text), prioritized optimization for type and vector graphics, and even output for WBMP, the image format used by many PDAs and wireless devices. The new Rollovers palette enables increasingly sophisticated Web graphics (see Figure 2). As if that's not enough, let's remember Photoshop's own Save for Web optimization capability.

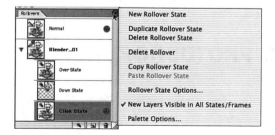

Figure 2
The new Rollovers palette shows that the Click state has an animation associated with it.

Digital Restoration and Retouching

Photoshop has long been the number-one name in image manipulation, and the new Healing Brush and Patch tool make doing your best even easier. Unlike the Clone Stamp, the Healing Brush can retain the color and shading while removing dust, scratches, blemishes, and wrinkles. The Patch tool enables you to use selections—even masks—to identify an area for healing. The source pixels retain the color, lighting, and shading of the pixels being repaired, and the texture is corrected.

Whether you're a professional photographer, a pro-sumer, or a digital hobbyist, Photoshop offers the most complete collection of image correction tools and commands available. Color correction can be achieved by working with the individual color channels themselves. Curves and Levels commands can also be applied to specific channels. Photoshop 7 adds a new Auto Color command, too.

Incredible Integration with Other Adobe Products

The Adobe family of products gives you a level of integration that's sure to ease any multiprogram workflow. Adobe GoLive creates Web pages with Photoshop-native graphics. Add the .psd file to the Web page as a SmartObject, and let GoLive handle the optimization. Need to update the image? GoLive will automatically open the image in Photoshop for you.

InDesign lets you say "page layout" and "variable transparency" in the same sentence without having to include the word "can't." In addition to adding .psd files directly to InDesign documents, you can use Photoshop alpha channels (masks) and paths to designate transparency and even to wrap text. InDesign also automatically reads embedded color profiles.

Illustrator and Photoshop can exchange files while retaining the editability of type. Illustrator recognizes Photoshop layers and maintains Photoshop blending modes and transparency.

Adobe After Effects, Premiere, LiveMotion, and AlterCast are just a few of the other members of the clan that work and play well with Photoshop. You'll find appendixes at the end of the book that discuss interoperability between Photoshop and a variety of Adobe and non-Adobe products.

Save in a Wide Variety of File Formats

Using Photoshop's Save As and Save for Web commands, you can create files in no fewer than two dozen file formats (when using the optional plug-ins supplied on the Photoshop CD). For print, you can choose among TIFF, EPS, PDF, and (if using InDesign) PSD. Web graphics can be created in GIF, JPEG, and PNG formats as well as the PDS/Wireless WBMP format. Paths can be exported to Illustrator, too, for use as clipping paths or to prepare trapping.

WHY UPGRADE TO PHOTOSHOP 7?

If you're reading this Introduction and have not yet upgraded to Photoshop 7, we think you should both upgrade and buy this book. (The book discusses the major differences between Photoshop 6 and Photoshop 7 as well as explaining where and how your interaction with Mac OS X or Windows XP will differ from earlier operating systems.)

When looking at the new features in this release of Photoshop, some may ask "Is that all there is?"

The answer is "There's more there than you think!" The new capabilities are strong, and they'll get a lot more use than it might seem. In addition, Photoshop 7 offers a compelling reason to upgrade: operating system compatibility. Whether you're on a Windows computer or a Macintosh, Photoshop 7 allows you to work in the most modern operating systems available.

Mac OS X and Windows XP

Windows XP is a major step forward for Microsoft, with its 32-bit kernel and improved stability and performance. Mac OS X, similarly, is a gigantic leap into the future. Although this book is not about operating systems and interfaces, you'll find everything you need to know to transition to Photoshop 7, no matter which OS you run. If your current operating system doesn't have "X" in the name, it soon will—Windows XP and Mac OS X are the future.

On the Mac side, one could honestly say that the most important new features in Photoshop are protected memory and pre-emptive multitasking. By rewriting the core code to take advantage of the best features of Mac OS X, Adobe provides a stable environment within which to run Photoshop. Photoshop 7 can also run in the Mac Classic (OS 9.2) mode as well as on Macs using OS 9 exclusively.

Windows users can run Photoshop 7 on computers running Windows 98, if desired. However, Windows XP offers tremendous advantages, including the stability and performance improvements mentioned. In most cases, if the hardware supports it, migrating to XP is recommended.

New Capabilities, Improved Capabilities

Perhaps the most visible of Photoshop's new capabilities are the File Browser, Tool Presets palette (both shown in Figure 3), Pattern Maker, Healing Brush, and Patch tool. However, look more closely, and you'll find that Photoshop has also added spell check and text find/replace, native support for Pantone metallic inks, document security, WBMP file format creation, and a wide variety of other new tricks.

Figure 3
The File Browser allows you to navigate and even update the contents of your disks and drives, and the Tool Presets palette gives you one-click access to various tool configurations and setting combinations.

In many cases, Photoshop users may be just as excited (or more excited) about improvements to existing features:

- The Brushes palette makes a stunning return as the interface for a whole new paint engine.

- Layers can be renamed directly in the Layers palette.

- The New dialog box offers a list of document size presets.

- Open image windows can be presented onscreen in tile arrangement as well as cascade.

- Many filters have larger preview windows.

- The Curves dialog box is resizable.

- The History palette can now be set to record up to 1,000 history states—10 times as many as Photoshop 6.

- ImageReady offers improved transparency support.

- In addition to saving the current palette locations, *workspaces* can be established, preserving palette arrangements and tool settings, too.

WINDOWS AND MACINTOSH

No matter which platform you use, Photoshop offers the same powerful features. The interface is as close to identical as possible, with virtually the same tools, palettes, and commands. Many of the images in this book show Macintosh interface elements, such as palettes, menus, and windows. In those few specific instances in which a difference exists between Macintosh and Windows, the differences have been shown or noted. Keyboard shortcuts are shown for both platforms throughout, with Macintosh appearing first in parentheses, followed by the Windows equivalent in brackets.

The abbreviations used in this book are as follows:

- **(Command) [Ctrl]**—This identifies the Command key for Macintosh and Control key for Windows. The Command and Control keys are modifier keys; they do nothing on their own. They are always used in combination with another key or a mouse click. The key must remain pressed while you press the other key or click the mouse button.

- **(Option) [Alt]**—This identifies the Option key for Macintosh and Alt key for Windows. The Option and Alt keys are modifier keys, and they too must always be used in combination with another key or a mouse click. The key must remain pressed while you press the other key or click the mouse button.

- **(Control-click) [Right+click]**—Macintosh users must press the Control key and click the mouse button; Windows users click the mouse's right button once.

HOW THIS BOOK IS ORGANIZED

Special Edition Using Adobe Photoshop 7 has eight parts, encompassing 31 chapters, plus a ninth part, consisting of three appendixes. Each of the eight parts is structured around a central theme, with the individual chapters developing the part's concept. (Each appendix addresses Photoshop's interoperability with one or more other programs.) Readers new to Photoshop should read the earlier parts before exploring the later chapters. Readers who have some familiarity with Photoshop 7 should also take a look at the first three parts. Although few high-level practitioners have the time to thoroughly explore a new version of a favorite program, often incredibly useful tools and techniques can be added to the reader's workflow.

Part I: Fundamental Photoshop 7

Five chapters develop a basic understanding of Photoshop 7, its interface, what you need to run it, and how to get pixels into and out of the program. Chapter 1, "What's New in Photoshop 7," is directed at those transitioning from Photoshop 6. If you've been working with this latest version for some time, you might still want to take a look—some of the improvements are not likely to catch your eye immediately. Chapter 2, "The Photoshop Interface," helps you develop a better understanding of how you, the user, manipulate the program. Among other things, you'll find a couple of tables of shortcuts that can speed your daily work.

The third chapter, "Hardware, System Setup, and Photoshop's Preferences," answers many common questions. What do I need to run Photoshop 7? What do I need to run Photoshop 7 *efficiently*? How do I set the Preferences? How do I recover from a corrupt Prefs file? (This last answer may be for some the most important information in this entire book—how to get Photoshop back up and running properly without going through the time and trouble of a full reinstall.)

Chapter 4, "Getting Pixels into Photoshop," looks at scanning, digital cameras, stock art, and other sources of images. Some Photoshop files start life as blank canvas, but most are based on previously existing imagery. This chapter helps you understand the basic concepts, leading to improved workflow and fewer problems later in the creative/productive process.

Part I ends with Chapter 5, "Photoshop's File Formats and Output Options." Very few (if any) images are created to simply view in Photoshop. Most need to be saved in a way or a file format that's appropriate for incorporation into a page layout program or a Web page, or for printing from an inkjet printer or a film recorder. (There are other options, too, and they are also reviewed in the chapter.) In each case, one or more specific files formats is required. Chapter 5 helps you choose the format (and its options) that is most appropriate for your needs.

Part II: Critical Concepts

When you consider the root level, Photoshop is all about color. Images are created primarily with pixels. Each pixel is a single color. Creating an image in Photoshop means assigning a *specific* color to each pixel. The four chapters in Part II help you understand pixels, color theory, creating color in Photoshop, and color management in Photoshop 7. Chapter 6, "Pixels, Vectors, and Resolution," looks at pixels, what they are, and how they differ from vector artwork. It also discusses the concept of resolution and what it means.

Chapter 7, "Color Theory and Practice," examines closely the various color modes in Photoshop, how they differ, and when to use which. You'll get a look at working with specific colors in Chapter 8, "Defining and Choosing Colors." Chapter 9, "Photoshop Color Management," shows you how to ensure that the specific color you want is the specific color you get, whether printing to an inkjet, outputting to the Web, or preparing for process printing.

Part III: Photoshop's Creative Tools

Just as the core theory of Photoshop is pixel color, so too are certain concepts key to the creative process in this program. Part III looks at selections and masks in Chapter 10, "Making Selections and Creating Masks." Chapter 11, "Type and Typography in Photoshop," develops the ideas central to adding text to an image. (This chapter is supplemented on the accompanying CD by additional material, which serves as a glossary of typographic terminology.)

Photoshop 7's new paint engine (and how you work with it) is the subject of Chapter 12, "Photoshop 7's Painting Tools and Brushes." In addition to the theory and practice of painting tools, it examines the new Brushes palette and how custom brushes are created and saved.

In Chapter 13, "The Pen Tools, Shape Layers, and Other Paths," Photoshop's vector capability is examined. (This chapter looks at the non-type vectors in Photoshop.)

Part IV: Photoshop's Advanced Creative Capabilities

Many of Photoshop's most powerful—and most complex—capabilities are examined in Part IV. Chapter 14, "Working with Layers and Layer Styles," shows you how to exploit both multiple layers and layer effects. You'll also learn how to combine (and save) layer effects as layer styles. Working directly with an image's color information is discussed in Chapter 15, "Channels: Color and More." Editing channels, adding spot color and alpha channels, and mixing channels will be explained.

Building on the color and color management chapters earlier in the book, Chapter 16, "Color Correction and the Adjustment Commands," is a practical look at how to use Photoshop's capabilities to get the correct colors and tonal range in your images.

See Chapter 17, "Using Blending Modes," for information on how blending modes determine how colors interact.

Chapter 18, "Applying Photoshop's Filters," and Chapter 19, "Extract, Liquify, and the Pattern Maker," explore ways in which you can enhance, alter, and distort images. For many Photoshop artists, the filters are the backbone of the program.

Part V: Image Composition, Retouching, and Compositing

Three of the most common procedures in image manipulation are explored in depth in Chapter 20, "Image Cropping, Resizing, and Sharpening." Most images passing through Photoshop undergo at least one of these three operations. Learning the theory behind the techniques helps ensure that they will be applied in the most effective, appropriate way.

Chapter 21, "Retouching and Restoration Basics," discusses the most important techniques for improving (and salvaging) photographic images. Essential topics in the chapter include Photoshop 7's new Healing Brush and Patch tool.

Going beyond image repair, Chapter 22, "Advanced Compositing and Collaging in Photoshop," looks at the core concepts of combining elements of multiple images.

Part VI: Photoshop, ImageReady, and the Web

In recent years, creating Web graphics has become one of the major uses of Photoshop. Photoshop users who just a few years ago had never accessed the Internet now produce graphics for it on a daily basis. Other Photoshop professionals are assuming these responsibilities as additional duties—creating Web graphics in addition to their jobs as prepress or photographic experts. Many are producing graphics for their own Web sites.

Chapter 23, "Photoshop, ImageReady, and Web Design," explores the core concepts of Web graphics. It looks at the capabilities available in Photoshop and ImageReady. (Even experienced Web professionals should take a look at Chapter 23 to see what's new in Photoshop and ImageReady.)

Producing the most effective Web graphics means balancing file appearance and file size. In Chapter 24, "Save for Web and Image Optimization," this art/science is dissected and examined. The chapter includes a look at the new capabilities of Save for Web (including creation of WBMP graphics for PDAs and wireless devices).

Working in ImageReady—and maximizing efficiency in the program—is the subject of Chapter 25, "ImageReady Basics." Among the new capabilities discussed are dithering to create transparency and optimizing with priority for text and vector graphics.

Part VII: Print and Prepress

Even if you do prepress daily, you'll want to take a glance at Chapter 26, "The Printing Process: A Primer." Photoshop now natively supports Pantone metallic inks. This chapter also discusses flexographic printing and explores Photoshop's Print with Preview dialog box.

Chapter 27, "Grayscale, Line Art, and Vectors," looks at three of the challenges facing print professionals who work with Photoshop. Getting the greatest tonal range in an image that uses only one ink, maintaining the integrity of artwork that uses only black and white, and ensuring that Bézier curves print at full resolution are the topics discussed.

Commercial printing presses can't function properly unless the printing plates are correctly prepared. Among the keys are working with halftone settings and producing color separations. Chapter 28, "Halftones, Screen Frequency, and Separations," explains the key concepts and how Photoshop implements them.

Part VIII: Power Photoshop

The final set of chapters gives you the ticket to faster, more productive Photoshop work. Chapter 29, "Actions and Automation," looks at Photoshop's Actions and the Automate commands. Chapter 30, "JavaScript, AppleScript, and Scripting with Visual Basic," explains how the operating system can be used to control some Photoshop operations. Chapter 31, "Efficiency Tips and Tricks," offers ways to improve your efficiency and quick tips to give you an edge.

Separate appendixes look at Photoshop's interaction with Illustrator 10, the major page layout programs (InDesign, Quark, and PageMaker), and the Web graphics programs LiveMotion and Flash. In addition to basic interoperability, you'll learn tips and tricks to make your work go more smoothly.

CD: Added Value

On the CD that accompanies this book, you'll find a variety of goodies. In addition to color versions of many of this book's images and illustrations, you'll find extra sections that we're supplying only electronically. (To put everything on paper would not only have made this book thicker and heavier, but also have increased the price—something of which we are all very conscious.) We've invited some friends and contacts to include other goodies for you. In addition to demo versions of some great commercial software, we solicited some additional useful, practical, and valuable contributions: actions, fonts, stock photography, and more. See the ReadMe file on the disk for instructions on how to load these extras on your computer.

On the Web

Space considerations did not allow us to fit all the chapters in the printed book. Because of this, additional chapters will be made available online. Go to http://www.quepublishing.com/, and type the book's ISBN (0789727609) into the search field to go to this book's Web page and download the additional material.

FUNDAMENTAL PHOTOSHOP 7

IN THIS PART

WHAT'S NEW IN PHOTOSHOP 7

IN THIS CHAPTER

WHAT'S DIFFERENT—OVERVIEW

The number and importance of the changes to Photoshop 7 certainly rank it as one of the top upgrades in the history of the program. Perhaps most important are the changes to the program's code that allow it to be fully compatible with Mac OS X and Windows XP. On the Macintosh side, a *Carbonized* (OS X native) Photoshop is perhaps as important as Microsoft Office for OS X. For PC users, XP compatibility means Photoshop is ready for the future, and for today.

Although the differences between Photoshop 6 and Photoshop 7 are perhaps not as dramatic as the inclusion of ImageReady in Photoshop 5.5, nor as constantly visible as the Options Bar in Photoshop 6, they certainly enable you to change the way you work—for the better. There are dozens of little changes as well as several rather sizable ones:

- **File Browser**—Provides more than just a look at what images are in what folders; you can actually move, delete, even rename files, all from within Photoshop.

- **Tool Presets**—Enables you to save sets of tool options. Want the Type tool to produce 14-point Adobe Garamond Pro, center aligned, 110% width, tracking at −10? No problem—it's just a click away. Need to switch to Arial 10-point, Sharp antialiasing, left aligned? One click to make the change. Preset the Crop tool to 4×6 inches at 300ppi, and set it to 8×10 inches at 240ppi. Then switch to either preset with a single click.

- **Saved Workspaces**—Just as habit-forming as tool presets. If you need certain palettes in certain locations for certain jobs, this feature is for you. Set up for Web production, and save the workspace. Set up for prepress, and save the workspace. Set up for photo restoration, and save the workspace. With one click, your palettes jump to the correct configuration—any configuration. Instead of saving just the last palette locations, Photoshop can save any arrangement.

- **Healing Brush** and **Patch tool**—Make short work of restoration and retouching work. Unlike the Clone Stamp tool, these tools preserve the target area's shadows, lighting, and texture. The Patch tool enables you to heal with selections, even masks.

- **Brushes palette**—Evidence of a new and improved paint engine. (And, yes, you can leave this Brushes palette open while you work.) Perhaps the most significant change is that any brush, even custom brushes, can be scaled.

- **Spell Checker** and **Find/Replace**—Long awaited and finally here for Photoshop's type engine. The spell checker can assign (and check) language on a word-by-word basis. You also have the option of using smart quotes now.

- **ImageReady**—Sees several improvements, including a new Rollovers palette, dithered transparency, and optimization priority for text and vectors.

- **Project Collaboration**—If you work in a collaborative environment, you'll see some new things, too. For example, PDF files generated in Photoshop can have the security such as that applied in Acrobat. And the File, Manage Workflow submenu becomes Workgroup, with more sophisticated commands and capabilities.

Improvements were also made to the Layers palette, Liquify, Extract, Canvas Size, Picture Package, Web Photo Gallery, the custom shape collections, and even the Open dialog box. Photoshop has added several new blending modes, too.

Whether new work or old, there are certain to be changes to the way work is done. Photoshop added several features that are likely to be quickly integrated into your working habits. The following sections describe in more detail these and many other of Photoshop 7's most important improvements. Dozens of other changes and updates are explained throughout this book.

THE FILE BROWSER: SAY GOODBYE TO THE OPEN COMMAND?

Now, in Photoshop, you can *really* preview images before opening. Indeed, the Open command gives you the option of showing a preview if one is available in the file, and only one at a time. With the File Browser (see Figure 1.1), you can do far more than simply see a thumbnail view.

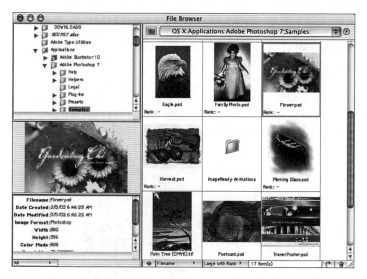

Figure 1.1
The File Browser is a palette when docked to the Palette Well and can also be a window, opened through the File or the Window menus.

The File Browser is far more than a glorified preview window, however. It can be used as a rather robust document management tool, too. Digital photographers will find Batch Rename especially useful (see Figure 1.2). For many, the File Browser may quickly become the most indispensable of all the improvements in Photoshop 7.

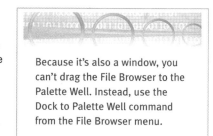

Because it's also a window, you can't drag the File Browser to the Palette Well. Instead, use the Dock to Palette Well command from the File Browser menu.

Figure 1.2
Batch Rename, opened through the File Browser menu, allows you to assign up to five components to filenames, in addition to the required file extension.

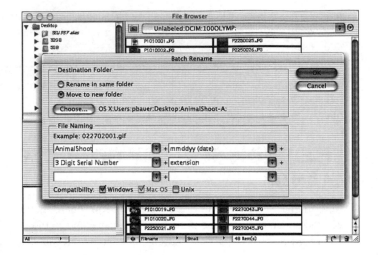

Looking at the Layout

The File Browser acts like a palette when docked to the Palette Well in Photoshop's Options Bar. When dragged from the well, it functions like a window. As such, it can be covered by floating palettes, minimized and maximized, and even hidden by open documents.

In the Expanded view, the File Browser offers four panes (see Figure 1.3). To the right in the preview pane are thumbnails of images in the currently selected folder as well as icons representing any subfolders. To the left, stacked in a column, are a navigation pane (called the *tree*), an additional preview pane, and a file data pane.

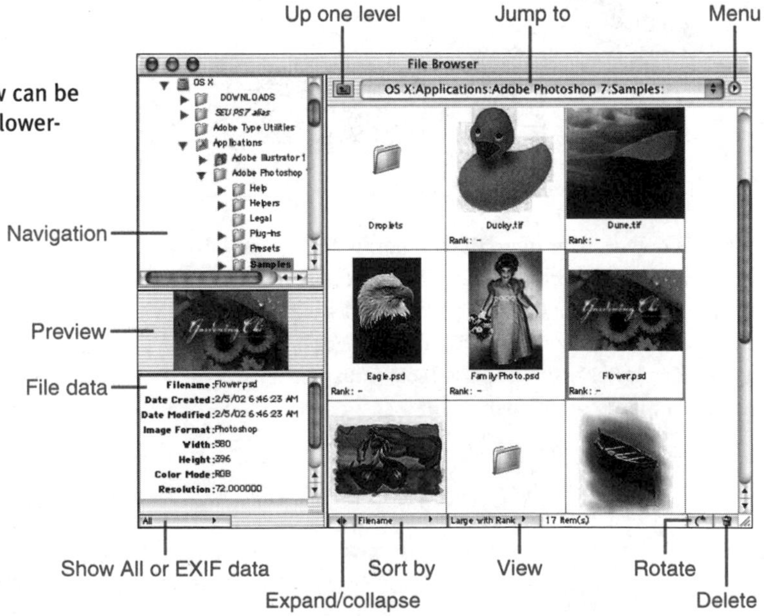

Up one level   Jump to   Menu

Figure 1.3
The File Browser window can be resized by dragging the lower-right corner.

Navigation

Preview

File data

Show All or EXIF data   Sort by   View   Rotate

Expand/collapse   Delete

Getting Around in File Browser

In the upper-left navigation pane you'll find the *tree*, a hierarchical display of the current folder's location. Much like the Folders view in Windows Explorer (or My Computer for Windows XP), you can click on a folder to jump to that location. You can also expand and collapse the folders by clicking on the triangles (Mac) or the plus/minus symbol (Windows). Jump to any folder by clicking on it. To move a file, drag its image from the preview pane on the right to a folder in the navigation pane.

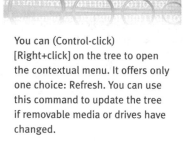

You can (Control-click) [Right+click] on the tree to open the contextual menu. It offers only one choice: Refresh. You can use this command to update the tree if removable media or drives have changed.

Click on any image in the preview pane on the right to select it. It appears in the center-left preview pane as a preview, and the file's information appears in the file data pane at the lower left. The dividing bars between the panes can be dragged to resize them (see Figure 1.4). The preview to the left of the selected image is resized to fill the available space.

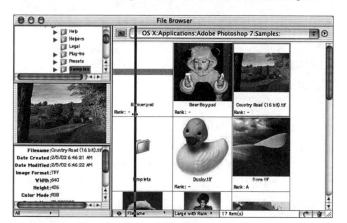

Figure 1.4
The horizontal bars can also be dragged to reapportion the left column.

The display in the preview pane on the right can be customized in a variety of ways. You can show the large thumbnail and the filename with the assigned rank (as shown in the preceding figures) or without the rank. (*Rank* is an assigned value, used to categorize or group images. Assigning rank is explained later in this chapter.) The pane can also be set to small or medium thumbnails with filenames (enabling you to view more images at the same time). A comparison of the Small and Medium Thumbnail views is shown in Figure 1.5.

Another File Browser view option, called Details, shows you a thumbnail somewhere in size between the large and medium, and also shows the file information. This view is especially useful when the File Browser in not in Expanded mode (see Figure 1.6).

At the top-center of the File Browser, you'll see an icon of a folder with an arrow, a symbol familiar to most Windows users. Click the button to move up one level in the hierarchy. The contents of the large preview pane are then updated to display the contents of the parent folder.

Immediately to the right of that button is a pop-up menu displaying the current folder (directory). Click on the menu, and you'll have access to the entire folder hierarchy and all available drives.

Figure 1.5
Although the Medium Thumbnail view shows more of the image, it displays less of the filename.

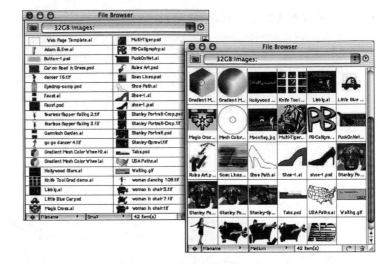

Figure 1.6
The information shown can include file size, dimensions, embedded color profile, and copyright info as well as the filename and the creation and modification dates.

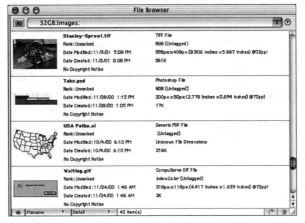

The File Browser's menu is used to change the browser's appearance. It is discussed later in this chapter, in the section "The File Browser Menu." (You can also make the change by using a pop-up menu at the bottom of the File Browser.)

Across the bottom of the File Browser window or palette, you'll find several more menus and buttons. To the left (in Expanded view only) is a choice of Show All or EXIF (Exchangeable Image Format) for the file data pane. Many digital cameras record EXIF data with the image (see Figure 1.7). The exact information recorded can vary from camera to camera.

⇨ *Uncertain about the EXIF data? See "Enter the EXIF" in the NAPP Help Desk section at the end of this chapter.*

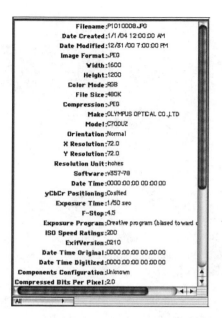

Figure 1.7
Among the most valuable EXIF data for use in Photoshop are image dimensions, resolution, and color space. Photographers might also be interested in such information as exposure, f-stop, ISO, flash, aperture, and focal length.

A handy button allows you to switch between the File Browser's Expanded and Collapsed views. When expanded, the button appears to the right of the vertical divider. When collapsed, it's in the lower-left corner. Another great feature of the File Browser is the capability of sorting images according to a variety of criteria (see Figure 1.8). Selecting a criterion from the Sort By pop-up menu starts the process.

Figure 1.8
Note the lowest entry in the menu: Ascending Order. When unchecked, the images are reversed in the File Browser.

You can change the view by using the pop-up menu (as well as the File Browser menu). The options are Small, Medium, Large (with or without ranking), and Details (as described earlier in this section).

Sorting by rank allows you to customize the sorting criteria. Photoshop has a built-in ranking system, from A through E, but that's just the start. When the Rank field is visible in the window (Large with Rank view only), you can click on it and type any value (see Figure 1.9).

Figure 1.9
When the File Browser is set to sort by rank, the images are sorted numerically, then alphabetically.

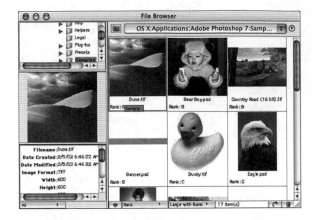

At the far right of the File Browser's bottom edge is the familiar Trash icon for deleting a selection (which actually deletes the selection—it doesn't just remove it from the File Browser). Just to the left of the Trash is a rotate button. You can rotate the selected image clockwise 90°. (To rotate counterclockwise, click three times.) File Browser rotates only the thumbnail, unless the image is opened in Photoshop (see Figure 1.10).

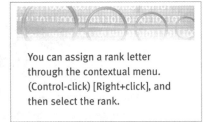

You can assign a rank letter through the contextual menu. (Control-click) [Right+click], and then select the rank.

Figure 1.10
Click OK to complete the rotation. Should you change your mind, the Esc key cancels the rotation.

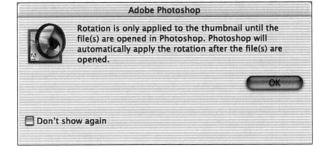

The File Browser Menu

The File Browser's menu (see Figure 1.11) can be opened by clicking the triangle in the upper-right corner of the palette or window.

The menu offers several commands that can also be accessed in the File Browser window or palette itself, and some that cannot.

When the File Browser is displayed as a window, you cannot drag it into the Palette Well; you can move it to the well only with the Dock to Palette Well command. (This command is grayed out when the monitor is set to 800×600 pixel resolution because the Palette Well is not available). When displayed as a palette from the well, the command appears as Show in Separate Window (see Figure 1.12).

Figure 1.11
Much of the menu is redundant, but some capabilities of the File Browser can be accessed only through the menu.

Figure 1.12
When the File Browser is displayed as a palette from the Palette Well, you can access the menu through the triangle in the palette's tab.

The Open command opens the selected file(s) in Photoshop. You can also double-click an image in the File Browser to open it. You can use the Rename command from the menu, or you can simply click on the filename in the File Browser. In either case, the file's name is highlighted, ready for you to retype it. In both cases, the file extension is *not* highlighted to avoid accidental deletion. Keep in mind that you cannot rename files on disks to which you cannot write. CDs and DVDs, for example, can't be rewritten from within File Browser, so you can't rename files on them. This also pertains to any drive or directory for which you haven't been granted write access.

The Batch Rename command is especially useful for digital photographers and those who batch scan images. It offers the capability of identifying folders of images with a few clicks.

Working with Batch Rename

If you're familiar with the Photoshop Batch command under the File, Automate menu, this dialog box should look familiar.

Batch Rename is available only if two or more images are selected in File Browser.

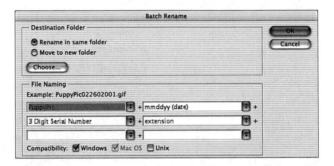

You have the option of saving the newly renamed images to the same folder or choosing a different folder as a destination. The new names can be constructed of up to six different elements. Each of the six text boxes has a pop-up menu offering the following choices: The existing document name in capital and small letters, all lowercase, or all uppercase; a one-, two-, three-, or four-digit serial number assigned sequentially (001, 002, 003, and so on); a serial letter (a, b, c, and so forth) in lowercase or uppercase; the date in any of seven formats; the required file extension as lowercase or uppercase; and the option of None, which simply bypasses that text box. As you can see in the preceding figure, you can also type anything you want into one or more of the text boxes. Photoshop does not allow you to rename files without the file extension. If you try to do so using Batch Rename, an error message appears.

The Delete command can be used from the File Browser menu to delete an image but not a folder. You can also drag the image to the Trash icon in the browser, click the Trash icon, or use the Delete (Backspace) key.

The Clear Ranking command is available when one or more selected files have had ranks assigned. This command simply empties the Rank field for the file(s).

New Folder adds an empty folder to the particular directory you're working in, assuming that you can write to that drive/directory. You can then move images into that new folder. Remember that you can't add folders in directories to which you cannot write, such as CDs and DVDs. If the Show Folders option isn't checked in the File Browser menu, folders don't appear in the preview pane on the right. They still appear in the tree in the upper-left navigation pane.

To select several contiguous images in the File Browser, click on the first and then Shift-click the last. To select multiple files that are *not* contiguous, (Command-click) [Ctrl+click] each. To deselect, click an empty area in the preview pane.

The rotation commands can be applied to one or more selected images. As noted earlier when discussing the Rotate button, the transformation applies only to the thumbnail until the image is opened in Photoshop.

The five view options determine what you'll see in the preview pane on the right in the File Browser. Using the File Browser's menu is the same as making a selection from the pop-up menu at the bottom of the window/palette.

If drives have been turned on or disks have been inserted since the File Browser was opened, the desktop might not immediately show them. To speed the process of making the new drives or disks available, you can use the Refresh Desktop View command.

The command Reveal Location in Finder (Windows: Reveal Location in Explorer) opens a window in the operating system (not Photoshop) that shows the selected file(s) in the appropriate folder.

Exporting the cache allows you to save the thumbnail images generated by File Browser. Because the thumbnails for a folder filled with many images take a long time to generate, this option may be a good idea. There are several things to keep in mind about exporting the cache. It can be exported only to the folder that contains the images, so you cannot export the cache to a read-only disk or a directory for which you haven't been granted write access. The cache is not automatically updated—if you add, delete, rename, rotate, or otherwise alter a file or the content of the folder, the cache does not reflect the change.

Purging the cache deletes the thumbnails being held in memory. This command allows File Browser to use the cache for a different folder or to regenerate the cache from more current information.

Caution

Deleting a file doesn't just remove it from the File Browser window—it actually moves the file to the Trash or Recycle. Remember that the File Browser isn't just a Photoshop tool; rather, it's a robust file management tool.

Many of the File Browser's menu commands are also available in the contextual menu. (Control-click) [Right+click] on an image to open the contextual menu.

When preparing images that will be burned to a CD or DVD, make exporting the cache one of your last steps. Including the cache allows File Browser to show thumbnails much more quickly; exporting it last ensures that it is correct.

SAVING WORKSPACES AND TOOL PRESETS

No matter what you do with Photoshop, it's probable that you have to switch settings for one or more tools while you do it. Likewise, to maximize efficiency, you need to arrange the floating palettes in a way that makes some palettes more accessible than others. Changing between tool options and palette arrangements is much quicker with Photoshop 7's new capabilities.

Arranging Your Screen

Photoshop's preferences have long been able to remember the last-used arrangement of palettes. That isn't lost in Photoshop 7—when the program is next started, the palettes return to their most recently used positions. However, the last-used palette locations might not be appropriate for the next task. Photoshop and ImageReady now enable you to save multiple palette arrangements and switch among them through the Window menu (see Figure 1.13).

Figure 1.13
The saved workspaces are listed alphabetically at the bottom of the Workspace submenu.

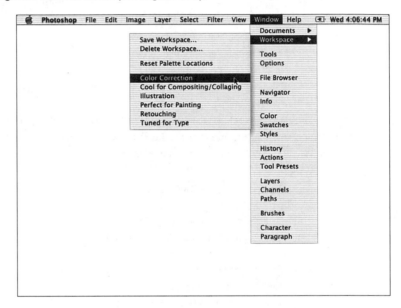

To save a workspace, simply arrange the palettes as desired and use the menu command Window, Workspace, Save Workspace. A dialog box gives you the opportunity to name the new saved workspace. The name can be up to 31 characters long (including spaces).

You can remove unwanted workspaces from the list by using the Window, Workspace, Delete Workspace command. A dialog box opens that contains a pop-up list of all the saved workspaces. Select a workspace from the list and click OK; you'll then be asked to confirm your choice. The pop-up menu also offers the option of deleting all saved workspaces.

The Tool Presets Palette

Consider, if you will, how convenient it would be to have Photoshop's Toolbox contain a unique tool for every purpose. There could be a Crop tool for creating images that are 8×10 at 240ppi, another that crops to 4×6 at 300ppi, a third for 600×45 pixels at 72ppi, and a half-dozen more for each possible use. Select the correct one, crop, done. No options to set.

When the File Browser is open as a window (not as a palette from the Palette Well), you can record its position in a workspace. What makes this feature truly valuable is that it also saves which folder is open. You can use saved workspaces as bookmarks or favorites for the File Browser.

But what if *each* of the tools in the Toolbox had a dozen or more variations? The Toolbox could get crowded, making it difficult to find precisely the tool you need.

Perhaps you have a Toolbox with a Rectangular Marquee tool at a specific size with feathering; one at the same size without feathering; a Rectangular Marquee tool at a different size with feathering; another at that same size without feathering; an Elliptical Marquee at one diameter, round, feathered; another round, unfeathered, and so on.

Rather than wading through near-endless tool variations, Photoshop's Options Bar enables you to customize a tool to your specific needs. And, new with Photoshop 7, is the Tool Presets palette, used to save customized tools and make them available at a single click.

Much like having a huge Toolbox with customized tools for every need, the presets enable you to save the tool configurations you regularly use. Unlike generic icons in a confusing Toolbox, with the Tool Presets palette, you can name each configuration in a recognizable manner (see Figure 1.14).

Figure 1.14
The Tool Presets can be opened through the Options Bar (left) or through the Window menu as a palette (right).

In addition to showing variations of a single tool, when the Current Tool Only check box is not selected, the Tool Presets palette displays saved presets for all of Photoshop's tools (see Figure 1.15).

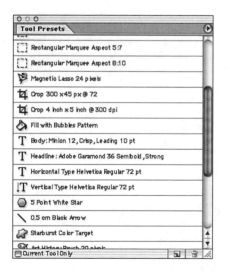

Figure 1.15
The Tool Presets palette can handle names up to 64 characters long. Rename an existing preset by double-clicking the name and retyping.

You can create a new tool preset by simply clicking the New Tool Preset button at the bottom of the palette. In the dialog box that opens, you can only name the preset. Make all the changes to the tool in the Options Bar and any related palettes before clicking the New Tool Preset button.

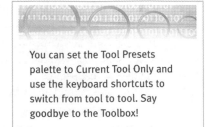

You can set the Tool Presets palette to Current Tool Only and use the keyboard shortcuts to switch from tool to tool. Say goodbye to the Toolbox!

Unsure about the value of tool presets? Check "Minimize Mousing" in the NAPP Help Desk section at the end of this chapter.

The Tool Presets menu, accessed through the triangle in the upper-right corner of the palette, gives you even greater control over this powerful capability:

- **Dock to Palette Well**—When the monitor is set to a screen resolution of over 800×600 pixels, the Palette Well is found at the right end of the Options Bar. Palettes placed in the well are easily accessible, yet out of the way.

- **New Tool Preset/Rename Tool Preset/Delete Tool Preset**—These three commands duplicate tasks that can be done directly in the palette. At the bottom of the palette are buttons that enable you to create a new preset (left) and delete a selected preset (right). To rename a preset, simply double-click its name in the palette and type.

- **Sort By Tool**—When a check mark appears next to this command and the palette is not set to Current Tool Only, the presets are grouped according to tool. When the option is not selected, new tool presets are added to the bottom of the palette.

- **Show All Tool Presets/Show Current Tool Presets**—This pair of commands duplicates the check box in the lower-left corner of the palette. One or the other has a check mark to the left, indicating the current content of the palette (which is also rather apparent from *looking at* the content of the palette).

- **Text Only/Small List/Large List**—In the two List views, the tool icons are visible. If you use either of these views, the tool name need not be part of the preset name—the icon tells you which tool is involved. However, if you use the Text Only view, a preset name such as "12 px" could refer to a selection tool, a painting tool, or any of a number of other tools. The three variations are shown in Figure 1.16.

Figure 1.16
You can change the appearance of the palette's content by selecting one of these three commands. The default is Small List.

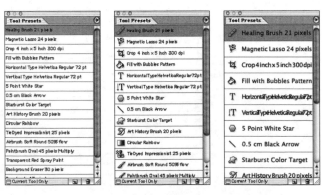

Text Only   Small List   Large List

- **Reset Tool/Reset All Tools**—Resetting the selected tool or all of the tools returns it or them to their default values. These commands have no effect on saved presets.

- **Preset Manager**—Photoshop's Preset Manager is used to determine what content is loaded into which palettes at startup. It can also be opened through the Edit menu. The dialog box (see Figure 1.17) enables you to select what will be in each of eight palettes. The Preset Manager's menu displays the appropriate commands and lists of sets for each of the eight menus (Figure 1.18 shows one example).

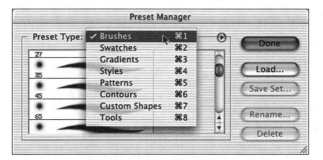

Figure 1.17
Each of Photoshop's palettes that use the Load and Save commands is listed. You can specify which sets to load and edit those sets by deleting or renaming individual entries in the palette.

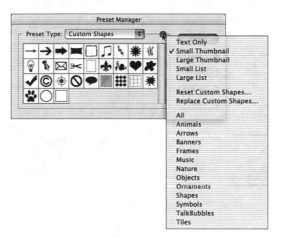

Figure 1.18
Note that you can select from any of the supplied sets from the bottom of the menu. The selected content can replace the current content or be added to it.

- **Reset/Load/Save/Replace Tool Presets**—Like several other palettes, the content of the Tool Presets palette can be saved. Set it up how you want it, and then use the palette's Save Tool Presets command. You can use Load Tool Presets at any time to restore the settings. You can also reset the palette to its default content and replace the existing content with any saved set of presets.

All sets of presets saved in the Presets, Tools folder are seen at the bottom of the Tool Presets palette menu. This list isn't updated until you quit and restart Photoshop.

Photoshop stores the Preset Manager settings in the same folder as Photoshop's preferences. Each of the eight palettes has its own .psp file. Deleting an individual .psp file resets the Preset Manager to the default for that palette; deleting the Adobe Photoshop 7.0 Prefs file resets all eight palettes (among other things).

NEW TOOLS AND CAPABILITIES

Among the most publicized and discussed features of Photoshop 7 are the new restoration tools. The Healing Brush and the Patch tool are far superior to the Clone Stamp tool in a variety of situations. There's also a lot of talk about the new Pattern Maker capability. There are a couple of other significant new additions as well.

⇨ *For an in-depth look at the Healing Brush and Patch tool,* **see** *Chapter 21, "Retouching and Restoration Basics," p. 645.*

⇨ *For additional information on the Pattern Maker,* **see** *Chapter 19, "Extract, Liquify, and the Pattern Maker," p. 587.*

Working with the Healing Brush

Just as you would with the Clone Stamp tool, you (Option-click) [Alt+click] to identify the area from which you want to copy. The Healing Brush is then dragged across the damaged area to repair it. The biggest difference between the two tools is that the Healing Brush retains the highlights and shadows of the area being repaired (see Figure 1.19).

Figure 1.19
Notice how natural the corrections look. The Healing Brush helps you avoid the artificiality sometimes introduced by the Clone Stamp tool.

A couple of differences between the Healing Brush and the Clone Stamp tools can be seen in the Options Bar. The Healing Brush has no Opacity field, and it uses only the blending modes Normal, Replace, Multiply, Screen, Darken, Lighten, Color, and Luminosity. In addition, the Healing Brush can be used to apply a pattern.

You can use the Edit, Fade command with the Healing Brush and the Patch tool. This allows you to lessen the effect of the tool by changing the opacity (but not the blending mode).

Patching Damaged Areas

Like the Healing Brush, the Patch tool protects the nature of the target area as it repairs. Unlike the Healing Brush, the Patch tool doesn't use a brush. Instead, a selection is made to identify either the area to be healed or the area from which you'll heal. Make the selection, and in the Options Bar, click on Source or Destination (see Figure 1.20). (Think of this choice as *to where* you're dragging the selection.) Drag with the Patch tool, and Photoshop will "heal" the area.

Like the Healing Brush, the Patch tool can add a pattern to the image. This feature can be especially useful for adding grass, sky, pavement, and other such detail to an image while preserving lighting.

Figure 1.20
Rather than telling Photoshop what you've selected, click a button in the Options Bar to tell Photoshop where you're going to drag the selection.

Making Patterns

With Photoshop 7's new Pattern Maker, found under the Filter menu, you create a piece of artwork and use the Pattern Maker window to customize the way it tiles. You can make a rectangular selection on which to base the pattern before or after opening the window. If a non-rectangular selection is active, Photoshop assumes a rectangle that encompasses the selection.

In the Pattern Maker (see Figure 1.21), you can choose a variety of options, including tile size, offset (vertical or horizontal, and the amount), smoothness, and sample detail. A border can be added around each tile, if desired. One capability that makes the Pattern Maker very practical is the ability to generate—even save—multiple variations of the pattern. Make changes to the options, and then click the Generate (or Generate Again) button. In the Tile History section, you can browse the generated patterns, delete unnecessary patterns, and save patterns for future use.

➡ *To learn more about saving patterns generated in the Pattern Maker, **see** "Pattern Maker Fundamentals," p. 601, in Chapter 19, "Extract, Liquify, and the Pattern Maker."*

After a pattern is applied by using the Pattern Maker's OK button, you can fade it, just as you would a filter or image adjustment command (see Figure 1.22). As with filters and adjustment, the Edit, Fade command is available only immediately after applying the pattern.

Figure 1.21
Earlier versions of Photoshop allowed you to save a single tile of a pattern, but didn't give you control over the tiling.

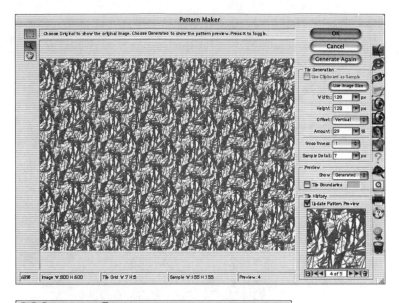

Figure 1.22
The opacity and blending mode of the pattern are changed, but the original artwork remains unaffected.

Auto Color

Located in the Image, Adjustments menu, Auto Color is designed to remove color casts from RGB images. Auto Levels and Auto Contrast work with an image's tonality, but Auto Color works to neutralize any unwanted tint in the image. It's available for both 8-bit and 16-bit images.

Although Auto Color can be as simple as selecting the command from the menu, you can have a great deal more control. The Auto Color Correction Options dialog box (see Figure 1.23) can be opened with the Options button in the Levels or the Curves dialog box.

*For a full discussion of Auto Color and the related commands, **see** Chapter 16, "Color Correction and the Adjustment Commands," p. 433.*

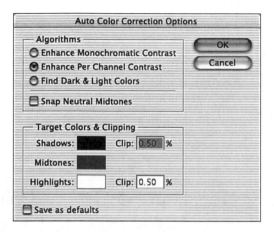

Figure 1.23
Changes made in this dialog box affect Curves, Levels, Auto Contrast, Auto Levels, and Auto Color when the Save as Defaults check box is selected.

Metallic Ink Support

Photoshop now includes native support for metallic inks. In the Color Picker, click the Custom button. From the Book pop-up menu, select PANTONE Metallic Coated (see Figure 1.24).

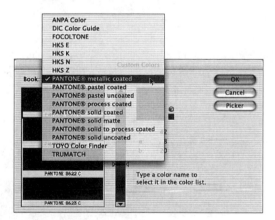

Figure 1.24
The metallic inks are used as spot colors in the printing industry.

THE PAINT ENGINE AND THE BRUSHES PALETTE

Among the most powerful changes to Photoshop is the way it works with brushes. You can now simulate fine art brushes and media as well as create special-effects brushes. All the painting tools, from the Paintbrush and Pencil to the Dodge and Blur tools, are affected.

Although they won't glitter like metal onscreen or when output to an inkjet, there's no reason you can't select one of these colors for use with an RGB image. It will be converted to the RGB equivalent.

⇨ *For more information about working with the new paint engine, **see** Chapter 12, "Photoshop 7's Painting Tools and Brushes," p. 311.*

Although mastering the new capabilities may require an investment in time, they can easily be integrated right away. Photoshop 7 also gives you the option of ignoring most of the changes by using its traditional Brushes palette. Among the changes that *can't* be ignored is the Airbrush. Instead of being a separate tool, it is now selected as a button in the Options Bar for several of the brush-using tools (see Table 1.1).

Table 1.1 Airbrush Capabilities

Airbrush-Capable	No Airbrush
Brush (formerly Paintbrush)	Pencil
Clone Stamp	Healing Brush
Pattern Stamp	Art History Brush
History Brush	Eraser tools
Burn	Blur
Dodge	Sharpen
Sponge	Smudge

When the button is selected, the active tool adopts an airbrush functionality: The longer the cursor is left in one spot (with the mouse button down), the more the foreground color is applied. Likewise, the slower the tool is dragged, the greater the effect (see Figure 1.25).

Figure 1.25
The Brush tool, with and without the Airbrush option. From the top: No Airbrush; Airbrush with Flow 100%; Airbrush with Flow 50%; Airbrush with Flow 25%.

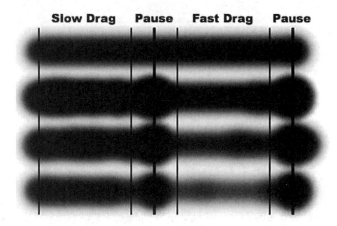

The Brushes Palette: New and Old

When Photoshop 6 was released, many long-time Photoshop artists were dismayed to find that they could no longer leave the Brushes palette open onscreen. Being able to instantly summon the palette through the contextual menu was no solace. They wanted to see what brush was in use and what others were available. Adobe listened when they complained, and Photoshop 7's Brushes palette can be left open for visual reference and easy access. However, there's a whole lot more to the Brushes palette now (see Figure 1.26).

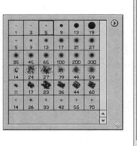

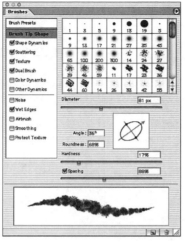

Figure 1.26
The Photoshop 6 Brushes palette is on the left. On the right, just one example of the potential complexity of the new Brushes palette.

When the additional features of the Brushes palette aren't required, or when the palette is too overwhelming, deselecting Expanded View from the palette's menu reduces it to a more manageable size and configuration (see Figure 1.27).

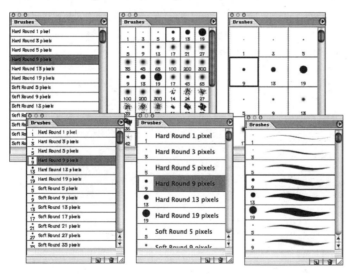

Figure 1.27
From left to right, the various unexpanded views of the Brushes palette: lists, simple thumbnails, or stroke thumbnails.

Brush Dynamics

Support for Wacom tablets (and other pressure-sensitive drawing devices) is also enhanced in Photoshop 7. In addition to the pressure applied to the tablet with the pen, Photoshop 7 supports Pen Tilt and Airbrush Wheel with appropriate hardware and tablet drivers (see Figure 1.28).

You can change the view of the Brushes palette only when it's set to Brush Presets. Expand the palette, click on Brush Presets, and then select the desired view in the Brush palette menu. When the palette is unexpanded, it retains the selected view.

Figure 1.28
If no tablet is attached, a warning triangle appears next to the brush dynamics pop-up menus in the Brushes palette (shown in the inset to the right).

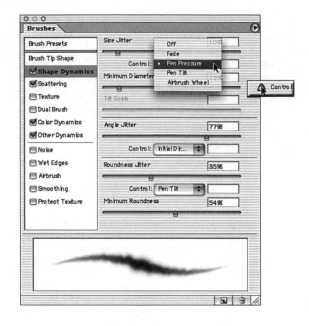

New Blending Modes

Photoshop 7 adds several blending modes and rearranges how they appear in the pop-up menus. Rather than grouping modes by how they work (Color Dodge and Color Burn versus Multiply and Screen), they are grouped by result (modes that darken versus modes that lighten). You'll find five new blending modes in several menus (see Figure 1.29).

Figure 1.29
The new blending modes are highlighted.

The new Linear Burn and Linear Dodge work with the brightness values of the base and blend colors. Vivid Light decreases contrast if the blend color is light and increases contrast if it is dark. Likewise, Linear Light works with brightness depending on the blending color. Pin Light replaces lighter pixels in the base color with the blend color, but leaves darker base color pixels untouched.

➪ *For full descriptions of how each blending mode works,* ***see*** *Chapter 17, "Using Blending Modes,"* ***p. 477.***

NEW TYPE-RELATED CAPABILITIES

Although Photoshop is not ready to challenge InDesign or QuarkXPress as a page layout tool, its type capabilities continue to improve. The addition of a spell checker and find/replace are welcome news, but Photoshop still lacks text wrapping, linked containers, and numerous other basic layout tools. Keep in mind, though, that Photoshop is an image editor and, as such, has incredibly powerful text-handling capabilities.

➪ *For an in-depth look at type and how to work with it,* ***see*** *Chapter 11, "Type and Typography in Photoshop,"* ***p. 273.***

Check Spelling

Just a few short versions ago, Photoshop text capability was restricted to creating selections in the shape of letters. It now has a rather sophisticated type engine with many powerful features. Among the newest features is the long-awaited spell checker (see Figure 1.30).

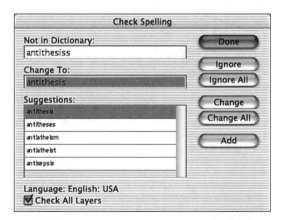

Figure 1.30
Note that the Check Spelling dialog box offers a check box for checking all type layers in the image.

Photoshop automatically switches dictionaries, even in the middle of a sentence, while checking spelling. The language (and dictionary) are set in the Character palette. (See the section "Improved Character Palette" later in this chapter.)

Find and Replace Text

Although not particularly sophisticated, the Find and Replace Text command is certainly adequate for an image-editing program. Enter the search target in the Find What text box and the desired replacement in the Change To text box (see Figure 1.31).

Figure 1.31
Searching one or all type layers is a powerful capability for Photoshop.

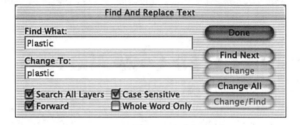

Improved Character Palette

In Photoshop 6's early days, many designers and artists (as well as production folk) lost countless hours because of Faux Bold. This type enhancement, buried in the Character palette menu, prevented the application of text warping. Faux Bold, as well as Faux Italic and six other type attributes, can be applied by using buttons in the Character palette (see Figure 1.32), and the button itself indicates whether the attribute is applied.

Figure 1.32
Note the pop-up menu in the lower-left corner that enables you to set the language and spell check dictionary on a word-by-word basis.

Notice in the lower-right corner of the dialog box the pop-up menu set to Sharp. This new antialiasing option is designed to help keep small Web text legible, but it's appropriate for a wide variety of type.

Smart Quotes

Smart quotation marks and apostrophes, also know as *printer's marks*, curve in toward the material being cited. The alternative (which can be called *dumb quotes*) are straight and identical at the beginning and end of the quoted material. A comparison is shown in Figure 1.33. Smart quotes are selected (or deselected) in the General pane of Photoshop's Preferences.

"Smart" quotes
"Dumb" quotes

Figure 1.33
The straight marks are appropriate for use as foot and inch marks.

OTHER NEW AND IMPROVED FEATURES

There are quite a few additional changes and improvements to both Photoshop and ImageReady. Some of the most significant are covered in the sections that follow.

Preset File Sizes

The New dialog box offers a pop-up menu of commonly used file sizes (see Figure 1.34). Web-oriented sizes automatically adjust the resolution to 72ppi, and print-related sizes use 300dpi.

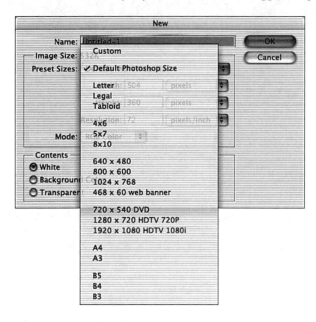

Figure 1.34
Although resolution is adjusted according to the most common use for each size, color mode is not changed.

Collaboration and Workgroups

If you work with others, the Workgroup advancements should be of particular interest. Photoshop can now create PDF files that use the same basic security available in Adobe Acrobat. Photoshop 6's Manage Workflow menu is now Workgroup. It has a number of new commands geared toward workgroups that share files stored on servers.

Web-Related Improvements

You'll find quite a few improvements, subtle and obvious, as you work more with ImageReady. Among the most significant changes are the following:

■ ImageReady jumps from version 3.0 (which was included with Photoshop 6) to ImageReady 7.0. The change was merely to bring the Photoshop and ImageReady version numbers in line.

■ The Rollovers palette improvements are quite substantial. The palette now enables you to see all states of an image at once and centralizes much of the work related to image maps and even animations (see Figure 1.35).

Figure 1.35
The new Rollovers palette is quite similar to the Layers palette.

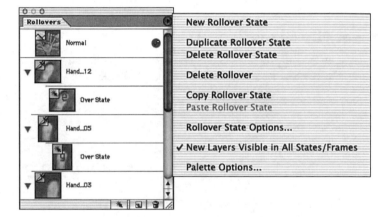

■ Dithered transparency allows images made for the Web to simulate such effects as drop shadows and glows. Instead of using partial transparency, a dithered pattern of opaque and transparent pixels is used.

⇨ *To learn more about using dithered transparency,* **see** *Chapter 25, "ImageReady Basics,"* **p. 763.**

■ Images can be optimized with priority assigned to vector artwork and type. This *weighted optimization* maintains their quality as well as possible, while still minimizing file size.

⇨ *For more depth on image optimization and Save for Web,* **see** *Chapter 24, "Save for Web and Image Optimization,"* **p. 725.**

■ Save for Web now offers support for the WBMP file format, used primarily for PDAs and wireless devices.

■ ZoomView images can be exported for use with Web-based technology from Viewpoint Corporation. ZoomView requires a browser plug-in to display and a license to create a ZoomView-capable Web site.

- Dynamic Data-Driven Graphics can automatically update a Web site (or other document) using images and text from a database. The Web pages incorporate *variables*, which in turn are linked to the database. To change a page, substitute another value in the database for a particular variable.

Simple, Yet Powerful Interface Changes

Some of the simplest changes to Photoshop can dramatically improve the way you work:

- **Direct Renaming**—Renaming a layer, style, Action, or any other element in a palette that shows names is as simple as possible now. Double-click the name to highlight it, and then type (see Figure 1.36). No dialog box required.

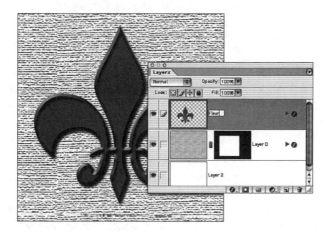

Figure 1.36
The same easy renaming applies to a variety of palettes when the palette is in List view. Styles, tool presets, Actions, spot and alpha channels, paths, swatches, and history snapshots can all be renamed directly in their palettes.

- **Rearrange Palette Content**—Using the Preset Manager, you can rearrange items in palettes. For example, you can reorder the brushes in the Brushes palette or change the arrangement of gradients in the Gradients palette.

- **Relative Canvas Size**—The Canvas Size dialog box now eliminates the need for on-the-fly math. Instead of trying to add 1.25 inches to 480 pixels, you can simply click the Relative check box and type the amount of canvas you'd like to add (see Figure 1.37).

- **Tile Image Windows**—Long familiar to Windows users, Photoshop now offers both window tiling and cascading. When multiple windows are open, you can automatically arrange them by using the commands under the Window, Documents menu.

- **Liquify Interface**—Zoom and Hand tools make Liquify a far more controllable (and powerful) capability.

- **Greater Curve Control**—A button in the lower-right corner of the Curves dialog box enables you to increase the size of the Curves grid to 125%. The larger grid gives you finer control and more precision.

- **Larger Filter Previews**—Many of Photoshop's filters have larger preview boxes.

1

Figure 1.37
You can also type a negative number to shrink an image in relation to its original size.

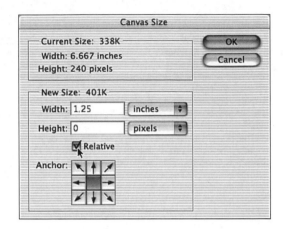

Other Improvements

No list of Photoshop's new or changed capabilities should overlook the following:

- **Scripting** with JavaScript, AppleScript, and Windows OLE Automation—This capability enables you to control Photoshop from *outside* Photoshop. For example, you could write a script that generates images in one scriptable program, then opens Photoshop, runs an Action on each of the images, saves them, closes Photoshop, and finally shuts down the computer.

- **Layer Blending Options**—In addition to the new blending modes, Photoshop has new blending options. In the Layer Style dialog box, the Blending Options pane now offers three new check boxes. Transparency Shapes Layer allows Photoshop to ignore transparent pixels, applying effects only to pixels with an opacity higher than zero. Layer Mask Hides Effects and Vector Mask Hides Effects determine whether a mask is applied before or after an effect. The difference is shown in Figure 1.38.

Figure 1.38
The Layers palette shows that drop shadows and bevels are applied to both layers. The mask for the leaf at the upper left does not hide the shadow, but the lower leaf's shadow is hidden by the layer mask.

- **Color Sampling Outside Photoshop**—The Eyedropper tool can now be used to select a color outside Photoshop—any color, anywhere onscreen can be sampled. Click inside an open Photoshop document window, hold the mouse button down, and drag to any color visible onscreen. Releasing the mouse button selects the color.

- **Custom Shape Collections**—Adobe is supplying a vastly more useful set of custom shapes with Photoshop. The new collections can be loaded into the Custom Shapes palette by using the palette's menu, just as you can load Actions or styles.

- **Improved Automated Tasks**—Last, but far from least, are the improvements to Picture Package and Web Photo Gallery. Picture Package enables you to create pages from two or more separate files and now offers the capability of adding labels to the images. Web Photo Gallery offers additional configurations and options.

FROM THE NAPP HELP DESK

The National Association of Photoshop Professionals (NAPP) offers e-mail assistance to its members. Here is some advice from the NAPP Help Desk related to issues in this chapter.

Enter the EXIF

What is this EXIF data I can access in the File Browser, and why do only some images have it?

EXIF (Exchangeable Image Format)is actually a file format that uses JPEG compression. It is readable by all programs that can display JPEG, including Web browsers. The EXIF data, which you see in the File Browser, is information recorded in the header of the JPEG. It is recorded by most digital cameras, although the specific fields can vary from camera to camera. EXIF data can also be seen in Photoshop through the menu command File, File Info.

You'll see EXIF data for almost all digital camera images and some stock images. Because it's recorded when the image is taken by a digital camera, you won't find it embedded in images not snapped digitally.

Minimize Mousing

Why should I establish tool presets? What's the value? They don't seem to do anything I can do otherwise.

Tool presets are merely a timesaver. Consider the number of clicks or drags it takes to change from the default Type tool options to the type you most often use. This can include changing the font, type style, size, leading, tracking, color, height, width, and antialiasing. There are actually some 19 different options that can be set in the Character palette. Instead of changing each of them, every time you add type, you can establish a preset with your own most commonly used options. Change from the default Type tool options to your usual options with one click instead of 6 or 10 or more.

THE PHOTOSHOP INTERFACE

IN THIS CHAPTER

PHOTOSHOP'S EVOLVING INTERFACE

Users of Photoshop 6 will feel right at home in Photoshop 7. There are some new tools and palettes, and some menus have been rearranged, but there should be a smooth transition.

Macintosh users transitioning to OS X will find differences in the operating system more extreme than changes in Photoshop. Windows XP users should move smoothly to Photoshop 7.

Rearranged Menus

A number of commands have been renamed or relocated in Photoshop 7. Here's a list:

- Under the File menu, Manage Workflow is now Workgroup. There have been several changes to the submenu.

- Also under the File menu, Print Options has now become Print with Preview—same dialog box, different name.

- The Edit menu now includes the commands Check Spelling and Find and Replace Text.

- Image, Adjustments now includes the new Auto Color command.

- The Image menu gets a little shorter, too, with Extract and Liquify moving to the Filter menu.

- The Layer menu sees Delete Layer shortened to just Delete.

- Add Layer Clipping Path and the companion command Enable Layer Clipping Path also have a semantic change, being replaced by Add Vector Mask and Enable Vector Mask.

- The Filter menu welcomes Extract and Liquify, as well as the new Pattern Maker command.

- In the View menu, you'll no longer find New View (it's moved to the Window, Documents menu and renamed New Window), and Show Extras becomes simply Extras.

- The Window menu had a more extensive make-over. It's discussed separately in the following section.

- The Help menu has also been rearranged. Mac OS X users no longer have Balloon Help available, some of the online options have new names, and there's a new System Info command that tells you everything Photoshop needs to know about your hardware and software.

If you'll be speaking with Adobe Tech Support, first open Help, System Info. With everything selected, click the Copy button. Switch to a word processor or text editor and paste, and then print the page—Tech Support will likely need at least some of the info.

The New Window Menu

The first thing you'll notice about the revamped Window menu is the addition of the Documents and Workspace submenus at the top. Documents gives you the opportunity to arrange open windows as well as bring to the front any open image. Arranging open documents onscreen is not new to Windows users, but a welcome addition to the Mac side. Figure 2.1 illustrates the difference between the Cascade and Tile options.

Figure 2.1
Familiar to many Windows users, cascading (left) and tiling (right) are convenient ways to arrange windows onscreen.

The command New Window replaces New View, found in earlier versions of Photoshop. At the bottom of the Window, Documents submenu, you'll find the names of currently open documents. (The list of open documents has moved from the bottom of the Window menu to the bottom of the Window, Documents submenu.)

The Workspace submenu allows you to save and load custom arrangements of palettes. Arrange the palettes the way you like, and then use the command Window, Workspace, Save Workspace. You can save a variety of palette arrangements, with various names, for use in different situations. All saved workspaces appear in a list at the bottom of the Window, Workspace menu. The Delete Workspace command opens a dialog box that includes a pop-up menu of all saved workspaces. You can remove unneeded workspaces or use the All option to clear the list.

Different procedures require access to different palettes. If you regularly perform certain tasks that require certain palettes, save workspaces for each. It's a snap to change from one arrangement to another.

You'll find three other commands added to the Window command. File Browser opens Photoshop's new image-viewing tool. The Tool Presets palette, also new to Photoshop 7, is opened through the Window menu. This version of Photoshop sees the revival of an independent (and greatly improved) Brushes palette (see Figure 2.2).

⇨ *File Browser is introduced in Chapter 1, "What's New in Photoshop 7," **p. 13**.*

Figure 2.2
The new Brushes palette not only can remain open while you work, but also can be used to create and edit brushes on-the-fly.

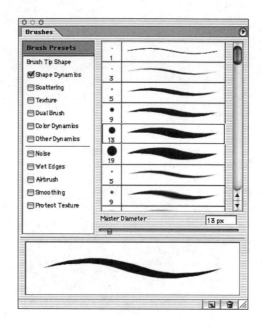

Tool Changes

In addition to introducing a couple of new tools (the Healing Brush and the Patch tool), Photoshop 7 made a couple of changes to some of the legacy tools. The tool formerly known as Paintbrush is now simply Brush, and the Airbrush has been rolled into it. Instead of being a separate tool, Airbrush is now an option in the Options Bar for the Brush tool, activated by clicking a button.

Photoshop 7 also marks the return of individual type tools for horizontal and vertical type, as well as type masks. Rather than buttons in the Options Bar, there are again individual tools for the four combinations of type layer/type mask, horizontal/vertical.

The Evolution of the Brushes Palettes

In Photoshop 6, the Brushes palette was available through the Options Bar or the contextual menu (Control-clicking) [Right+clicking]. The palette closed automatically after a brush was selected. Many Photoshop artists prefer having the palette open for inspection at all times, and Photoshop 7 gives them that option.

Photoshop 6's Brushes palette (see Figure 2.3) offered a selection of brushes (collections of which could be loaded through the palette's menu) and a New Brush dialog box, in which you could design a custom brush.

Photoshop 7 offers a far more sophisticated Brushes palette—or three (see Figure 2.4).

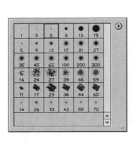

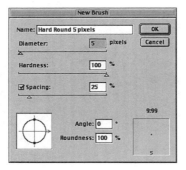

Figure 2.3
Photoshop 6's New Brush dialog box is accessed through the Brushes palette menu.

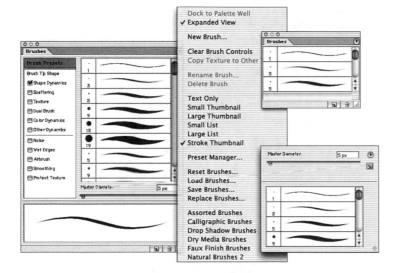

Figure 2.4
The Brushes palette's expanded view is shown to the left (with menu), the unexpanded view is shown to the upper right, and you can still change brushes on-the-fly through the contextual menu (lower right).

The various brush design options are explored in Chapter 12, "Photoshop 7's Painting Tools and Brushes," p. 311.

Mac OS X Changes

Perhaps most noticeably for Mac OS X users, Photoshop's Preferences and Color Settings commands have been relocated. You'll now find them under the Photoshop menu rather than Edit (see Figure 2.5).

You'll also find About Photoshop, which opens the Photoshop splash screen, and About Plug-In, which lists all the installed Photoshop plug-ins. Selecting a plug-in from the list opens its information box, allowing you to check the version number (and discover who to thank or blame for writing the plug-in).

Figure 2.5
Although not listed in the menu as a shortcut, Command-K still opens the General pane of the Preferences dialog box.

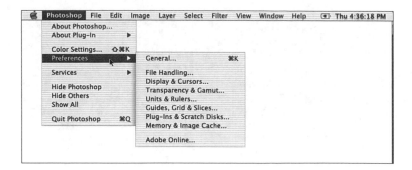

THE PHOTOSHOP INTERFACE: A CHEF'S TOUR

Photoshop is no different from many computer programs available. Almost every facet of creation and production in Photoshop is controlled through palettes, tools, and menu commands. Mouse clicks and drags and keystroke combinations are used to interact with the program's elements. Understanding the basics of that interface can improve your productivity.

Figures 2.6 through 2.8 show Photoshop 7 running on a monitor set to a resolution of 800×600 to show some of the program's interface detail. The difference between the minimum monitor setting and higher resolutions is discussed in the sidebar "Monitor Settings and the Photoshop Interface."

The Basic Interface

As you can see in Figures 2.6, 2.7, and 2.8, there is little difference in Photoshop among the three main operating systems.

Figure 2.6
This is the basic appearance of Photoshop when opened in Windows XP.

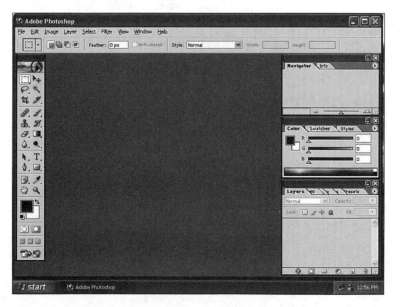

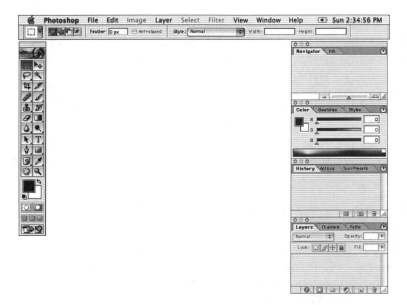

Figure 2.7
This is the basic appearance of Photoshop when opened in Macintosh OS X.

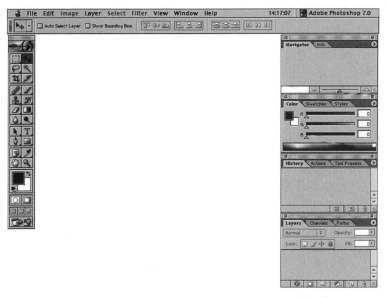

Figure 2.8
This is the basic appearance of Photoshop when opened in Macintosh OS 9.

In all three environments, Photoshop offers the same basic tools, palettes, and commands (although some commands are under different menus):

- Across the top of the window are the menus, in which you'll find the majority of Photoshop's commands.

■ Just below the menu bar you'll see the Options Bar, which is actually a palette. The Options Bar is contextual in nature, meaning its contents change with circumstances. The active tool generally determines what options are available, but the contents can also change depending on how the specific tool is being used (see Figure 2.9).

Figure 2.9
In the top example, the Options Bar shows the basic options for the Crop tool. In the lower example, the Crop tool is in use and the options have changed.

⇨ *Is the Options Bar partially obscuring your image window? See "Docking the Palettes" in the NAPP Help Desk section at the end of this chapter.*

■ To the left is the Toolbox. All of Photoshop's tools can be selected by clicking on the appropriate icon. Note that many tools are found on *flyout palettes*, which extend from the Toolbox when you click and hold on some tool icons (see Figure 2.10). Tools that include flyout palettes are indicated by small black triangles in the lower-right corner.

Figure 2.10
Click and hold on the Type tool and the additional type tools become visible. Switch tools by moving the cursor to the desired tool and releasing the mouse button.

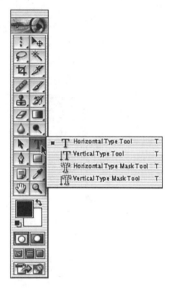

■ In the area to the right in Figures 2.6 through 2.8, you'll find the main palettes. They are called *floating palettes* because they are never obscured by the image window; they always appear above it. However, palettes can obscure other palettes. Click the tab (or any other visible part) of a partially hidden palette to bring it to the front.

Monitor Settings and the Photoshop Interface

Photoshop requires that your monitor be set to a minimum of 800×600 pixels to operate at all. To maximize detail, that resolution was used to capture the majority of the figures in this book that show Photoshop in action. However, when working at 800×600 pixels, you don't have access to Photoshop's Palette Well, which is discussed separately later in this chapter.

In addition to the Palette Well, higher resolutions give you additional working space. Because the screen's "real estate" includes more pixels in the same physical space, each pixel is smaller. The parts of Photoshop's interface (palettes, tools, and so forth) don't change size; rather, they retain the number of pixels at which they were designed. Therefore, they take up less space onscreen, but can be much smaller.

This is Photoshop's basic layout in Mac OS X with a monitor set to 1280×1024 pixels. Note the Palette Well at the right end of the Options Bar.

If your operating system and hardware allow, you can also use Photoshop on multiple monitors. In the following figure, the image is on one monitor while palettes are available on the other. The cursor can freely move back and forth between the monitors.

2

Using multiple monitors requires that each have a separate video card.

In addition to monitor resolution, the color depth must be suitable for the work being done. Photoshop requires that a monitor be capable of displaying a minimum of 8-bit color (256 colors). However, most Photoshop tasks require at least thousands of colors, if not millions. The computer's operating system controls the monitor settings.

Rearranging Palettes

Customizing your workspace by rearranging Photoshop's palettes can improve efficiency and provide a more pleasant working environment. If you'll need only a few palettes for the particular procedures you'll be doing, you can hide the rest to streamline the Photoshop interface and maximize the visible image. Here are the basic techniques for manipulating palettes in Photoshop:

- Tab shows and hides all palettes.

- Shift-Tab shows and hides all palettes except for the Toolbox and the Options Bar.

- Neither Tab nor Shift-Tab is available when a palette is open through the Palette Well.

- Individual palettes can be shown and hidden by using the Window menu.

- When several palettes share a window, click on a palette's tab to bring it to the front and make it active.

- By default, palettes appear along the edge of the screen. When you move a palette toward any screen edge, it will "snap" into place, indicating that it's *docked* to the edge. Normally, image windows cannot be opened or resized so that docked palettes overlap. (This behavior can be changed in the Options Bar with the Zoom tool active by selecting the Ignore Palettes check box.)

- Palettes can be restored to their default locations at any time by using the menu command Window, Workspace, Reset Palette Locations.

- Palettes can be minimized by double-clicking the palette's tab (see Figure 2.11).

Remember that monitors set to 800×600 resolution will not show the Palette Well.

Figure 2.11
Double-clicking a palette's tab shrinks it down, yet keeps it open. Double-clicking again expands the palette.

- The windows in which the palettes float also have buttons for minimizing and maximizing. Each of the three main operating system versions (Windows, Mac OS 9, and Mac OS X) has its own setup. In each case, the window has a button to minimize and/or maximize the palette's size and to close the palette. Photoshop uses the standard buttons that should be familiar to you on your operating system.

- Palettes can be sent to the Palette Well by using the appropriate command from the palette's menu or by dragging the palette's tab to the well. You can expand any palette in the well by clicking its tab.

- By default, Photoshop's palettes are *nested* or grouped into several windows. You can change the nesting groups by dragging a palette's tab from one window to another. When the destination window's palettes are surrounded by a thick black line, release the mouse button (see Figure 2.12).

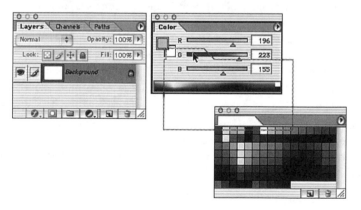

Figure 2.12
Note the heavy black line around the Color palette, indicating that the Swatches palette will be nested if the mouse button is released. Note that there is no black line around the Layers palette.

- Similar to nesting, palettes can also be *docked* to one another. By docking a palette to the bottom of another, you place them both in one window, but both can be visible at the same time. In contrast, palettes nested together in the same window have only the topmost palette visible.

To dock a palette to another window, drag the palette's tab to the bottom of the window and release the mouse button. When the palette is in the proper position, a thick black line appears at the bottom of the destination window. Contrast the line at the bottom of the palette in Figure 2.13 with the black line around the entire palette in Figure 2.12.

Figure 2.13
When the heavy black line is at the bottom only, the palette will dock. Note that the Layers and Channels palettes are both docked and minimized.

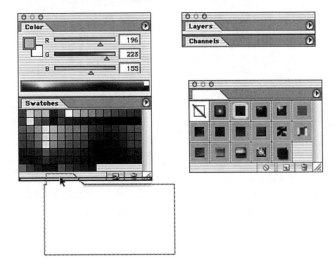

⇨ *Want one-click access to palette configurations? See "Workspace Hotkeys" in the NAPP Help Desk section at the end of this chapter.*

The Options Bar

The Options Bar appears by default across the top of the monitor, below the menu bar. It allows you to adjust a variety of settings for most tools. The Options Bar is *contextual*, meaning it changes content depending on which tool is active or what you are doing with the selected tool. (An example is shown in Figure 2.9 earlier in this chapter.) A couple of features of the Options Bar remain consistent from tool to tool. On the left end, you'll have access to the Tool Preset Picker; to the right, you'll see the Palette Well. (These two features are discussed individually in the following sections.)

As a floating palette, the Options Bar can be relocated onscreen for your convenience. Because it extends the width of the screen, it's usually at the top or bottom. To move the Options Bar, drag it by the tab at the left end. It can be shown or hidden with the rest of the palettes by using the Tab key. Shift-Tab leaves the Toolbox and the Options Bar visible. The menu command Window, Options shows and hides this palette individually.

Tool Presets

New in Photoshop 7 is the Tool Presets Picker, found at the left end of the Options Bar. The icon shows the currently selected tool, and clicking the down arrow next to the icon opens the picker.

The Tool Presets Picker operates along with the Tool Presets palette. Tool presets automatically set a tool to its predetermined settings. You can create presets for all tool configurations you normally use, saving the time it takes to adjust settings in the Options Bar.

There are two configurations for the picker: All Tools and Current Tool Only. In All Tools mode (see Figure 2.14), all presets for all tools are available in the list and in the Tool Presets palette.

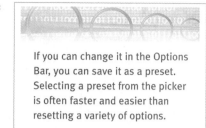

If you can change it in the Options Bar, you can save it as a preset. Selecting a preset from the picker is often faster and easier than resetting a variety of options.

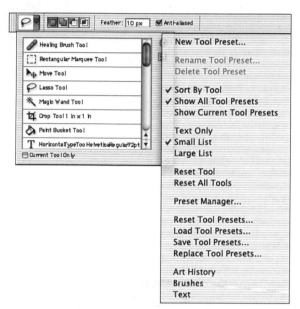

Figure 2.14
Click on the arrow in the upper-right corner of a palette to open its menu.

When the Current Tool Only check box is selected at the bottom of the picker, only saved presets for that tool are listed in the palette (see Figure 2.15).

Figure 2.15
When many presets are recorded for a variety of tools, selecting the Current Tool Only check box can simplify the list.

To create a new preset, simply select the desired tool from the Toolbox, set the configuration that you want to save, and either click the New Tool Preset button (directly under the triangle that opens the palette's menu) or use the picker's menu command New Tool Preset. You can use the picker's menu to rename or delete existing presets when no longer needed.

When set to All Tools, the Tool Presets Picker can replace the Toolbox. However, if there are many saved tool presets, the list might be unwieldy.

The Palette Well

The Palette Well, located at the right end of the Options Bar, is merely a convenience. It's a way to stash often-used palettes out of the way, yet have them readily available.

Drag the tab of a palette to the well to add it. Click on any tab in the well to expand the palette. You can also send palettes to the Palette Well by using a command from the palette's menu.

Don't forget the contextual menu! (Control-clicking) [Right+clicking] in the picker allows you to create, rename, or delete a tool preset.

The primary advantage of the Palette Well is screen space savings. By placing the palette in the well, it doesn't occupy screen space, yet can be expanded with a simple click. Alternatively, you can always nest or dock palettes and collapse/expand them by double-clicking their tabs.

The Title and Status Bars

The Title Bar appears at the top of an image window. It displays the name of the file, the zoom factor, the active layer, and the color mode. When the image's color mode is not the same as the working color mode, an asterisk appears to the right of the color mode.

Unfortunately, the Palette Well isn't there for you when you need it most. If a monitor is set to a resolution of 800×600 pixels, the Palette Well is not available. Yet it's when space is at a premium that it serves you best.

⇨ *Color modes are discussed in Chapter 9, "Photoshop Color Management," p. 219.*

The Status Bar is located at the bottom of the image window. Windows users can elect to show and hide the Status Bar through the Window menu, but that command is not available in Mac OS 9 or Mac OS X. To the left is the zoom field.

Hold down Shift when you press (Return) [Enter] to change the zoom. That leaves the field highlighted and ready for the next zoom change.

Typing a new zoom factor there zooms you in or out, depending on the difference between the new and previous percentages.

To the right of the zoom field is an icon used for accessing several of the commands under the File, Workgroup submenu. Unless the image is *checked out* (opened through the Workflow menu), the Workflow commands are not available.

Next is a field with variable content. If this area of the Status Bar isn't visible, expand the window by dragging the lower-right corner. To choose what the field will show, click the right arrow to display a menu of options (see Figure 2.16).

Figure 2.16
By default, Document Sizes is selected.

Here are the seven options:

- **Document Sizes**—Two numbers are located at the bottom of the image window. On the left is the file size if the image is flattened and without alpha channels; to the right is the file size with all layers and channels intact. Remember that the number on the right is the current size of the document *when open in Photoshop*. When the image is saved and the file closed, the actual file size on disk can be substantially smaller because Photoshop compresses alpha channels (masks). Likewise, the number on the left might not match the file size on disk of a flattened version of the file—file format and compression are two additional factors.

- **Document Profile**—The file's assigned color profile is displayed. Assign to Profile and Convert to Profile (under the Image, Mode submenu) can be used to change the document's profile.

- **Document Dimensions**—The document's dimensions are displayed in the unit of measure assigned to the rulers, which is selected in Photoshop's Preferences. Remember that you can change the unit of measure by showing the rulers (Command-R) [Ctrl+R] and using the contextual menu (Control-click) [Right+click] to select a new unit.

- **Scratch Sizes**—With Scratch Sizes displayed, a pair of numbers will be shown. To the left, Photoshop shows the amount of memory actually being used. To the right is the amount of memory allocated or assigned to Photoshop. If the left number is larger than that on the right, Photoshop is using the scratch disks to hold the excess data. Writing to and reading from hard drives (*scratch disks*) is far slower than using RAM. When the number on the left is larger, Photoshop is working slowly.

■ **Efficiency**—When Photoshop is performing at peak efficiency (100%), all possible operations are taking place in RAM. When the memory available to Photoshop is overloaded by data (several large images open, excess history states being recorded, and so on), the efficiency drops below 100% and performance suffers. Photoshop is forced to use the scratch disks rather than RAM. Closing unnecessary files, shutting down other programs running in the background, and using the command Edit, Purge to empty the memory are ways to restore Photoshop efficiency.

On Mac OS X, you'll also see a percentage in the Timing field, which tells you what percent of the processor's capability was devoted to the operation. If the percentage is low, you can speed up Photoshop by shutting down programs and utilities working in the background.

■ **Timing**—Although often seen as a curiosity or simply a way of comparing hardware, the Timing setting can be of practical use by displaying how long it took to perform the previous operation. This setting can be useful for planning such tasks as using the Batch command with an Action (giving you, perhaps, an idea of when to return to the office). It can also be used to show when an operation is complete. For example, the Smudge tool might seem to be delayed a second or more. Timing will stop updating when Photoshop has finished applying the smudge.

The Status Bar is not visible when Photoshop is in Full Screen Mode, with or without the menu bar. Those view modes hide the image window, removing the Title Bar, scrollbars, and the Status Bar.

Timing is cumulative with tools. If you select the Brush tool and begin painting in the image, the Timing field continues to run until you select and begin using another tool or command. When working with plug-ins, such as Liquify and Extract, Timing shows the entire amount of time you spent in the operation, not just how long it took to apply the changes to the image.

■ **Current Tool**—The active tool's name is displayed, which can be useful when the Toolbox is hidden and the cursors are set to Brush Size or Precise. For example, you might need to know whether you've used Shift-B to select the Brush tool or the Pencil tool.

In addition, if you click on the field itself rather than the triangle to the right, Photoshop shows you a diagram like that in Figure 2.17. This is a picture of how the image's print size compares to the paper on which it will be printed. Photoshop uses the print dimensions, which you can see or change in the Image Size dialog box, and the paper size selected in the Page Setup dialog box. The whitespace represents the page size, and the box with diagonal lines indicates the image size and placement. (The placement is determined by the margins selected in File, Print with Preview.)

Figure 2.17
Photoshop gives no indication of the actual page size or the image resolution, just comparative size and placement.

ZOOMING FOR IMPROVED PRODUCTION

In addition to good palette placement and management, Photoshop offers a number of other ways to improve your work environment onscreen. Familiarizing yourself with the basic zoom techniques is especially useful for working with laptops and other systems that have limited screen resolution.

Zooming In and Out

Some work is best done zoomed in so that each pixel is individually recognizable. Some portrait retouching and restoration jobs, for example, require close-up work. Refining icons and thumbnails might also need pixel-by-pixel perfection. Other work must be done at 100% zoom, such as proofing Web graphics and evaluating some filter previews. You can zoom to any factor between 0.13% and 1600% with double-decimal accuracy. Photoshop offers a number of ways to get back and forth between an overall look at the larger picture and the intimate look at the tiny colored squares that make up an image:

- **Zoom Tool**—Recognizable by the magnifying glass icon, this tool allows you to zoom both in and out. The keyboard shortcut to select the tool is Z. Click to zoom in, hold down the (Option) [Alt] key, and click to zoom out. The Options Bar also enables you to set the tool to Zoom Out mode, which reverses the behavior of the modifier key. Click-zooming always takes you to the next preset zoom factor.

  You can also drag with the Zoom tool to fill the window with a selected part of an image. When you drag-zoom, the magnification level is determined by how much of the image you choose to include within the zoom marquee.

  The Options Bar gives you some control over the tool's behavior. You can elect to have windows resize to match the zoom factor, and you can have windows expand beneath the palettes or stop at the edge. With the Zoom tool active, buttons in the Options Bar allow you to choose among some preset zoom factors.

■ **Zoom Field**—Located in the lower-left corner of the image window when the Status Bar is visible, you can highlight the zoom field and enter any desired zoom factor within Photoshop's range. Press Tab or (Return) [Enter] to perform the Zoom.

The zoom field always zooms you to or from the center of the image window.

■ **Navigator Palette**—The Navigator palette offers a number of ways to zoom. You can drag the slider, click on the small and large mountain icons, and enter a numeric value in the zoom field.

■ **View Menu**—Several commands in the View menu can zoom. Zoom In and Zoom Out work like clicking the Zoom tool. The commands Actual Pixels and Fit On Screen are also zoom commands. Actual Pixels changes the image to 100% zoom. Fit On Screen enlarges the image window to fit the available space on the monitor, and then fills the window with the image. The entire image will be visible.

The menu command Print Size and its companion button in the Options Bar use the image's print dimensions to simulate print size onscreen. Because the monitor resolution is a determining factor, consider this command to be a relative zoom factor. With experience, you can use it to compare other images viewed on the same monitor at the same resolution.

■ **Keyboard Shortcuts**—The (Command) [Ctrl] key used with the plus (+) and minus (-) keys zooms you in and out. Use the (Command) [Ctrl] key with the number zero to zoom to Fit On Screen, and add the (Option) [Alt] key for Actual Pixels.

Hold down Shift when you press (Return) [Enter], and the zoom field remains highlighted so that you can quickly type another zoom factor. This is a great way to zoom in and back out in just a few keystrokes.

The amount of monitor that Fit On Screen uses depends on the Ignore Palettes option in the Options Bar (Zoom tool). When this check box is selected, the image window extends to the right edge of the monitor. When it's not selected, the window expands only to the edge of palettes docked to the right edge. (The window does not expand under the Toolbox or the Options Bar when they are docked.)

Caution

Do not base any layout decisions on an image viewed by using Print Size. You cannot hold a ruler to the screen to determine the size at which the image will output on paper.

Navigating While Zoomed In

When zoomed in, Photoshop's Hand tool can be used to reposition an image in the window. Click and drag to shift the visible part of the image. You can access the Hand tool at almost any time by holding down the spacebar. (The notable exception is when the Type tool is being used to enter text. The spacebar then, of course, types spaces.)

The Navigator palette displays the part of the image that's visible in the image window. A red rectangle indicates what you see onscreen. You can drag that rectangle around in the Proxy Preview to reposition it, changing the view in the window (see Figure 2.18). Click at any point in the Proxy Preview to jump to that part of the image onscreen.

In addition, when Photoshop is in Standard Screen Mode, you can navigate around the image by using the scrollbars at the right and bottom edges of the image window. If one or both scrollbars are not available, the image fits within the dimension of the window. Remember that when Photoshop is in Full Screen Mode (with or without the menu bar), there are no window scrollbars.

Several commands under the Window menu also affect your view. The Window menu is discussed earlier in this chapter, in the section "The New Window Menu."

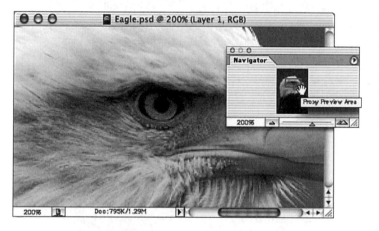

Figure 2.18
The cursor automatically changes to the Hand icon to allow you to drag the red rectangle. Away from the rectangle, the icon changes to indicate that you can click to jump to a different area of the image.

KEYBOARD SHORTCUTS

Keyboard shortcuts, those preprogrammed combinations of keystrokes that replace mouse clicks and menu commands, have been thoroughly integrated into Photoshop. There are literally hundreds of key combinations that perform various tasks. A tremendous number of tasks, from changing tools in the Toolbox to changing a tool's blending mode to adding a new layer to an image, can be done by using the keyboard. They can, of course, be done other ways, too, but the keystrokes are often handiest.

Palette Shortcuts

Keyboard shortcuts have been assigned to show and hide several of the palettes. These shortcuts toggle the visibility of the palettes (and any palettes nested or docked with them). The two primary keyboard shortcuts are Tab to show and hide all palettes and Shift-Tab to show/hide all but the Toolbox and Options Bar.

Table 2.1 shows some of the other shortcuts for use with Photoshop's palettes.

Note that palettes hidden by clicking the window's close button or by using the Window menu are not shown and hidden with the Tab key. This allows you to create custom arrangements of only those palettes you need for use with the Tab key.

Table 2.1   Keyboard Shortcuts for Palettes in Photoshop and ImageReady

Palette	Action	Mac Shortcut	Windows Shortcut
Actions	Show/hide	F9	F9
Animation	Show/hide (ImageReady)	F11	F11
Animation	New frame	Shift-Command-Opt-F	Shift+Ctrl+Alt+F
Brushes	Show/hide (Photoshop)	F5	F5
Character	Show/hide	Command-T (while entering text)	Ctrl+T (while entering text)
Color	Show/hide	F6	F6
Color	Set background color	Option-click	Alt+click color ramp
Color	Change color ramp	Shift-click color ramp	Shift+click color ramp
History	Move backward in history	Command-Option-Z	Ctrl+Alt+Z
History	Move forward in history	Shift-Command-Opt-Z	Shift+Ctrl+Alt+Z
Info	Show/hide	F8	F8
Info	Change color readout	Click eyedropper icon	Click eyedropper icon
Info	Change unit of measure	Click crosshair icon	Click crosshair icon
Layers	Show/hide	F7	F7
Layers	Move layer down	Command-Option-[	Ctrl+Alt+[
Layers	Move layer up	Command-Option-]	Ctrl+Alt+]
Layers	New layer with dialog box	Shift-Command-N	Shift+Ctrl+N
Layers	New layer, no dialog box	Shift-Command-Option-N	Shift+Ctrl+Alt+N
Layers	New layer via copy	Command-J	Ctrl+J
Layers	New layer via cut	Shift-Command-J	Shift+Ctrl+J
Optimize	Show/hide (ImageReady)	F10	F10
Swatches	Select foreground color	Click swatch	Click swatch
Swatches	Delete swatch	Option-click swatch	Alt+click swatch
Swatches	Select background color	Command-click swatch	Ctrl+click swatch

Selecting Tools with Keyboard Shortcuts

Instead of mousing to the Toolbox, you can select any of Photoshop's most commonly used tools with a single keystroke. In most cases, if tools share a flyout palette, they share a shortcut, and you can change between them by adding Shift to the shortcut key. (Note that there are no keyboard shortcuts for the Add Anchor Point, Delete Anchor Point, and Convert Point tools.) Other than using the Shift key with grouped tools, no modifiers are required—simply press the single letter indicated in Table 2.2 (unless, of course, you are entering text with the Type tool).

You can return the palettes to their default locations at any time by using the command Window, Workspace, Reset Palette Locations.

Table 2.2 Keystrokes to Select Tools

Tool	Shortcut
Rectangular Marquee	M
Elliptical Marquee	M
Alternate Marquee tools	Shift-M
Move	V
Lasso	L
Polygon Lasso	L
Magnetic Lasso	L
Rotate Lasso tools	Shift-L
Magic Wand	W
Crop	C
Slice	K
Slice Select	K
Alternate Slice tools	Shift-K
Healing Brush	J
Patch	J
Alternate Healing Brush and Patch tool	Shift-J
Brush	B
Pencil	B
Alternate Brush and Pencil	Shift-B
Clone Stamp	S
Pattern Stamp	S
Alternate Stamp tools	Shift-S
History Brush	Y
Art History Brush	Y
Alternate History brushes	Shift-Y
Eraser	E
Background Eraser	E
Magic Eraser	E
Rotate Eraser tools	Shift-E
Gradient	G
Paint Bucket	G
Alternate between Gradient and Paint Bucket	Shift-G

2

Table 2.2 Continued

Tool	Shortcut
Blur	R
Sharpen	R
Smudge	R
Rotate Focus tools	Shift-R
Dodge	O
Burn	O
Sponge	O
Rotate Toning tools	Shift-O
Path Selection	A
Direct Selection	A
Alternate Selection tools	Shift-A
Horizontal Type	T
Vertical Type	T
Horizontal Mask Type	T
Vertical Mask Type	T
Rotate Type tools	Shift-T
Pen	P
Freeform Pen	P
Alternate Pen and Freeform Pen	Shift-P
Each of the Shape tools	U or Shift-U
Notes	N
Audio Annotation	N
Alternate Notes and Audio Annotation	Shift-N
Eyedropper	I
Color Sampler	I
Measure	I
Rotate Eyedropper, Color Sampler, and Measure	Shift-I
Hand	H
Zoom	Z

There are a few other keyboard shortcuts, shown in Table 2.3, that pertain to the lower section of Photoshop's Toolbox.

Table 2.3 Additional Toolbox Shortcuts

Tool	Mac Shortcut	Windows Shortcut
Restore the default foreground (black) and background (white) colors	D	D
Swap the foreground and background colors (regardless of color)	X	X
Enter Quick Mask mode	Q	Q
Exit Quick Mask mode	Q	Q
Rotate Standard Screen Mode, Full Screen Mode with Menu Bar, and Full Screen Mode	F	F
Jump to and from ImageReady	Shift-Command-M	Shift+Ctrl+M

PHOTOSHOP IN FOCUS

Among the most powerful of Photoshop's new features is the capability to save tools with specific options. The Tool Presets, in fact, may soon rank with Layers and the History palette as "indispensable." Get a head start on Tool Presets by preparing the Type tool.

1. Start by looking at several of your most recent projects, and determine what type settings you're most likely to use.

2. Select the Type tool in the Toolbox.

3. In the Options Bar or Character and Paragraph palettes, set the tool to your typical settings for headline type.

4. In the Tool Presets palette menu, choose the command New Tool Preset. Save the settings as Headline Type.

5. Change the Type tool's settings to a typical body text configuration.

6. Save the preset as Body type.

7. Save additional Type tool configurations using settings that are common to your projects and recognizable names.

FROM THE NAPP HELP DESK

The National Association of Photoshop Professionals (NAPP) offers e-mail assistance to its members. Here is some advice from the NAPP Help Desk related to issues in this chapter.

2

Docking the Palettes

When I open an image in Photoshop, it's partially covered by the Options Bar. How do I prevent that?

Photoshop respects the territory of palettes that are docked to the edges of the screen. When palettes are docked, image windows won't open under them (by default). When palettes are floating free onscreen, Photoshop assumes that you want them on top of the image window.

It seems, in this case, that the Options Bar has been moved away from the upper-left corner of the screen. Grab it by the tab on the left end and drag it toward the middle of the screen. Now drag it back to the upper-left corner until it "snaps" into position. You might want to redock the Toolbox to the lower-left corner of the Options Bar, too.

The same pertains to Photoshop's other palettes. If they're docked to the right edge of the screen, image windows will not open with the palettes overlapping. If they're not docked to the edge of the screen, image windows can open beneath them. Don't forget the menu command Window, Workspace, Reset Palette Locations!

Workspace Hotkeys

There are some palettes that I want to have open all the time (Info, Navigator) and some that I need only sometimes (Color, Layers, Swatches). It's too much trouble to use the Window menu for each of the palettes, and Tab shows/hides all at once. Any suggestions?

Actually, a couple of suggestions. First, remember that some palettes have assigned keyboard shortcuts. The Layers palette, for example, can be shown and hidden with F7. That keystroke also shows and hides all palettes docked to or nested with Layers. Dock your sometimes-needed palettes to Layers (F7) or Color (F6), and use that key to show and hide them without disturbing the palettes you always want open.

Alternatively, you can set up the palettes exactly as you want, save the arrangement as a Workspace, and then record an Action to activate the Workspace. With an F-key combination assigned to the Action, you've got instant access to different workspaces.

Here's how to make it work:

1. Arrange your screen with just the Navigator and Info palettes visible.

2. Use the menu command Window, Workspace, Save Workspace. Name the new workspace "Nav-Info" or some such.

3. Arrange the screen with Navigator, Info, Layers, Color, and Swatches visible and in the appropriate locations.

4. Save this workspace as "All" or another descriptive name.

5. Open the Actions palette, and click the New Action button.

6. Name the Action "Nav-Info Workspace," and assign it an F-key combination.

7. With the Action recording, use the menu command Window, Workspace, Nav-Info.

8. Stop recording the Action.

9. Record another Action, with a different key combination, for the workspace named "All."

10. Use the assigned F-key combinations to run the Actions, which will activate the workspaces onscreen.

2

HARDWARE, SYSTEM SETUP, AND PHOTOSHOP'S PREFERENCES

IN THIS CHAPTER

PHOTOSHOP 7'S MINIMUM REQUIREMENTS

Photoshop 7 is a rather sophisticated piece of software. As such, it won't run on just any old computer. There are certain minimum requirements for both the computer's hardware and the operating system. Of course, in addition to the minimum requirements, it's good to know what you can do—both hardware and software—to make Photoshop run faster. This chapter looks at computer equipment that can make your production speedier, as well as Photoshop's Preferences and how to set them for improved efficiency.

Windows Requirements

Photoshop requires at least a Pentium III-class processor, 128MB of available RAM, a video card capable of 8-bit color (256 total colors), and a monitor capable of displaying a resolution of at least 800×600 pixels. Realistically, consider at least 192MB of RAM (128MB for Photoshop, 64MB for the operating system) and a video card with at least 16MB of on-board video memory (VRAM). In addition, you'll likely want a monitor displaying a minimum of thousands of colors with resolution set to at least 1024×768 pixels—with the minimum resolution, you'd not be able to take advantage of Photoshop's Palette Well.

In addition to the hardware requirements, the operating system must be one of the following:

- Windows XP

- Windows 2000

- Windows NT 4.0 (service pack 6a)

- Windows ME

- Windows 98 SE

- Windows 98

Note that Photoshop 7 will not run on Windows 95.

Macintosh Requirements

Adobe lists the minimum Macintosh requirements as any PowerPC G3 or G4 processor, 128MB of RAM, an 8-bit video card, and a monitor set to 800×600 pixel resolution. Photoshop also requires Mac OS 9.1 or later, or Mac OS X version 10.1 or later.

In reality, a suitable system starts with at least a G3 processor, preferably running at 350MHz or faster (Blue and White G3). With 256MB of physical RAM, both Photoshop and the operating system can fulfill their needs (although Virtual Memory would still be a good idea). The video board should have a minimum of 16MB of on-board VRAM and be capable of supporting a monitor displaying 800×600 pixels at thousands of colors. Remember that at 800×600, the Palette Well doesn't appear in the Options Bar.

IMAGE-EDITING SPEED DEMONS

If Photoshop is your business, and work is piling up, two things can make your life easier: techniques that improve your workflow and hardware that doesn't keep you waiting. Throughout this book, you'll find the former, and in this chapter, you'll find information on how various parts of your system work with Photoshop and how you can speed things up.

Dual Processor Prowess

The processor (technically, *central processing unit* or *CPU*) is the brain of the computer, the part that does the mathematical calculations on which virtually all computing is based. The faster the CPU, the sooner your work is done. Adding a second CPU to the machine can improve performance by allowing two "brains" to share the work, by simultaneously working on filters and performing other calculation-intensive processes.

Photoshop is tuned to take advantage of multiple processors in both Windows (except Windows 98, which does not recognize the second processor) and the Mac OS. Mac OS X itself is dual-processor aware, further improving performance. Most, but not all, of Photoshop's filters can take advantage of a second processor. However, the speed gains might not be noticeable except with very large files.

3

The Processor Wars

You might notice that this discussion studiously avoids the questions of Mac/Windows and Intel/AMD, and makes no mention whatsoever of specific processor speeds. Processor capabilities change with furious speed, so anything written the day this book is sent to the print shop will be outdated before copies hit the bookstore.

There are numerous resources on the Web (*some* of which are impartial and unbiased) that compare various processors and computers in both benchmark (laboratory) tests and real-world situations. Photoshop is often used in the testing because of the demands it places on a system as well as the number of high-end computers on which it runs.

A few words of advice: Ignore the megahertz (or gigahertz) rating when comparing different types of chips. A Pentium III and a Pentium 4 at similar clock speeds perform differently. A Celeron processor and an Intel processor at the same megahertz rating work differently. A Macintosh G4 at 1GHz is faster than a Pentium 4 at 1GHz. How much so depends on the tasks being performed. (Apparently, it also depends on who is doing the testing, which leads to the next point.) Be aware of the source—various manufacturers have a vested interest in making their product look good in testing. Likewise, some "independent" Web sites have links to a particular manufacturer or platform.

Among the most dependable sources of up-to-date information on Windows-compatible hardware are Tom's Hardware (www.tomshardware.com) and Upgrading and Repairing PCs (www.upgradingandrepairingpcs.com). For information on Macintosh computers, visit www.barefeats.com. You'll also find lots of information about both types of hardware at www.zdnet.com.

A number of factors other than the processor speed contribute to a computer's performance. System bus (the speed with which data moves to and from the processor), level 2 and level 3 cache (small amounts of memory immediately available to the processor), and a variety of other hardware all play their parts.

RAM Up

Often more important than processor speed is the amount of memory available to Photoshop. The CPU can process information only as fast as that data can move to and from the processor. Information that's available in the computer's memory can get to the processor far faster than information that must be read from the hard drive.

The price of RAM is extremely low. Many systems can be filled with their maximum amount of RAM for under $200. It's critical that the correct type of RAM be installed. Check the documentation that came with your computer for its specific requirements.

Like CPUs, memory comes in several different types. Which is faster, and by how much, is subject to change. Macintosh users have no choice; their computers use only one kind. When building or ordering a Windows-compatible machine, however, a decision may be necessary. Check the links mentioned earlier (see the sidebar "The Processor Wars") for current information.

Seeing the Big Picture

Monitors are available in a variety of sizes and a pair of technologies. Cathode ray tubes (CRTs) are the large, heavy, TV-looking monitors. Liquid crystal displays (LCDs) are the thin, elegant, lightweight monitors similar to those found in laptops and other portable computers. Each has advantages:

- CRTs are generally less expensive for a given monitor size.

- LCDs have more usable screen space at a given monitor size.

- Color calibration is still a young art for LCDs. However, some Apple LCDs are self-calibrating, and some hardware calibration equipment for LCDs is now available.

- LCDs are generally easier on the eyes and sharper than CRTs.

That having been said, the price of LCDs is rapidly coming down, and the technology continues to improve.

The monitor itself really doesn't have much of an impact on the speed with which Photoshop runs. Rather, it is the video card (the circuit board to which the monitor is attached) that may be a factor. Most modern monitors have multiple resolution and color depth settings available. (The monitor resolution is set through the operating system's control panels or system preferences.)

The higher the resolution, the greater the number of individual pixels that have to be *refreshed* (updated) to change the screen's appearance. The greater the *color depth* (the number of different colors an individual pixel is capable of displaying), the more information is required for each pixel. The greater these two requirements, the higher the demands on the computer's video card. There are several different *chip sets* (technologies) available. If you have a choice when ordering or designing a system, remember that Photoshop is primarily a 2D graphics program. If you also work with digital video, 3D, or games, you might want to make those requirements your priority.

Perhaps more important than the chip set is the amount of VRAM. VRAM is memory built into the video card for the purposes of speeding onscreen performance. Generally speaking, more is better.

Ensure that your chosen video card has enough VRAM to power your monitor of choice at the required resolution and color depth.

If you have multiple video cards (or a dual card), you can use multiple monitors with Photoshop. Two or more monitors can be set up to serve as one extended screen. Photoshop (and other programs) enables you to use the entire space of multiple monitors as one large work area. Multiple monitors are set up and controlled through the operating system.

Storage for Now and Later

Another factor that affects the speed at which Photoshop runs is data storage. Photoshop must write to and read from disks. The most obvious examples are opening and saving files. The speed of the hard drive is important, as is the technology linking it to the computer.

Internal Hard Drives

Internal hard drives are typically either *small computer system interface* (*SCSI*) or *advanced technology attachment* (*ATA*). Portable computers typically have ATA drives. ATA is the official name of Integrated Drive Electronics (IDE), which was developed by Western Digital and Compaq. SCSI is generally a faster interface technology, but ATA/IDE drives are considerably cheaper. Both SCSI and ATA come in different varieties, with a wide range of capabilities.

Keep in mind that not all SCSI drives are created equal. There are, give or take a few, eight varieties of SCSI available that differ in how fast they can transfer data. The original SCSI (SCSI-1) has a maximum burst speed of 1MB/sec, but the most recent SCSI implementation can reach 320MB/sec. Table 3.1 shows the maximum burst transmission speeds by SCSI type.

Table 3.1   Burst Transmission Speeds by SCSI Type

Version	Maximum Data Transfer Rate
SCSI-1	5MB/sec
SCSI-2 (Fast SCSI)	10MB/sec
Fast Wide SCSI	20MB/sec
Ultra SCSI	20MB/sec
Wide Ultra SCSI (aka Ultra Wide)	40MB/sec
Ultra-2 SCSI	80MB/sec
Ultra 160	160MB/sec
Ultra 320	320MB/sec

Likewise, there are varieties of ATA/IDE technology. Typically, you'll see ATA/33, ATA/66, or ATA/100, with the number signifying the maximum transfer rate in MB/sec.

Both SCSI and ATA can be used for other types of hardware, too, including CD and DVD drives and scanners. ATA allows only two devices per connector, but more recent versions of SCSI can link up to 15 devices.

External Hard Drives

External hard drives, drives not physically located within the computer itself, are easily added to most computer systems. In addition to SCSI, you have the option of drives using *Universal Serial Bus* (*USB*) and *FireWire* (also known as IEEE 1394). USB is also used for keyboards, mouse devices and trackballs, drawing tablets, digital cameras, scanners, printers, and more. You'll find FireWire connectors on hard drives, scanners, printers, digital still cameras, and digital camcorders. Both USB and FireWire enable devices to be connected and disconnected while the computer is running (unlike SCSI), but that's not a good idea with hard drives.

> Remember that USB and FireWire are connection technologies. The drives themselves are ATA/IDE. When shopping, check to see whether you're looking at an ATA/66 or an ATA/100 drive.

USB now comes in two varieties. USB-1 has a maximum data transfer rate of 12MB/sec, and you can attach as many as 127 devices in a single USB chain. USB-2 offers speeds up to 16MB/sec. FireWire's top speed is currently 400MB/sec. A chain of FireWire devices can include up to 63 pieces of hardware. Some portable hard drives have both USB and FireWire connectors.

RAID

When two or more hard drives are arranged in an *array* (the computer sees them as a single device), you can establish a RAID. *RAID*, which stands for redundant array of independent (or inexpensive) disks, can be used to provide increased data protection through redundancy or to speed system performance in read/write operations. There are several different types of RAID, as shown in Table 3.2.

Table 3.2   Possible RAID Configurations

Level	Description	Drives
RAID 0	Data striping, highest performance	2
RAID 1	Disk mirroring, data protection	2
RAID 0/1	Combines data striping and protection	4
RAID 5	Data striping with parity	3
RAID 0/5	Combines RAID 0 and RAID 5	6

The number of drives listed is the minimum necessary for each level of RAID. RAID 0/1 is also referred to as RAID 10; RAID 0/5 is also referred to as RAID 50.

For Photoshop, RAID Level 1 is most appropriate. It writes the identical data to two (or more) drives, providing data protection through redundancy. If one drive fails, the data is still safe (you hope) on the other RAID drive. RAID Level 0 is more appropriate for digital video and other applications in which it's necessary to record huge amounts of data as quickly as possible. It works by using the arrayed drives as a single drive, spreading the data among them. Because the data is being written to two (or more) drives simultaneously, it can be recorded almost twice as fast. It's rare to need this type of hard drive performance in Photoshop, but there might be some workplaces for which it is appropriate.

Recordable Media

Hard drives can be reserved for data that is used often. The operating system and your programs need to be on the hard drive(s). Files with which you're working should be on the local hard drive. However, there's no need to clutter your hard drive with archives of files. Older files can be recorded to recordable media, such as CD-R, CD-RW, DVD-R, Zip, Jaz, optical disks, tape drives, and, in some cases, even floppy disks.

The advantages of storing files on removable media include security, data protection, and convenience. The files can be kept safe and secure by storing them in an appropriate container and/or location. Labeling the media makes it easier to locate a specific file. In addition, your hard drive is less cluttered, making it simpler to find and work with current files.

The various types of media have their advantages (prices noted are, as always, subject to change):

- **3.5-inch Floppy Disks**—Floppies are virtually free these days. Ask a few friends and colleagues, and you might find yourself buried in old, reusable floppy disks. There is a reason for that, however. Floppies hold only about 1.3MB of data, are slow, and are not particularly reliable. Floppy drives are no longer standard on all computers, and Apple Computer no longer offers them at all. (There are, however, many third-party floppy drives available.)

- **Zip Disks**—Iomega is the manufacturer of both Zip and Jaz drives. Zip drives come in 100MB and 250MB varieties. The larger drives can read both types of disks, but the older drives work only with the 100MB disks. Basically oversized floppies, these drives are not fast. The 100MB disks cost $9–$10 each, and 250MB disks generally retail for $14–$15 each.

- **Jaz Disks**—Jaz drives and disks come in 1GB and 2GB varieties. The large amount of storage space is offset to some degree by a huge price tag. In addition to the cost of the drives, the media are very expensive. The 1GB disks cost about $80 each, with 2GB disks available for about $100 each.

- **CD-R**—These disks are write once/read forever. Once you record (or *burn*) a CD-R, the disk is permanently recorded. Recordable CDs hold about 650MB or 700MB each and can be purchased for as little as $0.25 each in bulk (without jewel cases or paper sleeves). Although recording is often slow, the disks can be read very quickly.

- **CD-RW**—The RW stands for "rewritable," meaning that you can record these disks over and over. You can write once and later add more info to the disk, or you can erase it and start over. CD-RW disks generally must be recorded and read at slower speeds than CD-Rs. They are also more expensive, costing between $1.25 and $2.00 each (with cases).

- **DVD-R**—Holding 4.7GB of data, these disks are the larger kid brother of CD-Rs. Like CD-Rs, DVD-Rs can be recorded only once. They can be purchased for $6–$10 each.

- **DVD-RAM**—As DVD-R is to CD-R, so DVD-RAM is to CD-RW. Think of them as a *very* large brother—double-sided DVD-RAM disks can hold as much as 9.4GB of information. (Single-sided DVD-RAMs hold 4.7GB.) Expect to pay $15 for one-sided and $35 for two-sided disks.

Tape back-up systems can also be used to store files, as can magnetic-optical (MO) drives.

> ### Caution
> If you're recording files to CD for archival purposes, don't buy discount media. The low-cost disks can be much less reliable. This is especially true if the CD will hold the only copy of an important file.

Dedicated Scratch Disks

Another way that hard drives affect Photoshop's performance is when serving as *scratch disks*, which are hard drive space set aside for Photoshop to support the memory. When Photoshop is idle, it copies the contents of the allocated memory to the scratch disks. In some cases, Photoshop has to handle more information than can fit into memory. The program then uses the scratch disk space as though it were additional memory.

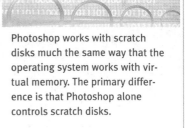

Photoshop works with scratch disks much the same way that the operating system works with virtual memory. The primary difference is that Photoshop alone controls scratch disks.

Scratch disks can be assigned by using Photoshop's Preferences (see Figure 3.1). By default, the startup drive is used as the scratch disk, although up to four drives can be assigned. Theoretically, there is no limit on the amount of scratch disk space. Photoshop accesses the drives in the order assigned.

Figure 3.1

If there is more than one hard drive or partition on the computer, use Preferences, Plug-Ins & Scratch Disks to assign scratch disks.

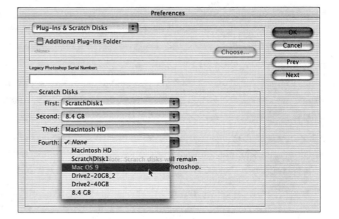

It's important that the amount of available scratch disk space be at least equal to the amount of memory allocated to Photoshop. If 512MB of RAM is available to the program, but only 50MB of free space on the scratch disk(s), Photoshop uses only 50MB of RAM.

For optimum performance, add a small, fast hard drive to your system and use it exclusively for Photoshop's scratch disk. The disk need be only somewhat larger than the memory allocated to Photoshop. (A 2GB drive should be adequate.) By dedicating a drive to scratch space, you ensure that there's never a delay in reading from or writing to the drive.

Here are some additional guidelines for Photoshop's scratch disks:

- If multiple hard drives are available, put Photoshop's primary scratch disk on a drive other than Startup. (That's the drive used by the operating system to support the memory. It's best if the OS and Photoshop are not trying to read/write at the same time to the same drive.)

- If there's only one physical drive, but it has multiple partitions, keep the scratch disk on Startup. (You don't want the OS and Photoshop trying to write to separate areas of the same drive at the same time.)

- If there are multiple drives available other than Startup, use the fastest drive as the first scratch disk.

- It's a very good idea to defragment drives used as scratch disk space. That eliminates the slowdowns caused by the drive jumping from place to place to find an area in which it can write.

> **Caution**
>
> Never use removable media or network drives for Photoshop's scratch disks. Using such drives can lead not only to slowdowns, but also to program failures.

SETTING PHOTOSHOP'S PREFERENCES

Much of how Photoshop looks and acts depends on a file called Adobe Photoshop 7.0 Prefs. This file contains such information as how you last arranged the palettes, the dimensions and color mode of the most recent new document, what style of cursors you prefer, and how you like to name files when saving.

> The preferences are updated and the file rewritten every time you quit Photoshop. Because this file is rewritten so often, it is subject to corruption. Fixing problems that stem from a bad Prefs file is discussed later in this chapter in the section "Photoshop Quick Fix—Replacing the Preferences."

Photoshop organizes the preferences in eight groups, each of which is displayed and changed in a separate pane of the Preferences dialog box. Windows and Mac OS 9 users can open the Preferences by using the menu command Edit, Preferences. Mac OS X users will find Preferences under the Photoshop menu. The first pane of the dialog box, General, can be opened with the keyboard shortcut (Command-K) [Ctrl+K]. You can move among the eight panes by using the Next and Prev buttons, which appear in all eight panes.

Preferences, General

The General preferences include a variety of settings that affect the way Photoshop operates. The General preferences are shown with their default settings in Figure 3.2.

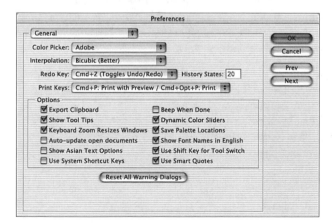

Figure 3.2
In Windows, the preference Keyboard Zoom Resizes Window is off by default; in Macintosh, it is on. The Windows Preferences also lack the Use System Shortcut Keys check box.

Here are the options available in the General preferences:

- **Color Picker**—You have the choice of using Adobe's Color Picker, the Photoshop standard, or the color picker supplied by your operating system.

▷ *For full information on the color pickers, including the Windows and Macintosh system color pickers,* **see** *"Working with Color Pickers," p. 209 in Chapter 8, "Defining and Choosing Colors."*

- **Interpolation**—When you transform a selection, Photoshop must add or subtract pixels to make the new size conform to the image's resolution. *Bicubic* interpolation looks at a range of surrounding pixel color values to determine what color to make new pixels. This option produces the highest quality for photographic and continuous tone images. *Bilinear* interpolation compares the adjacent pixels. It is faster than bicubic, but generally produces less satisfactory results. *Nearest Neighbor* interpolation is the fastest of the three, but should be avoided for photographic images. On the other hand, the Nearest Neighbor option is most appropriate for images that have large areas of solid color, especially in linear and rectangular shapes.

- **Redo Key**—Photoshop gives you the option of assigning a key for the menu command Edit, Redo (the opposite of Undo). After the Undo command or keystroke has been invoked, you can reverse that action by using Redo. The default, (Command-Z) [Ctrl+Z], is the same shortcut assigned to Undo. The shortcut, therefore, toggles between Undo and Redo. In effect, this is the same as clicking alternately on the two most recent states in the History palette. If the shortcut is assigned to either of the other choices, (Command-Shift-Z) [Ctrl+Shift+Z] or (Command-Y) [Ctrl+Y], the Undo and Redo shortcuts can be used to go backward and forward through all the available history states.

- **History States**—The history states, available through the Undo/Redo commands and the History palette, are saved in the memory allocated to Photoshop. Having more history states gives you increased flexibility and more "Undo's," and having fewer frees up memory for other Photoshop tasks.

- **Print Keys**—Print with Preview, comparable to Photoshop 6's Print Options dialog box, opens by default when you use the shortcut (Command-P) [Ctrl+P]. You can bypass this dialog box and go directly to your printer's Print dialog box by using the shortcut (Command-Option-P) [Ctrl+Alt+P]. This preference gives you the option of reversing that behavior so that (Command-P) [Ctrl+P] bypasses Print with Preview.

- **Export Clipboard**—If you'll need to use something you copied from Photoshop in another program after exiting Photoshop, leave this option selected. If you deselect it, the contents of the Clipboard will not be saved upon quitting Photoshop (and Photoshop will shut down somewhat faster.) This option has no effect on Photoshop while it is running.

- **Show Tool Tips**—When on, Tool Tips show you the name of any tool or button—simply leave the cursor over the tool icon or button for a second or two. If you find these little reminders annoying, deselect the option.

Changing the default Redo key changes the Step Forward and Step Backward shortcuts in the Edit menu. If you accept the default, you can still move forward and back through all history states by adding the Shift and (Option) [Alt] keys to the Undo shortcut (Command-Z) [Ctrl+Z].

- **Keyboard Zoom Resizes Windows**—When selected, zooming with keyboard shortcuts resizes the image window. If you use the keyboard to zoom out, the image window shrinks. If you zoom in, the window expands (to a maximum of the space available onscreen). The window resizes so that the image fills it.

- **Auto-Update Open Documents**—If a document that is open in Photoshop is also open in another program and a change is made there, this option allows the Photoshop version to be updated. When it is deselected, changes are not seen in Photoshop until the image is closed and reopened.

- **Show Asian Text Options**—This check box controls whether the options for Chinese, Japanese, and Korean (CJK) text are visible in the Character and Paragraph palettes. Figure 3.3 shows the difference. If you don't work with CJK fonts, there's no need to show these options.

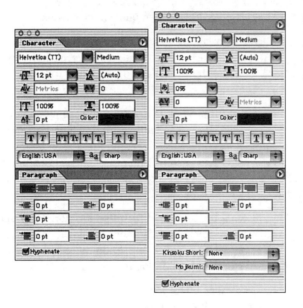

Figure 3.3
On the left, the palettes without the Asian options. On the right, the same palettes with the options visible.

3

- **Use System Shortcut Keys (Mac Only)**—When selected, this option overrides Photoshop's keyboard shortcuts when there's a conflict with the operating system's shortcuts. For example, if the Mac is set to use the F-keys, this option forces Photoshop to recognize the system's commands rather than the program's commands. In Mac OS X, the system's keyboard shortcuts are controlled through the System Prefs, Keyboard pane. Mac OS 9 uses the Keyboard control panel. (Windows also has a control panel named Keyboard, but the individual F-keys are not programmable through it.)

- **Beep When Done**—Photoshop can be set to give an audible announcement when it finishes a task. If Photoshop runs slowly on your system or if you work with extremely large files, this option may be of use (especially if you do other things while waiting for Photoshop). If the program runs quickly and efficiently, however, the beeps might be an annoyance.

■ **Dynamic Color Sliders**—This option allows the color bars above the sliders in the Color palette to be updated as you drag. Without this option, the color bars retain their basic color, no matter how the sliders are arranged. Dynamic sliders, the default, enable you to see how changes to a component color will affect the overall color.

■ **Save Palette Locations**—When this option is selected, Photoshop writes the location and visibility of each palette to the Prefs file, which is updated every time you quit Photoshop. With this option selected, the palettes will be restored to their most recently recorded positions at Photoshop's next startup. When the option's not selected, the palettes automatically return to their default locations when Photoshop is reopened.

> With Photoshop's capability to save workspaces (Window, Workspace, Save Workspace), the Save Palette Locations option is not nearly as important as it once was. You can record multiple sets of palette locations and easily switch between them.

■ **Show Font Names in English**—If you use non-Roman fonts, this option shows their name in English in the Font menu. If it's not selected, such fonts are listed only with their actual names. This preference is designed for use with the Chinese, Japanese, and Korean versions of Photoshop.

■ **Use Shift Key for Tool Switch**—When this option is active, you can rotate among tools that share a keyboard shortcut by holding down the Shift key and typing the assigned letter shortcut. When inactive, the Shift key is not required. For example, to change from the Lasso tool to the Magnetic Lasso tool by default requires pressing Shift+L twice. (The first keypress changes from the Lasso to the Polygon Lasso, and the second to the Magnetic Lasso.) With this preference box deselected, you need only press L twice.

■ **Use Smart Quotes**—Smart quotes is the term used for quotation marks that differ at the beginning and end of the quoted material, pointing inward toward the quote (see Figure 3.4). You'll also find the term *curly quotes* used to describe them. When this option is not selected, Photoshop uses the same character for the quotation marks in both locations.

■ **Reset All Warning Dialogs**—Photoshop offers you the opportunity to skip certain warning dialog boxes (see Figure 3.5). If you select the Don't Show Again check box in a warning, you don't have to see it again. However, you also don't get the reminder that you're making a substantial change, one that could affect your ability to edit or make changes to the image later. Clicking this button in the General preferences resets all warnings. If you share a computer or are using Photoshop on a particular computer for the first time, resetting the warnings is a good idea.

> You can manually add curly quotes, even when Smart Quotes is not selected in the Preferences dialog box. The keyboard shortcuts (for most fonts) are (Option-[) [Alt+[] and (Shift-Option-[) [Shift+Alt+[]. When Smart Quotes is active, straight quotes are not available.

"Smart Quotes"
"Smart Quotes"
"Smart Quotes"

"Dumb Quotes"
"Dumb Quotes"
"Dumb Quotes"

Figure 3.4
Changing the Smart Quotes preference does not affect type that has already been set.

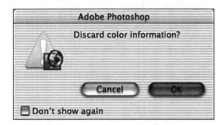

Figure 3.5
These are a couple of the warning messages that Photoshop allows you to turn off.

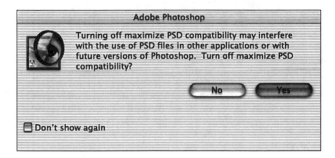

Preferences, File Handling

Because of differences in the way that Windows and Macintosh handle previews, Photoshop offers several more options on the Mac for saving files (see Figure 3.6).

Although the Image Preview options differ, the bottom portion of the File Handling pane is the same for Macintosh and Windows:

■ **Image Previews**—Windows users have the option of always saving previews, never saving previews, or making the decision at the time the image is saved (Ask When Saving). The difference is simply a check box in the Save dialog box. The Thumbnail check box will be deselected and grayed out (Never Save), selected and grayed out (Always Save), or available for you to select or deselect (Ask When Saving).

Figure 3.6
The upper portion of the Windows version of this pane has only the Image Previews pop-up menu and a choice of lowercase or uppercase letters for the file extension.

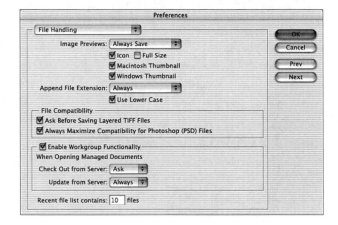

Macintosh users, on the other hand, have a variety of options and choices available in the Preferences (see Figure 3.7).

Figure 3.7
In addition to Always, Never, and Ask When Saving, Macintosh allows a choice of previews.

■ **File Extension (Append File Extension)**—This option also differs in Windows and Macintosh. Windows users have the option of including the file extension in lowercase or uppercase (but it must always be included). Macintosh users can choose among Always, Never, and Ask When Saving, and if the extension is added, have the option of lowercase or uppercase. For maximum file compatibility, append the file extension in lowercase.

■ **Ask Before Saving Layered TIFF Files**—The so-called Enhanced TIFF format (also known as Advanced TIFF) supports layers as well as annotations and transparency. If a layered TIFF file is open in a program that doesn't support Enhanced TIFF, a flattened version is used.

■ **Always Maximize Compatibility for Photoshop (PSD) Files**—When saving a file with maximum compatibility, a full-size, full-resolution flattened version is saved along with the actual Photoshop (.psd) file. The flattened version ensures that other programs that can use the Photoshop format show the image properly.

> **At this time, only Photoshop takes** advantage of the TIFF standard's more sophisticated capabilities. For that reason, there is little use for this option. If layers are important, save the file as .psd (Photoshop's native format) and skip layered TIFF.

Image Previews

Full-sized previews are used by some page layout programs. The Macintosh and Windows previews are used in the Open dialog boxes (and sometimes elsewhere). Many programs can generate previews from the image file itself, depending on file format, instead of relying on the presence of an embedded preview.

The embedded previews can have an effect on the size of a file. Using the file Eagle.psd from the Photoshop 7 Samples folder, the information in Table 3.3 was generated. (File size is listed in bytes.)

Table 3.3 Sample File Sizes

Icon	Full Size	Mac Thumbnail	Win Thumbnail	File Size
O	O	O	O	1,622,000
X	O	O	O	1,663,786
O	X	O	O	1,714,744
O	O	X	O	1,669,504
O	O	O	X	1,665,386
X	X	O	O	1,716,072
X	O	X	O	1,670,824
X	O	O	X	1,668,250
O	X	X	O	1,721,854
O	X	O	X	1,718,124
O	O	X	X	1,675,304
X	O	X	X	1,676,630
O	X	X	X	1,722,626
X	X	X	X	1,728,948

The difference between no previews and all optional previews is some 100KB in this instance. Keep in mind, however, that the size and complexity of the original image play a large part in how much the file size increases. The artwork for a simple Web button, 64×16 pixels, was saved without previews and with all previews. The file size increased from 35,556 bytes to 42,920 bytes.

Although embedded previews can increase a file's size, such factors as the file's format, compression (if any), and even the formatting of the disk can play far more important roles in file size.

- **Enable Workgroup Functionality**—Workgroup functionality is designed for use with a WebDAV server. Images stored on the server can be "checked out" (opened) by any member of a team working on a project. With workgroup management, you reduce the risk of different people trying to make conflicting changes to a single image. Like a book from the library, a second person can't check out a file until it's been checked back in by the first person. Deselecting this option in the File Handling preferences grays out the submenu command File, Workgroup.

- **Check Out from Server**—The options Always, Never, and Ask pertain to opening a managed document. If you will not be working on the document (opening only to look, for example), you need not check it out. When the document is checked out, no other member of the team can make changes to it.

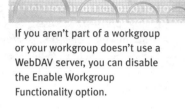

If you aren't part of a workgroup or your workgroup doesn't use a WebDAV server, you can disable the Enable Workgroup Functionality option.

- **Update from Server**—When opening a managed document, select this option to have Photoshop check the server to see whether the image requires updating.

- **Recent file list contains __ files**—You can specify a number from 0 to 30 for this list. The files can be opened by selecting them from the menu File, Open Recent. Tracking recent documents allows you to quickly locate and reopen an image on which you recently worked. However, making the list too long can reduce its usability.

Preferences, Display & Cursors

The options in this pane of Photoshop's Preferences are identical for Windows and Macintosh. They are shown in Figure 3.8.

Figure 3.8
All tools that use brushes are considered painting tools for the purposes of this dialog box.

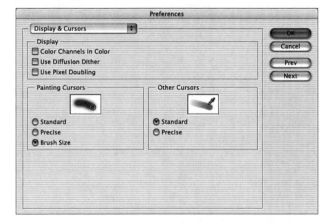

The choices you make in this pane can have a major impact on your interaction with Photoshop:

- **Color Channels in Color**—When this option is selected, Photoshop shows each of the color channels in its own color, rather than as a grayscale image. Although this display option can ensure that the correct channel is being edited, particularly with RGB images, the lack of contrast in yellow and cyan channels could be a problem. Showing color channels in color is often effective when multiple (but not all) channels are visible. The option includes spot channels but has no effect on alpha channels.

- **Use Diffusion Dither**—For use only with monitors showing 8-bit color (a total of 256 colors), diffusion dither allows Photoshop to simulate a higher color depth.

- **Use Pixel Doubling**—When dragging selected pixels onscreen, pixel doubling can speed screen redraw. By reducing the selection's resolution, this option reduces the amount of data required to refresh the screen. It can be of use with high-resolution images on low-power systems.

- **Painting Cursors**—Photoshop allows you to show the cursors for the painting tools in one of three ways: Standard, Precise, or Brush Size. Standard cursors show the tool's icon, which could be useful if you often change tools by using the keyboard shortcuts. Precise cursors use a crosshair to indicate the center of the tool's brush. Brush Size shows a circle the diameter of the selected brush for that tool.

    When a hard round brush is selected, the Brush Size option shows the cursor as a circle; the painting tool can affect pixels within that area. When a feathered (soft) brush is active, the affected area extends some distance beyond the circular cursor.

The Caps Lock key switches between Precise and Brush Size cursors. When either option is active, pressing Caps Lock swaps to the other. When Standard is selected, pressing Caps Lock switches between the tool icon and Precise cursors.

If keeping track of which tool is in use is critical, remember that the Status Bar can be set to Current Tool, leaving you free to use Precise (or Brush Size) for your cursors.

Remember, too, that non-circular cursors are included. When Brush Size is selected, you'll also see the cursor as irregularly shaped brushes.

- **Other Cursors**—Like the painting tool cursors, Photoshop's other tools can show the tool's icon or a crosshair. (Because non-painting tools don't use brushes, the third option—Brush Size—is not available.) The Caps Lock key toggles between the Standard and Precise options.

Preferences, Transparency & Gamut

Think of transparency as being able to see through a layer to the layer(s) below. When an area of an image has no opaque pixels on any layer, you see through to the next layer. That's where the transparency grid comes into play. Photoshop arranges a pattern of squares below an image to indicate where there is nothing opaque in an image. The transparency grid is nonprinting and does not appear in any final artwork. With reduced opacity (partial transparency), the grid is partially visible. You can set both size and color for the grid (see Figure 3.9).

The transparency grid can be customized to make it most appropriate for the image with which you're working:

- **Grid Size**—The options are Small, Medium, Large, and None, which turns off the transparency grid.

- **Grid Colors**—The pop-up menu offers grids of light gray/white, medium gray/light gray, and dark gray/medium gray. If gray interferes with your work—for example, when working on a grayscale image—you can also choose grids of white with one of five other colors. In addition, you can use the Color Picker to select the two grid colors; simply click on the swatches to open the Color Picker.

Figure 3.9
The default values, shown here, are the same for Macintosh and Windows.

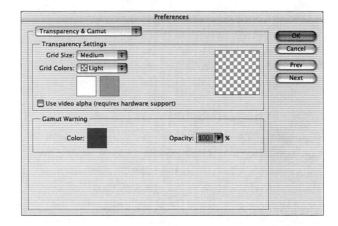

When this pane of the Preferences dialog box is open, you can also change the colors of the transparency grid by clicking and (Option-clicking) [Alt+clicking] in any open image. Click to change the first transparency color, and then (Option-click) [Alt-click] to change the second transparency color. Remember that the change affects all images, not just the one(s) in which you click.

⇨ *Transparency grid not visible? See "Transparency and Background Layers" in the NAPP Help Desk section at the end of this chapter.*

■ **Use Video Alpha (Requires Hardware Support)**—If your computer includes a video board that supports chroma-key, such hardware allows the video board to overlay an image from Photoshop onto a live video signal.

■ **Gamut Warning**—Click on the color swatch to choose a color; drag the slider or type a percentage to set the opacity. The gamut warning is used to identify colors in an image that cannot be reproduced in the selected CMYK gamut. To toggle this option, use the menu command View, Gamut Warning.

Although gray transparency grids are the least likely to interfere with color perception, it can sometimes be difficult to judge partial opacity with them. In those situations, a colored grid may make more sense.

If you have two prominent colors in an image, you can maximize the transparency grid's contrast like this: (Command-I) [Ctrl+I] to invert the image's colors. Open the Transparency & Gamut Preferences. Click and then (Option-click) [Alt+click] to set the grid colors, and then click OK. Press (Command-I) [Ctrl+I] again. The resulting transparency grid will have extreme contrast with your image's principle colors.

Preferences, Units & Rulers

This pane of the Preferences dialog box (see Figure 3.10) governs the units of measure used generally throughout Photoshop and for type.

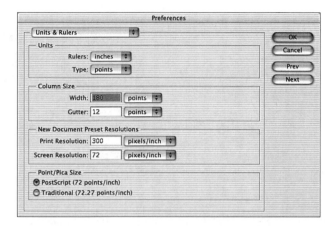

Figure 3.10
The default values of the Units &
Rulers pane are all print-oriented.

In addition, there are several settings that affect the dimensions of new documents:

- **Rulers**—In addition to Photoshop's rulers, this setting governs most units of measure, from dialog boxes to palettes to the Options Bar. The available units are pixels, inches, centimeters, millimeters, points, picas, and percent. (When percent is selected for rulers, absolute dimensions, such as those required when creating a new document, use inches.) You can also change this setting without opening the Preferences. (Control-click) [Right+click] on the ruler in any image, and select the new unit of measure from the pop-up list.

- **Type**—Type in Photoshop is governed separately from other units of measure. Type can be measured in points, pixels, or millimeters. Points are the standard unit of measure for type in print.

- **Column Size**—Photoshop's New dialog box allows you to specify the dimensions of a new document. One of the options is Columns (see Figure 3.11), which uses the width established in this setting.

  Columns can be used effectively when preparing an image to be placed into a multi-column page layout. The New dialog box calculates the width of such a document by multiplying the specified number of columns by this Width value and adding the amount specified by the Gutter value between the columns.

- **New Document Preset Resolutions**—Photoshop's New dialog box offers 19 preset sizes (see Figure 3.12). Some are designed for print, and some for Web or video. This pair of preferences allows you to specify which resolution is associated with each of the presets. It is simply a convenience—the resolutions can still be changed in the New dialog box.

- **Point/Pica Size**—With the advent of PostScript, the traditional measurement of a point was rounded down to 1/72 of an inch. In some press environments, it's important to maintain the conventional measurement by changing this preference to the Traditional option.

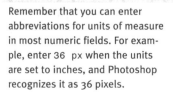

Remember that you can enter abbreviations for units of measure in most numeric fields. For example, enter 36 px when the units are set to inches, and Photoshop recognizes it as 36 pixels.

Figure 3.11
The width of a column is determined in the Units & Rulers Preferences.

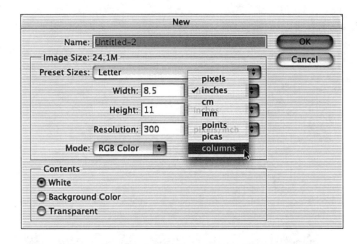

Figure 3.12
The Screen Resolution setting includes Web, DVD, and video presets.

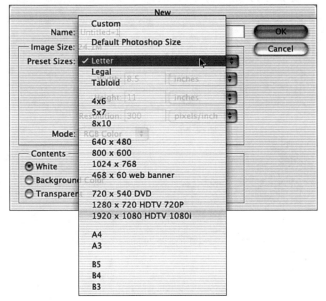

Preferences, Guides, Grid & Slices

In addition to setting the style and color for guides and grids, Photoshop now allows you to specify slice color globally. These preferences (see Figure 3.13) affect only the onscreen appearance; guides, grid, and slice lines are nonprinting. All three can be shown and hidden through the View menu.

The default values might not be appropriate for the images with which you work. These settings allow you to choose colors that may be more visible or perhaps less distracting:

- **Guides**—A pop-up menu offers nine preset color values, or you can choose Custom. You can also open the Color Picker by clicking on the swatch to the right. The Style menu allows you to set guides as lines or dashed lines.

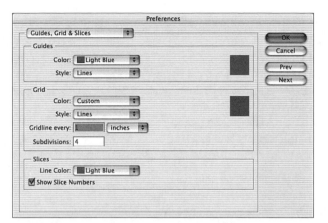

Figure 3.13
Photoshop's defaults show both guides and slice lines as Light Blue. You can customize one or the other (or both) to avoid visual confusion.

- **Grid**—The grid can also be set to one of nine presets or to a custom color. In addition to lines and dashed lines, the grid can be shown as a series of dots. This pane of the Preferences dialog box also enables you to specify the grid's spacing. Both major units and subunits can be entered, using any of Photoshop's units of measure. The gridlines are thicker than the subdivisions to differentiate between them onscreen.

- **Slices**—Used to define subdivisions of Web graphics, slices can be shown in one of the nine preset colors. You also have the option of hiding slice numbers while leaving the slice lines visible.

Preferences, Plug-Ins & Scratch Disks

Plug-ins are supplements to Photoshop's capabilities that you can run from within the program. Scratch disks are hard drive space used by Photoshop to supplement the allocated memory. This pane of the Preferences dialog box (see Figure 3.14) allows you to regulate what folders Photoshop uses for plug-ins and what hard drives are used for scratch disks.

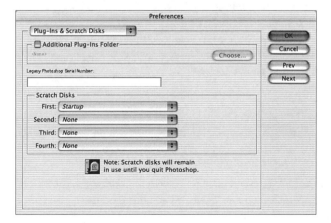

Figure 3.14
If you want Photoshop to load only the default plug-ins folder, leave the upper check box deselected. If you have only one hard drive, Startup is the appropriate scratch disk choice.

You can have several folders for plug-ins, but only one additional folder can be used at a time.

- **Additional Plug-Ins Folder/Directory**—If desired, you can have Photoshop load plug-ins from a second source when the program starts. (Macintosh uses "folder," and Windows uses "directory.") Click the check box, click the Choose button, and then navigate to the target folder. Select the folder in the window, and click the (Choose) [OK] button.

- **Legacy Photoshop Serial Number**—Some plug-ins require a valid Photoshop serial number. Older plug-ins won't recognize Photoshop 7's serial number. If you're loading plug-ins that need a previous version of Photoshop's old-style serial number, enter that number in this field.

- **Scratch Disks**—Scratch disks are hard drive space that Photoshop uses much as you might use a scratch pad—someplace to scribble and keep track of things. The assigned scratch disk or disks are used to support Photoshop's memory. If there's more data than Photoshop can hold in memory, it writes some to the disk for later retrieval. When things are slow, Photoshop can write the entire contents of memory to the scratch disks.

⇨ *For more information on scratch disks, see "Dedicated Scratch Disks," p. 76.*

You can assign up to four different disks and partitions as scratch disks. When multiple hard drives are available, you might see an increase in performance if the primary scratch disk is other than the startup disk. (Windows and Macintosh both use the startup disk to support memory. When the OS and Photoshop are both trying to write to the same disk, slowdowns are possible.) All available drives appear in each of the four pop-up menus.

Changes to the scratch disk preferences don't take effect until the next time Photoshop is started. To save time, you can change them *while* starting Photoshop. Hold down the (Option-Command) [Alt+Ctrl] keys during Photoshop startup to select scratch disks.

Caution

Never use removable media, such as Zip or Jaz drives, as scratch disks. In addition, network drives should never be assigned as scratch disks.

Remember the difference between a *partition* and a *drive*. A single hard drive can be partitioned into separate volumes, each of which your OS sees as a drive. Partitions are still physically part of the same drive, however, so the computer cannot write to multiple partitions at the same time.

Preferences, Memory & Image Cache

The image cache stores low-resolution versions of an image that can be used to speed screen redraw. The increased monitor response can come at the price of accurate detail, however. Photoshop also enables you to manage how the cache is used.

Windows and Mac OS X dynamically allocate memory to active programs as they need it. Mac OS 9 uses set memory allocations for each program. The more advanced operating systems allow you to use this Preferences pane (see Figure 3.15) to specify what percent of the *available* memory should be allocated to Photoshop.

Plug-Ins and Photoshop

Plug-ins can greatly expand Photoshop's capabilities, but some care must be taken. Here are some notes on using plug-ins:

- Remember that plug-ins load with Photoshop when you start the program. An excessive number of plug-ins can drastically increase the time required to start the program.

- A number of other programs use Photoshop-compatible plug-ins. You can use the Additional Plug-Ins Folder preference to load plug-ins from Painter, After Effects, Illustrator, and other programs' plug-ins folders.

- If you hold down the (Shift-Command) [Shift+Ctrl} keys while Photoshop is starting up, you can choose an additional plug-ins folder to load. With this capability, you can have several additional plug-ins folders and load only the set you'll need for that work session. This speeds loading and reduces the memory overhead required to run Photoshop.

- Plug-ins folders can have subfolders to keep plug-ins organized.

Hundreds of plug-ins from a variety of sources are available for Photoshop. Commercial third-party software companies generally provide high-quality products. However, some shareware and freeware plug-ins can cause stability problems or crashes. It's always a good idea to keep track of which plug-ins were installed when so that if problems develop, you can try to trace them to a specific plug-in. Likewise, it's a good idea to load new plug-ins singly or in small groups, and test them immediately.

Check with the manufacturers of legacy plug-ins for Photoshop 7 compatibility information.

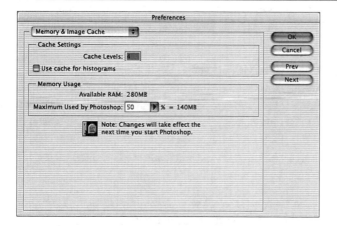

Figure 3.15
Note that because of the way Mac OS 9 handles memory, the OS does not show the Memory portion of the preferences, so the name of the pane is simply Image Cache.

These settings have an impact on how Photoshop performs:

- **Cache Settings**—When set to the default of four, Photoshop stores four low-resolution versions of a high-resolution image in memory. These four are at increasing zoom levels from 100%. When zoomed in, Photoshop uses the low-resolution images to redraw the image on the monitor more quickly. The cache, which uses memory allocated to Photoshop, can be set from one to eight.

Using the cache for histograms allows Photoshop to more quickly generate the histogram for such operations as Levels. Although using the low-resolution cached version of the image produces a less accurate histogram, the differences are rarely significant. If you need to check for posterization, it's best to use a histogram based on the entire image rather than a sampling. No matter what the cache setting is, you can view an accurate histogram by holding down the Shift key while selecting the menu command Image, Histogram.

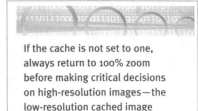

If the cache is not set to one, always return to 100% zoom before making critical decisions on high-resolution images—the low-resolution cached image might not be accurate.

- **Memory Usage**—This section of the Preferences, which is not used in Mac OS 9, shows you how much RAM is available and allows you to specify a preferred percentage. This setting, which can be changed by typing a value in the numeric field or by dragging the slider, puts a limit on the amount of memory you allow Photoshop to use. Changes are not put into effect until Photoshop is restarted.

PHOTOSHOP QUICK FIX—REPLACING THE PREFERENCES

Sometimes Photoshop doesn't seem to work quite right. Tools don't perform correctly, commands don't execute the way they should, the interface is mangled, Photoshop runs slowly or crashes often—these problems could all be signs of a corrupted preferences file. Instead of reinstalling the entire Photoshop program, you can often simply replace the "Prefs."

The Prefs: What They Are and How They Work

In addition to the options selected in the Preferences, the Prefs file stores such settings as the positions of the palettes, tool settings, guide and grid settings, scratch disk locations, and file saving settings. It is updated every time you quit Photoshop. (It is not updated during a crash.) Because the file is rewritten so often, it is subject to corruption.

When Photoshop is started, it looks for the Prefs file and loads the last settings. If it cannot find a Prefs file, Photoshop loads the default settings.

➪ *If you restarted Photoshop and your most recent settings weren't loaded, see "Unwritten Preferences" in the NAPP Help Desk section at the end of this chapter.*

Finding the Prefs

Photoshop's Prefs file is stored is different locations for different platforms. In the following list, folder names are separated by slashes. The notation [username] represents the name of your particular account on that computer. For example, in the Mac OS X hierarchy, [username] might be replaced by pbauer or jfoster.

- **Mac OS X**—Users\[username]\Library\Preferences\Adobe Photoshop 7.0 Settings\ Adobe Photoshop 7.0 Prefs

- **Mac OS 9**—System Folder\Preferences\Adobe Photoshop 7.0 Settings\Adobe Photoshop 7.0 Prefs

- **Windows XP**—Documents and Settings\[username]\Application Data\Adobe\ Photoshop\7.0\Adobe Photoshop 7.0 Settings\Adobe Photoshop 7.0 Prefs (see Figure 3.16)

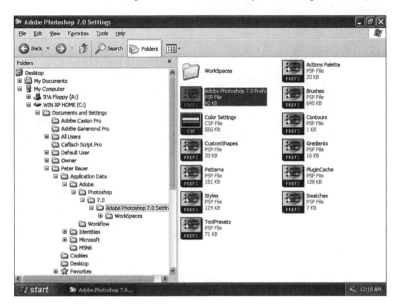

Figure 3.16
The path shown in the left frame is comparable for Windows NT and Windows 2000.

- **Windows 2000**—Documents and Settings\[username]\Application Data\Adobe\Photoshop\7.0\Adobe Photoshop 7.0 Settings\Adobe Photoshop 7.0 Prefs

- **Windows NT**—WinNT\profiles\[username]\Application Data\Adobe\Photoshop\7.0\ Adobe Photoshop 7.0 Settings\Adobe Photoshop 7.0 Prefs

- **Windows Me**—Windows\Application Data\Adobe\Photoshop\7.0\Adobe Photoshop 7 Settings\Adobe Photoshop 7 Prefs

- **Windows 98**—Windows\Application Data\Adobe\Photoshop\7.0\Adobe Photoshop 7 Settings\Adobe Photoshop 7 Prefs

Replacing the Prefs to Reset Photoshop

The easiest way to cure basic Photoshop ills is to replace a corrupted Prefs file. The easiest way to do that is simply delete the file and let Photoshop generate a new one to replace it. To restore Photoshop to its default settings, hold down (Command-Option-Shift) [Ctrl+Alt+Shift] when starting the program.

One way to help prevent corruption of the Photoshop Prefs is to lock the file with one of these methods:

- In Mac OS X, locate the file in the Finder and press Command-I to open Get Info. Click once on the Locked check box (see Figure 3.17).

Figure 3.17
Once locked, the Prefs file is less likely to become corrupted, but cannot be updated.

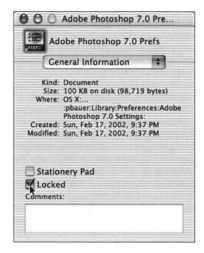

- In Mac OS 9, locate the Prefs file in the Finder and press Command-I to open Get Info. Select the Locked check box.

- Windows users should find the Prefs file in My Computer and click on it once to highlight it. From the File menu, select Properties. Select the Read-only check box, and click OK (see Figure 3.18).

The Additional Preferences Files

In addition to the Prefs, the Adobe Photoshop 7.0 Settings folder holds a variety of other files. You'll find separate files for the Actions palette, Brushes, Styles, Shapes, Swatches, and more. That's also the location of a folder called Workspaces, which holds your custom work setups.

What you *won't* find in the Settings folder are preferences for paths, Save for Web, or ImageReady. On the Macintosh platform, Save for Web and ImageReady generate their own preferences files, and a separate file is also created for Photoshop Paths. You'll find all three files in the same location as the Adobe Photoshop 7.0 Settings folder. Color Settings is a separate file within the Photoshop Settings folder.

On Windows, Save for Web and ImageReady must write to the Windows Registry instead of creating separate files. You'll find a separate Color Settings file with the Photoshop preferences in the Adobe Photoshop 7.0 Settings folder.

Caution
You are strongly advised to leave the Windows Registry undisturbed unless you are a Microsoft Certified Expert.

Figure 3.18
Windows XP is shown. The procedure is similar for other versions of Windows.

PHOTOSHOP IN FOCUS

Replacing the Photoshop Prefs file is often the fastest and easiest way to cure problems with the program—it's certainly easier than suffering through a full reinstall of the program. There are some things that can make this process easier. For example, rather than restore to the factory defaults, you can replace a corrupt preferences file with a copy that is preset to restore your preferred settings. Create a custom set of preferences, and copy that file as a backup. Use it to replace a corrupt file. Here's how to set it up:

1. Shut down Photoshop if it's running, and then delete the existing Prefs file.

2. Start Photoshop, and set up everything just the way you like it. Arrange palettes, select tool presets, and establish your preferred settings in the Preferences panes.

3. Immediately quit Photoshop.

4. Locate the new Prefs file.

5. Duplicate the file, and put it someplace other than the Photoshop Settings folder.

6. When you need to replace a corrupt Prefs file, simply delete the bad file and copy the duplicate into the Settings folder (make sure that the name is exactly the same).

FROM THE NAPP HELP DESK

The National Association of Photoshop Professionals (NAPP) offers e-mail assistance to its members. Here is some advice from the NAPP Help Desk related to issues in this chapter.

Transparency and Background Layers

No matter how I set the transparency grid, I can't see it. What's wrong?

Open the Layers palette and look for a layer named Background. A background layer does not support transparency, so you won't see the grid "behind" it. To correct the problem, convert the background layer to a regular layer by renaming it. Click on the word *Background* in the Layers palette and type the new name.

Unwritten Preferences

I set up all my palettes, tools, and settings just the way I wanted them and then immediately quit Photoshop. When I restarted the program, my custom settings weren't there, just the defaults. Any ideas?

Check the Prefs file to see if it's locked. Photoshop won't warn you when it can't update the Prefs, assuming that you've locked the file to protect it.

GETTING PIXELS INTO PHOTOSHOP

DIGITAL CAMERA BASICS

One of the most common sources of images for Photoshop now is the digital camera. Once reserved for big-budget journalism operations, digital photography is within the reach of virtually all Photoshop users. Ranging in price from under $100 to well over $10,000, there is quite a selection available. There is also a huge range of capabilities, involving such variables as the number of pixels captured, ISO simulation, lens range (and zooming), and even the hardware with which the image is actually captured.

Digital Versus Film

Some high-end digital cameras capture enough data that they can rival 35mm film cameras for detail. The majority of digital cameras, however, fall short of that level of precision. Some specialty digital backs for large-format cameras are even suitable for studio work.

The primary limitation for most digital cameras is the actual amount of detail that can be captured. The size of the individual pixels is determined by the number of pixels used to capture the image. If the number of pixels is low, each pixel must be large to capture an image. If, for example, that image is a landscape with power lines in the distance, extremely fine detail may be required. If each pixel is larger than the width of a power line, there are not enough pixels to capture all the detail.

Megapixels is the measure of how much information a digital camera will capture. Instead of measuring pixels per inch (ppi) at a certain physical size (such as 4×6 inches at 200 ppi), the number represents the millions of pixels captured, regardless of resolution or print size. (You'll see the abbreviation *MP* for megapixels.) Typical camera ratings range from 1.3 megapixels to over 6 megapixels. Table 4.1 explores the relationship among megapixels, pixel size, and print size.

Table 4.1   Megapixels Versus Print Size

Megapixel Rating	Pixel Dimensions	Print Size @ 240dpi
1.3	1280×960	5.33×4.0
2.1	1600×1200	6.67×5.0
2.3	1800×1200	7.5×5.0
3.1	2160×1440	9.0×6.0
3.3	2048×1536	8.53×6.4
4.0	2272×1704	9.47×7.1
5.2	2560×1920	10.67×8.0

For the sample print resolution, 240dpi was selected because it's the resolution at which many inkjet printers reach maximum quality.

Keep in mind that these are maximum pixel dimensions. Numerous other factors may play a role in whether you have suitable resolution for your desired print size. For example, many cameras can capture images at multiple resolutions. The lower resolutions are designed to reduce file size and can be used when you need less resolution or when you want to capture more individual images on the camera's storage medium.

Another factor to consider is cropping. It's fine to say that a 5.2MP camera can capture enough data for an 8×10-inch inkjet glossy. However, if the picture is taken at the wrong distance or with an improper zoom, the digital photo might need to be substantially cropped to compose it properly. Figure 4.1 shows an example.

> **Caution**
>
> Cramming too many pixels onto too small a CCD (the part of the digital camera that captures the image) is a bad idea. The pixels can be too small to record detail accurately. When shopping, compare both megapixels and CCD size.

Figure 4.1
The original image is 2560×1920 pixels. When cropped to the desired image area, it measures only 1440×1152.

Cropping can reduce an image to pixel dimensions that are unsuitable for reproduction at 8×10 inches. In this example, the cropped image would output to 8×10 inches at 144 pixels per inch, which is less than optimal for inkjet output. (If an image is worth printing at such a size, it's worth having appropriate resolution.) You could, of course, use Photoshop to resample the image to a higher resolution, but that can introduce softness. Sharpening can reduce softness, but generally it's better to use an image's original pixels. Images properly captured on film, on the other hand, lose very little quality when enlarged to reasonable sizes.

File Formats and Compression

Digital cameras often offer the choice of several compression levels and sometimes a choice of file formats. Suffice it to say that although compression helps reduce file size and enables you to capture more images on the same media, too much compression can seriously damage digital images.

➡ *JPEG compression (and its effect on file quality) is discussed in Chapter 5, "Photoshop's File Formats and Output Options," p. 119.*

To maintain quality, keep compression to a minimum. Capturing images in TIFF file format can maximize quality; however, many cameras cannot capture a large number of TIFF images on their storage media. Table 4.2 shows the storage capabilities of a sample 2.1MP camera.

Table 4.2 Storage Capabilities—2.1MP Camera

File Format	Pixel Dimensions	Images per 8MB SmartCard
TIFF	1600×1200	1
JPEG-SHQ	1600×1200	7
JPEG-HQ	1600×1200	16
JPEG-SQ	1024×768	38
JPEG-SQ	640×480	82

Obviously, the file format and pixel dimension options have a tremendous impact on the number of images that can be captured to a single card. (The numbers shown are for the Olympus C-700 Ultra Zoom.) Capabilities vary from camera to camera, so check the documentation for a specific camera (or the manufacturer's Web site).

FROM CAMERA TO PHOTOSHOP

Moving images from a digital camera to Photoshop can take any of several forms. Your camera, its software, and your computer's operating system all can play a role. The various combinations of camera, software, and OS are many; this section presents some generalities and uses one camera as an example. Consult the documentation for your camera, software, and OS, and use the Internet to get the latest information and software updates for your configuration.

Depending on the media that your camera uses to record and your camera's connection capability, you may be able to access the images directly from the camera. Alternatively, you might need to connect a media reader to your computer. Some cameras record directly to floppy disks or mini-CDs (Sony Mavica cameras, for example), which can be read directly by the computer.

Using the Camera's Software

A huge variety of software is supplied with digital cameras. Some software is designed only to download images from the camera to the hard drive. Other software is often provided to help you work with those images. Many cameras come bundled with Adobe Photoshop Elements or another image-editing program. These programs do not necessarily allow you to access the images while in the camera.

Many cameras are considered "auto connect" USB devices and require no software. The camera is seen as a hard drive and can be accessed as such (in a read-only configuration).

Even auto-connect cameras require a driver for use with Windows 98. Check your camera's documentation for more information.

Mac OS X and Digital Downloads

There are several ways to move digital photographs from a camera to the hard drive when using Mac OS X and Photoshop. OS X includes the Image Capture utility that can automatically sense and access your digital camera when attached to the computer.

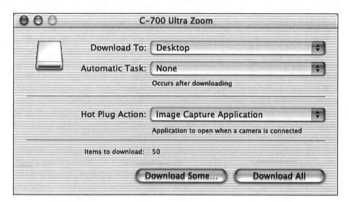

Image Capture can be set to automatically launch when a camera is connected or turned on.

Image Capture can perform a variety of operations, including thumbnail generation, color profile embedding, and deleting from the camera after downloading.

Photoshop's Open command can see many digital cameras as external hard drives in OS X. You can read from, but you cannot write to such "hard drives." The camera appears at the highest level of the computer, not on the user's desktop.

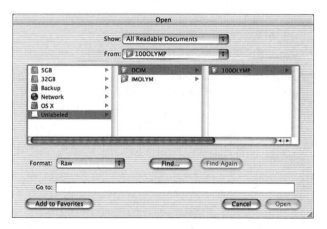

Scroll all the way to the left to see the drives that are available.

If you can see your camera in the Open dialog box, you can use Photoshop 7's File Browser. (File Browser is explored in depth in Chapter 1, "What's New in Photoshop 7.") With File Browser, you can not only open images, but also do some rather extensive file management. You can move images from the camera to folders on the hard drive, delete them, and even batch-rename a group of files. File Browser can display the images in a variety of ways, with or without basic file information.

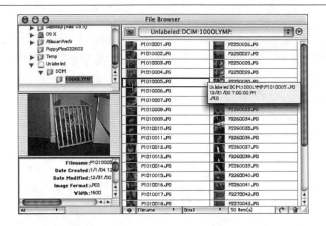

Moving the cursor over a thumbnail shows the location, date, and file format of the image.

Apple's iPhoto software can also be used to access images on a digital camera. If Photoshop can't see the camera, but iPhoto can, use iPhoto to import the images and then save them to the hard drive.

Resolution Adjustment

Most digital cameras capture and record pixels without regard to future use of the image. Photoshop opens these images and prepares them for viewing on the monitor. Because the camera typically doesn't record any printing instructions with the images, Photoshop assumes a monitor resolution of 72ppi. To maintain the highest image quality possible, follow these steps to change an image's resolution:

1. Open the image in Photoshop.

2. Open the Image Size dialog box by using the menu command Image, Image Size.

3. Deselect the Resample Image check box. This locks the upper part of the dialog box and prevents changes to the image's actual pixel size (see Figure 4.2).

Figure 4.2
When Resample Image is unchecked, Image Size merely changes the resolution instruction for printing. It makes no change to the image's actual pixels, preserving the picture's original quality.

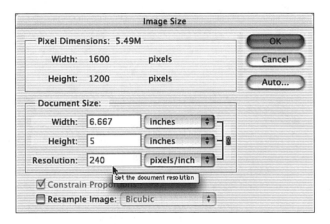

4. Enter the desired print resolution in the Resolution field, *or* enter the desired height or width and let Photoshop calculate the resolution.

5. Click OK.

Some cameras *can* record resolution with images. Photoshop reads the EXIF data and maintains it with the file.

By *not* resampling, you preserve the image's pixels exactly as captured. You can adjust the resolution and let Photoshop calculate the image's print dimensions, or you can enter the desired height and/or width and let the program determine the resolution.

⇨ *Not clear on resampling? See "Adding, Subtracting, and Preserving Pixels" in the NAPP Help Desk section at the end of this chapter.*

Remember that resolution refers only to a printing instruction, telling the output device the size of the pixels and, therefore, how tightly to pack them on the page. At 72ppi, each pixel is 1/72 of an inch square. If the same image is converted to 240ppi, each pixel is 1/240 of an inch. If the image isn't resampled, the same number of pixels fits into an area about 1/10 the size.

Consider an image 1600×1200 pixels in size. At 72ppi, printing would require a sheet of paper more than 22×16 inches, and the image would look pixilated because of the size of the individual pixels. Maintaining those same 1600×1200 pixels but printing at 240ppi yields an image 6.67×5 inches on paper, and the image's quality is greatly enhanced.

EXIF Data

Exchangeable Image Format (EXIF) is actually the file format used by digital still cameras. Originally developed in the mid-1990s by the Japan Electronic Industry Development Association (JEIDA), it now includes even audio format instructions. It requires the use of JPEG for compressed image files and TIFF (version 6.0) for uncompressed files.

One benefit of using EXIF is the image information that is stored with the picture. Date, time, camera settings, image pixel dimensions and resolution, and even data from a global positioning system (GPS) device are among the dozens of pieces of information that can be recorded with the file.

Photoshop 7 can access the EXIF information through the File Browser or with the menu command File, File Info (see Figure 4.3).

4

Figure 4.3
Photoshop can save file info as XMP, data embedded with the file in a format based on XML. The latest versions of Acrobat, InDesign, and Illustrator can also read XMP data.

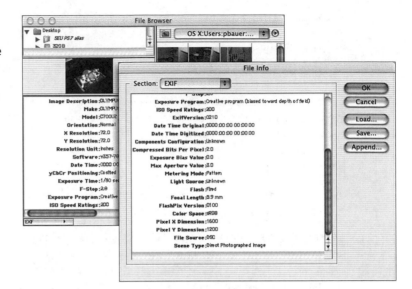

COMMON PROBLEMS WITH DIGITAL CAMERA IMAGES

There are two quite common problems with digital cameras: noise and color cast. Noise is viewed in the image as spots of blue, red, green, or gray scattered throughout the picture. Even in grayscale, the noise is evident in the zoomed view in Figure 4.4.

Figure 4.4
At 25% zoom, the noise doesn't show. However, when zoomed to 200%, the colored artifacts are noticeable as an irregular grain in the image.

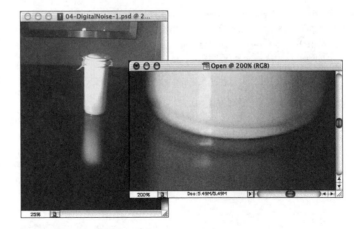

Digital noise is most commonly seen as blue artifacts. The Green channel is typically the least affected. In Figure 4.5, each of the channels is shown individually.

By using the Photoshop filters Blur, Gaussian Blur and Noise, Despeckle or Noise, Dust & Scratches, you can minimize the artifacts in the damaged channel or channels, leaving the remaining color channel(s) untouched.

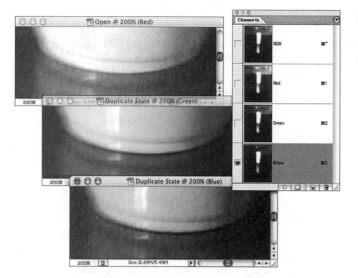

Figure 4.5
Especially in the lower-right area, the artifacts are most apparent in the Blue channel.

Photoshop also offers an easy fix for those unwanted tints known as color casts. When an image shows a distinct cast, using Image, Adjustments, Auto Color is often an easy solution. By balancing the highlights, midtones, and shadows, and then extending that correction throughout the image, you can remove unwanted tinting with a single click.

➡️ *To learn more about color correction, **see** Chapter 16, "Color Correction and the Adjustment Commands," **p. 433**.*

Should the Auto Color command not produce the result you want, remember that Curves and Levels can each be used on individual color channels. Just as blurring a single channel can remove unwanted artifacts, so too can correcting a single channel repair an overall color cast.

Rather than correct digital noise and color casts in Photoshop, avoid them in the first place. Make sure that your digital camera is set to the proper white balance, the proper light source, and the proper ISO for the conditions. Check your camera's documentation, and consider using Auto Exposure, if available.

4

SCANNERS: HARDWARE BASICS

Images can be digitized using scanners as well as digital cameras. Although hardware exists to make accurate three-dimensional scans, the vast majority of scanning for Photoshop involves flat, 2D originals. Most originals fall into one of two categories: reflective materials and transparencies.

Reflective, in this situation, indicates that light bounces off the original and is captured when it returns. Paper is the primary example of reflective material. Photographs, pages from books and magazines, and even samples of canvas or brick can be considered reflective.

Transparencies are film. Whether slides or negatives, in a variety of sizes (35mm, medium format, or large format), film is recorded somewhat differently by scanners. Instead of light bouncing off the surface and being collected, the light passes through the film and the image is captured on the other side.

Flatbed and Drum Scanners

Flatbed scanners are the most common and least expensive equipment for digitizing reflective art-work. Serviceable scans can be produced by equipment costing under $100. Drum scanners are far more expensive, much more complicated, and produce scans to much more exacting standards. Drum scanners are more likely to be found at service bureaus and print houses, while flatbed scanners are common in studios, offices, and homes. Some high-end flatbed scanners can achieve quality comparable to low-end drum scanners.

Flatbed scanners can be connected to your computer via USB, FireWire, or SCSI. FireWire is typically found only on high-end scanners that are designed and intended to capture large amounts of information. If you scan at high resolution on a regular basis, FireWire or USB-2 may be appropriate.

Flatbed Resolution and Bit Depth

When considering a flatbed scanner, several features should be considered. The size of the scanner's bed (the largest size it can scan) could be important. The software package that comes with the scanner can perhaps influence your decision. You should also consider the hardware's resolution and bit depth as well as the competence of the scanner's own software.

Resolution is often advertised with two pairs of numbers: the *optical* resolution and the *interpolated* resolution. The first tells you what the hardware can do; the second is all about software. Because you can perhaps more accurately interpolate images in Photoshop, the optical resolution is more important. Optical resolution is typically either 600 or 1200ppi. More accurately, scanner resolution should be measured in "samples per inch" (spi) (however, there's no practical difference between spi and ppi). Drum scanners can reach resolutions of 9600spi, but film scanners are typically either 2000 or 4000spi.

Color *bit depth* describes how much information the scanner records for each pixel. Although Photoshop can work with 16-bit color, the files are much larger, the program's capabilities are limited, and output options are restricted. Most images in Photoshop, whether RGB, CMYK, or grayscale, use 8-bit color depth.

That having been said, more color information from the scanner is generally better than less. Photoshop eventually discards the excess information, but there's a stronger probability of getting accurate color with a 48-bit scanner than with a 24-bit scanner. Remember, though, that bit depth is dependent on the quality of the scanner's hardware. Although a sub-$100 scanner might offer 42-bit color, that doesn't mean that it will produce more accurate scans than a $1,500 36-bit scanner.

The scanner's *dynamic range* should also be considered. The dynamic range, also referred to as the *density*, is the scanner's capability to capture tonal range. The higher the value, the better the scanner reproduces detail in shadow areas. Density rated below 3.2 is marginal. Very high-end flatbed and drum scanners can approach the theoretical maximum of 4.0.

Film Scanners Versus Transparency Adapters

Transparencies can be scanned by using film scanners or with transparency adapters for flatbed scanners. (Drum scanners can also digitize transparencies.) Dedicated film scanners generally produce higher-quality scans than do flatbed scanners. The image's tonal range is often captured much more accurately and completely with a film scanner.

If you work only with 35mm film, you'll find film scanners for under $1,000 that do excellent work. If your requirements include medium-format film, expect to pay $3,000 or more. Large-format film scanners cost upward of $10,000.

Consider dynamic range to be the thickness of a book and bit depth to be the number of pages. A book three inches thick that has only 30 very hefty pages is probably just as useless as a book one-tenth of an inch thick with 4,000 pages too flimsy to turn. Both dynamic range and color bit depth are required for a quality scanner.

Transparency adapters are often built into high-end flatbed scanners costing $1,000 or more. Less expensive flatbeds also offer integrated or add-on transparency capabilities, often at a substantial increase in price and with lower-quality results.

Scanning Software

The quality of the scanner's software is also important. Some scanners simply acquire images. Others have sophisticated software capable of removing dust and scratches. Online and magazine reviews are often valuable when evaluating scanner software. However, seeing is often believing. If you have the opportunity to put a scanner through its paces before buying, make sure you test its software. If it offers color correction, try it. If the scanner claims to be able to make repairs to damaged originals, give it a test drive.

Most scanners that would be of interest to a Photoshop user enable you to acquire images by using the Photoshop command File, Import, which opens the image directly in Photoshop. To operate the scanner from within Photoshop, the scanner's acquire module must be located in the correct Photoshop folder. This plug-in is the link between Photoshop and the scanner. In almost all cases, it should be installed or copied to the Import/Export folder within Photoshop's Plug-Ins folder. (Photoshop should not be running when plug-ins are added.)

SCANNING IMAGES INTO PHOTOSHOP

In most cases, you can use Photoshop's File, Import command to access a scanner's plug-in. The plug-in opens the scanner's software and allows you to control the hardware. Because such a wide range of scanner software is available, this section looks primarily at theory rather than specific examples.

When preparing to scan, always start from the endpoint: Determine the size and color depth requirements for the final image file before starting to scan.

Resolution

When scanning, the resolution determines the fineness of detail (and file size) of the captured image. In Figure 4.6, the same image has been scanned at four different resolutions.

Figure 4.6
The four windows have been "zoomed" to show the same area of the image.

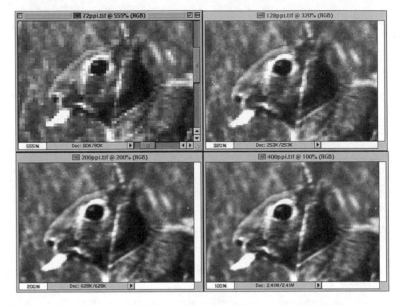

In the top-left corner, the image was scanned at 72ppi. The top-right image was scanned at 128ppi, a resolution that is suitable for many newsprint applications. In the lower-left corner, the image is at 200ppi, appropriate for many magazine printing jobs. The lower-right image was scanned at 400ppi. This resolution isn't typically used for print but can be used to resize an image while scanning.

Notice the difference in the relative size of the pixels at the various resolutions. When each image occupies the same space, the number of pixels available determines the size of each pixel. The very visible pixels in the 72ppi image (upper left) are more than five-and-a-half times as large as the pixels in the lower-right image. That means the lower-resolution image uses one pixel for an area of detail in the image that the high-resolution image displays with about 30 pixels. For example, the 72ppi image uses approximately 36 pixels to reproduce the rabbit's eye. The 400ppi image uses almost 1300 pixels for the eye.

Remember that the scanning resolution determines the actual number of pixels that will be in the image, which also plays a large role in the file size. In Figure 4.7, the same four scans are shown, each at 100% zoom.

At 100% zoom, each pixel in each image is exactly the same size. The higher-resolution scans require more space onscreen because they have more pixels. Higher-resolution scans also require more space on disk. Because more pixels are being captured, more file information needs to be recorded. Resolution (unless changed in Photoshop) also determines print size. See Table 4.3 for some comparative numbers.

Figure 4.7
From the back to the front, the scans are at 400ppi, 200ppi, 128ppi, and 72ppi.

Table 4.3 Relative Size at Various Resolutions

Resolution	File Size	Pixel Dimensions	Print Size at 200dpi
400ppi	2,410KB	1112×755	5.56×3.75 inches
200ppi	638KB	562×381	2.81×1.905 inches
128ppi	253KB	356×242	1.78×1.21 inches
72ppi	80KB	200×136	1.0×0.68 inches

Picking a Scan Resolution

The appropriate resolution for an image depends on its final purpose. Images intended to be thumbnails on a Web page don't need to be scanned at the same resolution as photographs that will be printed at 8×10 inches on glossy paper. Nor will either of those images have the same requirements as an image that will occupy three columns at four inches tall in the daily newspaper.

In all cases, the best start is at the end. Determine what the final image size must be *in pixels*, and then scan to that size. Here is one example:

1. An image will be output on a commercial printing press as part of a page layout program's document.

2. The document will be printed at a line screen frequency of 133lpi (lines per inch).

3. An appropriate image resolution for 133lpi is 200 dpi. (The general rule of thumb is 1.5 to 2 times the line screen is an appropriate image resolution.)

4. The image will occupy a space 4×6 inches in the document.

The terms ppi, dpi, and lpi all refer to *linear* inches. When we say 200 pixels per inch, that's the number of pixels side-by-side, not in a square inch.

5. The final pixel size must be 800×1200 pixels. (That's based on 200dpi times 4 inches, by 200dpi times 6 inches.)

6. The original photograph to be scanned measures 5×7.5 inches.

7. The appropriate scan resolution is a mere 160ppi. (800 divided by 5 equals 160; 1200 divided by 7.5 also equals 160.)

With some scanning software, you can simply input the desired print size and resolution. That eliminates the need to "do the math."

➭ *Print resolution is examined in Chapter 26, "The Printing Process: A Primer," p. 793.*

Alternatively, if the original photograph measured only 2×3 inches, the appropriate scan resolution would be 400ppi—800 divided by 2; 1200 divided by 3.

When you capture the appropriate number of pixels from the start, you eliminate the possibility of image degradation that can be caused by resizing and sharpening.

➭ *Uncertain about scan resolution for transparencies? See "Scanning Resolution for Film" in the NAPP Help Desk section at the end of this chapter.*

Image Resolution for Inkjets

There is a difference between the "resolution" of an inkjet printer and the appropriate image resolution. An inkjet's 1440×720 resolution, for example, refers to the ink droplets. It takes several droplets to replicate a colored pixel on a sheet of paper.

The image's resolution refers to the actual pixels in an image. To get the maximum quality from an inkjet printer, you need to use an image resolution of one-third the printer's stated resolution. When two numbers are given, divide the smaller. In the example of a 1440×720 inkjet resolution, an image resolution of 240 is optimal.

Remember, too, that most inkjet printers are rather limited in the file size they can handle. If your printer can produce 1440×1440 droplets per inch, the one-third rule would indicate an image resolution of 480dpi. Run a few tests, and you'll find that there might be no visual difference between 240 and 480dpi for your printer. There could be, however, a huge difference in output time or whether the image prints at all.

Scanning for Grayscale

Although most scanners can produce a grayscale image, it's often better to generate a color image and convert from RGB to grayscale in Photoshop. By capturing more color information, you increase the available tonal range. The tonal range determines, among other things, how much detail will be visible in the image's shadow and highlight areas.

➭ *To learn more about working with an image's appearance, **see** Chapter 16, "Color Correction and the Adjustment Commands," p. 433.*

There are a number of ways to convert an RGB image to grayscale in Photoshop. The easiest is to simply use Image, Mode, Grayscale. Better results are often achieved by using two steps: Image, Adjust, Desaturate, and then Image, Mode, Grayscale. However, for even greater control (and a better result), use Photoshop's Channel Mixer (see Figure 4.8).

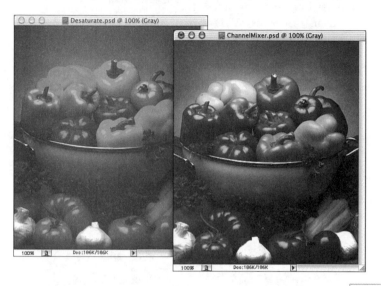

Figure 4.8
The image on the left was desaturated and then converted from RGB to Grayscale. On the right, the Channel Mixer was used before converting.

The Channel Mixer enables you to take the best parts of each color channel and combine them into a single grayscale channel. Open the dialog box with the menu command Image, Adjust, Channel Mixer. To create a grayscale image, click the Monochrome check box in the lower-left corner (see Figure 4.9). Adjust the sliders until you achieve the desired tonal range. Afterward, use the menu command Image, Mode, Grayscale.

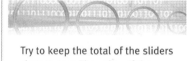

Try to keep the total of the sliders close to 100. The value of the Constant slider, negative or positive, should be multiplied by three when adding to 100.

Figure 4.9
The original image, Peppers.jpg, is found in the Samples folder installed by default with Photoshop 7.

Digitizing Line Art

Line art contains pixels that are either black or white, with no shades of gray. Scanning line art without *jaggies*, those visible pixel corners that make curves look ragged, requires very high resolution. Instead of scanning at 300ppi, line art should be scanned at 1200ppi. For a comparison, see Figure 4.10. Many scanners have special settings for line art, which might also be listed as "bitmap." Even with the higher resolution, the corners of the pixels will be there; they just won't be as visible. Remember that higher resolution means that each individual pixel is proportionally smaller.

> ### Caution
>
> Resist any temptation to scan line art as RGB. There is no advantage over grayscale, and the size of a 1200ppi RGB image can create problems.

Figure 4.10
The two zooms show the same area of the image, at 300ppi on the left and 1200ppi on the right. The difference in pixel size—and image detail—is apparent.

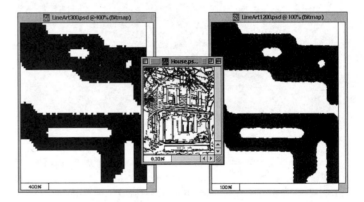

In addition to scanning at high resolution, you can exercise some control to improve the digitized line art. Scanning in grayscale and then applying the Threshold command can be very effective. The Threshold slider enables you to determine which of the gray pixels will be converted to black and which to white. (When scanning line art as black and white, the scanner's own setting determines the darkness at which any gray pixel is converted to black.) A comparison of Threshold settings is shown in Figure 4.11.

Moiré Patterns and How to Avoid Them

One of the most common problems encountered in scanning artwork is moiré patterns. These obvious patterns occur when scanning artwork printed in CMYK. The pattern of dots produced by the printing press, although not visible to the eye, appears quite exaggerated when scanned (see Figure 4.12).

Typically, the easiest way to avoid the appearance of any pattern in scanned artwork is to use the capability built into most scanners. Whether called "Descreening" or "Moire Removal," or perhaps activated by choosing "Magazine" or "Color Document" as the source, the scanner's software is usually the best way to avoid the problem.

Figure 4.11
The Threshold command converts all pixels to either black or white. You use the slider to determine the grayscale value at which the division is made.

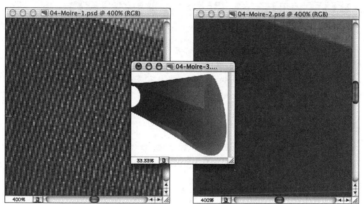

Figure 4.12
To the left, the moiré pattern is visible. To the right, the scanner's descreening option was used.

Placing printed artwork on the scanner's glass at a 15° angle can also help reduce moiré. Because the dot pattern no longer aligns with the path of the scan head, the pattern is diminished. In conjunction with this technique (or in place of it, if you have no control over the original scan), you can apply a Gaussian Blur filter to smooth the pattern. The more pronounced the pattern, the greater the blur required. The greater the blur, the more the image is softened.

Although sharpening can reduce the softness introduced by blurring, it can also reintroduce a moiré pattern. Striking a balance between blurring and moiré may be possible, but often it's more feasible to compromise on *where* rather than *how much*. Instead of blurring the entire image and then sharpening the entire image, consider where the focus should be. Work selectively to reduce moiré in key areas of the image, and blur the less important areas to a greater degree. Consider masks or selections to isolate areas of the image, and then use the Blur and Sharpen tools to fine-tune those areas.

Tuning Your Scanner

Just as all scanners are not created equal, so too are areas of the scanner's bed often unequal. Most scanners have a "sweet spot," an area where they seem to work best. Finding the prime position on your flatbed can be as easy as scanning a blank piece of paper at low resolution. Any gray areas in the resulting scan indicate where the image was captured inaccurately. Generally, you'll find that there's a rectangular area in the center of the scanner's bed that gives the best results.

To gain practical experience with scanning, let us recommend *The Scanning Workshop* (Que, ISBN 0-7897-2558-4), by our contributing author and technical editor, Richard Romano.

Scanning a blank sheet of paper can also indicate whether you need to clean the scanner's glass. (Always follow the manufacturer's instructions for cleaning the glass. Damaging the glass can render the scanner unusable.) Remember, too, that the minutes it takes to clean a scanner's glass can save hours in artifact removal in Photoshop.

STOCK PHOTOGRAPHY AND OTHER EXISTING ARTWORK

Another source of ready-made pixels is stock art. Available on the Web and in collections on CD or DVD, stock artwork consists of photographs, illustrations, clip art, and even audio and motion clips (which cannot be used in Photoshop) prepared by others and licensed for your use. Many programs, including Photoshop, ship with some stock art. (Photoshop 7's default installation includes the Samples folder, inside the Adobe Photoshop 7.0 folder.)

Artwork can also be found on the Internet, in books, and elsewhere. You should be aware of copyright laws before using any artwork not created by and for yourself.

Sources of Stock Images

Stock photography firms abound, and most of the major players have a Web presence. Comstock, SuperStock, PhotoSpin, EyeWire (a division of Getty Images), PhotoDisc, and DigitalVision are just some of the major sources of stock photos. You'll also find vector artwork and, in many cases, fonts.

You can search for images that fit your needs from their extensive collections, pay online by credit card or account, and download. You can also order collections of images on CD. If you use the same type of image regularly, but don't want to use the same specific image, collections can save you a lot of money.

The fine folks at PhotoSpin have allowed us to include some samples of their stock art on this book's CD. Please read the licensing agreement before incorporating any of these images into your own work.

Royalty-Free Versus Licensed Images

The images you pay for are not really purchased; rather, they are licensed. The copyright is not transferred, and you are not free to do whatever you want with the image.

Even the most lenient licensing arrangements prohibit you from reselling the images as stock art or from using them in defamatory ways. What you can do with the images is governed by the type of license for which you paid.

Royalty-free artwork is licensed to you to use as many times, in whatever manner (except as mentioned previously) you like. The same image can be reused in a variety of works and for whatever purposes you desire.

Traditionally licensed images (also called rights-protected) are much more tightly restricted. You purchase a license to use the image for a specific purpose, for a specific period of time.

Another major difference is availability of the images. Royalty-free images can be and are licensed repeatedly and can appear simultaneously in a variety of different works by different people or studios. You cannot control who else is using the images and for what. (Over the past several years, there has been a preponderance of "perspective" shots—photos taken from a ladder while looking downward at a person. One particular image of a young woman appeared in no fewer than 12 different advertising materials, for 12 different companies, in the space of four months. A couple of those companies were direct competitors.)

Rights-protected images can be licensed exclusively for a period of time—no one else will have access to or permission to use that specific image during the license period

Copyright Concerns

The licensing agreements for stock images are explicit (and should be read carefully), but rights to other images are not always as clear. Although there is no substitute for advice from a legal professional, there are certain guidelines you should consider when using artwork that might belong to another:

- If you didn't create it, you probably need to contact the person who did.

- *Derivative works*, those that are made from or include existing artwork, don't transfer copyright. You cannot include another's work in your art without permission.

- There need not be a copyright symbol © to indicate protected work. Creative work is automatically copyrighted as soon as it is created.

Other than a practicing legal professional, perhaps the best source of information about copyright law is the law itself. It can be accessed online through the Library of Congress at `www.loc.gov/copyright`.

PHOTOSHOP IN FOCUS

Whether working with a scanner, a digital camera, or stock photos downloaded via the Internet, it's always best to start with the correct pixel dimensions. The process of resampling—changing the pixel dimensions of an image without changing its content—can harm the appearance of your artwork. Here's a little exercise to show you what we mean:

1. Open Photoshop and choose the menu command File, Open.

2. Navigate to the Photoshop folder and open Samples.

3. Select the Eagle.psd image and open it.

4. Click twice on the leftmost button at the bottom of the History palette to create two identical copies of the file.

5. With either copy active, use the menu command Image, Image Size. Select the Resample (Bicubic) and Constrain Proportions check boxes, and enter a new width of 212 pixels. Click OK.

6. Switch to the other duplicate Eagle image and use Image Size to change the width to 848 pixels.

7. Zoom in on all three images, as shown in Figure 4.13.

Figure 4.13
The original is at the top, the reduced copy is in the middle, and the enlarged copy is at the bottom.

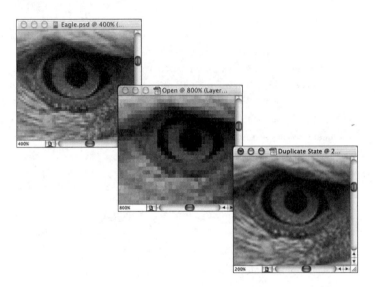

Notice the pixilization of the middle copy. The pupil of the eagle's eye is no longer round. Less noticeable, but nonetheless still there, is a substantial "softening" of the eye that was "upsampled" (the number of pixels in the image was increased). The softness can be reduced by using the Sharp filters; however, if the image had been scanned at a width of 848 pixels originally, there would be no softness.

FROM THE NAPP HELP DESK

The National Association of Photoshop Professionals (NAPP) offers e-mail assistance to its members. Here is some advice from the NAPP Help Desk related to issues in this chapter.

Adding, Subtracting, and Preserving Pixels

What is resampling and why should I avoid it?

Resampling is the process of increasing or decreasing the number of pixels in an image while attempting to maintain the overall look of the image. The content of the image (theoretically) remains the same, but it is created with more or fewer pixels. (This process is in contrast to cropping, which reduces the number of pixels but also changes the image's content.)

When you use Image, Image Size to increase an image's pixel dimensions, Photoshop has to create new pixels to place between (or in place of) the original pixels. It averages the color values of surrounding pixels to determine what color the new pixels should be.

When Image, Image Size is used to reduce the number of pixels in an image, Photoshop averages the color values of a group of pixels and uses that color value to create the replacement pixel(s).

The problem with resampling is that the process of averaging color values introduces a "softness," sort of an out-of-focus look, to the image. When you avoid resampling, you avoid introducing that blurriness.

Scanning Resolution for Film

How do I determine the target scan resolution when using a film scanner?

The formula is the same. Determine the required output size in pixels, measure the original, and divide those dimensions into the pixel dimensions. The only difference is that instead of measuring, say, a 4×6-inch photograph as the original, you may be measuring a portion of a 35mm negative. If you will be using the entire 35mm negative or slide, consider it to be 0.95×1.4 inches. If you'll be scanning only a portion of the film, be sure to place it in a protective sleeve before placing a ruler on it.

Copyright and "Fair Use"

I understand that I can use someone else's work in my own under "fair use" standards. What are they, and how is fair use determined?

As always, this is no substitute for professional legal advice, but here is a summary of the fair use doctrine:

- Under certain circumstances, you can use limited portions of another's work for certain purposes.

- Those purposes are generally held to be commentary, criticism, news reporting, and scholarly work.

- Copyright law states no specific percentage of a work or number of words or musical notes for what constitutes fair use.

- Incorporating someone else's work into your own, with the intent to sell or claim the entire work as your own, does not constitute fair use.

PHOTOSHOP'S FILE FORMATS AND OUTPUT OPTIONS

IN THIS CHAPTER

CHOOSING A FILE FORMAT

Selecting the proper file format for your final artwork can mean the difference between having a usable image and a worthless collection of zeros and ones recorded to magnetic media. The file format should be determined by the image's final destination; for example, the Web has different requirements than page layout programs. Even the Web design or page layout program you use can make a difference in what format to choose.

Within the broad categories of Web and print, there are additional choices to be made. The file content will help you determine which format to choose.

Basic Concepts

Different file formats have different capabilities. Photoshop's native .psd format supports all the program's features. Some formats restrict the number of colors that can be used in a file (GIF and PNG-8, for example), and many don't support the CMYK color mode. The capability of portraying transparency with clipping paths and/or alpha channels also varies among formats. Vector type and vector paths can be supported in only a few file formats. The choice of format may require that you consider such features.

Generally speaking, working in Photoshop's .psd file format until your artwork is complete is a good idea. Saving the original, with all layers intact and unrasterized type, in .psd format gives you the most flexibility for future editing, or *repurposing* of a file. Repurposing can be considered to be making another copy of a file in a different format, size, or color mode for a different purpose. For example, an image prepared as part of a print advertising campaign can be repurposed as a Web graphic for the advertiser's site.

It's also important to understand that file formats differ in how they record information. It's not enough to change the three letter extension at the end of a file's name; the file must be resaved or re-exported to change the format.

⇨ *Unsure about file formats and cross-platform issues? See "Formats and Platforms" in the NAPP Help Desk section at the end of this chapter.*

You might also find that several file formats are appropriate for your end use and image content. Which one you choose could depend on factors beyond your control. For example, your service bureau or print shop might have a preference, or perhaps the intended audience for your Web site could not be expected to have a plug-in required to see a particular format. However, in some cases there is no difference between formats, and you're free to choose as you will.

Save, Save As, Save for Web, and Exporting

The primary methods of assigning file formats in Photoshop are the menu commands File, Save As and File, Save for Web.

Save

If you create a document in Photoshop using the command File, New, the menu command Save is not available until a file format has been assigned by using Save As. Afterward, using the Save command updates the file on disk, maintaining the same format, if possible. If you've added layers or otherwise changed the file so that it can no longer be saved in the original format, using the Save command opens the Save As dialog box. You have the option of changing to the Photoshop file format or saving the file as a copy.

The Save As dialog box tells you which features force the file to be saved as a copy—small warning triangles appear next to the check boxes of features in the image.

Save As

Any time you select a file format in Save As that cannot support all the document's features, Photoshop defaults to saving a copy of the file. The As a Copy check box will be selected and grayed out to prevent deselection, the word *copy* will be appended to the filename, and a warning message will appear at the bottom of the dialog box (see Figure 5.1).

Common triggers for the As a Copy warning are layers and transparency, which are supported by only a few file formats. When you see the warning, you have the option of saving the image as a copy or selecting a different file format from the Format pop-up menu. If you select a file format that does support the features of the image being saved, the warning disappears.

Photoshop uses As a Copy to prevent accidental loss of image features. If, for example, you have numerous layers in an image and attempt to save in a format that doesn't support layers, Photoshop will, by default, attempt to make a copy. This preserves the layers in the original for continued editing.

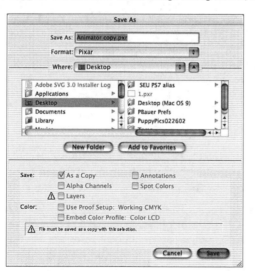

Figure 5.1
The image being saved contains layers, and the Pixar file format cannot support layers.

5

Save for Web

Save for Web is, as the name implies, a Web-oriented tool and, therefore, is restricted to the Web-related formats. (The difference between Web and print formats is explained in the section "Web Versus Print" later in this chapter.) Save As, on the other hand, enables you to convert a file to a variety of formats, including JPEG and GIF (see Figure 5.2). You cannot create a WBMP file using Save As.

Caution

In addition to Photoshop's native .psd file format, layers are supported in TIFF, but at some cost. The so-called advanced or enhanced TIFF features create files that might not be compatible with your page layout program. InDesign 2.0 supports layered TIFF files.

⇨ *For an in-depth look at Save for Web,* **see** *Chapter 24, "Save for Web and Image Optimization," p. 725.*

⇨ *For more information on preparing images for commercial printing,* **see** *Chapter 26, "The Printing Process: A Primer," p. 793.*

Figure 5.2
Each of the file format choices (and others) is explained individually later in this chapter.

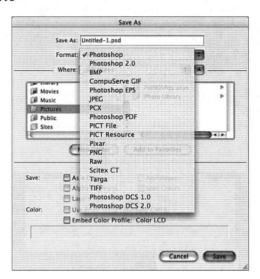

Export

Photoshop's Export command can generate paths for use with Adobe Illustrator. An Illustrator format file (.ai) is created. When opening the file in Illustrator, it contains only the unstroked, unfilled paths. The paths can be used to create objects or perhaps as clipping paths for an image.

Export can also create ZoomView files. ZoomView, from Viewpoint Corporation, is a sophisticated Web presentation technology that allows quick downloading of interactive graphics. The viewer can zoom and pan within the graphic without any additional hardware. For information on obtaining a license to broadcast ZoomView files over the Internet, contact Viewpoint (http://viewpoint.com).

Export Transparent Image

Another way Photoshop can assign a file format to an image is found under Photoshop's Help menu. The Export Transparent Image command walks you through the process of creating an image with a transparent background for use in a Web page or page layout document. You need answer only two questions, and an appropriate file is generated (see Figure 5.3).

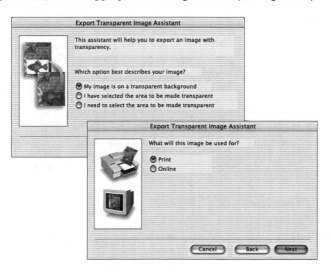

Figure 5.3
If you click the I Need to Select the Area to Be Made Transparent radio button, you will be instructed to make the selection before returning to the assistant.

If the image is not already on a transparent background, make a selection of the area before selecting the menu command. Depending on your needs, the automated assistant generates an EPS file with clipping path (for print) or a transparent GIF or PNG (for Web). After the file is created, the Save As dialog box opens. Do not change the file format in the Save As dialog box. The final file will have transparency defined as a matte (GIF) or by a clipping path (EPS).

⇨ *Clear on the difference between transparency created with clipping paths or mattes and that generated with masks? If not, see "Hard and Variable Transparency" in the NAPP Help Desk section at the end of this chapter.*

After you've saved the file created by the assistant, you'll be presented with a final dialog box. After clicking Finish, you can close the Photoshop file generated during the process. There's no need to save the file.

Photoshop's File-Handling Preferences

Several file-saving options can be set in Photoshop's Preferences. The top section of the File Handling pane (see Figure 5.4) enables you to determine what preview (if any) is saved with the file as well as whether the file extension is added to the name automatically.

Figure 5.4
The file extension is required for Windows, suggested for Mac OS X, and optional for Mac OS 9. Remember that many programs in which you place or view files require file extensions.

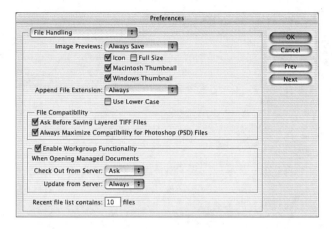

The File Compatibility section of the File Handling pane contains important options for file sharing and compatibility. Photoshop can create TIFF files that include layers, which might not be usable by other programs.

The option to maximize Photoshop compatibility adds a flattened composite of the image, which increases file size (often substantially). The composite is used by early versions of Photoshop (4.0 and before) and by some programs that can place Photoshop files.

Depending on compression, layered TIFFs can be somewhat smaller than layered Photoshop files. Otherwise, there is no real advantage to layered TIFF over layered .psd files.

Additional Considerations: Platforms and Compression

Although all the Web file formats and the major print-oriented formats are *cross-platform* (they can be viewed on both Macintosh and Windows computers), a number of the less common formats are primarily for use on one system or the other. In addition, such factors as file-naming conventions and media format could affect your ability to move a file from one operating system to another.

Windows requires that each file has an appropriate *extension*, a dot (period) and two- or three-letter suffix at the end of the filename. Lowercase extensions maximize compatibil-

If you move the cursor over the option to maximize Photoshop compatibility, you'll see a warning that without the flattened composite, the file may not be readable by *future* versions of Photoshop. However, later versions of the program devolving to the point where layers are not supported is inconceivable.

ity. This extension identifies the file format and tells the operating system which program to use to open the file. Mac OS X prefers a file extension, but if a file or file type has been associated with a particular program, the file can still be opened by double-clicking. When no program is associated with a file or file type, a warning dialog box appears, and you're asked to pick an application for opening the file (see Figure 5.5).

5

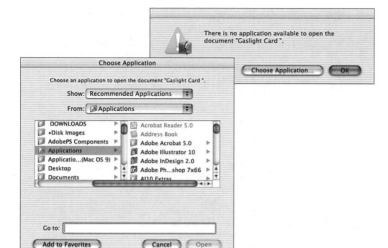

Figure 5.5
The warning message is shown in this example. When you click Choose Application, the dialog box is opened for you.

Mac OS 9 requires no file extension. However, using extensions is a good idea. Even if you never plan on sharing the file(s) with anyone using a different operating system, eventually you'll upgrade and want the files to still be usable.

▷ *You can change the program assigned to open a file format. See "Associating a File Type" in the NAPP Help Desk section at the end of this chapter.*

File compression can also be an issue. Compression schemes available in a file format are either *lossy* or *lossless*. Lossy compression reduces file size, in part, by discarding image data. When the file is reopened, the missing data is reconstructed from the surrounding image information. Lossless compression maintains all the original data. JPEG uses lossy compression, on a sliding scale, and PNG and GIF use lossless compression. Lossy compression can result in substantially smaller file sizes, but at the cost of some image quality.

The compression supplied by a file format should not be confused with that available through utilities. Compressed *archives* can be produced by such programs as StuffIt and from within Windows (see Figures 5.6 and 5.7).

Zipped, stuffed, and other archived files must be uncompressed by the same or another utility before a program can open them. In the archive, the file retains the format with which it was saved. These types of file compression can be considered lossless—that is, they do not degrade the image quality.

When archiving files, consider using a compression utility rather than the JPEG file format. The size of Photoshop and TIFF files can be substantially reduced, without losing any image quality.

5

Compression utilities are especially handy when transferring image files via e-mail. In addition to reducing the file size, which speeds transmission and helps avoid "over limit" message rejection, compression helps protect the files from corruption in transmission.

Figure 5.6
Utilities such as StuffIt can produce a variety of compressed files.

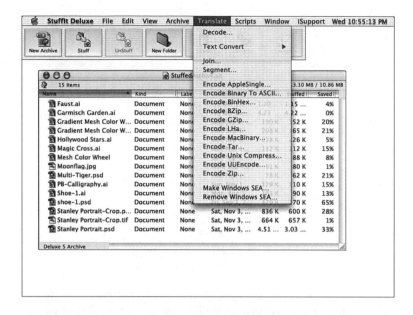

Figure 5.7
Windows XP can compress files, folders, and drives in a variety of ways. The inset shows the icon for a "zipped" folder.

Using the Photoshop Format in Other Programs

One of the greatest advantages to using the latest generation of Adobe products with Photoshop is SmartObjects. This feature enables you to insert Photoshop files in their native .psd format into Web pages and page layout documents. Adobe InDesign accepts .psd files directly into a page layout, flattening layers and applying masks, paths, and alpha channels. The original Photoshop file is untouched, and it can be reopened in Photoshop from within InDesign.

➪ *Interoperability between InDesign and Photoshop is discussed in more depth in an appendix to this book. **See** Appendix B, "Photoshop with InDesign, QuarkXPress, and Other Page Layout Programs," p. 905.*

Likewise, Adobe GoLive can place .psd files in a Web page, despite the fact that Web browsers cannot display them. You can continue to work with the original file in Photoshop and ImageReady, even changing slices. The image is updated in GoLive as necessary. When the Web page is finished, the file is optimized in GoLive with Save for Web.

SmartObjects not only gives you the convenience of using Photoshop's native .psd format in page layouts and Web pages, but also enables you to edit the original file and automatically update the image in the layout or Web page.

THE FILE FORMATS

Each file format that can be generated from Photoshop has its specific capabilities and intended purpose. Most offer one or more options as you save the file. Typically, a supplemental dialog box opens after you have selected a filename, format, and location in Save As.

In the following sections, the file formats are presented in the order in which they appear in Photoshop's Save As dialog box. At the end, you'll find a brief discussion of additional file formats for which you'll find plug-ins on the Photoshop CD.

Format Capabilities: The Overview

Different file formats have various capabilities. Table 5.1 shows a summary. The file formats (and their capabilities) are discussed individually in the sections that follow.

Table 5.1 File Format Capabilities

Format	Clipping Paths	Alpha Channels	Spot Channels	Paths	Vector Type	Layers	Primary Use
PSD	Y	Y	Y	Y	Y	Y	General
BMP	Y[1]	Y	N	Y	N	N	RGB
DCS 2.0	Y	Y	Y	N	N	N	Print
EPS	Y	N	N	N	Y[2]	N	Print
GIF	N[3]	N	N	N	N	N	Web
JPEG	Y	N	N	Y	N	N	Web/Archive
PCX	Y	N	N	Y	N	N	RGB
PDF	Y	Y	Y	Y	Y[2]	Y	(Various)
PICT	N	Y	N	Y	N	N	RGB
Pixar	Y	Y	N	Y	N	N	Video

5

Table 5.1 Continued

Format	Clipping Paths	Alpha Channels	Spot Channels	Paths	Vector Type	Layers	Primary Use
PNG	Y	N	N	Y	N	N	Web
RAW	Y	Y	Y	Y	N	N	Photo
SciTex	Y	N	N	Y	N	N	Scans
Targa	Y	N	N	Y	N	N	Video
TIFF	Y	Y	Y	Y	Y[4]	Y[4]	Print
WBMP	N	N	N	N	N	N	Web

1 Clipping masks are stored but not used by most other programs. Adobe InDesign does read the clipping path.

2 Type is rasterized if the file is reopened in Photoshop.

3 Transparent background can be maintained in GIF.

4 TIFF advanced mode preserves layers.

Photoshop (.psd)

Photoshop's native file format supports all of the program's capabilities. Files in this format can be placed in the latest versions of InDesign and GoLive as SmartObjects and can be opened in Adobe Illustrator. This is the default file format. Most workflows (but not all) benefit from maintaining a file in Photoshop format until it's time to create a final TIFF, EPS, JPEG, or other file. It's also usually a good idea to maintain the original image, with editable type and layers, for future use.

When saving in Photoshop format, the Save As dialog box indicates which features are used in the image (see Figure 5.8). If a check box is grayed out, that feature is unused. If you uncheck a box, the file is saved as a copy.

Figure 5.8
Selecting the As a Copy check box without changing other options simply appends "copy" to the original filename.

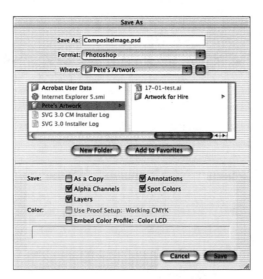

Photoshop 2.0

The Photoshop 2 file format does not support layers or spot colors. It does, however, allow you to retain an alpha channel with the image. Use this file format when preparing images for use with programs that support only the earliest .psd format.

BMP

The Windows Bitmap file format is a raster image format, used primarily in Windows. BMP files cannot be displayed with a Web browser, so they're not appropriate for Web design. Nor can BMP be used for commercial printing, because the format doesn't support CMYK. BMP files *can* be inserted into Microsoft Word and PowerPoint documents. The file format supports up to 24-bit color with an alpha channel. After choosing a name and location for the file and selecting BMP as the file format, the Save button moves you to the BMP Options dialog box, shown in the center of Figure 5.9.

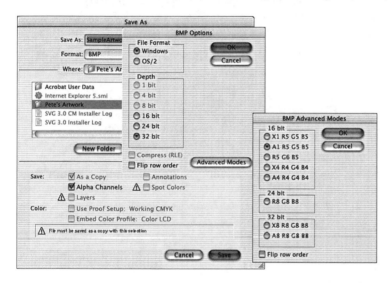

Figure 5.9
Files without alpha channels are saved as 24-bit.

The options include making the file Windows or OS/2 compatible and selecting the color bit depth. You can compress 4-bit and 8-bit BMP files by using Run Length Encoding (RLE), a lossless compression scheme. Clicking the Advanced Modes button opens the BMP Advanced Modes dialog box seen to the right. In that dialog box, you can determine how the selected number of color bits will be distributed among the channels.

CompuServe GIF

GIF is a common Web file format, suitable for illustrations and other images with large areas of solid color and no or few gradients or blends. Many logos and cartoons, as well as Web navigation items, such as banners and buttons, are appropriate for GIF. This file format is not appropriate for most photographs and other continuous tone images because it can record a maximum of only 256 distinct colors. (A photograph might have thousands or millions of individual colors.)

Although very small and adequately detailed thumbnails of photographs can be created as GIFs, a continuous tone image typically suffers from *posterization*. When areas of similar (but not identical) color are forced into a single tint, the image quality can suffer severely.

The color table (the list of specific colors included in the image) is controlled through the Indexed Color dialog box. This box opens after you select the CompuServe GIF file format, a name, and a location for the file, and then click OK.

*For full information on the color options available for GIF files, **see** "Indexed Color," **p. 186**, in Chapter 7, "Color Theory and Practice."*

Among GIF's capabilities are interlacing and animation. When a GIF image is interlaced, a Web browser displays every other line of pixels first, and then fills in the balance of the image. This allows the Web page's visitor to see the image loading, giving the impression that progress is being made and that the image is loading faster. Animated GIFs are created in ImageReady.

The GIF format supports transparency in a limited way: A specific pixel can be opaque or transparent. You cannot have any pixels that are partially transparent in a GIF image. If the image is on a transparent background, you need only select the Transparency check box in the Indexed Color dialog box (see Figure 5.10).

Figure 5.10
The Indexed Color dialog box opens automatically when you use Save As to create a GIF.

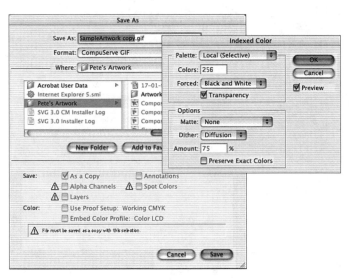

You can also specify a color to be made transparent by using the Matte options in the Indexed Color dialog box. Dithering allows an image in Indexed Color mode to simulate more colors than are actually contained in the color table by interspersing dots of two or more colors.

*GIFs can also be created with Save for Web. **See** Chapter 24, "Save for Web and Image Optimization," p. 725.*

The GIF standard is maintained by CompuServe, and software that creates or displays GIF images must be licensed by Unisys. (The licensing fee was paid by Adobe, and part of Photoshop's purchase price goes to the licensing.)

Photoshop EPS

PostScript is a page description language, developed by Adobe and at the heart of the desktop publishing revolution of the 1990s. An *Encapsulated PostScript* (*EPS*) file can contain any combination of text, graphics, or images and is designed to be included ("encapsulated") in a PostScript document. EPS files contain the description of a single page or an element of a page.

EPS is typically used for elements to be included in a page layout or PDF document. Because PDF files can be designed for onscreen display as well as print, EPS supports the RGB color mode in addition to CMYK and Grayscale modes. EPS files cannot be displayed by Web browsers (although they can be incorporated into PDF files, which can be shown through a browser plug-in).

One of the greatest advantages of EPS as a file format is the capability of including both raster and vector data and artwork.

➯ *To learn more about the difference between raster and vector images, **see** Chapter 6, "Pixels, Vectors, and Resolution," p. 155.*

EPS supports all color modes except Multichannel and does not support layers or alpha and spot channels. (The DCS variation of EPS supports both spot colors and masks. It is discussed separately, later in this chapter.) The EPS Options dialog box (shown in Figure 5.11) offers several options.

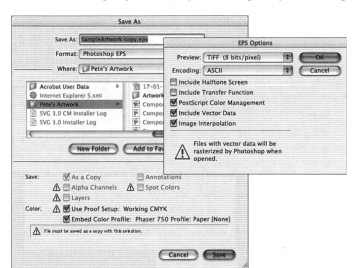

Figure 5.11
Note in the Save As dialog box that the warning triangles indicate which features are not supported by the EPS file format.

The Preview option determines what—if any—image will be shown in the page layout program where you're placing the file. The preview doesn't normally have any effect on the printed image and is used for onscreen display only. (Note that Windows offers only None and TIFF as preview options.)

- **None**—No image preview is saved. Although Photoshop's File Browser can still generate a thumbnail, files placed into a page layout document show on the screen as a box with diagonal lines.

- **TIFF (1 bit/pixel)**—A black-and-white version of the image is shown in a page layout document.

- **TIFF (8 bits/pixel)**—A color version of the image is displayed onscreen in page layout programs. This option provides a reasonably accurate preview and is cross-platform.

- **Macintosh (1 bit/pixel)**—A black-and-white PICT preview is included with the EPS file. The PICT file format is designed for use on Macintosh systems but can be used for Windows programs as well.

- **Macintosh (8 bits/pixel)**—A color PICT preview is prepared.

- **Macintosh (JPEG)**—Using a JPEG preview can reduce the file size but reduces compatibility.

The Encoding options include ASCII, Binary, and JPEG. ASCII is cross-platform and compatible with virtually all page layout programs. Binary is a Macintosh encoding system, and it can produce smaller files. JPEG encoding produces comparatively tiny files, but uses lossy compression (which can result in image degradation) and is not compatible with all page layout programs. In addition, JPEG encoding can prevent an image from properly separating to individual color plates. ASCII is certainly the safest choice when the image will be sent to a printer or service bureau.

Halftone screens and transfer functions are established through the Print Preview dialog box. Screen frequency, angle, and shape can be established for each ink. These criteria determine the distribution and appearance of the ink droplets applied to the paper. The transfer function compensates for a miscalibrated image-setter.

PostScript Color Management is available only for CMYK images outputting to devices with PostScript Level 3. This option should *not* be selected if the image will be placed into another document that itself will be color managed.

When the image contains unrasterized type and/or vector artwork or paths, select the Include Vector Data check box. When outputting to a PostScript device (such as a laser printer or imagesetter), the vector outlines will be preserved and the artwork will print more precisely. You need not include vector data when outputting to an inkjet printer.

Image Interpolation, when checked, allows a low-resolution image to be upsampled when printing to a PostScript Level 2 or 3 printer. Increasing the resolution during printing helps smooth edges and improve the general appearance of low-resolution images, but could introduce a slight out-of-focus appearance. If the output device isn't PostScript level 2 or higher, this option has no effect.

> **Caution**
>
> Never change the halftone screen settings or transfer functions unless specifically instructed to do so by your printer or service bureau. Incorrect data can result in project delays and additional costs.

> **Caution**
>
> The advantages of vector type and artwork are lost if an EPS file is reopened in Photoshop. Photoshop must rasterize an EPS file to work with it. If you've saved vector data, do *not* reopen the EPS file in Photoshop.

⇨ *For more information on upsampling, **see** "Two Types of Resampling," **p. 630,** Chapter 20, "Image Cropping, Resizing, and Sharpening."*

JPEG

Joint Photographic Experts Group (JPEG) is technically a file compression algorithm rather than a file format. The actual file format is JFIF (JPEG File Interchange Format), although JPEG is more commonly used. JPEG supports Grayscale, RGB, and CMYK color modes and can be used with files more than four times as large as Photoshop's 30,000×30,000 pixel maximum. JPEG does not support transparency, alpha channels, spot colors, or layers. Paths can be saved with a JPEG file, including clipping paths (although most programs can't use the clipping path, with the notable exception of InDesign). Type is rasterized when a file is saved as JPEG.

It's important to keep in mind that JPEG is a *lossy* compression system. Image data is thrown away when the file is saved. When the image is reopened, the missing data is re-created by averaging the colors of surrounding pixels. See the Sidebar "Digital Cameras and Resaving JPEGs" for more information.

JPEG is commonly used on the Web for photographs and other continuous tone images in which one color blends seamlessly into another. Because of its support for 24-bit color (in RGB mode), it is far better than GIF for displaying the subtle shifts in color that occur in nature. (Rather than GIF's maximum of 256 distinct colors, JPEG files can include more than 16.7 million colors.) JPEG is the most common file format for digital cameras because of the outstanding file size reduction capabilities.

When you choose JPEG as the file format and click OK, Photoshop's Save As dialog box is replaced with the JPEG Options dialog box (see Figure 5.12). You can select a matte color, a level of compression, and one of three options for Web browser display.

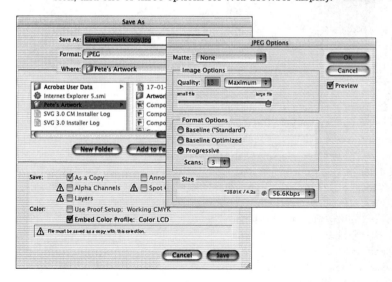

Figure 5.12
The bottom of the dialog box shows the estimate of the amount of time it will take, under optimal conditions, for the file to download at a given modem speed at the selected quality setting.

⇨ *JPEG files can also be created with the Save for Web option. **See** Chapter 24, "Save for Web and Image Optimization," **p. 725**.*

Simulating Transparency in JPEG Files

Although JPEG does not support transparency, you can use the Matte pop-up menu to help simulate it. From the menu, choose a color that matches the background of the Web page into which the image will be placed. By replacing transparent areas of the image with the selected color (rather than just flattening to white), those areas can match the Web page's background (see Figure 5.13).

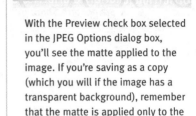

With the Preview check box selected in the JPEG Options dialog box, you'll see the matte applied to the image. If you're saving as a copy (which you will if the image has a transparent background), remember that the matte is applied only to the copy, not the original image.

Figure 5.13
The Photoshop image is shown at the top. To the left, it's been saved as a JPEG with a red matte and placed into a GoLive document with a red background. On the right is the image as it appears in a Web browser—a JPEG duck surrounded by "transparency."

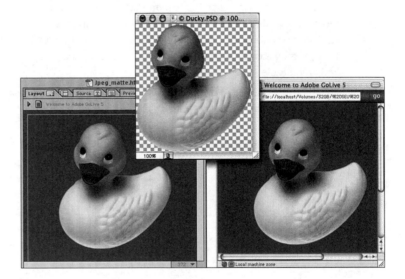

Optimization Options

The cornerstone of the JPEG format is image optimization. The JPEG Options dialog box presents you with the tools to strike a compromise between file size and image quality. The Preview check box enables you to monitor changes to the image's appearance. The slider ranges from 0 (very small file, possibly substantial quality loss) to 12 (large file, very little—if any—damage due to file compression). The Quality pop-up menu offers Low (3), Medium (5), High (8), and Maximum (10). Figure 5.14 shows a comparison of file sizes and file quality, using the duck image from the previous figure. The chart shows file format, compression type or level, and file size as reported by Mac OS X's Show Info command. (Different images might produce substantially different results.)

Caution

When preparing images for the Web, you should generally make final decisions based on the image's appearance at 100% zoom. With the exception of SVG images, Web browsers can display images only at 100%, so base your decisions on how the pictures will look to the Web page's visitor.

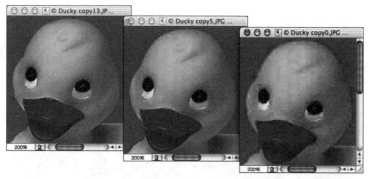

Figure 5.14
From left to right, the three images show JPEG quality settings of 12, 5, and 0. Note the substantial image quality degradation at the lowest quality setting.

Photoshop	Tiff	Tiff	JPEG	JPEG	JPEG	JPEG	JPEG	JPEG
uncompressed	uncompressed	LZW	13	10	8	5	3	0
248 KB	236 KB	104 KB	104 KB	60 KB	52 KB	48 KB	44 KB	44 KB

Format Options

The Format Options section offers three different variations from which to choose:

Different programs use differing JPEG quality/compression scales. Photoshop 7 uses a 13-step scale (0–12), Illustrator uses 0–10, and Save for Web works with 0–100%.

- **Baseline ("Standard")**—This is the most widely compatible version of JPEG, which can be displayed by all graphics-capable Web browsers. It's also the version to use for non-Web JPEG files.

- **Baseline Optimized**—Optimized JPEG can produce better color fidelity but is not compatible with all older Web browsers.

- **Progressive**—Like interlacing a GIF file, Progressive JPEG files appear in stages in a Web browser, providing visual feedback and the illusion of speed to the Web page's visitor. You can elect to have the image appear fully in three, four, or five passes. (Three is usually adequate.) Progressive JPEG files are typically (but not always) slightly larger that Baseline Standard versions of the same files.

At the bottom of the JPEG Options dialog box is an area that shows the size of the file that will be created with the selected options as well as how long such a file will take to download. The pop-up menu enables you to select modem speeds ranging from 14.4Kbps to 2MBps.

JPEG/JFIF became an ISO standard in 1990. Baseline JPEG is in the public domain, but many variations are patented and licensed. Variations of lossless and near-lossless JPEG are under development.

Resaving JPEG Images

Because JPEG is a lossy compression scheme (some data is thrown away when compressing), it's generally understood that files should be saved in the format only once (if at all). Resaving a JPEG file in JPEG format sends the image through the compression process again, possibly resulting in damage to the image's appearance because of the second round of data loss.

With the booming popularity of digital cameras, more and more images are being captured as JPEGs. To completely eliminate JPEG as a file format for resaving these images (and JPEGs created for the Web) after editing is unfeasible. To best understand how to avoid damaging an image when resaving as JPEG, you should know a little about *how* JPEG compresses.

Lossy compression, such as JPEG, can produce far smaller file sizes than lossless compression. That's because some image information is actually thrown away during the compression process. When the image is reopened, the existing data is averaged to re-create the missing pixels. However, the cost is image quality (see Figure 5.15).

Figure 5.15
As you can see, the image on the right (saved at Quality 1) has a much degraded appearance compared to the original (left) and the image saved at Quality 12 (middle). Note, however, that the lower quality produced a file size about one-third that of the higher-quality image.

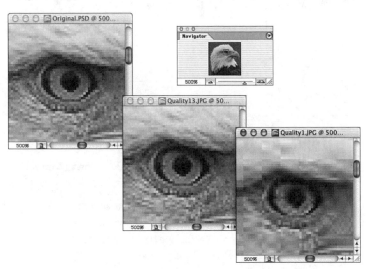

Zooming in to 800% shows one key aspect of how JPEG works. In the low-quality version of the image, JPEG's distinctive 8×8 blocks of pixels are visible (see Figure 5.16). Colors can be averaged or patterns determined based on the content of the blocks.

Figure 5.16
An image is broken down into these 8×8 pixel blocks starting from the top-left corner.

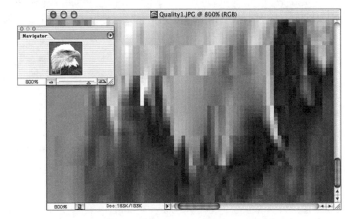

Because JPEG uses blocks of pixels to compress an image, cropping becomes important. If you must crop an image that has already been substantially compressed with JPEG, any cropping from the top and left should be in increments of 8 pixels. Two copies were made of the image saved at JPEG Quality 1 (see Figure 5.17). One copy (left) was cropped exactly 8 pixels from the top and 8 pixels from the left. The second copy (right) had 4 pixels cropped from the top and left. Both copies were then resaved at JPEG Quality 1.

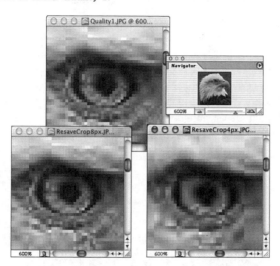

Figure 5.17
The image that was cropped in increments of 8 pixels (left) bears far more resemblance to the original (top). On the right, the image that was cropped in increments of 4 pixels looks much blurrier.

Perhaps the most precise way to crop an image in increments of 8 pixels is to use the Canvas Size dialog box. It not only allows you to specify an exact pixel size, but the Relative check box even eliminates the need to do math—select the check box and enter a negative number to reduce the canvas size (see Figure 5.18).

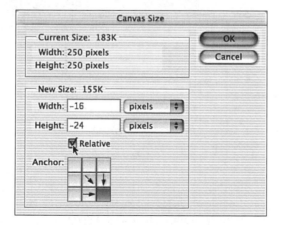

Figure 5.18
The grid, called the proxy, determines from where the canvas will be reduced or enlarged. If cropping from the center, remember to work in increments of 16 pixels— 8 for each edge.

Another technique for preserving image quality when resaving a JPEG file as a JPEG file is to use exactly the same compression setting as originally used. *If* the original quality/compression setting is known, and *if* the image is being recompressed in the same program, *then* this technique is valid.

However, keep in mind that different programs use different "scales" of JPEG compression. Saving a JPEG file at Quality 4 in Photoshop 7 is not the same as saving as Quality 4 in Illustrator 10, nor the same as using 40% in Save for Web. And there is no set formula to translate between compression settings from a digital camera to Photoshop.

When minimizing additional image degradation is important, consider resaving JPEG files at High or Maximum Quality, especially if the image has been cropped. The file size might be somewhat larger than the original JPEG, but quality will be maintained.

If you use a digital camera, a little experimentation can help determine which quality setting you should use. In the example shown in Figure 5.19, the image in the upper right was taken at SQ (Standard Quality), which captures 640×480 pixels for this camera. To the left is the same scene, shot at HQ (High Quality), which produces an image 1600×1200 pixels, compressed at approximately the equivalent of using JPEG Quality 7 in Photoshop. The image in the lower right was shot at SHQ (Super High Quality), 1600×1200 pixels, minimal compression.

Figure 5.19
The two lower images are zoomed to 300%. The upper-right image, because of the smaller pixel dimensions, is zoomed to 700%.

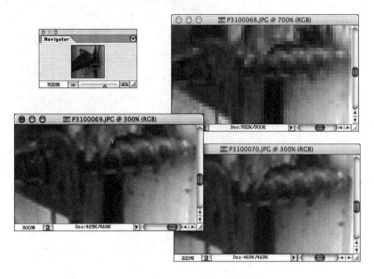

The two larger JPEG images are cropped to about 469KB when open in Photoshop. The original images as captured were 480KB (left) and 956KB (lower right). With the minimal difference in image quality and the substantial difference in file size between HQ and SHQ, for most purposes the more practical setting for this camera is HQ. Your camera may differ.

PCX

One of the original bitmap file formats for MS-DOS, PCX is readable by most graphic programs. PCX files can be RGB, Grayscale, Indexed Color, or Bitmap modes. The format doesn't support transparency, layers, alpha channels, spot colors, or vector artwork and type. It can support images in color depths of 1-, 4-, 8- and 24-bits. There are no options when saving as PCX. Generally, PCX is considered to be an outdated format, superseded by BMP.

Photoshop PDF

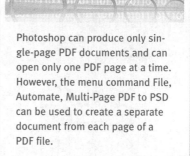

Adobe's Portable Document Format (PDF) is a cross-platform format that can be opened and viewed in the free Acrobat Reader, available for most computer operating systems. PDF is, at heart, a PostScript file format. Photoshop breaks PDF into two categories: Photoshop PDF and Generic PDF. Both can be opened, but only the former can be created.

Photoshop PDF supports all of Photoshop's color modes, transparency, vector type and artwork, spot and alpha channels, and compression (JPEG or ZIP, except for bitmap images, which use CCITT-4 compression).

The PDF Options dialog box (see Figure 5.20) offers a choice of compression schemes as well as several other choices.

Photoshop can produce only single-page PDF documents and can open only one PDF page at a time. However, the menu command File, Automate, Multi-Page PDF to PSD can be used to create a separate document from each page of a PDF file.

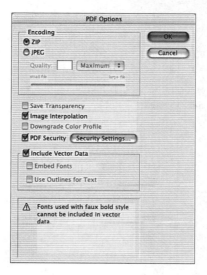

Figure 5.20
After selecting a filename, location, and Photoshop PDF as the file format, clicking OK opens this dialog box.

5

Although ZIP compression is most effective for images with large areas of solid color, it is also more reliable than JPEG for PDFs that are destined for process printing. (PDFs compressed with JPEG might not separate correctly.) JPEG, however, can produce substantially smaller files (at the cost of image quality).

Photoshop 7 also enables you to use standard PDF security, such as that added to PDFs in Adobe Acrobat (see Figure 5.21). Passwords can be required for opening the document as well as printing, selecting, changing, copying, or extracting the document's content.

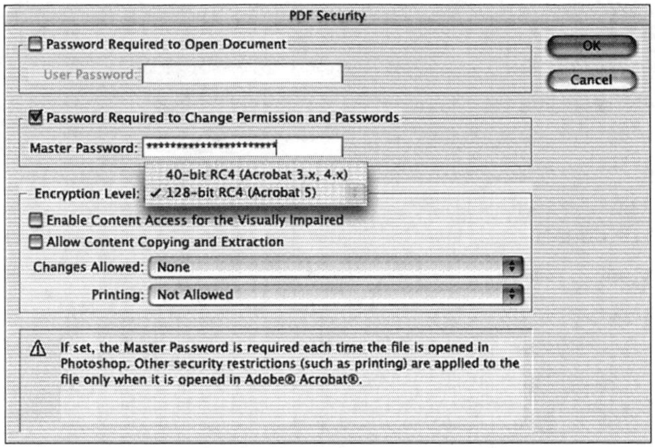

Figure 5.21
Other check boxes in the PDF Security dialog box are made available if they pertain to the file being saved.

PICT File

PICT is primarily a Macintosh file format. It is a versatile graphics format, supporting RGB, Grayscale, Indexed Color, and Bitmap color modes as well as 16-bit color in Grayscale and RGB. An alpha channel is supported in RGB mode, but layers and spot channels are not.

The options for PICT are restricted to bit depth and compression. PICT uses RLE compression, but with QuickTime installed, JPEG is also available.

PICT Resource (.rsr)

PICT Resources are found in a Macintosh file's resource fork. PICT Resource images might include a program's splash screen. Both the resource name and ID can be specified when saving a PICT Resource (see Figure 5.22).

Figure 5.22
Resolution and compression can also be set in this dialog box.

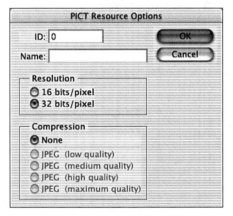

A single alpha channel is supported in RGB mode, but not in the other color modes. Layers and spot channels cannot be saved with PICT Resource files.

Pixar (.pxr)

Pixar Studios, creators of such animated films as *Toy Story* and *Monsters, Inc.*, has a graphics format for use with its workstations. The .pxr format supports Grayscale and RGB modes, in 8-bit color with an optional alpha channel, but without transparency, spot channels, or layers. There are no options when saving in Pixar format.

Single frames of a Pixar animation can be opened in Photoshop for *rotoscoping* (editing or masking individual frames of a sequence). The frames are then resaved as .pxr files for insertion back into the animation.

PNG

Developed as an alternative to GIF and JPEG for the Web, Portable Network Graphics come in both 8-bit (Indexed Color) and 24-bit (RGB) variations. JPEG's lossy compression and the licensing requirement associated with GIF's compression lead to the demand for an alternative. PNG-8 and PNG-24 are both now widely supported by Web browsers.

The Save As dialog box makes no distinction between PNG-8 and PNG-24, instead using the file's existing color mode. If the image is RGB, PNG-24 is automatically created. If the image is Indexed Color, PNG-8 is used. Grayscale is also 8-bit. (Save for Web allows you to specify whether you want to create an 8-bit or 24-bit PNG file.) Because PNG does not support CMYK, it is not appropriate for commercial printing applications.

Like interlaced GIF and progressive JPEG, PNG files can also be displayed incrementally in a Web browser. After selecting the PNG format, name, and location and clicking OK, the PNG Options dialog box enables you to make the selection (see Figure 5.23).

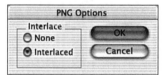

Figure 5.23
Interlacing can add slightly to the file's size. It's not necessary with small interface items but is often appropriate for larger images.

Images in Indexed Color mode are comparable in size and appearance when saved as GIF and as PNG-8. PNG-24 cannot match the file size reduction available in JPEG; however, the format does offer transparency (which is not available at all in JPEG) and uses a lossless compression algorithm, thus preserving image quality.

Raw

The Raw file format records pixel color and very little else. Each pixel is described in binary format by color. Because the file doesn't record such basic information as file dimensions and color mode, coordination and communication are important. If incorrect data is entered into the Raw Options dialog box when opening an image, an unrecognizable mess is likely (see Figure 5.24).

Figure 5.24
In the upper left, the image was opened properly. To the right, the Interleaved option wasn't selected. Below, the dimensions were incorrect. If the number of channels or the bit depth is wrong, you'll see a warning that the file size doesn't match.

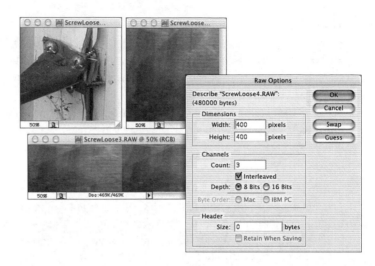

When saving an image in the Raw file format in Macintosh, you can specify the four-character file type, the four-character creator code, how many bytes of information appear in a header before the image data begins (if any), and in what order to save the color information (see Figure 5.25). When interleaved, color information is recorded sequentially for each pixel—the first pixel's red, green, and blue values are followed by those three values for the second pixel, and so on. The sequence is recorded as R,G,B, R,G,B, R,G,B…. Non-interleaved order records the red values for all the pixels, then the green values for each pixel, and then the blue values. The sequence is then R,R,R… G,G,G… B,B,B….

Figure 5.25
Before saving a file in the Raw format, make sure you know and understand the requirements for the program in which the file will be opened.

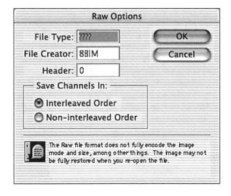

Some digital cameras offer Raw as an alternative to JPEG to avoid lossy compression. Check the documentation for information about the specifications for those files before opening.

Scitex CT (.sct)

Scitex Continuous Tone file format is used for some high-end image processing equipment. It can work with CMYK, Grayscale, and RGB images. When saving from Photoshop, the format does not support alpha or spot channels.

Scitex CT generally is appropriate only for use with Scitex equipment. The files sizes can be very large, especially for CMYK images, but the output can be extremely good. The Scitex Digital Printing division can provide additional information about the file format at www.scitexdpi.com.

Targa (.tga)

Targa is a file format designed for use on Windows computers that incorporate a Truevision video board. Targa supports RGB images with alpha channels as well as Indexed Color and Grayscale images without alpha channels.

TIFF (.tif)

Tagged Image File Format (TIFF) and EPS are the two most widely accepted image formats for commercial printing. TIFF files can be produced directly by most desktop scanners and many digital cameras. The format supports CMYK, RGB, Lab, Indexed Color, Grayscale, and Bitmap color modes. In Bitmap mode, alpha channels are not supported, but they are available in all other color modes. Spot channels are supported, and clipping paths can also be saved with TIFF images to denote areas of transparency.

Photoshop offers a variety of TIFF options, some of which are not supported in other programs. Background transparency, layers, and JPEG compression are three. Additional TIFF options are found in the TIFF Options dialog box, which appears following the Save As dialog box (see Figure 5.26).

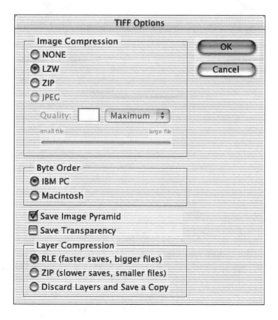

Figure 5.26
Some options in this dialog box might be grayed out and unavailable, depending on the image's content.

5

For maximum compatibility, choose LZW as the compression scheme. ZIP and JPEG are not supported by many programs that use TIFF files. JPEG offers the same 0–13 scale of quality available in the JPEG Options dialog box.

The Byte Order option determines compatibility with Macintosh or IBM PC computer systems. Because the Mac has no trouble reading the IBM version of TIFF files, that is the safest choice.

Although Photoshop itself doesn't read a TIFF file's image pyramid, the multi-resolution data can be saved for other programs, such as InDesign. *Image pyramid* refers to multiple versions of the same image being stored in one file, each at a different resolution. Photoshop reads only the highest resolution version of a TIFF file.

If the file contains background transparency, you can elect to save that transparency. As with other advanced TIFF features, the transparency option is not widely supported for TIFF files; however, it is supported by InDesign 2.0 (see Figure 5.27). (Remember that this transparency refers to the entire file, not layers above a background layer.)

When a file is saved with layers, you have the option of determining how those layers will be compressed. Because layers can greatly increase file size, ZIP may produce substantially smaller files. You can also choose at this point to disable layers in the TIFF file and save as a copy. In terms of the resulting file, there is no difference between discarding layers with this option and unchecking the Layers check box in the Save As dialog box.

Because not all other programs can read a TIFF file's layers, Photoshop saves a flattened version of the image as well. Saving layers in this file format triggers a warning message from Photoshop. Because a flattened version of the image is also saved in the TIFF file, the warning can be ignored.

Figure 5.27
If the image is to be used in a program that doesn't support transparency in TIFF files, a flattened version will be shown.

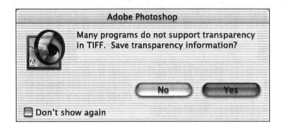

Photoshop DCS 1.0

Desktop Color Separations (DCS) is a version of EPS developed by Quark. (The file that's produced has the .eps extension.) Version 1.0 should be used only with older programs that don't read the DCS 2.0 standard. DCS 1.0 supports CMYK and Multichannel modes and creates a separate file for each color channel, plus an optional 8-bit color or grayscale composite. The DCS 1.0 Format dialog box appears after you click OK in the Save As dialog box (see Figure 5.28).

You can elect to save no preview, a 1- or 8-bit TIFF preview, and in Macintosh, a 1- or 8-bit Macintosh (PICT) preview or a JPEG preview. The 8-bit TIFF preview is the most widely supported. In addition to the preview, which is used primarily in dialog boxes, you have the option of including a grayscale or color composite image or no composite at all. The composite is used to show the image when a page layout document is viewed onscreen.

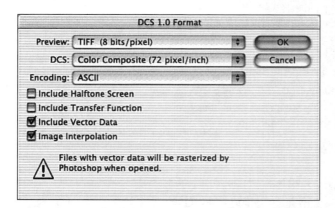

The encoding options include Binary, ASCII, and JPEG. As with EPS files, ASCII is used in Windows and can be read by Macintosh programs, Binary produces smaller files but is Mac-specific, and JPEG reduces both file size and compatibility. In addition, JPEG encoding can prevent an image from properly separating to individual color plates. ASCII is certainly the safest choice when the image will be sent to a printer or service bureau.

The Print Preview dialog box offers access to halftone screens and transfer functions for the file. These criteria determine the distribution and appearance of the ink droplets applied to the paper. The transfer function compensates for a miscalibrated imagesetter. Do not make changes to the screens or include a transfer function without explicit guidance from your printer or service bureau.

Photoshop DCS 2.0

DCS 2.0 is a more sophisticated version of Desktop Color Separations. The majority of its options are the same as those described for DCS 1.0. However, DCS 2.0 gives you several options when it comes to what file or files are actually produced (see Figure 5.29).

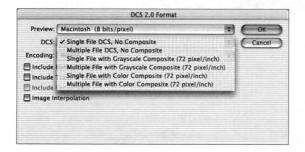

If you choose any of the three Multiple File options (no composite, grayscale composite, color composite), one file is generated for each color channel. The four process channels (if present in the image) use the channel's letter for a file extension. Spot channel extensions are numbers, starting with 5. The composite, if generated, will have the .eps extension.

For example, the file "Target" with two spot channels could be saved as DCS 2.0, with multiple files and a color composite. The files generated would be Target.C, Target.M, Target.Y, Target.K, Target.5, Target.6, and Target.eps.

DCS 2.0 should be selected over DCS 1.0 in any circumstance where both are supported. The single file saves disk space and can simplify file exchange and handling.

WBMP

Wireless Bitmap (WBMP) is generated in Photoshop only through Save for Web. It is a raster image format designed for use with mobile computing devices, such as portable digital assistants (PDAs) and wireless Internet handheld terminals. The file format supports only 1-bit images—each pixel is either black or white. However, you can use dithering to make the image appear to be grayscale rather than bitmap. There is no compression option.

WBMP optimization in Save for Web converts pixels darker than 50% gray to black, and those lighter, to white. If part (or all) of your image seems to be missing, select one of the three forms of dithering.

Photoshop can also open Photo CD files but cannot save them. High-resolution Pro Photo CD can also be opened in Photoshop.

Additional Plug-Ins

By default, Photoshop installs a folder of additional file format plug-ins (see Figure 5.30). If you need to use these formats, the appropriate plug-in can be added to the File Formats folder of Photoshop's Plug-Ins folder.

Figure 5.30
Even if you work with some of these programs, it's likely that you can use a more mainstream format to move your images.

THE FINAL DESTINATIONS

The vast majority of images created or prepared in Photoshop are destined for the World Wide Web or for print. The difference between the two is substantial, and the ultimate use of the image must be considered when selecting a file format.

Images created in Photoshop can also be used in a variety of other situations. For example, photographs or illustrations can be prepared for use in Microsoft PowerPoint or other presentation programs. Digital video productions can use Photoshop files for titling. Computer game production often involves Photoshop for creating textures. Templates and navigation elements for kiosk and terminal displays can be created in Photoshop, too. Word processing documents can accept images created in Photoshop.

Check the documentation for the program in which you'll be using the Photoshop artwork. You'll want to check for information on file formats that can be opened or placed in the program, color mode and bit depth requirements, limits on file sizes, applicability of alpha channels or clipping paths for transparency, and any other factors that could determine which file format is most appropriate.

Web Versus Print

The World Wide Web uses certain standards in an attempt to ensure that everybody can see everything, as long as they have a decent computer and a relatively recent Web browser. These standards include certain types of file formats for graphics so that all browsers can display images from the Web.

Page layout programs accept certain file formats that allow the best reproduction of the image with ink on paper. Illustration programs that you use with Photoshop are able to create graphics for both print and Web.

Because the requirements are different, and even the color mode differs between the Web (RGB) and print (CMYK), the file format you choose should depend on the image's final destination.

Generally speaking, the print file formats are TIFF, EPS, and PDF. For Web, Photoshop/ImageReady can produce GIF, JPEG, PNG, and WBMP files. In addition, a variety of other file formats are available for different purposes.

Commercial Printing Versus Inkjet Printers

Keep in mind that there's a huge difference between preparing an image for commercial printing and preparing an image for output to an inkjet printer. With the exception of those using a hardware or software RIP (raster image processor), inkjet printers require RGB color data. The vast majority of inkjet printers are used with programs that do not support CMYK color. (CMYK color mode is available only in professional-grade graphics and layout programs.)

Another important difference is that images prepared in Photoshop that eventually are printed commercially are typically placed into a page layout program. Inkjet-destined images are usually printed directly from Photoshop. Additionally, inkjet printers can output virtually any file format created from Photoshop.

Presentation and Word Processing Programs

Microsoft PowerPoint is the leading presentation program. The graphics file formats that it accepts vary from version to version. However, when creating images in Photoshop for use in PowerPoint, you can generally be sure that it will accept JPEG, GIF, PNG, TIFF, EPS, BMP, and PICT.

5

The most recent version of PowerPoint for Macintosh also accepts such files as PDF, TGA, and even Photoshop's own PSD format. PowerPoint also supports numerous file formats that cannot be created in Photoshop, such as WMF and EMF (vector-based clipart file formats).

In PowerPoint, graphics are added to a slide by using the menu command Insert, Picture, From File (see Figure 5.31).

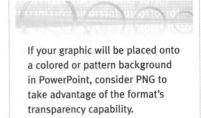

If your graphic will be placed onto a colored or pattern background in PowerPoint, consider PNG to take advantage of the format's transparency capability.

Figure 5.31
The dialog box that this command opens allows you to navigate to the folder or disk holding the required image.

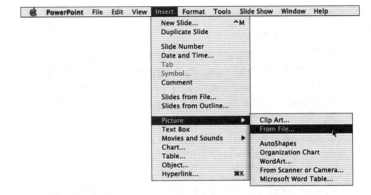

The presentation program Power Show from ScanSoft can import BMP, JPEG, PSD, TGA, and TIFF files.

Microsoft Word and other word processors can add a variety of raster and vector image formats to documents. Recent versions of Word can work with such formats as BMP, EPS, GIF, JPEG, PDF, PICT, PSD, and TIFF, among others. Because most word processing documents have a white background, transparency is less of an issue than it is with presentation programs.

Images can typically be scaled or resized numerically after they've been added to the presentation or word processing document. However, you should be aware of resolution issues. If a presentation is to be shown onscreen via computer, a resolution of 72ppi is probably adequate. Too high a resolution can lead to delays in the graphic appearing onscreen, slowing down slide changes.

Digital Video

A number of digital video programs accept various file formats that can be produced in Photoshop. Files can be created for textures, titling, and inserted still images.

Outputting to Film Recorders

Film recorders (sometimes referred to as *slide printers*) can be considered printers. However, instead of using paper, they print to photographic film. The most common recorders typically print to 35mm slide film. High-end professional models can print to negative as well as transparency film and can handle medium- and large-format film. Recorders designed for 35mm slide film often produce foggy images when photographic negative film is used. Images are often printed to slides for presentation purposes and printed to negative or positive for printing and archiving.

Graphic images to be output to film need to be measured a bit differently. Most film recorders measure resolution as a series of vertical lines across the film. The standard resolutions are 4,000, 8,000, and 16,000 lines. Note that these are not "lines per inch," but total lines. Each line represents a dot. The higher the number, the more information sent to the film.

The sharpness of the output can vary widely among film recorders of the same resolution. One recorder may use 4,000 lines on a cathode ray tube (CRT) measuring 4 inches wide. Another might place 4,000 lines on a 6-inch CRT. The actual size of the dots (measured in millimeters) can also vary from recorder to recorder. As the image is projected onto the CRT, each dot "blooms," or spreads. The more overlap, the softer the image. Typically (but not always), larger CRTs have less overlap. However, a smaller dot on a 4-inch CRT might produce a sharper image than a larger dot on a 6-inch CRT.

Another feature of film recorders is 33-bit or 36-bit color. This feature allows for a wider range of colors, often more than the source program can produce. Images being recorded to film almost always are RGB. The exceptions are usually CMYK images that are being archived or must be duplicated from film.

Depending on the film recorder's software, Photoshop can print directly to a film recorder, as it would to an imagesetter, laser printer, or inkjet printer. The film recorder is selected just as you would select a printer. The command File, Export is used with some film recorders. In other cases, the image must be prepared to be opened in or imported into a program that serves as the interface with the recorder. Among the most common file formats required are TIFF, EPS, BMP, PICT, and JPEG. PostScript is often an option on film recorders.

The documentation of many film recorders suggests appropriate sizes for images to be output in terms of file size. For example, the documentation may recommend that a 24-bit image be 5MB to fill a 35mm slide. If the image will occupy only part of a slide (in a presentation, for example), the file size can be reduced proportionally.

However, when you're preparing an image for a film recorder, it's better to know the actual *addressable* dimensions, in pixels. This is the number of pixels needed for an exact fit onto the film. A number of popular slide printers use the dimensions 4,096×2,732 pixels for 35mm film.

When you're working with film recorders to produce images that fill a frame, the aspect ratio is important. The ratio for 35mm film is 3:2. Film called 4×5 actually has an aspect ratio of 54:42, and 6×7 film is 11:9. (By convention, the larger number comes first when you're discussing aspect ratios. The names of the film sizes list height before width.)

If an image is not proportioned properly, you can resize it or add a border. When you're working with presentation slides, a border is often preferable to a blinding white reflection from the projection screen.

5

Some digital film recorders are designed to use 35mm or 16mm movie film. These cameras require aspect ratios appropriate for the film being used.

PHOTOSHOP IN FOCUS

JPEG is an important file format when you consider the number of such images on the Internet and those taken with digital cameras. The lossy compression algorithm that JPEG uses is worth exploring:

1. Open an image in Photoshop, any image.

2. Use the menu command File, Save As, and select JPEG as the file format.

3. Use an image quality value of zero and save the file to your desktop.

4. Close the open file and use the menu command File, Open to open the file you just saved.

5. Click the leftmost button at the bottom of the History palette to create a copy of the open image.

6. Save this copy, appending "-1" to the name. Again, use JPEG quality 0. Close and reopen the –1 file.

7. Position the two windows next to each other and zoom in to 500% on an area of detail. Compare the two. Although neither looks good, they should be nearly identical.

8. Use the menu command Image, Canvas Size. Click in the lower-right corner of the proxy (the 3×3 grid labeled Anchor). Switch the unit of measure to Pixels, and input a height and width, each 4 pixels smaller than the original value. Click OK.

9. Save the file as JPEG again, using the lowest quality setting.

10. Close and reopen the image.

11. Zoom in to 500% and compare this version to the original.

You should see that saving the same image at the same setting doesn't cause much harm, but using a low compression setting after cropping an image that has *already* been compressed with JPEG can cause severe quality reduction.

FROM THE NAPP HELP DESK

The National Association of Photoshop Professionals (NAPP) offers e-mail assistance to its members. Here is some advice from the NAPP Help Desk related to issues in this chapter.

Formats and Platforms

What makes .tif or .psd files different in Macintosh and Windows?

Actually, nothing. A file extension indicates a particular file type. File types are almost always standardized so that they work equally well on both Windows and Macintosh computers (assuming that the appropriate program is available). However, the file must be on a disk or drive that can be read by the computer. Macintosh computers can read and write Windows-formatted disks, but Windows computers can't read Mac-formatted disks without a utility.

Remember, too, that file formats can change with versions of the software. Just as a .psd file created by Photoshop 7 can have features that cannot be used in Photoshop 4, so, too, do the most recent .doc files from Microsoft Word have features unavailable in Word 4.2.

Hard and Variable Transparency

I want a soft drop shadow around my image, but Export Transparent Image always seems to leave a white halo below the shadow.

The transparency generated for EPS and GIF files is *hard-edged* transparency, in which a pixel is either completely transparent or completely opaque. Your drop shadow relies on *variable transparency*, in which pixels can be partially transparent.

Save for Web can now generate GIFs with dithered transparency, interspersing opaque pixels and transparent pixels. Print applications are a good bit trickier. InDesign 2.0 supports variable transparency, but other page layout programs do not. There are various techniques for simulating such effects as drop shadows, but generally it's easier to replicate the page's background in Photoshop.

Associating a File Type

When I double-click a file, it opens in the wrong program. Have any ideas?

In Mac OS X, find a file of that type and click on it once. Command-I opens Get Info. From the pop-up menu, choose Open with Application. Select the application and click Change All.

Mac OS 9 requires that you use the control panel File Exchange. Click on the PC Exchange tab. Find the file type (often listed more than once), and change the associated program (change all of that file type).

In Windows, click on one of the files of that type, and go to Properties (under the File menu or right-click). Change the associated program there. Don't forget to click Apply.

5

CRITICAL CONCEPTS

IN THIS PART

PIXELS, VECTORS, AND RESOLUTION

IN THIS CHAPTER

THE TWO TYPES OF COMPUTER GRAPHICS

Virtually all computer graphics can be classified as raster or vector artwork. Raster images (also known as *bitmap* images) are composed of tiny colored squares called *pixels* (short for *picture element*). The differences in color among pixels create the image. Vector images, on the other hand, consists of shapes and objects that are created by using lines called *paths*, which are colored to produce the artwork.

The two different types of digital images have their strong points and their weaknesses, and they are designed to do different jobs. One of Photoshop's strengths is the capability of combining raster and vector artwork in the same image.

Pixels and Raster Art

Raster refers to a grid—rows and columns in rectangular alignment. Raster artwork is created by using a series of pixels in those rows and columns. The pixel, the building block of raster imagery, is the lowest common denominator, sort of the "atom" of the artwork.

Each pixel can be exactly one color. That color can be changed at any time, but a pixel cannot be multicolored. The color value for the pixel can be recorded in several different ways, depending on the image's color mode. For RGB images, each color is recorded as the amount of red, green, and blue components. For CMYK, the proportions of the four inks (cyan, magenta, yellow, and black) are used to generate the color. Photoshop can also record pixel color using shades of gray (Grayscale color mode), black and white (Bitmap color mode), or luminosity and two color components (L*a*b color mode). If you think of a pixel as an atom, the color values recorded for a specific pixel are the protons, neutrons, and electrons.

➾ *Color is discussed in Chapter 7, "Color Theory and Practice," p. 173.*

As you can see in Figure 6.1 (even with the image reproduced in grayscale), each of the pixels is a single color. In some cases, adjoining pixels are the same color, and in many areas, the difference between neighboring pixels is small. However, in no instance is there a pixel divided into two colors, nor do any pixels blend from one color to another.

Also note that each pixel is square, and all pixels are exactly the same size. In any raster image, every pixel is the same size and shape. The actual size of the pixels can vary from image to image, but within each image, pixels are always the same dimensions.

➾ *For more discussion of the importance of pixel size, **see** "Image Resolution," p. 167, later in this chapter.*

The pixels in an image are independent. Although collectively they can represent a flower or a dog, they remain individual pixels. Photoshop enables you to manipulate some or all of the pixels simultaneously, but the image or selection remains a series of distinct pixels.

In some video applications, pixels can be rectangular rather than square. Each pixel in the file, however, is exactly the same shape and size.

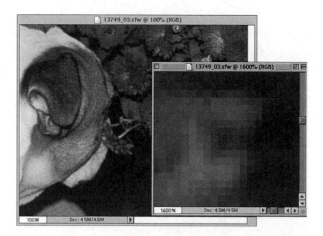

Figure 6.1
The inset is zoomed to 1600% to show the individual pixels.

⇨ *There's a way to make Photoshop treat a collection of pixels somewhat more like an object. See "Layers and Objects" in the NAPP Help Desk section at the end of this chapter.*

The basic raster image data in a file is recorded as the number of pixels, the arrangement of the pixels (width and height of the image), and the color values for each pixel. Additional information, such as print resolution and color profiles, can be saved with the file as well.

Paths and Vector Art

Vector artwork, such as that created in Adobe Illustrator, consists of objects. Each object is defined by a path, which can be *stroked* (color is applied along the path) and/or *filled* (color is applied within the path).

A path can be a straight or curved line, a circle or square, or a more complex object (see Figure 6.2).

Figure 6.2
Each of these objects is a single path in Photoshop's Paths palette.

⇨ *Creating and editing Bézier curves is discussed in Chapter 13, "The Pen Tools, Shape Layers, and Other Paths," p. 349.*

⇨ *Photoshop works with paths to create shapes but does not create actual vector artwork; **see** "Shape Layers" later in this chapter.*

Paths are actually mathematical descriptions in the file. Raster files record image data by noting the component colors of each pixel, but you can think of vector files as recording artwork by describing the starting point and shape of each path segment, along with the stroke and fill.

Vector paths are also known as *Bézier curves*, named for the French engineer Pierre Etienne Bézier (1910–1999), who pioneered their use in design. Each path segment is bordered by a pair of *anchor points*. Paths can consist of one or more path segments, with segments joined at their anchor points. The direction and shape of a curved path segment is determined by *direction lines* and *control points* at the anchor points. Anchor points can have one or two path segments connecting them, but no more than two. The anatomy of a Bézier curve is shown in Figure 6.3.

Figure 6.3
The control points and direction lines, like the path itself, are non-printing. Only the stroke and/or fill applied to a path is printed.

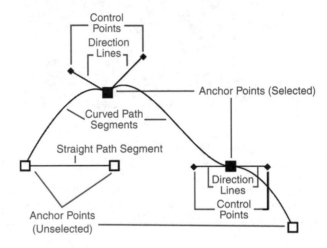

Anchor points with diametrically opposed direction lines are referred to as *smooth points* because the path continues smoothly, without changing direction, as it passes through the point. Anchor points without direction lines or those that contain direction lines that are not 180° from each other are *corner points*. The distance and angle of the direction line from the anchor point determine how the path will be shaped from that point. When there are smooth anchor points at either end of a segment, the direction lines and control points influence each other to create the curve. Compare the two curves in Figure 6.4.

Figure 6.4
The left anchor points for the two paths are identical. Notice how the path changes according to the difference between the direction lines to the right.

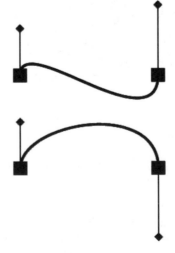

6

A straight path segment has corner anchor points at each end. The points can have no direction lines or control points, or can have one direction line (for a curved path segment bordering the straight segment). The straight path segment extends directly from one anchor point to the neighboring anchor point.

Paths can be *open* or *closed*. The anchor points at each end of an open path connect to only one path segment, but each anchor point in a closed path has a segment on either side. Consider the difference between a piece of string and a rubber band. The string has two distinct ends, while the rubber band (in most cases) forms a loop with no visible start or stop (see Figure 6.5).

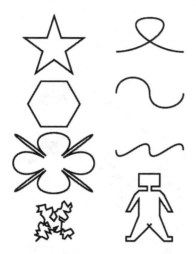

Figure 6.5
The paths to the left are closed paths. The paths to the right are open paths, even if the path crosses over itself.

Because vector artwork consists of path segments, you can manipulate an object in its entirety or change only a portion of it.

Comparing Raster and Vector

The greatest strength of raster artwork is its ability to reproduce photographic-quality images. It is certainly possible to produce vector illustrations that are photorealistic (the work of Bert Monroy immediately comes to mind). However, gradients in an illustration program, such as Adobe Illustrator, cannot easily reproduce the look of textures and surfaces in nature. That is one of the reasons that most photorealistic illustrators use Photoshop with their illustration program. Photoshop's capability of producing extremely subtle color transitions from pixel to pixel enables it to produce extraordinarily realistic textures and shadows. Gradients, gradient mesh objects, and patterns can all be used to simulate surfaces and textures in an illustration program. However, it's almost impossible to match the realism achieved by scanning actual objects into Photoshop.

Want a little more information on why it's tough to make illustrations look perfect? See "Texture in Nature" in the NAPP Help Desk section at the end of this chapter.

Vector artwork, on the other hand, can produce clean, crisp images that are easily and accurately resizable in a page layout program or when output to a PostScript printer. The ability to scale without loss of quality is a major advantage of vector art. It stems from the way the artwork is recorded.

6

A path is no more than a mathematical description of a shape and can easily be scaled by applying a little more math. *After* scaling, the colors are applied to the path's fill and stroke.

In addition, unlike the smooth curves of vector art, raster images are constructed of square pixels. The pixels are aligned in perfectly straight rows and columns. Because of that, when pixels are used to reproduce a curve, the corners of the pixels stick out. When this effect is obvious, the image is said to have the *jaggies* (see Figure 6.6). Jaggies can be visibly minimized by using anti-aliasing (discussed in the following section).

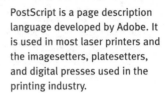

PostScript is a page description language developed by Adobe. It is used in most laser printers and the imagesetters, platesetters, and digital presses used in the printing industry.

Figure 6.6

The term "jaggies" comes from the stair-step appearance of the corners of pixels along a curve. Without anti-aliasing, the familiar copyright symbol is almost unrecognizable.

Figure 6.7 shows the difference between scaling a simple circle in raster and vector artwork. Both circles have been scaled to 400%. Although the original circles (at the top) look almost identical, there is a huge difference when they're scaled.

Figure 6.7

Raster artwork (right) can develop irregular edges along curves when scaled. Vector art (left) maintains its quality when resized.

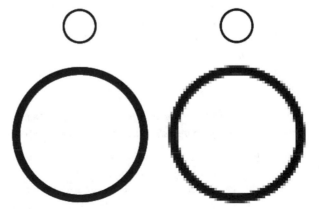

Remember that the vector artwork is an object, defined by a path and stroked and filled. On the other hand, the raster artwork is a series of pixels, selected and *interpolated* (changed in number and appearance) as a group. The vector circle in Figure 6.7 is an object, but in the raster image, there's no "circle," just some colored pixels.

Keep in mind, too, that Photoshop doesn't "resize" selected pixels. Rather, when a selection is enlarged, Photoshop spreads the appearance of the selection over more pixels. No pixels change size, no pixels are moved. Instead, existing pixels are recolored. When an entire image is interpolated, pixels can be added (to enlarge) or subtracted (to reduce), and the artwork is distributed across the new image size as accurately as possible.

Because raster artwork consists of pixels, various filters and effects can be applied to alter the image with incredible complexity and precision. Although Adobe Illustrator and similar programs provide filters and effects that can be applied to vector art, the vector object (or a copy of it) is often rasterized.

➪ *Filters are discussed in Chapter 18, "Applying Photoshop's Filters," p. 503.*

One area in which vector artwork is certainly superior to raster is text. In Figure 6.8, you can see a comparison of vector type and pixel-based type. The vector type not only has cleaner, smoother edges, it can be scaled without loss of quality. The bitmap (raster) type, on the other hand, is designed to be reproduced at a single point size.

Figure 6.8
Because pixels are square, they have trouble reproducing curves, especially in small type.

Anti-Aliasing Raster Type and Artwork

Anti-aliasing uses colored pixels to soften the edges of curves. The added pixels blend between the color of the type or shape and the background color. For example, a black shape on a white background would have shades of gray added to anti-alias (or soften) the curves (see Figure 6.9).

Notice, too, that without anti-aliasing, the straight edges of the pixels form perfect horizontal and vertical lines.

➪ *Photoshop's anti-aliasing options for type are discussed in Chapter 11, "Type and Typography in Photoshop," p. 273.*

A number of Photoshop's selection tools have anti-aliasing available in the Options Bar. The selections made with this option have a slight amount of feathering to avoid the jaggies.

Caution

Anti-aliasing can make small type and fine lines look fuzzy. Web graphics with small text, for example, should use sans serif, vertical fonts without anti-aliasing to maintain legibility.

6

Figure 6.9
On the left, the letter has no anti-aliasing. On the right, the curves appear smoother when viewed at 100% zoom (the frame at the top) because of the anti-aliasing.

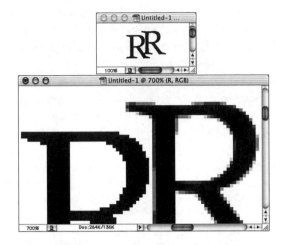

VECTORS IN PHOTOSHOP

Photoshop 7 uses vector paths in a variety of ways. For example, vector clipping paths are used to designate part of an image as transparent for a page layout program. Vector paths are also used with Photoshop's shape layers. Type in Photoshop is also vector.

*The following sections provide a brief overview of Photoshop's vector capabilities. For more in-depth discussions, **see** Chapter 11, "Type and Typography in Photoshop," **p. 273**, and Chapter 13, "The Pen Tools, Shape Layers, and Other Paths," **p. 349**.*

The Paths Palette

Photoshop's paths are nonprinting. They can be stroked and/or filled and can be used with shape layers to produce printable artwork, but the paths themselves do not print. In fact, unless selected in the Paths palette, paths are invisible in the image.

Photoshop uses the Paths palette (shown in Figure 6.10) to manage paths. Each path in an image is listed separately. To select a path and make it visible in the image, click on it in the Paths palette. Only one path can be active at a time, but as you can see from the thumbnail of Path 2 in Figure 6.10, a single path can consist of multiple subpaths.

The term *Work Path*, which is italicized in the Paths palette in Figure 6.10, refers to a temporary path. Work paths are created with the Pen tool or the Make Path from Selection button. An image can have only one work path—creating a new work path deletes any existing work path. A work path can be saved as a regular path by renaming it. To do this, double-click a work path to open the Save Path dialog box (see Figure 6.11). By default, Photoshop suggests the name Path 1 or the next available number. Paths, however, can be given any unique name.

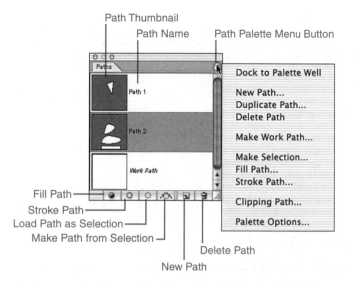

Path Thumbnail
Path Name
Path Palette Menu Button

Fill Path
Stroke Path
Load Path as Selection
Make Path from Selection
New Path
Delete Path

Figure 6.10
The Paths palette is set to the largest thumbnail view.

Figure 6.11
Naming a work path allows you to save it as a regular path.

Paths can be created in several ways:

- Make a selection, and then click the Make Work Path from Selection button at the bottom of the Paths palette. A new work path is created, replacing (not supplementing) any existing work path.

- Use the Pen tool (with the Paths option selected in the Options Bar) to create a new work path.

- Click the New Path button at the bottom of the palette, and then use the Pen tool to create the path.

- Create a shape layer by using one of Photoshop's Shape tools (see Figure 6.12).

Clipping paths are created by using the Paths palette menu command.

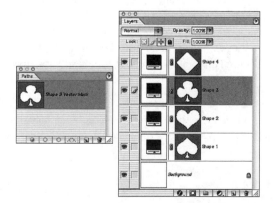

Figure 6.12
The Paths palette shows the path of the shape layer that's active in the Layers palette.

6

The Pen Tools

Incredibly precise paths can be created with Photoshop's Pen tools, and with the click of a button, these paths become incredibly precise selections. The Pen tools can also be used to edit existing paths, including those created with Photoshop's Shape tools.

Photoshop 7 offers several path-related tools, including two tools for creating paths and five for editing existing paths (see Figure 6.13).

Figure 6.13
The tools are selected from fly-out palettes in Photoshop's Toolbox.

Each of the path-related tools has one or more functions:

- **Path Selection Tool**—Identifiable by the black arrow icon, this tool is used to select and move paths. It can select only the path that is active in the Paths palette. When a path consists of multiple subpaths, each can be selected individually, or you can Shift-click to select more than one subpath. The Path Selection tool can be used to scale and otherwise transform a path when Show Bounding Box is selected in the Options Bar. The Options Bar also allows subpaths to be combined, intersected, excluded, and aligned.

- **Direct Selection Tool**—Individual anchor points can be selected and manipulated with the Direct Selection tool. Moving an anchor point with the Direct Selection tool, of course, alters the shape of the path. In addition to dragging anchor points, the Direct Selection tool can be used to drag path segments. When dragging a segment bordered by two corner anchor points, the points are dragged with the segment. When one or more bordering anchor points have direction lines, the anchor point remains stationary and the direction line is adjusted to meet the path segment's new shape. After you click on an anchor point to show the direction lines and control points, you can use the Direct Selection tool to drag the control points of smooth anchor points.

- **Pen Tool**—The primary tool for creating paths in Photoshop is the Pen tool. Each anchor point is individually placed with the tool by clicking. Dragging the Pen tool creates a curved path segment and a smooth anchor point. When Auto Add/Delete is selected in the Options Bar, the Pen tool automatically switches to the Add Anchor Point or Delete Anchor Point tool when positioned over a path segment or an anchor point. The Options Bar also enables you to conveniently switch to the Freeform Pen tool or any of Photoshop's Shape tools. You can also use it to combine subpaths.

- **Freeform Pen Tool**—Instead of clicking or dragging to establish anchor points and path segments with the Pen tool, you can use the Freeform Pen tool to simply draw a path. Drag the Freeform Pen tool, and Photoshop automatically places anchor points.

- **Add Anchor Point Tool**—When positioned over a path segment, this tool enables you to add corner anchor points (click) or smooth anchor points (drag) to the path. When positioned over an existing anchor point, the tool automatically switches to the Direct Selection tool.

- **Delete Anchor Point Tool**—You can delete an existing anchor point by clicking on it with this tool. When not positioned over an anchor point, the Delete Anchor Point tool functions as the Direct Selection tool.

- **Convert Point Tool**—Use this tool to convert a smooth anchor point to a corner point (click) or to convert a corner anchor point to a smooth point (drag). When not over an anchor point, the tool functions as the Direct Selection tool.

Shape Layers

Photoshop's shape layers simulate vector objects. Instead of being actual vector objects, each is a layer filled with a color, pattern, or gradient. In the Paths and Layers palettes, a shape layer is identifiable by the thumbnails of the filled layer (left) and the layer's vector mask (right) as well as by the default name "Shape" (see Figure 6.14).

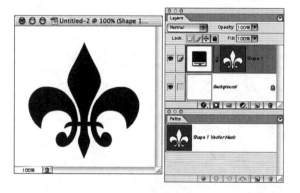

Figure 6.14
If the layer's name is changed in the Layers palette, the path name is automatically updated in the Paths palette.

In the Layers palette, the layer fill is visible in the thumbnail to the left, and the layer vector path is visible in the thumbnails of both the Layers and Paths palettes.

The primary method of creating shape layers in Photoshop is using the shape tools. However, the Pen tool can also be set (in the Options Bar) to create shape layers, and when pasting an object from Illustrator, you'll also have the option of creating a shape layer. (Illustrator's AICB clipboard option must be activated in the program's preferences.)

The "shape" is created with a vector path that selectively shows and hides areas of the layer. You can (Control-click) [right+click] on the layer vector mask's thumbnail in the Layers palette and select Disable Vector Mask from the contextual menu. With the mask disabled, you can see that there is fill color throughout the layer (see Figure 6.15).

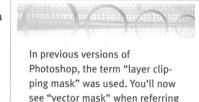

In previous versions of Photoshop, the term "layer clipping mask" was used. You'll now see "vector mask" when referring to a layer's clipping path.

Figure 6.15
The layer vector mask can be enabled through the same contextual menu. (Control-click) [Right+click] to restore the vector mask.

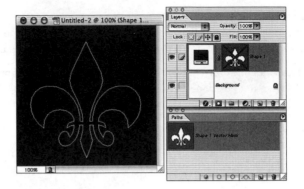

Whether enabled or disabled as a layer vector mask, the path can be selected in the Paths palette and edited with Photoshop selection and pen tools.

Shape layers can have layer styles in the same way as regular layers. In addition, the menu command Layer, Change Layer Content allows you to use gradients and patterns in addition to solid colors. Shape layers can even be converted to adjustment layers by using that command (see Figure 6.16).

The contextual menu also enables you to delete a vector mask or to convert it to a pixel-based layer mask (using the Rasterize Vector Mask command).

Figure 6.16
As you can see from the Layers palette, the shape layer is now a Curves adjustment layer, with layer effects applied.

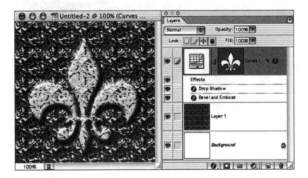

No matter the fill or type of layer, the layer mask remains a vector mask.

Vector Type

Using vector paths to create type outlines enables laser printers and other PostScript devices to produce sharp, clean-edged type that can be scaled. Because vector type (like vector artwork) uses mathematically defined outlines, even the printer itself can resize it, without losing quality. Bitmap type, on the other hand, is designed to be reproduced at a specific size. Although bitmap fonts often have multiple sizes, the type should not be scaled.

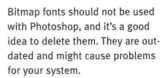

Bitmap fonts should not be used with Photoshop, and it's a good idea to delete them. They are outdated and might cause problems for your system.

Remember, too, that Photoshop's Type tool allows you to create letter-shaped selections. When in Type Mask mode (see Figure 6.17), Photoshop is not creating vector type. Rather, it is making a mask in the shape of the type. The selection created from the mask can then be filled, used as a layer vector mask, or otherwise used in Photoshop, but it is not vector-based.

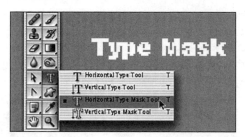

Figure 6.17
A red overlay, such as that used in Quick Mask mode, is created by a type mask tool. It is converted to a selection when you switch tools.

IMAGE RESOLUTION

An image's *resolution* is the relationship between its size in pixels and its size on a printed page. Resolution determines how large or small a raster image appears in print and the relative fineness or coarseness of detail. Although raster images are recorded and stored as a series of square pixels, they are printed as a series of dots.

The term "resolution" is also used to identify the capabilities and characteristics of various devices, such as monitors and scanners.

The Different Types of Resolution

Resolution is a term used for several different concepts. A computer monitor, for example, has a certain resolution, which refers to the number of pixels displayed on the screen. You might also hear the term *color resolution* when discussing monitors. That's actually the monitor's color bit depth—the number of different colors that the monitor is set to display. Figure 6.18 shows both Windows and Macintosh monitor resolution capabilities, which vary according to monitor and video card.

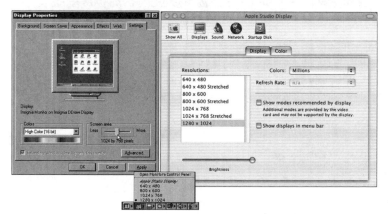

Figure 6.18
From the left, a Windows Display Properties dialog box, a Mac OS 9 Control Strip resolution menu, and a Mac OS X Display dialog box.

6

Resolution for a scanner or digital camera is the number of pixels per unit of measure that it can capture. For scanners, it is usually measured in pixels per inch (ppi). Digital cameras, on the other hand, are usually marketed by the overall number of pixels that can be acquired, which is measured in megapixels.

When scanning, the resolution determines the number of pixels captured for the image. The higher the resolution, the greater the number of pixels. Therefore, in a higher resolution image, the same area of an image is reproduced with more pixels than in a low-resolution image. Because there are more pixels reproducing a given area, the individual pixels must be smaller, and when the pixels are smaller, the image's detail is finer (see Figure 6.19).

Figure 6.19
On the left, an image scanned at 72ppi. On the right, the same image scanned at four times the resolution. The insets show the difference in detail.

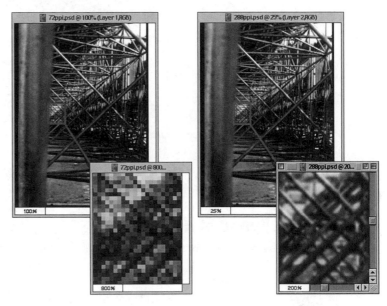

➩ *Scanning and digital cameras are discussed in greater detail in Chapter 4, "Getting Pixels into Photoshop," p. 97.*

Inkjet and laser printers have resolution, too. Printers can place a certain number of dots per inch (dpi) on a sheet of paper. The output of commercial printing presses, however, usually depends on their *line screen frequency*, measured in lines per inch (lpi). The line screen frequency is a measure of the size of the halftone cells used to print the image.

➩ *Commercial printing is discussed in Chapter 26, "The Printing Process: A Primer," p. 793.*

The terms ppi, dpi, and lpi all refer to *linear* inches. Therefore, 200 pixels per inch is the number of pixels side by side, not in a square inch.

Resolution with Raster and Vector

Resolution is critical to raster artwork. If the resolution is not appropriate, the project might not print correctly. Vector art, on the other hand, can be resolution-independent when printing to a PostScript device. Because vector art is defined mathematically and can be scaled without losing quality, resolution can be insignificant to the artwork itself. Keep in mind that non-PostScript printers and most file formats rasterize any vector artwork or type in a Photoshop image. If you're outputting to a non-PostScript printer (such as an inkjet) or using a file format that rasterizes your vectors, make sure that the image's resolution is high enough to maintain the quality of the artwork.

Determining Resolution for Print

The appropriate resolution for print is determined by the output device. Inkjet printers typically give maximum quality at 240dpi. Resolution for commercial printing presses is determined by the line screen frequency being used for the particular job, measured in lines per inch. Resolution should be 1.5 to 2 times the lpi.

Line screen frequencies are rather standard throughout the printing industry. For newsprint, you're likely to see 50, 85, or 100lpi. Uncoated paper can be printed at 110, 120, or 133lpi. Coated stock line screen values are often 120, 133, 150, or 175lpi. There are, however, often exceptions. Consult the print shop at the start of a project and have all images scanned or produced at the appropriate resolution.

Image Resolution for Inkjets

There is a difference between the "resolution" of an inkjet printer and the appropriate image resolution. An inkjet's advertised 1440×720 resolution, for example, refers to the ink droplets. It takes several droplets to replicate a colored pixel on a sheet of paper.

The image's resolution refers to the actual pixels in an image. To get the maximum quality from an inkjet printer, you should use an image resolution of one-third the printer's stated resolution. When two numbers are given, divide the smaller. In the example of 1440×720 inkjet resolution, an image resolution of 240 is optimal.

Remember, too, that inkjet printers are rather limited in the file size they can handle. If your printer can produce 1440×1440 droplets per inch, the one-third rule would indicate an image resolution of 480dpi. Run a few tests, and you might find no visual difference between 240 and 480dpi for your printer. There could be, however, a huge difference in output time—or whether the image prints at all.

6

Resolution and the Web

It's common to hear that Web graphics should be 72ppi. The rationale is that computer monitors reproduce images at 72ppi. However, if you hold a ruler to the screen and measure one inch, it's improbable that you'll find exactly 72 pixels.

A typical 17-inch CRT monitor has a viewing area approximately 12.5 inches wide. (The 17-inch designation comes from the diagonal measurement.) If that monitor is set to show 1024×768 pixels, there are about 82 pixels per linear inch (because 1204 divided by 12.5 is just a bit under 82). If the same monitor is set to 800×600 pixels, there are 64 pixels per inch.

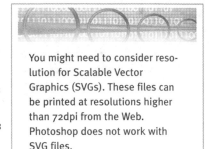

You might need to consider resolution for Scalable Vector Graphics (SVGs). These files can be printed at resolutions higher than 72dpi from the Web. Photoshop does not work with SVG files.

You can safely ignore resolution when creating raster images for the Web. Instead of thinking about a certain number of pixels per inch, consider only the pixels themselves. A Web page has certain dimensions, measured in pixels. Determine what part of the page should be occupied by the image, and size it to match those dimensions.

An image with print dimensions of 4 inches by 6 inches at 72dpi has pixel dimensions of 288 pixels by 432 pixels. It will occupy exactly 288×432 pixels in a Web page. If that image is resampled in Photoshop to 4×6 inches at 300dpi to improve print quality, the pixel dimensions change to 1200×1800 pixels. Instead of improving the image's appearance on the Web, the image simply occupies more space onscreen (see Figure 6.20).

Figure 6.20
Resampling an image in Photoshop changes the file's pixel dimensions, which affects the size of images on the Web.

PHOTOSHOP IN FOCUS

Although the general rule of thumb is that *most* inkjet printers reach maximum quality at 240 dpi *most* of the time, you can find your own printer's best balance between quality and file size.

1. Open a new Photoshop document. Make it RGB, filled with white, 6 inches wide, and 1 inch tall at 200ppi.

2. Select the Gradient tool from the Toolbox. In the Options Bar, choose Linear and the Spectrum gradient.

3. Drag from the upper-left corner of the document to the lower-right corner to create a diagonal gradient: red-magenta-blue-cyan-green-yellow-red.

4. In the Print with Preview dialog box, uncheck the Center Image box and input a top margin of 1 inch. Leave the left margin as it was set.

5. Print the gradient on glossy paper, using your printer's highest quality output settings.

6. Open another new Photoshop document, identical to the first but with a resolution of 240ppi.

7. Drag an identical gradient from the image's upper-left corner to the lower-right corner.

8. In the Print with Preview dialog box, again uncheck Center Image, but this time make the top margin 2 inches.

9. Reload the same sheet of glossy paper into the inkjet printer and print the second document.

10. Create a third new document at 300ppi and fill it with a gradient. Print the third gradient on the same sheet of paper, 3 inches from the top.

11. Print a fourth gradient, 400ppi, 4 inches from the top of that same sheet of paper. You should have a single sheet of paper with four near-identical gradients, as shown in Figure 6.21.

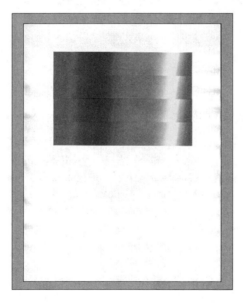

Figure 6.21
The gradients are identical, but the print quality can differ.

After the gradients are printed, use a magnifying glass or a loupe to examine the print quality. If you cannot see any improvement between the 240ppi and the 300 ppi samples, there's never a reason to use the higher resolution. If you do see a difference, or if you can't see any difference between the 200ppi and the 240ppi samples, you might want to consider flipping the paper around 180° and printing some additional samples on the other end at some different sample resolutions.

FROM THE NAPP HELP DESK

The National Association of Photoshop Professionals (NAPP) offers e-mail assistance to its members. Here are some questions from the NAPP Help Desk related to issues in this chapter.

Layers and Objects

You say that Photoshop doesn't recognize such things as circles and squares and other objects made from pixels. Yet I routinely drag a circle made from pixels around in an image. What's going on?

If the pixels that form the "circle" are on a separate layer, you can treat them as a separate object. You're not dragging an object; you're repositioning a layer. This, by the way, is an important concept for moving artwork back and forth between Photoshop and Illustrator. Illustrator recognizes objects. When you open a Photoshop file in Illustrator, you can have each layer become a separate object. You can then manipulate the "objects" individually in Illustrator. (The artwork will still be rasterized, however.)

Texture in Nature

I've seen some truly wonderful photorealistic illustration by such artists as Bert Monroy and Felix Nelson, but why can't I achieve that level of perfection?

That level of perfection comes from being less than perfect. The textures created and applied by computer often look *too* good. Textures, whether created manually or scanned, are typically applied to an area of an illustration from a sample, which can be quite small. For example, a wall in an image might be filled with a texture to simulate painted stucco. The actual texture that's applied could be only 100 pixels square to fill an area many times that size.

Because of the repeating pattern, the wall has a uniform look across its entire surface. In nature, walls have marks here and there, the paint possibly isn't applied uniformly, the surface could be chipped. Top photorealistic illustrators take time to "personalize" their surfaces to make them look more realistic. Photoshop has a collection of tools that are great for this job. The Burn, Dodge, Desaturate, Blur, and Sharpen tools can all be used to make surfaces a little less regular.

COLOR THEORY AND PRACTICE

IN THIS CHAPTER

PHOTOSHOP AND COLOR

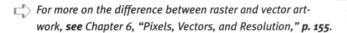

An image in Photoshop *is* color. Whether the image is in bright, vivid colors, various shades of gray, or even just black and white, it doesn't exist without color. At its heart, Photoshop is about assigning the correct color to each pixel.

How Photoshop Records Color

Photoshop works primarily with raster artwork, although it does have some sophisticated vector capabilities. Raster images, also known as bitmap images, consist of a rectangular pattern of pixels, with a single color assigned to each of the tiny squares. The differences in color among the pixels determine the appearance of the image.

> Be aware that the term "bitmap" can have two different meanings. It can be used as a synonym for raster ("That is not vector artwork; it's a bitmap image."). In this usage, it refers to an image consisting of pixels arranged in rows and columns. When talking about color, "bitmap" refers to black-and-white images. In Bitmap color mode (also called 1-bit color), each pixel is either black or white. There are no shades of gray or other colors.

🔖 For more on the difference between raster and vector artwork, **see** Chapter 6, "Pixels, Vectors, and Resolution," **p. 155**.

In simple terms, raster image file formats record image data pixel by pixel, keeping track of each pixel's location in the image and that particular pixel's color values. Theoretically, you could digitally re-create the *Mona Lisa* by assigning specific colors, one at a time, to each pixel. Remember that each pixel is a single color. The color can be changed, but a pixel can have only one color at any time (see Figure 7.1).

Figure 7.1
This zoomed-in look at pixels illustrates an important point: Each pixel can have only one color.

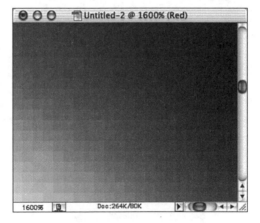

What Is a Color Model?

The actual recording of a pixel color or a vector object's assigned color depends on a couple of factors. The file format you select determines, of course, how the actual data is recorded. (Photoshop handles that process transparently as the file is saved.) The document's *color mode*, however, is assigned by the user and should depend on the image's final destination and its content.

7

The color mode (with the *color model*) determines what *component colors* are used to create the specific colors in the image.

The RGB color mode, for example, records the entire range of color as proportions of red, green, and blue (the RGB component colors). CMYK, on the other hand, records each color as percentages of cyan, magenta, yellow, and black (the CMYK component colors). A grayscale image is composed of grays, measured as percentages of black. Each of Photoshop's color modes and color models is discussed individually in this chapter.

Color Models and Color Modes

For these discussions, there is a difference between a *color model* and a *color mode*. For clarity, we will consider a color model to be a system of defining color. (It can also be referred to as a *color space*.) It is used to define the attributes or components of a specific color in order, perhaps, to add that color to an image. A color mode, on the other hand, refers to the image as a whole, specifying how the colors are recorded in the actual file.

The difference is this: A file can be in the RGB color mode, intended eventually for the World Wide Web, but colors within the file can be defined during editing by the color models RGB, Grayscale, Lab, and HSB (Hue, Saturation, Brightness). Although the artwork can be defined as you work using several color modes, the file itself actually is recorded with all colors in one color model.

You assign a color mode to an image with the menu command Image, Mode. Color models are used when defining a particular color, specifically when using the Color palette. RGB, CMYK, Grayscale, and Lab are both color modes and color models. Indexed Color, Bitmap, Duotone, and Multichannel are color modes but not color models. HSB is a color model but not a color mode in Photoshop.

⇨ *For more on the Color palette,* **see** *Chapter 8, "Defining and Choosing Colors," p. 201.*

THE TWO TYPES OF COLOR

Colors in Photoshop can be considered *additive* or *subtractive*. Additive colors produce white when all colors are combined (added) at full strength. Subtractive colors produce white by removing (subtracting) all component colors. Conversely, a lack of color in an additive model produces black, while combining all colors in a subtractive model produces black.

Consider spotlights in a theater. The more spotlights you train on a specific area of the stage, the more brightly lit that area is—this is additive color. Now consider preparing paint for a blank canvas. Without any paint, the canvas is white. As with subtractive color, when you start mixing various paints together, they get darker. (The result is more likely to be muddy brown than black, but the concept is the same.)

Although there are lots of ways to classify color (for example, primary colors, warm and cool colors, earthtones, pastels), for Photoshop the largest determining factor is how colors are reproduced. The resulting color can be similar, but the differences in how additive and subtractive colors are created result in different treatment in Photoshop.

7

Additive Colors

Additive color is produced from a light source that's typically filtered to present color. For example, a household light bulb (which emits "white" light) behind a blue lampshade gives you blue. Behind a yellow lampshade, the same bulb gives you yellow. A stage spotlight can be filtered with a gel, a translucent piece of colored gelatin, to produce colored light. Multiple gels can be combined to create a wide range of colors.

Televisions and computer monitors produce additive color. The light is viewed directly or near directly, preferably without interference from other light sources. The light is filtered into red, green, and blue components that, in combination, produce all the colors that can be created with that device. Many large front-projection TVs actually use three synchronized lights, one of each of these colors, to produce images onscreen. Televisions, computer cathode ray tube (CRT) monitors, and computer (and other) liquid crystal display (LCD) monitors use red, green, and blue light in combination to produce the colors of the spectrum.

There are several key concepts about additive colors:

- The component colors (red, green, blue) combined in full intensity produce white.

- The complete lack of the component colors produces black.

- The light is seen directly, reaching the eye either from a colored source or from a source through a colored filter.

- In theory, by varying the amount of each component color (red, green, blue), virtually all colors of the visible spectrum can be reproduced. (In reality, not all colors can be reproduced because of limitations of the devices.)

- Because the component colors are red, green, and blue, additive color is referred to as *RGB* in Photoshop and other graphics programs.

Subtractive Colors

Subtractive colors are, generally speaking, seen with reflected light. A white or colored light source reflects off a colored surface to the eye. The color that's visible to the eye is that part of the spectrum not absorbed by the colored surface. For example, if you shine a white light on a wall painted yellow, you see yellow because all other colors are absorbed by the paint, and yellow is reflected back to the eye. The wall itself is not a light source; rather, it reflects light to the eye.

Like the wall's yellow paint, subtractive colors are applied to a surface. The visible color of the paint or ink is that part of the spectrum that is reflected rather than absorbed. Subtractive color in Photoshop is used to design for print, where ink is applied to paper to reproduce the artwork.

For Photoshop, subtractive color is reproduced by using cyan, magenta, yellow, and black inks. The color mode is called CMYK. Theoretically, the entire range of color can be produced with varying amounts of CMY inks, but it's necessary to add black to reach the darkest colors.

K is used for black to differentiate it from blue, represented by *B*. *K* can also be thought of as standing for *key color*, from the days when black was printed first to assist in registering the other colors.

There are several key concepts about subtractive colors:

- The component colors (cyan, magenta, yellow) can theoretically be combined to produce the full visible spectrum. However, in reality, printing inks are limited in the range of color they can reproduce.

- The lack of component colors results in white.

- Combined at full intensity, CMY should theoretically produce black. However, once again, there are limitations with real-world inks. Because mixing cyan, magenta, and yellow inks produces a dark brown rather than black, printers must add black ink (K) to CMYK printing.

- With subtractive colors, light is reflected rather than seen directly. The color perceived by the eye is that portion of the visible spectrum that the colored surface doesn't absorb. For example, when looking at a red wall, all parts of the spectrum *except* red are absorbed, and red is reflected to the eye.

- Printing on a press with CMYK inks is often referred to as *four-color process printing*, and the four inks are called the *process colors*.

- In printing, CMYK inks can be supplemented with additional inks, often called *spot colors*. Spot colors are usually predetermined, premixed inks of a specific color. They are typically applied to a specific area (spot) on the image. It is not unusual to use one or more spot colors in place of CMY inks to create two- or three-color images.

▷ *Unsure about why the difference between additive and subtractive color is important? See "How Color Is Made" in the NAPP Help Desk section at the end of this chapter.*

RGB, CMYK, AND SPOT COLORS

The vast majority of work in Photoshop is done in RGB or CMYK color modes. Virtually all output is done in RGB, CMYK, or Grayscale modes, although Photoshop actually supports eight color modes.

▷ *For more on the other color modes, **see** "Photoshop's Other Color Modes," p. 183, later in this chapter.*

The Relationship between RGB and CMY

Theoretically (but not in practice), all RGB colors could be replicated by using cyan, magenta, and yellow. Likewise (and also theoretically), all CMY colors could be reproduced by using red, green, and blue. (Black [K], remember, is added to CMY to compensate for impurities in the inks. It is not one of the theoretical component colors.) The relationship among the six component colors is shown in Figure 7.2.

One of the biggest differences between RGB and CMYK color modes is the number of channels. Each component color is recorded in a separate color channel. Because RGB has three component colors, it has three color channels (plus a composite channel). CMYK has four component colors, so there is one more color channel.

7

Figure 7.2
Notice that RGB and CMY alternate.

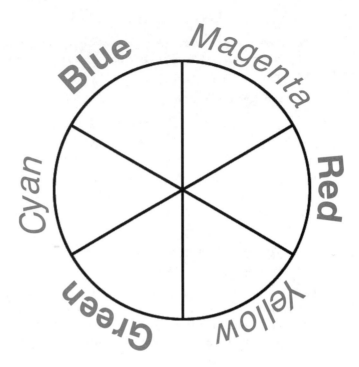

The relationship is also shown in Table 7.1.

Table 7.1 RGB and CMY Relationships

Combine	And	To Create
Red	Green	Yellow
Red	Blue	Magenta
Green	Blue	Cyan
Cyan	Magenta	Blue
Cyan	Yellow	Green
Magenta	Yellow	Red

These relationships may not be the same as those you learned in preschool, or even art school, but they are the relationships among component colors in Photoshop (and other digital imaging and illustration programs).

When displayed in a *color wheel*, a circular arrangement of colors, the relationships among the component colors is clear. A color wheel, such as that in Figure 7.3, shows the way that the component colors interact with each other. Red is at zero degrees, the "three o'clock" position on the circle.

In a color wheel, each of the RGB colors is opposite a CMY color. These opposites represent the *inverse relationship* among colors. The inverse colors are also easily summarized (see Table 7.2).

7

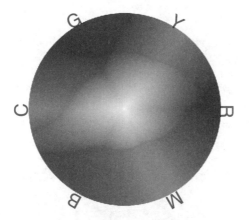

Figure 7.3
The 0° point is typically to the right of a color wheel. This figure is also in the color insert of this book.

Table 7.2 Inverse Relationships

Color	Inverse
Red	Cyan
Green	Magenta
Blue	Yellow
Cyan	Red
Magenta	Green
Yellow	Blue

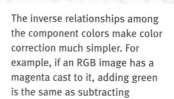

The inverse relationships among the component colors make color correction much simpler. For example, if an RGB image has a magenta cast to it, adding green is the same as subtracting magenta.

Choosing a Color Mode

An image's color mode should be dependent on the image's final destination. The two major color modes, RGB and CMYK, are intended for different applications. CMYK is for use with commercial four-color printing presses and those smaller printers specifically designed for the color mode. These devices include color laser printers, "proofers" (printers that simulate a print press's output), and high-end inkjet printers used for fine-art prints.

RGB is intended for use on the Internet, on monitors and kiosks, with film recorders, for broadcast and digital video, and with most inkjet printers. Virtually all Photoshop work not destined for a commercial printing press should be done in RGB mode.

In the following discussions, Photoshop's 8-bit color mode is assumed. Photoshop also permits you to work in 16-bit color. You'll find more information on that subject in the section "A Note on Color Bit Depth" later in this chapter.

Caution

When using the terms *print*, *printing*, and *printer* in Photoshop, always keep in mind that there are differences between the inkjet printers likely to be found in studios, offices, or home and commercial offset printing presses; color laser printers; and high-end inkjet proofers and fine-art printers. When designing for home/office inkjets, remember to use RGB rather than CMYK. Although these printers actually use cyan, magenta, yellow, and black ink, the printers' software requires RGB image data.

7

RGB Color Notation

RGB colors are designated as proportions of the three component colors: red, green, and blue. Each value can range from 0 to 255. These 256 possible values for each component color are a product of 8-bit color depth. The standard notation is (red value)/(green value)/(blue value). For example, 35/120/57 means that the red value is 35, green is 120, and blue is 57. Keep in mind that when all three component colors are 0, black results, and when all three are 255, you get pure white. When the component color values are equal and between 0 and 255, you get shades of gray.

The specific color for each pixel is broken down into the three component colors. Each component color value is recorded in the appropriate color channel. In practice, each color channel is a grayscale copy of the image, with only the component color values recorded in the channel. Figure 7.4 shows the red, green, and blue channels for an image.

Figure 7.4
Each channel records the amount of the component color for each pixel.

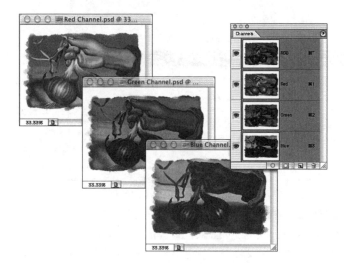

In Figure 7.4, a separate document is shown for each of the color channels. In addition, the Channels palette is visible, containing one channel for each component color and, at the top, the composite channel (named RGB).

Because each color channel can have 256 possible values, the total number of different colors that can be reproduced in 8-bit RGB is 16,777,216. That's $256 \times 256 \times 256$. Consider, if you will, the sequence of colors 0/0/0, 0/0/1, 0/0/2, 0/0/3 through 135/87/42, 135/87/43, 135/87/44, 135/87/45 all the way to 255/255/252, 255/255/253, 255/255/254, 255/255/255. The difference between 135/87/42 and 135/87/43 is too subtle for the human eye to see. In fact, variations of as much as five in a single color component are difficult to detect in most circumstances. A variance of five in two color components can, on the other hand, be very noticeable.

CMYK Color Notation

Like RGB colors, CMYK colors are recorded as proportions of the component colors. Unlike RGB, CMYK has four components. Therefore, the notation is a bit longer. If you have a green color recorded in RGB as 35/120/57, a comparable shade of green could be recorded as 85/29/100/17 in CMYK.

(Depending on the color settings selected in Photoshop, there could be considerable variation. Also note that several different combinations of CMYK colors could produce similar shades of green.)

Besides the additional component, CMYK notation differs from RGB notation in a very significant way: RGB values range from 0 to 255, but CMYK components are measured in percentages. Each of the four values can range from 0% to 100%. In practical terms, the percentage represents the ink density for that particular color. Values less than 100% can be thought of as "thinning the ink."

Although in theory a particular spot on the page could have 100% each of cyan, magenta, yellow, and black ink, in practice, that is not done. Depending on the paper used, maximum ink density is typically between 250% and 300%.

Like RGB color mode, CMYK records the component color value for each pixel in a separate color channel. CMYK images have one channel for each of the component colors, plus a composite channel.

Identifying Spot Colors

Photoshop also enables you to specify a particular color using *spot colors*. These predesignated colors chosen from a library of color represent premixed inks for use in commercial printing. Spot colors are used in addition to, or in place of, CMYK inks. The color is identified by name in the image, and the press operator mixes the exact color, using a specific formula or a premixed ink.

Photoshop supports a variety of spot color collections. Most common in North America are the Pantone collections. These and other spot color collections can be accessed through Photoshop's Swatches palette (see Figure 7.5).

⇨ *The Swatches palette is discussed in the section "The Swatches Palette," **p. 207**, in Chapter 8, "Defining and Choosing Colors."*

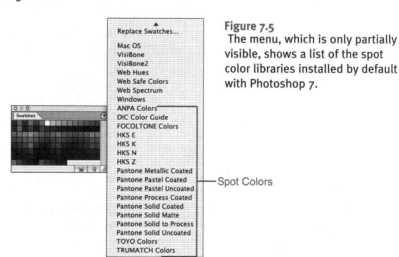

Figure 7.5
The menu, which is only partially visible, shows a list of the spot color libraries installed by default with Photoshop 7.

7

One of the most common uses of spot colors is to ensure an exact color match. For example, the specific red of the Adobe logo can be specified in a print image as Pantone 485, Toyo 8096, or Dainippon 2497. This particular shade of red can also be reproduced by using CMYK 0/100/100/0.

Spot colors can also be used to supplement an image's tonal or color range. They can also provide a cost-effective printing method, using black ink and one spot color rather than all four process (CMYK) colors. Keep in mind that although most spot colors can be reproduced by using process colors, the premixed inks require only a single pass through the press, instead of three or four.

Some colors cannot be reproduced on press using the CMYK inks, so other spot colors are added. Metallic and neon colors, for example, can be added to an image only through the use of spot colors. These inks cannot be duplicated with process inks.

In print, you might see *PANTONE*, in all capital letters, indicating a registered trade name.

Although you could specify a spot color when working in RGB color mode, spot colors are designed for use with CMYK.

Spot color names are assigned by the company that produces the inks. The notation varies from company to company (and within brands, to some extent). Pantone inks for use with uncoated paper have a three- or four-digit number, followed by the letter *U*. Inks for use with coated paper have the letter *C* following the number. A specific color has the same number, whether the ink is for use with coated or uncoated paper. Most other manufacturers also use numeric designations for their inks.

Here are descriptions of the various spot color collections installed with Photoshop 7:

- **ANPA Colors**—These 300 colors are designed for use on newsprint. The name comes from the American Newspaper Publishers Association, now known as the Newspaper Association of America.

- **DIC Color Guide**—This is a collection of 1280 CMYK spot colors that can be matched against the *DIC Color Guide* from Dainippon Ink & Chemicals. These spot colors are most commonly used in Japan.

- **FOCOLTONE Colors**—Focoltone colors are designed to be used with the parent company's charts showing overprint and absorbency characteristics with different stocks. Focoltone International, Ltd., of the United Kingdom provides these 830 CMYK colors.

- **HKS E**—HKS-Farben is a German firm with four different collections of colors for use with inks from BASF or Hostmann-Steinberg. The "E" series (from the German *Endlospapiere*) is the 88 colors designed for use with continuous forms papers.

- **HKS K**—The "K" (*Kunstdruckpapiere*) series is for use with gloss art papers. This set also has 88 colors.

In previous versions, Photoshop's General Preferences offered the choice of using "Short PANTONE Names." That option was designed to improve communication with page layout and illustration programs into which a Photoshop image might be placed. That option is no longer required.

- **HKS N**—These 86 colors are for uncoated paper (*Naturpapiere* in German).

- **HKS Z**—The *Z* stands for *die Zeitung* (German for "newspaper"), and this collection of 50 spot colors is for newsprint.

- **TOYO Colors**—These colors are as common in Japan as the Pantone colors are in the United States. There are 550 predesignated colors in this set.

- **TRUMATCH Colors**—Trumatch is a system for designating CMYK colors. The first digit of each color's name represents one of 50 hues. The next pair of digits represent the saturation (*a* through *h*) and the amount of gray (1 through 7).

PHOTOSHOP'S OTHER COLOR MODES

Photoshop enables you to work in six color modes in addition to RGB and CMYK. Each of the color modes has specific characteristics and can be used for specific purposes.

Grayscale

Often referred to (incorrectly) as "black and white," this color mode offers 256 shades of gray, including black and white. Grayscale mode uses one color channel. Although Grayscale is an 8-bit color mode (with 256 shades of gray), Photoshop measures each pixel's color as a percentage of black. Grayscale can be used in commercial printing, on the Web, or for output to other devices, such as inkjet printers and film recorders. Photoshop also permits you to work with 16-bit grayscale images (see "A Note on Color Bit Depth" later in this chapter).

When converting color images to grayscale, all color information is lost. The image retains only the brightness value of each pixel, expressed in varying shades of gray. Converting a grayscale image to RGB or CMYK mode does not add color to the image; rather, it adds color channels, allowing you to add color.

➡ *When outputting grayscale images to an inkjet printer, sometimes the output has a slight color tint, usually magenta or cyan. For advice on how to avoid this problem, see "Inkjet Grayscale" in the NAPP Help Desk section at the end of this chapter.*

Bitmap

Bitmap color mode is true black and white. Perhaps clearer would be the phrase "black *or* white." Each pixel in such an image is either black *or* white; there are no shades of gray and no colors.

> **Caution**
>
> Do not confuse "bitmap color mode" with "bitmap image." Bitmap color mode refers to the possible colors of an image's pixels, and is in contrast to terms such as RGB, CMYK, and Grayscale modes. Bitmap image, on the other hand, is the same as "raster image" and means that the image is made up of pixels. It is used in contrast to *vector art*, in which the image is constructed of mathematically defined objects. Bitmap images can be of any color mode. (For more on the difference between raster/bitmap and vector artwork, see Chapter 6.)

7

As you can see in Figure 7.6, each pixel is either white or black. The Navigator palette indicates the area of the image that is shown in the document window. In addition, note that the Channels palette shows only a single channel (and the image is somewhat identifiable in the palette thumbnail).

Figure 7.6
The image is shown at 300% zoom so that individual pixels are recognizable.

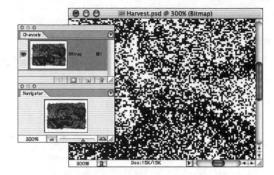

Bitmap color mode can be used effectively with certain line art and for special effects, and greatly reduces file size, but generally is not appropriate for most images.

A file must be in Grayscale mode or Duotone mode to convert to bitmap. When converting from Grayscale to Bitmap mode, you have several options for how the gray pixels are converted to black or white (see Figure 7.7).

Figure 7.7
The results of four different bitmap conversions are shown.

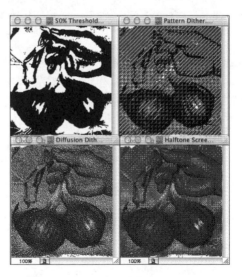

Photoshop uses different criteria for the four types of bitmap conversion:

- **50% Threshold**—Pixels with gray values higher than 128 (50% gray) are converted to white. Pixels with gray values lower than middle gray are converted to black (see Figure 7.7, upper left).

- **Pattern Dither**—Geometric patterns of black and white dots are created to represent the image's general appearance (see Figure 7.7, upper right).

- **Diffusion Dither**—This technique bases the conversion on the color of the pixel in the upper-left corner of the image. Unless that pixel is pure white or pure black, the transformation to either white or black produces some margin of error. That error is transferred among the surrounding pixels, and so "diffused" throughout the image (see Figure 7.7, lower left).

- **Halftone Screen**—By specifying a halftone screen, you create a bitmap image that simulates reproduction with halftone dots. You can specify the line screen frequency

Caution

Once an image is converted from Grayscale to Bitmap, converting back to Grayscale does not restore the image to its prior appearance. Each pixel is still black or white, until editing the image changes the color value.

(up to 999 lines per inch, *lpi*) and the dot shape. (Typically, newspapers are printed at 85lpi and magazines at 133 or 150lpi.) The example in Figure 7.7 at the lower right uses 133lpi and a diamond-shaped dot to convert a grayscale original at 72dpi.

A closer look at the results of the four bitmap conversions shows the different distributions of black and white pixels (see Figure 7.8).

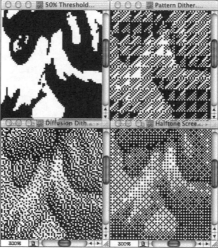

Figure 7.8
Each of the bitmap images is zoomed to 300% at the center of the image.

In Photoshop, you can also specify custom screens when converting to Bitmap mode, but you must create a pattern first. If the pattern is smaller than the image, it is tiled. The Custom Pattern option simulates shades of gray by making the halftone pattern thicker and thinner.

L*a*b

This color mode, often called simply Lab, uses three channels. Unlike RGB and CMYK modes, the channels do not contain component color information. In contrast, one channel contains only the lightness value for each pixel, and the additional channels split the color spectrum into two pieces (see Figure 7.9).

7

Figure 7.9
Notice that the Lightness channel is a beautiful grayscale representation of the image.

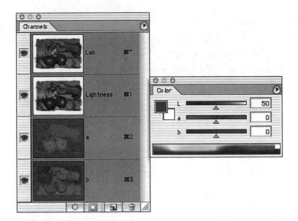

The *L* (lightness) channel controls the brightness of a pixel, with a range of 0 to 100. The *a* channel contains the color value of the pixel along a red-green axis. The value normally ranges from –120 (green) to +120 (red). The *b* channel contains color information running along a blue-yellow axis. This value, also normally –120 (blue) to +120 (yellow), is combined with the *L* and *a* channels to produce the pixel's color.

The Lab color gamut is wider than RGB or CMYK, containing a range of colors not otherwise reproducible. When Photoshop converts between RGB and CMYK, it uses Lab as an intermediate color model.

Lab images can be printed to many PostScript devices (Level 2 and 3 only), and can be used to edit Photo CD images. In addition, converting from RGB or CMYK to Lab enables you to work directly with the luminance values in the image.

Indexed Color

Indexed Color mode is a subset of RGB. Rather than 8 bits of information for each of the color channels, files in Indexed Color mode contain only a total of 8 bits of color information for each pixel. For that reason, each image can contain a maximum of 256 different colors. They can be any colors, even 256 different shades of blue or red or yellow, but there can be only 256 different colors.

Indexed Color mode is used with GIF and PNG-8 file formats, and can be specified for some other formats. The advantage of 8-bit color is smaller file sizes, but that is often outweighed by the sometimes drastic degradation in image quality. Many photographic images cannot be accurately reproduced with such a limited palette.

> Can't edit an image in Indexed Color mode? See "Index Editing" in the NAPP Help Desk section at the end of this chapter.

Caution

Don't submit Lab images or place them into a page layout document without prior approval from your service bureau or printer. If they can't work with the color mode, additional expenses can be incurred.

Many basic Photoshop capabilities are not available in Indexed Color mode. For example, the image is restricted to a single layer and most filters cannot be used.

An image in Indexed Color mode has a single color channel, called Index, in the Channels palette. Photoshop records the colors used in an Indexed Color mode image in a *color lookup table* (*CLUT*). The color table is recorded with the file and might be unique to that file or a standardized color table. If you attempt to add a color to the image that isn't among the 256 available colors, it is converted to the nearest color.

Only RGB and Grayscale mode images can be converted to Indexed Color. Grayscale conversions happen automatically because there are a maximum of 256 shades of gray in an 8-bit grayscale image. When converting an RGB image, however, the Indexed Color dialog box appears (see Figure 7.10).

Caution

Images must be flattened before converting to Indexed Color mode. Make sure that you don't have any necessary layers hidden at the time of conversion—they will be lost.

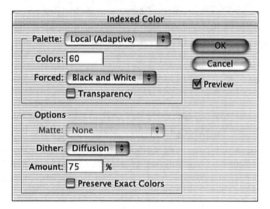

Figure 7.10
The Indexed Color dialog box offers some control over an image's reduction to 256 colors.

The Palette pop-up menu offers a dozen options:

- **Exact**—If the RGB image contains 256 or fewer colors before conversion, the Exact option lets you create a color table using those colors. The image's appearance is maintained.

- **System (Mac OS)**—The image's colors are converted to the Macintosh system's 8-bit palette.

- **System (Windows)**—The 8-bit palette standard for Windows is used to produce the color table.

- **Web**—The Web-safe palette of 216 colors common to both the Macintosh and Windows system palettes is used.

- **Uniform**—The color table is created by taking samples from the RGB spectrum. Six evenly spaced values for red, green, and blue are taken: 6×6×6=216. If the total number of colors is limited to fewer than 216 in the dialog box, the next smallest perfect cube (125, 64, 27, or 8) is used.

- **Perceptual**—The color table is created giving priority to those colors for which the human eye has greater sensitivity. (Local emphasizes colors within the image, and Master relies on the RGB gamut.)

- **Selective**—Large areas of consistent color are taken into account when creating the palette with this option. Otherwise, it generally follows the guidelines for Perceptual. Generally, this option does the best job of preserving an image's appearance.

- **Adaptive**—An adaptive palette is created by using the colors that appear most frequently in the image. If the color of a specific area of the image is most important, you can make a selection of that area before converting and choose Adaptive.

- **Custom**—This option enables you to edit the color table directly. It opens with the adaptive palette. You also have the option to load a previously saved palette.

- **Previous**—The most recently used custom palette is used to create the color table. This option enables you to convert numerous images using the same palette.

The difference between Local and Master for the Perceptual, Selective, and Adaptive options is most apparent when the color table is reduced from 256 to a smaller number of colors. Local emphasizes colors that exist in the image, but Master looks at the RGB gamut. Dithering can be critical when using the Master options.

You can enter a specific value in the Colors field to shrink file size even more by choosing to retain fewer than 256 colors.

The Forced pop-up menu enables you to specify colors that must be maintained in or added to the image's color table. Forcing black and white adds those two colors to the table, whether used in the image or not. The Primaries option adds black, white, red, green, blue, cyan, magenta, and yellow. Web adds the 216 Web-safe colors (see the following section, "Web-Safe RGB," for more information on the Web-safe palette). If you select Forced: Custom, you can specify colors that must be added to the image's color table.

Selecting the Transparency check box maintains any areas of transparency that exist in the image. When this option is not selected, any existing transparent pixels are filled with the specified matte color or, if no matte color is selected, with white.

Selecting a matte color helps edges along a transparency blend with the designated color by using anti-aliasing. If, for example, the image will be placed on a Web page with a specific background color, using that color as the matte color helps the edges blend into the background. Choosing None in the Matte pop-up menu results in a hard-edged transparency or, if Transparency isn't selected, a white fill for transparent pixels.

You can also select the type and amount of dithering to apply. Dithering simulates colors missing from the color table. Pixels of colors that *are* in the color table are interspersed to simulate the missing color. Diffusion, Pattern, and Noise dithering are all available (as is the choice of None). Here's how they differ:

- **None**—Instead of attempting to simulate a color, the nearest color in the color table is substituted.

- **Diffusion**—An error-diffusion method of dithering is applied, which results in a less structured appearance than does Pattern dithering.

■ **Pattern**—A pattern of dots similar to a halftone pattern is used to simulate colors that are not in the color table.

■ **Noise**—Adding noise along edges helps break up potentially visible seams in sliced images. (Slices are used with Web graphics to control optimization and downloading.)

The option Preserve Exact Colors, which is available with Diffusion dithering, ensures that colors already existing in the color table are not dithered. It is helpful for preserving fine lines and type. Preserve Exact Colors is not available for Pattern dithering and is mandatory for Noise dithering.

An image's color table can be edited directly by using the menu command Image, Mode, Color Table. The dialog box, shown in Figure 7.11, enables you to make changes to the individual colors saved with the file.

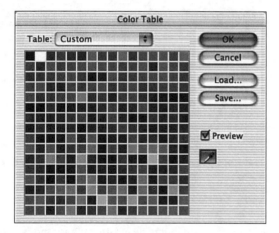

Figure 7.11
This color table shows the maximum 256 unique colors allowed for any image in Indexed Color mode.

You have several options when editing a color table:

■ Select the Preview check box to see the effect of your changes on the image.

■ Select a standardized color table in the Table pop-up menu, if desired. Leave Table set to Custom to use the color table created during the color mode conversion.

■ Click on any color in the color table to select it and open the Color Picker. In the Color Picker, you can designate a new color to replace the selected color throughout the image.

■ Drag the cursor through the table to select multiple colors. You can then use the Color Picker to assign a range of colors to replace those selected. When the Color Picker opens, select the first color. After you click OK, the Color Picker reopens so that you can pick the ending color. A gradient is then generated, with each step replacing one of the selected colors.

■ (Command-click) [Ctrl+click] to delete a color from the table.

■ (Option-click) [Alt+click] a color to designate that color for transparency. You can also click on the Eyedropper tool in the dialog box and use it to designate the transparent color.

7

■ Custom color tables can be saved and loaded. Color tables should be saved with the file extension .act. Tables can be loaded from .act files or from GIF files.

Web-Safe RGB

The term "Web safe" refers to that subset of an 8-bit RGB gamut (indexed color) that is common to both the Macintosh and Windows system palettes. The two operating systems have built-in color palettes for use with 8-bit color (256 maximum colors, not 8 bits per channel). Color values are recorded in a single color channel (see Figure 7.12).

Figure 7.12
In this image, both the Color palette's sliders and ramp are set to Web-safe colors.

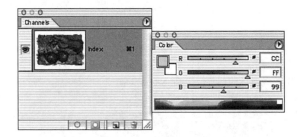

Both the Macintosh and Windows system palettes contain 256 colors (the maximum allowed under 8-bit color), but only 216 of the colors are common to both palettes. These are the Web-safe colors.

HTML, the basic language used with the World Wide Web, records color as a base-16 (hexadecimal) value. Rather than 10 possible values for each digit (the numerals 0 through 9), hexadecimal notation permits 16 different values for each digit. In addition to the 10 numerals, the letters *A* through *F* are used.

In Figure 7.12, notice that the Color palette's sliders have vertical lines indicating stops. The sliders automatically click to the stops for each color component to ensure that the selected color is Web safe. In addition, when set to Web safe, the color ramp in the Color palette lets you select from only the 216 specified colors.

Web-Safe Colors: Desirable or Dinosaur?

In the days when many computer monitors (especially laptops) were capable of displaying only 256 colors, the Web-safe palette allowed Web designers to produce graphics that would theoretically look the same on both Windows and Macintosh computers. (However, because the designer had no control over monitor calibration and dozens of other factors that determine color fidelity, using Web-safe colors was at most a "best effort.")

With more and more color PDAs (personal digital assistants) capable of Web surfing, the Web-safe palette is perhaps more important now than it has been since the mid-'90s. However, the determination of whether to restrict an image to the smaller gamut rests with the designer. The primary consideration should perhaps be the expected Web site visitor. Sites that are likely to attract traffic from PDAs, such as those that specialize in certain types of business information, might want to consider using the Web-safe palette. A Web site devoted to fine art reproductions, on the other hand, would do itself a disservice by restricting the available palette in such a way.

Duotone

Duotone color mode in Photoshop actually refers to four different types of color images. *Monotones* use a single colored ink, much like printing a grayscale image with an ink other than black. *Duotones* use two inks, typically black and a color. *Tritones* use three inks, and *quadtones* use four. In practice, unless an ink's curve is edited, each image appears as a tinted grayscale image (see Figure 7.13).

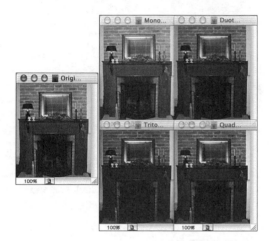

Figure 7.13
The original image is on the left. This figure is reproduced in the color insert of this book.

What sets these color modes apart is that the inks are used throughout the image, rather than placed in specific areas. Each of the inks is, by default, distributed according to the single color channel.

Duotones can be created only from grayscale images. To convert an RGB, CYMK, or other color mode to Duotone, first use the menu command Image, Mode, Grayscale. The Duotone Options dialog box (see Figure 7.14) enables you to select mono-, duo-, tri-, or quadtone in the Type pop-up menu.

Clicking on a color swatch to the left of a color name opens the Color Picker in Custom Color mode. A Pantone or other custom color can be selected.

⤵ *For more information on the Color Picker, **see** "Working with Color Pickers," **p. 209**, in Chapter 8, "Defining and Choosing Colors."*

Clicking on the thumbnail in the left column, which by default has a diagonal line, opens the Duotone Curve dialog box for that ink. Adjusting the curve gives you control over the distribution of the ink in the image. By default, each ink is printed at the gray value of each pixel. For example, a 50% gray midtone pixel is printed at 50% tint of the ink, while a darker pixel in a shadow area is printed with a higher tint. The straight-line curve uses the pixel's brightness value as the tint percentage for each ink.

The term "duotone" is used generically throughout this discussion to refer to monotones, duotones, tritones, and quadtones. When a point refers specifically to monotones, tritones, or quadtones, that term is used.

7

Figure 7.14
As you can see in the Channels palette, this image has already been converted to Duotone and the dialog box is reopened, enabling a change of color if necessary.

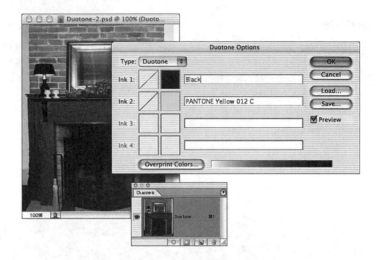

The curve can be modified to change the distribution of an ink. Reopen the Duotone Options dialog box by using the menu command Image, Mode, Duotone. In Figure 7.15, the curve has been changed to eliminate the yellow ink from the image's highlights and shadows, and to print yellow at a darker tint in the midtones. Note that both the curve thumbnail and the image preview are automatically updated.

Figure 7.15
In this example, the yellow ink will be printed only in the image's midtones.

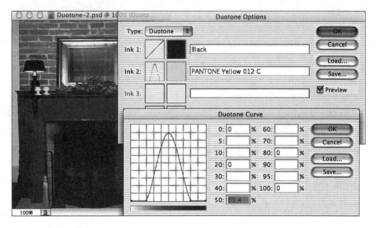

Note that custom curves can be saved and loaded in the Duotone Curves dialog box. The Duotone Options dialog box also has Load and Save buttons. Photoshop 7 ships with a variety of predesigned duotones, tritones, and quadtones. You'll find them all in the Duotones folder, inside the Presets folder, within the Photoshop folder (see Figure 7.17).

The Info palette will show you the "before" and "after" values while modifying a duotone curve. Move the cursor around the image to get the ink percentages at any point (see Figure 7.16).

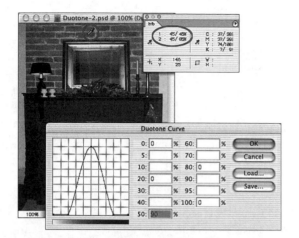

Figure 7.16
The cursor changes to the Eyedropper when moved in the image window. The Info palette tells you each ink's tint percentage before (left) and after (right) the new curve is applied.

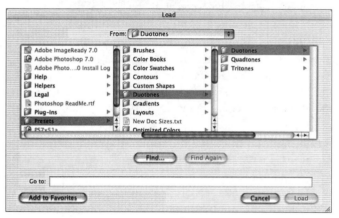

Figure 7.17
By default, Photoshop 7 installs folders filled with preset duotones, tritones, and quadtones.

The presets include a variety of duotones, tritones, and quadtones in shades of gray, with Pantone custom colors, and with process (CMYK) inks.

The Overprint Colors button in the Duotone Options dialog box shows you how the inks will interact (see Figure 7.18). Clicking a color swatch in the Overprint Colors dialog box opens the Color Picker, allowing you to modify the overprint color.

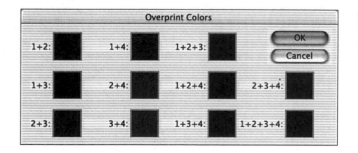

Figure 7.18
With a duotone, only 1+2 is available. With a tritone, 1+2, 1+3, 2+3, and 1+2+3 are available.

7

Images in Duotone color mode can be saved and printed in Photoshop (.psd), EPS, PDF, or Raw file formats. When in .psd format, all of Photoshop's capabilities are available, including spot channels, layers, and filters.

Multichannel

Multichannel color mode uses a separate color channel for each of the image's component colors, just as RGB and CMYK color modes do. However, Multichannel mode does not include a composite channel, so each color channel can be considered a spot color.

Multichannel mode is designed for use with some specialized image printing (such as some Scitex CT format images) and can be used to edit individual color channels. In Photoshop, it is typically used with images destined for commercial printing, including CMYK and duotone images.

Although most of Photoshop's capabilities are available for Multichannel mode images, they can be used on only one color channel at a time. Because there is no composite channel as there is in RGB or CMYK mode, the entire image cannot be manipulated at once.

Multichannel images can be created from CMYK, RGB, Lab, Duotone, and Grayscale files. Converting a CMYK image creates spot channels from each of the four color channels and deletes the composite channel. The four resulting channels are cyan, magenta, yellow, and black. There might be some color shift during the conversion. RGB images converted to Multichannel mode typically undergo a large color shift. During the conversion, the red, green, and blue channels are changed to cyan, magenta, and yellow. Figure 7.19 shows the difference between creating a Multichannel mode image from CMYK and from RGB.

Converting an image from Lab color mode to Multichannel creates three alpha channels, rather than spot channels. Because a grayscale image starts with only one color channel, converting to Multichannel mode results in an image with only one channel. The channel's name is switched from Gray in Grayscale mode to Black in Multichannel mode, but is otherwise identical.

> **Caution**
>
> Modifying an overprint color with the Color Picker can produce an unprintable image. If you select a color that cannot be reproduced with the designated colors, your preview will not match the printed result.

> Some of Photoshop's filters produce unexpected results with duotones because of the lack of color channels. For example, the filter Pixelate, Color Halftone cannot produce color halftone dots without color channels with which to work.

> When working in Multichannel mode, you can't apply a filter to the entire image at once because there's no composite channel. Remember that a filter can be repeated on each channel individually with the keyboard shortcut (Command-F) [Ctrl+F]. Apply the filter to one channel, and then switch to the next and use the keyboard shortcut to apply the same filter with the same settings. Repeat for each channel.

> *Alpha channels are discussed in Chapter 10, "Making Selections and Creating Masks," p. 243.*

Figure 7.19
Note that converting an RGB image to Multichannel mode (bottom) creates cyan, magenta, and yellow spot channels, not red, green, and blue. This figure is also reproduced in the color insert of this book.

A duotone image can be converted to Multichannel mode, creating one color channel for each of the inks. This allows direct editing of the color placement, which is not possible in Duotone mode.

HSB: The Non-Mode Color Model

Photoshop offers one additional way to define color, but it's not found under the Image, Mode menu. *HSB* stands for hue, saturation, brightness. Rather than a color mode, it is a *color model* used with the Color palette and the Color Picker. Images themselves are not recorded as HSB, but this color model can be used to define colors in the file in RGB, CMYK, Indexed Color, Lab, or Multichannel modes. (HSB is not available for images in Grayscale, Bitmap, or Duotone color modes.)

> **Caution**
>
> An image converted from Duotone to Multichannel mode cannot be converted back to Duotone mode. It can be converted to Grayscale and then to Duotone. Doing so, however, eliminates any changes made to the color channels in Multichannel mode.

HSB is designed to replicate the way human eyes (and the brain) recognize color, breaking it down into color, purity, and brightness. Hue (color) is based on the color wheel and measured in degrees. The six primary component colors (RGB and CMY) are found evenly spaced around the wheel (see Table 7.3 and Figure 7.20).

Table 7.3   Hue Values for Photoshop's Primary Colors

Color	Hue Value
Red	0°
Green	120°
Blue	240°
Cyan	180°
Magenta	300°
Yellow	60°

Figure 7.20
The hue values for the primary colors are typically measured from the 3 o'clock position on the color wheel.

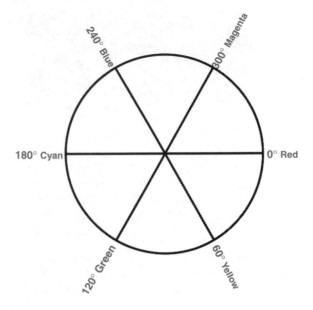

Saturation determines the purity of the color, from gray (0%) to pure or fully saturated (100%). Brightness (also sometimes called *lightness*) is the relative darkness (0%) or lightness (100%) of the color. When brightness is at 0%, the hue and saturation are insignificant—black results. When brightness and saturation are both at 100%, the result is white, regardless of the hue.

Most Photoshop users employ HSB on a regular basis, perhaps without recognizing it. By default, Photoshop's Color Picker is set to Hue (see Figure 7.21).

Figure 7.21
The H stands for hue. The Color Picker can also be set to use saturation (S), brightness (B), the RGB colors, or the Lab components as the basis for color selection. As you can tell from the lack of radio buttons, the CMYK colors cannot be used as a basis for color definition.

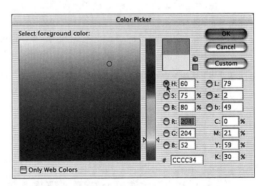

Color Modes Compared

A number of Photoshop's capabilities cannot be used in certain color modes. Table 7.4 summarizes what features are and are not available for images in the various color modes.

Table 7.4   Photoshop Features for the Color Modes

Color Mode	Channels	Layers	Paint Tools	Filters
RGB	3 (R, G, B)	Yes	All	All
CMYK	4 (C, M, Y, K)	Yes	All	Most
L*a*b	3 (L, a, b)	Yes	All	Most
Indexed Color	1 (Index)	No	Most	No
Grayscale	1 (Gray)	Yes	All	Most
Bitmap	1 (Bitmap)	No	Some	No
Duotone	1 to 4	Yes	All	Most
Multichannel	Varies	No	All	Most

A Note on Color Bit Depth

In addition to the various color modes, Photoshop permits you to work in 16-bit color for RGB, CMYK, and grayscale. Rather than 256 possible values for each pixel in each color channel, 65,536 possible values are available. With over 65,000 possible values for each of the three channels, the number of colors available is overwhelming.

Although most output devices can't handle the additional color information, or don't have the capability of reproducing such fine variations among similar colors, 16-bit mode can be printed. Some film recorders, especially with grayscale images, can show improved tonal range.

The disadvantages of 16-bit color usually outweigh the improved color depth; for example, 16-bit files are twice as large as 8-bit images. In addition, 16-bit mode does not support Photoshop's layers, filters, some color adjustment commands, and many tools.

PHOTOSHOP IN FOCUS

The terms *8-bit color* and *16-bit color* refer to the actual amount of computer data recorded for each pixel's color. A *bit* is a single piece of digital information. Groups of eight bits of related data are called a *byte*. (A group of eight bits of unrelated data is better called an *octet*.) Think of bits as letters of the alphabet, bytes as words, and an entire computer file as a book.

Each bit can be a zero or a one, but can have no other value. Computers are—for now, anyway—binary machines. Each bit can be either value and must be one or the other. Consider the difference between a standard household light switch and a dimmer switch. The typical light switch is either on or off, but the dimmer switch can be set to any of a variety of "on" positions. With binary systems, there are no dimmer switches, just the old-fashioned on/off.

In Photoshop, 8-bit color uses 8 bits (one byte) for each component color of each pixel. A pixel in an RGB image has 8 bits of information for each of the three colors. A CMYK pixel has 8 bits of color information for each of four component colors. Grayscale images have only 8 bits of information for each pixel's color. In 16-bit color, each component color can have 16 bits of color data, whether RGB, CMYK, or Grayscale.

7

How does it actually work? With 8-bit color, each of the bits can be a zero or a one, and the values work together. Because each of the 8 bits can be only one of two possible values, you can calculate the number of possible combinations like this:

2×2×2×2×2×2×2×2=256

For example, let's create a fictional set of colors in Table 7.5.

Table 7.5 A Simulated 8-Bit Color Notation

8-Bit Color	Color Name
00000000	White
00000001	1/254 Gray
00000010	2/254 Gray
00000100	3/254 Gray
00001000	4/254 Gray
00010000	5/254 Gray
00100000	6/254 Gray
01000000	7/254 Gray
10000000	8/254 Gray
00000011	9/254 Gray
00000101	10/254 Gray
00001001	11/254 Gray
...	
11101111	251/254 Gray
11011111	252/254 Gray
10111111	253/254 Gray
01111111	254/254 Gray
11111111	Black

Now if you consider an RGB pixel, the possible colors are based on combinations of 8 bits of information for each of the three channels. For example, one pixel might be

00000000/00000000/00000000

while another pixel could have this combination:

11101111/00001001/10000000

The first, using the color notation from Table 7.5, would be RGB 255/255/255, pure white. The second would be 4/244/247, a bright cyan.

Keep in mind that the terms *8-bit* and *16-bit* as used here refer to the number of bits *per channel* in an image. In contrast, Indexed Color mode, like Grayscale mode, records a total of 8 bits of information for each pixel, and that byte's worth of information can represent a totally different color from image to image. The eight-character string records a reference to a place in that particular image's color table, not a reference to an objective color mode.

FROM THE NAPP HELP DESK

The National Association of Photoshop Professionals (NAPP) offers e-mail assistance to its members. Here are some questions from the NAPP Help Desk related to issues in this chapter.

How Color Is Made

What is the big deal about additive and subtractive? How does it relate to RGB and CMYK?

The key to both additive/subtractive and RGB/CMYK is how color is actually created. (You use RGB for the additive colors and CMYK for the subtractive colors.) Additive color is created by and viewed from an active light source. Computer monitors are active color sources, as are televisions, projectors, and candles. Subtractive color is seen "on the bounce." It is reflected light, coming from a painted or printed surface. The printed page of a book, the walls in a room, the computer's keyboard—all are seen because light reflects from them to the eye. They appear to have color because parts of the light are absorbed and parts are reflected. You see the reflected light.

When working with color modes in Photoshop, consider whether the colors will be seen directly from a light source, such as colors on a monitor, or whether they'll be seen on a surface, such as a sheet of paper. Remember, though, that inkjet printers are the exception. Although the end product is subtractive (CMYK), the print driver typically assumes RGB input and converts the colors for you automatically.

Inkjet Grayscale

When printing to my inkjet printer, my grayscale images come out either magenta or cyan. How can I get them to print only in shades of gray?

Your printer supplements black ink with a mix of CMY inks to maintain detail in shadows. This *rich black* (also called *process black*) enables the printer to produce a wider number of "blacks" in the darker areas of an image. To print with only black ink, check your Print dialog box. A sample dialog box, from an Epson printer, is shown in Figure 7.22.

7

Figure 7.22
Your printer's dialog box might differ. Look for an option to print in black or color.

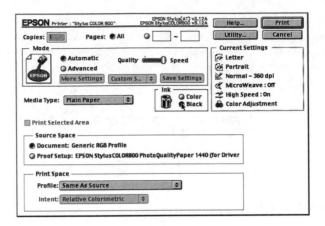

Index Editing

I can't use the Layers palette, filters aren't available, I can't even add text. What's going on?

Check the image mode (Image, Mode on the menu bar), and convert the image from Indexed Color mode to RGB. After editing, convert back to Indexed Color. That color mode doesn't support the features you're trying to use because of the restricted color table.

DEFINING AND CHOOSING COLORS

IN THIS CHAPTER

WORKING WITH COLORS IN PHOTOSHOP

8

To apply a color to pixels in an image in Photoshop, the color must first be selected. This process of identifying the specific color with which you would like to work can be considered "activating" the color. After a color is selected, it can be added to the image by using a variety of tools and commands.

Colors must also be selected for a variety of other operations in Photoshop. For example, as discussed in Chapter 7, "Color Theory and Practice," often duotone images and those in Indexed Color mode also require that you work with specific colors.

Color Handling Capabilities: Overview

There are always two colors ready to be applied in Photoshop: the foreground and background colors. Found in both the Toolbox and the Color palette, they are represented by color swatches (see Figure 8.1). Photoshop's default colors are black (foreground) and white (background).

Among the handiest of Photoshop's keyboard shortcuts are those that restore the default foreground/background colors and swap the two colors. Press D on the keyboard (no modifier keys) to return to black and white; press X (no modifiers) to swap the foreground and background colors (regardless of the current color). Of course, these shortcuts are not available when you are using the Type tool to add text. Clicking the small black and white squares to the lower left of the swatches in the Toolbox also restores the default colors. The two-headed arrow to the upper-right swaps foreground and background.

Figure 8.1
Both sets of swatches are updated when you change the foreground or background color.

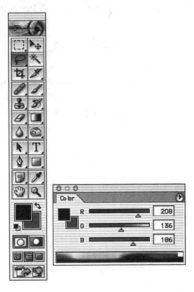

Photoshop has three primary methods of selecting or designating other foreground and background colors:

■ **Color Palette**—The Color palette, shown in Figure 8.2, can be shown or hidden with the keyboard shortcut F6. (Like other palettes, it can also be shown and hidden through the Window menu, docked to the Palette Well, and expanded and contracted by clicking its tab.)

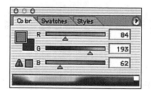

Figure 8.2
The Color palette is shown with the RGB sliders and color ramp.

The Color palette has one or more sliders and numeric fields (depending on the color model selected in the palette's menu) and a *color ramp*, a bar at the bottom of the palette showing available colors as a gradient. The foreground and background colors are shown as small swatches, and the palette can warn if a color cannot be printed by standard four-color inks. Notice that, in addition to not being resizable, the Color palette has no icons or buttons at the bottom.

■ **Swatches Palette**—Predefined colors can be stored in the Swatches palette (see Figure 8.3), making them available at a single click. When you click a color swatch in the palette, it becomes the foreground color. (Command-clicking) [Ctrl+clicking] a swatch makes it the background color.

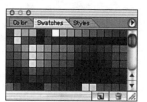

Figure 8.3
By default, the Swatches palette is docked with the Color and Styles palettes.

Photoshop ships with a variety of swatch collections, most representing spot colors. You can also add and delete swatches from the palette as well as create and save custom sets of swatches.

For a discussion of spot colors, **see** "RGB, CMYK, and Spot Colors," **p. 177**, in Chapter 7, "Color Theory and Practice."

■ **Color Picker**—Photoshop lets you select its native color picker, the system (Macintosh or Windows) color picker, or a third-party plug-in. Although the features of each differ, they all have the same basic capability: selecting color. How you create a specific color varies depending on the color model. Some color models use component colors; others use different attributes. The color pickers allow you to specify the components or attributes to achieve the desired color. (Color models are discussed in Chapter 7.)

Specific characteristics of the Adobe, Macintosh, and Windows color pickers are described in the section "Working with Color Pickers" later in this chapter.

⇨ *Sometimes the color being applied in the image doesn't seem to match the foreground color swatch. Check out "Swatches: Only Half the Story" in the NAPP Help Desk section at the end of this chapter.*

PHOTOSHOP'S COLOR PALETTE

Quick and easy access to color is available through Photoshop's Color palette, which enables you to change the foreground or background color almost instantly. The palette holds one or more sliders (depending on the color model you select) that are used to adjust the amount of each component color (see Figure 8.4). In addition, the color ramp, the multicolored bar at the bottom of the palette, can be used to select a color.

Figure 8.4
The Color palette's menu is used to select the color mode for both the sliders and the ramp. Note that the two can be set for different color modes.

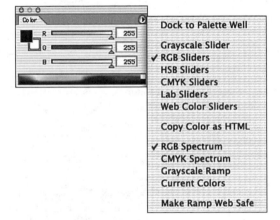

Changing Color with the Color Palette

To change the foreground or background color using the Color palette, use this procedure:

1. Make the Color palette visible by clicking on its tab or by selecting Color from the Window menu.

2. Click once on the foreground or background swatch in the palette to indicate which color you are changing.

3. Use one of the following options to change the color:

   ■ Use the sliders (or the slider for Grayscale) to change the proportion of each of the component colors.

   ■ Enter values into the numeric fields to the right of the slider(s).

   ■ Click anywhere in the color ramp to select a color.

   ■ Click on the white or black swatches to the right of the color ramp.

Selecting Color with the Eyedropper

Click with the Eyedropper anywhere in an image to select a specific color as the foreground or background color (whichever is active in the Color palette). Hold down the (Option) [Alt] key, and click to change whichever swatch is not active in the palette.

Using the Options Bar, you can set the Eyedropper to select the color of the exact pixel on which you click (point sample) or to average surrounding pixels. The 3 by 3 Average setting looks at a radius of one pixel and determines a blend. The 5 by 5 Average setting looks at a total of 25 pixels, almost double the radius. Generally, the 3×3 setting is appropriate for low-resolution images, and 5×5 is best for high-res images.

> You can also use the Eyedropper tool to select a color *outside* Photoshop. Click in the image window, drag to the color you want, and release the mouse button.

Choosing a Color Model for the Palette

You can use the Color palette's menu, accessed by clicking the triangle in the palette's upper-right corner, to change the sliders and color ramp to various color models. The menu choices are shown in Figure 8.4, and the results of selecting a color model are shown in Figure 8.5.

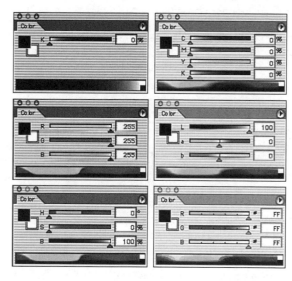

Figure 8.5
Various configurations of the Color palette.

Selecting a color model from the menu results in the following configurations:

- Left, top: Grayscale slider with grayscale ramp

- Left, middle: RGB sliders with RGB ramp

- Left, bottom: HSB sliders with RGB ramp

- Right, top: CMYK sliders with CMYK ramp

8

■ Right, middle: Lab sliders with RGB ramp

■ Right, bottom: Web-safe sliders with Web-safe RGB ramp

The sliders and the color ramp need not be set to the same color model, offering increased flexibility in color selection. Note that the color ramp does not show HSB or Lab. In Web-safe mode, the sliders can be set only to the positions indicated by the marks on the sliders. This ensures that the color selected is part of the Web-safe palette.

⇨ *Not sure about the difference between the Color palette's sliders and the color ramp? See "Choosing a Model" in the NAPP Help Desk section at the end of this chapter.*

The Color Palette Menu

In addition to the slider and ramp color model options, the Color palette menu holds a few other commands:

■ **Dock to Palette Well**—Photoshop's Palette Well, located at the right end of the Options Bar, is a handy place to store frequently used palettes. Putting the Color palette in the Palette Well leaves it accessible without taking up valuable screen space. (The Palette Well is available only when the monitor is set to a resolution above 800×600 pixels.)

■ **Copy Color as HTML**—When this command is invoked, Photoshop records to the Clipboard the hexadecimal value of the currently selected color (foreground or background). That value can then be pasted into an HTML document in the format:

COLOR="#33FFFF"

The character string 33FFFF represents the hexadecimal value of the color (in this example, cyan). To use this command, click the foreground or background swatch in the Color palette to select it, and then use the palette's menu command Copy Color as HTML. Open the appropriate HTML page in a Web tool or text editor, and use the Paste command to insert the color's hexadecimal value.

■ **Current Colors**—This is actually a color ramp command. When you select this command, Photoshop changes the color ramp to a gradient that runs from the foreground color to the background color.

■ **Make Ramp Web Safe**—When active in the Color palette menu, the color ramp contains only Web-safe colors. It can be used with any of the color ramp's modes, including Grayscale, CMYK, and Current Colors. A check mark appears next to the command in the menu when it's active. To return to the standard color ramp, deselect the command in the Color palette menu.

Color values can also be copied to the Clipboard by using the Eyedropper tool. (Control-click) [right+click] with the Eyedropper on any color and select the menu command Copy Color as HTML. You can then paste the hexadecimal notation into a Web page's HTML code.

THE SWATCHES PALETTE

The Swatches palette is a convenient way to select colors. Clicking on a swatch makes it the foreground color, and (Command-clicking) [Ctrl+clicking] makes it the background color. Sets of colors can be loaded into the palette, and colors you designate in the Color palette or Color Picker can be added. The palette, with its menu open, is shown in Figure 8.6.

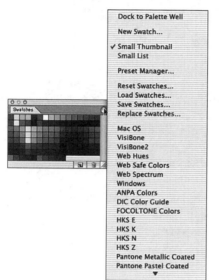

Figure 8.6
Selecting a color from the Swatches palette ensures that it's an exact match every time and enables you to access custom colors without opening the Custom Color dialog box.

Loading the Swatches Palette

Sets of spot colors can be loaded by selecting the name from the list in the palette's menu. Photoshop gives you the option of adding the swatches to the bottom of the palette (Append) or replacing the colors already in the palette with the new set (OK). At the bottom of the palette are icons that allow you to customize the palette by adding and deleting swatches. The New Swatch button adds the foreground color.

The Swatches Palette Menu

In addition to the spot color collections seen in the Swatches palette menu, there are a variety of other commands. Like Photoshop's other palettes, Swatches can be added to the Palette Well. The New Swatch command creates a swatch from the current foreground color and opens a dialog box that enables you to name the swatch.

The palette can be viewed as swatches (the default) or by name. The Small List view, shown in Figure 8.7, includes a thumbnail of each swatch as well as the name.

Showing the Swatches palette content in list view offers the capability of selecting a Pantone (or other) spot color by name.

Figure 8.7
Small List view offers both the thumbnail and the name of each swatch, but shows only a fraction as many swatches in the same palette space.

The next command in the Swatches palette menu opens the Preset Manager. The Preset Manager, which is discussed in Chapter 2, "The Photoshop Interface," enables you to determine what content is shown by default in a variety of palettes. Using the Preset Manager with the Swatches palette establishes which swatches will be available every time Photoshop is opened.

The final four non–spot color commands in the Swatches palette menu can be considered "housekeeping" commands. Reset Swatches returns the palette to the default (as set in Preset Manager). The Load and Save Swatches commands can be used to prepare and use customized collections of swatches. Files must be saved with the .aco extension for Photoshop to recognize them as swatches. The Replace Swatches command empties the Swatches palette and then adds the selected set of swatches.

Pausing your cursor over a swatch in the palette shows the swatch's name. To change the name, double-click the swatch to open the Color Swatch Name dialog box (see Figure 8.8).

Caution

Renaming Pantone and other spot colors can lead to confusion if the image is placed in a page layout program or sent to the printer. It's best to use the original name.

Except when working with spot colors, renaming swatches can be a great idea. You may know that "Pale Green" was used for the underside of the leaves in an image, but a year from now, a swatch name such as "Under Leaves" might seem like a better idea.

Figure 8.8
Every swatch in the Swatches palette can be renamed.

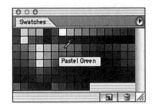

WORKING WITH COLOR PICKERS

Photoshop enables you to choose a color by using a color picker. Somewhat more sophisticated than the Color palette, Adobe's Color Picker is the default. However, you also have the option of using the color picker that comes with your operating system or a third-party plug-in color picker.

Choosing a Color Picker in Photoshop's Preferences

Using a color picker can give you greater control and more options for designating color. Both Macintosh and Windows offer their own system color pickers. Photoshop's General Preferences pane offers the option of using the system color picker, the Adobe Color Picker, or any appropriate third-party plug-ins installed on the system (see Figure 8.9).

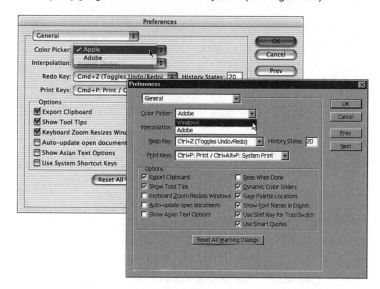

Figure 8.9
Both Macintosh and Windows offer a choice of color pickers in General Preferences.

Creating Color with the Adobe Color Picker

By default, Photoshop uses the Adobe Color Picker. The capabilities and options for the Color Picker are the same on Macintosh and Windows computers. All of the Color Picker's options and capabilities are available, regardless of an image's color mode. However, you should consider the document's color mode when choosing a color. For example, the Color Picker allows you to select a vivid red in the RGB model. If you paint with that red in an image in Grayscale mode, the result is gray. The parts of the Color Picker are identified in Figure 8.10.

8

Figure 8.10
The configuration of the Color
Picker is the same for both
Macintosh and Windows.

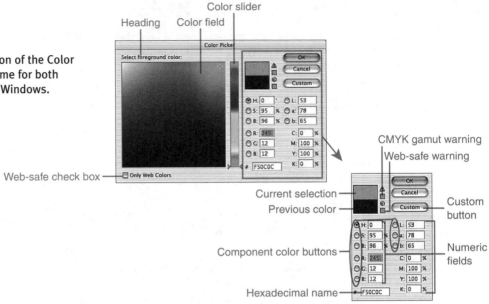

Here's how the components work:

- **Heading**—This shows either "Select foreground color" or "Select background color" to indicate which color you are changing.

- **Color Field**—You click or drag the cursor in this area to change the color values, and the preview and numeric fields are updated as you drag. The color field and the color slider work together to define a color. (Their interaction is explained later in this section.)

- **Web-Safe Check Box**—Clicking this check box forces the color field to Web-safe colors. Instead of continuous gradients in each direction, the field consists of a series of colored shapes. Each shape is a Web-safe color, with no gradients between.

- **Color Slider**—The slider works with the color field to define the color. (Their interaction is explained later in this section.)

- **Previous Color**—The lower color swatch shows the previous color. If you click Cancel rather than OK, this color is retained.

- **Current Selection**—The upper color swatch reflects the Color Picker's current settings. As you change the color field and color slider (or make changes in the numeric fields), the swatch is automatically updated. The change does not take effect until you click OK.

- **Web-Safe Warning**—When a color is not part of the Web-safe palette, this cube-shaped warning appears. The small color swatch below the cube is the nearest Web-safe color. Clicking the swatch loads that color in the Color Picker. When not preparing images for Web-safe output, this warning can be ignored. The icon is shaped like a cube, which represents one of the common methods of arranging the Web-safe palette.

- **CMYK Gamut Warning**—Any time that the current color falls outside the CMYK gamut (that is, cannot be reproduced in CMYK), the warning triangle appears here. Underneath is a small color swatch of the nearest CMYK color. Clicking on the swatch loads it as the current selection and updates the color field, slider, and numeric fields. When not preparing an image for CMYK output, this warning can be ignored.

The CMYK gamut warning is only as accurate as your color settings. It is based on the CMYK profile loaded in your Photoshop Color Settings.

➪ *For more about the color settings,* **see** *Chapter 9, "Photoshop Color Management," p. 219.*

- **Custom Button**—This button switches the Color Picker from the standard mode to the Custom Color mode. (See the following section "Selecting Custom Colors" for complete information.)

- **Component Buttons**—The nine component buttons allow you to select which color attribute appears in the color slider. Click on any button to use that color component or attribute as the basis of selection. When H (hue) is selected (the default), the color's hue is determined with the color slider and the saturation and brightness are selected in the color field. When S is selected, saturation is determined with the slider, and hue and brightness in the color field. HSB work together, as do RGB and the Lab attributes. CMYK colors cannot be directly defined with the slider and color field because they have four components, not three.

The Color Picker enables you to enter values into the a and b fields that range from −128 to +127, but the Color palette in Lab mode restricts you to −120 to +120. There can be a color difference, although small, between the extreme values. If you enter numbers beyond −120 or +120 in the Color Picker, the values are shown (and used) in the Color palette.

- **Numeric Fields**—Colors can be defined numerically by entering values into these fields. After you've clicked in one of the fields, you can use Tab and Shift+Tab to move among them. Hue is measured in degrees and can range from 0 to 360; saturation and brightness are measured in percentages and can range from 0 to 100. R, G, and B can range from 0 to 255. L is measured in percentages and ranges from 0 to 100; a and b can range from −128 to +127. C, M, Y, and K are measured in percentages and can range from 0 to 100.

Although called the "Adobe" Color Picker, this particular version is unique to Photoshop. Illustrator's color picker doesn't offer the Lab fields. ImageReady's color picker offers only HSB and RGB. LiveMotion uses a palette that incorporates the features of Photoshop's Color palette and its Color Picker.

- **Hexadecimal Name**—The color's hexadecimal value is shown in this field, whether Web-safe or not. You can highlight this value to copy and paste it into an HTML document.

8

Selecting Custom Colors

When you click the Custom button in the Color Picker, it switches to the Custom Colors dialog box (see Figure 8.11). This custom color picker is used to select the preset colors usually referred to as "spot colors." The Color Picker opens to the spot color that most closely matches the current color.

The collections of custom colors available are shown in the Book pop-up menu. Select the appropriate group of colors in the list, and then select the specific color you want from the list of swatches on the left side of the Custom Colors picker. You can type a color's numeric designation to jump to it in the list, or use the vertical slider to move through the swatch list.

You can drag the indicators along the side of the slider, click on the arrows at the top or bottom, or simply click anywhere in the slider. All three techniques will change the visible colors in the swatch list to the left of the slider.

You'll often see the term *book* used to refer to collections of spot colors because actual books can, in fact, be used to select the colors. A spot color book contains samples of each of the colors. Designers can use the book to see how the colors look on paper and to select the appropriate one. That color sample is labeled with the color's name or number, which is then selected in Photoshop's Custom Colors dialog box. Spot color collections can also be viewed on swatch cards and other guides. Books and swatch cards can be purchased from Pantone and other ink manufacturers.

Figure 8.11
You can return to the Color Picker from the Custom Colors dialog box by clicking the Picker button.

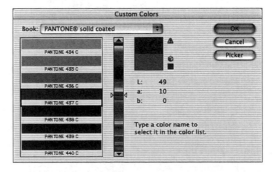

Like the Color Picker, the Custom Colors picker shows you swatches of both the currently selected color and the color to be replaced as the foreground or background color. It also has CMYK and Web-safe warnings. Below the swatches, you'll see the Lab or CMYK equivalent of the selected color.

CMYK is used for Pantone Process Coated, Pantone Solid to Process Coated, Trumatch, Focoltone, and any other spot color collections consisting of CMYK colors. Other books show the Lab values for the selected color.

The Windows Color Picker

The Windows color picker offers 48 basic colors, plus space to define and easily access 16 more custom colors (see Figure 8.12). You can click on any color swatch in the (basic or custom) Color dialog box and then click OK to make the selected color active in Photoshop.

Click the Define Custom Colors button to open the right side of the Color dialog box (see Figure 8.13).

The CMYK and Web warnings can usually be ignored when using the Custom Colors dialog box. If the book consists of process colors, the warning won't show. If it's another spot color book, you've likely selected it because you *can't* use a CMYK equivalent. And because spot colors are not normally used on the Web (and certainly not with a Web-safe palette), the cube-shaped warning can also be ignored.

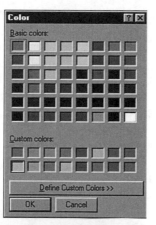

Figure 8.12
The Windows Color dialog box offers 48 standard colors and space for 16 user-defined custom colors.

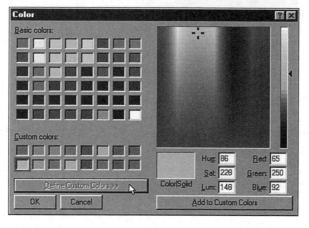

Figure 8.13
The right side of the color picker is used to define custom colors.

To define a custom color, drag the crosshairs in the large color field, and then drag the vertical slider found to the right of the color field to change the luminosity (brightness). The slider changes the luminosity of the selected color without affecting the hue or saturation. (The HSL model used in the Windows Color dialog box is equivalent to Photoshop's HSB color model. The terms *luminosity*, *lightness*, and *brightness* represent the same concept.) Numeric values can also be entered directly into the HSL or RGB fields.

After the 16 custom color swatches in the Color dialog box are filled, defining additional colors replaces them in the order in which they were defined. For example, when you define the 17th custom color, the first custom color is overwritten.

An existing custom color can also be edited. Click once on the color swatch, and then make any changes to the hue, saturation, and luminosity. Click the Add to Custom Colors button to finalize the change.

The Apple Color Picker

When Macintosh users select Apple as the color picker in Photoshop's General Preferences, they have a choice of five options. When the Apple Color Picker is open, users can select any of these color pickers at any time during the color selection process.

The first option uses CMYK sliders, much like those in Photoshop's Color palette (see Figure 8.14).

Figure 8.14
Clicking on CMYK at the top of the left column changes the color picker to the configuration shown.

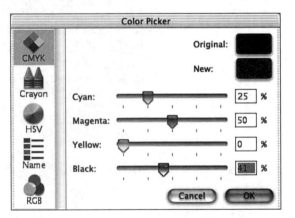

The second option, Crayon (see Figure 8.15), offers 48 preset colors. Clicking on a "crayon" selects that color; clicking OK makes it the active color in Photoshop.

When a color has been selected in another color picker that does not exactly match one of Apple's crayons, Crayon adds "-ish" to the name of the nearest color (as shown in Figure 8.15).

Some of the crayon names are useful, such as Maroon, Magenta, Teal, and Lavender. Others are very descriptive, including Lemon, Lime, Tangerine, and Salmon. Some color names are quite whimsical, such as Spindrift (CMYK 60/0/20/0), Orchid (60/60/0/0), and Flora (60/0/60/0).

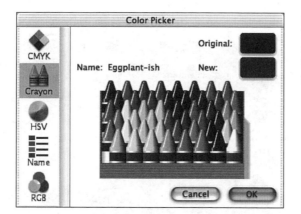

Figure 8.15
The Crayon color picker offers only 48 colors, comparable to the Windows Color dialog box, but without custom colors.

The various shades of gray are named for metals: Mercury (10%), Silver (20%), Magnesium (30%), Aluminum (40%), Nickel (50%), Steel (60%), Iron (70%), Tungsten (80%), and Lead (90%). (Interestingly, the colors named Nickel and Tin are both 50% gray.) Black and white are Licorice and Snow.

Apple's HSV color model is comparable to Photoshop's HSB and Window's HSL. V (value) is equivalent to B (brightness) or L (luminescence/luminosity/lightness). The HSV color picker, shown in Figure 8.16, uses the color wheel for hue and saturation and a slider for value (brightness).

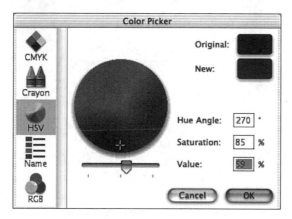

Figure 8.16
The Hue Angle is measured in degrees from red (at 3 o'clock), and Saturation and Value are measured in percentages.

To determine hue and saturation, you can drag the crosshairs in the color wheel. Moving the crosshairs toward the center of the wheel reduces saturation, and moving around the wheel changes hue. The Value slider at the bottom is independent of the color wheel. You can also enter values directly into the numeric fields.

The Apple Color Picker's Name option offers the Web-safe colors by default, identified by their hexadecimal name (see Figure 8.17).

8

Figure 8.17
By default, the pop-up menu at
the top offers only Web Safe
Colors.

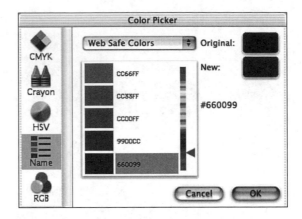

The fifth option for the Apple Color Picker is RGB. This version offers three sliders, one each for the component colors red, green, and blue (see Figure 8.18). Unlike Adobe's Color Picker, which lets you specify 256 levels of each color, Apple's RGB sliders use percentage, restricting you to 100 different levels of each color. Rather than having 16.7 million colors available, this limits you to one million (which is typically more than adequate for situations in which colors must be defined manually).

Figure 8.18
RGB colors can be created by
using the sliders or entering percentages in the numeric fields.

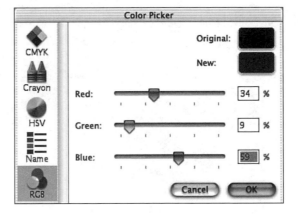

Besides the obvious difference between CMYK and RGB, you might find that some color pickers are better than others under different circumstances. For example, after you learn the CMYK and RGB equivalents of Apple's crayons, you might find them an easy way to pick a color or shade of gray. On the other hand, trying to select a pure gray with Apple's HSV Color Picker requires trying to drag the crosshairs into the exact center of the color wheel, which is not nearly as efficient as numeric input in the CMYK or RGB color pickers.

PHOTOSHOP IN FOCUS

The Swatches palette can be a great time saver—not only can you easily and quickly use the exact color in a variety of places in an image, but you can also find many of those hard-to-mix colors already prepared. You can also use the Swatches palette to find the RGB or CMYK equivalent of a specific color.

1. Drag Photoshop's Swatches palette to the top-left corner of your screen, and drag the lower-right corner down and to the right. Open the palette wide, ready for filling.

2. Use the Swatches palette menu to load the following swatch sets: Pantone Metallic Coated, Pantone Pastel Coated, and Pantone Solid Coated. (Skip Pantone Process Coated.)

3. Position the Info palette so that it's visible.

4. Select Palette Options from the Info palette menu.

5. Set the first readout to RGB and the second readout to CMYK.

6. Press I on the keyboard to select the Eyedropper tool.

7. Move the Eyedropper around the Swatches palette and check the RGB and CMYK readings for various swatches. Compare various "gold" swatches from the metallic set to similar-looking swatches from the other Pantone collections. Note the exclamation marks to the right of the CMYK values for some of the metallic golds. That's the Info palette's gamut warning, comparable to the warning triangle in the Color palette.

FROM THE NAPP HELP DESK

The National Association of Photoshop Professionals (NAPP) offers e-mail assistance to its members. Here are some questions from the NAPP Help Desk related to issues in this chapter.

Swatches: Only Half the Story

Sometimes it seems that the foreground color swatch in the Toolbox and the Color palette doesn't match the color that's being added to my image. Why is that?

The color designated in the Color palette or the Color Picker, or selected in the Swatches palette, is only part of the story. That's the color you're adding to the image. However, what you see onscreen and what prints might be totally different. In addition to the color with which you're painting (or otherwise adding to the image), there's the question of how the color interacts with other colors already in the image. Here are some of the factors:

- Check the document's color mode. If the mode is CMYK but you're using the RGB color model in the Color palette, you could be adding an out-of-gamut color. ("Out of gamut" means that the color cannot be reproduced accurately.) You'll see it onscreen if you've selected Proof Colors from the View menu.

- What is the blending mode of the layer where you're adding color? The blending mode, selected in Layer Style or the Layers palette, determines how pixels on that layer interact with pixels below. Any blending mode other than Normal can result in a change to the appearance of the color.

- Check the layer's opacity, too. If the opacity of the layer is reduced, the color you apply isn't "solid," so the color or colors below might show through.

8

■ In addition to the layer blending mode and opacity, the painting tools have their own controls. If, for example, the paintbrush is set to Multiply, it's comparable to painting in Normal mode on a layer set to Multiply.

Choosing a Model

In the Color Palette, do I have to use the same color model for the sliders and the ramp?

No. In fact, it's often very convenient to have the sliders and the ramp set to different color models. The Color palette menu lets you select each color model independently. (Don't forget that the color ramp can't show HSB or Lab.) If you're working in both color and grays, setting the sliders to RGB and the ramp to Grayscale can save a lot of time when choosing grays. It's much easier to select a gray from the ramp than it is to pick out a specific color.

9

PHOTOSHOP COLOR MANAGEMENT

IN THIS CHAPTER

9

WHAT IS COLOR MANAGEMENT?

The term "color management" has been known to strike fear into the hearts of even hard-core Photoshop professionals. Starting with Photoshop 5, the program offered a great deal more control over the process of ensuring that an image looked the same onscreen as it did on paper. Photoshop 6 simplified the process considerably and made it more versatile, but it remains one of the most misunderstood aspects of Photoshop. Photoshop 7 continues the trend toward simplification.

It should be noted that the depth and breadth of this subject cannot possibly be covered adequately in this arena. Creating custom CMYK profiles using a densitometer, the peculiar characteristics of third-party color spaces, the nuts and bolts of each hardware calibration system available—these subjects are far too broad to be covered in the space available. This chapter explains the concepts and theory of color management and looks at the application for the mid-range user. Print facilities and service bureaus that work with high-end glossy publications will find the theory here useful, but might require additional resource material.

Setting the Table: Terminology

The various terms used in color management should be clarified before the discussion begins. Many of the terms are similar, but refer to different aspects of the color management process or theory.

- **Calibration**—Calibration is the process of adjusting a specific device to ensure that it produces the most accurate color possible. This process can involve the knobs and buttons on a monitor and/or external hardware used to precisely measure the output of a monitor's phosphors and the density of ink on a page. Calibration is intended to make the device produce colors that are *as close as possible* to an objective standard. The Adobe Gamma control panel doesn't actually calibrate a monitor; rather, it makes some adjustments while producing a profile of the monitor's behavior. (See also *profiling*.)

- **Characterizing**—See *profiling*.

- **CIE**—Headquartered in Austria, the Commission Internationale de l'Eclairage/The International Commission on Illumination (www.cie.co.at) is a technical/scientific/cultural, nonprofit autonomous organization. Founded in the 1920s, it is accepted as the best authority on the subject of lighting and is recognized as such by the ISO (International Standards Organization) as an international standardization body. In the 1930s, it developed a way to assign numbers to every color visible to the human eye. (See also *L*a*b, CIELAB, Lab.*)

- **CMM**—The Color Management Module is the software that translates color information from one profile to another. Adobe Color Engine (ACE) is a CMM. (See also *CMS* and *color management engine*.)

- **CMS**—The color management system is the conglomeration of color engine, ICC profiles, color settings, and other bits and pieces that you use to manage color. You can select an established CMS, such as ColorSync, or you can choose to use custom profiles that are specific to the devices (monitors, printers, scanners) you have on hand. Apple's ColorSync and Microsoft ICM for Windows are system-level color management systems, and Kodak CMS is a program-level CMS. (See also *color management engine* and *ICC profile*.)

- **CMYK Profile**—Loaded into Photoshop's Color Settings dialog box, this profile identifies to the color management engine the capabilities of your output device or the press on which the image will be printed. Profiles for inkjet printers, which require RGB images, are also loaded as CMYK profiles. The CMYK profile determines the CMYK working space.

- **Color Gamut**—See *gamut*.

- **Color Management Engine**—Also known simply as the color engine, this software serves as the translator between devices, mapping color from one device profile to another. It reads the color data in the file and the color profile for the monitor and converts the colors to the color space of another device. For example, when you output to a printer, the color engine adapts the colors you saw onscreen to the closest colors that the printer can produce. Likewise, if you open an image created on another computer with a different monitor profile, the image can be converted to your RGB working space when you open it on your computer.

- **Color Management Policies**—Selected in Color Settings, these options determine what Photoshop does when you open a file with an embedded profile that doesn't match your working space. You can retain the embedded profile, which could result in an inaccurate appearance on your screen, convert to your working profile, or simply ignore the profile entirely.

- **Color Model**—A color model is the system of notation used to describe numerically the specific colors within a gamut. RGB, CMYK, Grayscale, Lab, and HSB are color models. (See also *color space* and *gamut*.)

- **Color Profile**—See *embedded profile*.

- **Color Settings**—This term refers to both the options you've selected for color management and the Photoshop dialog box where you make those choices.

- **Color Space**—The collection of possible colors that can be created by a specific technique or device is the color space. In Photoshop, Lab has the widest theoretical color space, encompassing all the colors that the human eye can see. RGB includes all the colors that can be reproduced by using combinations of red, green, and blue light. The CMYK color space includes only those colors that can be re-created by using the four process color inks. However, the color space is restricted by the capabilities of the specific devices you use. (See also *color model* and *gamut*.)

- **Embedded Profile**—When a file contains information about the devices with which or for which it was prepared, the RGB or CMYK profile is embedded into the file itself. This is also called *tagging* a document. A document with an embedded profile is *tagged*, and one without is *untagged*. When the file is opened or output, the color management engine reads the embedded profile(s) and applies the color management policies, either converting the image's colors to your working space or not. ICC-aware file formats (such as Photoshop's PSD, TIFF, and EPS, among others) give you the option of embedding a profile in the Save As dialog box. Profiles can be changed by using Image, Mode, Assign Profile and Image, Mode, Convert to Profile. (See also *profiling*.)

- **Gamut**—The gamut for a particular color model (RGB, CMYK, Lab) is the collection of colors that exist within that color space. The gamut for a device is the subset of colors that can be reproduced by that monitor or printer. (See also *color model* and *color space*.)

9

9

- **ICC**—The International Color Consortium (www.color.org) was founded in 1993 by a group of eight companies, including Apple, Microsoft, Agfa, Adobe, and Kodak. The intent was to establish a system whereby color could be standardized from computer to computer, program to program, printer to printer. The .icc file format was developed as a way to store and provide access to information about a specific device's capabilities.

- **ICC Profile**—The .icc (Macintosh) or .icm (Windows) file records the device-specific information for a monitor, printer, or scanner profile. ICC profiles are loaded in Photoshop's Color Settings dialog box as working spaces. (See also *working space*.)

- **L*a*b, CIELAB, Lab**—Developed by the CIE in the 1930s, Lab is a color model that numerically defines every color visible to the human eye. (See also *CIE*.)

- **Mapping, Color Mapping**—Translating color information from one profile to another is known as mapping or color mapping. The color engine looks at the image's color data, takes into account the source profile embedded in the file, and then maps the color information to the destination profile. (See also *color management engine*.)

- **Profiling**—After a device is calibrated, it is profiled. Profiling, also called *characterizing*, creates a record of how close a device comes to matching an objective standard for color reproduction. This record is the device's ICC profile. Calibration gets the device as close as possible, and profiling measures the shortfall. (No device is expected to be 100% accurate.) The Adobe Gamma control panel adjusts and profiles a monitor, instead of actually calibrating it. Third-party hardware/software products often calibrate and profile in the same procedure. (See also *calibration* and *ICC profile*.)

- **RGB Profile**—The gamut that your monitor is capable of reproducing, along with any vagaries in performance, are recorded as the RGB profile in an .icc (Macintosh) or .icm (Windows) file. The profile is used by the color engine. Creating a profile is called *profiling* or *characterizing* a device. (See also *gamut*.)

- **Working Space**—The working space is the gamut of the image's color model, as restricted by the device profile. For CMYK images, the working space is defined by the CMYK profile. For RGB images, it is defined by the RGB profile. (See also *color model* and *gamut*.)

The filename in the image window tells you if no profile is embedded in the image or if there's a profile mismatch between the image and your working space. When an asterisk appears after the color mode in the title bar, there's a profile mismatch. When a pound sign appears, the image is not color managed and no profile is embedded.

The Quest for Perfect Color

In an ideal world, every device would show color exactly as your eyes see it. Regardless of monitor or offset press or inkjet printer or Web browser, an apple or an orange would always look just like it does in real life.

Unfortunately, that can't happen. The limitations of how color is reproduced—and the vagaries of individual devices—produce a wide range of appearances for a single image.

Rather, we use the capabilities of Photoshop and other software to attempt to control these differences. Color management can be considered a system of compensating for the individual characteristics of devices to produce uniform color. Think of the goal as "what you see is what you get."

Not that you can't get accurate color output from a printer in other ways! Rather than WYSIWYG (what you see is what you get), you can have "Kentucky windage," an attempt to make corrections based on best guesses and trial and error. For example, suppose you know that your particular printer always produces output that's a little light. You could make your images darker before printing. They'd look too dark onscreen, but would look fine in print. Or perhaps the printer is too heavy with cyan. You could reduce the cyan in the image to ensure proper images on paper. If you know a rifle shoots a little to the left, aim a little to the right. However, it is certainly preferable to aim at the bull's-eye and hit the bull's-eye—and that's the purpose of color management.

To carry the rifle analogy further, consider various printing presses, inkjet printers, and monitors as targets at different distances. Just as a marksman's rifle scope can be adjusted for a particular distance, so, too, do you need to apply different settings for different output. As the marksman calibrates his scope for specific ranges, so must you have the appropriate profile for a specific device. Setting the rifle's scope for 500 meters when shooting at a target 300 meters away sends the bullet too high. Likewise, using a profile for an inkjet printer produces lousy output from a Heidelberg press.

Do You Need Color Management?

You can determine whether you need color management in Photoshop by answering a single question. If you answer *yes*, you should manage your color. The question is this:

Do you use Photoshop?

If you use Photoshop, you should manage color. Whether you create images to be printed in full-color coffee table books, produce fine art or print photos from an inkjet printer, or create buttons for Web pages, you should use the color management tools built into Photoshop. Some images and some workflows require more stringent color management than others, but all Photoshop users should enable at least the minimum capabilities. If you're not seeing accurate color on your own monitor, it's likely that the images you produce are no closer to reality.

Caution

It is important to remember that color management is designed to accurately reproduce *accurate* color. If your image contains a color cast or other color fault, proper color management doesn't correct the problem; rather, it ensures that the problem is reproduced exactly. Color management is not a substitute for color correction.

The range of color management requirements varies greatly among Photoshop users. Print shops and service bureaus, especially those that produce high-end glossy materials, have extreme needs. Folks who produce Web graphics have a different set of requirements.

Theoretically, you could even do CMYK color correction on a grayscale monitor. If you relied totally on the numbers available to you in Photoshop's Info and Color palettes, you could produce accurate color. Although checking the numeric values of key colors is a good idea, attempting to do all your work exclusively by the numbers is counterproductive.

You're happy with your output and don't want to manage color? See "Riding the Wave" in the NAPP Help Desk section at the end of this chapter.

An Overview of the Process

Color management revolves around a color management system (CMS). The CMS is based on the *color engine*, the software that actually translates from one set of color values to another. The engine uses *color profiles* embedded in the image files, which describe how a particular piece of hardware reproduces color. When the profile is applied to the image, the color values are skewed for the particular characteristics of the specific device. When the color values need to be prepared for output to a different device, the engine translates the colors so that they appear in the final product as precisely as possible.

For example, say you have a monitor with a slight blue cast to the colors onscreen. (This cast could be caused by design, settings, or even age.) You calibrate or adjust the monitor to show—onscreen—the most accurate color possible. You then *characterize* the monitor, creating a profile (the RGB setting). That profile is used to ensure that when you add red (for example) to the image, the color recorded in the file is the same hue and tint as what you see onscreen.

Say you're preparing this image for commercial printing at your local print shop. You need to make sure that the red you choose is a red that can be reproduced by the printing press on which the job will be run, using the proper inks and on the paper selected for the job. For that, you use an appropriate CMYK setting, a profile for the specific press and job parameters.

Because the RGB gamut can display colors that cannot be output on press, you tell the color engine how to handle the translation. Working just in the RGB space, you might come up with a design incorporating several shades of red that are beyond the capability of the press. You tell the color engine how you want those reds to be squished down into the CMYK color space.

You could theoretically simply "clip" the unprintable reds and not use them in your image. Or you can have all reds outside the space brought into *gamut* (the printable color space, in this case) in a couple of different ways. All the reds can be shifted so that the most extreme RGB red becomes the most extreme CMYK red, the second most extreme RGB red becomes the second most extreme CMYK red, and so on. Think of this as a *perceptual* shift. Alternatively, you can compress the out-of-gamut reds into the nearest printable color, a *relative* conversion of the colors. (This is a simplification of the relationship between *perceptual* and *relative* rendering.) Figure 9.1 shows a comparison.

Take another look at Figure 9.1 and carry the analogy a little further:

- The first column, RGB (Original), represents what the monitor shows, which depends on the monitor's capabilities and the profile used. One monitor may show a different range of reds, perhaps only from Red-2 to Red-13. Another monitor might not have such even steps among the reds.

- The CMYK profile, used to define the printing press's capabilities, might be substantially different. The point where the CMYK gamut starts could be above Red-3 or below Red-6, for example. This information can determine how you decide to handle the color conversion.

If an image doesn't have extremely bright or extremely saturated colors—colors that are likely to fall out of the CMYK gamut—this discussion still applies. Color spaces can have different gamma settings, which affect image brightness.

- There might be very few pixels in your image that are out of gamut, perhaps few enough to ignore. In the "relative" example in Figure 9.1, five different "RGB reds" are being squished into a single "print red." If your image doesn't use those extreme reds, there's no reason to worry.

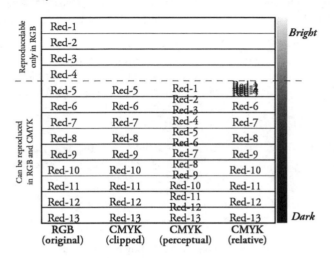

Figure 9.1
The "reds" are labeled by name. You can perhaps visualize how the four images would compare.

It's important that you have both the correct profiles and an appropriate rendering intent. Both are discussed later in this chapter.

⇨ *Unsure about how this discussion pertains to inkjet printers? See "When RGB Is CMYK" in the NAPP Help Desk section at the end of this chapter.*

Preparing the Work Environment

Perhaps the key to effective color management is ensuring that you see onscreen the same colors that are recorded in the file. You want the screen to accurately portray the image. Not only must the monitor show you the colors, but also you must be able to *see* those colors accurately.

If color accuracy is critical to your work, you must create an environment conducive to color viewing. It's obvious that your monitor's colors look more saturated (richer) when the office lights are off and the shades are down. In a dark room, the monitor's glow isn't competing with other lights. The more ambient light in the room, the more competition for the monitor.

Consider an office with a beautiful view. During the day, as the sun changes position, the amount of light coming through the windows changes. Colors onscreen look different in the morning than they do in the afternoon. Ceiling lights, desk lamps, even light tables and proofing lamps can have substantial impact on how colors on your monitor are perceived by your eyes.

On the flip side, working in a completely dark office, using just the glow of the monitor, hour after hour, day after day, is also not particularly conducive to making the best color decisions. In addition, such environments can substantially reduce productivity.

The compromise? Control ambient lighting when doing color correction; enjoy your work environment (as much as possible) otherwise. Let your calibrated monitor and your color management system perform at their best when you need them most.

9

You should consider several other issues when preparing an environment suitable for proper color management:

- The monitor can be shielded from ambient light by using a hood. Although hoods are available commercially, they can also be produced in-house. Shield the top and sides of the monitor to a distance of at least 12 inches, and paint the inside of the hood matte black.

- The computer's desktop should be neutral gray. Avoid colorful family pictures and beautiful scenery. Alternatively, you can create a temporary background in Photoshop simply by pressing the F key. Photoshop's Full Screen Mode with Menu Bar creates a gray background around your image. If you want to work in Standard Screen Mode, try this: Open a new document, and fill it with 50% gray. Press F to put that image into Full Screen Mode with Menu Bar. Zoom a couple of times until the image fills the screen. Now open your work image(s).

- Objects on and around the monitor should be removed. Unless you use Post-It Notes that are 50% gray, they should not appear on the bezel of a monitor used for color correction. Additionally, leave the desktop as clear as possible.

- Walls within sight when you're looking at the monitor should also be free of colorful decoration and painted a neutral gray.

How critical are these adaptations to the work environment? Only as critical as the accuracy of your color. The more important a color match, the more important the environment in which that match is made.

SYSTEM-LEVEL COLOR MANAGEMENT

A good place to start your color management is at the system level. Both Macintosh and Windows offer color management systems (CMSs) that can work across programs and with monitors, printers, scanners, and digital cameras.

Macintosh CMS: ColorSync

In Mac OS X, ColorSync is found in the System Preferences. You can specify ICC profiles for Input, Output, Display, and Proof (see Figure 9.2). The selected profiles are the *assumed* profiles—Photoshop defaults to these profiles, but you can change them on a document-by-document basis if necessary.

The second panel (the Document Profiles tab) tells ColorSync (and the programs that use it as the CMS) how to handle images without embedded profiles (see Figure 9.3).

When multiple color management modules are available, ColorSync offers you the opportunity to specify one CMM to handle all color conversion (see Figure 9.4).

In-depth information about ColorSync, as well as a variety of useful resources, are available at www.apple.com/ colorsync.

Even if you don't use ColorSync color management, remember the ColorSync utility. Found in the Applications, Utilities folder, it can verify—and repair—ICC profiles.

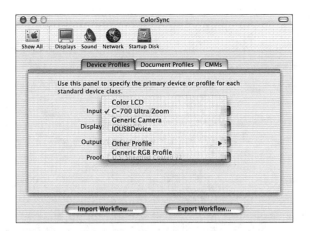

Figure 9.2
The menus show the appropriate ICC profiles for each category.

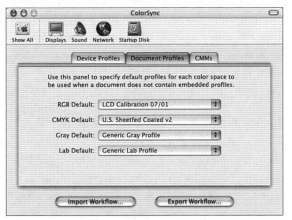

Figure 9.3
These settings do not affect images that contain embedded ICC profiles for color management.

Figure 9.4
Unless there's an overriding reason to pick a third-party CMM, stick with the Automatic option.

9

Measuring Onscreen Color for Mac OS

Mac OS X and OS 9 include a utility called DigitalColor Meter that can help you determine how accurately your monitor is producing color:

1. Profile your monitor using Adobe Gamma or another utility. (See "Calibrating and Profiling the Monitor," later in this chapter.)

2. Open Photoshop's Color Settings and load your monitor profile as the RGB setting.

3. Open the Swatches palette and move it to the center of the screen. Use the palette's menu command Reset Swatches. Replace (the OK button) rather than append.

4. Open DigitalColor Meter. In Mac OS X, look in the folder Applications, Utilities. For OS 9, look in Applications (Mac OS 9), Apple Extras, Monitors Extras folder.

5. Set the readout to RGB As Percentage and make sure that Aperture Size is set to one of the three leftmost settings. If it's not, press Command-Shift-H, change it, and then press Command-Shift-H again.

6. Position the DigitalColor Meter window where it will be visible while you work.

7. In Mac OS X, use the Dock to make Photoshop active again. In Mac OS 9, use the Application Switcher menu in the upper-right corner of the screen.

8. Position the cursor over the upper-left swatch. If your monitor is showing accurate color *and* is calibrated correctly *and* your RGB profile is good, DigitalColor Meter will read R:100, G:0, B:0. Try the other swatches. Make sure to include the grayscale swatches.

9. For comparison, in Photoshop's Color Settings, switch to Adobe RGB as the RGB profile. Measure the swatches again. Typically, your custom monitor profile will be more accurate.

The first six swatches should give the following readings: 100/0/0 (RGB Red), 100/100/0 (RGB Yellow), 0/100/0 (RGB Green), 0/100/100 (RGB Cyan), 0/0/100 (RGB Blue), and 100/0/100 (RGB Magenta). The gray swatches in the top and second rows should be close to the appropriate percent, but more important, the amounts of each of the three component colors should be equal.

When using your custom monitor profile as the RGB setting, if your readings vary substantially or show a consistent discrepancy in one particular color, recalibrate, re-profile, and try again.

Windows CMS:

The Image Color Management (ICM) component of Windows is designed to work with ICM-aware programs and devices to standardize color. It is not used directly from Photoshop. However, if you use other programs that are ICM aware, set them to use ICM. In those programs, choose Color Management from the File menu.

Caution

Some monitors, printers, and other devices include color management systems that might not be compatible with Photoshop. If you choose to install a third-party CMS, make sure that you don't override the Windows InstallShield—you may need to remove the CMS to run Photoshop.

CALIBRATING AND PROFILING THE MONITOR

A properly calibrated monitor provides you with an accurate view of color. If you have calibration hardware from such companies as Gretag Macbeth (www.gretagmacbeth.com), ColorVision (www.colorpar.com), or X-Rite (www.xrite.com), you can accurately adjust your monitor. Prepress professionals and other Photoshop users who rely on color accuracy should invest in hardware calibration equipment. If you output to a home/office inkjet printer or are a Web specialist, you might not benefit as much from the expenditure. If you don't have access to calibration hardware, you can adjust your monitor during the profiling process.

Whether you use Adobe Gamma, ColorSync, or a third-party product, make a note of where you save the profile and what name you use (the monitor name and date, for example). Mac users should include the file extension .icc; in Windows, it's .icm.

You can navigate to any drive or folder when loading your RGB profile, so there's no need to put it in a specific place. In fact, if you create a separate folder, there's less chance of losing the profile during a reinstall of Photoshop or the system software.

9

Caution

Do not use the Adobe Gamma control panel to profile an LCD monitor—it works only with CRTs. Third-party hardware calibration/profiling packages are available, and your LCD monitor's manufacturer may have included a utility.

Profiling with Adobe Gamma

Photoshop installs the Adobe Gamma control panel for Windows in the Control Panel, accessed through Settings in the Start menu. For Mac OS 9, it's accessed through the Apple menu, where you choose Control Panels, Adobe Gamma (see Figure 9.5 for both Windows and Mac OS 9). Adobe Gamma is not compatible with Mac OS X (see the following section).

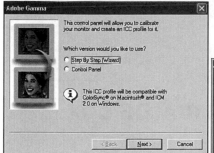

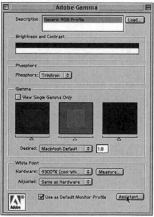

Figure 9.5
Although you'll see the word "calibrate" associated with Adobe Gamma, think of it more as a tool for profiling a monitor.

When you open Adobe Gamma, you'll be offered the choice of working directly in the control panel or walking through the profiling, step by step. Unless you're familiar with the procedure, use the wizard (Windows) or assistant (Mac).

To get an accurate profile of the monitor, you should work with Adobe Gamma in the same conditions under which you'll be correcting and evaluating color. Control the ambient lighting and remove from view anything that could influence your perception of the screen.

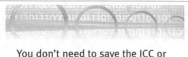

You don't need to save the ICC or ICM profile in a specific location for Windows or Macintosh. In the Color Settings dialog box, select the Advanced Mode check box and Load RGB will be available—you can navigate to any folder available to your computer.

Monitor Profiling in Mac OS X

The System Preferences, Displays window has a pair of tabs, unless you're using multiple monitors, in which case it has three tabs. Click on the Color tab and then the Calibrate button to access the Display Calibrator Assistant utility (see Figure 9.6). Like Adobe Gamma's Assistant mode, this utility walks you through the process of creating a monitor profile.

Figure 9.6
Select the Expert Mode check box for access to all the calibration options.

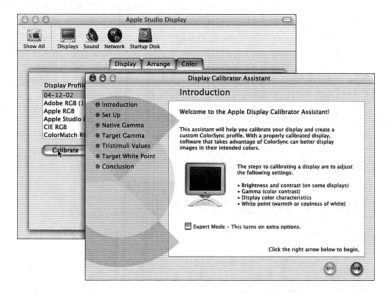

PHOTOSHOP'S COLOR SETTINGS DIALOG BOX

The first time you open Photoshop 7, you have the opportunity to customize your color settings (see Figure 9.7). Whether you do so then or not, you can always revisit your settings and make changes. In Windows and Mac OS 9, use the Edit, Color Settings command. In Mac OS X, you'll find Color Settings under the Photoshop menu. Your color settings are stored in a file of that name in the Adobe Photoshop 7.0 Settings folder. Deleting the file restores Photoshop to its default color settings.

Different operations and different Photoshop tasks require different setting for proper color management. This section gives general guidance for the majority of Photoshop users.

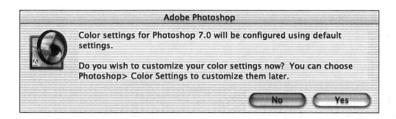

Figure 9.7
If you click No, Photoshop loads color settings appropriate for the Web. Clicking Yes takes you immediately to the Color Settings dialog box.

The Settings Menu

At the top of the Color Settings dialog box is the Settings pop-up menu. This menu lists preset packages of color settings, generally appropriate for specific categories of work (see Figure 9.8).

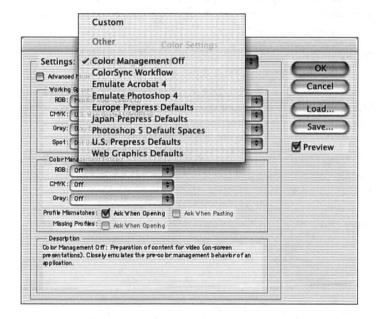

Figure 9.8
Choosing any package of settings from this menu automatically configures the remaining options in the dialog box. The Windows list does not include ColorSync.

Using these prepackaged sets of profiles is worthwhile only in a workflow that is geared toward them. Even then, more appropriate profiles should be assigned later.

RGB Working Spaces

The selection made in the RGB working space defines your RGB working space. When you embed a color profile in an RGB image, this is what you're including.

If you have a perfectly calibrated monitor (using hardware calibration) and work in a production environment with several other perfectly calibrated monitors, it might make sense for all systems to use Adobe RGB (or another large gamut) as the RGB profile. If you have Radius Pressview monitors, ColorMatch RGB should be the choice. Wide-gamut dye sublimation printers and many photo-quality printer operations might benefit from ProPhoto RGB. If you send images to a service bureau or print shop as RGB, they may prefer one gamut over another.

9

Photoshop users who don't send out RGB images (including Web professionals) are typically best served by using the custom monitor profile they created with Adobe Gamma or other calibration/profiling procedures. Your profile is geared for your monitor. It produces the most accurate color onscreen. This situation includes many Photoshop users who output only to inkjet printers. If you profiled your monitor with Adobe Gamma, your custom profile is available in the menu as Monitor RGB.

Macintosh users can refer to the sidebar "Measuring Onscreen Color for Mac OS" earlier in this chapter for a procedure through which they can measure a profile's accuracy. (Windows users don't have a built-in utility comparable to DigitalColor Meter.)

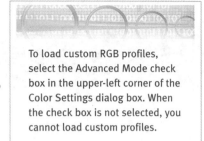

To load custom RGB profiles, select the Advanced Mode check box in the upper-left corner of the Color Settings dialog box. When the check box is not selected, you cannot load custom profiles.

CMYK Working Spaces

Even if you output only to inkjet printers, you need to have the proper profile assigned for your CMYK setting. Although inkjet printers use RGB color data from the image, they are actually CMYK devices at heart. Many inkjet printers install several different ICC profiles for various combinations of resolution and paper quality. Choose the one you normally use, and change the profile if you print to a different paper.

If you're preparing images for output to a specific printing press, contact your print shop or service bureau to see if there's a custom CMYK profile available. If not, or if you don't know what printer will be handling the job, choose the stock profile that best fits the specs of your job—coated or uncoated paper or newsprint, web-fed or sheet-fed press. Some service bureaus and print shops don't care what profile you embed because they simply strip it out anyway and use their own.

When you know the specifications of a press, you can create a profile for it by using the Custom CMYK selection from the menu. Talk with your print shop to get the correct values for each field (see Figure 9.9).

Figure 9.9
A profile created with Custom CMYK can be tailored for a specific printing press. However, it should be created only with information from the print shop or service bureau.

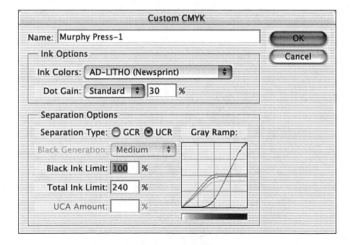

Gray: Gamma, Dot Gain, or Profile?

The Gray working space affects only the onscreen appearance of a grayscale image. It enables you to see the effects of dot gain or gamma on an image. If you work in prepress, especially newspapers, use your standard dot gain. Web professionals, Mac and Windows, are best served by gamma 2.2 (the Windows setting), unless the primary audience for the graphic is Mac-oriented. If you use a strict ColorSync workflow, choose that profile.

Spot Dot Gain

The dot gain for spot channels is typically that of the press in general. The default is 20%. Dot gain refers to the amount of "spread" a drop of ink produces on a given quality of paper. Coated papers, including glossy stock, typically produce very little dot gain because the paper isn't particularly absorbent (due to the coating). Uncoated papers, especially newsprint, absorb far more ink, so they exhibit more spreading or gain for each drop of ink. The dot gain settings compensate for the amount of spread by reducing the size of the ink dot.

Photoshop's Color Management Policies

One of the keys to color management is the capability of converting an image from one ICC profile to another. This section of the Color Settings dialog box is a two-edged sword. *Generally* speaking, the following guidelines hold true:

- If you will be looking at or working on an image and then returning it to the source (or the originating computer), do *not* convert to your working space, whether it's RGB or CMYK. Rather, use the command Image, Mode, Assign Profile to change the appearance onscreen while you review or work. (The Assign Profile command is discussed in the section "Changing Embedded Profiles" later in this chapter.) Converting an image and then converting back to another profile can cause needless color shifts and clipping of the image's tonal range. Instead, assign your profile, review or edit, return the image, and let the receiver know that the original profile should be reassigned.

- If your computer is the last machine to handle the image and the final output will be prepared on your computer, convert to your working space.

- Turn off color management completely for grayscale images. Assigning profiles and converting images are unlikely to improve the appearance or output and *are* likely to clip the grayscale tonal range.

- Remember that you can make decisions on a case-by-case basis by using the Profile Mismatches options (described in the next section).

If you're a prepress professional and receive files from outside sources, generally you will want to preserve the embedded CMYK profile until you have had a chance to evaluate it. If it's the correct profile, there's no need to strip it out and add it back later. (However, it is the policy of many production operations to automatically strip any CMYK profile from any image submitted.)

If you work with Web graphics, it's usually acceptable to convert to your working space. Digital photographers might notice that Photoshop 7 reads the EXIF data embedded by many cameras. If you're confident that the embedded profile is correct, you might want to keep it when opening the image and later assign or convert to your working space. That gives you the luxury of Undo should you notice color shifts or clipping.

Mismatch Notification Options

Most Photoshop users should use the mismatch notifications. This option gives you the opportunity to evaluate the situation and choose whether to save the embedded profile, convert to your working space, or discard the profile completely (see Figure 9.10).

Figure 9.10
This dialog box not only gives you the flexibility of overriding your color management policies, but also tells you what profiles are involved.

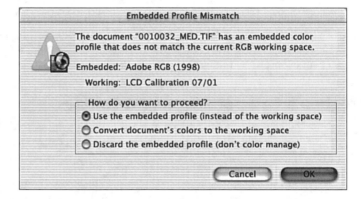

You should, however, uncheck the boxes for mismatch notification in some situations:

- You'll be opening a series of images that you know must be converted to your working space.
- You must strip incorrect profiles from a series of images.
- You'll be batch processing a folder of images, and you have decided that they all must be handled the same.

Loading and Saving Color Settings

After you've determined your color management needs, selected your working spaces, and chosen your options, you can save the collection. Name the color settings (include the .csf file extension) and save the file. You can later use the Load button to return to those settings.

You can also establish a number of different configurations, any of which can be selected with the Load button—often faster than navigating to find a custom CMYK profile and swapping options.

The Advanced Color Settings

Selecting the Advanced Mode check box in the upper-left corner of the Color Settings dialog box presents some additional options.

Color Engine

All the available color engines do a good job of converting color from one profile to another. Adobe (ACE) is the usual choice. Macintosh users have the option of ColorSync or Apple CMM, and Windows offers the Windows ICM engine.

Intent

Your choice for Intent determines how the color engine deals with colors that fall outside the destination gamut. When converting from one profile to another, it's possible that your image will be going from a larger gamut to a smaller one. Or, perhaps, certain colors are possible in the fringe area of one gamut that cannot be achieved in the other gamut. In either case, the engine needs to have instruction. Here are the options:

- **Perceptual**—The result of the color conversion will be as close as possible to the original for the human eye. If the source gamut is larger than the destination gamut, all colors will be shifted. For example, the brightest red will remain the brightest red, the second brightest is the second brightest, and so on. If the first red is not reproducible in the new gamut, but the second is, they will both shift anyway (as will all the other reds in the image).

  Use Perceptual when you want to maintain the image's overall appearance and don't need to retain any specific colors within the image.

- **Saturation**—Any colors that are out of the destination gamut retain their saturation values and are brought into gamut by adjusting the lightness and hue. Colors that are in the destination gamut are unchanged.

  Use Saturation for very richly saturated artwork, such as clipart, graphs, and logos.

- **Relative Colorimetric**—Colors reproducible in the destination gamut are unchanged. The colors that fall outside the new gamut are brought into gamut by adjusting hue and saturation. This option preserves the image's overall tonality.

  Use Relative for most images. Only those colors on the fringe of the gamut are affected, and they maintain their lightness value. Remember that the human eye is far more sensitive to tonal changes than to changes in hue.

- **Absolute Colorimetric**—The absolute Lab coordinates of the source colors are mapped to the destination gamut without regard for white point mapping. Some very unusual color shifts are possible.

  Use Absolute for one- or two-color logos or, in some situations, when preparing hard proofs. Absolute is not generally acceptable for conversion of continuous tone images, such as photographs.

You can refer back to Figure 9.1 for a comparison of Perceptual and Relative color conversions.

Remember that Intent comes into play primarily when converting from a larger gamut to a smaller gamut. You are unlikely to see any color shift when converting from, for example, sRGB (a very small gamut) to Adobe RGB (one of the largest RGB gamuts). You are *very* likely to perceive color shifting when converting a bright and colorful image from Adobe RGB to any CMYK gamut.

9

Black Point Compensation

When this check box is selected, the darkest neutral pixels in the source gamut are mapped to the darkest neutral color in the target gamut. When unchecked, the neutral shadow is mapped to black. When converting from RGB to CMYK, normally you want to have the option selected.

Monitor Dithering

Dithering during conversion can increase file size, but it can also reduce banding in a continuous tone image. If too many related colors are mapped to too few colors in the destination gamut, visible stripes of colors can appear in gradients and other areas of blended color. Dithering reduces the potential problem. The Use Dither option doesn't have any impact when converting 16-bit and Indexed Color images.

Desaturating Monitor Colors

Desaturating the monitor colors enables you to see a bit more detail in highlight areas of images in very large RGB spaces, such as Adobe RGB. It should be selected only when actually working in those highlight areas and only if that part of the gamut is not being portrayed onscreen. If the Info palette shows that there are variations in the very lightest areas, but you can't see them onscreen, try selecting this check box. Remember to uncheck it afterward because it skews all colors.

Blend RGB Colors Using a Different Gamma

Another option to be used only if your onscreen representation is obviously flawed, changing the gamma can reduce artifacts along distinct edges in an image. By default, Photoshop uses the assigned monitor gamma to blend red, green, and blue onscreen. When you're zoomed in very close, if the monitor shows artifacts that the Info palette tells you shouldn't be there, try this option. Increase or decrease the gamma to smooth the RGB blending. Remember to deselect the option before resuming your regular work.

CHANGING EMBEDDED PROFILES

The profile embedded in an image can be changed in a variety of ways. You can convert an image to your working space on opening. You can change the color mode of the document. You can strip the profile from the image by selecting Discard the Embedded Profile when notified of a mismatch. You can also change the embedded profile or the profile and the image's color space.

Image, Mode, Assign Profile

The Assign Profile command enables you to strip the embedded profile from a document, tag the document with the working profile (RGB, CMYK, or Grayscale), or choose another profile of the appropriate color mode (see Figure 9.11).

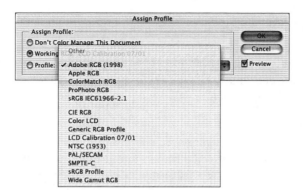

Figure 9.11
The menu shows all available profiles for the document's color mode. The working space is identified by name in the dialog box.

9

Assigning a new working space does *not* change the color values in the image. Rather, it simply embeds a new profile in the document and shows you onscreen what the image will look like in that gamut. The Preview option enables you to see what the new profile will look like without actually assigning it. If the preview looks unacceptable—or if you just wanted a quick peek at the possible conversion—click Cancel to retain the document's original embedded profile.

Image, Mode, Convert to Profile

Unlike Assign Profile, Convert to Profile *does* change the color values in the image. The image's colors are mapped from the embedded profile to the profile you select in the Convert to Profile dialog box (see Figure 9.12).

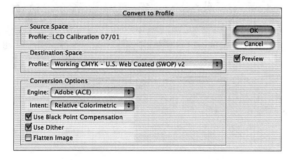

Figure 9.12
The options selected in this dialog box override those that are active in Color Settings.

Convert to Profile attempts to maintain image appearance as closely as possible when remapping, using the engine and intent specified in the dialog box.

SOFT PROOFING IN PHOTOSHOP 7

With proper calibration and custom profiles, you can get a good idea of what a printed image will look like by using Photoshop's View, Proof Colors command. Keep in mind, however, that *soft proofing*, previewing images onscreen, is no substitute for an actual printed proof.

Soft Proofing Versus Hard Proofing

Soft proofing, in a perfect world, would enable you to see onscreen exactly what comes off the press or, for that matter, what visitors to your Web site see. In reality, even with expert calibration and precise custom profiles, simulating the CMYK of ink on paper with the RGB of a monitor is still at best a simulation. Hard proofs, whether laminates or wet prints, are still necessary for most jobs.

Proof Setup

Before selecting the menu command View, Proof Colors, you must tell Photoshop what you want to simulate onscreen. Use the View, Proof Setup command to make that selection (see Figure 9.13).

Figure 9.13
In addition to your selected CMYK profile, you can inspect individual color channels or view different RGB gamuts.

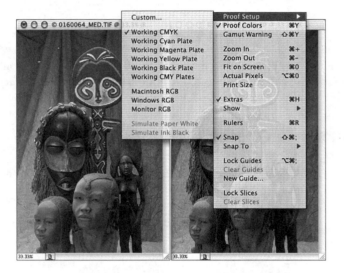

Proof Colors is normally used to view how your RGB image will convert to the selected CMYK working space. However, you can also use the Custom option from the View, Proof Setup menu to view how the image would look with any available profile (see Figure 9.14).

Note that you have two additional options: Simulate Paper White and Simulate Ink Black. These options, when selected, attempt to display onscreen the physical characteristics of paper and the black generation information recorded in the profile.

Using the Window, Document, New View command opens a second window of the same image. Proof Colors is applied only to the active window, giving you a side-by-side comparison, as you can see in the background of Figure 9.13.

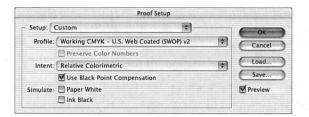

Figure 9.14
The Profile pop-up menu includes all available profiles, including RGB, CMYK, Grayscale, and the Photoshop 4 and Photoshop 5 emulations.

Selecting an individual CMYK working plate for proofing is comparable to converting the document to CMYK and viewing a single channel in the Channels palette. The image is portrayed in grayscale onscreen, unless you have selected View Color Channels in Color in the Display & Cursors pane of the Preferences dialog box.

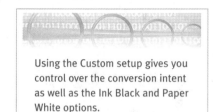

Using the Custom setup gives you control over the conversion intent as well as the Ink Black and Paper White options.

PHOTOSHOP IN FOCUS

To see what effect profiles can have on an image, compare different profiles with a single image. However, instead of placing them side-by-side, let Photoshop's blending modes show you how they differ. Before you get started, pop into Photoshop's Color Settings and set the RGB color management policy to Off.

1. Pick an RGB image, any photo, and open it in Photoshop. Flatten, if necessary.

2. In the History palette, click twice on the New Document from Current History State button to make two copies of the image.

3. Use Convert to Profile to assign sRGB to one copy and Adobe RGB to another copy, and strip any existing profile from the third image with Assign Profile.

4. Position the images around the screen and take a look. Now open the Layers palette.

5. Make the sRGB image active and Shift-drag the Background layer from the Layers palette to the untagged image's window. The Shift key ensures that the new layer will be perfectly centered. Rename the layer sRGB. Close, but don't save, the sRGB image.

6. Shift-drag the Background layer from the Adobe RGB image's Layers palette to the untagged image's window. Name this layer Adobe RGB. Close, but don't save, the Adobe RGB image.

7. In the last remaining window, you should have three layers, named Background (the original untagged image), sRGB, and Adobe RGB. Rename the Background layer Untagged, which also converts it to a regular layer.

8. In the Layers palette, click the eyeball icons in the left column to show and hide the three layers. Watch the appearance of the image change as you view the different profiles.

9. In the Layers palette, drag the Untagged layer to the New Layer button to duplicate it. Hide the sRGB and Adobe RGB layers. Change the Untagged Copy layer's blending mode to Difference. The image should turn flat black. The Layers palette should show two hidden layers and two visible layers, with the Difference (Untagged Copy) layer on top.

10. Now that you've seen what the image looks like when two identical layers are overlaid with the Difference blending mode, it's time to compare profiles. Hide the Untagged Copy layer. Click on the sRGB layer to show it and make it the active layer, and then change that layer's blending mode to Difference.

11. Hide the sRGB layer. Activate and show the Adobe RGB layer by clicking on it, and change its blending mode to Difference.

12. Hide Untagged, switch sRGB to Normal, and put it under Adobe RGB (if it's not already there).

13. Flip-flop both the stacking order and the blending modes of the sRGB and Adobe RGB images. Put Adobe RGB on the bottom, blending mode Normal. Put sRGB on top, blending mode Difference.

The Difference blending mode shows you how the color values on two layers differ. When two identical layers (the two Untagged layers) are the only layers visible, the image is black. When two *different* layers—or in this example, two images with different profiles—are overlaid, Difference shows you where they are not identical.

The next step in the progression, if you're interested, is to compare (using the same technique) how different rendering intents affect conversion to the same profile.

FROM THE NAPP HELP DESK

The National Association of Photoshop Professionals (NAPP) offers e-mail assistance to its members. Here is some advice from the NAPP Help Desk related to issues in this chapter.

Riding the Wave

I'm quite pleased with the colors I get from my inkjet printer. They look just like the colors on my monitor. Should I still color-manage my workflow?

If you're satisfied with what you're getting, don't change a thing! Photoshop's defaults and your hardware are, in fact, managing your color and apparently doing a fine job of it. If your monitor and your printer agree, you've reached that happy place, the one where color management wants to take us.

When RGB Is CMYK

You've written that inkjet printers require RGB data to print properly. Do I need to use CMYK profiles?

Indeed you do—but only if you want the most accurate color possible. Yes, you should send RGB image data to most inkjet printers. The printer's software (the print driver) expects RGB. However, the printer probably came with one or more printer profiles, which have an .icc file extension for Mac or .icm for Windows. Load them as the CMYK profile in Color Settings. Think of the CYMK setting as the "output" profile.

PHOTOSHOP'S CREATIVE TOOLS

IN THIS PART

MAKING SELECTIONS AND CREATING MASKS

SELECTIONS AND MASKS: TELLING PHOTOSHOP WHERE TO WORK

Whether it's deleting part of an image, adding color, or perhaps applying a filter, you need to let Photoshop know which pixels you want to change. Using a painting tool (or other tool that works with brushes), you need simply select a brush and drag. The size, shape, and hardness of the brush, combined with the course along which the tool is dragged, control what happens.

When working with adjustments, filters, and many other menu commands, you must first identify the target area. You can, of course, apply a filter or other command to an entire layer. By not isolating a section of the layer, you have, in effect, identified where you want the filter to work: the entire layer. However, often you need to apply a filter to only a section of a layer. That's when you need to use selections and masks.

Selections Defined

Experienced Photoshop users understand that selections are critical to effective use of the program. Understanding the theory behind selections can be a key to mastering their application.

Photoshop has a variety of tools and menu commands available to make *selections*. Consider a selection to be an area of an image that is activated, the part on which you're working. Pixels within the selection can be changed; those outside the selection are protected. Selections can be made with tools and commands and from paths and masks.

Generally speaking, a pixel is either inside a selection or outside a selection. However, under a variety of circumstances, a pixel can be *partially selected*. Any filter or adjustment command applied to the selection is partially applied to any partially selected pixels—the filter or effect is applied with less intensity. Selections that are anti-aliased or feathered can have partially selected pixels along their edges. Selections made from masks can have up to 256 variations of "selected" among the pixels.

As an example, consider two selections. One has no feathering or anti-aliasing: A pixel is either inside the selection or outside. The second selection has 2 pixels partially selected on either side of the line of selection. When the two selections are filled with black, there are two different results (see Figure 10.1).

⇨ *Selection border not visible? See "Showing and Hiding Edges" in the NAPP Help Desk section at the end of this chapter.*

The flashing dashed line that indicates the edge of a selection in Photoshop is technically referred to as a *selection border*, *selection marquee*, or *selection edge*, but you are far more likely to hear the term "marching ants."

When selecting, keep in mind that sometimes it's easier to select the pixels that you *don't* want and then use the command Select, Inverse to swap the selection to the portion that you do want.

When a selection is feathered, anti-aliased, or otherwise contains partially selected pixels, the selection marquee indicates which pixels are at least 50% selected. It is certainly possible to have selections that contain *only* pixels that are less than 50% selected, for example, when the feathering is set to an amount greater than the radius of a selection. In such cases, the pixels will indeed be affected by whatever additional steps you take (fill, delete, filter, and so on), but the marching ants will not be visible. Photoshop provides a warning when no selection border will appear (see Figure 10.2).

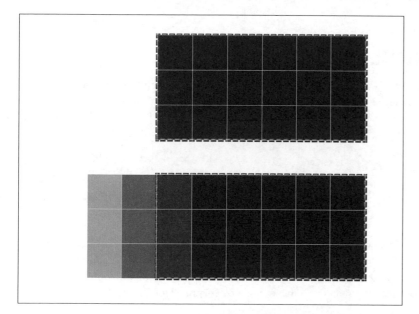

Figure 10.1
At the top, the black fill is consistent and stops at the edge of the selection. Below, the partially selected pixels get filled with black but are partially transparent.

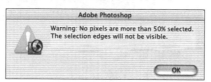

Figure 10.2
Even if all the pixels are selected at less than 50%, your additional steps will be performed on them. The effect of a filter or an adjustment on partially selected pixels might be extremely subtle, but the command is executed nonetheless.

Masks Unmasked

Just as a painter uses masking tape to protect parts of a surface and expose others, so, too, can you use *masks* in Photoshop. Masks are used to create and store selections. (Until a mask is loaded and used as a selection, it has no effect on the appearance of an image.)

Masks can be created from selections or created from scratch. In either case, masks are stored in *alpha channels*. Alpha channels are grayscale representations of an image. The shades of gray determine levels of selection for individual pixels.

You can use painting tools, selection tools, and even adjustment commands and filters to alter masks. Virtually anything you can do with a grayscale image can be done with an alpha channel.

Photoshop also offers Quick Mask mode, which enables you to make a selection with all the flexibility of masks, but without creating an additional channel.

For more information on creating masks without creating channels, **see** *"Quick Mask Mode," p. 264, later in this chapter.*

THE SELECTION TOOLS

Photoshop has a collection of tools used to make selections. There are eight primary selection tools (see Figure 10.3): four marquee selection tools, three lasso tools, and the Magic Wand.

Figure 10.3
Click and hold on an icon to show the tools on the flyout palettes. Hold down the Shift key and use the keyboard shortcut shown in the flyout to rotate among the related tools.

When creating a selection, remember that the Shift key can be used with selection tools to add to an existing selection. Likewise, the (Option) [Alt] key can be used with a selection tool to subtract from an existing selection. When both modifier keys are used with a selection tool, anything outside the new selection border is deselected, and anything inside remains selected (see Figure 10.4).

Figure 10.4
The Shift and (Option) [Alt] keys are pressed down; therefore, when the mouse button is released, nothing outside the loop being dragged will be selected. Within the loop, only what is already selected will stay selected.

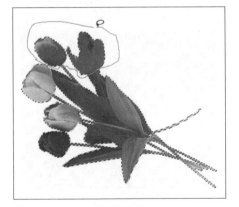

The Marquee Tools

Photoshop offers two major and two minor marquee selection tools. The Rectangular Marquee and Elliptical Marquee tools have several options and a great deal of flexibility. The Single Row Marquee and Single Column Marquee selection tools are one-trick ponies, with a specific job to do and few options.

The Rectangular and Elliptical Selection Tools

The Rectangular Marquee tool is used to make rectangular and square selections. Its round counterpart, the Elliptical Marquee Tool, creates oval and circular selections. To select squares and circles, hold down the Shift key while dragging. That constrains the selection to a 1:1 aspect ratio, forcing identical width and height. You can also hold down the (Option) [Alt] key to drag the selection from the center with either tool. The Options Bar lets you use the tools in several modes (see Figure 10.5).

Remember that any selection can be converted to a path by using the Make Work Path button at the bottom of the Paths palette. Likewise, any selection can be converted to a mask by using the Select, Save Selection command.

Figure 10.5
The pop-up menu is part of the Options Bar when the Rectangular or Elliptical Marquee tool is active.

In Normal mode, the tool can be dragged as you wish, creating a selection of whatever proportions you desire. The Fixed Aspect Ratio option gives you the opportunity to establish a width-to-height ratio in the numeric fields to the right. A ratio of 1:1 creates a square (Rectangular Marquee) or a circle (Elliptical Marquee). You can specify any ratio, constraining the shape of the selection. Using this option, no matter what size the marquee, the proportions remain the same.

The Fixed Size option not only restricts the selection to a set aspect ratio, but also determines the selection's actual dimensions. Rather than drag the marquee tool, you click once. The selection is made to the lower right of the clicked point. Input the desired selection size, which assumes the unit of measure specified in Photoshop's preferences, or use another unit of measure by including the appropriate abbreviation in the field.

▷ *Is your Rectangular Marquee giving you fits? See "Check the Options" in the NAPP Help Desk section at the end of this chapter.*

The Options Bar also offers several other variables for the marquee selection tools. Normally, the tools are used to create a selection. If a selection already exists in the image, the tool can be set to add to, subtract from, or intersect with that selection (see Figure 10.6).

You can reposition a selection border while creating it. Continue to hold down the mouse button when using a marquee tool and press the spacebar. You can now move the selection in the image. Release the spacebar and continue dragging. Release the mouse button to finish the selection.

The Fixed Aspect Ratio option is invaluable in preparing images for Picture Package and other photograph printing. Dragging with a 5:7 or 4:6 aspect ratio ensures that the image can be properly cropped with the menu command Image, Crop.

10

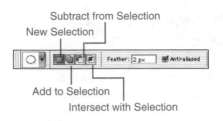

Figure 10.6
Feathering and the tool behavior options are the same for both the Rectangular Marquee tool and the Elliptical Marquee tool. With no active selection, the tools create a new selection with any of the four behaviors selected.

The Feather field lets you specify how "soft" to make the edges of the selection. (Remember that feathering lessens the effect of whatever you do on the edges of a selection, whether it's adding a fill, deleting, or applying a filter or an adjustment.) Feathering can be as high as 250 pixels and is always measured in pixels, regardless of the document's unit of measure. Keep in mind that feathering actually affects several times as many pixels as the number specified. To ensure that the effect appears seamless, a feather of two pixels actually affects a band that is approximately 10 pixels wide along the selection border.

In Figure 10.7, a square selection border is visible, measuring slightly more than 100×100 pixels. With feathering set to 50 pixels, the actual selection border when the mouse button is released is shown by the circular selection within. (Remember that the marching ants are drawn around pixels at least 50% selected.) When the heavily feathered selection is filled with white on a black background, the impact extends far beyond the selection border, as you can see.

Figure 10.7
The square selection border indicates where the Rectangular Marquee tool (set to Feather: 50 pixels) was dragged. The circular selection edges indicate pixels at least 50% selected. Filling with white affects pixels almost to the corners of the 300×300 pixel black square.

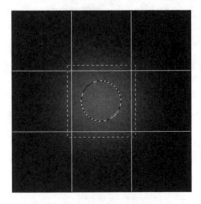

Anti-aliasing softens the edges of curves. It is not available for the Rectangular Marquee, the Single Row Marquee, and the Single Column Marquee selection tools because these tools make selections with straight edges. When an anti-aliased selection is filled with color or deleted, the appearance of the edges is softened by using pixels that are intermediate in color between the selected area and the background. For example, filling an anti-aliased selection with black on a white background results in gray pixels to soften the curves (see Figure 10.8).

The stair-step appearance of curves without anti-aliasing is often referred to as *the jaggies*.

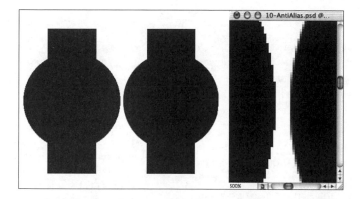

Notice, too, that the straight edges of the filled selections form perfect horizontal and vertical lines with and without anti-aliasing.

Selecting Single Rows and Columns

Photoshop offers two additional marquee selection tools, the Single Row Marquee and the Single Column Marquee. As their names indicate, they select a row or column of pixels exactly 1 pixel high or wide. The row or column extends from edge to edge of the image and is made at the point where you click the mouse.

These tools, set to Feather: 0, are excellent for creating grid lines 1-pixel thick. Click to place the first line and fill with the foreground color. With the tool still selected and the selection still active, you can use the arrow keys (with or without the Shift key) to reposition the selection for the second line. Each line will be perfectly horizontal or vertical and exactly 1 pixel in width or height.

Although designed to work with 1-pixel selections, the Single Row and Single Column tools do offer the option of feathering. Examples of feathering 1-pixel selections are shown in Figure 10.9.

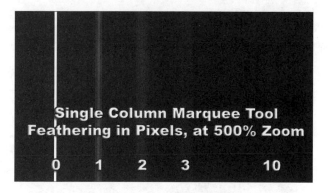

Single Column Marquee Tool
Feathering in Pixels, at 500% Zoom
0   1   2   3   10

Figure 10.9
When Feather is set to zero, a clean-edged, 1-pixel selection is made. Any feathering with these tools generates a warning that no pixels are more than 50% selected.

Making Irregularly Shaped Selections

The marquee selection tools are fine for making regularly shaped selections. However, they lack the kind of flexibility needed for many selection jobs. Photoshop's lasso tools are designed to help you make irregular selections, with and without assistance.

The Lasso Tool

The Lasso tool itself is a free-form tool. Drag it in any shape or direction. When you release the mouse button, the selection will be established. You need not mouse back to the point from which you started—the Lasso finishes a selection with a straight line from the point where you release the mouse button to the point where you started to drag.

Like the marquee selection tools, the three lassos offer buttons in the Options Bar to make new selections or to have the tools add to, subtract from, or intersect with an existing selection. Anti-aliasing and feathering are also options for the lasso tools.

Use the (Option) [Alt] key to switch between the Lasso tool and the Polygonal Lasso tool on-the-fly. While dragging the Lasso, hold down the modifier key and click-move-click to place straight selection edges. When working with the Polygonal Lasso tool, hold down the key and drag to make free-form selections.

The Polygonal Lasso Tool

The Polygonal Lasso tool is not a free-form tool. Rather than drag the tool, you click, move, click, move, click to establish a selection with straight sides. Although the edges of the selection are straight, they can be at any angle, not just horizontal and vertical. Using the anti-aliasing option can help prevent jaggies along angled edges.

To complete a selection with the Polygonal Lasso tool, position the tool over the start point and click. When the cursor is directly over the start point, a small circle appears to the lower right of the tool's icon. Alternatively, double-click or press the (Return) [Enter] key to complete the selection with a straight segment from the cursor's location to the selection start point. (Command-clicking) [Ctrl+clicking] does the same. The Escape key can be used to leave the selection process before a selection is complete.

The Magnetic Lasso Tool

The third lasso tool is a bit more complex. The Magnetic Lasso tool attempts to follow existing edges in an image to make a selection. Using contrast to identify edges, the Magnetic Lasso is best suited for use on images that have uncomplicated backgrounds (see Figure 10.10).

Figure 10.10
This image is a perfect candidate for the Magnetic Lasso because of the strong contrast between the foreground and background.

While working, the Magnetic Lasso places a series of temporary anchor points as it follows the path you trace. (Note that the tool does not create a path; the anchor points disappear when the selection is completed.) Double-clicking, clicking on the start point, and pressing the (Return) [Enter] keys all close the selection.

As you drag, you can click the mouse button to manually place anchor points at spots where the edge you're tracing takes a sharp turn. If the tool places an anchor point in an incorrect location, press (Delete) [Backspace] to remove it. You can also back up along the edge to retrace a segment.

The (Option) [Alt] key with the Magnetic Lasso gives you access to both the Lasso and the Polygonal Lasso tools. With the key pressed, drag for a free-form selection or click-move-click to create straight selection edges.

In addition to the options common to all three lasso tools, the Magnetic Lasso has four options of its own (see Figure 10.11).

Figure 10.11
The first three of these four options are unique to the Magnetic Lasso tool.

Width determines the Magnetic Lasso's search area. It is always measured in pixels and can range from 1 to 256. It follows the line of pixels with the highest contrast within this radius. If the image has few edges, a high Width setting allows you to move quickly and requires less precision. If there are multiple areas of contrast closely placed in the image, a lower width is required, forcing you to keep the cursor precisely along the desired edge. When Photoshop's Preferences are set to Precise for Other Cursors, the width is displayed as a circle around the tool's crosshair. If you see the tool's icon as the cursor, you need not change the Preferences. Before you start working with the tool, press the Caps Lock key to show the width cursor.

Edge Contrast can be considered the sensitivity setting for the Magnetic Lasso. It ranges from 1% to 100%. Lower values reduce the amount of contrast required to define an edge. However, that can also lead to the selection border being placed along false edges—areas where a texture or shadow/highlight create contrast. Likewise, too high a setting might lead to the tool not finding any edge at all and a very confused selection border.

Frequency determines the automatic placement of anchor points as you drag. Ranging from 0% to 100%, the higher numbers produce more anchor points. Remember that you can manually add anchor points by clicking.

The Pen Pressure check box is used with pressure sensitive tablets, such as those from Wacom. Increased pressure on the tablet constricts the tool's width and increases the frequency of the anchor points, and lighter pressure results in a higher Width setting and fewer anchor points. The width varies from twice the value in the Options Bar (very light pressure) to 1 (very hard pressure).

You can change the Width setting for the Magnetic Lasso on-the-fly. Think of it as a brush size. The left and right bracket keys increase and decrease the Width by one pixel. Add the Shift key to jump to the maximum (256 pixels) and minimum (1 pixel) widths.

10

Magic Wand

The Magic Wand tool has its fans and its detractors. Some love it; some find it useless. Designed to select similar colors throughout an image, the Magic Wand enables you to specify a *tolerance* (the range of sensitivity) and click on a sample. Depending on choices in the Options Bar, you can restrict the Magic Wand to the active layer or use all visible layers. (Although the check box is labeled Use All Layers, hidden layers are excluded.) It can also create a selection of all similar pixels throughout the image or only those similar pixels contiguous to the pixel on which you click.

When Contiguous is selected in the Options Bar, to be selected, pixels must adjoin pixels of the selected color. If pixels of another color are between the clicked pixel and similarly colored pixels, those pixels are not selected (see Figure 10.12).

Figure 10.12
To the left, the Magic Wand was set to Contiguous—only similarly colored pixels adjacent to the clicked pixel are selected. On the right, Contiguous was not selected—all similarly colored pixels throughout the image were selected.

The Tolerance setting for the Magic Wand can range from 0 to 255. Photoshop compares the pixel clicked with the tool to all other pixels in the image. Each color channel value is compared to the clicked pixel. To be included in the selection, each component color for a specific pixel must fall within the tolerance range when compared to the clicked pixel.

For example, if the Magic Wand is set to Tolerance: 32 and then clicked on a pixel with the RGB values 200/150/100, the range of color values included in the selection are as follows:

- Red: 168 to 232

- Green: 118 to 182

- Blue: 68 to 132

To be selected, a pixel must meet *all three* of the criteria. Therefore, included in the selection would be pixels with such different RGB values as 168/18/68 and 232/182/132. However, not included would be pixels with color values of 200/150/133 or 200/150/67, because the Blue component is beyond the tolerance.

Because the Magic Wand selects in a range that extends to both the high and low, click on a pixel that's in the midtones of the color you want to select.

You can Shift-click with the Magic Wand to add to a selection and (Option-click) [Alt+click] to subtract from a selection. The Options Bar also enables you to set the tool to add to or subtract from a selection. The tolerance can be changed between clicks as well.

Selections from Paths

Paths can be used to create extremely precise selections. Any path, including work paths and those created with Photoshop's shape tools, can be used to create selections. With the path selected in the Paths palette, either click the Load Path as a Selection button at the bottom of the palette or use the Paths palette menu command Make Selection (see Figure 10.13).

When selecting a uniformly colored background for deletion or to extract an image, it's usually a good idea to use the menu command Select, Modify, Expand with a setting of 1 or 2 pixels. This helps eliminate any fringe or halo from anti-aliasing.

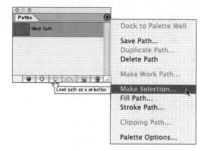

Figure 10.13
Simply clicking the button makes an active selection from the path; the menu command opens a dialog box.

You can also (Command-click) [Ctrl+click] a path in the Paths palette to load it as a selection. Adding the Shift and (Option) [Alt] key adds the path to or subtracts the path from an active selection.

When you choose the Make Selection command, you'll be presented with the Make Selection dialog box. If a selection is already active in the image, you'll be able to add to, subtract from, intersect with, or replace the selection (see Figure 10.14). You'll also be able to specify feathering and choose or forgo anti-aliasing.

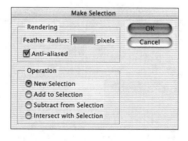

Figure 10.14
The Make Selection dialog box can also be opened by (Option-clicking) [Alt+clicking] the Load Path as a Selection button at the bottom of the Paths palette.

⇨ For an in-depth look at creating and editing paths, **see** Chapter 13, "The Pen Tools, Shape Layers, and Other Paths," **p. 349**.

The Type Mask Tools

Although the tools have the word *mask* in their names, no alpha channel is added to the Channels palette. Unlike Quick Mask mode (discussed later in this chapter), there is no mask to save when using these tools. Therefore, you should consider them to be selection tools of a special nature.

The type mask tools do not create vector type, nor do they generate type layers. In addition, their product is not "live"—you cannot return to the letter-shaped selections and edit them as you would type by changing fonts or correcting typographical errors.

You can select the Horizontal Type Mask tool or the Vertical Type Mask tool from the Toolbox (see Figure 10.15). All the options for the regular type tools are available when creating type masks.

Figure 10.15
The Options Bar, Character palette, and Paragraph palette give you the same control over type set as a selection as they do over type set as vectors.

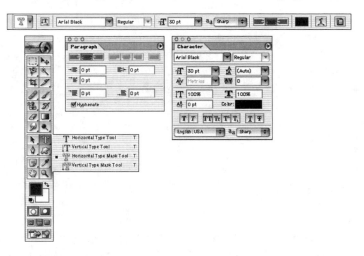

Photoshop offers both point type and area type masks. To set point type, click once anywhere in the document. A translucent red overlay will appear, much like working in Quick Mask mode (see Figure 10.16). The type mask tools cut holes in this overlay. When you drag the tool, a bounding box will show, indicating a type container—a rectangle into which you can place type. Remember that the bounding box can be resized while you work by dragging a handle.

Figure 10.16
Area type is currently being set. The "Point Type" selection was an existing selection when a type mask tool was dragged.

When you click the check mark icon at the right end of the Options Bar or press (Command-Return) [Ctrl+Enter], the type is accepted, the red overlay disappears, and a selection border ("marching ants") appears in the shape of the type. You can then fill, delete, apply adjustments or filters, or do anything else that you can do to a selection in Photoshop.

The type mask tools do *not* create layers when you use them. Also unlike the regular type tools, they are not vector tools—there are no paths for crisp output to a PostScript printer.

➡️ *To learn the full capabilities of the type tools,* **see** *Chapter 11, "Type and Typography in Photoshop," p. 273.*

SELECTION COMMANDS

Photoshop's Select menu includes commands in five basic categories (see Figure 10.17). The commands All, Deselect, Reselect, and Inverse can be thought of as the "macro" commands—they work on a large scale. In contrast, the modification commands, Feather, Modify, Grow, and Similar, can be considered the "micro" commands—they fine-tune or adjust an existing selection.

Keep in mind when working with the type mask tools that you can create a mask from any selection by using the Select, Save Selection command. Likewise, you can generate a work path from the active selection by clicking the Make Work Path button at the bottom of the Paths palette.

10

Transform Selection also modifies an existing selection, but does so on the basis of selection shape, rather than content. Selections can be saved as alpha channels (masks) and loaded later. This method is especially useful for protecting the work that went into a complex selection and for modifying a selection as a mask.

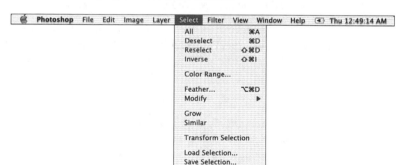

Figure 10.17
Although this image shows no commands grayed out for illustrative purposes, not all commands are available at the same time. For example, the command Reselect is grayed out when there is an active selection, so it can't be available at the same time as Deselect.

The Color Range command is also a "macro" selection command, but is far more complex than simply selecting all or deselecting. It offers the capability of selecting based on one or more colors within an image.

Basic Selection Commands

The four basic selection commands are rather simple in nature. Select, All makes a selection of the entire active layer. If the layer contains transparency, the transparent pixels are selected with the others. If you were to press (Option-Delete) [Alt+Backspace] next, the entire layer would be filled with the foreground color.

Deselect does exactly what you would expect from the name. It is available only when there is an active selection in the image. After using this command, no pixels in the image are selected.

Reselect is extremely useful for those occasions, among others, when an unintended click inadvertently deselects. Although you can use the Undo command immediately after deselecting to restore the selection, Reselect is available until another selection is made or the image is closed (or the history purged).

Select, Inverse reverses an active selection—pixels that had been selected are deselected, or pixels that had not been selected are selected. Inverse also recognizes anti-aliasing, feathering, and other partially selected pixels. If, for example, you load a mask containing pixels selected at 25%, Inverse switches them to 75% selected.

Modifying Existing Selections with Commands

The Select menu offers a number of commands that enable you to modify an existing selection. Feathering softens the edges of a selection, which results in a reduced effect on those pixels. Whether deleting, filling, filtering, or adjusting, feathering produces a subtle transition between those pixels 100% affected by the command or tool and those pixels that are unaffected. Selecting this command opens a dialog box in which you enter the amount of feathering, which is always measured in pixels.

▭▷ *Feathering is discussed in more detail earlier in this chapter; **see** "The Marquee Tools," **p. 246.***

The Modify commands, accessed through the Modify submenu of the Select menu, are rather clumsy tools and are best applied using very small pixel values. Like Feather, they open dialog boxes into which you enter a value in pixels.

Border

The Border command creates a new selection and discards the original selection. The new selection is centered on the original selection border, with or without anti-aliasing and feathering, at the width specified in the Border dialog box. That width, however, extends both inward and outward from the original selection border, so the term "width" is somewhat misleading. The affected area is actually twice the Width value.

The selection created by Border is feathered. Only the two pixels immediately on either side of the original selection border are 100% selected, with the balance of the width tapering to 0% selected. If, for example, you drag a square selection with the Rectangular Marquee tool, use Border with a Width value of 10, and then press (Option-Delete) [Alt+Backspace] to fill with the foreground color, you will not get a beautiful frame around the original selection.

Instead of Border to create a frame, consider using the menu command Edit, Stroke. If the pixels to be framed are on a separate layer, Layer Style, Stroke is an even better alternative.

Instead, you'll see a line of color that fades inward and outward, with angled corners rather than square.

Smooth

The Smooth command is designed to eliminate jagged edges in selections. It uses the pixel value you enter into the Sample Radius field to see which pixels should be included in the active selection. It rounds the corners of a rectangular or angular selection.

The Smooth command can be used effectively with the Magic Wand tool and the Color Range command. If your initial selection has numerous unselected pixels scattered around within it, try Smooth at 1 or 2 pixels.

Expand

You can move a selection border outward by as much as 100 pixels by using the Expand command. However, any rectangular corners in the original selection become angles (and angles will be rounded) when a selection is greatly expanded. The number of pixels you enter into the Expand By field can be considered a radius from the center rather than a linear measure from the selection border.

The Expand command can be very effective in eliminating a *halo*. When a background is selected for deletion, expanding 1 or 2 pixels can eliminate any fringe pixels.

Caution

When a selection extends to the edge of the canvas, neither Expand nor Contract is effective along that edge. A selection cannot be expanded beyond the edge of the canvas, and any selection border on the edge is not affected by the Contract command.

Contract

The Contract command brings in a selection border toward its center. If the active selection consists of a variety of discrete areas, each is contracted individually. Just as Expand can help eliminate a fringe when a background is selected, so, too, can Contract help eliminate a fringe when a foreground is selected.

Other Selection Commands

In addition to the commands under the Modify submenu, Photoshop's Select menu offers the Grow and Similar commands. Grow searches for, and adds to the active selection, pixels of a similar color to those already selected. The command uses the Tolerance value set for the Magic Wand tool. Only adjacent pixels are considered for inclusion in the selection. The Grow command can be applied multiple times to achieve a desired selection.

The Similar command is identical to Grow with one exception: The pixels need not be contiguous. All similarly colored pixels in an image are included in the selection, regardless of their location in the image.

Transforming Selections

An active selection can be scaled, rotated, skewed, and distorted by using the Select, Transform Selection command. A bounding box is created around the active selection (see Figure 10.18).

Figure 10.18
The bounding box originates as a rectangle surrounding the selection. You can manipulate it in a variety of ways with the cursor and modifier keys.

You can drag within the bounding box to move the selection, drag an anchor point to scale, (Option-drag) [Alt+drag] to scale from the center, and Shift-drag to scale proportionally. Adding the (Command) [Ctrl] key allows you to skew, distort, or add perspective to a transformation. The Options Bar is also available for numeric transformations.

After manipulating the selection boundary, you can accept the changes by clicking the check mark icon in the Options Bar, double-clicking within the selection, or using the (Return) [Enter] key. The Escape key cancels a transformation.

After you choose the Select, Transform Selection menu command, look again at the menu bar. The Edit menu offers all the standard Transform commands to make transforming a selection much more predictable.

Saving and Loading Selections

Any selection that took more than a couple of keystrokes and a drag to create is worth saving. Recreating a selection might not produce the exact results. It could also be time consuming. Photoshop has the capability to store any selection as an alpha channel—a mask—that can be reloaded at will.

The menu commands Save Selection and Load Selection enable you to create an alpha channel from a selection and to load that channel as a selection. Alpha channels are discussed in the "Alpha Channels and Masks" section, later in this chapter.

The Color Range Command

With the Color Range command, you can create a selection that encompasses all pixels of one or more colors within an image. It is ideal for selecting a range of similar colors, such as the blues in a sky or flesh tones. The Color Range dialog box (shown in Figure 10.19) enables you to fine-tune your selection much like the Magic Wand's Tolerance setting determines what will be selected.

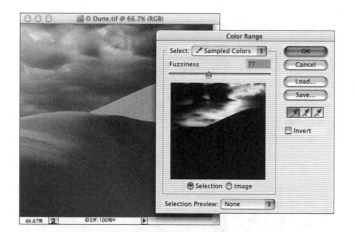

Figure 10.19
In this example, the grayscale preview shows that the sky (white and grays) will be selected, but the dunes (black) will not.

The leftmost Eyedropper tool is used to select the primary color of the selection. To add similar colors or even different colors to the selection, you can use the Shift key with the Eyedropper or use the Add Eyedropper (the eyedropper tool with a plus sign). Likewise, to remove colors from the selection, you can use the (Option) [Alt] key with the Eyedropper or use the Subtract Eyedropper (the eyedropper tool with the minus sign).

You can make a selection before opening the Color Range dialog box. Doing so restricts the final selection to areas within the initial selection. Color Range selects like-colored pixels only within the original selection.

Use the Fuzziness slider to determine a range of selected pixels, based on the clicked pixel. Dragging the slider to the right increases the number of pixels selected by increasing the amount of color variation allowed. Dragging the slider to the left restricts the selection to pixels that more closely match the selected color.

Below the preview window are radio buttons labeled Selection and Image. Selection presents a grayscale representation of the selection, much like a mask, in the preview window. The preview is updated when you click with an eyedropper tool or drag the Fuzziness slider. Clicking the Image radio button shows you the original image. That preview shows no indication of what areas will be selected, but you can click in the Image preview with any of the eyedropper tools to change your selection.

The Selection Preview pop-up menu offers five choices. They determine how the image window (not the Color Range preview window) will appear while you make your selection. Especially with very large files, the None option can make Color Range updates a bit snappier. The other four options, shown in Figure 10.20, are Grayscale (upper left), Black Matte (upper right), White Matte (lower left), and Quick Mask (lower right).

The Color Range dialog box also offers buttons labeled Load and Save. These options do not save the selection, but rather the selection *criteria*—the color range information. If you have a series of images that require the same correction (because of a color tint or a light leak, for example), saving a range of selection can also save a lot of work.

Figure 10.20
In all four examples, the dunes are selected. The selection, in this case, is seen most accurately in the grayscale preview to the upper left.

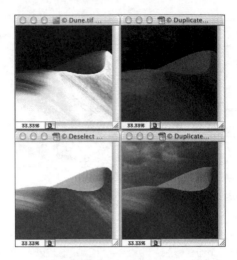

One other capability of Color Range deserves discussion. At the top of the dialog box is the Select pop-up menu. In the discussion to this point, Color Range has been shown (and described) using Sampled Colors mode. However, Color Range can also be used to select predetermined color ranges (see Figure 10.21).

Pixels are selected based on their content of the target color. For example, a pixel with an RGB value of 64/128/75 will be 50% selected when Green is chosen, but only 25% selected if Red is chosen. Neither the Fuzziness slider nor the eyedropper tools are available when using the presets from the pop-up menu.

Color Range can be especially useful for making selections of hair, branches, and other complex images. It works best when there's a strong contrast between the subject and the background.

Figure 10.21
The Out of Gamut option is available only for RGB and Lab color mode images.

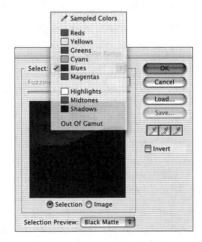

Selection Tips

Accurate selections, with appropriate feathering or anti-aliasing, can make or break a project. Quick and efficient selection can make or break deadlines. Here are some tips that can improve your selection procedures:

- (Command-click) [Ctrl+click] on a layer in the Layers palette to make a selection of all non-transparent pixels on the layer. (This cannot be done on a layer named *Background* because it relies on transparency, which is not supported on background layers.)

- Open the Channels palette and look at each color channel individually. Your intended selection area may stand out in better contrast on one layer or another. Working with just that layer active improves the performance of the Magic Wand, Color Range, or Magnetic Lasso. After creating the selection, remember to make the composite channel active again in the Channels palette.

- The Extract command, which has been moved to the Filter menu in Photoshop 7, is an automated way of creating a selection—and deleting the inverse, all in one step. You can use the command to make a selection, too. Duplicate the target layer and hide all other layers. Use Extract on the duplicate layer. Click once in the now-transparent background with the Magic Wand. Delete that layer and restore the visibility of others. To finish selecting the subject, use the menu command Select, Inverse.

➡ *To learn how to work with Extract, **see** "Using the Extract Command," **p. 588**, in Chapter 19, "Extract, Liquify, and the Pattern Maker."*

- If you do a lot of complex selecting that involves hair, fur, glass, clouds, fabric, and the like, you may be best served by a special-purpose plug-in or program. Mask Pro from Extensis is a capable tool that is Photoshop 7 compatible. (At the time of Photoshop 7's release, no Mac OS X version of Mask Pro was available.) Procreate offers KnockOut, another excellent masking/selection choice, which is Photoshop 7 compatible and runs under Mac OS X.

- When a subject has been removed from a background and your selection wasn't perfect, you might see a "halo" around the edges. The command Layer, Matting, Defringe can be used to clean up the selection.

- Showing the Grid and/or Guides and using Snap can give you an added level of precision when working with selection tools.

- A selection can be dragged from one open document to another. You can copy your document, use Levels or Curves to create extreme contrast, make a selection, and then drag that selection back to the original document. With a selection active, use any selection tool to drag from one window to the other.

10

ALPHA CHANNELS AND MASKS

When you use the command Select, Save Selection, you're creating an *alpha channel*. Like other channels, an alpha channel is an 8-bit grayscale representation. As an 8-bit image, there are a maximum of 256 shades of gray in the channel. The levels of gray represent the level of selection for each pixel. For example, a pixel colored 50% gray in an alpha channel is 50% selected when the channel is loaded again as a selection.

Alpha channels can be created from scratch as well as from an existing selection. As a channel, they can also be edited as though they were grayscale images, with tools, filters, adjustments, and more.

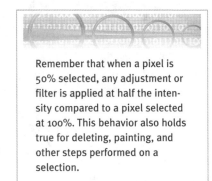

Remember that when a pixel is 50% selected, any adjustment or filter is applied at half the intensity compared to a pixel selected at 100%. This behavior also holds true for deleting, painting, and other steps performed on a selection.

➯ *For a full discussion of channels, **see** Chapter 15, "Channels: Color and More," p. 409.*

Basic Alpha Channel Creation

The easiest way to create an alpha channel to store a selection is to make the selection first. With any selection active in the image, use the menu command Select, Save Selection to open the Save Selection dialog box (see Figure 10.22).

Figure 10.22
The Destination area of the dialog box is where you choose both the document and the channel in which to save the selection. You can also select a name when creating a new channel.

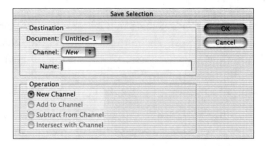

The Document pop-up menu lists all files open in Photoshop that have *exactly* the same pixel dimensions; it also includes the option to create a new document. (Open files that are a different size than the document in which you made the selection do not appear in the list.) Selecting New creates a new document with the same dimensions and resolution as the original. The document consists of only the single alpha channel and is in Multichannel mode. Although the new image contains no color channels and holds only the saved selection, you can convert the document to any color mode (after first converting it to Grayscale). The name selected in the Save Selection dialog box is applied to the channel, not to the new document.

The Channel pop-up menu lists all available alpha channels in the image selected in the Document field. You can create a new channel or add to, subtract from, or intersect with an existing alpha channel. When working with an existing channel, the Name field is grayed out.

With a selection active in the image, you can also create a new alpha channel through the Channels palette (see Figure 10.23). Clicking the Save Selection as Channel button at the bottom of the palette creates a new alpha channel and bypasses the Save Selection dialog box. (The new channel is named Alpha 1 or the next available number.)

The third technique for adding an alpha channel from an existing selection is through the Channels palette menu. Select the command New Channel (not New Spot Channel). You'll have an opportunity to name the channel and decide the channel's options (see Figure 10.24).

In terms of the actual content of a newly created alpha channel, there is no difference among the Select, Save Selection menu command, the Channels palette Save Selection as Channel button, and the palette menu command New Channel. Each generates the same channel from the same selection.

Figure 10.23
A new channel added with the Save Selection as Channel button can be renamed by double-clicking the name in the Channels palette.

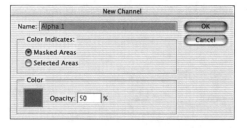

Figure 10.24
The Color Indicates and Color options determine the appearance of the mask when it is activated over one or more channels.

Editing Masks

Whether an alpha channel is saved from a selection or created empty, you can alter its content as though it were a grayscale image. In the Channels palette, click on the alpha channel to make it the only active channel. Use all of Photoshop's power to manipulate the shades of gray. Remember that the changes you make in the alpha channel will be reflected in the selection after the channel is reloaded.

For example, applying a Gaussian Blur filter to an alpha channel softens edges, much like controlled feathering. If a selection is made within the alpha channel first, the blur can be even further controlled.

The basic tools for adjusting an alpha channel remain the Brush and the Eraser. Using the Brush tool, you can add black to hide areas in the alpha channel, removing them from the selection when the channel is loaded. Likewise, you can erase or paint with white to add areas or an image to a selection. Various shades of gray can be used to create areas of partial selection or feathering (see Figure 10.25).

Figure 10.25
Painting with gray results in pixels that will be partially selected when the alpha channel is loaded as a selection.

You can also work on an alpha channel with the image visible behind it. Click on the alpha channel in the Channels palette to make it active. Next, click in the visibility column (the "eyeball" icons) next to the image's composite channel to make the color channels visible. (The channel will be named either RGB or CMYK for those color modes.) By default, the areas that are outside the selection when the channel is loaded are covered with a 50% opaque red overlay (see Figure 10.26).

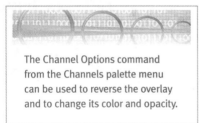

The Channel Options command from the Channels palette menu can be used to reverse the overlay and to change its color and opacity.

Figure 10.26
Although not apparent in the grayscale version of this image, the background and beak, as well as parts of the eye, are covered by the red overlay.

Quick Mask Mode

Photoshop offers a convenient way to edit selections through the use of masks—without ever having to look at the Channels palette. Quick Mask mode takes you directly to a red overlay that is active and ready to be edited as an alpha channel. Simply press Q on the keyboard or click the button in the Toolbox to enter Quick Mask mode (see Figure 10.27). After editing the mask, press Q again or click the opposite button to exit Quick Mask mode.

Figure 10.27
The button to the left of the cursor returns you to Standard mode.

When in Quick Mask mode, a temporary channel is created in the Channels palette. Just as a work path disappears when no longer needed, so, too, is a quick mask deleted when you exit Quick Mask mode. After exiting Quick Mask mode, there is a selection active in the image and you can, of course, save that selection as a regular alpha channel.

When in Quick Mask mode, the Channels palette menu also offers the Quick Mask Options command. You can change the overlay's opacity or color and even decide whether it shows or hides the masked areas.

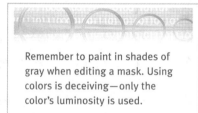

Remember to paint in shades of gray when editing a mask. Using colors is deceiving—only the color's luminosity is used.

Masking Tips

Masks can provide incredible control over selections. With 256 levels of selection available, all through a simple change in gray value, you can create extraordinarily complex selections. Remember that virtually all of Photoshop's capabilities are available to you when editing alpha channels. Here are some suggestions:

- Alpha channels are grayscale—edit them with shades of gray. Set the Color palette to Grayscale and use the preset grays in the Swatches palette. Remember that Photoshop 7 can save workspaces for you. Position the palettes you need for mask editing, and use the menu command Window, Workspace, Save Workspace. Name it Mask Editing. Select it when you need to work on an alpha channel.

- The D key sets the foreground color to black and the background color to white. The X key swaps them. When editing a mask, you can quickly switch between "add to" and "subtract from" by switching from white to black and vice versa.

- Set up the Brush tool with one brush, the Pencil with another, and the Eraser with a third. Switch between them with keyboard shortcuts to speed up editing masks. Remember that erasing to black is the same as painting with black—the only difference being a simple press of the X key.

- Although a selection border cannot accurately show feathering, a mask can. To take a quick look at the feathering of a selection, press Q to enter Quick Mask mode, and then Q again to exit.

- The filter Sharpen, Unsharp Mask can work wonders on detailed and complex masks. However, you might want to isolate certain areas of the channel before applying the filter to avoid harsh edge transitions.

- You can soften the edges of an extremely detailed mask to simulate anti-aliasing without blurring. Rotate the mask one or two degrees by using Edit, Transform, Rotate and entering the value in the Options Bar. Then rotate it back to the original position, again using the command and Options Bar (not Undo). The effect will be subtle, and that's generally what you want.

- You can create a selection using a type mask tool and save that selection as an alpha channel. You can edit the mask, load it as a selection, and have customized text. Keep in mind, however, that you can't edit the text, and it won't output as vector to a PostScript printer.

Alpha Channels and File Formats

Alpha channels can be stored in several file formats. Photoshop's native format (.psd) supports multiple alpha channels. TIFF images in RGB and CMYK mode can support multiple alpha channels, as can PDF files created in Photoshop. The RAW file format can support numerous channels, but presents problems of its own. For example, when reopening a RAW file, you must know the exact dimensions of the image, the correct number of channels, and whether the color data was interleaved when saved.

A single alpha channel can be saved with BMP, PICT, and Pixar files. The PNG-24 file format can generate an alpha channel to store transparency in an image, but that information cannot be accessed directly or edited. Rather, it is updated if you change the transparency of the image.

→ *To learn more about the capabilities—and restrictions—of the various file formats, **see** "The File Formats," p. 127, in Chapter 5, "Photoshop's File Formats and Output Options."*

LAYER MASKS, VECTOR MASKS, AND CLIPPING GROUPS

Alpha channels are used to store masks (and, in some cases, to store transparency information), but masks can also be used to show and hide certain areas of a layer. Layer masks are pixel-based masks, much like alpha channels. They support variable transparency and can be edited with painting tools. Vector masks, on the other hand, use paths to define the visible areas of a layer. They use paths and support only *hard-edged* transparency. (The term "hard-edged" is used in contrast to variable transparency—a pixel is either completely opaque or completely transparent with vector path transparency.)

Creating a Layer Mask

You can hide areas of a layer easily with a layer mask. At its simplest, you need only make a selection and click the Add Layer Mask button at the bottom of the Layers palette (see Figure 10.28).

Figure 10.28
Clicking the Add Layer Mask button leaves the selection visible. (Option-clicking) [Alt+clicking] hides the selection and reveals the rest of the layer.

Layer masks can also be added to the active layer by using the commands in the Layer, Add Layer Mask menu. You can choose to add a mask that hides the entire layer, reveals the entire layer, hides the active selection (if any), or reveals the selection.

⇨ *Want to get rid of a mask? See "Deleting or Applying?" in the NAPP Help Desk section at the end of this chapter.*

Each layer can have only one layer mask (in addition to a clipping mask). Layer masks cannot be applied to *Background* layers. Layer masks create transparency, which background layers do not support.

After a mask has been added to the layer, it appears in the Layers palette, linked to the layer thumbnail (see Figure 10.29). In the mask's thumbnail, white indicates visible areas of the layer, black is used for hidden areas, and shades of gray show areas of partial transparency.

Figure 10.29
The icon to the right of the visibility eyeball indicates that the layer mask is selected for editing. If the layer itself were active, a paintbrush icon would appear in the second column.

Creating a Vector Mask

10

In previous versions of Photoshop, the terms "clipping mask" and "layer clipping path" were used. *Vector mask* more accurately reflects the nature of the capability. (It also avoids confusion with clipping paths created to selectively show and hide areas of an image in a page layout program, which are still called clipping paths.) A vector path is used to determine visibility on a layer. The term "visibility" is used in lieu of "opacity" because there is no variable transparency with a vector mask—a pixel is either inside the path and visible or outside the path and invisible. This does not mean, however, that the *content* of the layer can't have reduced opacity, simply that variable transparency cannot be controlled through a vector mask.

The two biggest differences between vector masks and layer masks are variable transparency (layer masks provide it, vector masks do not) and PostScript output (vector masks provide it, layer masks do not). Vector paths, when output to PostScript-enabled printers, produce crisp, clean edges. This advantage is lost when printing to an inkjet printer, which cannot process the mathematical path description and rasterizes the image.

➡️ *For a complete discussion of the differences between vector and raster, **see** "The Two Types of Computer Graphics," p. 156, in Chapter 6, "Pixels, Vectors, and Resolution."*

The process of creating a vector mask is reversed from the layer mask procedure. Instead of identifying the area to be masked and then clicking a button, you click the button *first*, and then create the path. To add a vector mask, hold down the (Option–Command) [Alt+Ctrl] buttons, and then click the Add Layer Mask button at the bottom of the Layers palette. You can then use the Pen tool or a shape tool (set to Make Work Path), or paste a path to form the mask. It will appear in the Layers palette to the right of the layer thumbnail or to the right of a layer mask thumbnail, if one is present (see Figure 10.30).

To temporarily disable a mask and show the entire content of a layer, Shift-click on the thumbnail in the Layers palette. A large red X will appear across the thumbnail, and the layer will be completely visible. To re-enable the mask, Shift-click the thumbnail again.

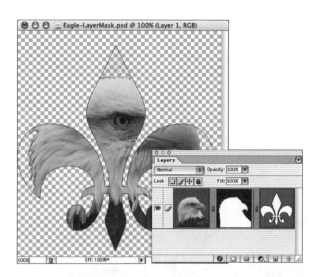

Editing Layer and Vector Masks

Click on a mask thumbnail in the Layers palette to make it active and prepare it for editing. Alternatively, both vector masks and layer masks can be edited from the mask's own appropriate palette. Vector masks appear in the Paths palette, and layer masks are found in the Channels palette (see Figure 10.31).

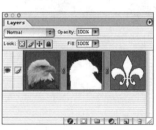

Figure 10.31
Select the mask in its "home" palette to edit it. Note that a vector mask's path will be visible in the Paths palette only when its layer is active in the Layers palette.

A layer mask can be edited much like an alpha channel. You can use shades of gray (as well as black and white) in the image window to edit the mask. Paint and erase in the image to show and hide parts of the layer.

Vector masks are edited with the Pen tools, the Direct Selection tool, and the Path Component Selection tool. When the path is selected in the Paths palette, a vector mask can also be manipulated with the Edit, Transform commands.

A layer can have both a layer mask *and* a vector mask. The masks can be created in either order, using the procedures described earlier in this chapter.

You can also click the link icon between two thumbnails in the Layers palette to unlink a mask from the layer's content. The mask can then be repositioned in the window. Click on the thumbnail and use the Move tool. Click between the thumbnails again to restore the link between the layer and the mask.

Clipping Groups

A *clipping group* is formed when two (or more) layers are joined to selectively show/hide artwork. The opacity on the lowest layer is used to determine what areas of the upper layer(s) are visible. Completely transparent pixels are ignored on the clipping layer, and the rest are used to determine visibility for the upper layers of the clipping group.

To create a clipping group, hold down the (Option) [Alt] key and click on the line between the two layers in the Layers palette (see Figure 10.32). With the modifier key pressed and the cursor properly positioned, the cursor changes to "wedding rings."

10

Figure 10.32
The "wedding rings" cursor is shown in the inset.

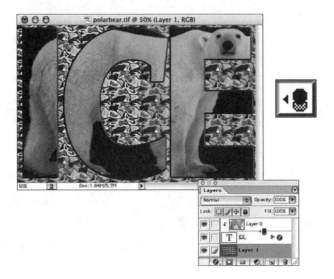

In addition to clicking in the Layers palette, you can create a clipping group in several ways. Make sure the upper layer is active in the Layers palette and use the menu command Layer, Group with Previous. When creating a new layer, you can have it automatically grouped with the previous layer. Hold down the (Option) [Alt] key when clicking the New Layer button, or choose the Layers palette menu command New Layer. In the New Layer dialog box, select the Group with Previous Layer check box. You can also drag a layer into an existing clipping group in the Layers palette.

To clip a number of layers at the same time, you can link the layers in the Layers palette and use the menu command Layer, Group Linked (see Figure 10.33).

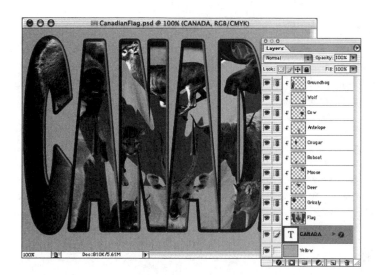

Figure 10.33
The linked layers are clipped to the lowermost. Any nonlinked layer would not be clipped.

PHOTOSHOP IN FOCUS

To get a feel for the difference between vector and raster layer masks, try this:

1. Open an image, any image. If the image is flattened, convert the background layer to a regular layer by renaming it.

2. Select the Custom Shape tool and pick a shape from the Custom Shape palette.

3. In the Options Bar, click the Make Work Path button. (It's the second of three buttons at the left end of the Options Bar.)

4. Drag the shape, creating a path that covers most of the image.

5. Choose the Layer, Add Vector Mask, Current Path menu command.

6. At the bottom of the Layers palette, click the Add Layer Mask button (again, second from left). The layer mask icon will appear in the Layers palette between the layer thumbnail and the vector mask thumbnail. Do not deselect the layer mask thumbnail.

7. Select a gradient tool and set the gradient to black-to-white in the Options Bar.

8. Drag a gradient within your vector mask.

9. In the Layers palette, Shift-click on the mask thumbnails to hide one, then the other, and then both.

10. Use the Direct Selection tool to drag anchor points of the vector mask.

FROM THE NAPP HELP DESK

The National Association of Photoshop Professionals (NAPP) offers e-mail assistance to its members. Here is some advice from the NAPP Help Desk related to issues in this chapter.

Showing and Hiding Edges

I dragged the Rectangular Marquee tool in my image but didn't see any marching ants. I hit the Delete key to find out if anything was selected and, sure enough, all the pixels in the area I'd selected disappeared. Where did the ants go?

The keyboard shortcut (Command-H) [Ctrl+H] is used to show and hide "Extras." Among the extras is Selection Edges. You can also use the menu command View, Extras to toggle between visible and invisible. To determine what gets included in the Extras, open the Show Extras Options dialog box with the menu command View, Show, Show Extras Options. Choose from among Selection Edges, Target Path, Annotations, Grid, Guides, and Slices. Whatever is checked will be hidden and shown with the keyboard shortcut.

Check the Options

I can't get the Rectangular Marquee to behave. Sometimes I try to drag, but it makes a box and I just drag the box around. Other times it lets me drag, but only certain shapes. Now and then, it doesn't have square corners. What's going on?

Check the Options Bar. This is good advice for any tool that isn't doing what it used to do. When you're just dragging a box around, it's set to Fixed Size. If the proportions are constant but the size changes, it's in Fixed Aspect Ratio mode. A rectangular selection border with rounded corners is a function of feathering.

Deleting or Applying?

I tried to drag a layer mask to the Trash in the Layers palette to get rid of it, but I got a scary warning message, so I canceled instead. What's the difference between "Discard" and "Apply" for masks?

If you drag a layer mask or a vector mask to the Trash icon in the Layers palette, Photoshop asks if you want to keep the layer appearance and throw away the mask, or throw away the mask and the masking, too. The warning dialog box asks "Apply mask to layer before removing?" It offers three buttons: Discard, Cancel, and Apply. If you discard the mask, it's gone as though it never existed, and the layer is restored to full visibility. If you click Cancel, the mask is retained as it was before you dragged it to the Trash. Clicking Apply uses the mask to edit the layer, and then discards the mask. Hidden pixels on the layer are deleted, and areas of partial transparency get reduced opacity. The layer retains the appearance it had with the layer active, but the layer itself is no longer needed.

TYPE AND TYPOGRAPHY IN PHOTOSHOP

IN THIS CHAPTER

PHOTOSHOP'S TYPE CAPABILITY

As the subject of type and text in Photoshop is discussed, it's important to keep one basic concept in mind: Photoshop is an image-editing program. It is not designed to be a page layout program, nor a word processor. As such, don't consider Photoshop's type-handling capabilities to be substandard; rather, think of them as a bonus. If you have large amounts of text to add to a document, or need to work with very small type, consider Adobe InDesign or Adobe Illustrator.

Just a few versions in the past, Photoshop's type capability was restricted to creating masks in the shape of letters. (The biggest problem with type masks is that the type isn't *live*. You can't edit the words or change the typographic attributes without re-creating the entire type element (see Figure 11.1).

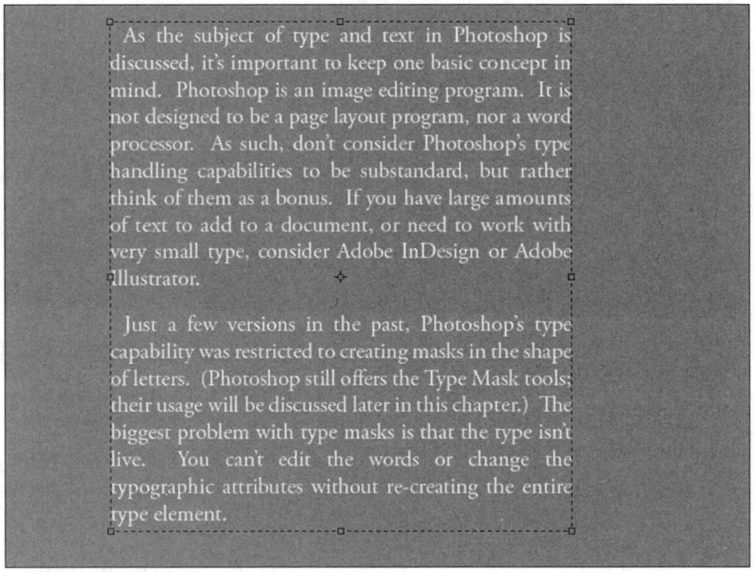

Figure 11.1

After the type is set, it becomes nothing more than filled pixels. Changing the font or even one misspelling might mean re-creating the entire image when type is added as a mask.

As the subject of type and text in Photoshop is discussed, it's important to keep one basic concept in mind. Photoshop is an image editing program. It is not designed to be a page layout program, nor a word processor. As such, don't consider Photoshop's type handling capabilities to be substandard, but rather think of them as a bonus. If you have large amounts of text to add to a document, or need to work with very small type, consider Adobe InDesign or Adobe Illustrator.

Just a few versions in the past, Photoshop's type capability was restricted to creating masks in the shape of letters. (Photoshop still offers the Type Mask tools; their usage will be discussed later in this chapter.) The biggest problem with type masks is that the type isn't live. You can't edit the words or change the typographic attributes without re-creating the entire type element.

⇨ *Photoshop still offers type masks; their use is discussed in "The Type Tools," later in this chapter.*

Photoshop 5 introduced type layers and Photoshop 6 added vector type. Photoshop 7 refines the type engine and adds both a spell checker and a find/replace capability.

Vector Type

As discussed in Chapter 6, "Pixels, Vectors, and Resolution," there are numerous advantages to vector artwork. For example, when printed with a PostScript output device, the edges remain crisp and clean, without the so-called *jaggies*—the visible stair-step edges of pixels along a curve. Vector artwork can be scaled in an illustration program or by a PostScript printer and still retain those high-quality edges. Because it consists of mathematically defined paths, it can also be manipulated in ways impossible with raster art. Figure 11.2 shows the difference between scaling vector type and raster type.

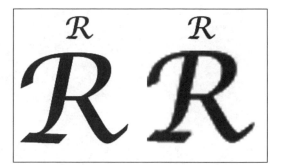

Figure 11.2
The original letters are shown for comparison. Notice the dramatic difference in quality when vector and rasterized type are scaled to 400%.

The primary advantage of raster art is its capability of reproducing fine transitions and gradations in color. Because type is usually a single color, that is not of particular value. However, Photoshop's vector type can be rasterized whenever necessary.

Saving Images with Type

The difference between vector and rasterized type is primarily of importance during the creation process and when preparing artwork for placement in a page layout program. In most other circumstances, the type is automatically rasterized. Remember that with the exception of scalable vector graphics (SVG), a format that is not supported by Photoshop, Web artwork is raster. Similarly, inkjet printers don't take advantage of vector type. (Only PostScript printers can actually work with vectors as such.) When outputting to an inkjet printer, saving images for the Web, or using a non-PostScript file format, type is automatically rasterized.

In Photoshop, the PostScript file formats, those that support vectors, are limited to Photoshop (.psd), Encapsulated PostScript (.eps), Portable Document Format (.pdf), and Desktop Color Separations (.dcs). The enhanced TIFF file format can also support vector type layers, but full implementation of the format's advanced features outside Photoshop is virtually nonexistent.

⇨ *For more on enhanced TIFF, **see** Chapter 5, "Photoshop's File Formats and Output Options," p. 119.*

When saving in a format that can maintain vector artwork or type, you'll need to ensure that the Include Vector Data option is selected. In Figure 11.3, you can see the check boxes for the various PostScript file format options. Note that both the EPS and the DCS option dialog boxes warn about reopening files in Photoshop, but the PDF dialog box does not.

11

Caution

EPS, PDF, and DCS support vector type when saving from Photoshop. However, reopening any of these image formats in Photoshop results in rasterization. After you save a file with vector text in one of these formats, don't reopen it in Photoshop. It's a good idea to keep the original in Photoshop's own .psd format.

When saving files as TIFF, Photoshop offers the option of saving layers. Unless your print shop specifically approves, don't use layers in TIFF images. And if you won't be sending the image out, there's little advantage to enhanced TIFF over Photoshop's .psd format.

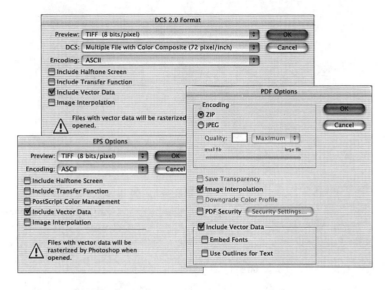

Figure 11.3
EPS, PDF, and DCS file formats all offer (but don't require) saving vector data in a file. If there are no vector paths in the image, the option is grayed out.

These three file formats (and enhanced TIFF) are the only formats supported by Photoshop that do not rasterize type.

Point and Paragraph Type

In addition to the differentiation between vector and raster, type in Photoshop can be categorized as *point type* or *paragraph type*. Point type is added to a document at a specific location (or point) in the image. In contrast, paragraph type (also called *area type*) fills a portion (or area) of the image. Figure 11.4 illustrates the difference.

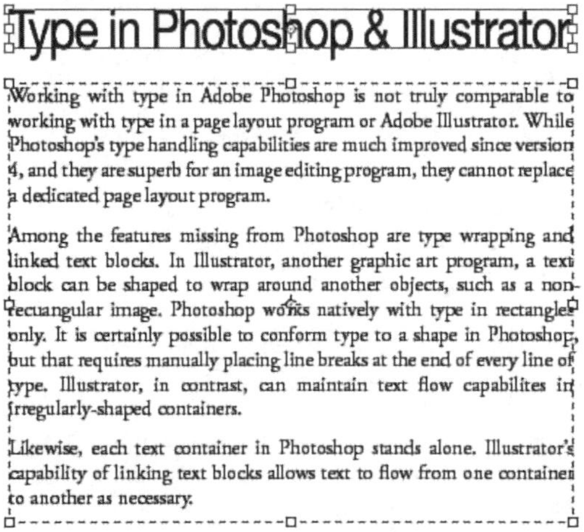

Figure 11.4
Point type is often used for single lines of text, such as headlines, and paragraph type is used for large blocks of text. Note the difference between the transform bounding box (top) and the paragraph type container (bottom).

Type in Photoshop & Illustrator

Working with type in Adobe Photoshop is not truly comparable to working with type in a page layout program or Adobe Illustrator. While Photoshop's type handling capabilities are much improved since version 4, and they are superb for an image editing program, they cannot replace a dedicated page layout program.

Among the features missing from Photoshop are type wrapping and linked text blocks. In Illustrator, another graphic art program, a text block can be shaped to wrap around another objects, such as a non-rectangular image. Photoshop works natively with type in rectangles only. It is certainly possible to conform type to a shape in Photoshop, but that requires manually placing line breaks at the end of every line of type. Illustrator, in contrast, can maintain text flow capabilites in irregularly-shaped containers.

Likewise, each text container in Photoshop stands alone. Illustrator's capability of linking text blocks allows text to flow from one container to another as necessary.

There are a number of important differences between the two types of type:

- Point type continues in a straight line unless you press the (Return) [Enter] key to insert a line break. Paragraph type automatically wraps to the next line when the text reaches the boundary of its box.

- The space occupied by point type continues to expand as more characters are added. Paragraph type is restricted to the designated rectangle; characters that don't fit in the rectangle are hidden.

- Point type is added from the specific spot in the image where the Type tool was clicked. Paragraph type is added from the top of the bounding box.

- To add point type, click with a Type tool. For paragraph type, drag with a Type tool to create a rectangle to fill with the type.

- Resizing the bounding box around point type scales the type. Resizing the container rectangle for paragraph type forces the text to reflow within the container; the type maintains its original size and proportion.

Consider point type to be similar to headlines in a newspaper or magazine. It typically occupies one line, but might require two or three lines. To add lines, type to the desired width, press (Return) [Enter] to move to the next line, and continue typing.

Paragraph type, on the other hand, can be compared to the body text of a newspaper or magazine. It flows from one line to the next, and if you go back to the beginning and add a word, the text repositions itself, automatically adjusting the line breaks. This is called *reflowing*.

Think, if you will, of the difference (or one of the differences) between a typewriter and a word processor. With a typewriter, you must be aware of the warning bell that indicates you've reached the end of a line, the edge of the paper. You then advance the paper, return to the left margin, and begin typing on the next line. With a word processor, you can continue typing and the text will automatically wrap from line to line.

With a typewriter, if you need to go back to the first line to add a word, the length of that line is thrown off. If it's a long word, you can't just erase the top line and retype it; you have to retype the entire paragraph. Adding a word to the opening line with a word processor simply moves all the text to the right and, if necessary, down to the next line—the text reflows. A comparison is shown in Figure 11.5.

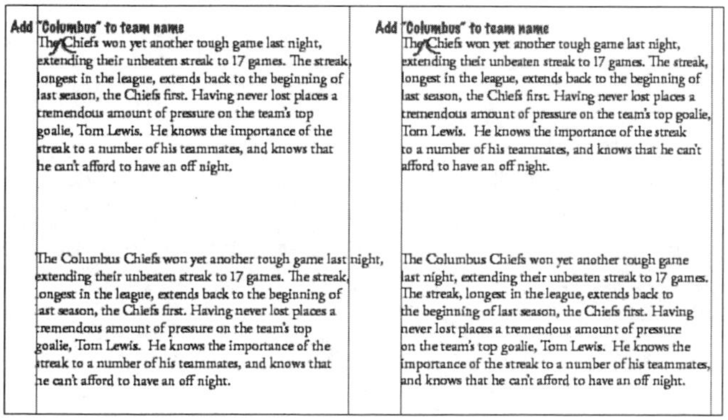

Figure 11.5
Compare the pairs. Observe how adding a single word extends the point type past the acceptable boundary, but simply causes the paragraph type to reflow without affecting the width of the type container.

Working with Type Layers

As long as type remains part of a type layer, it remains editable. You can return to the type layer at any time and make changes to the character and paragraph characteristics, or edit the text itself. After the layer is rasterized or merged or the image is flattened, the type can no longer be edited as type. (You can, of course, edit the pixels, but you cannot, for example, highlight a word with the Type tool and overtype to correct a spelling error.)

In many ways, type layers are comparable to other non-background layers. Layer styles can be applied, type layers can be moved in the Layers palette, they can become part of a layer set, and adjustment layers can be applied (see Figure 11.6).

Figure 11.6
The Layers palette indicates what effects and adjustments have been applied to the type layers.

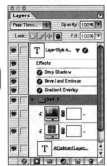

Layer Style Applied

Adjustment Layers Applied

A type layer is always indicated by the letter *T* in place of a layer thumbnail in the Layers palette. Like other layers, you can click on the layer's name and rename it. (By default, Photoshop names a type layer using the first characters of the layer's content.) You can change the blending mode and opacity of a type layer and create layer-based slices from type layers.

Unlike other non-background layers, you cannot add pixels to a type layer. You cannot paint on a type layer, nor can you stroke or fill a selection. The adjustment tools (Blur, Sharpen, Dodge, Burn, Sponge, Smudge) cannot be used on type layers.

Warping Type

Among the most fun tools in Photoshop is Warp Text. You can apply preset distortions to type and customize their effects, and the type remains completely editable. You can apply layer styles to the warped text as well (see Figure 11.7).

The Warp Text dialog box can be opened with the button to the right of the color swatch in the Options Bar (when a Type tool is active) or with the menu command Layer, Type, Warp Text. The dialog box allows you to select any of 15 shapes and then use three sliders to adjust the result (see Figure 11.8).

Figure 11.7
Each of the five examples is on a separate type layer.

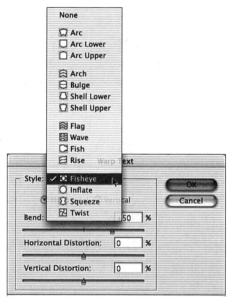

Figure 11.8
To remove an existing warp effect, select None from the top of the Style pop-up menu.

11

THE TYPE TOOLS

Photoshop offers four related tools for adding type to an image. The Horizontal Type tool (usually referred to as simply the Type tool), the Vertical Type tool, the Horizontal Type Mask tool, and the Vertical Type Mask tool are shown in their flyout palette in Figure 11.9.

Figure 11.9
To open the flyout palette, click
and hold on whichever Type tool
icon is visible in the Toolbox.

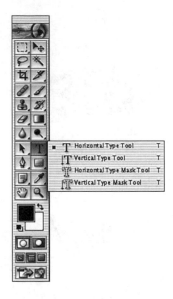

The Horizontal and Vertical Type Tools

The only difference between the Horizontal Type and Vertical Type tools is the orientation of the characters added to the image. Note in Figure 11.10 the difference between vertical type and horizontal type that has been rotated.

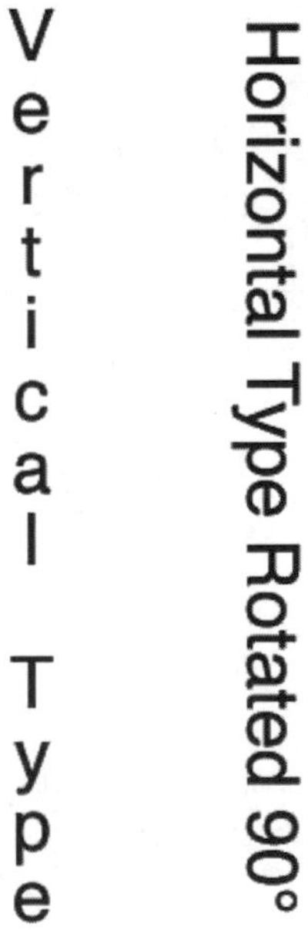

Figure 11.10
Consider vertical and horizontal
to be references to the relationship among letters.

Vertical Type

Horizontal Type Rotated 90°

Both the Horizontal and Vertical Type tools create type layers when used. Unless you rasterized the type, and as long as the file remains in Photoshop's native format (.psd), the type remains editable. You can change the font, size, or other attributes as well as change the content of the text. You can click with either tool anywhere in an image window to create a new type layer and add point type. You can also drag with either tool to create a type layer and add paragraph type.

To edit existing type, click and drag with either tool to make a type selection. Changes are restricted to the selected type. There are a few shortcuts available when selecting type:

- Click twice in a word with the Type tool to select the whole word.

- Click three times to select the entire line of type.

- Clicking four times selects the entire paragraph.

- After clicking in existing type with the Type tool, hold down Shift and use the left and right arrow keys to add letters to the selection. The up and down arrow keys select all characters to the same location in the next line above or below the blinking cursor.

- (Shift-Command) [Shift-Ctrl] and the right and left arrow keys add or subtract adjacent words from a selection.

- Clicking at one point and Shift-clicking at another selects all characters in between.

To make changes to an entire type layer, don't select any type; merely select the type layer in the Layers palette. You can change any attributes in the Character or Paragraph palettes, and the change is applied throughout the type layer.

To better evaluate changes being made to selected type, especially color changes, use (Command-H) [Ctrl+H] to hide the selection highlighting.

11

The Type Mask Tools

Also available for horizontal and vertical type, the Type Mask tools do not create type layers. Rather, they create masks in the shape of the letters. (A non-type layer must be active in the Layers palette.) These masks become selections when you change tools, click the check mark in the Options Bar, or press (Command-Return) [Ctrl+Enter].

Using the Type Mask tools is comparable to using Photoshop's Quick Mask mode. Like Quick Mask, the temporary mask that is created is not retained after the selection is made. You'll see the translucent red overlay while adding the type, but the mask itself is lost when converted to a selection (see Figure 11.11).

Figure 11.11
On the left, the mask is visible while the type is being set. On the right, the type is a selection and the mask is discarded. This happens automatically when you change tools or otherwise accept the type.

⇨ *For a full discussion of Quick Mask mode, **see** "Quick Mask Mode," p. 264, in Chapter 10, "Making Selections and Creating Masks."*

Type masks are often used to create layer masks in the shape of letters. It is usually not the tool of choice for creating large amounts of text and is especially inappropriate for small type sizes.

If you want to save the type mask, choose Select, Save Selection immediately after changing tools or otherwise accepting the type mask input.

THE TYPE PALETTES AND COMMANDS

In addition to the Type tools in the Toolbox and the Options Bar, some 16 menu commands and two palettes are designed for use specifically with type. Some of the commands duplicate options found in the Options Bar (such as anti-aliasing), which allows you to access the capabilities without having the Type tool active. Two of the menu commands, found under the Edit menu, are new to Photoshop 7. Check Spelling and Find and Replace Text will be discussed separately later in this chapter.

In addition, virtually all other commands and palettes can be used with type in one way or another. Styles can be applied, colors can be changed, transformations are available—these are just some of the ways that Photoshop enables you to work with type.

Type Commands Under the Layer Menu

The Type submenu found under the Layer menu offers 13 commands, each of which is available only when a type layer is active in the Layers palette. Two of the commands can be used to convert the editable type into vector paths, either as work paths or as shape layers.

Create Work Path

This command converts the type layer from editable type to a work path. The work path consists of all the subpaths used to create the vector type. Photoshop does nothing with the work path, nor does it change your type layer in any way. You can, however, open the Paths palette and save the work path, you can use it to create a layer mask or clipping mask, you can stroke the paths (on a separate layer, not on the original type layer), or you can use the work path as a basis for a selection. Paths created from type can also be exported to Illustrator. In addition, you can edit the individual anchor points of the subpaths to customize the type (see Figure 11.12).

In Figure 11.13, you can see the number of anchor points for the converted type. Note the density of points in the type.

Caution

Be aware that paths created from type are very complex. When created from large amounts of text, they can be complex enough to cause output problems for image-setters and printers. Unlike Illustrator, Photoshop has no Simplify command to reduce the complexity of paths.

Figure 11.12
The type has been converted to a work path, and the Direct Selection tool is being used to edit the letterforms. The path can be converted to a selection and filled or stroked.

Figure 11.13
The type is set at a relatively large 18 points. The density of anchor points would be increased at lower font sizes because the number of points per character remains the same.

The font used can play a major role in the number of anchor points created when type is converted to work paths. Serif fonts and some script fonts often require a substantially higher number of anchor points to reproduce as editable paths. Multiply the increased number of anchor points, as seen in Figure 11.14, by the number of letters in a several-word type layer, and you can calculate the increased complexity of the work path.

Figure 11.14
The fonts are Arial (27 anchor points), Times New Roman (38 anchor points), Brush Script (74 anchor points), and Lucida Calligraphy (34 anchor points).

11

Convert to Shape

Like the command Create Work Path, this command uses a vector type layer to create paths. However, rather than creating a work path, a shape layer is produced. The original type layer becomes a layer comparable to those produced by Photoshop Shape tools. A shape layer consists of a filled layer with a layer clipping mask. The clipping mask selectively reveals areas of the filled layer (see Figure 11.15).

Take a look at the Layers palette in Figure 11.15. Note that the original type layer is still there, but hidden. (Hide the original type layer by clicking its eyeball icon in the Layers palette.) It's always a good idea to create a shape layer from a *copy* of the type layer.

⇨ *Shape layers and the Shape tools are discussed in Chapter 13, "The Pen Tools, Shape Layers, and Other Paths," p. 349.*

Figure 11.15
The Layers palette shows the layer thumbnail as well as the layer clipping path created from the type layer. The Paths palette shows the clipping path as a vector mask.

The new shape layer is filled with the same color that was originally applied to the type. If more than one color is applied to the type, the shape layer is filled with the color of the first character. When a style has been applied to the type layer, it is retained in the shape layer.

The paths created by the Convert to Shape command are identical to those created by the Create Work Path command. The caution presented earlier also applies to the shape layer path—paths with too many anchor points can create output problems.

Other Type Commands

A number of additional commands in the Layer, Type submenu can be used to change the orientation, anti-aliasing, and a couple of other attributes of the selected type or type layer. The submenu also holds commands that enable you to compensate for missing fonts.

Both Convert to Shape and Create Work Path are available for type that has been warped. The paths that are created, whether work paths or layer clipping paths, follow the contours of the warped type.

- **Horizontal**—A check mark appears next to this command when the type layer contains horizontal type.

If the check mark does not appear, you can select this command to convert the type from vertical to horizontal.

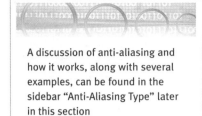

A discussion of anti-aliasing and how it works, along with several examples, can be found in the sidebar "Anti-Aliasing Type" later in this section

■ **Vertical**—A check mark appears next to this command when the type layer contains vertical type. If the check mark does not appear, you can select this command to convert the type from horizontal to vertical.

■ **Anti-Alias None**—Anti-aliasing smoothes the edges of type onscreen. This command removes all anti-aliasing, which can result in jagged-edged type (see Figure 11.16). However, None is often the appropriate choice for very small type and small type at low resolution.

Figure 11.16
Although the differences in the other four types of anti-aliasing are virtually impossible to spot in this sample, None (at the upper left) is certainly apparent.

■ **Anti-Alias Sharp**—This option results is the lowest amount of anti-aliasing. If the type appears rough or jagged along curves, select another option.

■ **Anti-Alias Crisp**—High contrast edges take precedence over smoothing with the Crisp option.

■ **Anti-Alias Strong**—The Strong option adds anti-aliasing outside the character in an attempt to maintain the individual character's width.

■ **Anti-Alias Smooth**—The greatest amount of anti-aliasing is applied with this option. If characters become blurry, consider Crisp or Sharp. If the characters seem to lose optical weight (the strokes appear too thin), opt for Strong.

■ **Convert to Paragraph Text/Convert to Point Text**—As discussed earlier in this chapter, there are several key differences between point type and paragraph or area type. Perhaps most important, paragraph type can automatically reflow, adjusting the placement of words on each line, if the type container is changed or if text is added or subtracted. Multiple lines of point type, in contrast, must have line breaks (returns) manually entered at the end of each line. These commands allows you to convert between the two. Which command is visible in the menu depends on the content of the active type layer.

■ **Warp Text**—Using this command is equivalent to clicking the Warp Text button in the Options Bar. Unlike the button, this command is available even when no Type tool is selected. The Warp Text dialog box and the effects of warping are discussed in the section "Warping Type" earlier in this chapter.

11

- **Update All Text Layers**—When you open a Photoshop file containing type from a prior version or from Photoshop Elements, you might get a message saying that the type layers need to be updated before they can be output as vector type. If you don't update the type layers upon opening, this command gives you another opportunity. Be aware that all type layers in the image will be converted to vector, not just the active layer.

- **Replace All Missing Fonts**—If an image is opened that contains one or more fonts that are not available to Photoshop (for example, not present on the computer), a warning will appear. Layers containing one or more missing fonts are not updated.

When a font is missing, you have the option of selecting the type layer in the Layers palette and assigning a font. If you choose to have Photoshop replace the missing font(s) using this command, the results could be less than satisfactory (see Figure 11.17).

Figure 11.17
Substituting Helvetica for Ponderosa has less-than-effective results. Manually replacing a missing font can be far preferable to using the command Replace All Missing Fonts.

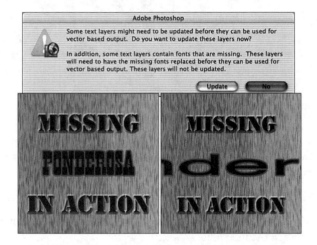

One other command deserves special attention. The menu command Layer, Rasterize, Type converts a vector type layer to pixels, and the type is rasterized at the image's resolution. This command is not available if the active layer in the Layers palette is not a type layer (identifiable by the *T* symbol in place of the layer thumbnail).

Anti-Aliasing Type

Anti-aliasing is the process of adding transitional pixels along edges to soften the appearance of curves. These pixels are added in intermediary colors between the subject and the background colors. It is used with selection tools as well as type.

Selection tools offer the option of anti-aliasing or not, but Photoshop's type engine is more sophisticated, offering several levels of anti-aliasing. Because the appearance of type is usually critical, and because different fonts and type sizes have different requirements, Photoshop's type engine offers Sharp, Crisp, Strong, Smooth, and None as anti-aliasing options.

Anti-aliasing makes curves and angled lines appear smoother by adding colored pixels along edges. Think of the transitional pixels as a mini gradient, blending from the foreground color to the background color. When you look at black type on a white background, the added pixels are shades of gray.

The number 2 has no anti-aliasing applied, but the letter S is set to Crisp. The inset is at 100%, and the image behind is at 800% zoom.

At 100% zoom, the jagged edges of the character without anti-aliasing are visible. With Crisp anti-aliasing, the curves appear smoother.

The colors used for the transitional pixels depend on the colors of the type and the background. For example, if the type is yellow (RGB 255/255/0) and placed on a background that's blue (0/0/255), the transitional pixels could be RGB 238/238/17, 187/187/68, 136/136/119, 119/119/136, 68/68/187, and 17/17/238.

The differences among the four type anti-aliasing options are subtle. Even when zoomed to 1200%, it takes a close look to see variations.

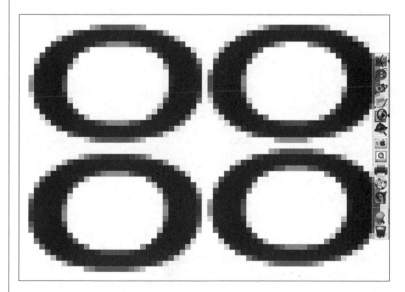

The top row shows Sharp and Crisp, and the bottom shows Strong and Smooth.

11

In this particular example, the area of greatest variation is the left edge of the letter *O*. The Strong anti-aliasing (bottom left) is substantially darker than the others. Sharp (top left) and Smooth (bottom right) are nearly identical in both placement and coloring of the transitional pixels.

Keep in mind that anti-aliasing is not always a good idea. Very small type can become quite blurry onscreen when anti-aliased. Especially when preparing images for the Web, think carefully about anti-aliasing. Using larger type, particularly the more linear sans serif fonts, such as Arial, can do far more to approve legibility and appearance than anti-aliasing. In addition, if the image is to be saved as a GIF or PNG-8 file, remember that anti-aliasing introduces several new colors to the color table, potentially increasing file size.

Remember, too, that anti-aliasing is not used when you print vector type to a PostScript printer.

The Options Bar and the Type Tools

Photoshop's improved Options Bar includes the capability to save tool presets. This is a great way to speed your work with the Type tool. If you regularly use certain fonts at certain sizes, they can be saved as presets in the Tool Presets Picker at the left end of the Options Bar (see Figure 11.18).

Figure 11.18
Select the font, size, anti-aliasing, alignment, and color, and then use the palette's menu command New Tool Preset. You'll have the opportunity to name the new configuration.

Each of the settings in the Options Bar can be changed for a preset. The values in the Character and Paragraph palettes are recorded as well. Note that the Horizontal Type tool and the Vertical Type tool have separate presets. The Tool Presets palette is available only when the Type tool is selected, but not in the act of adding type to the image. (When you're actually adding type, the preset palette's button is grayed out.)

⇨ *Presets gone haywire? Not sure why the type you add doesn't look like the type you want? See "Character Check" in the NAPP Help Desk section at the end of this chapter.*

Immediately to the right of the Tool Presets Picker button is a button that allows you to switch existing type between horizontal and vertical. The button is available when a type layer is active in the Layers palette, whether the type itself is selected in the window or not. Swapping the type orientation applies to the entire type layer; you cannot change part of a sentence from horizontal to vertical.

With a Type tool active, you can use the Options Bar to change the font, font style (when the font has multiple styles available), type size, anti-aliasing, alignment, and color. To the right, the Options Bar offers four additional buttons. Just to the right of the color swatch is a button to open the Warp Text dialog box. The only difference between using this button and the menu command Layer, Type, Warp Text is convenience. To the right of Warp Text is a button that toggles the visibility of the Character and Paragraph palettes. Again, this is comparable to using the appropriate commands in the Window menu to show and hide the palettes. Next are the Cancel Current Edits and Commit Current Edits buttons, which are visible only while a Type tool is in action. Clicking the Cancel button returns the type layer to its previous state (or cancels a new type layer), and the Commit button accepts the type entry or edit. The keyboard shortcuts for these two buttons are Escape and (Command-Return) [Ctrl+Enter].

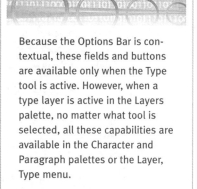

Because the Options Bar is contextual, these fields and buttons are available only when the Type tool is active. However, when a type layer is active in the Layers palette, no matter what tool is selected, all these capabilities are available in the Character and Paragraph palettes or the Layer, Type menu.

The far right end of the Options bar is occupied by the Palette Well on monitors set to resolutions higher than 800×600 pixels. At 800×600, the Palette Well is not available.

The Character Palette

You can show and hide the Character palette (see Figure 11.19) through the Window menu or a button in the Options Bar when a Type tool is active. The palette replicates many of the fields and options available in the Options Bar for Type tools. Unlike the type-related fields in the Options Bar, the Character palette is also available when a non-Type tool is active

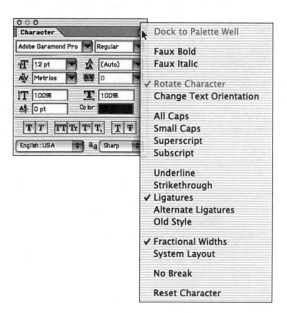

Figure 11.19
Not all menu options are available at the same time.

The Character palette can be used in several ways:

- It can be used without any active type layer to establish presets for the Type tools. This affects all type that is entered later, until additional changes are made in the Character palette or the Options Bar.

- With a type layer active in the Layers palette but no type selected in the image, changes can be made to the entire layer. These changes affect all type on the layer, but only type on that layer. The changes remain in effect in the Character palette and Options Bar.

- When some type on a type layer is selected with a Type tool, changes can be made to that portion of the type without affecting the rest of the type layer. Such changes affect only the selected type and remain in effect.

- If a Type tool is active and in use, the Character palette can be used to set the characteristics of type that has not yet been entered. All type entered from that point on has the new characteristics, but previously entered type is unaffected.

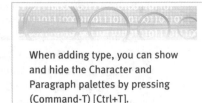

When adding type, you can show and hide the Character and Paragraph palettes by pressing (Command-T) [Ctrl+T].

In the Style field, you can jump only to styles available for that font. If you type *I* for italic and the current font doesn't offer italic, you'll hear an error tone.

There are 12 fields and eight style buttons in the Character palette. (The eight buttons are duplicated by commands in the palette's menu.) You can navigate among the fields in the Character palette with the Tab key. Tab advances you to the next field, and Shift-Tab returns to the previous one. Note that this method works even with the Font Family (name) and Font Style fields. In these fields, you can type the first letter of an entry in the pop-up list to jump to it

Font Family

The Font Family pop-up menu includes a list of all fonts available to Photoshop on your system. Font families include Helvetica, Times New Roman, Arial, and so on. All properly installed TrueType, Type 1, and OpenType fonts should appear. This menu selects only the font family.

Font Style

The Font Style pop-up menu shows the font styles and weights built into the font itself. The options can include Regular or Roman, Bold, Italic, Semibold, Condensed, Expanded, and combinations of those options, such as Semibold Italic. Some fonts, such as Stencil and Techno, are designed at a single weight and style, in which case the menu's arrow is grayed out.

You can navigate in the Font Family field by typing the first letter of a font's name or by using the arrow keys. The change is then applied to any selected type or to an active type layer. Using the arrow keys is a great way to preview fonts, but take a snapshot in the History palette first because the History palette will rapidly fill with "Set Character Style" entries.

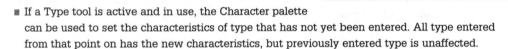

Styles and Weights

When we talk about *style* for variations in a font's appearance, we're often misusing the term. Styles include condensed, extended, italic, Roman, small caps, strikethrough, and underline. The terms bold, light, regular, and semibold are actually referring to a font's *weight*. Think of weight as the thickness of the stroke used to create the character. Consider style to be what you do to the characters: pushing and pulling, tilting and leaning, adding lines through and under.

There's no real reason to differentiate between style and weight in Photoshop, but typographers know the difference.

Font Size

The Font Size field determines how large the font will appear in the image. In addition to the preset values in the pop-up menu, you can type any size between 1/10 of a point and 1296 points. By default, Photoshop uses points as the unit of measure for font size. One point is equal to 1/72 inch. You can change the unit in Photoshop's Preferences. In addition, you can type any unit of measure directly into the field. For example, typing 28 px makes the font size 28 pixels. The other available abbreviations are in (inches), cm (centimeters), pica (picas), and pt (points). Fractional values can be entered as decimals.

For really large projects, you can work around Photoshop's font size limitation. Enter the text at 1296 points, and choose Edit, Transform, Scale. Make the type larger than you need. You can now return to the Font Size field and enter any point size up to the scaled size.

11

Character and Line Spacing

In addition to controlling the appearance of type through fonts, you can determine positioning among characters and between lines of type.

- **Leading**—Pronounced like the metal rather than the verb *to lead*, this measurement determines the distance between lines of type. Like size, it is normally set in points, but you can enter values in any unit of measure. The pop-up menu defaults to Auto, which sets the leading at 120% of the font size (although this can be changed in the Justification dialog box opened through the Paragraph palette's menu). You'll find that the values in the pop-up menu mirror those of the Font Size field. Remember that leading is based on the tallest character in a line.

  ⇨ *Changing the leading doesn't change anything? See "Adjusting Line Spacing" in the NAPP Help Desk section at the end of this chapter.*

- **Kerning**—Kerning is the space between a pair of characters. It affects only those two adjoining characters. Each font is designed with specific kerning for various pairs of characters, applied with the default setting of Metrics, but you can fine-tune the appearance of type with judicious use of kerning. Kerning is especially valuable when letters of different font size adjoin (see Figure 11.20).

Figure 11.20
The top example shows the default kerning. By manually changing the value, the overall appearance is improved.

There once was a lady from
There once was a lady from

To adjust kerning, select a Type tool and click between the letters that need adjustment. Use the pop-up menu or enter a numeric value in the Kerning field. Pressing (Return) [Enter] will commit the change. If you change your mind while still in the numeric field, you can use (Command-Z) [Ctrl+Z] to undo, or simply hit Escape to cancel.

Kerning is measured in 1/1000 em, a unit of measure based on the particular font's size. One em in a 24-point font is equal to 24 points.

Reducing the tracking can be an excellent way of squeezing type into a space that's just a little too small. Whether paragraph or point type, tightening the tracking can be far preferable to scaling or resizing the type.

- **Tracking**—Kerning sets the distance between two letters, but tracking adjusts the spacing among a group of selected letters. Tracking is measured like kerning. It can also be applied to an entire type layer by selecting the layer in the Layers palette and then making the change. When tracking is adjusted for a group of letters in a selection, the first letter doesn't move. All selected letters beyond it (by default, to the right) shift to meet the adjustment. Consider tracking to be the addition or reduction of space to the right of selected characters.

Unsure of all the typesetter's terms being tossed about? See "Typographic Terminology" in the NAPP Help Desk section at the end of this chapter.

Changing Scale, Shifting, Coloring, and Styling

Photoshop's Character palette enables you to change the vertical and horizontal scaling of one or more characters, and move a character up or down in relation to the baseline. You can also assign a specific color to a character or block of type and add style characteristics not built into the font, such as bold, italic, strikethrough, and even anti-aliasing.

- **Vertical Scale**—Because Photoshop's type is vector based, you can scale it without loss of quality. The Character palette allows you to adjust the height of selected characters from 0% (invisible) to 1000%. The font's default appearance is always 100%. You can apply vertical scaling to selected type or to an entire type layer. Keep in mind that this scaling is independent of the menu command Edit, Transform, Scale. The Character palette still shows 100% after a scale transformation.

- **Horizontal Scale**—Useful for simulating expanded or compressed font styles, horizontal scaling can be adjusted from 0% to 1000%. When used proportionally with vertical scaling, the effect is comparable to changing the font size.

■ **Baseline Shift**—The *baseline* is the imaginary line on which most letters in a font rest. (Some letters, of course, extend well below the baseline, such as *g*, *j*, *p*, *q*, and *y*; others extend slightly below the baseline, such as *e* and *o*.) Shifting a letter above the baseline creates *superscript*; shifting below the baseline produces *subscript* (see Figure 11.21).

True superscript and subscript are typically smaller than the other characters in the text. Shifting the baseline changes the position of the character(s) without changing the size.

$$H_2O$$

$$e = mc^2$$

Figure 11.21
These "2" examples show a common example of subscript and perhaps an equally familiar superscript.

Baseline shift can be adjusted by using (Option-Shift) [Alt+Shift] with the up and down arrow keys. Adding the (Command) [Ctrl] key changes the increment from 2 points to 10 points.

■ **Text Color**—The swatch in the Character palette indicates the current type color. Click it to open the Color Picker. Remember that Photoshop allows multiple colors in a single type layer, so each letter can be a different color, if desired. Use a type to select text to change, or select a type layer in the Layers palette to apply the change to the entire layer.

■ **Style Buttons**—From the left, the buttons are Faux Bold, Faux Italic, All Caps, Small Caps, Superscript, Subscript, Underline, and Strikethrough.

When the selected font offers a bold weight or an italic style, it's definitely preferable to choose it in the Font Style pop-up menu than to apply the faux style. On the flip side, using Photoshop's Superscript and Subscript buttons is usually easier than working with Baseline Shift and then scaling the character. Remember, too, that Photoshop does not allow you to warp type to which faux bold has been applied (see Figure 11.22).

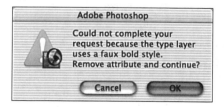

Figure 11.22
Unlike Photoshop 6, you can now remove the style and continue to the Warp Text dialog box with a single click.

- **Language**—You use this pop-up menu to select the dictionary to use for spell checking and hyphenation (paragraph type only). All available dictionaries will be listed. Photoshop allows you to mix languages on a type layer. Select a word or words with a Type tool, and then select a language in the pop-up menu.

- **Anti-Aliasing**—You have the option of applying one of four types of anti-aliasing to selected type or a type layer, or having no anti-aliasing applied. (Anti-aliasing is discussed earlier in this chapter and in the sidebar "Anti-Aliasing Type.")

Character Palette Shortcuts

A number of keyboard shortcuts, listed in Table 11.1, can be used to adjust type, even when the Character palette isn't visible.

Table 11.1   Type Shortcuts

To:	Macintosh	Windows
Increase font size by 2 pts (selected text)	Command+Shift+period	Ctrl+Shift+period
Increase font size by 10 pts (selected text)	Command+Option+ Shift+period	Ctrl+Alt+Shift+period
Decrease font size by 2 pts (selected text)	Command+Shift+comma	Ctrl+Shift+comma
Decrease font size by 10 pts (selected text)	Command+Option+ Shift+comma	Ctrl+Alt+Shift+comma
Increase leading by 2 pts (one or more lines of type selected)	Option+down arrow	Alt+down arrow
Increase leading by 10 pts (one or more lines of type selected)	Command+Option+ down arrow	Ctrl+Alt+down arrow
Decrease leading by 2 pts (one or more lines of type selected)	Option+up arrow	Alt+up arrow
Decrease leading by 10 pts (one or more lines of type selected)	Command+Option+ up arrow	Ctrl+Alt+up arrow
Increase kerning by 20 pts (insertion point between two characters)	Option+right arrow	Alt+right arrow
Increase kerning by 100 pts (insertion point between two characters)	Command+Option+ right arrow	Ctrl+Alt+right arrow
Decrease kerning by 20 pts (insertion point between two characters)	Option+left arrow	Alt+left arrow
Decrease kerning by 100 pts (insertion point between two characters)	Command+Option+ left arrow	Ctrl+Alt+left arrow
Increase tracking by 20 pts (one or more characters selected)	Option+right arrow	Alt+right arrow
Increase tracking by 100 pts (one or more characters selected)	Command+Option+ right arrow	Ctrl+Alt+right arrow

Table 11.1   Continued

To:	Macintosh	Windows
Decrease tracking by 20 pts (one or more characters selected)	Option+left arrow	Alt+left arrow
Decrease tracking by 100 pts (one or more characters selected)	Command+Option+ left arrow	Ctrl+Alt+left arrow
Increase baseline shift by 2 pts (one or more characters selected)	Shift+Option+up arrow	Shift+Alt+up arrow
Increase baseline shift by 10 pts (one or more characters selected)	Command+Shift+ Option+up arrow	Ctrl+Shift+Alt+up arrow
Decrease baseline shift by 2 pts (one or more characters selected)	Shift+Option+down arrow	Shift+Alt+down arrow
Decrease baseline shift by 10 pts (one or more characters selected)	Command+Shift+ Option+down arrow	Ctrl+Shift+Alt+down arrow

Remember that the difference between changing kerning and changing tracking is the selection. If the cursor is between two characters and there is no selection, the shortcuts adjust kerning. If one or more letters are selected, the tracking is changed. Otherwise, the keystrokes are identical.

Also keep in mind that adjusting leading might show no effect unless the entire line is selected. If part of a line has leading set to 24 and another part of the same line has leading of 48, the entire line appears as 48-point leading. Leading is applied to an entire line, but baseline shift can be applied to individual characters.

The Character Palette Menu

The Character palette's menu contains a number of commands that simply duplicate the style buttons found in the palette itself. Faux Bold, Faux Italic, All Caps, Small Caps, Superscript, Subscript, Underline, and Strikethrough show a check mark to the left when the style is applied to the selected type or type layer. To select or deselect, simply choose the style from the menu or use the palette's button.

The palette's other menu commands deserve additional attention:

When type is rotated, you bring the individual letters closer together by using tracking rather than leading. Photoshop still considers the type to be on a single line, and characters are not above and below each other; rather, they are next to each other, as with unrotated vertical type and horizontal type.

- **Dock to Palette Well**—When grayed out, as in Figure 11.19, it indicates that the monitor's resolution is too low (800×600) to support that feature of the Options Bar. Docking the Character palette to the well makes it easily accessible.

- **Rotate Character**—Rotate Character is used with vertical type. An entire type layer can be rotated, or just selected characters. Rotation determines the orientation of the individual characters, as shown in Figure 11.23.

11

Figure 11.23
With Rotate Character selected, the individual characters are aligned to the bottom of the image. When it's deselected, characters align to the type's baseline.

Vertical ROTATED Mixed Rotation

■ **Change Text Orientation**—This command swaps horizontal and vertical type. The Rotate Character command has no effect on conversion from vertical to horizontal. The command must be applied to all type on a layer; there cannot be both vertical and horizontal type on a single type layer.

■ **Ligatures, Alternate Ligatures, Old Style**—These options are available only for those fonts that have the specific capabilities built in, primarily OpenType fonts. (OpenType fonts are often identifiable by the work "Pro" in the name.) *Ligatures* are two letters combined into one charac-ter to improve the look of certain letter combinations (see Figure 11.24). Old Style refers to num-ber characters. These are lowercase numbers, used primarily with lowercase type. Many old-style numerals have ascenders and descenders, as shown in Figure 11.24.

Figure 11.24
The top two lines compare the same letter combinations without and with ligatures. The lowest line shows old-style numerals with their natural baseline. (The font is Adobe Garamond Pro.)

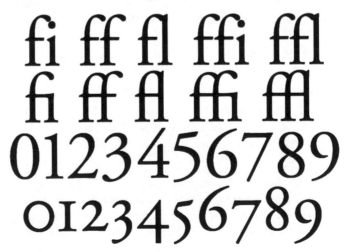

- **Fractional Widths**—When selected, Photoshop can adjust spacing between letters on an individual basis, using fractions of a pixel. Although this method often improves legibility for large type (20 points and over), it can cause problems for smaller type sizes. It is especially inappropriate for small type destined for the Web. Fractional widths can be applied only to entire type layers.

> Many non-OpenType fonts have the *fi* and *fl* ligatures built in, and you can add them with (Shift-Option-5) [Shift+Alt+5] and (Shift-Option-6) [Shift+Alt+6]. You'll find ligatures in such common fonts as Times and Geneva, but not in many others, including Arial, Helvetica, and any all-caps fonts.

- **System Layout**—Selecting this option simplifies the characteristics of the selected type layer to match as closely as possible the type of Windows Notepad or Apple's SimpleText and TextEdit. The settings include Kerning:0, Tracking:0, Vertical Scaling:100%, Horizontal Scaling:100%, Baseline Shift:0, and Anti-Aliasing:None, and it disables the Fractional Widths option. It does not change font, font size, leading, character style settings, color, or dictionary. System layout is used primarily for screen mockups and user interface elements.

- **No Break**—This option disables hyphenation in paragraph type. It can be applied on a word-by-word basis by selecting the type with a Type tool and then selecting the command from the menu. No Break can be applied to specific letter combinations to force the break to occur elsewhere in the word. It can also be applied to a group of words to force Photoshop to keep those words on the same line. It is not used with point type because all breaks are inserted manually with the (Return) [Enter] keys.

- **Reset Character**—This command returns the Character palette (and any selected type or type layer) to the default settings. You can reset selected type or an entire type layer. Either use a Type tool to highlight type on a type layer, or select the type layer in the Layers palette. The default settings are not user-definable. Figure 11.25 shows the defaults for Macintosh and Windows.

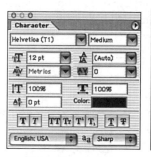 

Figure 11.25
The Mac OS X and Windows XP Character palettes are shown with their default settings.

The Paragraph Palette

Nested by default with the Character palette, the Paragraph palette can be shown and hidden by using the button in the Options Bar, the command in the Window menu, or the (Command-T) [Ctrl+T] shortcut while editing or inputting type. This palette and its menu (see Figure 11.26) govern the appearance of a body of type. Photoshop considers a "paragraph" to be any amount of text followed by a return.

Figure 11.26
The Paragraph palette is shown with its default settings.

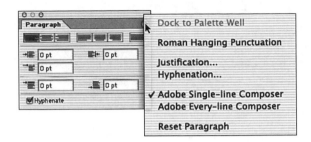

All options in the Paragraph palette can be set individually for each paragraph. The entire paragraph need not be selected; simply click with the Type tool in a paragraph to indicate that it's the target of the changes. You can highlight one or more characters from several paragraphs to select them all. If you don't click in the text, Photoshop assumes that changes made in the Paragraph palette should be applied to the entire type layer. If no type layer is active in the Layers palette, any changes made are used the next time type is added to the image.

Point type that appears on a single line without a return at the end is considered a paragraph for Photoshop's alignment options.

Across the top of the palette are seven buttons that govern alignment and justification of paragraphs. What they do to a paragraph of text is apparent from the button icons. The first three buttons are alignment, arranging the text to have an even margin on the left, have each line centered, or have an even margin on the right. In each case, the text remains within the boundaries of its rectangle. Photoshop's criteria for justifying text are set in the Justification dialog box opened through the Paragraph palette's menu. (Justification rules are discussed in the next section.)

The four remaining buttons at the top of the Paragraph palette determine justification. Justified text has even margins on both the left and right. These four options govern the last line of a paragraph. When the final line is not full—that is, it does not naturally stretch from the left to the right margin—Photoshop offers several options. The final line can be aligned left, centered, aligned right, or justified. To justify the final line, space is added between words and, if necessary, letters. Should the final line be substantially shorter than the others, the amount of whitespace added can be unsightly and interfere with legibility (see Figure 11.27).

Figure 11.27
The same text is shown with Justify Last Left and with Justify Last All. Note the difference in the final line of each paragraph.

Alignment Also called (incorrectly) "justification," this terms refers to the positioning of lines of text within a paragraph. Text can be flush left, centered, flush right, or justified (flush left and right). Illustrator allows you to choose two types of justification: All Full Lines and All Lines. The difference is the last line of a paragraph. Under the first option, the last line (if it doesn't extend from margin to margin) will be aligned left. With the second option, the word spacing will be extended to stretch the line from margin to margin. Text that is flush left, centered, or flush right is sometimes referred to as "unjustified."

Alignment Also called (incorrectly) "justification," this terms refers to the positioning of lines of text within a paragraph. Text can be flush left, centered, flush right, or justified (flush left and right). Illustrator allows you to choose two types of justification: All Full Lines and All Lines. The difference is the last line of a paragraph. Under the first option, the last line (if it doesn't extend from margin to margin) will be aligned left. With the second option, the word spacing will be extended to stretch the line from margin to margin. Text that is flush left, centered, or flush right is sometimes referred to as "unjustified."

The second section of the Paragraph palette governs indenting. Entire paragraphs can be indented to the left, to the right, or both (the upper pair of buttons), and you can specify indenting separately for the first line of a paragraph (the lower button in the middle section of the palette). By default, the unit of measure for indenting is points. That can be changed in Photoshop's preferences under Units & Rulers. The Paragraph palette uses the unit of measure specified under Type. A visual comparison of paragraph and first line indenting is shown in Figure 11.28.

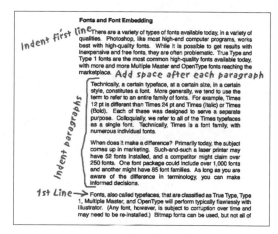

Figure 11.28
The middle paragraphs are indented both left and right.

Also visible in Figure 11.28 is paragraph spacing. Using the lower set of buttons in the Paragraph palette, you can specify spacing before a paragraph (left), or space can be added after a paragraph (right). Like indenting, the unit of measure specified for type in the Preferences is used.

At the bottom of the palette is a check box that turns hyphenation on and off in the paragraph. Like the other Paragraph palette options, hyphenation can be set on a paragraph-by-paragraph basis. Specific rules for hyphenation are set by using the Paragraph palette's menu command of the same name (discussed in the following section).

The Paragraph Palette Menu

Several commands appear in the Paragraph palette's menu. Like most palettes, the top command, Dock to Palette Well, enables you to add the palette to the Palette Well. (Remember that the Palette Well is not available unless the monitor's resolution is set to display more than 800×600 pixels.)

Roman hanging punctuation is an advanced typesetting option. With paragraph type, certain punctuation marks fall outside the margins to the left and right, creating a "cleaner" look to the margins (see Figure 11.29).

The Justification dialog box (shown in Figure 11.30) controls how Photoshop justifies paragraphs. Making changes here allows you to make tiny adjustments to how Photoshop spaces words and letters to create full justification.

Figure 11.29
Hanging punctuation allows the larger letterforms to align to the margins. This option gives the text more of a "block" look, producing the illusion of straighter margins.

"Work," he said, "is but another of life's little comforts. Without it, one would feel uneasy, rudderless.

"Yes," she replied, "yet the thought of endless vacation holds some certain attraction, does it not?"

"Never! It is outrageous to even suggest such a thing!" His hrumph could be heard throughout the room. "To think that a man in this day and age would not feel a desire—nay a need for work is beyond belief."

"Work," he said, "is but another of life's little comforts. Without it, one would feel uneasy, rudderless.

"Yes," she replied, "yet the thought of endless vacation holds some certain attraction, does it not?"

"Never! It is outrageous to even suggest such a thing!" His hrumph could be heard throughout the room. "To think that a man in this day and age would not feel a desire—nay a need for work is beyond belief."

Figure 11.30
Other than Auto Leading, these values are applied only when text is justified.

Justification	Minimum	Desired	Maximum	
Word Spacing:	80%	100%	133%	OK
Letter Spacing:	0%	0%	0%	Cancel
Glyph Scaling:	100%	100%	100%	☐ Preview
Auto Leading:	120%			

Word Spacing establishes minimum, maximum, and target amounts for space between words. The 100% represents the font's built-in spacing plus any changes you've made to tracking in the Character palette. Values can range from 0% to 133%.

Letter Spacing determines how much change Photoshop can make to spaces between letters within words. Justifying relies on letter spacing only after word spacing has been applied and only if necessary. Although percents are shown in the dialog box, the unit of measure is actually fractions of an em. Inputting 0% in all three fields turns off letter spacing.

Glyph Scaling, a method of last resort, actually changes the width of individual characters to create justification. Sacrificing the appearance of the letters for the appearance of the margins is rarely a good idea. A value of 100% represents the original width of each character.

At the bottom of the dialog box, you can specify what percentage of a font's size will be used for the Auto setting in the Character palette's Leading pop-up menu.

The Hyphenation dialog box (see Figure 11.31), opened with the Hyphenation command on the Paragraph palette's menu, controls what rules Photoshop applies when breaking words at the end of a line. Photoshop uses the assigned dictionary to determine where a word is hyphenated; these settings determine whether a word is hyphenated at all.

Figure 11.31
Remember that only paragraph type can be automatically hyphenated.

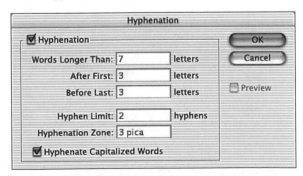

Hyphenation			
☑ Hyphenation			OK
Words Longer Than:	7	letters	Cancel
After First:	3	letters	
Before Last:	3	letters	☐ Preview
Hyphen Limit:	2	hyphens	
Hyphenation Zone:	3 pica		
☑ Hyphenate Capitalized Words			

11

You use the Hyphen Limit field to control how many consecutive lines can end with hyphens and the Hyphenation Zone field to establish a distance from the right margin in which words will not be hyphenated. For example, if the preceding word enters the designated zone, the following word is moved in its entirety to the following line. Likewise, if a word to be broken does not have a dictionary-defined break within the zone, the word remains unhyphenated.

If you deselect the Hyphenate Capitalized Words check box at the bottom of the dialog box, words that begin with a capital letter cannot be hyphenated. This includes proper nouns as well as words that start sentences. (The possibility that a word is long enough to both start a sentence and require hyphenation in Photoshop indicates very narrow columns or very long words.) This setting has no effect on type set in all caps or entered with the Caps Lock key locked down.

The difference between the Adobe Single-line Composer and the Adobe Multi-line Composer commands is the approach to hyphenation. Single-line looks at one line and decides the appropriate hyphenation, and then moves to the next line. Multi-line examines all the selected text before making decisions, which usually produces fewer word breaks and a generally more pleasing look to the text.

The Reset Paragraph command restores the Paragraph palette to its default settings.

SPELL CHECK AND FIND/REPLACE

New in Photoshop 7 are a spell checker and a find/replace tool. Spell checking has been one of the most requested features for Photoshop over the past several years.

The Spell Checker

The menu command Edit, Check Spelling opens Photoshop's Check Spelling dialog box (see Figure 11.32). Similar to spell checking systems found in many word processing programs, this tool offers suggestions and allows you to input your own changes in the dialog box. In addition, you have the choice of ignoring that particular word, ignoring all instances of that word in the image, changing that instance to a suggested spelling or a word you type in the Change To field, changing all instances to the selected new spelling, or adding the word to the dictionary.

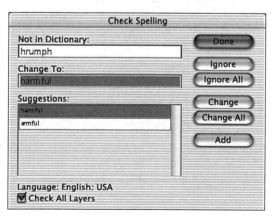

Figure 11.32
The spell checker is rather basic, but it certainly is a welcome addition for many Photoshop users.

The spell checker uses the dictionary assigned to the selected text. If more than one dictionary is assigned, it automatically switches to the appropriate dictionary on the fly. The spell checker does not check grammar.

> ⇨ *Photoshop's spell checking dictionaries are not user-editable. For a handy tip that could save hours down the road, see "Dictionary Backup" in the NAPP Help Desk section at the end of this chapter.*

Caution

Think twice about using the Add button in Photoshop's spell checker because the dictionaries are not editable. After you add a word, it's there for good. Instead, rely on the Ignore and Ignore All buttons unless the word will appear often—and you're absolutely certain the spelling is correct.

Find/Replace

The Find and Replace Text command, also located under Photoshop's Edit menu, functions much like that in a basic word processor (see Figure 11.33). Unlike MS Word, it doesn't offer search by format or style, nor can it search for special characters.

Figure 11.33
To find without replacing, simply enter the word or phrase and click Find Next. You can then click Done without making any changes.

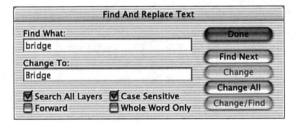

Enter the word or phrase that you want to find, and enter a replacement word or phrase. The Find Next button initiates the search. When an instance of the word or phrase is located, it is highlighted in the text. You have the option of changing that instance, changing all instances in the image, or changing and continuing the search for the next instance (Change/Find). You can also click Change All immediately after entering the target and replacement words.

You have the option of restricting the search to the active type layer or searching all type layers. You can make the search case sensitive, requiring a match in capitalization as well as spelling. When you select the Forward check box, Photoshop searches from the current Type tool insertion point to the end of the text. Selecting the Whole Word Only check box prevents Photoshop from finding matches within longer words. For example, when this option is deselected, a search for *ten* also returns such words as *often*, *intent*, *tension*, and *tents*.

FONTS AND FONT EMBEDDING

Many types of fonts are currently available in various qualities. Photoshop, like most high-end computer programs, works best with high-quality fonts. Although you can get good results with inexpensive and free fonts, they are often troublesome. TrueType and Type 1 fonts are the most common high-quality fonts available, with more and more multiple master and OpenType fonts reaching the marketplace.

Fonts (also called typefaces) classified as TrueType, Type 1, multiple master, and OpenType typically perform flawlessly with Photoshop. (Any font, however, is subject to corruption over time and might need to be reinstalled.) Bitmap fonts should not be used with Photoshop.

Although Photoshop can use multiple master fonts, it cannot take advantage of the special characteristics of these fonts. Unlike Illustrator, Photoshop has no provisions for customizing the appearance of multiple master fonts.

Fonts and Font Families

Technically, a certain typeface at a certain size in a certain style constitutes a *font*. More generally, we tend to use the term to refer to an entire family of fonts. For example, Times 12 pt is different from Times 24 pt and Times (Italic) or Times (Bold). Each was designed to serve a separate purpose. Colloquially, we refer to all the Times typefaces as a single font. Technically, Times is a font family, with numerous individual fonts.

Many fonts come in both Macintosh and Windows versions. Make sure you install the appropriate font. OpenType fonts can use the same font file on either platform.

When does terminology make a difference? Primarily, the subject comes up in marketing. Such-and-such a laser printer may have 52 fonts installed, and a competitor might claim more than 250 fonts. One font package could include more than 1,000 fonts, and another might have 85 font families. As long as you are aware of the difference in terminology, you can make informed decisions.

11

Sources of Fonts

Photoshop ships with a number of fonts, which are installed by default. In addition, other installed software likely added fonts to your computer. Free and low-cost fonts can be purchased as collections on CD or downloaded from a variety of sites on the Internet. Because Web sites come and go so fast, it's impossible to provide a current and accurate list.

Commercial Web sites that offer high-quality fonts for sale, on the other hand, are reasonably stable, and many of these sources are likely to be around for quite some time. You'll find fonts on a wide variety of Web sites. Here are some notable sites:

- **Adobe** (www.adobe.com/type)   In addition to one of the largest collections of top-quality fonts, you'll find a wealth of information about how fonts work—and how to use them effectively.

- **Agfa | Monotype** (www.agfamonotype.com)   Over 8,000 fonts are available. You'll find fonts from Adobe, ITC, and other major foundries.

- **Berthold** (www.bertholdtypes.com)   Another of the top foundries, where you'll find a large collection of fonts.

- **Letraset** (www.letraset.com)   To an entire generation, this company's name is synonymous with rub-on letters. It also has an extensive collection of digital fonts.

■ **Xerox** (www.font.net)   In addition to a wide variety of fonts, you'll find a wealth of background information.

Most of the major stock photography sites also offer fonts. Some collections are quite extensive. Specialty fonts are available at independent sites as well. A huge list of links can be found at www.microsoft.com/typography. Here are several exceptional sites:

■ **The Chank Company** (www.chank.com)   Chank Diesel's work includes custom fonts for a variety of packaging. A walk down the aisles of your local supermarket will take you past many examples. Chank.com offers a variety of fun and quirky fonts, perfect for grabbing attention.

■ **House Industries** (www.houseindustries.com)   Fun, funky, powerful fonts are available individually or in collections.

■ **Linguist's Software** (www.linguistsoftware.com)   Fonts for over 600 languages are available from this organization.

■ **ParaType** (www.paratype.com)   This site specializes in foreign language fonts. A large selection of Cyrillic, Hebrew, Greek, Arabic, Armenian, and Georgian are available. You'll also find a wide variety of more familiar Latin alphabet fonts and even some experimental fonts.

If you are inclined to create your own fonts, you can explore Macromedia's Fontographer (www.macromedia.com/software/fontographer) and FontLab (www.fontlab.com) as well as software from such companies as DTPSoft (www.dptsoftware.de) and High Logic (www.highlogic.com).

Adding and Removing Fonts

Generally speaking, if a font is properly installed on your computer (and it is a PostScript font), it will appear in Photoshop's Font menu.

Font installation in Mac OS 9 is easy: Simply drag the font files to the Fonts folder inside the System folder. This is best done with no applications running. If programs are running at the time, restart them to ensure that they can properly identify the new fonts.

Mac OS X users have fonts in three or more locations (see Figure 11.34).

Normally, fonts should be installed in the Library/Fonts folder. That makes them available to all applications and users. The Application Support/Adobe/Fonts folder holds those fonts critical for Adobe programs to run properly. If multiple individuals are using a computer but a font is licensed to only one user, install the font in the Users/<username>/Library/Fonts folder.

As in Mac OS 9, font files can be dragged and dropped into the appropriate font folder to install them. Likewise, it's a good idea to restart any programs that are running at the time of font installation.

Windows users should open the Control Panel. In Windows XP, the Control Panel is directly accessible through the Start menu. Earlier versions of Windows use the path Start/Settings/Control Panel.

Windows XP users can click on the button that switches to Classic View mode if they prefer (see Figure 11.35.)

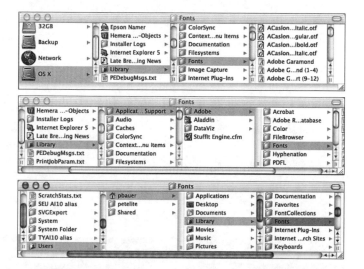

Figure 11.34
The top two windows show font locations in a pair of locations in the same Library folder. The Users folder, seen in the bottom window, is also on the startup disk.

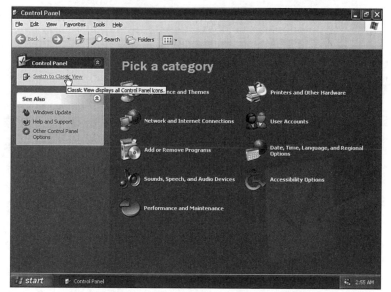

Figure 11.35
In Windows XP's default view, the Fonts icon is not visible.

11

The Fonts pane of the Windows Control panel shows all installed fonts. To add a font, use the menu command File, Install New Font (see Figure 11.36).

Figure 11.36
It's important that new fonts be installed properly, not just for Photoshop, but to ensure that Windows runs correctly.

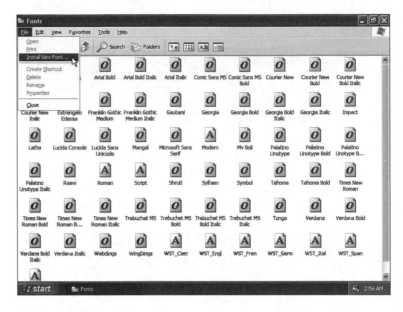

To install a new font, follow these steps:

1. In the Fonts pane of the Control Panel, navigate to the location of the new fonts.

2. Open the folder that holds the font you want to install.

3. Click the Select All button or Ctrl-click to select individual fonts from the list shown in the upper pane (see Figure 11.37).

Figure 11.37
In this instance, several varieties of an OpenType font are listed as available in the selected folder.

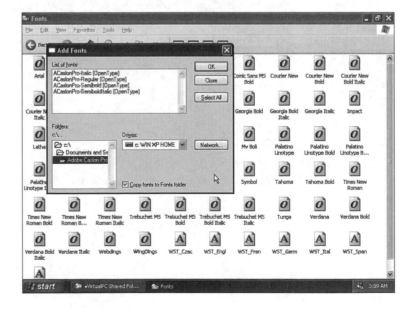

4. Select the Copy Fonts to Fonts Folder check box to leave the originals undisturbed, or deselect the check box to move the original files, deleting them from their original locations.

5. Click OK to move/copy the fonts to the Fonts folder.

6. Restart any program running during font installation to ensure that the new fonts are available to the program. It is not necessary to restart Windows.

Font Management

Too many installed fonts can slow Photoshop (and other programs) to a crawl. There are a number of font management utilities available for all platforms. Typically, a font management utility creates collections of fonts that can be activated when needed. This allows the system (and programs) to run without the overhead of hundreds of fonts that may or may not be needed during a particular work session.

Windows users and users of Mac OS 9 can opt for Adobe's Type Manager Deluxe. They can also choose Extensis Suitcase or Font Reserve from Diamondsoft, which are also available for Mac OS X.

PHOTOSHOP IN FOCUS

There are many options that need to be precisely set to make your type look "just right." After you find a combination of settings that produce what you want, you'll likely want to use them in other projects. Photoshop 7's Tool Presets can make reproducing a specific look a snap.

1. Select the Type tool from the Toolbox.

2. In the Options Bar, select a font that you typically use for large type.

3. Select options that are appropriate for large type. Font size, tracking, scaling, color, and leading are some of the choices you need to make.

4. Click on the Tool Presets palette tab or use the Window menu command Tool Presets to bring the palette forward.

5. From the Tool Presets palette menu, choose New Tool Preset or click the New Preset button at the bottom of the palette.

6. Name the new preset appropriately. The name might contain such words as *Headline* or *Large* and the font name.

7. Change all parameters necessary, including font and size, to set the Type tool for body text.

8. Save the new settings, using the Tool Presets palette menu.

9. Open the Presets Manager by using the Edit menu or the Tool Presets palette menu.

10. Shift-click on your Type tool presets. Click the Save button to create a set of type tools for future projects.

11

Remember that creating tool presets doesn't save them. Should you need to reset your Tool Presets palette, your custom tool presets are lost unless saved as a set.

FROM THE NAPP HELP DESK

The National Association of Photoshop Professionals (NAPP) offers e-mail assistance to its members. Here is some advice from the NAPP Help Desk related to issues in this chapter.

Character Check

I've established presets for my type tools using the Options Bar, but when I actually try to add type to an image by using the presets, the text is distorted. What's the problem?

It's a good idea to have the Character and Paragraph palettes open when establishing presets. The settings there are included in the preset, whether the palette is visible or not. It sounds as though the character height and width were not set to 100% when you created your presets. Every field and button in each of the two palettes is also recordable in a preset, including the spell check dictionary.

Adjusting Line Spacing

I've changed the leading for a line of type, but don't see any change. What's wrong?

Make sure you've selected the entire line of type—it's not enough to simply click in a word. If you're reducing the leading, it's also very important that you select the *entire* line of type. Just one letter at the higher leading setting forces the whole line to that value.

Typographic Terminology

Leading? Kerning? Ascenders? Descenders? Where can I learn more about all these technical terms?

The CD that came with this book includes some nifty extras. Among them you'll find a PDF document called *A Typography Primer*, which is a glossary of typographic terminology. The anatomy of type and various layout terms are explained.

Dictionary Backup

Having read that I can't go into Photoshop's spell checking dictionaries and delete words, I'm afraid to use the Add button. Any ideas?

Always an idea! Start a text document in your favorite word processor. Type in all the words that you want to add to Photoshop's dictionary. Check them carefully, and then use the Select All command and copy them. Open a document in Photoshop. Select the Type tool, drag a type container in the document, and then paste. (It doesn't matter if the text exceeds the container size.) Now run the spell checker and click the Add button to put these terms into the dictionary. (If you work in multiple languages, make sure you're adding the terms to the correct dictionary.)

Save the document for future use, just in case you need to reinstall Photoshop or replace the dictionaries. You can add to or subtract from the word processing document as much as you'd like. If you have to remove words from the dictionary, follow these steps:

1. Put the Photoshop 7 CD into your drive.

2. Start the Installer.

3. Elect to do a Custom install rather than an Easy install.

4. In the Installer, choose to reinstall only the dictionaries (see Figure 11.38).

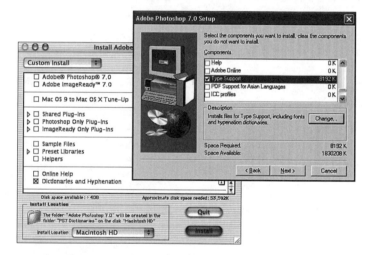

Figure 11.38
The Custom install options for Mac and Windows are shown. Note that in the Mac installer, the dictionaries are not part of Type Support.

11

5. After the dictionaries have been reinstalled, repeat the process described earlier to add your custom terms to the dictionary.

PHOTOSHOP 7'S PAINTING TOOLS AND BRUSHES

IN THIS CHAPTER

PAINTING IN PHOTOSHOP

At its heart, *painting* in Photoshop is nothing more than applying color to pixels using tools. Unlike many other Photoshop techniques that require a selection to identify where pixels will be edited, painting tools use *brushes*. Consider a brush to be sort of a moving selection. The brush defines an area within which pixels are altered. Like a selection, a brush can be round, square, or irregularly shaped, and it can be feathered or hard edged.

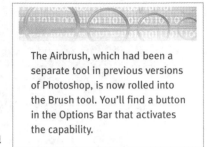

The Airbrush, which had been a separate tool in previous versions of Photoshop, is now rolled into the Brush tool. You'll find a button in the Options Bar that activates the capability.

More broadly, the term "painting" can also encompass some menu commands, including Stroke and Fill and the comparable commands in the Paths palette menu. These commands apply color to the image along selection edges or paths, using painting tools or a specific pixel width, comparable to using a brush.

There are three primary painting tools (Brush, Pencil, Eraser), a couple of painting tools that don't use brushes (Gradient, Paint Bucket), and a number of tools that use brushes but modify pixels rather than paint them. All these tools are grouped in the Toolbox (see Figure 12.1).

Figure 12.1
These tools are grouped in the Toolbox because they use brushes, are painting tools, or are related to a tool that falls into either category.

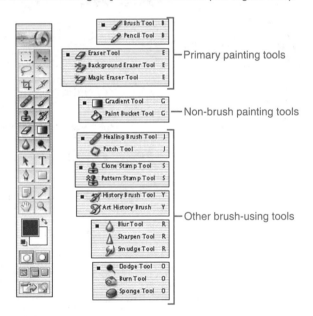

Basic Painting Terms and Concepts

Before starting a discussion of painting capabilities in Photoshop, certain terms must be clarified:

- **Airbrush**—The Airbrush is an option for the Brush tool. It enables the tool to function much like a traditional airbrush, regulating the application of color through movement of the tool.

- **Blending**—The painting tools can have assigned blending modes. The selected mode determines how color applied by the tool interacts with color already applied to that layer.

- **Brush**—The Brush tool succeeds the Paintbrush tool as Photoshop's primary painting tool. The name change reflects the incorporation of the Airbrush as a tool option.

- **Brush Tip**—Selected from and customized in the Brushes palette, the brush tip determines the area affected by the brush-using tools. (Using the Brushes palette is discussed thoroughly in "The New Brushes Palette," later in this chapter.) There are a variety of characteristics that can be modified:

  - **Angle**—Changing the angle of a non-round brush tip produces a calligraphic tool. The line you create changes shape, depending on the direction you drag the tool.

  - **Dynamics**—The dynamics settings control variations in the brush tip as the tool is used.

  - **Hardness**—The Hardness setting (0%–100%) determines the sharpness of a brush tip's edges. The higher the setting, the sharper the edge. The lower the setting, the greater the feathering of the edges. The term *soft-edged brush* is often used to describe a tool using a brush tip with a low Hardness setting. Hardness is used only with round brushes.

  - **Roundness**—Brush tips designed in the Brushes palette can be round or elliptical. Roundness (0%–100%) determines the relationship between width and height of all brush tips, not just round tips.

  - **Shape**—A brush tip can be round or elliptical when created in the Brushes palette or can be any other shape or pattern when created from artwork by using the menu command Edit, Define Brush.

  - **Spacing**—Clicking the mouse with a brush-using tool active is comparable to tapping the point of a pencil on paper. The mark created is the shape of the tip. Spacing determines how closely positioned the "marks," or *instances* of the brush tip pattern, will be when the tool is dragged rather than clicked.

- **Diameter**—Using the Brushes palette, you can scale any brush tip, round, square, or otherwise. The Diameter slider controls the size.

- **Instance or Brush Instance**—An instance is a single impression of the selected brush tip. If the selected tip is round, a circle results from a single instance. If a custom brush is selected, you get a single impression of the artwork from which you defined the brush. The brush's spacing determines the proximity of the instances when you drag the cursor in an image. When the instances are spaced at less than 100%, they overlap. When they overlap enough, the result appears to be a continuous line rather than a series of instances. (See also *spacing*.)

- **Jitter**—Variation or change. When jitter is greater than 0%, you introduce variation in the placement or appearance of the individual instances of a brush's tip.

- **Media Brushes**—Brush tips that simulate traditional painting techniques and effects include the "media brushes." Such brushes replicate the behavior of such media as charcoal, crayon, and watercolor, among others.

- **Paintbrush**—See *brush*.

12

- **Scattering**—The distribution of the individual instances of the brush tip can be controlled. Instead of aligning each mark left by the brush tip along the path of the cursor, Scattering enables you to vary them along the cursor's path.

- **Spacing**—The Spacing setting in the Brushes palette determines how closely each brush tip shape will be placed. When placed very close together, the brush appears to create a continuous line. Actually, however, dragging the cursor with a painting tool creates a series of instances of the brush tip. When the Spacing amount is high, the individual instances are visible. (See also *instance*.)

- **Texture**—Brush tips can have a specific texture built in so that they replicate the appearance of ink or paint on a specific surface.

- **Tip**—See *brush tip*.

The Primary Painting Tools

The Brush and the Pencil tools use brushes to define the area where they will affect the image. As you drag the tool in the image window, the foreground color is added to the image within the area defined by the brush, according to the opacity and blending mode specified in the Options Bar.

➡ *For specific information on selecting and defining brushes, **see** "The New Brushes Palette," **p. 326**, later in this chapter.*

Opacity and Blending for Painting Tools

The opacity of the tool is *combined with* the opacity of the layer on which you use it. Compare the contents on the two upper layers in Figure 12.2. On the left side of the image, the Brush's opacity is 50% and the layer's opacity is 50%. On the right, the Brush's opacity is again 50%, but the layer's opacity is 100%.

Many of the brushes used as samples in this chapter can be found on the CD that accompanies this book.

Unlike opacity, the blending modes of the tool and the layer are not combined. Rather, the opacity of the Brush or Pencil is applied only on that layer—the tool's blending mode affects how it interacts with colors already on the layer, and then the layer's blending mode determines how the layer interacts with those below. The exception is Dissolve, which appears to interact with lower layers, regardless of the layer's blending mode. Dissolve, however, is less a blending mode and more a dispersal pattern.

The contextual menu gives you instant access to the Brushes palette. You can also change blending modes by holding down the Shift key when you open the contextual menu. Remember, too, that Mac OS X, like Windows, can use a multibutton mouse.

➡ *For information about Photoshop's blending modes and how they affect color, **see** Chapter 17, "Using Blending Modes," **p. 477**.*

Figure 12.2
To determine the effective transparency of the Brush or Pencil tool, multiply the layer's opacity by the tool's opacity. On the left 50%×50% is 25%. On the right, 100%×50% is 50%.

The Brush Tool's Airbrush and Flow Options

The Options Bar for the Brush has, in addition to blending mode and opacity, a pair of controls. Flow is designed for use with the Airbrush option but can be used alone. The Airbrush button in the Options Bar (see Figure 12.3) replaces the standalone tool of previous versions of Photoshop. When the option is selected, the button appears darkened.

Figure 12.3
The lower Airbrush button shows you how it appears when the option is selected.

12

Flow influences how the brush applies color according to the brush's Spacing option. When you reduce flow, the brush, with or without the Airbrush option, treats each brush instance (using Spacing) as a separate application of the brush. In Figure 12.4, you can see a comparison of reduced opacity and reduced flow. In all three examples, the foreground color was black and the brush tip was set to 50% Spacing.

With 50% Spacing, the brush tip is applied at an interval of one half the brush's diameter. With Flow set to 100%, the tool applies a continuous color, with the brush tip's shape (round) visible at the specified interval. With reduced flow, however, each instance of the brush tip (using Spacing) is treated as a separate application of the tool visually (not in the History palette). The areas of overlap darken, as though the Brush tool had been applied repeatedly. The appearance is the same as though you had set the option to Flow: 100%, clicked the Brush tool, moved it slightly, clicked it again, moved it slightly, clicked, and so on.

When the Airbrush option is selected, Flow governs the density of color applied by the Brush tool. Think of it as how quickly "paint" is applied. Figure 12.5 shows basic airbrush application.

Figure 12.4
The Brush was applied along three identical paths. At the top, the tool was set to 100% Opacity and 100% Flow. In the middle, the Opacity was reduced to 50%, with Flow at 100%. At the bottom, the Opacity was 100% and Flow was reduced to 50%.

Figure 12.5
Where you drag the Airbrush slowly, more color is applied. Where you pause the tool while dragging, color builds up.

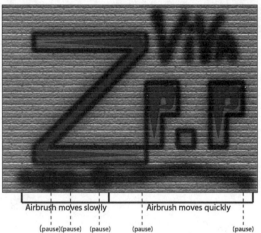

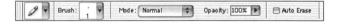

The Pencil Tool and Auto Erase

The Pencil tool is designed to be used with hard-edged brush tips but can be used with any brush. The Pencil doesn't offer the Airbrush or Flow options but does have Auto Erase (see Figure 12.6).

Figure 12.6
The term Auto Erase is slightly deceptive. Instead of erasing, the option enables you to replace the foreground color with the background color.

With the Auto Erase option selected, if the center of the Pencil's cursor is over the foreground color when you drag, the tool uses the background color. If the cursor is over any color other than the foreground color, it applies the foreground color. If you click with the tool on an area of the foreground color and begin dragging, the background color is applied wherever you drag, not just over the existing foreground color.

The Art History Brush: Painting or Not?

Although it uses brushes and applies color, the Art History Brush can't quite be put into the same category as the Brush and Pencil tools. Like the History Brush, it uses data from a specified history state to modify the image. However, the History Brush re-creates the data, and the Art History Brush uses it in combination with various options to stylize the image (see Figure 12.7).

Figure 12.7
The original is shown in the background. The Open state (the original) is used here as the source history state.

The Art History Brush cannot use Scattering, Dual Brush, Airbrush, or Smoothing, but the Color Dynamics option is available.

➡ *For more information on the History Brush,* **see** *"Working with History," **p. 660** in Chapter 21, "Retouching and Restoration Basics."*

The Non-Brush Painting Tools

Photoshop includes two other tools that can be considered "painting" tools: the Paint Bucket and the Gradient tools. Both tools add color to the image, but do so in ways that don't use brushes.

The Paint Bucket

The Paint Bucket applies the foreground color or a pattern to the image. By default, it fills all contiguous pixels of the clicked color with the foreground color. The Options Bar enables you to select a pattern for the fill, deselect the Contiguous option, and choose a blending mode and opacity for the tool. In addition, you can set the Tolerance field to specify how closely colors must match to be filled with the Paint Bucket.

You might find the effect of the Art History Brush to be more controllable at high resolution. Using the Image, Image Size command to triple the pixel dimensions and then downsampling can be effective. Remember, too, that you can copy a selection of the image to a new document, work with the Art History Brush, and then paste back into the original.

To constrain the Paint Bucket to a certain part of an image, you can make a selection first, enclosing the areas of color you want to change.

12

The Paint Bucket can be anti-aliased, and you can elect to fill target color on all layers or just the active layer.

The Anatomy of a Gradient

Gradients are areas of multiple colors that smoothly blend from one color to the next. No matter how many colors are assigned to the gradient, only adjacent colors will blend (see Figure 12.8).

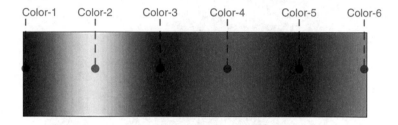

Figure 12.8
Color-1 blends to Color-2, but not past. In no case does a color blend through an adjacent color to the color beyond.

The structure of a gradient is defined in the Gradient Editor. To open the dialog box, select the Gradient tool in the Toolbox, and click on the sample of the gradient in the Options Bar (see Figure 12.9).

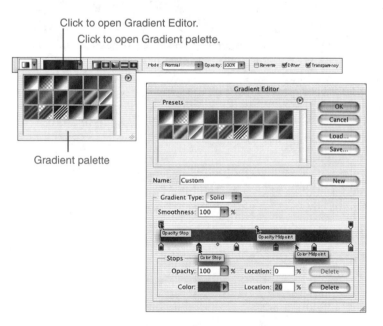

Figure 12.9
Click on the arrow to the right in the Options Bar to open the Gradient palette; click on the gradient itself to open the Gradient Editor.

Although the Gradient Editor might appear to be complicated, it's actually reasonably simple. The upper portion shows all the gradients currently available in the Gradient palette. You can click on any to use it as the basis for your custom gradient. Note that to the left of the OK button there's a little triangle. It gives you access to the Gradient palette menu, including the sets of gradients that you can load into the palette. You will not see, however, the Load, Save, Replace, Delete, and New commands. (Load, Save, and New are represented by buttons in the Gradient Editor.)

Here are the options available to you as you edit gradients:

- **Load and Save**—Sets of gradients can be saved and loaded into the Gradient Editor and Gradient palette. Photoshop 7, by default, installs several sets of gradients in the Presets folder in your Photoshop 7 folder.

- **Gradient Type**—You can create the familiar Solid gradients, which are bands of color that blend into each other, or you can create Noise gradients. A Noise gradient uses a randomly generated series of colors within parameters you set. (See "Noise Gradients" later in this chapter for more information.)

- **Smoothness**—Smoothness, which ranges from 0%–100%, governs the abruptness of the transition between colors in the gradient. The lower the number, the sharper the transition. At the highest settings, the transition is gradual. The Smoothness setting is universal for the gradient—you can't specify different smoothness values for different parts of the gradient. You can, however, create a sharper transition by using two color stops of the same color next to each other on either end of the transition. Positioning the middle two stops close together creates a sharper transition.

- **Opacity Stop**—Opacity stops regulate the transparency for a particular section of the gradient. To add a stop, click above the sample gradient. To duplicate an existing stop, hold down the (Option) [Alt] key and drag the stop to the new location. When a stop is selected, the little triangle of the slider is filled. Unselected stops have hollow triangles. At the bottom of the Gradient Editor, you can input numeric values for a selected stop's opacity and location. The arrow to the right of the Opacity field opens a slider. The Location field represents the distance from the left end of the gradient in percents. You can remove an opacity stop by dragging it straight up or down away from the gradient sample.

- **Opacity Midpoint**—The opacity midpoint represents the point between two opacity stops where their influence is balanced. By default, the midpoint is at the 50% point, halfway between the two stops. You can, however, drag the stop to a new location or click it to make it active (the diamond is filled for the active midpoint) and specify a numeric value for the position in the Location field.

- **Color Stop**—Color stops are the heart of the Gradient Editor. You use them to assign colors to the gradient and to determine where the blends occur (via the Location field or by dragging the color stop). Like an opacity stop, you click on a color stop to make it active, and also like opacity stops, the stop's triangle becomes black when selected. You click on the color swatch to open the Color Picker. Alternatively, you can assign the foreground color or the background color by using the triangle to the right of the Color field. When Foreground or Background is selected from the menu, the gradient automatically assumes the appropriate color from the Color palette when selected. You can also designate the color as User Color from the menu, in which case the color remains static, regardless of the current foreground and background colors.

- **Color Midpoint**—Like an opacity midpoint, the diamonds between color stops determine where the blending is balanced. You can skew a blend toward one or the other color stop, or you can accept the default value of 50%, which balances the blend between the two stops.

12

⇨ *Unsure about how the Foreground and Background designations affect gradients? See "Auto Gradients" in the NAPP Help Desk section at the end of this chapter.*

Working With Gradients

Gradients can be applied to selections or the active layer. The Gradient tool has five variations, which you can select through the Options Bar (see Figure 12.10). They differ in the pattern used to apply the selected gradient.

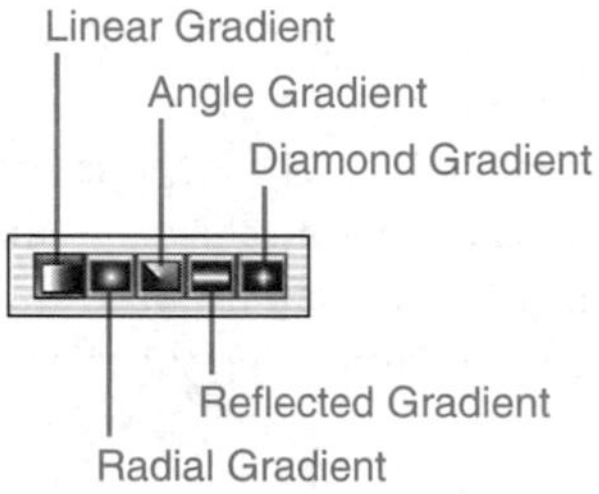

Figure 12.10
The five gradient variations all apply the selected gradient; they just apply it in different directions.

Linear Gradient
Angle Gradient
Diamond Gradient
Reflected Gradient
Radial Gradient

The appearance of the gradient depends both on which tool is selected in the Options Bar and on how you drag the tool through the selection or layer. Here are the basic capabilities of the five gradient tools:

■ **Linear Gradient tool**—When you drag a linear gradient, the colors are distributed perpendicularly to the line of drag (see Figure 12.11, top left). The distribution of color starts where the drag begins and ends where the button is released (or stylus lifted). Any selected areas outside the drag are filled with the first and last colors of the gradient (or transparency, if built into the gradient). Everything before the drag is the first color; everything after is the last color. The Linear Gradient tool is typically dragged all the way across a selection.

■ **Radial Gradient tool**—The colors in the gradient form concentric circles from the start to the end of the drag (Figure 12.11, top center). Any areas beyond the drag are filled with the last color. Remember that transparency in the gradient and selections can limit the outer fill. The Radial Gradient tool is typically dragged from the center (or somewhat off center) of a selection to the edge.

■ **Angle Gradient tool**—The Angle Gradient tool "wraps" the gradient around the line of drag (Figure 12.11, top right). Consider the line of drag to be the minute hand of a clock. The gradient is applied clockwise, centering on the point where you started the drag. Like the Radial Gradient tool, the Angle Gradient tool is typically dragged from the center to the edge of a selection.

■ **Reflected Gradient tool**—The Reflected Gradient tool produces the same gradient extending outward from either side of the line of drag (Figure 12.11, bottom center). Think of the start of the drag as the point from which the reflection will begin and the length and direction of drag as the extent of the gradient. For that reason, the Reflected Gradient tool is typically dragged from the center of a selection outward.

■ **Diamond Gradient tool**—The Diamond Gradient tool is somewhat of a cross between the Reflected Gradient and Angle Gradient tools (Figure 12.11, bottom right). Multiple copies of the gradient are produced (like the Reflected Gradient tool), but they rotate around the line of drag (like the Angle Gradient tool). Regardless of the shape of the selection, the Diamond Gradient tool always produces gradients along straight lines. Note that in the sample image, if the tool had been dragged to a side of the selection rather than a corner, the pattern would be a diamond rather than a square—picture the gradient rotated 90° with the square selection remaining oriented to the page.

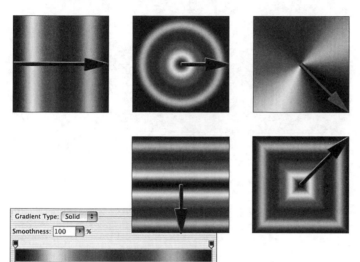

Figure 12.11
The arrows show the start and direction of drag. The sample gradient is shown in the lower-left corner.

The Options Bar offers three additional gradient tool options. Reverse simply switches the order of the colors in the gradient. (You can simply drag the Linear Gradient tool in the opposite direction, but the same trick doesn't work with the other four tools.) Dither helps reduce banding in very large gradients and for gradients in images that will be changed to Indexed Color mode. The Transparency option works with opacity stops in the gradient. If the gradient is designed with reduced opacity at one or more places, this check box must be selected to accurately apply the gradient. If the option is not selected, transparency in the gradient is ignored, and the adjacent colors are used at 100% opacity.

Shading with Gradients

Gradients, especially those using black, white, and shades of gray, can be very valuable for simulating depth and 3D. Figure 12.12 shows three examples.

Compare the two sets of circles. When all the circles are selected (left), the gradient is spread throughout the selection—the circles are shaded as a group. The second set of circles appears to be a group of individual objects because the gradient was applied individually to each.

Figure 12.12
The circles in the upper left were all selected at the time the gradient was applied. The circles to the right have gradients applied individually. Below, gradients are used with drop shadows.

Noise Gradients

Instead of blending between pairs of colors, noise gradients are patterns of color, randomly selected within parameters you specify. When you select Noise for the Gradient Editor's Gradient Type, the dialog box changes (see Figure 12.13).

Figure 12.13
Several noise gradient examples are visible, including the background.

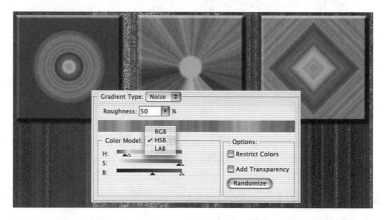

Use the Roughness slider to specify the spread of the individual colors within the noise gradient (0%–100%). High settings result in definite, identifiable stripes of color, and very low settings can smooth the gradient to the point where the noise isn't apparent (see Figure 12.14).

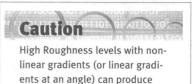

Caution

High Roughness levels with non-linear gradients (or linear gradients at an angle) can produce severe pixelation.

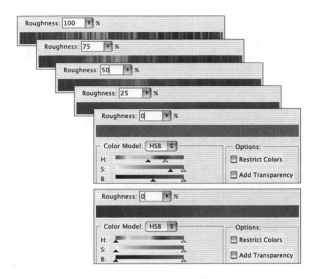

Figure 12.14
The only difference among the upper gradients is the Roughness setting. The lowest gradient shows a Roughness of 0% with a broader range of colors.

Use the Color Model pop-up menu to determine how you define the color range for the noise gradient. HSB and Lab are more appropriate for gradients that concentrate the colors within a specific range. RGB is better for noise gradients with a large variety of colors. If you switch color models, the sliders remain in position—they do not shift to select comparable values because the color models do not have comparable sliders.

The Restrict Colors option prevents oversaturation of colors, which keeps most colors within the CMYK gamut. The Add Transparency option introduces variable opacity to the gradient. When you click the Randomize button, the gradient is regenerated with the specified settings—if you don't see a gradient you like, keep clicking Randomize until the sample shows a gradient that is close your needs. You can fine-tune by dragging the sliders after Randomize has created a gradient.

To create a grayscale noise gradient, use HSB color mode and drag both triangles for the S slider all the way to the left—no saturation produces gray.

Remember that the New button adds your noise gradient to the palette, just as with any other gradient, making it available for future use.

Other Brush-Using Tools

A variety of other tools in Photoshop also use brushes. The basic concepts of brushes remain the same, but some of the brush options do not apply. The specific options are discussed later in this chapter and the various tools elsewhere in the book. Here is a summary of which brush options are available for the various brush-using tools:

- **Healing Brush**—Only the Brush Tip Shape options can be modified for the Healing Brush. Access the options through the Options Bar rather than the Brushes palette.

- **Clone Stamp and Pattern Stamp**—All brush options except Color Dynamics and Smoothing are available for both of these tools.

- **History Brush**—All brush options except Color Dynamics are available for the History Brush.

- **Eraser tools**—The Eraser cannot use Color Dynamics or Wet Edges. The Background Eraser uses only Brush Tip Shape variables and accesses them through the Options Bar rather than the Brushes palette. (The Magic Eraser is not a brush-using tool; rather, it relies on a Tolerance setting, as the Magic Wand does.)

- **Focus tools**—The Blur and Sharpen tools can be adjusted for Brush Tip Shape, Shape Dynamics, Scattering, Strength Jitter (Other Dynamics), and Noise. The Smudge tool uses Brush Tip Shape, Shape Dynamics, and Strength Jitter.

- **Toning tools**—The Dodge, Burn, and Sponge tools are adjustable for all brush options except Color Dynamics and Opacity Jitter (Other Dynamics).

In place of Flow Jitter (Other Dynamics), you will see Strength Jitter and Exposure Jitter for tools whose options are so named.

Painting Tools in ImageReady

ImageReady 7 doesn't use the sophisticated painting engine found in Photoshop 7. Rather, its painting tools function like Photoshop 6, using a simplified Brushes palette and, in some cases, fewer tool options. The Brushes palette menu includes the Load Brushes command, but only sets of brushes compatible with the simplified painting engine can be loaded. If you see the error message in Figure 12.15 when trying to load brushes, the set contains one or more brushes that are more complex than ImageReady can handle.

Figure 12.15
The brushes at the bottom of the Brushes palette menu can be loaded, but no sets defined in Photoshop 7 can be loaded.

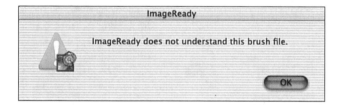

Figure 12.16 shows which brush-related tools are available in ImageReady, along with the Brushes palette.

Here's a list of the major options (in addition to brush size and hardness) for ImageReady's painting and other brush tools:

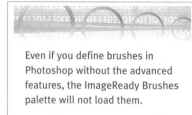

Even if you define brushes in Photoshop without the advanced features, the ImageReady Brushes palette will not load them.

- **Paintbrush**—Blending mode, opacity. Airbrush: blending mode, flow. Pencil: blending mode, opacity, auto erase.

- **Eraser**—Mode (Paintbrush, Airbrush, Pencil, Block), opacity. Magic Eraser: not a brush-using tool.

- **Clone Stamp**—Blending mode, opacity, alignment, Use All Layers.

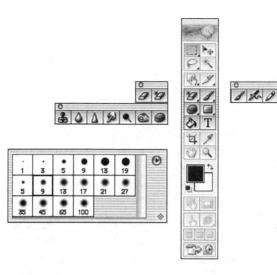

Figure 12.16
The Brushes palette menu enables you load various sets of brushes.

The Paint Commands

Two menu commands and two palette commands serve as "painting commands." In the Edit menu, you'll find both Fill and Stroke. The Stroke command is available only when there's an active selection in the image. Each command opens a dialog box, shown in Figure 12.17.

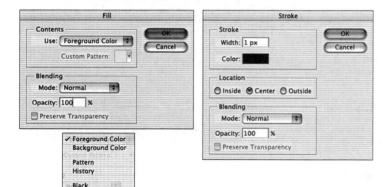

Figure 12.17
The menu below the Fill dialog box shows the basic choices for the Use option.

Both the Edit, Fill and Edit, Stroke commands respect anti-aliasing and feathering of the selection. With the Stroke command, feathering overrides the specified stroke width. If, for example, you stroke a heavily feathered selection with a 1-pixel width, the resulting stroke fades gradually over a distance of several dozen pixels.

Similar to the commands under Edit, the Paths palette menu has its own Stroke and Fill commands. These commands are available only with an active path in the Paths palette. They can be used with work paths or saved paths and vector clipping masks, but they are not available for shape layer vector masks. In Figure 12.18, you'll see two major differences between filling/stroking selections and filling/stroking paths.

Figure 12.18
Filling and stroking paths rather than selections offers additional control.

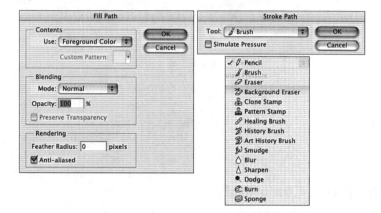

When filling a path, the Contents and Blending options are the same as when filling a selection. However, filling a path also enables you to specify anti-aliasing and/or feathering for the fill. This is comparable to converting the path to a selection, feathering the selection, and then filling.

When stroking a path, instead of specifying a width and location in relationship to a selection border, you choose a tool. The command then uses the brush, blending mode, and opacity currently selected for that tool.

THE NEW BRUSHES PALETTE

At the heart of Photoshop's painting capabilities is a new painting engine. The difference is most visible in the Brushes palette. This palette is the doorway to an exciting new level of creativity in Photoshop. Understanding how the palette works—and what it offers—is the key to that doorway.

The buttons at the bottom of the Paths palette enable you to convert selections to paths and paths to selections.

Set up a brush-using tool before using the Paths palette menu command Stroke Path. Also, remember that the focus, toning, stamp, and history tools, as well as the new Healing Brush, can be applied along a stroke.

The Palette Layout

Like the Layer Style dialog box, the Brushes palette's Expanded View mode uses a two-column configuration (Figure 12.19).

Like the Layer Style dialog box, you click on a heading in the left column to show its options in the right column. (A preview is shown at the bottom.) Also like the Layer Style dialog box, you can click a check box on the left to activate the option with the current settings. To see the settings, however, you must click on the name.

Perhaps the most impressive feature of the new painting engine is the capability to scale any brush—round, square, or custom—by using a slider. Remember, however, that scaling custom brushes far below the size at which they were defined can seriously degrade their appearance.

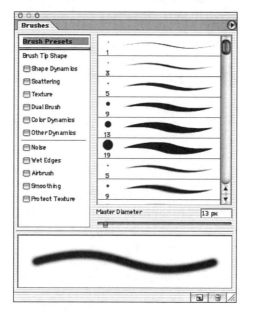

Figure 12.19
Use the palette's menu to select and deselect the Expanded View. When Expanded View is not selected, only the brush thumbnails or names are visible.

The Brushes Palette Menu

To access the Brushes palette menu when the palette is docked in the Palette Well, click on the arrow in the Brushes tab. When the palette is free-floating in a window, click the triangle in the upper-right corner of the palette. The only difference in the menu between the configurations is the Dock to Palette Well command, which is logically not available when the palette is already docked (see Figure 12.20).

If the Brushes palette content is grayed out and unavailable, select a brush-using tool from the Toolbox. You can also use keyboard shortcuts to activate a tool, such as B for the Brush tool.

12

Figure 12.20
The list of brush sets at the bottom of the menu contains all the sets available in the Presets, Brushes folder in the Photoshop 7 folder.

Although most of the menu commands are straightforward, a few require additional clarification.

Expanded View

The default Expanded View mode for the Brushes palette, seen earlier in this section, enables you to customize brushes using all the brush options. If you have already created all the brushes you'll need and selected their options, you can simplify the palette by deselecting this option from the menu.

When Expanded View is not selected, the Brushes palette reverts to a simplified version, similar to that in ImageReady 7, in any of the six configurations listed in the menu (see Figure 12.21).

Figure 12.21
From left to right, top to bottom, the configurations are Text Only, Small Thumbnail, Large Thumbnail, Small List, Large List, and Stroke Thumbnail.

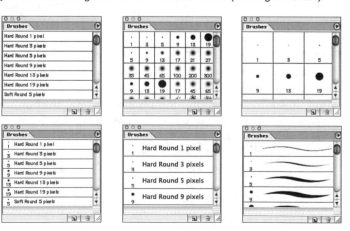

You select a preset brush by clicking on it. Double-clicking enables you to change the brush's name. The content of the palette can be changed by using the palette's menu, but in the simplified view, the brushes themselves cannot be edited.

The six configurations shown in Figure 12.21 are the same six available in the Expanded View mode for the right column of the Brushes palette.

Clear Brush Controls

The Clear Brush Controls command deselects all the user-definable settings for the selected brush. The brush reverts to the basic brush tip shape, using the Angle, Roundness, Hardness, and Spacing settings with which it was originally defined. (See "Brush Settings, Pane by Pane," later in this chapter, for specific information about each of the options.)

Clearing the controls does not permanently change the brush, but you can clear the controls and then use the New Brush command to save the changes.

⇨ *Cleared a brush's controls and can't reset them? See "Restoring Cleared Brush Controls" in the NAPP Help Desk section at the end of this chapter.*

Copy Texture to Other Tools

When you painstakingly prepare a texture for a specific brush, you can use the New Brush command to save your work. However, if you quickly whip up a texture for a little touch-up to an image, you might want to simply use the Copy Texture to Other Tools command to make that texture available for the editing job at hand. For example, if you match the grain of an image for the Burn tool, instead of going through the process again for the Dodge tool, you can use this command. The tools to which the texture will be matched are Brush, Pencil, Eraser, Clone Stamp, Pattern Stamp, History Brush, Art History Brush, Dodge, Burn, and Sponge.

Copying a custom texture doesn't *apply* it to the other tools; rather, it makes it available to the tools. If you change tools, you might still need to open the Brushes palette and select the Texture check box to activate your custom texture.

Preset Manager

This command opens the Preset Manager, which enables you to customize the content of the Brushes palette. You can also open the Preset Manager through the Edit menu. Customizing the Brushes palette can streamline the search for the appropriate brush. Remember, too, that you can save sets of brushes that can be loaded through the Brushes palette menu or selected as the default in the Preset Manager.

12

BRUSH SETTINGS, PANE BY PANE

In the Expanded View, the new Brushes palette contains eight different panes or windows, and an additional five options that have no variables. Each pane is selected in the left frame or column of the palette, and the variables appear on the right. At the bottom of the palette is a preview that updates automatically as you change settings. Remember that you can click on a check box to activate or deactivate a set of options, or you can click directly on the name to open the options pane (see Figure 12.22).

Click the box to activate/deactivate the options.

Figure 12.22
The five lowest entries in the left column do not have separate panes because they have no variables to change. Clicking the name or the check box activates/deactivates the option.

Click the name to open the options pane.

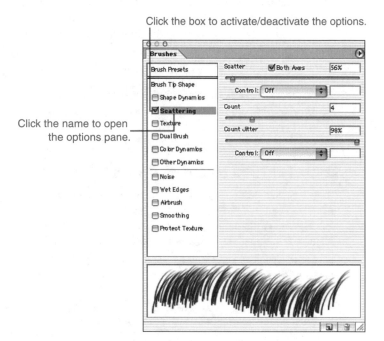

⇨ *Can't find the Brushes palette options? See "Expanding the Brushes Palette" in the NAPP Help Desk section at the end of this chapter.*

Brush Presets

At the top of the left column in the Brushes palette is the Brush Presets option. Click on the name to open the current palette contents in the right column (see Figure 12.23). (Note that there is no check box for Brush Presets—this is not an option, but a pane in which you select from the available brushes.)

To change the content of the Brush Presets, use the following palette menu commands:

- **Reset Brushes**—Restores the default set as specified in Preset Manager.

- **Load Brushes**—Adds to or replaces the content of the palette.

- **Save Brushes**—Creates a set that can be loaded at another time.

- **Replace Brushes**—Deletes the current content and adds a different set of brushes.

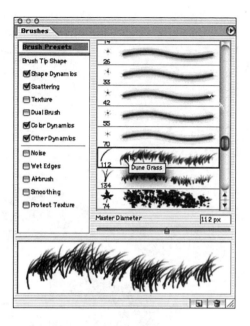

Figure 12.23
The preview window does not show the brush to scale beyond 48 pixels in diameter.

The Brush Presets pane is the only one in which these menu commands are active. You can delete and rename individual brushes by using the palette menu.

After you have selected a brush, you can adjust its size by using the Master Diameter slider in the Brush Presets pane. You can also move to other panes of the Brushes palette to modify the brush's appearance and behavior.

Brush Tip Shape

The Brush Tip Shape pane includes thumbnails of the brushes currently loaded in the palette (which can make the Brush Presets pane unnecessary when working with brushes that are already loaded). Click on a thumbnail to select the brush. You can then modify the diameter, angle, roundness, hardness, and spacing values by entering numeric values or, for three options, using sliders. As you can see to the right in Figure 12.24, you can also modify the roundness (top) and angle (middle) by dragging in the preview.

When a custom or square brush is selected, the Use Sample Size button is visible (Figure 12.24, bottom right). When not grayed out, you can click it to reset the brush to the size at which it was designed.

The Spacing variable determines the distance between instances of the brush tip. Rather than a continuous flow of ink from a pen, think of Photoshop's brushes as a series of imprints of the brush tip (see Figure 12.25).

When experimenting with the various brush capabilities, it's easiest to see what each does when you disable all the others. For example, when determining optimal spacing for a brush tip, uncheck the dynamics options in the Brushes palette.

Figure 12.24
The Hardness slider determines feathering for the brush tip. It is available only for round brushes.

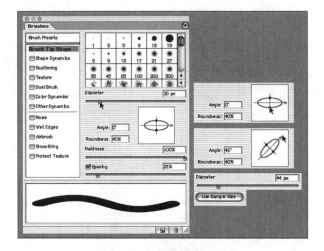

Figure 12.25
Instead of a continuous stream of ink, think of the brush as a stamp or pattern wheel.

When the brush tip instances are very closely spaced, they overlap and you see what appears to be a continuous line of color. When spacing is increased, you see the individual instances (see Figure 12.26).

When the Spacing option is turned off in the Brush Tip Shape pane of the Brushes palette, the spacing is governed by the speed of your drag. The faster you drag, the greater the spacing (see Figure 12.27).

You can create dashed lines in Photoshop. Select a square brush of the appropriate size, reduce the Roundness setting to 10%–25%, and increase the Spacing variable to 110%–200%. Shift-drag (or click and Shift-click) to create straight dashed lines.

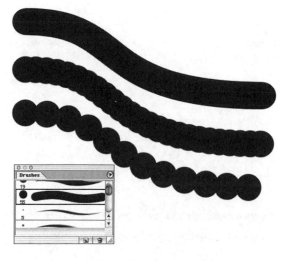

Figure 12.26
From the top, three identical paths are stroked with a 55-pixel hard round brush with spacing of 1%, 40%, and 83%.

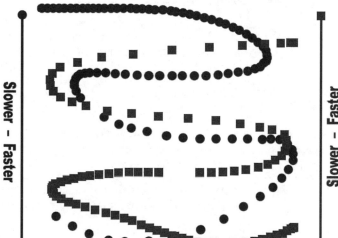

Figure 12.27
As indicated, the mouse was dragged at increasing speed through the curves.

Controlling the Dynamic Options

Before discussing the additional Brushes palette panes, an explanation of the Control pop-up menus is appropriate. Many of the options explained in the following sections are "dynamic" options—they produce variations in the brush as the brush is used. The variety of brush instances adds a randomness to the stroke that would be time-consuming to create manually. You can use the Fade option to taper off the effect on the brush. Photoshop 7 enables you to exercise even more control over the "randomness" of the variations when you use a drawing tablet.

Off

When Control is set to Off, Photoshop applies the selected jitter randomly and throughout the length of the brush stroke. The stroke is unregulated.

Fade

Fade is available with or without a pressure-sensitive tablet. When Fade is selected, the field immediately to the right of the Control pop-up menu is active. You specify a value between 1 and 9999. If you set a jitter slider to 0% and specify a value, the Fade command specifies either the value to which the stroke fades or when the specific jitter ends along the stroke. Figure 12.28 shows the difference.

Figure 12.28
All three examples use the same brush, with Fade set to 25. Only one jitter option is active for each sample.

The only difference among the three strokes shown in Figure 12.28 is one jitter setting. The brush uses the same tip and a Spacing of 100% to best illustrate the differences in the effects of the Fade setting.

- The top sample shows Size Jitter set to 25%, with a minimum diameter of 50%. Note that the Fade option forces the brush tip size to the 50% diameter after 25 instances of the brush.

- The middle sample shows a stroke with the Angle Jitter set to 0% and Control set to Fade, 25. The brush tip "angles" 360° over the first 25 instances. After completing the selected jitter, the stroke returns to its original appearance for the 26th instance and beyond.

- The bottom stroke has Roundness Jitter set to 0%, Fade at 25 as the Control, and a Minimum Roundness setting of 20%. Like the top example, the stroke reaches the desired Roundness (20%) after 25 instances.

For the first and third examples, the Fade field's value represents the number of instances the stroke uses to reach the value specified for the jitter. In the middle example, the stroke uses the number entered in the Fade field as the extent or duration of the jitter.

The best way to learn how each option works is to isolate it. Deselect all but one brush option, and set that option's jitter slider to 0% and the Control pop-up menu to Fade. Now drag the brush around a blank layer and see how it works. Remember, too, that the Spacing setting plays a large role in any brush's appearance.

Pen Pressure

The Pen Pressure option is used with a pressure-sensitive tablet, such as those from Wacom. Increasing the pressure of the stylus on the tablet *decreases* the amount of jitter—the greater the pen's push, the less variation in the stroke. Figure 12.29 shows examples of Size, Angle, and Roundness Jitter with Pen Pressure activated.

Figure 12.29
In all three examples, the pen pressure is light on the ends and heavy in the middle.

Pen Tilt

Pen Tilt reads the angle rather than the pressure of the stylus on the tablet to adjust the jitter. It is especially useful for airbrush artists using the Brush tool with the Airbrush option.

Stylus Wheel

Some tablet accessories, such as Wacom's Intuous and Intuous2 Airbrushes, include a fingerwheel. When available, the wheel can be used to regulate the amount of variation when Stylus Wheel is selected in the Control pop-up menu.

Initial Direction

Available for the Angle Jitter option only, the Initial Direction option determines the orientation of the brush instances as you drag. In Figure 12.30, the settings are identical for both samples. The Angle Jitter is set to 25%, constraining the brush angles to –90° to +90°. The top sample, created from left to right, varies the angle in relation to the top of the page. The lower sample, dragged from right to left, reverses the orientation.

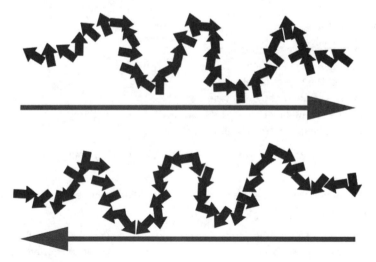

Figure 12.30
The 25% setting for Angle Jitter restricts the brush tip angle to one quarter of a circle (90°) in either direction from the original brush orientation.

12

Direction

Also available for the Angle Jitter option only, the Direction option orients the brush tip to the path rather than to the page. In Figure 12.31, the Angle Jitter is set to 0% to best show the orientation of the brush to the paths.

Figure 12.31
The initial direction of drag when using Direction determines which way the brush tip instances are pointed. The two examples to the right illustrate the difference.

Shape Dynamics

The Shape Dynamics pane of the Brushes palette, shown in Figure 12.32, controls three aspects of the stroke appearance: size, rotation, and perspective. The variations for each parameter are specified with sliders.

These are the Shape Dynamics settings:

Using an Angle Jitter of 0% and Control set to Direction keeps the brush tip oriented to the path. This is a great way to use custom brushes to draw borders, dividing lines, even railroad tracks and roads.

- **Size Jitter**—This slider determines the variation in the individual incidents of the brush's tip. At the maximum of 100% variation, instances of the brush tip can be as small as 10% or smaller of the diameter set. In no case will Size Jitter create instances of the brush tip larger than the Diameter selected in Brush Tip Shape or the Master Diameter selected in Brush Presets.

- **Minimum Diameter**—You can constrain the size of the smallest instances by using the Minimum Diameter slider.

- **Tilt Scale**—When the Control pop-up menu is set to Pen Tilt, this slider regulates how much the angle of the stylus affects the brush stroke.

- **Angle Jitter**—With non-round brush tips, the angle of application can be varied. The Angle Jitter setting determines the degree of variation. At a setting of 25%, the brush tip's orientation varies from −90° to +90° Remember that, by default, the angle is relative to orientation of the page rather than the path of the stroke—even if you drag a circular stroke, the variation in angle remains relative to the top of the image. Orient the brush tip to the path by changing the Control pop-up menu under Angle Jitter to Direction. (You don't need to change the Angle Jitter from 0%.)

- **Roundness Jitter**—The Roundness slider controls variation in the proportion of a brush tip. When set to 0%, each instance of the brush has the same width-to-height relationship. As you increase Roundness Jitter, you add variation. At 100% jitter, the height of the brush instances varies between approximately 5% and 100% of the size specified in the Brushes palette. Roundness never increases the height beyond that selected with the Diameter or Master Diameter sliders.

- **Minimum Roundness**—You can constrain the Roundness variations by using this slider. It sets the smallest instance that the brush will produce when Roundness Jitter is activated.

> When working with the dynamic brush options, think of the slider as representing the amount of variation/variety/change in the individual brush instances along the stroke and the pop-up menu as the control for that variation.

Examples of the shape dynamics are shown in Figure 12.32.

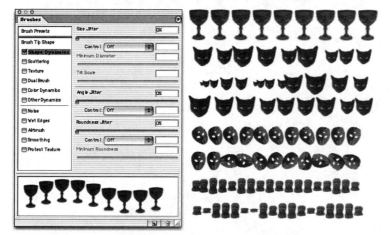

Figure 12.32
The top stroke has no shape dynamics applied; the bottom row has the shape dynamics shown in the palette's settings. In all cases, Spacing was set to 110% for each custom brush.

The cat face brush shows the size jitter. The first cat stroke has Size Jitter set to 50%. The second has Size Jitter at 100%, and the third shows the effect of Size Jitter at 100% combined with a Minimum Diameter of 50%.

The hockey mask strokes illustrate Angle Jitter. The first has a variance of 10%, and the second shows an Angle Jitter of 50%.

The strokes using the statue brush show a Roundness Jitter of 50% and a Roundness of 100% restricted to a minimum of 20%. Note the difference between Roundness and Size jitters. With Roundness, the width of each brush instance remains the same—only the height is varied.

Scattering

Scattering spreads copies of the brush tip as instances along the path of the stroke. Figure 12.33 illustrates how spacing affects Scattering and shows the influence of the Count and Count Jitter options.

Figure 12.33
The four samples use the same brush with the settings identified in the numbered list in the text, going from top to bottom.

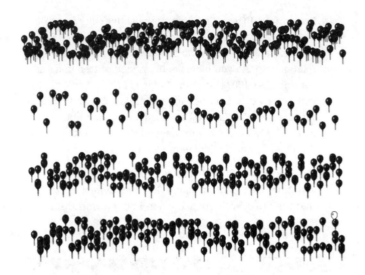

In Figure 12.33, the following settings are used:

1. Spacing 25%, Scatter 220%, Count 0, Count Jitter 0%

2. Spacing 100%, Scatter 220%, Count 0, Count Jitter 0%

3. Spacing 100%, Scatter 220%, Count 3, Count Jitter 0%

4. Spacing 100%, Scatter 220%, Count 3, Count Jitter 60%

Using Spacing to create a specific density of brush instances results in substantial overlap in places as well as some areas of "clumping," where many instances occur in a small space. Using the Scattering and Count options, especially along with Count Jitter, produces the appearance of random distribution, yet does a better job of preserving individual brush instances.

The Scattering pane of the Brushes palette also offers the Both Axes check box. In the first set of examples, only one axis is used for distributing the brush instances. The scattering is perpendicular to the path. Adding the second axis enables you to randomize the scattering along the path as well (see Figure 12.34).

These are the settings used in Figure 12.34, going from top to bottom:

1. No scattering

2. Scatter 100%, one axis

3. Scatter 100%, both axes

4. Scatter 250%, one axis

5. Scatter 250%, both axes

When Count and Count Jitter are used and Scatter is set to Both Axes, a very random pattern can be produced, but you're likely to see brush instances bunched together in groups. Add some Roundness Jitter (in Shape Dynamics) to produce an illusion of depth.

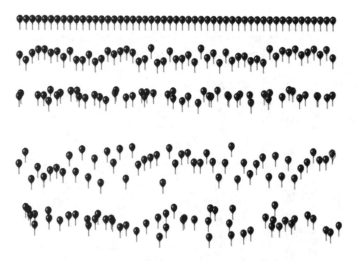

Figure 12.34
These five examples, all set to Spacing 100%, do not use the Count option, so they better illustrate the effect of adding a second axis of distribution.

Enabling the Both Axes option produces a result much like using a reduced Spacing setting—some clumping of the brush instances occurs as the distribution is varied along the path of the stroke.

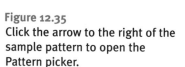

The Pattern picker menu enables you to load sets of patterns. Some of the patterns in the Artist Surfaces set are especially appropriate for use as brush textures.

Texture

Instead of a texture such as that applied with the Filter, Texture, Texturizer menu command, the Texture option in the Brushes palette applies a pattern to your stroke. Any pattern available in the Pattern picker for the Edit, Fill command or for the Paint Bucket is also available as a brush texture (see Figure 12.35). You can invert the pattern by selecting the Invert check box to the right of the pattern sample. Inverting reverses the pattern's grayscale values.

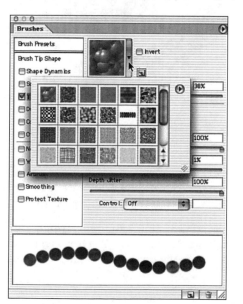

Figure 12.35
Click the arrow to the right of the sample pattern to open the Pattern picker.

12

Figure 12.36 shows the additional options available for texturing a brush. To the left are samples of the Dark Coarse Weave pattern at a variety of scale factors. From the left, the pattern is scaled to 15%, 30%, 50%, 100%, 150%, and 200%. The maximum scale factor is 1000%.

Figure 12.36
The Mode and the various Depth options are available only when Texture Each Tip is selected.

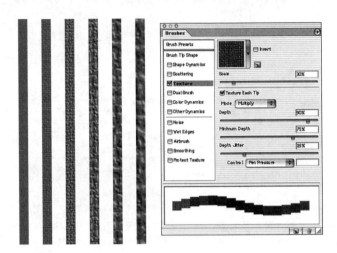

The Texture Each Tip option applies the pattern individually to each instance of the brush tip. Instead of treating the brush stroke as a whole, this option treats each application of the brush tip separately (see Figure 12.37).

Figure 12.37
A single instance of the brush tip is shown to the upper right. The pattern for the brush texture is Burlap.

The upper example shows how Photoshop applies a pattern to a stroke as a whole. Below, Texture Each Tip is activated. Note the areas of overlap from instance to instance. The pattern is applied over itself. There are several options available for Texture Each Tip:

- **Mode**—The blending modes available for Texture are Multiply, Subtract, Darken, Overlay, Color Dodge, Color Burn, Linear Burn, and Hard Mix. The blending mode affects how the overlapping brush instances interact and how the brush itself interacts with other colors already on the layer.

- **Depth**—Depth looks at the texture as a three-dimensional object, with the light and dark areas representing high and low points. Changing the Depth setting alters what grayscale values are affected. At 0%, the pattern is completely eliminated. At 100% Depth, the texture is reproduced normally.

- **Minimum Depth**—Used with Depth Jitter, this slider restricts the lowest jitter value.

- **Depth Jitter**—This slider regulates the amount of variation in depth over the course of the stroke. At 0%, there is no variation and the Depth slider determines the appearance of the brush. The Control options are discussed earlier in this chapter in the section "Controlling the Dynamic Options."

The Hard Mix blending mode is available only in the Texture and Dual Brush panes of the Brushes palette. Each of the brush's component color values is compared to the existing color on the layer. If the brush's component color is darker, the existing color is darkened. If it's lighter, the existing color is lightened.

Dual Brush

The Dual Brush option adds another brush tip to the tip selected in Brush Presets or Brush Tip Shape. The second tip is overlaid using the blending mode at the top of the Dual Brush pane of the Brushes palette (see Figure 12.38).

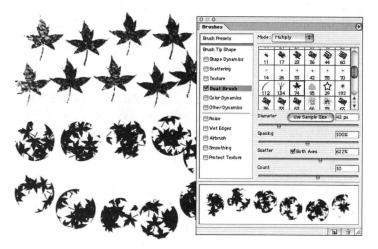

Figure 12.38
You can use Dual Brush to add a texture to a brush (top two rows) or to add a custom brush within a shape defined by the initial brush tip (bottom two rows).

12

The Dual Brush pane is a cross between the Brush Tip Shape and Scattering panes. In addition to selecting the second brush tip and blending mode, you adjust the second tip for diameter, spacing, scatter, and count.

Color Dynamics

The Color Dynamics pane gives you the opportunity to blend the foreground and background colors for the brush. Each instance of the brush uses only one color, but you can vary the proportions of the foreground and background colors with the sliders.

If you leave Control set to Fade and the Foreground/Background Jitter slider at 0%, the color reverts to the background color after the specified number of steps.

The Foreground/Background Jitter slider enables you to vary the color of the brush instances between the foreground and background colors, using various colors that are combinations of the two. When Control is set to Fade, the number specified is the number of different colored brush instances that occur before the color reverts to the foreground. (The Control options are discussed earlier in this chapter in the section "Controlling the Dynamic Options.")

When the Hue Jitter slider is set to a low percent, the stroke's hue remains close to the foreground color. As the percent grows, the background color is introduced. By about 25%, some additional color can be detected. At 100%, all the hues of the color wheel are used.

The Saturation Jitter slider affects only the saturation of the stroke. When the slider is toward the left (low percent), the saturation remains close to that of the foreground color. Likewise, the Brightness Jitter slider varies from that of the foreground color (left) to the full range of brightness (right).

The Purity slider is not, you will note, a "jitter" option. Rather, it works directly with the saturation value of the stroke. Set to 0%, the slider has no effect. Negative numbers reduce the saturation, with −100% creating a completely desaturated (gray) stroke. At +100, the stroke is completely saturated. Purity does not override the Saturation Jitter slider; rather, it restricts the setting.

Other Dynamics

The options in the Other Dynamics pane can be considered the paint dynamics or the tool option dynamics. The Opacity Jitter and Flow Jitter sliders vary the stroke's appearance up to but not beyond the values specified in the Options Bar for the Brush tool. These options are not available for other brush-using tools.

Additional Brush Palette Options

The five options at the bottom of the left column in the Brushes palette don't have separate panes. You activate them on an on/off basis and can click on the check box or the name. These are the available options:

- **Noise**—Noise is added to gray areas of the brush. Brushes defined as solid black are not affected.

- **Wet Edges**—Simulating watercolors, the paint collects along the edges of the brush stroke.

- **Airbrush**—The Airbrush option in the Brushes palette activates and deactivates the Airbrush button on the Options Bar for the Brush tool.

- **Smoothing**—Designed for use with drawing tablets, this option reduces the sharpness of some curves. If your stroke *should* have sharp angles, don't enable this option. Also be aware that it can reduce system responsiveness—your screen redraw might be slower.

- **Protect Texture**—Just as the Global Light option in Layer Style ensures consistency in lighting effects, so, too, does Protect Texture protect against anomalies in your image. Select this check box, and all the brushes that can use textures will use the same texture.

> **Caution**
>
> If you have an underpowered system or your video card is strained by your monitor resolution and color depth, make sure to disable Smoothing. The slower your system, the greater the delay you will experience with this option.

Using Brush Options in Combination

After you know how each of the options works, you are better prepared to combine them in a single brush stroke. For example, foliage in nature has leaves of different sizes and colors, at different angles and distances. You combine Shape Dynamics, Scattering, and Color Dynamics to create those variations (see Figure 12.39).

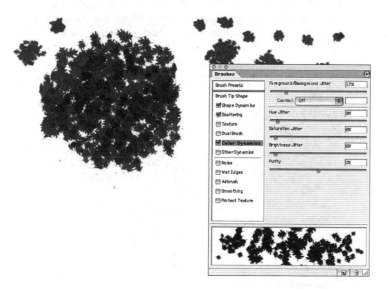

Figure 12.39
Color Dynamics replicates not only the shades of leaves, but also the angle of the leaves to the sun. Size, Angle, and Roundness jittering simulate not only differences in size, but also the positioning of individual leaves.

Changing the Diameter (in the Brush Tip Shape pane) along with Scatter and Count (in the Scattering pane) enables you to produce different sizes of your artwork, as shown in Figure 12.39. Adding in some single clicks of another brush at appropriate sizes on a lower layer can finish the image (see Figure 12.40).

Remember that you can balance Scatter and Count (in Scattering) with the Spacing slider (in Brush Tip Shape).

12

Figure 12.40
The "trunks" of the trees are created with single clicks of a brush using that shape. Scaling the trunks is simple—reduce the diameter in Brush Tip Shape or the Master Diameter in Brush Presets.

In addition, you can use the Dual Brush in combination with Scatter. In Figure 12.41, you can see the brush settings (right), the Dual Brush settings (inset), and a single stroke with those settings. By adding Scattering, you create a wide swath of randomly distributed coins as you drag.

Figure 12.41
The rectangle to the lower left is the rectangular brush. Using the settings shown in the Brushes palette to the right, the rectangle is 200 pixels wide by 100 pixels (50%) high.

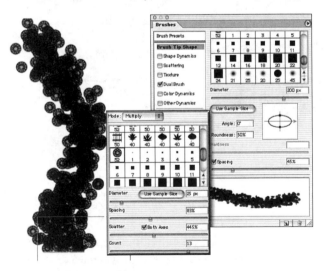

DEFINING BRUSHES AND BRUSH SETS

To take full advantage of Photoshop's new paint engine, you need to use custom brushes. You can load existing sets of brushes into the Brushes palette, or you can create your own.

Defining a Custom Brush

Photoshop's menu command Edit, Define Brush creates a custom brush from artwork you designate. The brush itself is always grayscale, so it's best to either work in Grayscale mode or desaturate your colored artwork (Image, Adjustments, Desaturate). If the artwork for the brush tip is alone on the layer, you need only use the Edit, Define Brush command. If there is other artwork on the layer, isolate the brush tip with a selection.

When you define a mask, Photoshop considers black to be 100% opaque, white to be transparent, and all other shades of gray (and colors) to be partially opaque. Where you add black to the artwork that will become a brush, you will later be painting with 100% opacity of the foreground color (allowing for tool and Brushes palette options, of course). In that respect, defining a brush is much like creating a mask, filter texture, or spot color channel—black is 100%, white is 0%, and everything else is in between. When you paint with the brush, that's how the foreground color will be added.

Unlike previous versions of Photoshop, you can define a brush on a layer filled with white or a background layer, and you can use irregularly shaped and feathered selections to define brushes.

Remember that your custom brushes are not permanently recorded until saved in a brush set. If you replace the content of the palette before saving, your custom brushes are lost.

Loading and Saving Brush Sets

Both the full-sized Brushes palette and the mini-palette available in the Options Bar enable you to load and save sets of brushes. The brush sets found in Photoshop's Presets folder (inside the Photoshop folder) appear at the bottom of the Brushes palette's menu. To add one of those sets to the palette, simply select its name from the menu. You'll be asked if you want to append the brush set (adding the new brushes to the bottom of the palette) or replace the palette's current content.

Save your custom brushes someplace outside the Photoshop folder—you don't want to lose them should you ever need to reinstall the program. It's always a good idea to keep a backup copy.

12

Although you cannot add individual brushes to the palette (unless they are saved as a set of one), you can delete brushes from the palette. Deleting removes them only from the palette, leaving them intact in their original set. The palette menu and the contextual menu both include Delete Brush commands. In the Preset Manager or the Brushes palette's Brush Presets pane, you can also (Option-click) [Alt+click] a brush to delete it.

The palette menu also offers the Save Brushes command. The current content of the palette, whether the brushes already belong to a set or not, will be saved together. Delete the default and other extraneous brushes from the palette before saving your custom brushes as a set. That keeps your new set tidy and makes the custom brushes easier to locate. You can reload the other brushes afterward.

On This Book's CD

A number of custom brushes have been included on the CD that accompanies this book. Load them as you would any other set of brushes. You're free to use them in your own work, but they cannot be further distributed.

PHOTOSHOP IN FOCUS

It seems that at one point or another, everyone who uses Photoshop needs to create foliage in an image. It's easy to prepare for that day ahead of time and, at the same time, get some practice managing brush sets.

1. Open the Photoshop Brushes palette.

2. From the palette menu, choose Reset Brushes.

3. Click the OK button rather than the Append button.

4. Put the *Special Edition Using Adobe Photoshop 7* CD into your optical drive and let it mount.

5. From the Brushes palette menu, choose Load Brushes.

6. Navigate to the Brushes folder on the CD and load Pete's Custom Brushes.

7. In the Brushes palette, (Option-click) [Alt+click] on all non-leaf, non-grass brushes to remove them from the palette. *Tip:* Start with the first brush, and the palette will bring the next to you—you don't have to move the cursor until it's time to skip a brush you want to keep.

8. For each of the brushes, set appropriate Shape Dynamics, Scattering, and Color Dynamics options.

9. Use the Brushes palette menu command Save Brushes. Name the set Foliage.abr (don't skip the file extension), and save the set to a location where you'll be able to find it when you need it.

FROM THE NAPP HELP DESK

The National Association of Photoshop Professionals (NAPP) offers e-mail assistance to its members. Here is some advice from the NAPP Help Desk related to issues in this chapter.

Auto Gradients

How do the Foreground and Background options for color stops work?

When Foreground or Background is assigned to a color swatch in the Gradient Editor, the gradient automatically updates itself when selected. For example, say that a gradient was defined with black and white as the foreground and background colors. Later, perhaps even in another project, that gradient is selected from the Gradient palette. If the foreground color happens to be red and the background color is blue, for example, the gradient is updated to reflect those colors for any color stops for which Foreground or Background is assigned.

Using Foreground and Background rather than specific colors can make a gradient far more flexible. These options are also very useful for complex gradients designed to integrate a subject and a background. Instead of having to identify and assign prominent colors from the image, simply use the Eyedropper tool and the Color palette to make those colors the foreground and background before selecting your gradient.

Restoring Cleared Brush Controls

I used the Brushes palette menu command Clear Brush Controls on one of the preset brushes, and I need to get the scattering back. Any way of doing it?

If you were in the Brushes palette's Brush Presets pane, simply click on the brush again—the controls will be restored. If you were in the Brush Tip Shape pane, change to Brush Presets and click on any other brush, and then return to Brush Tip Shape and click on the brush you need to restore. If all else fails, remember that you can reload any brush set.

Expanding the Brushes Palette

I can't find any of Photoshop's new brush options. All I see is the old-fashioned Brushes palette.

From the Brushes palette menu, choose Expanded View to show the options. When the Brushes palette is docked to the Palette Well, click the tab to open the palette, and then click the small arrow in the tab. Remember that ImageReady doesn't use the new painting engine—you'll see only the "old fashioned" palette.

12

THE PEN TOOLS, SHAPE LAYERS, AND OTHER PATHS

IN THIS CHAPTER

PHOTOSHOP'S PATHS

Photoshop uses vector paths in a variety of ways, for a variety of purposes. These nonprinting, mathematical descriptions of shapes and lines are called *Bézier curves*. They can be used to precisely define selections, create "objects" in the artwork, and even show a page layout program what should be visible in an image.

The paths used in vector art are referred to as Bézier curves after the French engineer who pioneered their application, Pierre Etienne Bézier (1910–1999).

Vectors in a Strange Land

Photoshop is primarily a raster image-editing program, designed to work with the pixels that make up a digital image. However, it does offer some rather powerful vector capabilities. Vector type, clipping masks and vector masks for layers, and Photoshop's shape layers are examples of vectors in raster images.

Briefly, vector artwork is based on paths that are recorded in a file as mathematical descriptions. The advantage of vectors is that artwork and images can be scaled to any size without loss of quality. Raster images, in contrast, can be drastically degraded when scaled either up or down (see Figure 13.1).

Figure 13.1
The X or circle on the left of each pair of images is raster; those on the right are vector. The lower pairs have been scaled to 300%. Vector artwork retains its appearance better than raster when scaled.

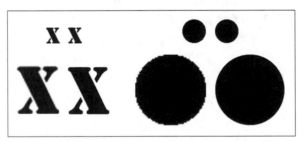

▷ *For more information on the differences between raster and vector,* **see** *"Shapes Versus Objects,"* **p. 367,** *later in this chapter.*

Programs such as Adobe Illustrator are designed to work with vector art and have some capability to edit raster images. Illustrator's artwork consists primarily of vector-based objects, with the capability to incorporate placed raster artwork. Photoshop, on the other hand, incorporates its vectors into its raster images. Illustrator doesn't have Photoshop's incredible image-editing power, nor does Photoshop have Illustrator's vector-manipulation capability—two programs, two purposes, some overlap.

If you use Illustrator, don't overlook the companion book, *Special Edition Using Adobe Illustrator* (Que Publishing), available for both Illustrator 9 and Illustrator 10.

▷ *To learn how to use Photoshop and Illustrator together to maximize your creative arsenal,* **see** *Appendix A, "Photoshop 7 and Illustrator 10,"* **p. 893.**

13

The Many Faces of Paths

Vector paths in Photoshop can exist independent of a layer, or they can be tied to a layer to create artwork. Vector type layers, for example, must contain nothing but the vector type. Likewise, shape layers can have no other artwork unless the layer is rasterized. Paths not used directly to create vector shapes or type can be used to create selections or masks for layers and can be stroked or filled.

Keep in mind that the Paths palette commands Stroke Path or Fill Path do not create vector objects. Rather, they color pixels on a layer according to the shape of the path. These commands are comparable to using a painting tool to draw a shape and to filling a selection with the Paint Bucket tool. They are also comparable to using the menu commands Edit, Stroke and Edit, Fill with selections.

⇨ *Unsure about the difference between vector objects and stroked and filled paths? See "The Chicken or the Egg?" in the NAPP Help Desk section at the end of this chapter.*

Photoshop can use vector paths in a variety of ways:

- **Type Layers**—Although you can't edit the paths directly, type on a type layer consists of filled vector paths. (However, don't overlook the command Layer, Type, Create Work Path. It creates editable paths from the letters.)

- **Shape Layers**—Photoshop's shape layers are actually layers filled with color, a gradient, or a pattern and selectively exposed using vector masks. When a shape layer is selected in the Layers palette, the path is visible (and selectable) in the Paths palette. When the layer is not active, its path is not visible in the Paths palette.

- **Clipping Paths**—The term *clipping path* is now used exclusively for those vector paths that determine areas of visibility for raster images placed into page layout documents. (*Clipping path* and *clipping mask* were also used in earlier versions of Photoshop as the name for paths used to show/hide areas of a layer. The term *vector mask* is now used.) When placing a raster image into a page layout program, you can use a clipping path to selectively hide the background (see Figure 13.2).

- **Vector Mask**—Paths can be used to selectively show and hide areas on a layer, much as a clipping path is used for an image as a whole.

- **Selection Definition**—A path can be used to precisely define a selection in Photoshop. The Paths palette offers a button that will convert any selected path to a selection.

- **Stroke and Fill**—Using the Paths palette menu, you can place color along an active path. Consider these commands to be ways to precisely control a painting tool. Remember that unlike true vector objects, if you stroke and/or fill a path and then move the path, the colored pixels remain behind. A path retains no connection to a stroke or fill in Photoshop.

⇨ *To learn more about vector masks and using paths to create selections, **see** "Layer Masks, Vector Masks, and Clipping Groups," **p. 267** in Chapter 10, "Making Selections and Creating Masks."*

13

Figure 13.2
The left image was placed into a page layout document with a clipping path. To the right, the same image was placed without a clipping path.

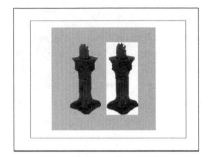

The Anatomy of a Path

The term *path* in Photoshop actually applies to an entry in the Paths palette. The path might or might not contain several subpaths, which work together to form the path (see Figure 13.3). In contrast, Illustrator considers any independent series of path segments to be a distinct path, even if there is but a single path segment.

Figure 13.3
The Paths palette shows a single path, although there are four distinct subpaths.

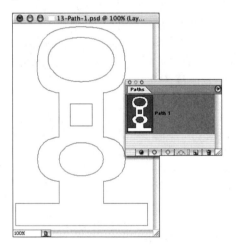

A path consists of one or more *path segments*, the lines you see on the screen. Each segment can be curved or straight. The path itself can be closed, with no discernable endpoints, or open, with two recognizable ends. When filling an open path or creating a vector mask, Photoshop assumes a connecting segment that runs straight between the endpoints. When stroked, only the existing path segments will be colored. Open paths cannot be used as clipping paths.

A path's shape is determined by *anchor points*. There is one anchor point on either end of each path segment. When path segments are connected, they are joined at a single anchor point. Each anchor point in a closed path has a path segment extending on either side. The endpoints of open paths have only one path segment connected. No anchor point can have more than two segments adjoining.

The position of the anchor points is not key to a path's shape; rather, the relationship among the points determines the path shape. Remember that paths are vector artwork and can be scaled to any size.

13

The relative positions, rather than the exact positions, are the key. In Figure 13.4, the two paths are identical except for size. Although the distance between anchor points is different, the relationship among them is the same—you could scale the smaller path up or the larger path down to create identical objects.

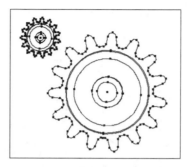

Figure 13.4
The smaller path is an exact copy of the larger one, simply scaled to one-third size.

The same path can often be drawn with different numbers of anchor points. In Figure 13.5, three paths have different numbers of anchor points yet present the same shape.

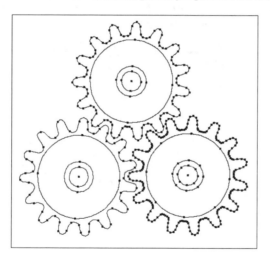

Figure 13.5
The top gear has 122 points, the gear on the left has half as many, and that on the right has twice as many. The shapes on the top and right are identical; that on the left is nearly identical.

How Anchor Points Work

There are two types of anchor points in Photoshop: smooth and corner. A smooth point is one through which the adjoining path segments flow in an uninterrupted curve. At a corner point, the path typically (but not always) changes direction. Smooth anchor points are always abutted by a curved path segment on either side. Corner points can have two straight path segments, two curved path segments, one of each, or—as an endpoint—only one of either type. Anchor points are visible when a path is being created or edited.

All smooth anchor points and some corner anchor points have *direction lines*. Direction lines extend from anchor points (smooth or corner) when the point is bordered by a curved path segment (see Figure 13.6). Direction lines determine the shape of the adjoining curved path segment.

They are visible only when an anchor point for a curved path segment (or the segment itself) is selected in the image. Selected anchor points are seen as filled squares, and unselected points are hollow squares.

Figure 13.6
There are 12 anchor points for this path. Two are selected. The corner point has no direction lines, but the selected smooth point has a direction line for each of the bordering curved path segments.

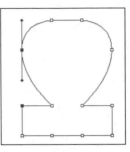

At the end of each direction line is a *direction point*, which is used to manipulate the direction line and, therefore, the shape of the curved path segment. The Direct Selection tool is used to drag direction points. Both the length and angle of direction lines affect the curve of a path segment.

➯ *Corner points through which a path runs smoothly? How can this be? See "Smooth Corner Points" in the NAPP Help Desk section at the end of this chapter.*

When a direction point for a smooth anchor point is dragged, the direction lines—and curves—on both sides of the anchor point are affected (see Figure 13.7).

Figure 13.7
The original curve is shown at the top. As the Direct Selection tool drags a direction point, the curves are altered.

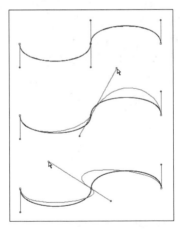

Note that in the lower examples in Figure 13.7, the direction line on the opposite side of the anchor point changes angle to stay 180° opposed but does not change length.

Direction lines for curves on either side of a corner anchor point function independently. In Figure 13.8, a smooth anchor point (top) and a corner anchor point are compared.

13

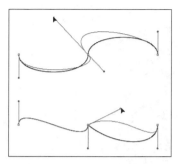

Figure 13.8
Dragging a direction point for a corner anchor point alters only one path segment.

CREATING PATHS IN PHOTOSHOP

Paths can be created in a variety of ways. The pen tools can be used to create paths from scratch, selections can form the basis of paths, shape layers are created with paths, and type can be converted to paths. Photoshop uses the Paths palette to manage paths.

A path is called "Work Path" until saved. There can be only one work path at a time. With a work path selected in the Paths palette, you continue to add subpaths. If the existing work path is *not* active in the Paths palette when you begin to create a new path, it will be replaced by the new path (which then assumes the name "Work Path"). The prior work path is lost. Renaming a work path saves it. Change the name by double-clicking "Work Path" in the Paths palette and overtyping, or by using the Paths palette menu command Save Path.

Remember that when a path is active in the Paths palette, creating another path with the Pen tool adds a subpath. Converting a selection into a path replaces an existing work path or, if the active path has been saved, starts a new work path.

The Paths Palette

The appearance of a path's name in the Paths palette gives you a good indication of what type of path it is. The palette also offers several buttons for use with paths (see Figure 13.9).

The Paths palette menu offers commands to create a new path or new work path; duplicate, delete, fill, and stroke a selected path; and convert a path to a selection or a clipping path. When a work path is selected in the palette, you can also use a menu command to save it, which opens a dialog box in which you can assign a name. However, you can achieve the same result by double-clicking the name "Work Path" in the Paths palette and typing a new name.

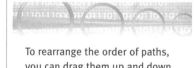

To rearrange the order of paths, you can drag them up and down in the palette. This has no effect on their appearance.

13

Figure 13.9
The Shape 1 Vector Mask path and the Layer 1 Vector Mask path would not normally be visible at the same time—only one layer can be active, and an inactive layer's vector mask is not shown in the palette.

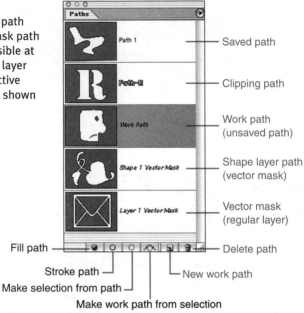

Saved path

Clipping path

Work path (unsaved path)

Shape layer path (vector mask)

Vector mask (regular layer)

Fill path — Delete path

Stroke path — New work path

Make selection from path —

Make work path from selection

Using the Pen Tool

The Pen tool enables you to place each anchor point individually as you work, deciding between corner and smooth points on-the-fly.

There are a few basic concepts behind the Pen tool:

- To place a corner anchor point with the Pen tool, simply click.

- To create a smooth point, click and drag. The direction and distance dragged set the anchor point's direction line and determine the appearance of the curved path segment.

- To close a path, click (or click and drag) on the first endpoint. The Pen tool cursor shows a small circle to the lower right when it's directly over the path's start point. Clicking elsewhere with the Pen tool then starts a new subpath.

- To end an open path, either switch tools or (Command-click) [Ctrl+click] away from the open path.

- To add to an existing open path, select the path in the Paths palette, click once with the Pen tool on an endpoint, and then continue creating anchor points.

Creating a path with the Pen tool can be as simple as clicking in two different locations—a straight path segment will be created between the points. More complex paths can be created by clicking and dragging. The key to creation with the Pen tool is understanding how dragging affects curved path segments. In Figure 13.10, four paths were created by clicking and dragging with the Pen tool. In each case, the Pen was clicked and dragged straight down to form the left anchor point.

13

Figure 13.10
The dashed lines show the direction and distance of drag for each anchor point. Note that the left points for each of the path segments were created with identical drags.

The only difference among the four path segments is the direction in which the Pen tool was dragged when creating the right-hand anchor point. (The distance is identical in each case.)

Multiple-segment paths show the difference between dragging in opposite directions at each end of a path segment and dragging in the same direction (see Figure 13.11). On the left, each anchor point was created by dragging the Pen tool in the same direction. The second path was created by dragging in alternating directions. However, as you can see on the right, the actual direction lines for the anchor points between path segments look identical.

Both sets of curves in Figure 13.11 are excellent examples of smooth anchor points. Observe that the direction lines for both selected anchor points are 180° apart— parallel to each other—and the path flows smoothly through the anchor points.

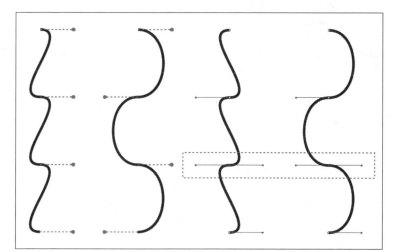

Figure 13.11
On the left, the dashed lines show the direction and distance of drag for each anchor point. The pair on the right show the direction lines for the anchor points.

Note on the right that although only the two anchor points within the dashed box are selected (their squares are filled), one direction line for each of the neighboring points is visible. Even though those neighboring points aren't selected, the direction line for the path segment bordering the selected anchor point is available. This enables you to use the Direct Selection tool to modify the path segments from either end.

Pen Tool Options

When the Pen tool is active, the left part of Photoshop's Options Bar offers you the choice of creating a work path or a shape layer (see Figure 13.12). (The option to create an area filled with the foreground color isn't available with the Pen tool.) You can also easily switch to the Freeform Pen tool or any of the shape tools.

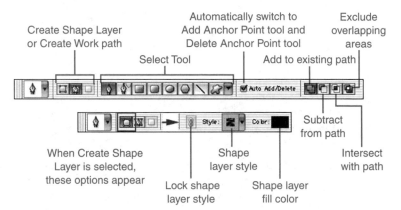

Figure 13.12
The Options Bar differs, depending on whether Create Shape Layer or Create Work Path is selected.

When set to create a work path and a path is active in the Paths palette, the right side of the Options Bar offers several different behaviors for a new subpath. You can add to, subtract from, intersect with, or exclude overlapping areas. The icons in the Options Bar show the differences.

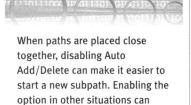

When paths are placed close together, disabling Auto Add/Delete can make it easier to start a new subpath. Enabling the option in other situations can save time switching tools.

Selecting the Auto Add/Delete check box in the Options Bar enables the Pen tool to automatically change to the Add Anchor Point or Delete Anchor Point tools. If the option is selected and the Pen is positioned over a path segment, it automatically prepares to add an anchor point if the tool is clicked. When activated and the tool is positioned over an existing anchor point, it can delete the point.

When the Pen tool is set to create or edit shape layers, additional options enable you to apply a style and color directly in the Options Bar. You'll notice a "link" icon to the left of the Style example in the Options Bar. Clicking the style link button (it will appear darkened) links the Style pop-up palette to the active layer. Changes made to the style through the pop-up palette in the Options Bar are applied to the active layer. When the link is not selected (it has the normal light gray appearance), changes to the style made in the Options Bar do not affect the active layer.

The style link button in the Options Bar (available with a pen tool or a shape tool active) applies only to the Style pop-up palette in the Options Bar. Changes made using the regular Styles palette are unaffected by the link status.

Clicking the down arrow to the right of the shape tools in the Options Bar exposes some additional tool-related options.

For the Pen tool, you have the Rubber Band check box. With Rubber Band activated, the Pen tool previews the path that will be created by tracking the cursor's movement with the mouse button up. Without Rubber Band, you won't see the path until you click and drag. Additional options for the Freeform Pen tool are discussed in the following section.

The Other Pen Tools

In addition to the Pen tool, Photoshop offers the Freeform Pen, Add Anchor Point, Delete Anchor Point, and Convert Anchor Point tools. The Freeform Pen tool can be used to drag a path, much like using the Pencil or Brush tool. Instead of clicking to add anchor points, the points are added automatically as you drag. (You can also add an anchor point to the path manually by clicking.) How closely the path follows the cursor's movement is a function of the additional tool options (accessed through the arrow to the right of the shape tool icons in the Options Bar). The default Curve Fit setting of 2 pixels is usually a good balance between path accuracy and complexity. Higher numbers (to a maximum of 10 pixels) reduce the number of anchor points, but accuracy can suffer (see Figure 13.13).

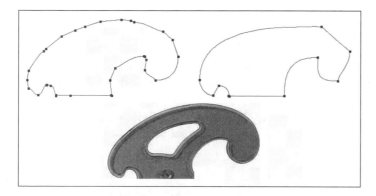

Figure 13.13
The image at the bottom was traced with the Freeform Pen tool twice. On the left, Curve Fit was set to 2 pixels. On the right, the setting was 10 pixels.

The Magnetic option for the Freeform Pen tool enables it to follow edges. It uses contrast to determine where an edge exists. It is best suited for images with plain backgrounds.

When working with the Magnetic option, the Freeform Pen places a series of anchor points as it follows the path you trace. As you drag, you can click the mouse button to manually place anchor points at spots where the edge you're tracing takes a sharp turn. If the tool places an anchor point in an incorrect location, press (Delete) [Backspace] to remove it. You can also back up along the edge to retrace a segment. Clicking on the start point closes the path. Double-click the tool, and it will attempt to follow the nearest edge back to the start point. Using the (Return) [Enter] key finishes the path and leaves it as an open path.

When using the Freeform Pen tool with the Magnetic option, you can temporarily disable the capability by holding down the (Option) [Alt] key. With the key pressed, drag a free-form path without regard for following edges. Release the modifier key to resume using the Magnetic option.

13

With the Freeform Pen tool selected, click the arrow to the right of the shapes in the Options Bar to set the Magnetic option's behavior. Width determines the radius within which the tool will search for an edge to follow. Contrast, measured in percent, governs how different the pixel color must be to constitute an edge. Frequency controls how often an anchor point will be placed as you drag.

With an existing path selected in the image, the Add Anchor Point tool enables you to add both corner (click) and smooth (drag) anchor points to the path. Similarly, the Delete Anchor Point tool removes existing anchor points from a selected path when you click on them. The Convert Anchor Point tool can change a smooth anchor point to a corner point (click on it) or convert a corner point to a smooth point (click on the point and drag).

🖝 *Wondering about the Auto Add/Delete option? See "Shutting Down the Auto" in the NAPP Help Desk section at the end of this chapter.*

The (Option) [Alt] key converts the Pen tool to the Convert Anchor Point tool when the cursor is over an anchor point. You can use it to convert corner anchor points to smooth, and vice versa. Click and drag on a corner point to create direction lines for a smooth point. Click once on a smooth point to change it to a corner point.

Editing Paths

Paths as a whole can be edited, or you can work with subpaths or even individual anchor points and path segments. To select an entire path, click on it in the Paths palette. You can stroke, fill, delete, and use the Edit, Transform commands.

To isolate a subpath from the entire path, use the Path Selection tool, whose icon is a plain black arrow (see Figure 13.14). Click on the subpath in the image window to select it.

Figure 13.14
The path must be selected in the Paths palette to make it visible. You can then use the Path Selection tool to select a subpath, making its anchor points visible.

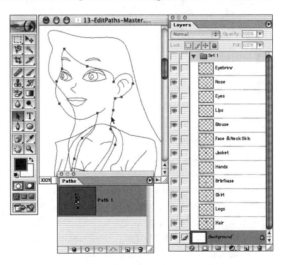

When you use the Path Selection tool to select a subpath, all the anchor points are selected. If you drag with the tool, you can reposition the subpath. You can also use the Paths palette menu commands to stroke or fill a selected subpath.

You can control the operation of the Path Selection tool in the Options Bar:

- When Show Bounding Box is selected, you can manipulate a path with the Path Selection tool much like using the bounding box with the Free Transform command. Drag a side or corner anchor to scale the path. Holding down the Shift key while dragging constrains the proportions, maintaining the original height-to-width ratio. The (Option) [Alt] key enables you to scale from the center and can be used with the Shift key. The (Command) [Ctrl] key can be added for skew and perspective transformations. The Edit, Transform commands are available with paths, and when transforming, the Options Bar can be used for numeric transformations.

- Shift-clicking on multiple subpaths with the Path Selection tool activates several buttons in the Options Bar. You can combine the paths by adding, subtracting, intersecting, or excluding areas of overlap. Select the preferred operation, and then click the Combine button.

- Multiple subpaths can also be aligned or distributed, according to their centers or any side. Shift-click the subpaths or drag across them with the Path Selection tool, and then use the appropriate buttons in the Options Bar.

To select an individual anchor point or path segment to edit the shape of a path, use the Direct Selection tool, identified by the white arrow icon (see Figure 13.15). The Direct Selection tool has no options in the Options Bar. Selected anchor points are identified as filled squares, and anchor points in the same subpath that are *not* selected appear as hollow squares. (Other subpaths are visible, but their anchor points are not.) If a selected anchor point has direction lines, they will be visible.

Figure 13.15
The direction lines for the selected anchor point are visible, as are one direction line from each of the neighboring points. The additional direction lines are visible so that you can edit the path segments connected to the selected anchor point.

The Direct Selection tool can be used to drag an anchor point or a path segment or to drag direction points, which alters the shape of a curve. Remember that dragging a direction point for a smooth anchor point affects the direction lines—and curves—on *both* sides of the anchor, but changing a direction line for a corner point alters only the curve on that side (see Figure 13.16).

Figure 13.16
On the left is the original curve. In the center, you can see how dragging either of a smooth anchor point's direction lines changes the path segments on each side. On the right, the same curve with a corner anchor point has independent path segments.

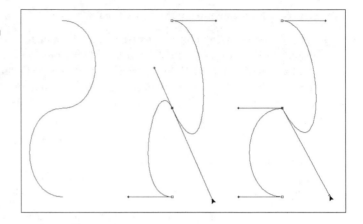

The Direct Selection tool can also be used to drag path segments. When a straight path segment is dragged, the neighboring anchor points move as well, altering not only the segment dragged, but also those on either side. When you drag a curved path segment, the adjoining anchor points remain in place and the neighboring path segments are undisturbed. Note that dragging a curved path segment automatically converts any adjoining smooth anchor point to a corner point. In Figure 13.17, dashed lines represent the original paths, and you can see how dragging path segments affects shapes.

To alter a curve connected to a smooth anchor point without disturbing the adjoining curve, hold down the (Option) [Alt] key and drag a direction point. The smooth anchor point is converted to a corner anchor point with direction lines.

Figure 13.17
To the left, a straight path segment is being dragged. In the center, a curved path segment is being dragged straight up. On the right, you can see one example of what can go horribly wrong when dragging a curved path segment. To avoid the unexpected, click and drag in the middle of a path segment.

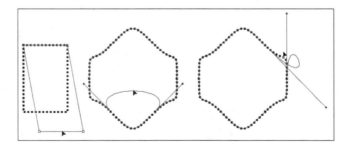

Stroking and Filling Paths and Subpaths

To add color to an image, you can stroke and fill paths and subpaths. Use the Path Selection or Direct Selection tool to make the target path active. Make sure that you're on the correct layer in the Layers palette. Use the Paths palette buttons or the commands from the Paths palette menu (see Figure 13.18), which open dialog boxes.

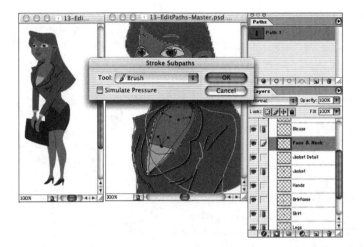

Figure 13.18
The buttons at the bottom of the Paths palette use the settings selected in the Stroke and Fill dialog boxes. Open the dialog boxes using the Paths palette menu, select the appropriate options, and afterward you can simply click the buttons to use the same settings.

The Stroke Path dialog box (or Stroke Subpath, depending on the active selection) offers all the tools that use brushes. You can even apply the Healing Brush, Clone Stamp, and Pattern Stamp tools along paths for incredible precision.

The Fill Path (or Fill Subpath) options include filling with the foreground or background color or with a pattern, history state, black, white, or 50% gray. You can select a blending mode, opacity, feather radius, and anti-aliasing for the fill. Remember that filling an *open path*—a path with two identifiable ends—fills an area that includes a straight line between the start and end anchor points.

In Figure 13.18 a second window is open to show the effect of stroking and filling without the distraction of the visible paths. Choose Window, Documents, New Window to create the second window. It will automatically be updated with changes made to the working window.

Changeable Names

When your path consists of a single subpath, the commands are Fill Path and Stroke Path. When you have multiple subpaths and all are selected, the commands and dialog boxes also show Fill Path and Stroke Path. When there are multiple subpaths and only one is selected, the commands and dialog boxes are Fill Subpath and Stroke Subpath. When you have multiple subpaths and some but not all are selected, the commands and dialog boxes adapt themselves grammatically and read Fill Subpaths and Stroke Subpaths.

Paths from Selections

The Paths palette offers two ways to create a path from a selection. At the bottom of the Paths palette, the dashed-circle button (Make Work Path from Selection) loads an active selection as a work path. Alternatively, the Paths palette menu offers the Make Work Path command, which opens a dialog box where you can specify a tolerance setting. Ranging from 0 to 10 pixels, it determines the accuracy with which the path will be created as well as the complexity of the final path.

If a selection is heavily feathered or created from a mask, the path will follow the marching ants (selection border), which indicates pixels at least 50% selected. If no pixels are at least 50% selected and you attempt to create a work path, a work path appears in the Paths palette, but there will be no anchor points or path segments.

Compound paths can be created from selections, such as that shown in Figure 13.19. You can create the selection with selection tools, from a mask, or by using selection commands.

Compound paths can be used as vector masks for layers and as clipping paths for images to be placed in page layout programs (see Figure 13.20).

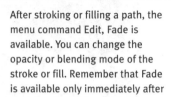

After stroking or filling a path, the menu command Edit, Fade is available. You can change the opacity or blending mode of the stroke or fill. Remember that Fade is available only immediately after applying the stroke or fill.

Caution

Remember that when you create a path from a selection, you're creating a work path. It will replace any existing work path in the Paths palette. And, unless saved, it will be lost as soon as you start another work path (although you can add additional subpaths). Save a work path by renaming it in the Paths palette.

Figure 13.19
When the (Option) [Alt] key is used along with a selection tool, areas within a selection can be deselected. The Options Bar also offers this capability for selection tools.

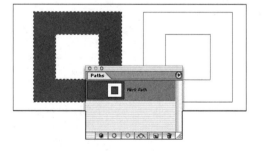

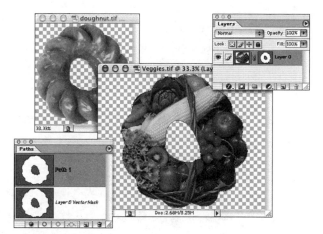

Figure 13.20
A compound path was created from a selection of the doughnut and used to mask an image of vegetables. Then the path was duplicated in the Paths palette and the copy converted to a clipping path. When placed into a page layout program, only the pixels between the paths are visible.

Converting Type to Paths

Editable paths can also be created from vector type. With a type layer selected in the Layers palette, use the menu command Layer, Type, Create Work Path. The original type layer is untouched, and a work path is created in the shape of the letters (see Figure 13.21). Although the original type layer remains editable as text, the work path is no longer type. Before filling or stroking a work path, make sure that you are on the appropriate layer.

Caution

Creating paths from large amounts of small type can cause problems. The paths can be too complex to output properly.

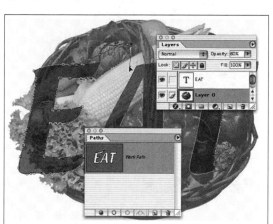

Figure 13.21
The two existing layers have reduced opacity to better show the work path. The Direct Selection tool can be used to move anchor points and direction points, customizing the letter shapes. The paths can then be filled or stroked.

13

A Note About Illustrator Paths

You can copy and paste paths between Photoshop and Illustrator. However, when copying from Illustrator, it's important that the Illustrator Preferences be set correctly. In Illustrator's Files & Clipboard preferences pane, select AICB (Adobe Illustrator Clipboard) in the Copy As area. If you'll be copying paths, click on Preserve Paths.

The PDF option can be used along with AICB, but when working with Photoshop, AICB must be selected.

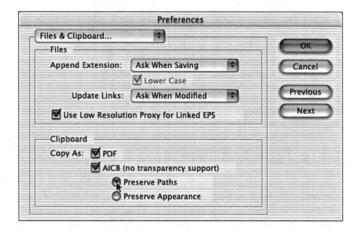

When you've copied one or more objects from Illustrator and switched to Photoshop, the Paste command opens a small dialog box. You have the option of pasting from the Clipboard as pixels, as just paths, or as a shape layer.

You can, in fact, use the Paste command twice—once to paste the path, and again to paste the pixels. The two will remain separate, and they don't become a vector object, but you'll have both the substance (paths) and appearance (pixels) of the original object.

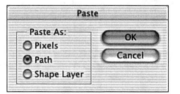

PHOTOSHOP'S SHAPE LAYERS

Photoshop simulates vector objects with shape layers. A shape layer is actually a layer in the image, completely filled with the selected color or pattern. The layer is selectively shown and hidden by a path called a vector mask. The pixels on the layer inside the path are visible; those outside the path are hidden (see Figure 13.22).

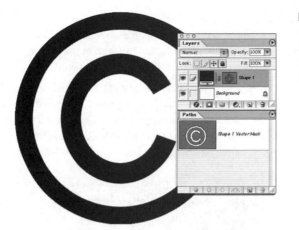

Figure 13.22
A shape layer's vector mask is visible in the Paths palette when the layer is selected in the Layers palette.

In the Options Bar, you can assign a color for a shape layer. With the shape layer selected in the Layers palette, you can use the menu command Layer, Change Layer Content to assign a gradient or pattern to the layer, or to convert the layer to an adjustment layer. You can also use the Layer, Layer Content Options command to adjust the fill of a shape layer.

Shapes Versus Objects

Unlike the vector objects created in Illustrator (and other vector-based programs), Photoshop's shape layers are actually pixel-based. The layers are clipped with a vector mask, but they contain pixels. The path itself can be scaled without risking output quality, but the pixels used to stroke or fill remain raster.

➡️ *For more information on the differences between raster and vector artwork, **see** "The Two Types of Computer Graphics," **p. 156** in Chapter 6, "Pixels, Vectors, and Resolution."*

Unlike filled paths, altering the vector mask of a shape layer actually *does* change the appearance of the artwork (see Figure 13.23). Because altering the path changes where the layer's fill is shown and hidden, in appearance it is somewhat akin to editing a true vector object.

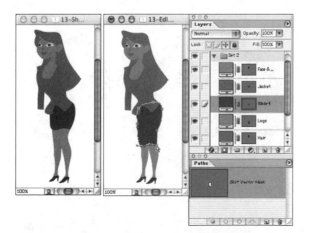

Figure 13.23
The original is on the left. Using Photoshop's Direct Selection tool to select and drag anchor points, the artwork can be changed when working with shape layers.

13

Shape layer paths in Photoshop can be stroked only by using the Layer Styles command. They can have only one of each layer effect, limiting them to a single stroke and one each of the Satin, Color Overlay, Gradient Overlay, and Pattern Overlay effects. (Other than the stroke, these effects are applied only to the fill of the shape layer and are in addition to the layer's own fill.)

Because of these limitations, Photoshop's shape layers cannot be stroked and filled in the same way that you can change a path's appearance in Illustrator. In Figure 13.24, the same object has been created in both programs. In Photoshop, the shape layer path was duplicated and, on a new layer, the Fill Subpaths and Stroke Subpaths commands were used (the latter, three times). The Illustrator object was created with the Appearance palette's menu command Add New Stroke.

Figure 13.24
Although the appearance is identical, the nature of the artwork differs. In Photoshop, there are pixels on a layer and a path. In Illustrator, there is an object.

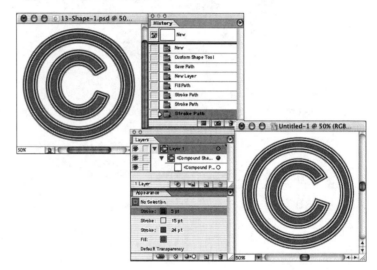

One of the biggest differences between these two "objects" is what happens when the path is edited. In Photoshop, the image's appearance is unaffected by editing the path—the pixels remain in place and only the path is changed. In Illustrator, editing the path results in changes to the object itself (see Figure 13.25).

Figure 13.25
On the left, selecting anchor points and dragging them in Photoshop doesn't change the artwork's appearance. On the right, a true vector object is changed when the path is manipulated.

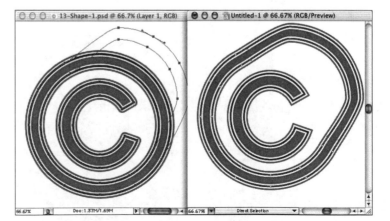

13

Using the Shape Tools

The shape tools are, at their heart, scalable paths. When you use a shape tool, you create one of three things: a shape layer, a work path, or colored pixels in a specific shape on an existing layer. The choice is made by selecting one of the three buttons to the left in the Options Bar.

The shape that is created can be selected in the Toolbox or the Options Bar (see Figure 13.26). The standard preset tools include Rectangle, Rounded Rectangle, Ellipse, Polygon, and Line. Custom shapes can also be selected from a palette, which can be loaded with Photoshop-supplied shapes, third-party shapes, or custom shapes you define.

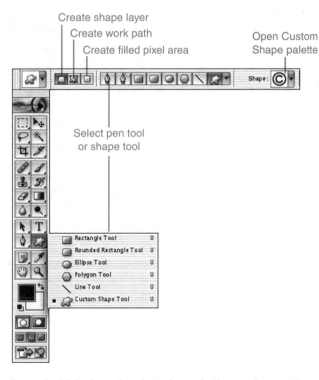

Create shape layer
Create work path
Create filled pixel area

Open Custom
Shape palette

Select pen tool
or shape tool

Rectangle Tool   U
Rounded Rectangle Tool   U
Ellipse Tool   U
Polygon Tool   U
Line Tool   U
Custom Shape Tool   U

Figure 13.26
There is no difference between selecting the tool in the Toolbox or the Options Bar. The shape tools are available in the Options Bar with any shape tool or a pen tool active.

Regardless of which shape is selected, or whether you're creating a shape layer, a work path, or a filled region, the basic operation of the shape tools is the same: Click and drag. (When size options are selected, you need only click.) Use the Shift key to constrain the shape to its original height-width ratio; use the (Option) [Alt] key to create from the center. The two modifier keys can be used together.

Each of the individual shape tools has characteristics that you can control through the Geometry palette of the Options Bar (see Figure 13.27).

13

Figure 13.27
To open the Geometry palette, click on the down arrow to the right of the Custom Shape tool icon.

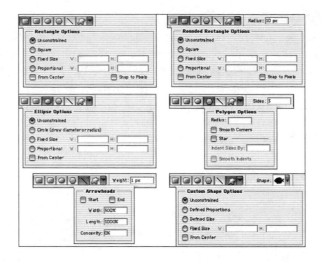

Most of the geometry options are self-explanatory, but several deserve explanation:

- When the Rounded Rectangle tool is selected, you'll see the Radius field in the Options Bar. The value entered there determines the curve of the corners.

- Snap to Pixels is primarily used when creating Web graphics. By snapping the horizontal and vertical edges of the shape to pixels, this option ensures that Web graphics will be crisp. The option is used only with the Rectangle and Rounded Rectangle tools and is not available for the shapes that don't have horizontal and vertical edges.

- The Polygon tool offers the option to create stars. When it's checked, you have the opportunity to specify the indentation of the star's arms. Percent is the unit of measure.

- The Line tool can have arrowheads at either or both ends. However, when you have arrowheads at both ends, they must be identical. (You can, of course, transform the line later.)

- The Defined Proportions and Defined Size options for the Custom Shape tool refer to the size and proportions at which the custom shape was originally created.

13 Editing Shape Vector Masks

The vector masks that selectively show and hide the fill of a shape layer can be edited like any other path in Photoshop. The path, of course, must be selected in the Paths palette. For the path to be visible in the palette, the shape layer must be selected in the Layers palette. The Path Selection tool selects all the anchor points in a path or subpath, enabling you to move the entire path or subpath as a unit.

The Direct Selection tool enables you to select one or more individual path segments or anchor points to manipulate. It is also used to drag the direction points of anchor points adjoining curved path segments.

For full information on editing paths in Photoshop, **see** "Editing Paths" earlier in this chapter, **p. 360**.

Using, Creating, and Saving Custom Shapes

Custom shapes are selected from the Custom Shape picker (see Figure 13.28). This palette, opened through the Options Bar, is available only when the Custom Shape tool has been selected in the Toolbox or the Options Bar.

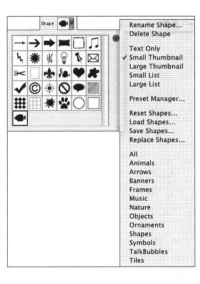

Figure 13.28
The Custom Shape picker's menu offers available sets of custom shapes at the bottom. The newly added shapes can be added to or replace those already in the picker.

After you have selected a custom shape from the picker and set options in the Geometry palette, it can be added to the image like any other shape. Shape layers, work paths, and filled pixel regions can all be added with custom shape tools.

You can create custom shapes and add them to the Custom Shape picker. Create a path or select an existing path, and use the menu command Edit, Define Custom Shape. You'll have the opportunity to name the new custom shape (see Figure 13.29).

Figure 13.29
Naming the shape is the only option. It is saved at the size created.

13

Remember that custom shapes are not saved when you add them to the picker. Rather, you must use the picker's menu command Save Shapes. The shapes are, by default, added to Photoshop's Custom Shapes folder within the Presets folder, but you have the option of choosing another location.

CLIPPING PATHS AND VECTOR MASKS

Clipping paths and vector paths serve the same purpose—identifying what will be visible or invisible—but they do so at two different levels. Clipping paths are used with images destined for page layout programs, delineating areas of visibility for the image as a whole. Vector masks are used in a similar manner to show and hide areas of individual layers within an image.

Open, closed, and compound paths can all be used to create both clipping paths and vector masks. You must name a work path to save it before you can convert it to a clipping path. Double-clicking a work path in the Paths palette and renaming it will save it, and you can then use the Paths palette menu command Clipping Path.

You can create a vector mask for a layer in either of two ways. You can first create the path and then assign it as a vector mask, or you can create the vector mask and then define it with a path. With or without an active path, use the menu command Layer, Add Vector Mask, or you can (Command-Option-click) [Ctrl+Alt+click] on the Add Layer Mask button at the bottom of the Layers palette.

⇨ *To learn more about creating vector masks and clipping paths, see "Layer Masks, Vector Masks, and Clipping Groups," p. 267 in Chapter 10, "Making Selections and Creating Masks."*

Be aware that all the shapes in the picker at the time are saved in the set—if you want to create a set that consists exclusively of your custom shapes, you'll have to delete the pre-existing shapes first.

In previous versions of Photoshop, vector masks were referred to as "layer clipping paths." Although the old term was accurate, the new term avoids possible confusion with the clipping paths used with page layout programs.

Caution

The Clipping Path dialog box includes a Flatness field. Never enter a value for flatness unless your imagesetter is having trouble outputting curves. The field overrides the device's native setting for vector reproduction.

PHOTOSHOP IN FOCUS

A shape layer in and of itself is rather boring—a layer filled with color and a vector mask—but styles can be applied, the mask can be edited, and once rasterized, even filters can be applied to a shape layer. Here's how:

1. Open a new document in Photoshop, 500×500 pixels, set the resolution to 72, and fill with white, RGB color mode.

2. Select the Custom Shape tool from the Toolbox.

3. Pick a custom shape from the Custom Shape picker in the Options Bar.

4. In the Options Bar, click on the first of the buttons to the left in the Options Bar. The tool is now set to create a shape layer.

5. Drag the Custom Shape tool in the image, starting in the upper-left corner and ending in the lower right. This fills the image with the new custom shape. (The foreground color is insignificant because a layer style will be applied.)

6. In the Options Bar, select the style Color Target (Button) from the Style pop-up palette. It will be applied to the shape layer.

7. Use the Layer, Rasterize, Layer menu command to convert the shape layer to a regular layer of pixels. The layer style is unaffected.

8. Select the Smudge tool from the Toolbox and choose a hard-edged brush of about 40 pixels diameter. In the Options Bar, set it to Mode: Normal, Strength: 100%.

9. Click in the visible pixels on the layer and drag. Repeat, smudging a couple of different areas.

10. Change the Strength to 50% and drag again.

11. In the Layers palette, use the Merge Down menu command to create a single layer of pixels in this image.

12. Apply the filter Pixelate, Crystallize with a cell size of 15.

Creating a shape layer and applying a style can be just the beginning of the creative process. When rasterized or merged, the content of the shape layer can become pixels on which you can apply filters, adjustments, and more.

FROM THE NAPP HELP DESK

The National Association of Photoshop Professionals (NAPP) offers e-mail assistance to its members. Here is some advice from the NAPP Help Desk related to issues in this chapter.

The Chicken or the Egg?

I'm not sure that I understand the fundamental difference between the way Illustrator and Photoshop handle paths to which color is applied. Which comes first, the color or the path?

Unlike the never-ending question about the order of appearance between the chicken and the egg, the path comes first with both Photoshop's stroked/filled paths and Illustrator's objects. In Photoshop, the path tells the program where to apply pixels—along the path for a stroke and within the paths for a fill. In Illustrator, it's basically the same—the path is defined and then color is applied.

The difference lies in what happens afterward. When working with true vector objects, the colors are bound to the path and are not applied until the path is defined in the image. If the path needs to be scaled because the print size changes, there's no change in the overall appearance of the image— the stroke and fill are applied *after* the path is recalculated and added to the image. In Photoshop, on the contrary, once the stroke or fill is applied, it's there for good. Yes, you can scale the pixels, but they are not tied to the path and can therefore lose quality.

Smooth Corner Points

My friend bet me that I can't create a corner anchor point through which a path runs smoothly—she doesn't think my stylus hand is steady enough. Can I win this bet?

The bet is a lead-pipe cinch! You don't even need your Wacom tablet. Straight is smooth, isn't it? Use Show Grid and Snap to Grid. Click once with the Pen tool. Move to the right and up a bit. Click again. Move back down and add a third anchor point to the right and horizontal to the first. End the path by pressing (Return) [Enter]. Now press A (or Shift-A) to activate the Direct Selection tool. Drag that middle point down until it's in line with the other two points. The path now flows smoothly (straight) through the three points, although none are smooth points.

Shutting Down the Auto

Why would I want to turn off the Auto Add/Delete function of the Pen tool in the Options Bar? It seems to me that this is a very useful function.

If paths are placed very closely together in an image, at times you might find that you're trying to start a path, but the Pen tool is converting to the Add Anchor Point or Delete Anchor Point tool. Unchecking the option in the Options Bar enables you to start that new path.

PHOTOSHOP'S ADVANCED CREATIVE CAPABILITIES

IN THIS PART

14

WORKING WITH LAYERS AND LAYER STYLES

by Jeff Foster

IN THIS CHAPTER

UNDERSTANDING THE CONCEPT OF WORKING ON LAYERS

Layers—and understanding how layers work with each other—are what make Photoshop such a powerful tool for the digital imagist. Everything else you do in Photoshop is affected by what you do on specific layers.

The clear, logical layout of the Layers palette, with the "stacking" of layers one on top of the other, helps you keep track of the images and elements you have on each layer. The topmost layers are the most visible. If the top layer is full-screen and set to Normal blending mode and 100% Opacity, nothing beneath it is visible.

Look at Figure 14.1 and imagine you're starting with a white piece of paper as the background. Add to that your base image, and then the shadow of your subject added on a piece of clear plastic film. Continue with your subject(s) on stacked layers of plastic film.

Figure 14.1
Consider the arrangement of layers in the Layers palette as images on stacks of film.

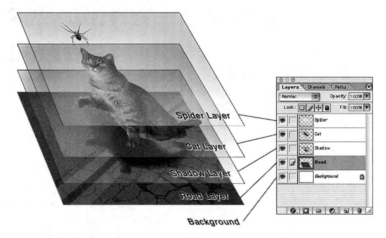

The topmost layer is in the foreground, and the subsequent layers are viewed as being beneath it, creating a complete, composited image. In this example, the spider is the topmost layer and visible in the foreground (see Figure 14.2).

If the topmost image layer is moved beneath the next layer down, it appears to be behind the object in the next layer—just as though you were shuffling stacks of clear film. To reorder layers, click on the layer's name in the Layers palette and drag it beneath the next layer in the stack. In this case, the Spider layer is moved under (or behind) the Cat layer (see Figure 14.3).

➪ *Unsure about "above," "below," "in front," "in back," "over," "under," and the related concepts? See "Relatively Speaking" in the NAPP Help Desk section at the end of this chapter.*

When a layer is named *Background* (in italics) in the Layers palette, it represents a solid layer. Background layers differ from regular layers in a number of ways: They don't support transparency, no layer can be moved below a background layer, and by default they cannot be moved. Convert a background layer to a regular layer by renaming it in the Layers palette.

Figure 14.2
A composite can have several layers that make up the final image, with the topmost layers visible in the foreground.

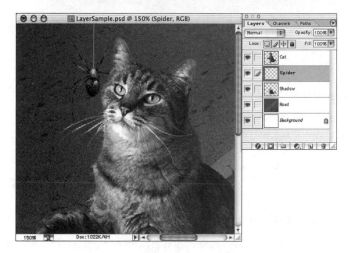

Figure 14.3
The Spider layer is moved down one step in the "stack" of layers, so that it looks like it is behind the cat's head.

LAYERS PALETTE OVERVIEW

Only a few items have been moved or changed on the Layers palette in Photoshop 7 (see Figure 14.4). Best of all, it's been streamlined and is easier to use than previous versions, as the location of frequently used icons and pop-up menus have been added. In addition, the most popular method of changing a layer name has reverted to the pre–version 6.0 double-click-on-the-name method.

Figure 14.4
The Layers palette is one of Photoshop's most powerful features.

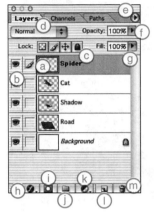

a   Paintbrush icon indicates that the layer is "active" and anything you choose to do will happen directly to this layer.

b   Eye icon indicates whether layer is visible or hidden. Click on this icon to hide the layer, or click on empty space to make it visible again.

c   Lock icons allow you to lock individual layers of transparency, paint or editing, movement or lock all.

d   Blending modes that can be applied to each layer.

e   Layer palette pop-up menu selector.

f   Sets Opacity of layer and Layer Styles, effects and masks.

g   Sets the Fill opacity of the layer, excluding Layer Styles, effects or masks.

h   Adds a Layer Style to the active layer.

i   Adds a Layer Mask to the active layer.

j   Creates a new Layer Set.

k   Creates a new Adjustment or Fill layer.

l   Creates a new Layer. You can also drag a layer to this icon to duplicate it directly.

m   Deletes the active layer. You can also drag a layer to this icon to delete it directly.

Showing and Hiding Layers

To hide layers, simply click on the eye icon of each layer you want to hide. Click on the empty box in the leftmost column to make it visible again. Making a layer visible does not select it or make it active. You must click on the layer name itself to make a layer active.

You can show or hide many layers quickly by dragging through the left column.

Linking Other Layers to the Active Layer

One common problem is not realizing that you're trying to add an effect or paint on a layer that's not selected, or "active." The selected layer is highlighted in the Layers palette and displays the paint-brush icon to indicate it's active. When a link icon appears in this column, the layer is *linked* to the active layer. If you move the active layer, the linked layer or layers move, too. As long as they are linked, the layers maintain their relative positions. You might also link layers to align or distribute them, to merge them, or to create a layer set.

To link a layer to the active layer, click in the second column next to the layer's name. You can link only to the active layer; however, links are maintained when you make another layer active.

Locking Layers

You can lock the active layer's transparency by clicking on the square checkered box in the Lock area of the Layers palette. To lock editing of a layer, click on the paintbrush in the Lock icons.

Click the four-headed arrow icon to lock the location of the layer's content or transforming of a layer, and click on the padlock icon to lock everything on a layer.

Choosing a Blending Mode

You use the Blending Mode pop-up menu to select the layer's methods of interacting with the layers beneath it. The default mode is Normal (see Figure 14.5). Try going down the list and selecting the different blending modes to see what effect they have on your image. In Photoshop 7, the blending modes have been categorized more logically than in previous versions, and there are many more modes to choose from. The Multiply, Darken, Color Burn, and Linear Burn modes are grouped together, as are the Lighten, Screen, Color Dodge, and Linear Dodge modes. Some new modes have been added, such as Linear Light, Vivid Light, and Pin Light. They create very different effects from each other, but all still work in a lightening capacity and are grouped with Overlay, Soft Light, and Hard Light modes.

➡ *The individual blending modes—and how they work—are discussed in "Blending Modes, One by One," p. 487, in Chapter 17, "Using Blending Modes."*

Figure 14.5
Select the blending mode in the pop-up menu.

The Layers Palette Menu

The Layers palette menu contains some commands and options similar to those available with the icons at the bottom of the Layers palette, but it also offers some additional options (see Figure 14.6). You can create new layers, duplicate layers, create layer sets from linked layers, merge layers together, and delete selected individual or grouped layers. You can also dock the palette to the Palette Well at the top of the screen or set palette options from this menu.

14

⇨ *Layer sets, merging layers, flattening images—all are different concepts. Check "Fewer Layers" in the NAPP Help Desk section at the end of this chapter.*

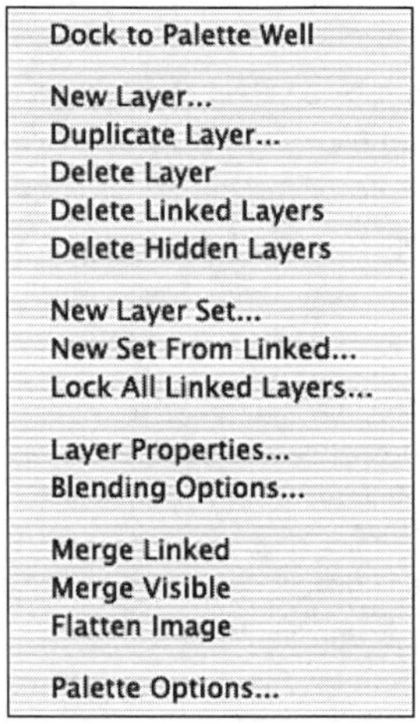

Figure 14.6
The Layers palette menu offers
several options.

Dock to Palette Well

New Layer...
Duplicate Layer...
Delete Layer
Delete Linked Layers
Delete Hidden Layers

New Layer Set...
New Set From Linked...
Lock All Linked Layers...

Layer Properties...
Blending Options...

Merge Linked
Merge Visible
Flatten Image

Palette Options...

The Opacity and Fill Settings

There is a fundamental difference between the layer's Opacity and Fill settings. The Opacity setting affects the entire layer—including any masks or layer styles applied to it; the Fill settings apply only to the layer's content, without affecting anything that's been applied, masked, or stylized. The same is true for adjustment, type, and shape layers as well.

The Layer Palette Buttons

Across the bottom of the Layers palette are several buttons. Although they duplicate commands in the Layer menu and the Layers palette menu, they are easily accessible doorways to incredible creative power.

Adding Layer Styles

Layer styles are applied to the pixels of a layer—the layer's content—and incorporate a combination of light, shadow, color, texture, and gradients. You can use layer styles to create 3D and other effects for the image layer. When a layer style is applied, the Layer Style icon is added next to the layer's name in the Layers palette.

When you click the Add Layer Style icon at the bottom of the Layers palette and select an item from the menu (see Figure 14.7), the Layer Style dialog box opens with the selected effect's settings (see Figure 14.8). You can also double-click the layer in the Layers palette (away from the layer name) to open the dialog box.

⇨ *For more information on working with layer styles, see "Layer Style Effects Overview," p. 398.*

14

Figure 14.7
In the Layer Style menu, select an effect to apply to a layer.

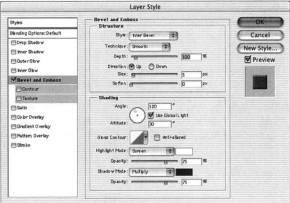

Figure 14.8
The selected layer style appears in the dialog box, where you can adjust the settings.

Adding Layer Masks

Clicking on the Add Layer Mask icon once gives you a rasterized (pixel-based) layer mask that you can paint, edit, and fill with selections. Click on the icon a second time to create a linked vector mask that can be filled with custom shapes or vectors drawn with the Pen tool. When you click the button, any active selection is used as the basis for the mask.

➪ *For a full discussion of layer masks, **see** "Layer Masks, Vector Masks, and Clipping Groups," **p. 267**, in Chapter 10, "Making Selections and Creating Masks."*

14

Layer Sets

Click the Create Layer Set icon to organize multiple layers into groups that can be easily hidden or made visible and arranged into folders. You can then move groups of layers within your document's layer hierarchy. (See "Organizing Layers with Layer Sets," later in this chapter.)

In addition to using layers to streamline the Layers palette, you can use them to isolate the effects of adjustment layers. Normally, an adjustment layer affects all layers below it in the Layers palette. Likewise, by default, an adjustment layer within a layer set affects *all* layers below it, whether they're in the set and not. Changing the layer set's blending mode from Pass Through to Normal prevents any adjustment layer in the set from having an effect on layers outside the set.

You can perform several menu functions by simply (Control-clicking) [right+clicking] on a layer in the Layers palette. This displays the contextual menu, which enables you to access Layer Properties, Blending Options, Duplicate or Delete Layer, Enable Layer Mask, Rasterize Layer, Copy Layer Style, Paste Layer Style, Paste Layer Style to Linked, or Clear Layer Style.

Selecting a Fill or Adjustment Layer

Fill layers can be filled with a solid color, gradient, or pattern. They are often used with a layer mask and a layer style. Click the Layers palette button and select the type of fill layer from the top of the pop-up menu. When you select Color, the Color Picker opens. Select Gradient and the Gradient Fill dialog box opens. When you select Pattern, the Pattern Fill dialog box appears. A pattern is tiled throughout the layer or an active selection.

Using an adjustment layer is the best way to color-correct the layers beneath it without permanently damaging the image layers. You can reverse or eliminate any modifications, corrections, or effects applied to the adjustment layer without any impact on the original image. Adjustment layers can be reopened at any time to change the settings, unlike changes made with the Adjustments commands. Click on the button and select the type of adjustment layer required from the pop-up menu.

Adding and Deleting Layers

Among the most basic layer-related steps are creating and deleting layers. The familiar buttons to the right of the Layers palette handle these tasks. You can add a new layer by clicking on the New Layer button or using the keyboard shortcut (Command-N) [Ctrl+N]. You can quickly duplicate an existing layer—and its content—by dragging the layer from its position in the Layers palette to the button.

Delete the active layer by clicking the Trash icon. Alternatively, you can drag a layer (or a layer mask) to the button to eliminate it.

LAYER BLENDING MODES, OPACITY, AND TRANSPARENCY

A layer's blending mode determines how it interacts with visible layers beneath it, including the layer's Opacity and Fill as well.

(Control-click) [right+click] on a layer and select Blending Options from the contextual menu to open the Layer Style dialog box (see Figure 14.9). Although this dialog box has the same name as the one that opens when you select a layer style, choosing Blending Options displays the Blending Options section at the top with the default settings.

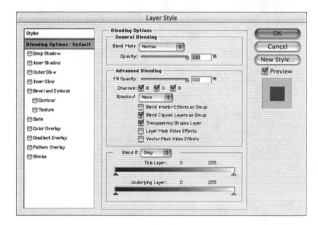

Figure 14.9
The Layer Style dialog box doubles as the Blending Options dialog box, with the default settings visible at the top.

The Advanced Blending section includes options for Fill Opacity (same as Fill in the Layers palette) as well as selectable RGB channels and more. To control the Fill Opacity setting, either type in a percentage for the selected layer or use the slider, as shown in Figure 14.10.

Figure 14.10
The Fill Opacity slider set to 100% makes the selected layer fully opaque.

Setting the Fill Opacity slider lower decreases the entire layer's opacity, even for the layer styles applied to the layer (see Figure 14.11).

Adjusting the Fill Opacity slider (or entering a percentage number in the numeric field) affects only the contents of the layer, not the layer styles applied to it. Notice how the stroke outline and drop shadow are still visible, but the layer content is totally transparent (see Figure 14.12).

14

Figure 14.11
The Fill Opacity slider set to 50% adjusts the opacity of the selected layer and its elements.

Figure 14.12
Only the filled contents of a layer are affected by adjusting the Fill Opacity slider on the selected layer.

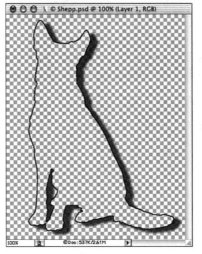 

You can set a layer's blending mode in the Blending Mode dialog box or by simply clicking the Blending Mode pop-up menu in the Layers palette and selecting a mode.

The blending modes are organized into the following groups:

- Normal, Dissolve

- Darken, Multiply, Color Burn, Linear Burn

- Lighten, Screen, Color Dodge, Linear Dodge

- Overlay, Soft Light, Hard Light, Vivid Light, Linear Light, Pin Light

- Difference, Exclusion

- Hue, Saturation, Color, Luminosity

The following figures show a few examples of the various blending mode effects. In Figure 14.13, the Plastic Wrap filter was added to the image layer to create contrast and the blending mode was set to Normal (the default setting). The layer is positioned directly above a nonfiltered layer of the same image.

Figure 14.13
No animals were actually shrink-wrapped in this example.

With the Multiply mode, the filtered layer increases the saturation of the image layer below and darkens the highlights and midtones so that very little of the filtered effect appears (see Figure 14.14).

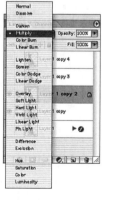

Figure 14.14
The Multiply blending mode applied to the filtered layer darkens and saturates the image layer beneath it.

Applying the Lighten blending mode adds the highlights of the applied Plastic Wrap filter. It also lightens the highlights and saturates the midtones of the underlying image (see Figure 14.15).

14

Figure 14.15
Only the highlights of the applied filter are visible when the Lighten blending mode is selected.

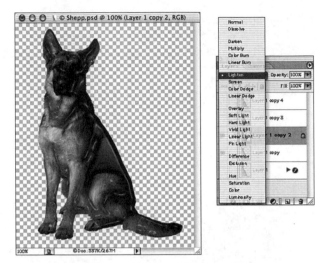

The Screen blending mode lightens the highlights and midtones and desaturates the image underneath (see Figure 14.16).

Figure 14.16
The Screen blending mode lightens and desaturates the underlying image layer.

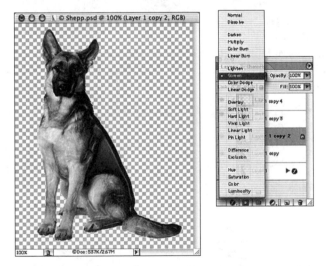

Selecting the Difference blending mode shows the differences between the filtered image and the underlying original image layer (see Figure 14.17).

Luminosity looks similar to the Normal blending mode, working with the blending mode's highlights and midtones, but is actually just the opposite of the Color blending mode (see Figure 14.18).

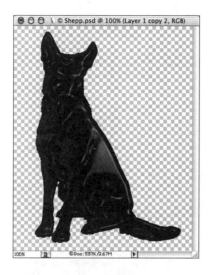

Figure 14.17
The difference between the filtered layer and the original image layer is visible when the Difference blending mode is selected.

Figure 14.18
The Luminosity blending mode looks similar to Normal but is based on the underlying layer's hue and saturation.

ORGANIZING LAYERS WITH LAYER SETS

In addition to placing layers in relation to each other, you can organize groups of layers into layer sets, which are "folders" you can create in the Layers palette. You can create a new layer set or create one from existing linked layers.

Layer sets can be used to sort large files with multiple layers and can be color-coded for easier organization. To hide or show large layer sets, simply click on the eye icon associated with the layer set. This method is especially helpful when designing multiple-stage button rollovers and animation sequences involving multiple layers.

14

To create a layer set, select New Layer Set or New Set From Linked from the Layers palette menu, as shown in Figure 14.19.

Give each layer set a unique name and color when you create it to make organization and navigation through your document layers much easier (see Figure 14.20).

The default blending mode for a new layer set is Pass Through. This is a simple folder that is selectable on or off and has no other effect on the layers inside it.

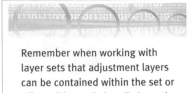

Remember when working with layer sets that adjustment layers can be contained within the set or affect all layers below. To keep the effect of an adjustment layer within the layer set, change the set's blending mode from Pass Through to Normal.

Figure 14.19
Create a new layer set from linked layers.

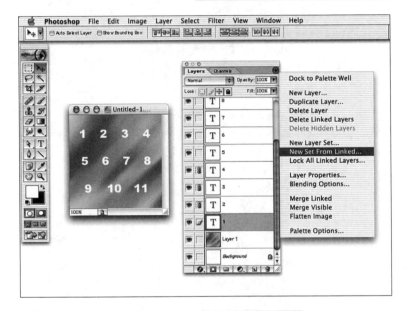

Figure 14.20
Name the new layer set and assign it a color for easier organization.

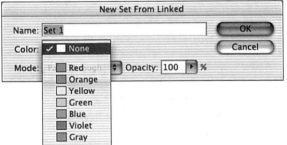

You can select other blending modes that affect all the layers in the layer set and set the opacity for the entire set (see Figure 14.21).

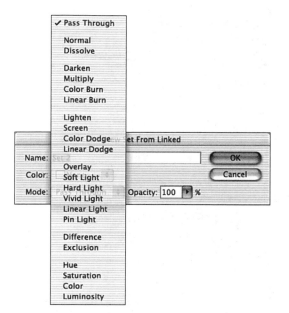

Figure 14.21
Configure the layer set's blending mode and opacity to affect all layers inside the set.

Clicking the arrow to the left of the folder icon opens the layer set in the Layers palette. This enables you to continue working with the content of the layers it contains, including layer styles and individual blending modes (see Figure 14.22).

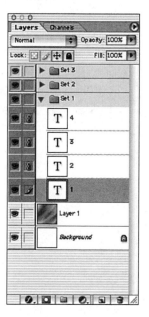

Figure 14.22
You can still work on the individual layers inside a layer set.

To duplicate or delete layer sets, use the corresponding commands in the Layers palette menu. The layers inside a layer set can be locked as a group or merged into one layer, eliminating the layer set and creating a single merged layer (see Figure 14.23).

14

Figure 14.23
Layer sets can be easily duplicated, locked, merged, or deleted
from the Layers palette menu.

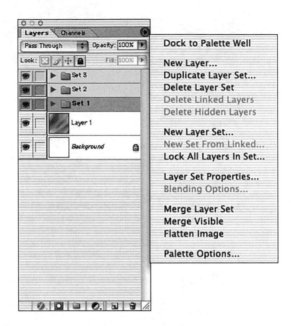

(Right-clicking) [Ctrl+clicking] on a layer set produces a contextual menu, where you can quickly duplicate, delete, or set layer set properties (see Figure 14.24). You can also duplicate a layer set by click-dragging it to the Create New Layer Set icon at the bottom of the Layers palette or delete it by click-dragging to the Trash icon.

Figure 14.24
(Right-click) [Ctrl+click] a layer
set to make quick edits or
changes to its properties.

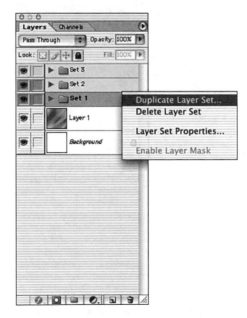

PHOTOSHOP'S SPECIALTY LAYERS

In addition to layers that contain your artwork's pixels, Photoshop uses a number of other types of layers. Adjustment and fill layers change the appearance of regular layers below without actually changing their pixels. Type layers contain any text you add to an image. As long as the type layer is not converted to a regular layer (using the Layer, Rasterize, Type command), the text remains editable and vector-based for sharp output to PostScript devices. Shape layers, which simulate vector objects, are filled with a color, pattern, or gradient and selectively exposed by using one or more vector paths.

Adjustment and Fill Layers

Using fill and adjustment layers over a regular layer enables you to create effects and color corrections nondestructively—no pixels are permanently changed. Fill layers can be added to create overall tonal shifting and colorization, patterns, and effects. Adjustment layers are used in place of the Edit, Adjustment commands (which make permanent changes to the image). They affect all the layers beneath, not just the adjoining layer, so more layers can be affected globally by the placement of your adjustment layer. You can restrict the effect of an adjustment layer to the one layer immediately below by (Option-clicking) [Alt+clicking] on the line between the layer and the adjustment layer in the Layers palette.

The nondestructive nature of adjustment and fill layers means you can experiment with an image until you're satisfied with the results, without actually changing the original image data or risking a burning contrast or oversaturation that can destroy an image. You can always remove or replace an adjustment layer later with no permanent effects to your image or drastic increases in the image size. In addition, each adjustment can always be changed, so you can go back and tweak your layers again—you won't have to start over.

Selecting a fill layer gives you the choice of Solid Color, Gradient, or Pattern for the fill. These layers can be used to quickly create a background color or texture. You can use the Gradient fill layer as an editable gradient that floats above the image layer so that you can modify it at any time (see Figures 14.25 and 14.26).

For more information on adjustment layers, **see** *"Adjustment Layers: The Live Corrections," **p. 468**, in Chapter 16, "Color Correction and the Adjustment Commands."*

14

Figure 14.25
A fill layer with a solid color, gradient, or pattern can be added to any image.

Figure 14.26
Use the Gradient Editor to select the appropriate gradient fill for your adjustment layer.

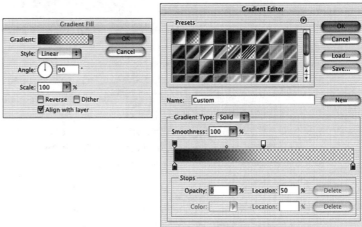

Type Layers

Type layers are created with the Type tool. Clicking in the image automatically creates a new layer that contains the vector-based type. The type's appearance is regulated through the Options Bar and the Character and Paragraph palettes. You can rasterize type layers or convert them to shape layers that can be modified as paths. To rasterize the type layer, use the Layer, Rasterize, Type command or (Control-click) [right+click] on the layer and select Rasterize Type from the contextual menu (see Figure 14.27).

To convert text to an editable custom vector shape, choose the Layer, Type, Convert to Shape command or use the contextual menu's Convert to Shape command. After the text is converted to an outline vector shape, notice that the thumbnails in the Layers palette have changed to a solid fill with a vector mask attached (see Figure 14.28).

When type is converted to outline vector shapes, it can no longer be edited in the Character or Paragraph palettes, including font style and size or spell check. However, you can edit the individual character shapes with the Direct Selection, Path Selection, and pen tools (see Figure 14.29).

There are two contextual menus for the Type tool and type layers. When text is selected or the Type tool is being used to edit, the contextual menu contains font-related and editing options. To access commands that enable you to convert the layer to paths or a shape layer, as well as check spelling and find/replace, make sure the type layer is active in the Layers palette but no text is selected, and then (Control-click) [right+click] directly on a character with the Type tool.

*For more information on working with text, **see** Chapter 11, "Type and Typography in Photoshop," p. 273.*

Figure 14.27
Type layers can be rasterized so that you can apply filters and Liquify effects to them.

Figure 14.28
The text layer converted to an outline shape displays a solid fill with a vector mask.

14

Figure 14.29
After the font layers are converted to vector shapes, every
aspect of the font can be modified with the pen tools.

Figure 14.29
After the font layers are converted to vector shapes, every
aspect of the font can be modified with the pen tools.

Shape Layers

Vector shape layers are layers filled with colors, patterns, or gradients that use vector masks on selective exposed parts of the layer. The exposed parts simulate vector objects and appear as artwork in your image. The individual path segments and anchor points of the vector mask can be edited with the Direct Selection, Path Selection, and pen tools (see Figure 14.30).

The Pen tool can also produce a vector mask on a fill layer (see Figure 14.31). Change the behavior of the Pen tool in the Options Bar.

You can save custom shapes, whether created by converting a type layer or with the Pen tool, in the Custom Shapes Library. Use the Edit, Define Custom Shape command. You can later reuse these shapes with the Custom Shape tool by selecting them from the Custom Shape picker.

The advantage to maintaining type and shape layers as vector (unrasterized) layers is twofold. Vector artwork can be scaled to any size without losing quality, and when outputting to a PostScript device, such as an imagesetter or a laser printer, the edges remain crisp and jaggie-free. For more information on the differences between raster and vector artwork, see Chapter 6, "Pixels, Vectors, and Resolution."

Figure 14.30
Create a shape with the Custom
Shape tool to produce editable
vector points on a vector mask.

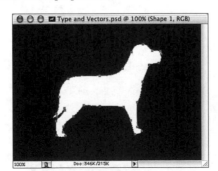

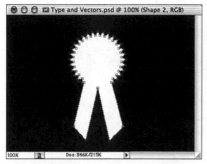

Figure 14.31
Use the Pen tool to create solid fill layers with a vector mask custom shape.

To learn more about the Pen tool and other vector objects in Photoshop, **see** Chapter 13, "The Pen Tools, Shape Layers, and Other Paths," **p. 349.**

USING LAYER STYLES

Quickly add three-dimensional effects and realism to raster and vector image layers by applying a layer style. Choose from a large variety of layer styles in the Preset Library or create one of your own. You can even modify existing or saved layer styles to create a look that's just right for your project, and save the customized style as a preset in your library. You can trade and e-mail custom layer style preset libraries to colleagues or clients. Saved Photoshop files retain the applied style effect on any layer.

Layer style effects range from simple drop shadows and embossed edges to transparent glass and textured 3D patterns. The effects remain with the layer even while editing, whether it's type, a vector shape, or a paint layer. Not all effects can be applied to Background layers, locked layers, or layer sets.

A layer style can have several effects, and each is fully editable after it's been applied because the layer effects don't degrade or destroy the image layer data (see Figures 14.32 and 14.33). The layer with the layer style effects applied has the Layer Style icon next to the layer name in the Layers palette.

Figure 14.32
No effects are applied to this type layer.

Figure 14.33
A layer style with four effects has been applied to this type layer.

Layer Style Effects Overview

When applying a layer style effect to a layer, the Layer Style dialog box opens with the Blending Options section displayed at the top. Click on one of the Styles options in the list to the left to apply an effect and modify its settings. You can then create and customize your own layer style effects.

Drop Shadow

The default Drop Shadow settings, as shown in Figure 14.34, have Multiply as the blending mode, with black as the shadow color and Opacity set to 75%. Generally, these settings are good for most applications. For the angle of the lighting, the Use Global Light option has been selected, which means that all effects lighting is linked together. The distance and size are scalable to the image layer and effect you want to achieve.

Figure 14.34
The default Drop Shadow settings in the Layer Style dialog box are adequate for most applications.

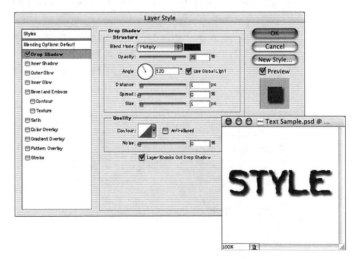

Inner Shadow

The Inner Shadow effect places a drop shadow along the inside edges of the image's fill area—such as cutout text—maintaining the layer's fill color and texture (see Figure 14.35). The default blending mode is Multiply, with black as the shadow color and Opacity set to 75%, which is the same as the default Drop Shadow settings.

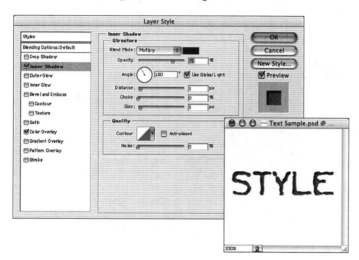

Figure 14.35
The Inner Shadow simulates a cutout effect from the background layer.

Outer Glow

Outer Glow can be used to add a splash of color around an object or a type layer to give it some definition against the background layer. Its primary use is to produce a glow against a dark background, with a default blending mode of Screen; for this example, however, the blending mode has been changed to Normal (see Figure 14.36).

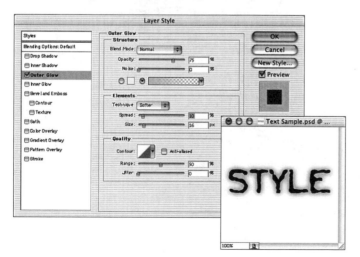

Figure 14.36
Outer Glow produces a splash of color around an image layer's fill edges.

14

Inner Glow

Like its counterpart, Outer Glow, the Inner Glow effect adds a glow around the inside edges of the image layer's fill area. The blending mode is set to Screen with Opacity at 75% for its default, the same default settings as Outer Glow's (see Figure 14.37).

Figure 14.37
Inner Glow adds a glowing rim around the inside of an object image's fill edges.

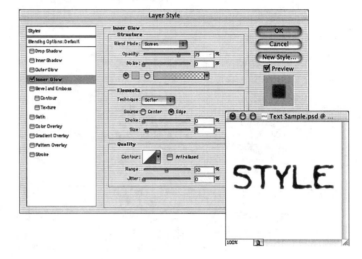

Bevel and Emboss

The Bevel and Emboss effect gives an object layer the most 3D effect of all the layer style effects. Simply applying the default setting to an image layer gives it a beveled plastic appearance (see Figure 14.38). This effect is usually best accompanied by the Drop Shadow layer style to complete the 3D effect.

Figure 14.38
The Bevel and Emboss default settings create a basic 3D effect.

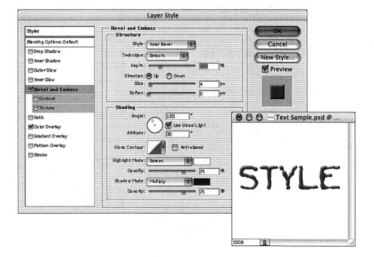

To further enhance the 3D effect of the Bevel and Emboss layer style, you can make adjustments to the Contour settings and apply a texture. Similar to the method that sophisticated 3D rendering programs use, adding a texture to the Bevel and Emboss layer style affects the way light hits the surface of the object layer's content. The texture does not affect the image layer's current fill color (see Figure 14.39).

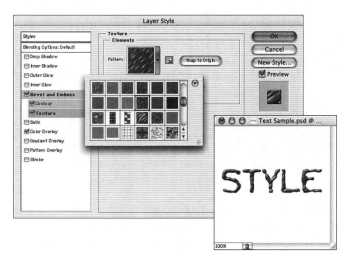

Figure 14.39
Adding a texture to the Bevel and Emboss layer style produces a realistic 3D surface-rendering effect.

Satin

Creating more of a two-dimensional surface effect, the Satin layer style uses the edges of the object layer's fill area to produce "waves" across the surface (see Figure 14.40).

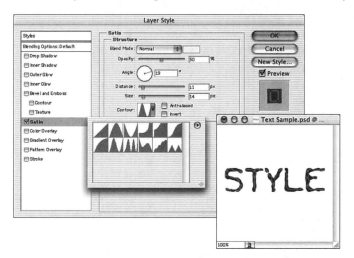

Figure 14.40
The Satin layer style produces a wavelike satin finish on the surface.

14

To edit the contour shape, click on the Contour thumbnail in the Structure section to open the Contour Editor (see Figure 14.41).

Figure 14.41
The Contour Editor enables you to customize the Satin effect for your image.

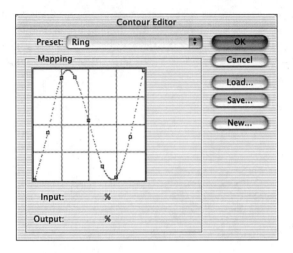

Color Overlay

The Color Overlay layer style is a simple but useful feature that enables you to apply a different color to your object layer without changing the layer's fill color (see Figure 14.42). Using the blending mode options gives you the same versatility to work with other layer style effects so that they show through or work together.

Figure 14.42
The most versatile and simplest of all layer style effects is Color Overlay.

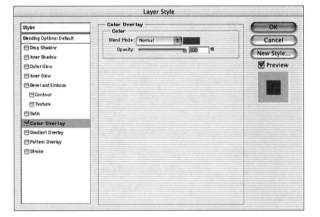

Gradient Overlay

The Gradient Overlay layer style simply applies gradients from the Preset Manager Gradients Library to the image layer's fill area (see Figure 14.43).

Clicking on the gradient thumbnail in the dialog box opens the Gradient Editor, where you can fine-tune your gradients (see Figure 14.44).

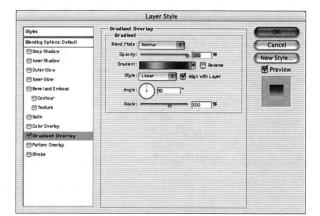

Figure 14.43
Scale and angle adjustments enhance the features of the Gradient Overlay layer style.

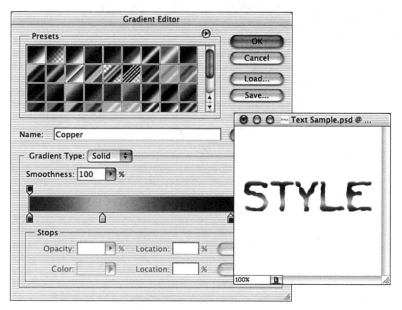

Figure 14.44
Modify existing gradients or create new ones in the Gradient Editor dialog box.

Pattern Overlay

The Pattern Overlay layer style works with other layer style effects, especially if the object layer's fill is solid and needs some texture to bring it to life. To apply the Pattern Overlay, select a pattern from the Preset Manager (see Figure 14.45).

The patterns can be scaled to your image layer's content and often produce interesting results (see Figure 14.46). In addition, clicking and dragging inside the image window moves the pattern around inside the object's fill area, so you can align the pattern to its best viewing position.

14

Figure 14.45
Select a pattern from the Preset Manager.

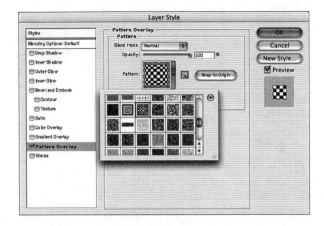

Figure 14.46
Adjusting the scale of the Pattern Overlay layer style.

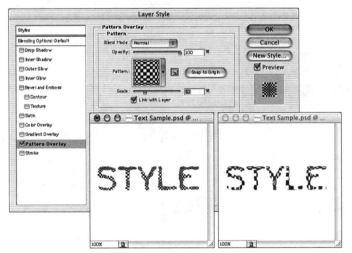

Stroke

The Stroke layer style simply creates a smooth outline of the object's fill edges. You can use the Size slider to adjust the pixel width of the stroke and modify the edge orientation in the Position pop-up menu—the choices are Inside, Outside, or Middle. Other options are typical of any color fill, such as Opacity, Blend Mode, and Color (see Figure 14.47).

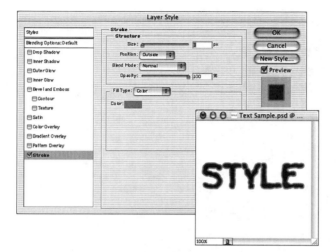

Figure 14.47
The Stroke layer style applies a smooth outline on the object layer's edges.

Combined Layer Style Effects

The best effects are usually combinations of layer style effects that work together to create a realistic 3D rendered image effect. In Figure 14.48, Drop Shadow, Bevel and Emboss with Texture, and Color Overlay are combined.

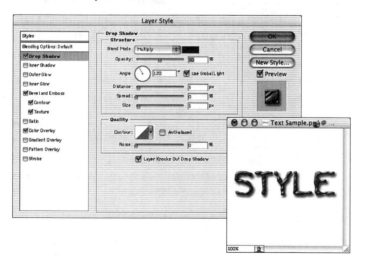

Figure 14.48
Combined layer style effects work together to create a 3D effect.

Selecting Custom Layer Styles from the Preset Library

Many custom layer styles ship with Photoshop 7, and most of them are a good starting point for creating your own special-effects modifications. Remember, you can save any modifications as a new layer style that you can recall for use later or share with colleagues (see Figure 14.49).

14

Figure 14.49
Select saved layer style presets from the library in the Styles palette.

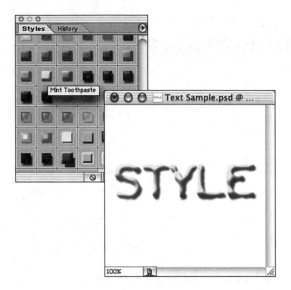

PHOTOSHOP IN FOCUS

The most common reason for linking layers is to preserve their relative positions. When layers are linked, their content can be moved as a unit. You've also seen how to create a new layer set from linked layers. However, you can also link layers to align or distribute them or to merge them.

- Here's how to align or distribute linked layers:

    1. In the Layers palette, make one layer active by clicking on it. Remember that if you're aligning the content of a Background layer, it must be an active layer—it can't move, so it must be the *key* layer.

    2. Position that layer exactly where you want it in the image (unless you're using a Background layer as the key layer).

    3. Leave that layer active and click in the second column next to the layers you want to align to the active layer. You should see a link icon in the column.

    4. Select the Move tool from the Toolbox or press V on the keyboard.

    5. In the Options Bar, click the appropriate button. The buttons' symbols show how they will align the layers.

- Here's how to merge linked layers:

    1. Click in the second column next to all the layers you want to combine.

    2. From the Layers palette menu or the Layer menu, choose the Merge Linked command. The keyboard shortcut is (Command-E) [Ctrl+E].

FROM THE NAPP HELP DESK

The National Association of Photoshop Professionals (NAPP) offers e-mail assistance to its members. Here is some advice from the NAPP Help Desk related to issues in this chapter.

Relatively Speaking

I'm a little confused by all the layers lingo and how layers are arranged.

When we discuss the relative order of layers, we're talking about the *stacking order*. Think of the layers as pieces of paper—or, perhaps better, sheets of transparent plastic. When they're placed on top of each other, it's easy to determine which is on top. If you draw on each sheet of plastic and stack the sheets, artwork on an upper sheet might block artwork on a lower sheet. Moving a sheet below another one changes which artwork hides other artwork.

The Layers palette is arranged the same way: The lowest sheet is on the bottom. When you change the order of layers in the Layers palette, you change the stacking order. Dragging a layer downward in the palette moves the layer's content below in the image.

Fewer Layers

My Layers palette is too full. What's the difference between merging and flattening layers? Do layer sets do the same thing?

Merging layers combines the content of two or more layers into a single layer. The image might still have multiple layers, but the merged layers become one. Merging all the layers of an image differs from flattening the image in an important way: Flattened images don't support transparency. On the flip side, many file formats don't support transparency, either, so an image must be flattened or saved as a copy.

Layer sets are unrelated to merging or flattening. Think of them as a way to organize the Layers palette. Because you can expand and collapse layer sets to show and hide the layers within, they are an excellent way to streamline the Layers palette without losing information. If you need to reduce the number of layers rather than simply hide them, merging is a possibility. Remember, though, that if the layers have overlapping artwork, the lower pixels might be lost. Both merging and flattening limit future editing possibilities.

14

CHANNELS: COLOR AND MORE

IN THIS CHAPTER

15

THE THREE TYPES OF CHANNELS

Channels are used by Photoshop to store image information. Every image has at least one channel, just as it has at least one layer. The layers hold artwork, and the channels hold the color information for that artwork. When an image has only a single layer and a single channel, the palettes may look the same, but they hold different information.

An image can have up to 24 total channels. There are three types of channels, two of which contain color data and one for storing selections.

Component Color Channels

Each color mode has different requirements for the Channels palette, but they all have one thing in common: The data that makes up each pixel's color is stored in one or more channels. The basic content of the Channels palette is always one channel for each of a color mode's *component colors*. Consider the component colors to be the ingredients from which an image is put together. In the case of an RGB image, each pixel's color is a function of the red, green, and blue components.

➡️ *For information on each of the color modes and how they work,* **see** *Chapter 7, "Color Theory and Practice," p. 173, and Chapter 8, "Defining and Choosing Colors," p. 201.*

The Channels palette always has one channel for each component color and, in some cases, a *composite channel* (see Figure 15.1). The composite channel isn't really a channel, in that it doesn't store color information. Rather, its purpose is to enable you to manipulate or edit all the component channels at the same time.

Figure 15.1
Photoshop offers eight basic color modes, with Monotone, Duotone, Tritone, and Quadtone lumped together under the label Duotone.

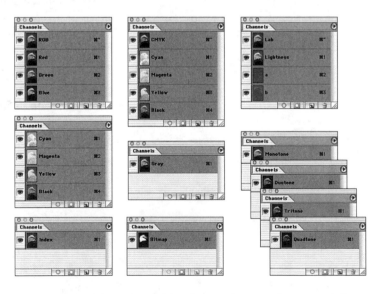

Three of the color modes include composite channels, and four have only one color channel. The basic channels of each color mode are described in the following sections as they are presented in Figure 15.1, from left to right, top to bottom.

RGB

The component color channels are Red, Green, and Blue, and the composite channel is RGB. Each pixel's color is determined by the amount of the three component colors, represented by the gray value of the pixel in each of the color channels. The lighter the pixel in a component color channel, the more of that color. When a pixel has high levels of all component colors, it is very bright. Low levels produce darker pixels. Equal amounts of each color, whether high or low, produce shades of gray. The amount of each component color is measured from 0 to 255, with higher numbers representing more of that color. Typical RGB notation shows the red, green, and blue values for a pixel in order. Examples of RGB notation include 140/133/70 and R:138 G:189 B:212. RGB is used for onscreen work (including Web graphics) and video.

CMYK

The component channels, named for the four primary inks used in commercial printing, are Cyan, Magenta, Yellow, and Black. (Black is abbreviated K to avoid confusion with Blue.) This color mode has a composite color channel, named CMYK. The amount of each ink that will be applied to paper is recorded from 0% to 100%. The more of each ink, the darker the pixel. CMYK values are always recorded in order, such as 21/18/79/28 or 47C 3M 9Y 0K. This color mode is used almost exclusively for preparing images for commercial printing.

Lab

Technically known as CIE Lab and also seen as L*a*b, this color mode is somewhat different. Instead of having component colors that are combined to create a pixel's color, Lab separates the color into two components and records the lightness of the pixels separately. The lightness is recorded in the L channel. The a channel represents the color value on a scale from green to magenta, and the b channel represents blue to yellow. On a standard color wheel, green and magenta are opposite each other, as are blue and yellow. Think of the four points of the compass, all pulling on an object. When North and West pull hardest, the object moves to the northwest. When North and South exert equal pull, and East pulls harder than West, the object moves due east. This is how the a and b channels influence color. When all are equal, the pixel is in the center of the color wheel, the proportions of the colors are equal, and the pixel is gray. The specific shade of gray (or any other color, for that matter) is determined by the L value, the brightness of the pixel. Lightness (L) is measured from 0 (black) to 100 (white). The a value ranges from −120 (green) to +120 (magenta), and b ranges from −120 (blue) to +120 (yellow). Lab notation typically records a pixel's color value as 56/-3/39 or 73L −23a −20b, although you might also see negative numbers in parentheses. Lab color mode is used in Photoshop primarily for image correction and as an interim mode during color conversions.

Multichannel

Pictured in the middle left of Figure 15.1, the Channels palette in Multichannel mode holds one channel for each color and does not have a composite channel. Because the color mode is designed primarily for printing, conversion from RGB produces CMY channels, and conversion from CMYK results in only the loss of the composite channel. (However, because Multichannel mode is not color-managed like CMYK, a color shift is likely.) Conversion from Lab mode produces three alpha channels.

When a Duotone image is converted to Multichannel mode, the original color channel is split into a separate spot channel for each assigned color. There is no standard notation for color values of a Multichannel mode because the number and color of the channels vary from image to image. Multichannel documents can consist exclusively of spot color channels. It is used primarily for print, including as a way of gaining direct control of the channels in a Duotone image.

Grayscale

Grayscale images have only one component color and, therefore, only one component channel, Gray. Because there's only one channel, there is no need for a composite channel. The gray value of each pixel is recorded as a percent, with 0 representing white and 100 representing black. (This is similar to the K channel of a CMYK image.) Grayscale mode is extremely versatile and can be used for Web and print.

Duotone

A blanket term for Monotone, Tritone, and Quadtone images as well as Duotone, this color mode has only one channel, no matter whether one, two, three, or four colors are used in the image. Each of the colors is applied to each pixel. The proportions of the colors are controlled through duotone curves.

➡️ *Adjusting duotone curves is discussed later in this chapter.* **See** *"Working with Duotone Channels,"*
    p. 424.

Indexed Color

Instead of having component color channels, Indexed Color mode relies on a *color table*, a listing of up to 256 individual colors that can be included in an image. The Index color channel seen in the palette can be considered comparable to a composite color channel—it enables you to manipulate all the pixels in the image at one time. Only RGB and Grayscale images can be converted to Indexed Color mode. A pixel's specific color is recorded as its RGB or Grayscale value. Indexed Color mode is used almost exclusively with Web graphics, in the file formats GIF and PNG-8.

Bitmap

Each pixel in a Bitmap color mode image is either black or white—there are truly no shades of gray. A pixel's color is recorded, therefore, as black or white or as 0% gray or 100% gray. Bitmap mode is used for some print and Web images.

Caution

If you ever need to use the Eyedropper tool with an image in Bitmap color mode, ensure that it is set to Point Sample. Using 3 by 3 Average or 5 by 5 Average is likely to show gray values, which do not exist in the image. However, because the pixels are either black or white, sampling isn't typically required.

Spot Color Channels

Spot color channels are primarily used with CMYK and Multichannel documents. They are designed to provide a channel for additional inks to be used in commercial printing. The location in the image where the ink should be applied is stored in the spot channel. A separate printing plate is generated, and an additional run through the press is required. This usually increases the cost of the print job.

If you need to ensure an exact match for a corporate logo, you might want to use a spot color. Another typical use is extending an image's color range beyond what can be produced by using CMYK inks. You can also add neon and metallic colors to an image with spot channels. Spot channels are also used to identify areas of an image over which a varnish will be applied.

> ## Caution
>
> Images containing spot channels should be placed into a page layout program in the DCS 2.0 file format. Although the advanced TIFF format supports spot colors, your page layout program might not recognize the additional channels or generate color separations from them.

⇨ *Want to know how to make spot colors* lower *your printing costs? See "Stop Some Presses" in the NAPP Help Desk section at the end of this chapter.*

A spot channel is added to the image—and to the Channels palette—by using the Channels palette menu command New Spot Channel. In the dialog box, click the color swatch to open the Color Picker (see Figure 15.2).

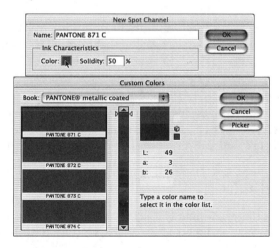

Figure 15.2
Spot colors are typically selected from a Custom book in the Color Picker.

The name of the color selected is automatically updated in the New Spot Channel dialog box, as is the swatch. Solidity refers to how the spot channel will be viewed onscreen—it has no effect on printing at all. When set to 100% solidity, the spot color will be completely opaque onscreen in areas where it will be printed at 100% ink density. (Lesser tints of the ink, identified in the channel by gray values under 100%, will be proportionately reduced in opacity.) Setting the solidity to 0%, however, does *not* make the spot color transparent. Rather, it simply reduces the opacity of the spot color areas. Solidity has no effect when the spot channel is the only visible channel.

15

The Solidity field is previewed live in the image, so you can experiment with various settings before closing the dialog box. You can also reopen the spot color options to change the setting by double-clicking the spot channel in the Channels palette.

There are three basic techniques for identifying where a spot color will be applied:

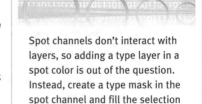

Spot channels don't interact with layers, so adding a type layer in a spot color is out of the question. Instead, create a type mask in the spot channel and fill the selection with black.

- Make a selection in the image before using the New Spot Channel command.

- Create the new spot channel, and then use Photoshop's various tools and commands to create a grayscale representation of the spot color.

- Make a selection with one or more channels active, copy, and then paste into the spot channel.

Spot channel information does not appear in the Layers palette. You edit the spot color information by editing the spot channel. Remember that the spot channel is a grayscale representation (even when the Preferences are set to show it in color). Paint with shades of gray, not the spot color itself, in the spot channel. Painting with black produces areas of 100% spot color tint. To show onscreen where the spot color will print, the spot channel must be visible in the Channels palette.

Alpha Channels

Instead of being used to record color information, alpha channels are masks. Each alpha channel represents a selection. They can be created by using the Channel palette's menu command New Channel, the New Channel button at the bottom of the palette, the palette's Save Selection as Channel button, or the menu command Select, Save Selection. The third and fourth techniques require that you have an active selection to create the alpha channel.

Like any channel, you can edit an alpha channel as a grayscale image. By default, areas of the channel that are black will be completely excluded from the selection, and white areas will be completely selected. Use shades of gray to create partially selected areas or gradients and feathering.

➪ *To learn more about creating alpha channels,* **see** *"Alpha Channels and Masks,"* **p. 262** *in Chapter 10, "Making Selections and Creating Masks."*

The New Channel dialog box shown in Figure 15.3 enables you to name the channel, determine whether to reverse black and white, and choose how the mask will appear onscreen when active with one or more color channels.

When you choose Color Indicates Selected Areas, the mask is reversed. Painting with black includes areas within the mask, and they will be selected when the channel is loaded as a selection. This option also reverses the appearance of the mask's overlay (see Figure 15.4). The dialog box offers a choice of color for the mask overlay as well as variable opacity.

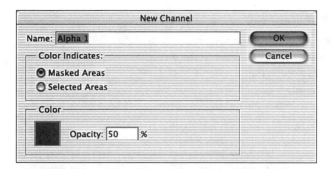

Figure 15.3
The color and opacity you select in the dialog box affect only the onscreen appearance of the mask when color channels are also visible.

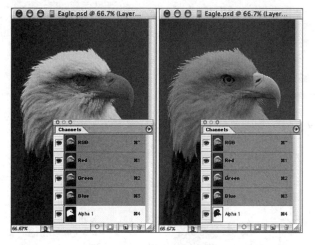

Figure 15.4
On the left, the overlay indicates masked areas. On the right, the overlay indicates selected areas. As you can see, the thumbnail in the Channels palette is also reversed.

In Figure 15.4, in both examples, the mask is visible, but the color channels are active. To edit the mask, click on the alpha channel in the Channels palette to activate it.

The selection represented by the alpha channel is activated by using the menu command Select, Load Selection and then choosing the alpha channel from the pop-up menu. You can also load a mask as a selection directly from the Channels palette—(Command-click) [Ctrl+click] the alpha channel in the palette.

Sometimes it is easier to edit a mask if you switch back and forth between Color Indicates Masked Areas and Color Indicates Selected Areas.

⇨ *Need to save a Quick Mask as an alpha channel? See "Quick Channels" in the NAPP Help Desk section at the end of this chapter.*

THE CHANNELS PALETTE

Both color channels and alpha channels are stored and managed in the Channels palette. Understanding the mechanics of the palette simplifies working with channels.

The Anatomy of the Palette

The component color channels—those channels that are built into the document's color mode—always appear at the top of the Channels palette. Any spot color channels or alpha channels also stored in the palette appear below the component colors. To make a channel active, click on it in the palette. You can Shift-click to activate multiple channels. Clicking on the composite channel (when the color mode has one) activates all component color channels, but not alpha or spot channels. An alpha channel appears as a grayscale image when it is the only active channel, but as a translucent red overlay (by default) when one or more color channels are also visible.

The Channels palette identifies the individual channels by name and shows a thumbnail of the content (see Figure 15.5). Spot channels and alpha channels can be renamed, but the component color channels and the composite channel cannot. To rename a spot or alpha channel, double-click its name in the Channels palette and type the new name.

Remember that keyboard short-cuts can be used to activate individual channels. When the image has a composite channel (RGB, CMYK, and Lab modes), use (Command) [Ctrl] and the tilde key (~), located to the left of the number 1 on standard keyboards. The other channels are activated with (Command) [Ctrl] and the number keys, in the order in which the channels appear in the Channels palette.

Figure 15.5
Using the Palette Options command from the palette menu, you can choose any of three thumbnail sizes or no thumbnail. The palette is shown here with Small thumbnails, the default.

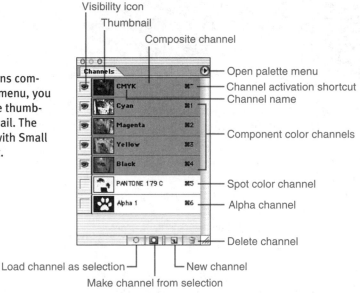

Visibility icon
Thumbnail
Composite channel
Open palette menu
Channel activation shortcut
Channel name
Component color channels
Spot color channel
Alpha channel
Delete channel
Load channel as selection
Make channel from selection
New channel

In the Channels palette, composite channels (including the Index and Duotone channels) are shown in color. Component color channels for RGB, CMYK, Lab, and Multichannel images are, by default, shown as grayscale. (The Gray channel of a Grayscale document and the Bitmap channel of a Bitmap image are, of course, shown in their respective color modes.) Photoshop's Display & Cursors preferences offer the option of showing the color channels in color. In addition to the thumbnails in the Channels palette, this affects the display when a single channel is active in the palette.

Rather than a grayscale image, the channel is portrayed as shades of the component color. When working with RGB images, you may find this option helpful. However, the yellow and cyan channels of most CMYK images are too pale to be of much use when displayed in color.

The Channel Palette Menu

In addition to duplicating the functions of the buttons at the bottom of the palette, the Channels palette menu provides a couple of powerful tools (see Figure 15.6).

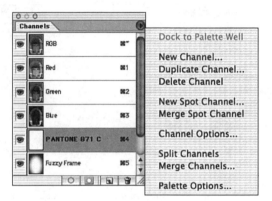

Figure 15.6
Not all menu commands will be visible at the same time. For example, Split Channels requires a multichannel document to be open, and Merge Channels is available only with multiple single-channel images open.

➡️ *The Split Channels and Merge Channels commands are discussed later in this chapter.* **See** *"Splitting and Merging Channels," p. 428.*

The New Channel command opens the New Channel dialog box and creates a new alpha channel. If there is no selection active at the time, the mask fills the image. Duplicating a channel by using the menu command is the same as dragging a channel to the New Channel button at the bottom of the palette—a copy of the channel is created as an alpha channel. Using the Delete Channel command removes the channel from the palette, just like dragging a channel to the trash icon in the palette.

The New Spot Channel command opens the dialog box shown previously in Figure 15.2, in which you choose the spot color, name, and solidity for onscreen viewing. Merging a spot channel removes the channel from the palette and attempts to duplicate the appearance using the component color channels. Photoshop calculates the nearest equivalent color using the CMYK or RGB component colors and adds appropriately to each of those channels. Merge Spot Channel is available only for CMYK and RGB color modes. The Solidity value selected in the channel options also plays a part in the image's appearance after the merge. Photoshop attempts to maintain the image's *onscreen* appearance—when solidity is reduced, the spot channel is semi-opaque. Also be aware that Merge Spot Channel requires a flattened image.

The Channel Options command is available only when a single channel is active in the palette. It opens the Spot Channel Options dialog box or the Channel Options dialog box, depending on whether a spot or alpha channel is active (see Figure 15.7).

To create a spot channel from an existing color channel, duplicate the channel, and then use the Channel Options command to convert it from an alpha channel to a spot color channel.

15

Figure 15.7
The Color for a spot channel is the ink color, but an alpha channel's Color option refers only to the onscreen overlay when editing the mask with other channels visible.

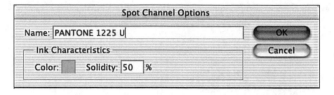

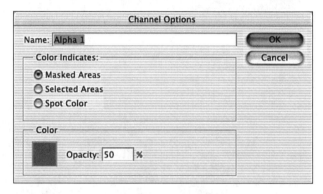

The Palette Options command offers a choice of thumbnail sizes for the Channels palette. You can show small (the default), medium, large, or no thumbnails. You can also change thumbnail size by (Control-clicking) [right+clicking] in an empty area below the channels in the palette and selecting from the contextual menu (see Figure 15.8).

Figure 15.8
The Channels Palette Options dialog box is opened through the palette menu, and the small contextual menu is opened by (Control-clicking) [right+clicking] at the bottom of the palette, as shown.

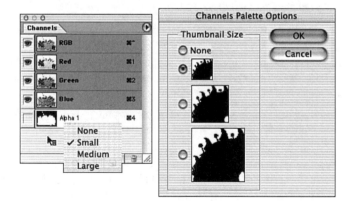

The Channels Palette Content by Color Mode

The basic content of the Channels palette varies depending on the document's color mode. All color modes have one or more component color channels, and some modes also have a composite channel. The composite channel actually represents the activation of all the document's component channels at the same time. Color modes without a composite channel can have only one channel active at a time. In addition to the component color channels, some color modes can have spot color channels and alpha channels. Table 15.1 shows the content of the Channels palette by color mode.

Table 15.1 Color Mode and the Channels Palette

Color Mode	Number of Component Colors	Composite Channel	Spot Channels	Alpha Channels
Bitmap	1	No	No	No
Grayscale	1	No	Yes	Yes
Duotone	1*	No	Yes	Yes
Indexed Color	1	No	Yes	Yes
RGB	3	Yes	Yes	Yes
CMYK	4	Yes	Yes	Yes
Lab	3**	Yes	Yes	Yes
Multichannel	***	No	Yes	Yes
16-Bit Grayscale	1	No	No	No
16-Bit RGB	3	Yes	No	No
16-Bit CMYK	4	Yes	No	No
16-Bit Lab	3**	Yes	No	No

*Duotone color mode includes Monotone, Duotone, Tritone, and Quadtone images. Each has only one color channel.

**Rather than component color channels, Lab mode has two channels for color and one channel for the luminosity value of each pixel.

***Multichannel mode contains one channel for each color.

⇨ *Confused about spot channels in nonprint color modes? See "Spot Colors in RGB and Lab" in the NAPP Help Desk section at the end of this chapter.*

A Note About 16-Bit Color

Photoshop permits you to work in 16-bit color for RGB, CMYK, Lab, and Grayscale color modes. When each component color is recorded with 16 bits of information rather than 8 bits, the file size doubles. However, the number of possible colors for each pixel increases exponentially. Instead of 256 possible values for each pixel in each color channel, 65,536 possible values are available. With more than 65,000 possible values for each of the three channels in an RGB image, the theoretical number of colors available is overwhelming.

Although most output devices can't handle the additional color information or don't have the capability of reproducing such fine variations among similar colors, 16-bit mode can be printed. Some film recorders, especially with grayscale images, can show improved tonal range.

The disadvantages of 16-bit color usually outweigh the improved color depth. In addition to doubling the file size, 16-bit mode does not support Photoshop's layers, filters, some color adjustment commands, and many tools.

Channels Palette Shortcuts

Using shortcuts can simplify and speed work with channels. Table 15.2 presents the most common Channels palette shortcuts.

Table 15.2 Channels Palette Shortcuts

Procedure	Shortcut
Show/hide the Channels palette	Press F7 (when docked with the Layers palette).
Skip the New Channel dialog box	(Command-click) [Ctrl+click] the New Channel button.
Convert an alpha channel to a spot color channel	Use the Channel Options dialog box.
Activate a channel	Use the shortcut shown to the right of the channel name in the Channels palette.
Rename a spot or alpha channel	Double-click the channel's name in the Channels Palette (component and composite channels cannot be renamed).
Change thumbnail size	(Control-click) [right+click] in the empty area below the channels in the palette.
Load a channel as a selection	Click the Load Channel button in the Channels palette.
(Command-click) [Ctrl+click] the channel in the palette.	Hold down (Option) [Alt] and use the channel activation shortcut.
Add channel to a selection	(Command-Shift-click) [Ctrl+Shift+click) the channel in the palette.
Subtract a channel from a selection	(Command-Option-click) [Ctrl+Alt+click] the channel in the palette.
Intersect the channel with a selection	(Command-Option-Shift-click) [Ctrl+Alt+Shift+click] the channel in the palette.

WORKING WITH CHANNELS

Editing channels in Photoshop gives you perhaps the ultimate control over an image's appearance. You can individually manipulate each component color value of each pixel or change a single component color for all pixels. You can even change *all* color values for *every* pixel.

Even if you've never opened the Channels palette, you've worked with channels before. Every time you've used Levels or Curves, you've directly manipulated the channels. At a more basic level, every time you change any pixel in any way, you're making a change to one or more color channels. Remember that without the channels, the pixel doesn't have color. Without color, the pixel is invisible.

Color Channels: Grayscale at Heart

The key to working directly in the Channels palette is remembering that each channel is nothing more than a grayscale image. Treat the channel as a single-layer grayscale image and use the same tools and commands that you would use on the layer of a grayscale image. Each pixel can be any of 256 different "gray" or brightness values. When considered with the other component color channels of the image, that value is actually the proportion of the channel's color.

Photoshop's Display & Cursors preferences offer the option of showing individual channels in color. When one channel is active, you'll see a monotone image in that channel's color rather than a grayscale image.

➡️ *The Grayscale slider in the Color palette uses 0%–100%. Want to know how to take advantage of all 256 levels of gray? See "Increasing the Gray Range" in the NAPP Help Desk section at the end of this chapter.*

When modifying a channel, click in the left column next to the composite channel so that you can monitor the effect of your changes on the image's overall appearance.

To edit an individual channel, click on it in the Channels palette. By default, the image will appear in grayscale, with only the values of the selected channel visible. Changes made are applied to only that active channel.

You can also make two or more channels active at the same time by Shift-clicking on them. When multiple color channels are active, the image appears in color, using a blend of the selected colors (see Figure 15.9).

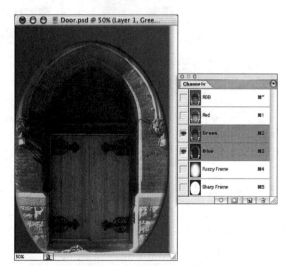

Figure 15.9
The Green and Blue channels are active in the Channels palette, so the window displays the image in a combination of greens and blues rather than grayscale.

You can also work with one or more channels active and all channels visible. By clicking in the left column next to the composite channel, or next to any channels of your choice, you can make them visible without being active. Likewise, you can hide the active channel by clicking the eyeball icon. At least one channel must be visible at all times.

15

The Relationship Between Channels and Layers

The color channels in the Channels palette show the content of the currently visible layer or layers. Remember that you can edit only one layer at a time, so the appearance of the Channels palette might not match the pixels with which you're actually working. Likewise, when working with the Layers palette visible, you must be aware of which channel or channels are active.

For example, compare the Layers and Channels palettes in Figure 15.10. On the left, the layer with the five blue balloons is active, as is the composite channel. If you edit the layer, you're editing all color channels. On the right, only the Blue channel is active—changes made to the layer will affect only the blue component of each pixel.

Figure 15.10
On the right, only the Blue channel is active, but all channels are visible. Unless the Channels palette is open, it's not immediately evident that changes will be made to only one channel.

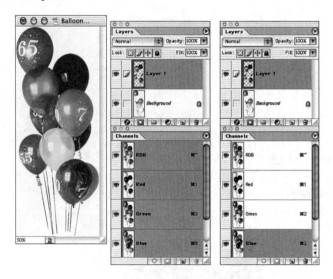

Remember, too, that a layer can be active but not visible or visible but not active. Likewise, you can have a single channel active but not visible—although this makes it impossible to judge the effect of your actions.

Remember that spot color channels are a different story. The pixels for a spot channel don't exist in the Layers palette—they're only a function of the spot channel itself. To edit the spot color in the image, you work with black, white, and shades of gray directly in the spot channel.

Filtering and Adjusting Individual Channels

Photoshop's filters can be applied to channels individually. You might do this to control the impact of a filter, to produce a special effect, or to fix a problem that occurs in only one or two channels.

Digital camera images often have a lot of noise. When you examine the channels individually, you'll often find that the noise is primarily or exclusively in the Blue channel. Instead of applying a Gaussian Blur or Dust & Scratches filter to the entire image, which results in a general softening of detail, you can filter only the noisy channel, retaining detail in the other channels. Figure 15.11 shows one example.

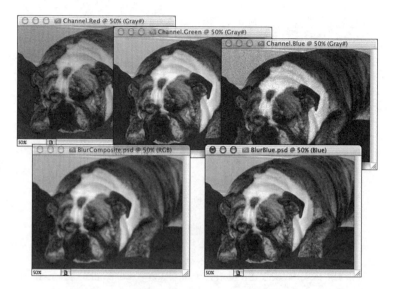

Figure 15.11
The original three channels are shown. The Blue channel contains the noise. Blurring the composite channel (left) degraded the image far more than blurring only the Blue channel (right).

Likewise, image adjustments can be applied to one channel rather than the entire image. In Figure 15.12, the darkness of the Blue channel thumbnail in comparison to the Green and Red channels is an indication that the skin tones are too yellow.

You can approach single-channel correction in a pair of ways. You can select the channel in the Channels palette to make it the only active channel and make your corrections, or you can use the adjustment dialog boxes to work with a single channel (see Figure 15.13).

Multichannel color mode doesn't have a composite channel, so to apply a filter you can Shift-click each channel in the Channels palette, or apply the filter to each channel individually. Use (Command-F) [Ctrl+F] to reapply a filter with the same settings to each additional channel.

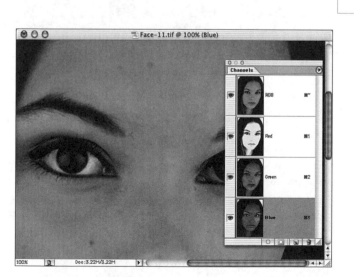

Figure 15.12
You don't need to see this image in color to recognize a problem—the thumbnails in the Channels palette tell the tale.

15

Figure 15.13
The image adjustment dialog boxes include menus from which you can select the channel to adjust.

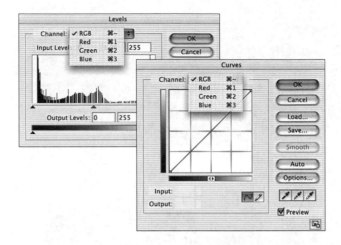

When multiple channels (but not the composite channel) are selected in the Channels palette, the dialog boxes show which channels are selected and the menu includes only those selected channels (see Figure 15.14).

Figure 15.14
If the Red and Blue channels were selected, the dialog box would show RB and list only those two channels.

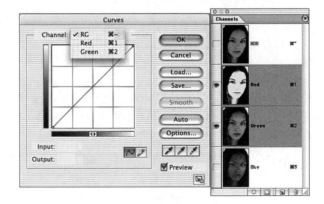

Working with Duotone Channels

Duotone images use channels differently than other color modes. You can make changes to the image's appearance by using the Channels palette, but the application of color is done through the Duotone Options dialog box (see Figure 15.15).

You can change the curve for each ink independently. Typically, a duotone image uses black and one other ink. The black ink creates a grayscale image, which is tinted with the second color. By adjusting the curve of the second color, you can customize the appearance of the duotone. Figure 15.16 shows three variations of the same image.

Remember, too, that you can convert a duotone image to Multichannel mode, which creates a regular color channel for each ink. Multichannel images can be saved as Photoshop (.psd) or prepared for print using DCS 2.0.

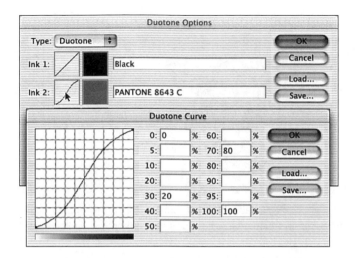

Figure 15.15
Clicking the curve thumbnail in the Duotone Options dialog box opens the Duotone Curve for that ink.

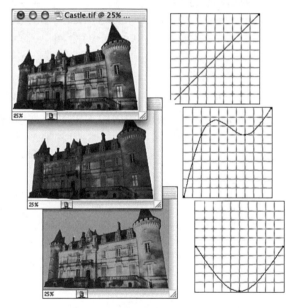

Figure 15.16
The black ink curve is identical for each image. The top image retained the default curve for the second ink. The lower two images use the curves shown.

ADVANCED CHANNEL MANIPULATION

Photoshop includes some very sophisticated tools for manipulating channels. You can use them to modify existing channels or even to create new documents from channels.

Channel Mixer

The menu command Image, Adjustment, Channel Mixer opens the dialog box shown in Figure 15.17. You can adjust the content of a color channel by using the content of the other channels as source material. In Figure 15.17, the gorilla is too red. The content of the channel can be modified by copying some of the information from the Green and Blue channels.

Figure 15.17
In this example, the Channel Mixer reduces the intensity of red by making that channel's content closer to that of the other channels—"neutralizing" the overly intense reds.

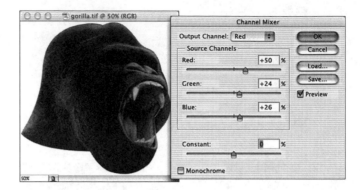

You can use Channel Mixer to completely replace the content of one channel with that of another channel. Select the target channel from the menu at the top of the dialog box, and then move its slider to 0% and the replacement channel's slider to 100%.

The Channel Mixer gives you incredible control when creating a grayscale image from a color image. Select the Monochrome check box, and the output channel automatically switches to Gray. Adjust the sliders to take the best of each channel. After you click OK, use the menu command Image, Mode, Grayscale to complete the transformation.

Here are some tips for using the Channel Mixer:

- Channel Mixer is available only when the composite channel is active in the Channels palette.

- You can make adjustments to one channel, and then switch to another to change it without leaving the dialog box. All channels can be adjusted before you click OK.

- Using a negative number inverts the channel's content before adding it to the output channel.

- Reducing the Constant slider adds black uniformly across the output channel; increasing the value adds white.

- You can select the Monochrome check box to desaturate the image and then uncheck the box to add a tint to the image.

- To maintain the overall tonality of the image, try to keep the output channel's value close to 100%. If you adjust the Constant slider, multiply its value by three when adding to or subtracting from the total percentage.

- Make a selection before opening the dialog box to restrict the change to part of an image. You can use this technique along with the Monochrome check box to force parts of a CMYK to appear only in the Black channel. This is an excellent way to ensure that shadows print with black ink only.

Calculations and Apply Image

The menu command Image, Calculations creates an alpha channel, a selection, or a new document (consisting of a single alpha channel). You blend the values of two channels, with or without a mask, to create the final product (see Figure 15.18).

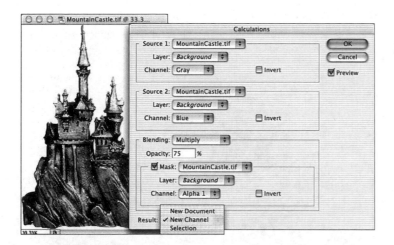

Figure 15.18
The Gray channel used as Source 1 is equivalent to a grayscale copy of the RGB image. Calculations also has the capability of using channel information from a single layer or from Merged, a composite of all layers.

Calculations can also be used with multiple images—but they must have exactly the same pixel dimensions (see Figure 15.19). Two images can supply source channels, and a mask can be created from an alpha channel in a third image.

Figure 15.19
In this example, Calculations used a channel from each image and a mask from the Bride image to create the new document on the right.

The Apply Image command, also found under the Image menu, is similar to using Calculations with two documents. You specify a target layer and channel before opening the dialog box, and then choose the source layer and channel from another (or the same) image (see Figure 15.20).

The Calculations and Apply Image commands do very little that you can't do manually in the Layers and Channels palettes. One difference between them and copying and pasting layers and channels are two additional blending modes. These commands offer the Add and Subtract blending modes, found nowhere else in Photoshop.

Add and Subtract blending modes (see Figure 15.21) perform simple mathematical calculations on the channel values for each pixel. The value from each channel (0 to 255 for RGB images) is added or subtracted. The Scale factor is then applied. Ranging from 1.0 to 2.0, consider it the divisor.

15

When set to 2, the combined value is averaged. The Offset field enables you to supply a constant that is either added to (positive) or subtracted from (negative) each pixel value. Offset can range from −255 to +255. When Scale is set to 1, use Offset to prevent too many of the pixel values from being either 0 (black) or 255 (white).

Figure 15.20
If the target image has multiple layers, flatten or select a specific layer before you open the dialog box.

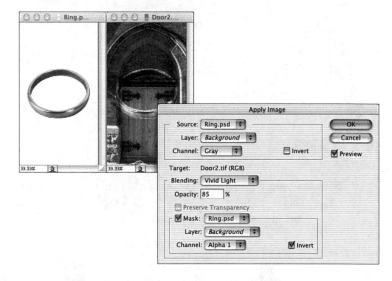

Figure 15.21
The Subtract blending mode also offers Scale and Offset.

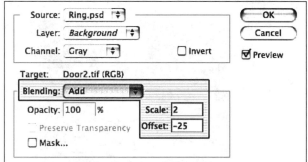

Splitting and Merging Channels

The Channels palette menu contains a pair of very powerful commands: Split Channels and Merge Channels. The Split Channels command creates a grayscale document from each of the channels in the Channels palette (except the composite channel, which is not truly a color channel). The original image is not retained, and your result is a series of one-channel grayscale images. Every color, spot color, and alpha channel is converted to a separate document. Split Channels requires a flattened image and is not available for Indexed Color or Bitmap color mode images. Duotones, regardless of the number of colors, create a single grayscale image from the Duotone channel, plus an image for each spot or alpha channels.

The resulting channels are named for the original image, followed by a dot and the channel name. If you'll be recomposing the image using Merge Channels, retain these filenames. If you'll be using the individual files separately, remember to assign a more reasonable name. For example, if you split an RGB image named Door.psd, the resulting files will have working names of Door.psd.Red, Door.psd.Green, and Door.psd.Blue. You'll want to assign filenames that have a dot only at the end of the filename, immediately before the file extension, if the image will stand alone.

The Merge Channels command is designed to re-create a document that's been divided by using the Split Channels command. However, it can be used on any open grayscale documents that have identical pixel dimensions, are flattened, and have only a single channel (see Figure 15.22).

Whether working with documents created by Split Channels or other grayscale images, the Merge Channels command opens two dialog boxes in sequence (see Figure 15.23).

If Multichannel mode is selected for the merged document, a series of dialog boxes, such as that shown in the center of Figure 15.23, appear. You assign a document to each channel. If you choose RGB, CMYK, or Lab color mode, a single dialog box is used to assign documents to channels. You can click the Mode button to change your selection for the merged document's color mode. Merge Channels uses the Split Channels names, if available, to automatically assign the images to their original color channels (see Figure 15.24).

If you have an image that's too large to fit on the available removable media or to send as an e-mail attachment, Split Channels may be the answer. Each of the resulting documents is substantially smaller than the original. The separate files can be combined later by using the Merge Channels command.

Caution

There is no Undo with Split Channels—not even the History palette can reverse this command. Remember that the original image is lost (unless saved on disk) and can be re-created only with the Merge Channels command.

Figure 15.22
The three images can be combined by using Merge Channels because they all are flattened grayscale images with only one channel and have exactly the same pixel dimensions.

Figure 15.23
The top dialog box appears first. The CMYK Color option is available if four or more appropriate images are open.

Figure 15.24
Merge Channels uses the dot-channel-name suffixes created by Split Channels to assign the images to their original channels.

PHOTOSHOP IN FOCUS

One statement in this chapter deserves a bit more attention. The Channel Mixer is touted as an excellent way to create grayscale images from color pictures. To see for yourself, try this:

1. Open a copy of an RGB image.

2. If it has multiple layers, flatten it.

3. Click twice on the leftmost button at the bottom of the History palette. That makes a pair of copies of the image. Zoom out, if necessary, and position the windows so that you can view all three onscreen at the same time.

4. Use the Image, Mode, Grayscale menu command to convert one image.

5. Click on another copy of the image. Use the Image, Adjustments, Desaturate menu command followed by Image, Mode, Grayscale.

6. Switch to the third copy, and use Image, Adjustments, Channel Mixer to open the dialog box.

7. Select the Monochrome check box.

8. Set the Red, Green, and Blue fields to 40, and change the Constant slider to -7.

9. Concentrate on an area of extreme highlight or extreme shadow. Slowly move the sliders back and forth, juggling the amounts of each channel you add or subtract. Watch how you can target certain tonal ranges, depending on the content of each channel.

10. As you work, compare this image with the others. Look for a balance in your mix that makes the image "pop" and provides the best tonal range.

FROM THE NAPP HELP DESK

The National Association of Photoshop Professionals (NAPP) offers e-mail assistance to its members. Here is some advice from the NAPP Help Desk related to issues in this chapter.

Stop Some Presses

I want to use spot colors in my design, but the client doesn't want to pay for a fifth or sixth color. How can I keep the cost down?

Consider skipping CMYK and using just one or two spot colors and black. Work in a monotone or duotone, and add a splash of spot color for a logo or other point of emphasis. The results can be striking and less expensive than a full four-color press run because you're using fewer colors. Check with the print shop before getting too far into the project.

Quick Channels

I like to work in Quick Mask mode, but when I exit, I lose my channel. Can I save it?

Quick Mask mode deletes the temporary channel when you return to normal editing mode, but you can create an alpha channel from the Quick Mask channel. After exiting Quick Mask mode, use the Select, Save Selection menu command. Even easier, however, is creating the alpha channel *before* exiting Quick Mask mode. Simply duplicate the Quick Mask channel by dragging it to the New Channel button in the Channels palette, or select Duplicate Channel from the Channels palette menu or the contextual menu. Don't duplicate the channel until you've finished editing it, or it won't be an exact copy of the Quick Mask.

Spot Colors in RGB and Lab

Spot colors are for commercial printing, so why can I add them to RGB and Lab images?

Remember that conversion to CMYK color mode often happens late in a workflow. You can add the spot color channels at any time—they're maintained when you do your final preprint color conversion. In addition, you can use a spot channel as an interim step in an RGB image. Create the spot channel, and apply the color. Because the spot color is in a separate channel, it is protected while you continue editing and adjusting the rest of the image. Later, use the Channels palette menu command Merge Spot Channel to integrate that channel into the RGB channels.

Increasing the Gray Range

The Grayscale slider in the Color palette gives me only 101 different levels of gray (0%–100%). How can I use all 256 levels available?

Work in Grayscale, but set the color palette to RGB. As long as all three component values are identical, you've got gray. When you define your grays in RGB, you can take advantage of the full 8 bits of grayscale available. As a handy reference, Table 15.3 is a Grayscale/RGB Gray conversion table.

Table 15.3 Grayscale–RGB Conversion

Gray Percent	RGB Gray
0% (white)	255/255/255
10%	229/229/229
20%	204/204/204
30%	179/179/179
40%	153/153/153
50%	128/128/128
60%	102/102/102
70%	76/76/76
80%	51/51/51
90%	26/26/26
100% (black)	0/0/0

16

COLOR CORRECTION AND THE
ADJUSTMENT COMMANDS

IN THIS CHAPTER

COLOR ADJUSTMENT THEORY

Whether your goal is exact reproduction of an image on paper or screen, or creating a special effect, manipulating the tonality and color of an image can be key. *Tonality*, the brightness of an image's pixels, can be the cumulative product of an image's component color channels or controlled through a separate channel (Lab color mode). Color (and grayscale and black-and-white values) is always stored in color channels. Manipulating these values can improve—or at least *change*—the appearance of your image.

↪ To learn more about color channels and how they work, **see** Chapter 15, "Channels: Color and More," p. 409.

Why Adjust?

In the vast majority of situations, you adjust color and tonality to produce an image that most closely reflects reality. You want the skin tones to match those of the person photographed, and you want the sky to be blue. The shadows should be black rather than dark purple. You want white highlights, not pale yellow or cyan or red.

The untrained human eye, in many circumstances, is very forgiving color-wise. Generally speaking, a shopper doesn't care if the type on laundry soap packaging is Pantone 1935 or Pantone 193. Nor can the eye tell the difference between the two shades when they stand alone.

On the other hand, slightly too much yellow in a skin tone or a bit too much blue in foliage can be disturbing, even to an inexperienced viewer. When an image portrays nature, whether flora or fauna, normally you want your image to be reproduced as exactly as possible. The goal is accurate output, whether to paper or screen.

↪ Looking for information about making people in your images look natural? See "The Skinny on Skin" in the NAPP Help Desk section at the end of this chapter.

You'll hear and read a variety of terms used to refer to the same thing. Brightness, luminosity, and lightness all refer to how close a pixel is to black or white.

The Need for Calibration and Color Management

You can't adjust what you can't evaluate. If your monitor shows bright red (RGB 255/0/0) as pink or magenta, you can't use your image's onscreen representation to make decisions. Certainly you can do all your corrections "by the numbers," evaluating color only through the Info palette, but that is not particularly efficient. Your monitor should be properly calibrated before attempting to color-correct any image.

Unless you have disabled color management, virtually every color and tonality correction you make relies on the profiles you've selected in Color Settings.

Color management is also important. Consider it to be correcting for the vagaries of various devices. Just as a golfer compensates for the pitch of a green when putting, or a sailor tacks against the wind, so, too, does color management help you produce the result you want by adjusting to meet circumstances. If, for example, a printer tends to make images a little too dark, you can lighten the originals before printing to produce perfect output.

➡️ *For information on preparing your equipment and settings for accurate color reproduction,* **see** *"What Is Color Management?"* **p. 220** *in Chapter 9, "Photoshop Color Management."*

The Eyes Have It

Even if you use color samplers and the Info palette to determine exact color values in an image, the final decision still rests with your eyes. The Info palette might indicate that the subject's skin is within your target range, but it's your *eyes* that have determined what that range should be. In the end, you use your own judgment when deciding whether an image or a print is acceptable.

EVALUATING IMAGES

Photoshop has a number of tools that can help you evaluate images. Some, such as the Proof Colors command, rely on accurate monitor calibration and proper color management. Others, such as the Info palette and the Histogram command, objectively measure color but are still dependent on profiles selected in Color Settings.

The Info Palette

The Info palette (see Figure 16.1) can give you two different color readings for the cursor location and color readings for up to four separately designated points in an image.

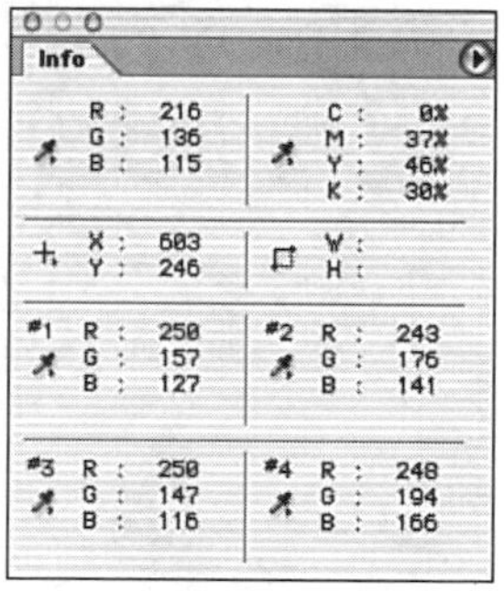

Figure 16.1
Regardless of which tool is active, the Info palette displays your choice of color readouts in the top two fields.

The four numbered fields at the bottom of the Info palette display readings for *color samplers*, which can be considered bookmarks placed in the image to track color at specific locations. (Color samplers are discussed in the following section.)

You choose what color information is displayed in the top two fields by using the Info palette menu command Palette Options (see Figure 16.2).

16

Figure 16.2
The First Color Readout and
Second Color Readout menus
offer the same list of options.

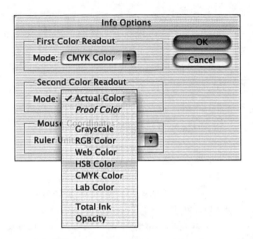

The color readings shown in the Info palette are tied to the Eyedropper tool. The tool's options determine the sample for the readings. If the Eyedropper is set to Point Sample in the Options Bar, a single pixel's value is displayed. To avoid false readings, set the Eyedropper to 3×3 Average for low-resolution images and 5×5 Average for high-resolution images.

While a color adjustment is being made, the Info palette displays a pair of values for each color reading (see Figure 16.3). The value on the left is the original; the value on the right is updated as you make the adjustments.

Figure 16.3
Observe the position of the cursor. The Info palette shows the values for the image pixels below the cursor, despite the dialog box. The dialog box is transparent to the Info palette.

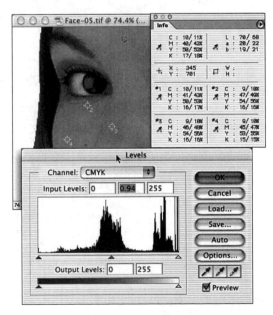

Color Samplers

Color samplers represent points in an image that you designate for color evaluation. The samplers appear in the image as numbered crosshairs (see Figure 16.4). You can place them or drag to move them by using the Color Sampler tool or by holding down the Shift key and using the Eyedropper. The Color Sampler tool is found in the Toolbox, grouped with the Eyedropper.

Color samplers are visible onscreen when painting, focus, toning, Hand, and Zoom tools are active. They are hidden when selection, pen, or type tools are active.

In photographs, objects are rarely a single color. A face, an apple, a sky—they all have a series of similar colors rather than a single color. Place color samplers in several areas to properly evaluate your work.

16

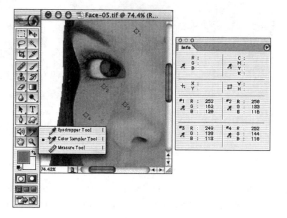

Figure 16.4
The color sampler icons adapt their own color to contrast with the pixels behind them.

By default, the Info palette shows values for each color sampler in the document's color mode. Change that reading by clicking on the eyedropper icon for that sampler in the palette (see Figure 16.5). You can also change the two upper readouts by clicking their icons.

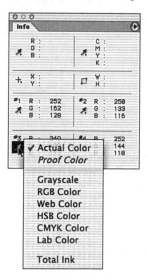

Figure 16.5
Each sampler's color mode can be adjusted independently. That enables you to place two samplers, set to different color modes, to monitor a single area of an image.

Remember that, like the top readings in the Info palette, the color sampler readings use the sample size specified for the Eyedropper tool in the Options Bar. The reading updates automatically if you change the sample size. Likewise, color samplers display dual readings during an image adjustment.

Histograms

Histograms show the distribution of pixels at various luminosity values for an image or an active selection. The Image, Histogram command opens the dialog box shown in Figure 16.6.

16

Figure 16.6
You use this histogram only to evaluate the image—you cannot make any changes to the image. You can position the cursor at any point in the histogram to get specific information for that particular value or, as shown, you can drag to get information for a range of values.

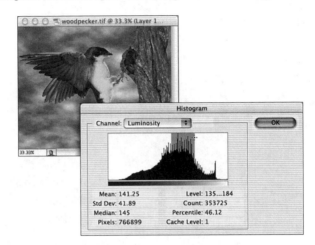

In addition to the luminosity of all the image's pixels, the histogram can show the values for a single color channel. Change the display by using the Channel pop-up menu at the top of the dialog box.

The histogram is used primarily for evaluating an image. It shows the distribution of pixels at each of the 256 possible values of brightness (composited for Luminosity or as computed for the individual color channel selected). The taller a black column at a given level, the more pixels in the image share that value.

When the bulk of the information in the histogram is to the right end, the image is very bright and said to be *high-key*. When the concentration is to the left, the image is dark—*low-key*. Figure 16.7 shows a comparison.

You can use the histogram to check for *posterization* as you correct images. Posterization occurs when similar color or luminosity values are consolidated in a single value. Gaps in the histogram appear, as shown in Figure 16.8.

The Memory & Image Cache pane of Photoshop's Preferences includes the Use Cache for Histograms check box. When it's selected, the histogram can be generated from low-resolution copies of the image stored in the cache. Histograms generated from the cache are typically less accurate, but the difference is usually insignificant. The advantage is a slight increase in the speed with which the histogram is generated.

Figure 16.7
The image on the left is low-key. On the right is an example of a high-key image.

16

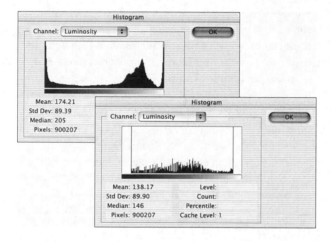

Figure 16.8
The lower histogram shows signs of posterization (gaps in the data) as well as clipping—the data ends before the lightest and darkest values.

Remember to look at the *relative* heights of the columns in a histogram. The tallest column always goes to the top of the box. If there is a much greater concentration of pixels at one value, all the other columns look short in comparison. Look at the two histograms in Figure 16.9. Both histograms represent the same black-to-white gradient. The only difference is that before the lower histogram was recorded, a 10-pixel-wide stripe of 50% gray was added to the image.

The single tallest column determines the histogram's overall appearance. Although it looks like there is a substantial difference in the two histograms, only one column is significantly different—all the other columns have the same *relative* heights in both histograms.

⇨ *If your histogram is showing a wildly impossible distribution, see "Evaluate What You're Evaluating" in the NAPP Help Desk section at the end of this chapter.*

You'll also find histograms in the Levels and Threshold dialog boxes. They function as part of those image adjustments and are discussed with their respective commands.

Figure 16.9
Every value in the image is nearly identical except for luminosity 128, which contains six times as many pixels in the lower histogram.

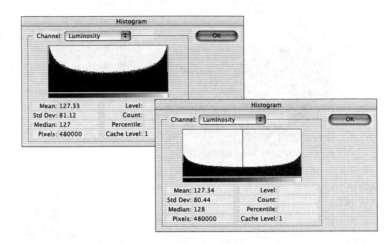

Proofing Colors

Photoshop's View menu includes a couple of commands used for *soft proofing*. Soft proofing is the process of evaluating onscreen how an image will appear when printed. Even with the most accurately calibrated monitor and most precise device profiles, soft proofing can never be 100% perfect. Remember that the monitor must use RGB color to simulate CMYK inks and that the way the light reaches your eye is different. However, you can use soft proofing to get a general idea of how an image will print, and it might show potential problems before they become serious.

The View, Proof Setup command determines what color setup you'll be using with the Proof Colors command. Your options include the currently selected CMYK working space, each of the individual color plates for that space, the combined working space CMY plates, and three RGB color spaces: Windows, Macintosh, and your monitor's profile. You can also prepare to proof in another color profile by choosing Custom from the Setup pop-up menu (see Figure 16.10).

Figure 16.10
All the available ICC profiles appear in the Profile menu.

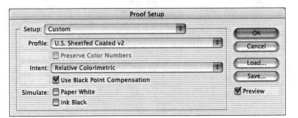

Depending on the profile that's selected, Photoshop can also attempt to simulate how CMYK inks will interact with paper (Simulate Paper White) and how black will be generated (Simulate Ink Black).

Selecting View, Proof Colors shows onscreen what the image should look like when output. A check mark appears next to the command name when active. To return to your normal working view, deselect Proof Colors.

You'll also find the Gamut Warning command under the View menu. Instead of simulating how an image will appear in print, it shows you what RGB colors in the image cannot be reproduced using the device whose CMYK profile you've loaded. By default, an opaque gray is shown for problem areas. You can change the gamut warning in the Transparency & Gamut pane of Photoshop's Preferences.

ADJUSTING TONALITY

16

The range of lightness and darkness in an image is often critical to its appearance. If the whites aren't bright enough, they look gray. If the brighter parts of the image are *too* bright, the highlights are "blown out" and lack detail. Likewise, if too many pixels are too dark, you get muddy, detail-less shadows. Photoshop offers quite a few tools for correcting the brightness of an image. You'll find several powerful tools in the Image, Adjustments menu. Adjusting the tones of an image is often referred to as *remapping*.

Remember that you can use the menu command Edit, Fade immediately after applying a tonal adjustment. The Fade command can lessen the impact of the adjustment and apply a blending mode.

Highlights and Shadows

It's important to understand the concept of highlights and shadows before adjusting an image's tonality. The key is knowing that shadow and highlight areas of an image are *not* completely black and white. They *should* have some detail. Even pictures of clouds and snow have some detail, and only the deepest shadows hold no detail.

Hold down the (Option) [Alt] key when selecting the Adjustments commands that have dialog boxes to open them with the most recently used settings.

When preparing images, especially for offset printing, consider the capabilities of the press. If the smallest dot that can be printed is 8%, your highlight areas should be filled with a very light gray pattern, created with 8% dots. Likewise, if the largest dot that can be reproduced without spreading into a solid area of black ink is 90%, that's where your shadows should be mapped.

➪ *Controlling the highlight and shadow points, the endpoints of an image, is discussed in the section "The Levels Eyedroppers," p. 445.*

Brightness/Contrast and Auto Contrast

The easiest to understand and use of the tonal adjustments, Brightness/Contrast is also the least flexible and the least powerful. The Brightness/Contrast dialog box (see Figure 16.11) consists of a pair of sliders and their related numeric fields, along with OK and Cancel buttons and a Preview check box.

There are actually two types of highlights in many images. *Specular highlights* are the pure white flashes of light created by reflections from metal or glass or otherwise occurring in a photograph. Specular highlights have no color information and are typically very small areas of pure white. *Diffuse highlights* are the "real" highlights of an image and should be reproduced with faint detail.

It can be used on the active layer or an active selection. It always affects all selected color channels equally, but you can apply it to channels individually by selecting the target channel(s) in the Channels palette.

Figure 16.11
Each of the sliders ranges from
–100 to +100.

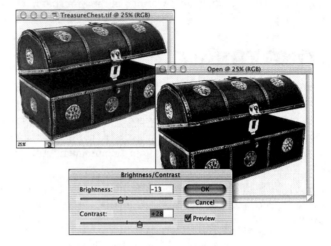

Dragging the Brightness slider to the right lightens the image (or selection), and dragging to the left darkens the image. The Contrast slider, in effect, increases or decreases the difference between light and dark pixels. Dragging the slider to the left (reducing the contrast) makes the image more gray and consolidates the pixels' luminosity values in the midranges; dragging the slider to the right distributes the luminosity values (see Figure 16.12).

Figure 16.12
The top image represents the original. In the middle, Contrast has been changed to –50. At the bottom, Contrast is changed to +50. Note that Brightness/ Contrast was applied only to the subject, not the white background.

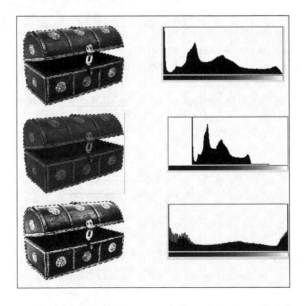

The Auto Contrast command adjusts image tonality by making light pixels brighter and shadows darker. It attempts to preserve the overall color relationship in the image while making the change.

Levels and Auto Levels

The Levels adjustment dialog box (see Figure 16.13) works with shadows, highlights, and overall gamma (the brightness of an image's midtones) independently. It also gives you separate control over input and output values, includes special eyedropper tools for identifying the highlight and shadow areas of an image, and offers a neutral gray eyedropper for removing color casts.

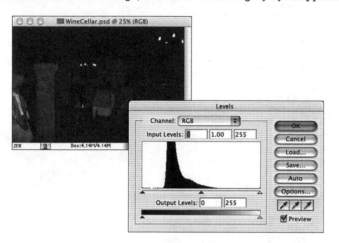

Figure 16.13
The image's tonal range is very compressed. Using Levels spreads the range out by moving values apart.

16

Input Levels

One of the most common uses of Levels is to expand an image's tonal range. Typically, the left and right sliders are dragged inward to the beginning of the image data in the Levels histogram. The middle slider is repositioned under what is likely to be the "center mass" of the histogram—the average value, the mean rather than the median (see Figure 16.14).

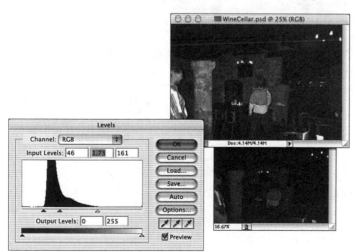

Figure 16.14
Note that the few stray pixels to the far left and right of the histogram are ignored.

Levels works by adjusting the brightness of pixels. The left and right sliders, and their corresponding Input Levels fields, are used to define where black and white begin. In Figure 16.15, the left slider is at 25—any pixels that had a brightness between 0 and 25 will be changed to 0 and become black. The right slider is at 225, so any pixels with a brightness higher than that become white (255).

As the left and right sliders are brought closer together, the number of possible brightness values in the image decreases. In Figure 16.15, the image will go from 256 possible tones (0–255) to 201 possible tones. Figure 16.16 shows what the histogram looks like *after* the adjustment in the previous figure is applied. The 201 values that were retained in the previous adjustment (25–225) are now spread over 256 total tonal values (0–255).

The histogram in Levels differs from that displayed with the Image, Histogram command. This histogram examines the composite color channel (or an individual color channel value). The graph in the Histogram dialog box looks at each pixel's brightness (or an individual component color value).

Figure 16.15
The middle slider, gamma, repositions itself automatically and remains set to 1.00 as the left and right sliders are changed.

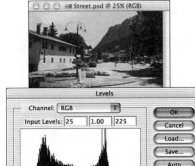

Figure 16.16
Notice the new empty columns in the histogram. Levels didn't create any new brightness values; rather, it redistributed the values that were retained in the previous adjustment.

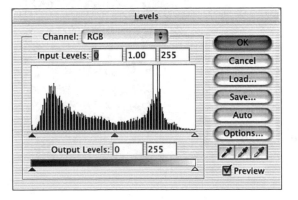

Output Levels

The lower slider in the Levels dialog box controls the tonal range of an image from a different direction. It is used to compress the range (which reduces contrast) and to *clip* highlights and shadows. These sliders can be used very effectively with the gamma (middle) slider below the histogram. In Figure 16.17, the correction is being made to the foreground only. This method not only provides a more accurate histogram, but also maintains the brightness of the white background.

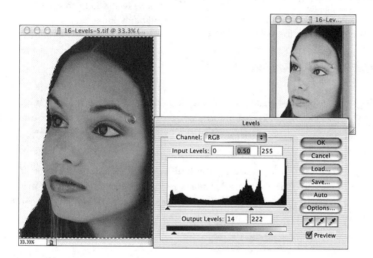

Figure 16.17
The original image, shown in the upper right, is skewed to brightness. Changing the Output slider on the right trims the highlights, and using the middle slider below the histogram adjusts the overall gamma.

Adjusting the Output sliders prevents pixels from becoming completely black or white. By bringing the left slider to level 14, the darkest a pixel can be is approximately 95% gray. Similarly, dragging the right slider from 255 to 222 results in the brightest pixel *in the selection* being 16% gray. (The white background is not affected because it is not selected.)

The Levels Eyedroppers

Using the Output sliders to determine an image's shadow and highlight points can compress the tonal range. Using the eyedropper tools in Levels to set the black and white points enables you to specify which *pixels* should be black and white, rather than which *tones*.

The first step is to identify the actual shadow and highlight pixels. In the Levels dialog box, you can find them by using the (Option) [Alt] key and the Input sliders. Hold down the modifier key and begin dragging the right slider. The image (or selection) will turn black. As you drag to the left, the first white areas you see will be your highlights—ignore colors and drag until you see white. Ignore any specular highlights, too. You want to identify the diffuse highlights.

When you identify the shadow and highlight pixels with the Input sliders, you can release the (Option) [Alt] key—keeping an eye on your target point—and move the cursor to those pixels. Shift-click to place a color sampler for later reference.

Similarly, hold down (Option) [Alt] and drag the left slider to the right. Again, ignore color and drag until you see black appear. Those areas are your image's darkest points.

> The Threshold command offers another way to find highlights and shadows. **See** "Threshold," **p. 465,** later in this chapter.

After you've identified the shadow and highlight points, you can click with the black and white eyedropper tools. The histogram changes to reflect the new distribution of tonal values. You still have the option of adjusting the gamma slider separately.

There is one advantage to using the Output sliders rather than the eyedroppers to establish black and white points: Output Levels can be recorded in an Action. Although not as precise as selecting pixels with the eyedroppers, it can be far more practical in a production environment.

The middle eyedropper tool is used for color balance. If the image contains an area that you know should be a neutral gray, you can click on it with the middle eyedropper. Remember that you can leave the Info palette open and maneuver the cursor around the image to check existing color values.

The values that you assign with the eyedroppers are set by double-clicking each of the tools' icons in the Levels dialog box. That opens the Color Picker. For average-key images intended for print, black points can be set to RGB 10/10/10 or CMYK 65/53/51/95 for a rich black. White points can be set to RGB 244/244/244 or CMYK 5/3/3/0. High-key images can have a higher black point, which reserves additional tonal steps for detail in the highlights. Likewise, low-key images can get better shadow detail when the white point is set somewhat lower.

The Auto Button and Auto Levels

Clicking the Auto button in the Levels dialog box is comparable to using the menu command Image, Adjustments, Auto Levels. The tonal range of each component color channel is maximized. By correcting each channel individually, rather than working with just brightness, as does Auto Contrast, this command can correct (or introduce) color casts. The lightest and darkest values for each channel in the image are mapped to the Shadows and Highlights values assigned in the Auto Color Correction Options dialog box.

Auto Color Correction Options

You'll find Options buttons in both the Levels and Curves dialog boxes. (In Photoshop 6, you had to hold down the (Option) [Alt] key to see the Options buttons.) The dialog box, shown in Figure 16.18, controls how the Auto buttons in Levels and Curves work as well as the performance of the Auto Contrast, Auto Levels, and Auto Color commands.

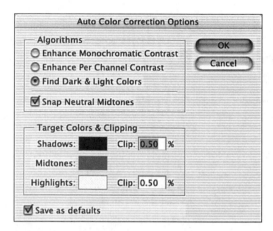

Figure 16.18
This dialog box is far more powerful than the Photoshop 6 version, which offered only clipping percentage fields.

These are the options available for the Auto commands and buttons:

■ **Enhance Monochromatic Contrast**—Used by the Auto Contrast command, this option adjusts the image by preserving the existing color relationships in the image and increasing the contrast. Highlights get brighter, and shadows get darker. All component color channels receive the same correction to avoid introducing a color cast. This adjustment is rather simplistic, best suited for images that already show good color and perhaps simply need a bit of a contrast boost. The Auto Contrast command can be recorded in an Action for a production environment.

■ **Enhance Per Channel Contrast**—Instead of adjusting the image as a whole, each channel is adjusted individually, maximizing the tonal range within the channel. This is the technique applied by Auto Levels. Because each channel is adjusted individually, color casts can be eliminated with this option. However, color casts can also be *introduced* if one component channel is substantially restricted. This option, which can be recorded in an Action through Auto Levels, is appropriate for images that need to look good but don't require exact color correction.

■ **Find Dark & Light Colors**—This option minimizes unintentional clipping of highlights and shadows while still increasing an image's tonal range. The brightest pixels are averaged, as are the darkest, to determine the adjustment. This is the algorithm used by Photoshop 7's Auto Colors command. It is generally effective on most photographic images, but can produce unacceptable results in some radically colored images.

■ **Snap Neutral Midtones**—Comparable in some respects to using the gray eyedropper in the Levels or Curves dialog box, this option finds a near-neutral color in an image and maps the gamma to it. The color is made truly neutral, and other colors in the image are adjusted accordingly. The option, used by the Auto Color command, can substantially reduce or eliminate color casts.

- **Shadows**—Click the swatch to open the Color Picker. Typically, a shadow value of RGB 10/10/10 (CMYK 65/53/51/95) is appropriate for print; Web designers are better served by a shadow value of 0/0/0. This is the color to which your image's black will be mapped.

- **Clip Shadows**—Clipping eliminates stray pixels from the determination of what constitutes a shadow. By clipping extremes, theoretically, the true shadows are identified. Clipping prevents a single pixel or two from being recognized as black in an image. Generally, 0.5% to 1% clipping is acceptable.

- **Midtones**—The neutral gray value for an image is almost always RGB 128/128/128. If you need to make an adjustment, click the swatch to open the Color Picker. To ensure that the gray is "neutral" and won't introduce a color cast to your image, enter equal values for red, green, and blue. It's best to define neutral gray in RGB or as 50% gray, even when working with a CMYK image.

- **Highlights**—Click the swatch to open the Color Picker and assign a highlight value. Images to be printed are likely to benefit from a highlight of RGB 244/244/244 (CMYK 5/3/3/0); Web-oriented images should use RGB 255/255/255.

- **Clip Highlights**—The clipping percent, which should be between 0.5% and 1.0%, identifies "white" in the image. The clipping value tells Photoshop which pixels it can ignore. This setting prevents a situation in which the highlight for an entire image is established by a single out-of-whack pixel.

- **Save as Defaults**—When this option is selected, clicking OK establishes the values in the dialog box for the appropriate menu commands and the Auto buttons of the Levels and Curves dialog boxes. When this check box is not selected, you're prompted to save the options nonetheless.

The Auto Color Correction settings, once saved, are used for all the commands—you cannot set different options for the various Auto commands.

Curves

The most powerful of Photoshop's image correction tools is, without a doubt, Curves. However, that power comes from complexity. The dialog box itself (see Figure 16.19), however, is not particularly complicated after a few basic techniques and concepts are clear.

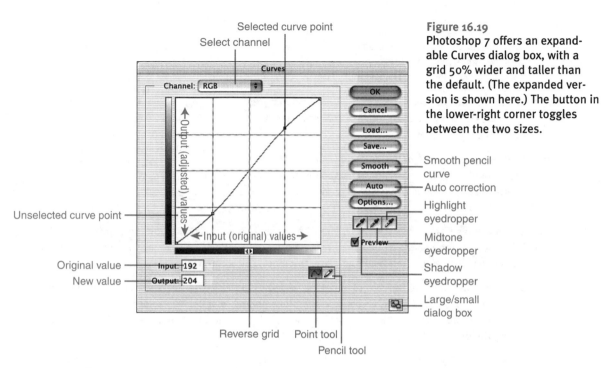

Selected curve point
Select channel

Channel: RGB

Output (adjusted) values

Unselected curve point

Input (original) values

Original value — Input: 192
New value — Output: 204

OK
Cancel
Load...
Save...
Smooth — Smooth pencil curve
Auto — Auto correction
Options... — Highlight eyedropper
Preview — Midtone eyedropper
Shadow eyedropper
Large/small dialog box

Reverse grid   Point tool
Pencil tool

Figure 16.19
Photoshop 7 offers an expandable Curves dialog box, with a grid 50% wider and taller than the default. (The expanded version is shown here.) The button in the lower-right corner toggles between the two sizes.

16

Here are the basics of working with Curves:

- Curves can be applied to a flattened image, an active layer, or a selection.

- Curves adjusts images much as Levels does but uses 256 separate values (RGB) or 100 values (other color modes) rather than just the three available in Levels.

- The horizontal axis represents the original value, and the vertical axis represents the new value. When you first open the dialog box, the "curve" is a diagonal line because each input value is equal to its corresponding output value.

- You select an input level by clicking on the curve itself, and then you drag the point up or down to change the image's appearance.

- Points can be used to make adjustments by dragging them up or down, and they can be used as anchors. Click once (or twice close together) on the curve to protect part of the curve from change.

- The grid's default three vertical lines represent the quarter tones, midtones, and three-quarter tones of the image. (Option-click) [Alt+click] on the grid to switch to a 10×10 grid.

- The Pencil tool can be used to replace a section of the curve with a custom adjustment. Simply select the tool and draw the segment you want.

16

- The Smooth button progressively straightens a curve drawn with the Pencil tool to ease the transitions. You can click multiple times, and only the segments of the curve created with the Pencil are affected.

Simplify the Curves dialog box in your mind: Picture it *without* the horizontal grid lines. The vertical grid lines help you identify input values, but the horizontal lines are unnecessary—drag points straight up and down and watch the Output field.

- A curve can have up to 16 distinct points (including the endpoints). Drag a point to reposition it, and drag it out of the box to delete it.

- Curves can be saved and later loaded to apply the same adjustment to another image. This option is especially useful when a scanner or digital camera regularly produces a color cast.

- When Curves is set to the image's composite channel (RGB or CMYK), you are adjusting the brightness of the image. When set to a single color channel, you're working only with that color component throughout the image and are, therefore, correcting color.

- When working with an RGB or a Lab image, shadows are to the left of the grid and highlights are to the right. With CMYK, Grayscale, and Multichannel images, brightness is to the left and shadows to the right. You can reverse the grid by clicking the two-headed arrow in the gradient below the grid.

- When working with RGB, the input and output values range from 0 to 255. For all other color modes, you're working with 0 to 100.

- Curves is available for 16-bit images as well as 8-bit images.

- The eyedropper tools in Curves work the same way they do in Levels.

There are also a number of shortcuts that make working with Curves easier:

- Shift-click to select multiple points. (Command-D) [Ctrl+D] deselects all points. You can also deselect by clicking away from the curve in the grid.

- Ctrl+Tab and Shift+Ctrl+Tab move through the existing points on a curve.

- Use the arrow keys to adjust selected points. Add the Shift key to increase the increment of movement.

- Move the cursor over the image and click to identify where that area falls in the curve. (Remember that you're using the Eyedropper tool's setting—Point Sample, 3×3 Average, or 5×5 Average.) Shift-click to add a color sampler to the image.

- (Command-click) [Ctrl+click] in the image to add a point to the curve. Add the Shift key to place the points in the color channels but not in the composite channel.

- Hold down the (Option) [Alt] key and the dialog box's Cancel button becomes Reset.

- You can manipulate two (or three) color channels at the same time by Shift-clicking them in the Channels palette before opening Curves.

Making Tonal Adjustments with Curves

Images that already look good can often benefit from some additional help. Typically, adjusting the *quarters* (the quarter tones and the three-quarter tones) is all that is necessary. The quarter and three-quarter marks are easily identifiable when the Curves dialog box is set to its default four-column/four-row configuration (see Figure 16.20).

Figure 16.21 shows a pair of common Curves adjustments. The adjustment shown in the upper figure tones down hot highlights and lightens dark shadows. In the lower example, the contrast of the image is increased by moving the quarters away from each other.

When working with RGB images, the Input and Output fields are calculated from 0–255 rather than 0–100. The 25% equivalent is 64, 50% is equal to 128, and 75% is comparable to 191.

16

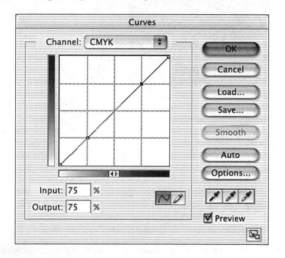

Figure 16.20
By default, vertical grid lines appear at the 25%, 50%, and 75% levels.

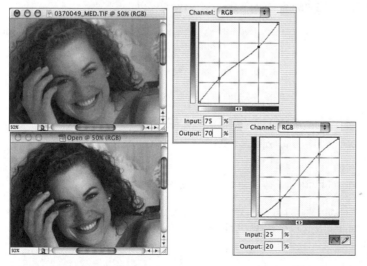

Figure 16.21
In each example, the adjustments are small—25% to 20 or 30, 75% to 80 or 70.

You can also make more complex adjustments, even targeting specific groups of pixels in an image. Shift-clicking in the image with the Curves dialog box open places color samplers, which can be used with the Info palette to track adjustments as you make them. In Figure 16.22, as you can see from the smaller original in the upper-right corner, the highlights on the forehead are too light and the shadows lack detail. The Curves adjustment targets those specific areas.

Figure 16.22
In the Info palette, the numbers to the left are the original color values, and those to the right are the values after the correction is applied.

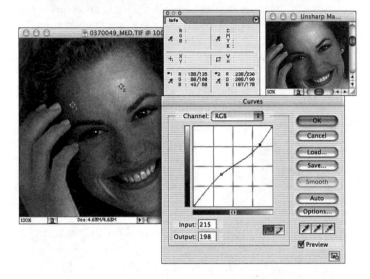

Hold down the (Command) [Ctrl] key and click in an image to place a point on the curve at that value. In this example, you can (Command-click) [Ctrl+click] on the color samplers to add points.

Color Correction with Curves

The Channel menu at the top of the Curves dialog box enables you to target a correction to a single component color in an image. Color casts can be removed by adjusting the individual channels. Keep in mind the relationship among the RGB and CMYK component colors:

- When working in RGB, you can increase or decrease yellow in an image by adjusting both the Red and Green channels (R+G=Y).

- In an RGB image, cyan can be adjusted by increasing or decreasing green and blue (G+B=C).

- Magenta in an RGB image is a function of red and blue (R+B=M).

- In a CMYK image, a blue cast can be corrected by reducing both cyan and magenta (C+M=B).

- The amount of red in a CMYK image is adjusted through the Magenta and Yellow channels (M+Y=R).

- Green in a CMYK image is a function of cyan and yellow (C+Y=G).

Curves can also be used with channels in combination. In Figure 16.23, the RGB image has yellow accent lighting that is too prominent. To adjust the yellow lighting without destroying the color in the remainder of the image, isolate it by using Select, Color Range.

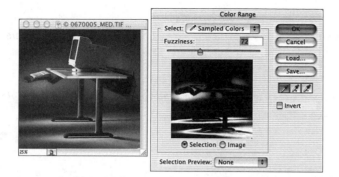

Figure 16.23
Curves can be applied to a selection. Color Range is an excellent tool for creating that selection.

In Figure 16.24, you can see that the Red and Green channels are active in the Channels palette, but that all channels are visible. That allows you to work on a pair of channels and continue to monitor the overall effect on the image. In this example, the Red and Green channels are active because *combined*, they are responsible for the yellow content of an RGB image.

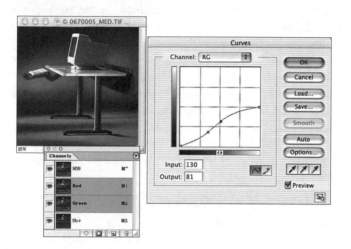

Figure 16.24
In the Channels palette, select the channels on which you'll be working before you open the Curves dialog box. The Channel pop-up menu shows RG, indicating that both the Red and Green channels are active.

The Curves Eyedroppers

The shadow, midtone, and highlight eyedroppers in the Curves dialog box function much like those in the Levels dialog box. First, you identify the darkest shadow and the brightest diffuse highlight (not specular highlight). Next, click with the appropriate eyedropper. The midtone eyedropper can be used to correct a color cast *if* there is a neutral gray in the image.

Auto Color

Photoshop's new Auto Color command is much more powerful than Auto Contrast or Auto Levels. The key to its accuracy in color correction is based on its method of evaluating the image. Instead of looking at the histogram to determine shadows, highlights, and midtones, it examines the image itself.

Using the values you specify in the Auto Color Correction Options dialog box, it clips the highlights and shadows, identifies the image's midtone, and neutralizes the color by balancing the component color values. You can open the Auto Color Correction Options by clicking the Options button in the Curves or Levels dialog box.

⇨ *For information on establishing the parameters for the Auto Color command, **see** "Auto Color Correction Options," **p. 446,** earlier in this chapter.*

The Toning Tools

Photoshop offers a pair of tools, known as the *toning tools*, for touching up the tonality of an image. The Dodge and Burn tools selectively lighten and darken areas of an image as you drag. The settings in the Options Bar enable you to concentrate on the shadows, midtones, or highlights as well as set an exposure value, which determines the strength of the tools. The toning tools are brush-based—you select a brush appropriate for the size and shape of the area you are adjusting.

The Dodge tool is used to selectively lighten an image or selection. It takes its name and icon from the darkroom technique used to lighten an area of an image during exposure. By using an opaque piece of cardboard on a stick and a circular motion, a photographer is able to block some of the light, lightening the final image in those areas. Similarly, photographers burn or darken an area of an image with their hand by selectively exposing an area to more light in the darkroom.

Be aware that choosing shadows, midtones, or highlights for the Dodge and Burn tools does not *restrict* the tool to the selected tonal range; rather, it concentrates the effect in that range. In Figure 16.25, the Dodge tool was used on a black-to-white gradient. At the top, the tool was set to Shadows; in the middle, to Midtones; and at the bottom, to Highlights. In all three cases the Exposure setting was 100%. Note that even when set to Highlights, the Dodge tool lightened the darkest areas of the image slightly.

Figure 16.25
The Dodge tool's options have an impact on how strongly it affects a particular tonal range, but the tool can affect the entire range, no matter the setting.

A third tool is grouped with the toning tools in the Toolbox and is sometimes considered with them. The Sponge tool can saturate or desaturate areas of an image. It, too, is a brush-based tool, with an option that determines the strength of its impact (Flow). When used on a Grayscale image, the Sponge tool increases or decreases contrast.

Pre-Photoshop Image Preparation

The best way to make sure you've got great tonal range and color in your output is to start with good input. You can do a number of things to make your color and tonal corrections easier *before* the image arrives in Photoshop:

- **Including Black, White, and Gray Swatches**—When you control the environment, add a target card in the bottom or side of the subject area before you snap the shot. It should have three squares of equal size: one black, one neutral gray, one white. (Keep them the same size to avoid skewing your histogram.) The card need not be large; actually, it should be as small as possible. Place it in the image near the subject, and take the picture. When you bring the image into Photoshop, use the eyedropper tools in the Curves dialog box on the squares to correct the image, and then crop to remove the swatches.

  The target card should be printed on the brightest white stock available and mounted on a stiff board. To prevent reflections, don't use glossy paper. The targets can be printed from a black-and-white laser printer to avoid any color cast.

- **Scanning Adjustments**—Scan your target card into Photoshop and check the black and neutral gray squares with the Eyedropper tool. If they show a color cast (the RGB values aren't equal), you can create a correction curve that can be loaded and applied to every scan. For more accuracy, create an 11-step black-to-white gradient.

  In addition, try scanning a blank white sheet of paper. See how evenly the scanner scans. Most flatbed scanners have a "sweet spot" in the middle where they produce the brightest, most accurate scans.

- **Know Your Digital Camera**—If you shoot with a digital camera, learn about and experiment with its settings. Read the manual and any electronic documents available from the camera manufacturer's Web site. Find out what capabilities it has and use them.

  Although it is easy and convenient to shoot with the camera in Auto mode, that might not be appropriate for your needs. Remember, too, that taking an hour to read the manual and experiment with the controls could save hundreds of hours in color correction and noise reduction later.

- **Set the Set**—When possible, set up your photo shoot with an eye toward your computer. Take the lenses out of eyeglasses. A little hairspray on highly reflective surfaces can tone them down. Use fill lighting and reflectors to avoid too-dark shadows.

16

COLOR ADJUSTMENT AND EFFECTS COMMANDS

Photoshop has a number of commands for directly altering the color of an image. Consolidated under the Image, Adjustments menu, they offer a variety of techniques and procedures to give you ultimate control over the appearance of your image. They can be used with Curves and Levels. Remember that proper monitor calibration and appropriate color management settings are critical to getting good results with these commands. If you are not accurately seeing color onscreen, your decisions are not based on the actual image content. Likewise, if your color management profiles are inappropriate for the image's destination, the colors you see are unlikely to be the colors actually produced.

⇨ *For a discussion of ensuring accurate color,* **see** *Chapter 9, "Photoshop Color Management," p. 219.*

Color Balance

The Color Balance command is available only when the composite channel is active in the Channels palette. The selection you make in the Tone Balance section of the dialog box (see Figure 16.26) enables you to concentrate (but not restrict) the effect in shadows, midtones, or highlights. The Preserve Luminosity option protects the image's tonality.

Typically, this command is used to compensate for color casts. Note that each of the sliders represents a pair of color opposites. Moving the top slider to the right increases red in the image, which is the same as reducing the amount of cyan. The other sliders work similarly. Color Balance can be used with a flattened image, an active layer, or a selection.

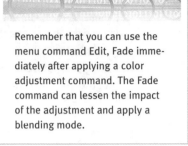

Remember that you can use the menu command Edit, Fade immediately after applying a color adjustment command. The Fade command can lessen the impact of the adjustment and apply a blending mode.

If you ever forget the relationship among the RGB and CMY component colors, open Color Balance. The inverse color pairs are evident in the slider labels.

Figure 16.26
The numeric fields across the top correspond to the three sliders from top to bottom.

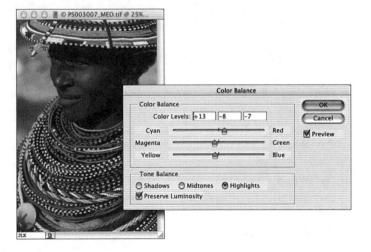

With Preserve Luminosity selected, moving all three sliders to the right equally has no effect on the image. Without the option, such a change would lighten the image by uniformly increasing the amounts of red, green, and blue throughout the image. Likewise, moving the three sliders equal distances to the left darkens the image when luminosity is not preserved.

Hue/Saturation

The Hue/Saturation command actually works with hue, saturation, and lightness. It can be used with flattened images, active layers, and selections, and you can manipulate the composite channel (all colors at once) or individually selected colors (see Figure 16.27).

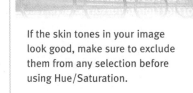

If the skin tones in your image look good, make sure to exclude them from any selection before using Hue/Saturation.

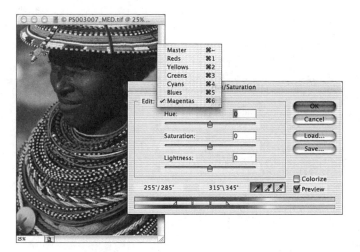

Figure 16.27
All six component colors can be adjusted individually, regardless of whether the image is RGB, CMYK, Lab, or Indexed Color mode. You can use Hue/Saturation with 16-bit images in appropriate color modes, too.

The Hue Slider

When Hue/Saturation is set to Edit: Master, you change the entire image or selection. Think of the Hue slider as a color substitution slider. At the bottom of the dialog box, the two gradient bars represent the original color (top) and the color that you'll be substituting (bottom). As the Hue slider is dragged, the lower gradient bar shifts. Moving it realigns the two bars so that you can see the color substitution. (When a specific color range is selected rather than Master, the substitution is limited to that color. The other hues in the image remain unchanged.)

For example, at +120, red (in the center of the top bar) is replaced by green throughout the image. Likewise, blue is replaced with red, cyan is replaced by magenta, and so on. At –120, the color shift is in the opposite direction, with red being replaced by blue, blue by green, and cyan by yellow.

The Hue slider is based on the standard color wheel, so it ranges in value from –180 to +180. Think of degrees around the circle. The key values for the Hue slider—and their results—are shown in Table 16.1.

Table 16.1 Color Changes with the Hue Slider

Hue Value	Original Color	Substituted Color
-180	Red	Cyan
	Green	Magenta
	Blue	Yellow
	Cyan	Red
	Magenta	Green
	Yellow	Blue
-120	Red	Blue
	Green	Red
	Blue	Green
	Cyan	Yellow
	Magenta	Cyan
	Yellow	Magenta
-60	Red	Magenta
	Green	Yellow
	Blue	Cyan
	Cyan	Green
	Magenta	Blue
	Yellow	Red
0	(no changes)	
+60	Red	Yellow
	Green	Cyan
	Blue	Magenta
	Cyan	Blue
	Magenta	Red
	Yellow	Green
+120	Red	Green
	Green	Blue
	Blue	Red
	Cyan	Magenta
	Magenta	Yellow
	Yellow	Cyan
+180	Red	Cyan
	Green	Magenta
	Blue	Yellow
	Cyan	Red
	Magenta	Green
	Yellow	Blue

Note that the −180 and +180 settings have identical results and, in effect, simply invert the image's colors.

Chapter 4

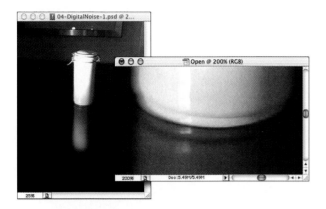

Figure 4.4

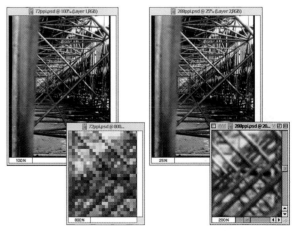

Figure 4.12

Chapter 6

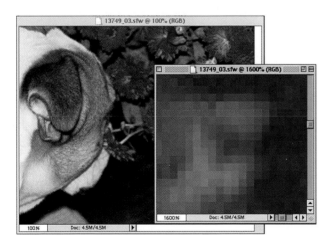

Figure 6.1

Figure 6.19

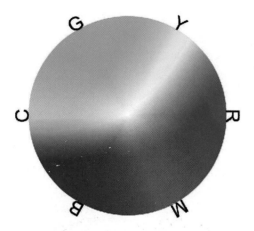

Chapter 7

Figure 7.3

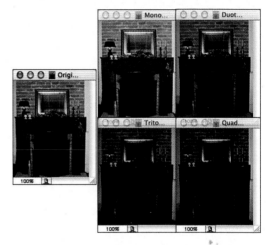

Figure 7.13

Figure 7.19

Chapter 10

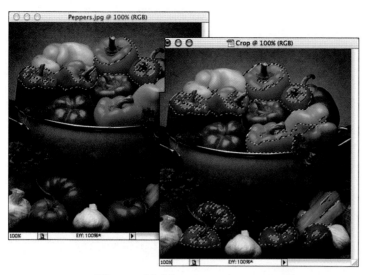

Figure 10.12

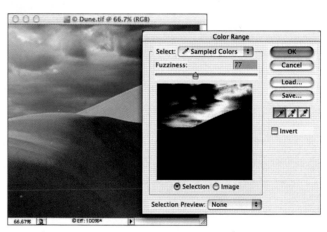

Figure 10.19

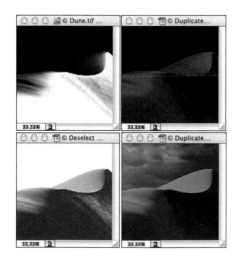

Figure 10.20

Figure 10.26

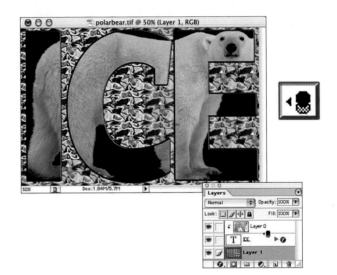

Figure 10.32

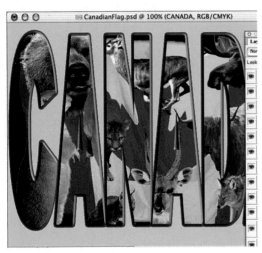

Figure 10.33

Chapter 11

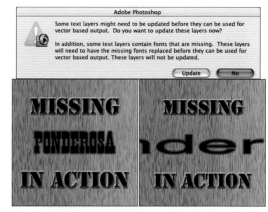

Figure 11.6

Figure 11.17

Chapter 12

Figure 12.5

Figure 12.7

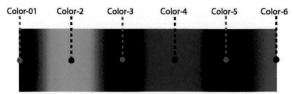

Figure 12.8

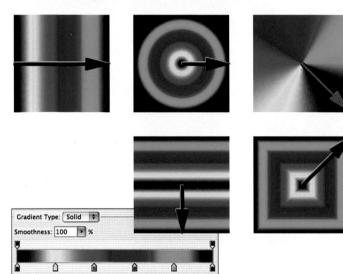

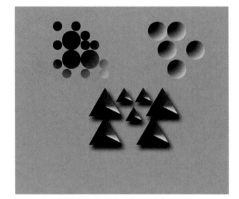

Figure 12.11

Figure 12.12

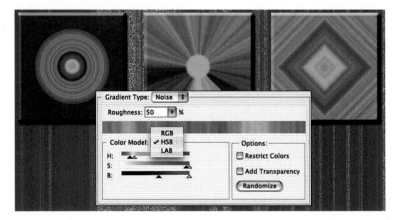

Figure 12.13

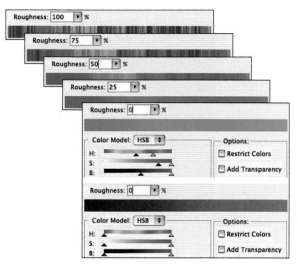

Figure 12.14

Figure 12.25

Chapter 13

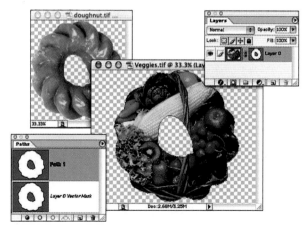

Figure 13.20

Figure 13.21

Chapter 14

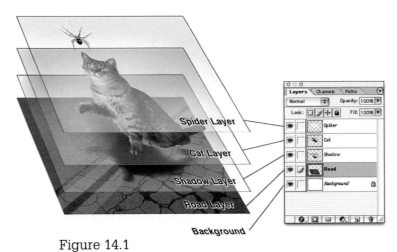

Figure 14.1

Figure 14.2

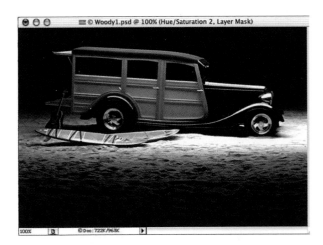

Figure 14.31

Figure 14.34

Chapter 15

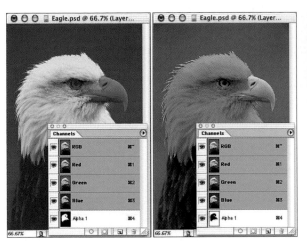

Figure 15.4

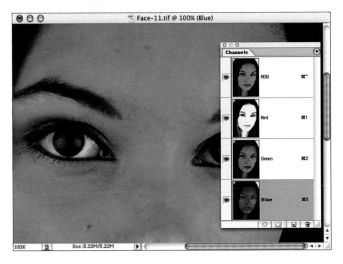

Figure 15.9

Figure 15.12

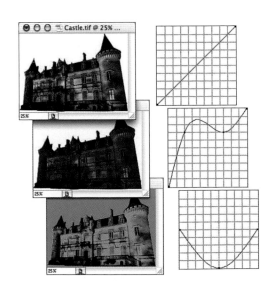

Figure 15.16

Chapter 16

Figure 16.7

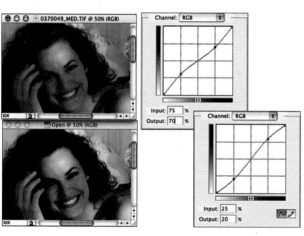

Figure 16.21

Figure 16.30

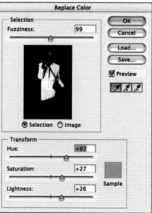

Figure 16.31

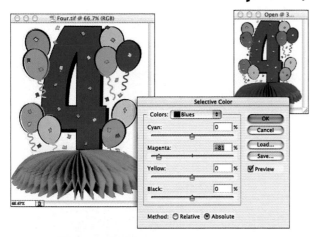

Figure 16.32

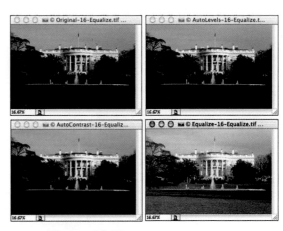

Figure 16.33

Figure 16.35

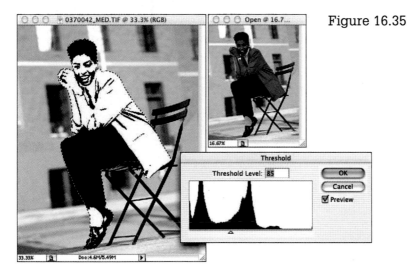

Figure 16.38

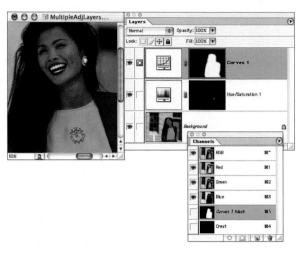

Figure 16.41

Figure 16.45

Chapter 17

Figure 17.1

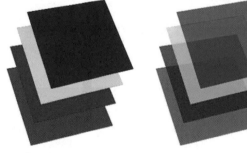

Figure 17.2

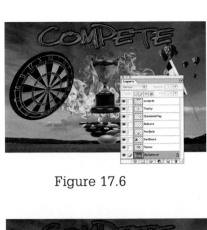

Figure 17.6

Figure 17.7

Figure 17.8

Figure 17.9

Figure 17.10

Figure 17.11

Figure 17.12

Figure 17.13

Figure 17.14

Figure 17.15

Figure 17.16

Figure 17.17

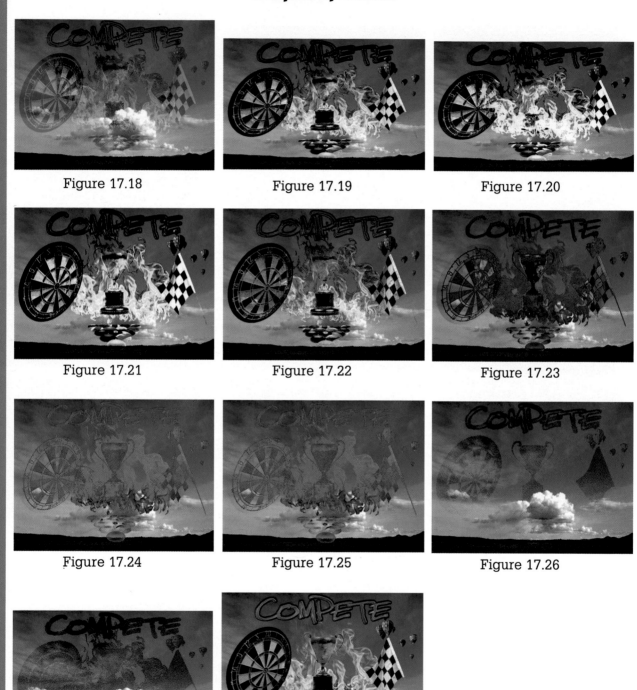

Figure 17.18

Figure 17.19

Figure 17.20

Figure 17.21

Figure 17.22

Figure 17.23

Figure 17.24

Figure 17.25

Figure 17.26

Figure 17.27

Figure 17.28

Figure 18.17

Figure 18.28

Figure 18.18

Figure 18.32

Figure 18.34

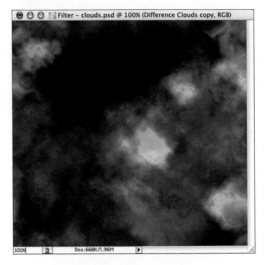

Figure 18.84

Figure 18.87

Figure 18.109

The Saturation Slider

The Saturation slider works in absolutes. Ranging from –100 (completely desaturated, grayscale) to +100 (completely saturated), it adjusts the vividness of the colors in the image or selection.

When the Saturation slider is dragged to the right, the primary component color (or colors) in a hue is increased, and the other colors (or color) are decreased to compensate. For example, if a pixel is RGB 220/60/60 (red) and the Saturation slider is dragged to +50, the resulting color is RGB 250/30/30 (without compensation for color profiles). A yellow pixel with a CMYK value of 2/17/73/0, on the other hand, would not likely be affected much by Saturation: +50 because it is already about as saturated as most CMYK profiles can produce.

Dragging the Saturation slider to the left reduces the primary component color(s) and increases the other component color(s). The closer that all the component colors get to equal values, the closer the pixel is to gray. When all three component colors meet, gray is the result.

If you need to simulate dusk or dawn, or even night, try reducing Lightness *and* increasing Saturation. Instead of just making the image dark, it makes the image dark and vivid—often a more realistic effect.

The Lightness Slider

Like the Saturation slider, Lightness works in absolutes. A setting of +100 turns every pixel pure white; -100 turns every pixel pure black. Smaller adjustments, in effect, increase the brightness of pixels by raising all three RGB component values or lowering the CMYK values (depending on the color mode).

Adjusting a Specific Color Range

When you select a color from the Edit pop-up menu, the Hue/Saturation dialog box adds some controls to the lower part of the dialog box (see Figure 16.28).

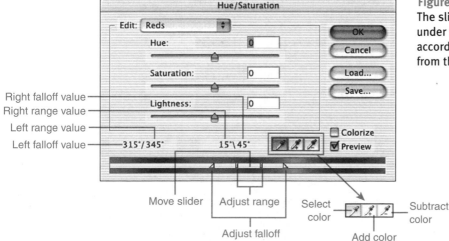

Figure 16.28
The slider is initially positioned under the top gradient bar according to the color selected from the Edit pop-up menu.

16

The slider consists of a pair of vertical bars bracketing the selected color range and a pair of wedge-shaped icons that adjust *falloff*. Think of falloff as a sort of feathering for color— it gradually fades the adjustment from the selected core color to the colors adjacent in the color wheel. The degree readings above the top gradient bar enable you to track the number of degrees of falloff to the left (the left pair), the actual range of color (the middle two numbers), and the right falloff (the right pair).

Falloff prevents posterization or visible banding when you make substantial adjustments to a color range in Hue/Saturation. The default value of 30° on either side is typically very good. However, to restrict the effect of your adjustment, you might need to reduce falloff on one side or both.

Dragging the middle portion of the slider repositions the entire slider without changing range or falloff amounts. If you drag it to another color, the menu at the top of the dialog box is updated to reflect the new position. Dragging the outer wedge-shaped icons inward reduces the amount of falloff, and dragging them outward increases it. Repositioning the vertical bars changes the targeted range of color.

If you need to adjust similar colors but must leave an intermediate hue untouched, you can create related color ranges. In Figure 16.29, the oranges and purples are selected, but the reds are not. Notice, however, that the Edit pop-up menu has named the two selections Reds and Reds 2. You could even have all six selection ranges within one color name.

Figure 16.29
Despite the related names, each color selection is manipulated individually in the Hue/Saturation dialog box. Change the selection, change the slider, switch to the next selection, change the sliders again, and then click OK.

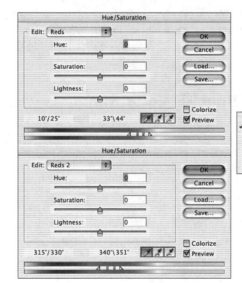

Colorizing with Hue/Saturation

Selecting the Colorize check box in the Hue/Saturation dialog box enables you to create the equivalent of a duotone image while retaining the original color channels. When you select the check box, the preview shows a desaturated image with a second color applied. You can adjust the sliders in the dialog box to change the appearance of the pseudo-duotone (see Figure 16.30).

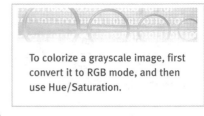

To colorize a grayscale image, first convert it to RGB mode, and then use Hue/Saturation.

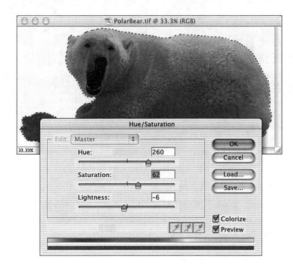

Figure 16.30
The original RGB channels are retained and updated. The image is not converted to Duotone color mode.

Desaturate

The Image, Adjustments, Desaturate menu command removes the color from an image, but does not convert the image to Grayscale mode. The original channels are retained. Using this command is equivalent to reducing Saturation to –100 in the Hue/Saturation dialog box. The brightness values of the pixels are retained, but the component colors RGB or CMY are equalized to create gray. Desaturate can be applied to a flattened image, an active layer, or a selection.

Selective use of Desaturate can be an excellent way to simulate a spot color in an RGB or a CMYK image. Simply make a selection of an area you want to keep in color, invert the selection, and desaturate. You can invert again and use the Hue/Saturation Colorize feature as well.

Replace Color

Photoshop's Replace Color capability is an incredibly powerful feature that combines Color Range with Hue/Saturation. You select a range of color in an image and change it, all in one step (see Figure 16.31).

You can choose the color to replace by clicking with the Eyedropper tool in the preview window or the image window. Additional colors can be added or subtracted with the plus and minus eyedropper tools, and the selection can be fine-tuned by using the Fuzziness slider.

16

Figure 16.31
The original suit was red, but Replace Color has produced several different color variations, while leaving the rest of the image virtually untouched.

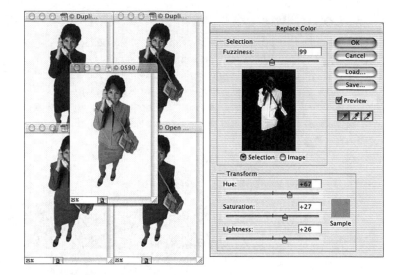

Selective Color

Selective color replacement is a technique that controls the amount of each component ink used to create a primary color. For example, blue in a CMYK image is primarily a blend of cyan and magenta inks. However, magenta is also one of the primary components of red in a CMYK image. Selective Color enables you to adjust the magenta in the blues without affecting the reds at all (see Figure 16.32).

Figure 16.32
The original image is in the upper right. Substantially reducing the magenta component of the blues turns them to cyan. Note that the reds are untouched.

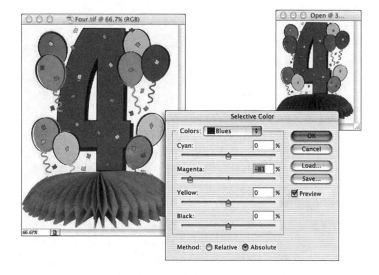

In addition to the six primary component colors (red, green. blue, cyan, magenta, and yellow), you can use Selective Color to adjust an image's highlights (Whites), midtones (Neutrals), or shadows (Blacks) by selecting the appropriate "color" from the pop-up menu in the dialog box.

Using the Relative adjustment option changes the color content based on the original content, and the Absolute adjustment option uses the actual ink values. For example, if a color will be reproduced with 80% magenta, a –25% Relative adjustment reduces the ink to 60% (80×0.75=60). On the other hand, a –25% Absolute adjustment would reduce the magenta to 55% (80–25=55).

Channel Mixer

You can adjust the content of a color channel by using the content of the other channels as sources. You make the adjustments with sliders. You can also completely replace the content of one channel with that of another channel. Select the target channel from the pop-up menu at the top of the dialog box, and then move its slider to 0% and the replacement channel's slider to 100%.

The Channel Mixer also gives you incredible control when creating a grayscale image from a color image. Select the Monochrome check box, and the output channel automatically switches to Gray. Adjust the sliders to take the best of each channel. After you click OK, use the Image, Mode, Grayscale menu command to complete the transformation.

➥ *For a full discussion of the Channel Mixer,* **see** *"Advanced Channel Manipulation," p. 425 in Chapter 15, "Channels: Color and More."*

Gradient Map

Gradient Map creates a new image from a color image, using two or more colors identified in a gradient. The gradient can use as many colors as you want, but the feature is designed for use with two-color gradients.

The leftmost color in the gradient is mapped to the image's shadows, and the rightmost is mapped to the highlights. If there are additional color stops in the gradient, they're apportioned according to their position in the gradient and the image's tonal range. The Gradient Map dialog box offers the options of dithering and reversing the gradient.

Invert

Invert is used primarily to create grayscale images from scanned black-and-white negatives. It is not appropriate for use with scanned color negatives because of their orange mask. When used with a color image, each channel is calculated independently.

Using the 256 possible values for each pixel in each color channel, Invert simply flips the color across the midpoint. Pixels with high values in one channel get low values, and vice versa. For example, a pixel with an RGB value of 240/130/65 changes to 15/126/190. To calculate, subtract the beginning value from 255 and you'll get the resulting value.

Generally speaking, you'll want a dark color on the left end of the gradient and a lighter color on the right. Reversing the setup can produce a "night vision" effect, however.

Equalize

The Equalize command identifies the darkest and lightest pixels in an image and maps them to black and white. The pixels in between are evenly distributed throughout the tonal range. In Figure 16.33, you can see a comparison of Auto Levels, Auto Contrast, and Equalize.

In Figure 16.34, the histograms for the four sample images are shown. Note that Equalize has distributed the pixels much more evenly than Auto Levels or Auto Contrast.

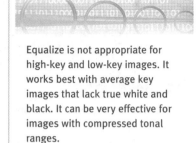

Equalize is not appropriate for high-key and low-key images. It works best with average key images that lack true white and black. It can be very effective for images with compressed tonal ranges.

Figure 16.33
The original image is in the upper left. Auto Levels was applied to the image in the upper right, Auto Contrast to the image in the lower left, and Equalize to the image in the lower right.

Figure 16.34
The histograms are shown in the positions of their images from Figure 16.33.

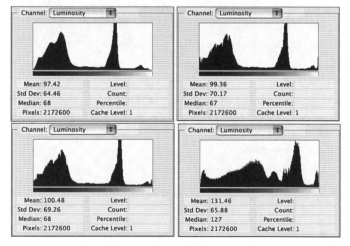

Threshold

The Threshold command converts every pixel in an image to black or white. You set the level at which the conversion is made in the Threshold dialog box with the slider or by entering a value in the numeric field (see Figure 16.35).

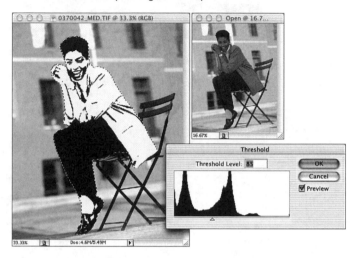

Figure 16.35
Threshold can be applied to a selection (as shown), a flattened image, or an active layer.

16

If an image is to be printed as line art, it should be converted to Bitmap mode (Image, Mode, Bitmap) after applying Threshold. The Threshold command does not change the number of color channels; rather, it forces the content of the channels to black and white. Remember, too, that resampling or blurring an image after applying Threshold converts some pixel values to grayscale unless the image has been changed to Bitmap mode.

You can use this grayscale blurring to your advantage if the image will not be printed as line art. In Figure 16.36, Threshold has been applied to the same picture. In the upper left, Threshold was used and then the image was downsampled to its current size. In the bottom center, the image was downsized and then Threshold was applied. To the upper right, the image was downsized, Threshold was used, and then a very slight Gaussian Blur was applied (0.3 pixel radius).

Figure 16.36
The top-left image has smooth edges but isn't blurred, a result of the resampling process. The image in the bottom center has the jagged edges of bitmap art. In the upper right, the blur has softened not only the edges (as in the first image), but also the overall look of the image.

16

Threshold is also the method of choice for finding an image's true shadow and highlight points. Instead of using the Levels sliders, you can use Threshold to easily identify the diffuse highlights and the shadows in an image (see Figure 16.37).

Figure 16.37
The top image illustrates identifying highlights, and the bottom example shows finding shadows.

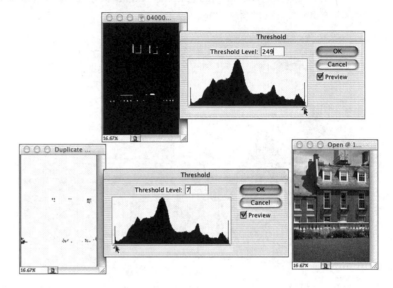

Here's how to do it:

1. Open the image in Photoshop.

2. Choose Image, Adjustments, Threshold.

3. Drag the slider to the far right.

4. Slowly drag the slider to the left until white areas begin to appear. These are the highlights of the image.

5. You can Shift-click on a highlight area to mark it with a color sampler. Make sure you choose a diffuse highlight rather than a specular highlight (an area of pure white, such as a reflection off glass or metal). Don't click the OK button.

6. Drag the slider to the far left and slowly bring it to the right until shadows appear.

7. Use a color sampler to mark a shadow point.

8. Click Cancel rather than OK.

Accurately identifying the highlight and shadow points in an image can be important for using the eyedropper tools in the Curves or Levels dialog box.

Posterize

The Posterize command works similarly to Threshold, but instead of reducing the image to two brightness values (0 and 255), you can specify a number of tones (see Figure 16.38).

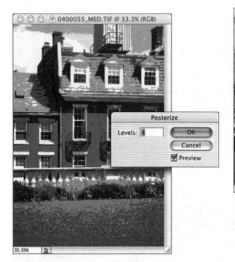

Figure 16.38
The number you specify is per channel. Using four levels on an RGB image results in four possible brightness values for each component color.

Variations

The Variations command helps you make tonal and color-correction decisions by presenting different choices head-to-head in a gigantic dialog box (see Figure 16.39).

Although the dialog box looks busy and complicated, using variations is actually quite simple:

You can produce a watercolor effect with Posterize. For best results, blur the image a bit before applying the adjustment. You can also use Posterize to simplify an image's colors for better results when creating vector art with Adobe Streamline.

- Your original image, the picture before you opened Variations, is always available for reference in the upper-left corner.

- Next to Original is Current Pick. This version shows what you'll get if you click OK.

- Current Pick is also displayed in the center of the color correction area to the lower left and the tonal correction area on the right.

- To make a change to the image, click on the preview image that looks best. It then becomes Current Pick and all the other previews are updated.

- In the upper right, you choose whether to work with the image's shadows, midtones, or highlights. You can adjust only one range at a time. Remember, though, that selecting Shadows doesn't mean that your choices won't affect the highlights, too, but that the changes will be concentrated in the shadows.

- Selecting Saturation strips out all previews except the pair at the top and three in the middle. You'll see Less Saturation, Current Pick, and More Saturation. Click on the left or right preview to change the image's saturation.

- The Fine—Coarse adjustment determines how radical the proposed changes will be. Each step on the scale doubles the amount of difference each preview shows.

16

- When Show Clipping is selected, Variations indicates with neon color any pixels that will be clipped. This includes pixels that will be forced to black or white as well as pixels that will become oversaturated.

- Holding down the (Option) [Alt] key changes the Cancel button to Reset. Clicking Reset enables you to start over without exiting the dialog box.

- You can save corrections and apply them later to similar images by using the Load button.

Note that the previews around the Current Pick in the main Variations area are arranged in the order of the color wheel. Opposites are directly across from each other— Red/Cyan, Green/Magenta, Blue/Yellow.

Figure 16.39
This dialog box does not fit on a monitor set to display 800×600 pixels. It is not resizable, nor is there an option for smaller previews.

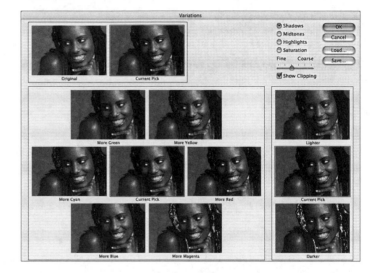

ADJUSTMENT LAYERS: THE LIVE CORRECTIONS

Most of the commands in the Image, Adjustments menu can be applied as *adjustment layers*. An adjustment layer changes the image's appearance without actually changing any pixel color values. In addition to preserving the original image data, adjustment layers can be reopened and settings changed. They can also be deleted at any time.

Adding an Adjustment Layer

You can add an adjustment layer through the Layers palette or the Layer menu (see Figure 16.40). Click and hold on the Add Adjustment Layer button at the bottom of the palette and select the type of adjustment from the list. Alternatively, use the menu command Layer, New Adjustment Layer and choose from the submenu.

An adjustment layer is always accompanied by a mask. If there's a selection active when you create the adjustment layer, the selection automatically forms the basis for the mask. If there's no selection, the adjustment layer is applied to the entire image.

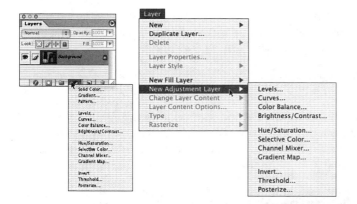

Figure 16.40
After you select the type of adjustment layer, the appropriate dialog box opens. Note that you can't add adjustment layers for the Auto commands, Desaturate, Replace Color, Equalize, or Variations.

After you've made the adjustment and clicked OK in the adjustment dialog box, the adjustment layer appears in the Layers palette. By default, it is added above the active layer. The Layers palette shows two thumbnails for each adjustment layer (see Figure 16.41). To the left, you'll see an icon representing the type of adjustment layer, and to the right, a thumbnail of the layer's mask. The Channels palette shows the mask of an adjustment layer only when that layer is selected in the Layers palette.

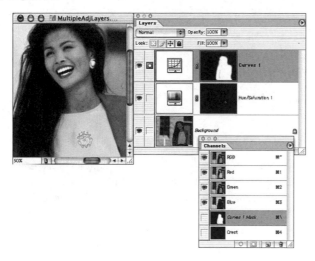

Figure 16.41
In this example, if you click on the Hue/Saturation adjustment layer in the Layers palette, the Channels palette hides the Curves 1 Mask alpha channel and shows Hue/Saturation 1 Mask in its place.

Adjustment layers can be hidden and their effects temporarily removed by clicking the visibility column (the eye icon) in the Layers palette. You can lock adjustment layers to prevent movement, but because they don't contain pixels, there's no need to lock them for transparency or editing.

Changing an Adjustment Layer

You can double-click the left-hand thumbnail of an adjustment layer in the Layers palette to reopen the dialog box and change your settings. The dialog box opens with the original settings, and the image is automatically updated when you click OK. The dialog box can also be opened with the Layer, Layer Content Options menu command. You can change the type of adjustment layer with Layer, Change Layer Content.

You can edit an adjustment layer's mask by clicking once on its thumbnail in the Layers palette and then painting in the image window with black, white, or gray. The mask itself won't be visible unless you show it by clicking next to it in the visibility column of the Channels palette.

➡️ *To learn more about creating and editing masks, **see** "The Three Types of Channels," p. 410, in Chapter 15, "Channels: Color and More."*

If you click on the link icon between the adjustment layer icon and the mask thumbnail in the Layers palette, you unlink the mask from the adjustment. Click on the mask thumbnail and use the Move tool to reposition the mask in the image window. Click between the icon and the thumbnail again to relink the mask and adjustment layer.

Restricting the Effect of an Adjustment Layer

By default, an adjustment layer affects all layers below it, including any other adjustment layers. To restrict the adjustment layer's effect to a single layer, group the adjustment layer with the layer below it in the Layers palette. (Option-click) [Alt+click] on the line between the layers to link them (see Figure 16.42).

Figure 16.42
The cursor shows the "wedding rings" icon (shown below the word "Gradient") when positioned correctly to group two layers. Note that the grouped layer is indented in the Layers palette to indicate its status.

The menu command Layer, Group With Previous also restricts the adjustment layer's effect to the layer or layers with which it's grouped. Additional layers can be added to the group by (Option-clicking) [Alt+clicking] the dividing lines. Adjustment layers can also be used with layer sets. To restrict the effect of an adjustment layer in a layer set, you can group all the layers or change the layer set's blending mode from Pass Through to Normal.

You can also use the Layers palette menu command Merge Down to permanently combine an adjustment layer with the layer below. The effect of the adjustment layer is applied to the layer with which it is merged and removed from any other layers below it.

Fill Layers

Using the New Adjustment Layer button in the Layers palette, you can also add *fill layers* to an image. A fill layer has no effect on underlying layers, except through blending modes (as do regular layers). A fill layer can be filled with a solid color, a gradient, or a pattern. You can create a fill layer with a selection or closed path active in the image to create a layer mask.

The advantage of using a fill layer over a regular layer and the Edit, Fill command is that the fill layer is "live." Like an adjustment layer, you can reopen the dialog box to change the content of the layer.

A Powerful Alternative: nik Color Efex Pro!

Photoshop has some incredibly powerful tools for color and tonal correction. However, if you do this type of work a lot, you'll likely find nik Color Efex! to be a worthwhile investment. It's available in a variety of configurations, at a variety of prices. The pro bundle includes the entire collection of filters and offers CMYK capability as well as Save and Load features.

Many of the filters are designed to help you reproduce effects that are difficult—if not impossible—in Photoshop. Simply dragging a folder from the product's CD to the Photoshop Plug-Ins folder and restarting Photoshop adds the filters to your Filter menu (see Figure 16.43).

Figure 16.43
A pair of submenus is added to the Filter menu. The Abstract Efex are designed for stylizing images, and the more mainstream filters are in the Color Efex submenu.

Each filter opens in its own windows, complete with zoomable preview (see Figure 16.44). You drag sliders, and the preview is updated in the window.

Of greatest interest for color correction and enhancement may be the Sunshine and Polarization filters. Sunshine uses a variety of algorithms to emphasize existing light, both outdoor and indoor. Polarization is an extremely capable filter that digitally mimics many of a photographer's favorite twists. As nik is quick to point out, however, this filter is applied *after* a photo is taken, so it cannot prevent reflection and surface glare.

To have the preview update as you drag, hold down the (Option) [Alt] key. Less powerful machines might experience a little delay when using this technique. You don't have to use the sliders—click directly on a number in a filter dialog box and type the new value.

Figure 16.44
The available sliders differ, depending on which filter is selected.

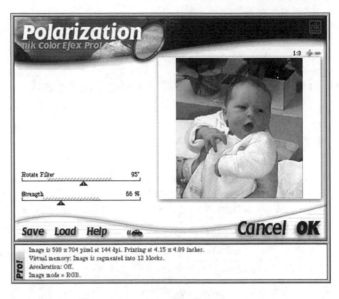

The true power of nik Color Efex! comes through when filters are used in combination. Figure 16.45 shows the result of a quick application of several filters, including Sunshine, Contrast Filter: Green, Graduated 201h (Sky Blue), and Graduated 213h (Dark Blue).

Figure 16.45
The filters were applied to the entire image. However, like Photoshop's own filters, nik Color Efex! can be applied to selections.

PHOTOSHOP IN FOCUS

Another excellent technique for creating eye-catching grayscale images from color pictures uses the Gradient Map command:

1. Open a copy of an RGB or CMYK image in Photoshop and position to one side of the screen. Hide your palettes with the Tab key if your monitor isn't huge.

2. Use the menu command Image, Adjustments, Gradient Map. Position the dialog box off in a corner, even partially hanging off the edge of the screen if necessary, so that you can see your image.

3. In the dialog box, click once directly on the gradient to open the Gradient Editor.

4. Create a gradient with the following color stops:

   - Location: 0%, Color: RGB 0/0/0

   - Location: 25%, Color: 64/64/64

   - Location: 50%, Color: 128/128/128

   - Location: 75%, Color: 191/191/191

   - Location: 100%, Color: 255/255/255

5. Move the Gradient Editor dialog box to the side so that you can see your image. Drag the color stops back and forth to see the effect on the image.

6. Click on the center color stop to make it active.

7. Click on the Color swatch to open the Color Picker. Move the Color Picker to the side so that your image is visible.

8. Try RGB 125/120/60. Experiment with other colors for a variety of highly controllable pseudo-duotones.

FROM THE NAPP HELP DESK

The National Association of Photoshop Professionals (NAPP) offers e-mail assistance to its members. Here is some advice from the NAPP Help Desk related to issues in this chapter.

The Skinny on Skin

Is there a magic formula for correcting skin tones? The people in my images never seem to look right.

Flesh tones are among the greatest challenges in Photoshop. One of the reasons for the difficulty is that we see and evaluate skin colors constantly. "You look a little pale." "Too much sun this weekend?" "You must be freezing!" In part because of how aware we are of the appearance of people around us, we are sensitive to the appearance of skin in images, too.

There is no single color mix for skin. There is no single relationship among component colors for skin. There is a tremendous range of skin tones in nature and, therefore, in images. Remember, too, that an individual's skin has a range of colors. The top and bottom of the forearm are typically different, as are the area beneath the chin and the chin itself. Parts of the body exposed to sun are typically darker, and how much darker often depends on the time of year.

In addition, the way an image is captured presents differences in skin tones. Because of reflections and lighting, foreheads, cheekbones, and noses might be lighter than the areas below the eyes, along the jaw, and the neck.

That having been said, here is some *general* guidance on skin color:

- Even when working with RGB images, evaluate skin in terms of CMYK. Set the Info palette's second color reading to CMYK. Also use color samplers set to CMYK in key areas, such as the forehead, the side of the nose, cheeks, and chin.

- The key component is magenta. Determine appropriate cyan and yellow proportions based on the magenta content.

- Too much yellow makes the skin look jaundiced. Too little yellow creates sunburn. In Caucasians, too much cyan produces grayish skin.

- Don't think in terms of specific percent values for each of the component colors; rather, consider the relationship among the three values. The actual percent of each CMY ink depends on the image's tonality.

- The skin of babies and northern Europeans can have a yellow content only slightly higher than the magenta. Southern Europeans may range to 25% more yellow than magenta. American blacks might have only slightly more yellow than magenta. African blacks may show equal values. Asians may have 30%–50% again as much yellow as magenta. Native American skin might even show more magenta than yellow, but only slightly.

- Cyan values should be very low for pale skin and babies. The cyan component might be only 10% of the magenta. Darker Caucasian and Asian skin may have cyan equal to 30% of the magenta. Cyan for Africans and African–Americans can range from 50%–75% of the magenta value. Tanned skin typically needs a higher cyan value than "winter-white" skin.

- With the exception of shadow areas, there should be little if any black ink in northern European and Asian skin tones. There may be trace amounts in darker Caucasian tones. African-Americans and Africans can range from 25% of the magenta value to as much as 75%.

Against my better judgment, I am providing a table of *sample* skin tone values that *may or may not* be comparable to the values you find in your image (see Table 16.2). These CMYK values are for illustrative purposes only and are based on studio lighting, proper calibration, and appropriate color management.

Table 16.2 Hypothetical Flesh Tone CMYK Values

Skin	Location	CMYK
Pale Caucasian	Highlights	4/17/15/0
	Midtones	14/35/35/0
	Shadows	31/63/71/31
Dark Caucasian	Highlights	11/35/42/0
	Midtones	14/38/49/0
	Shadows	35/64/73/27
African-American	Highlights	5/14/22/0
	Midtones	23/50/63/5
	Shadows	35/67/72/52
Asian	Highlights	3/11/13/0
	Midtones	12/35/42/0
	Shadows	29/60/56/25

There are two schools of thought when it comes to skin tone correction:

- Get a good monitor, calibrate it properly, work with controlled lighting, and trust your eyeballs.

- Ignore the onscreen appearance and work with the CMYK values.

I will confess to being from the first school, although I do keep my Eyedropper handy and my Info palette open. The skin tones usually are only *part* of an image—they must look appropriate within the context of the entire image. With the exception of portrait work, the skin is not usually the focus of the image. Although unnatural skin tones are certainly noticeable, make sure that you're not sacrificing the image's overall appearance to apply a formula.

Evaluate What You're Evaluating

My histogram can't possibly be right! It's showing that my image is high-key, with all the pixels stacked to the right. Yet the image itself is rather dark. What's going on?

Check to see if there's an active selection. If so, the histogram reflects only those pixels. If you're looking at the histogram in the Levels dialog box, remember that it shows only the active layer.

USING BLENDING MODES

IN THIS CHAPTER

UNDERSTANDING BLENDING MODES

Any time two colors overlap, whether on separate layers or when a second color is added with a painting tool, one of two things can happen: The upper color can block (or replace) the lower completely, or the two colors can interact. Opacity and blending modes determine how one color interacts with colors below it.

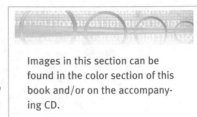

Images in this section can be found in the color section of this book and/or on the accompanying CD.

Color and Pixels

When a file is saved or outputted (either to screen or in print), each pixel can be only one color. (File formats that support transparency can also have pixels with *no* color—invisible pixels.) The color of a pixel can be changed in a variety of ways in Photoshop. Painting tools can apply a color or alter an existing color. Adjustment commands and layers can be applied. Layers can be added, with colors overlapping colors.

Photoshop's native file format (.psd) and the advanced capabilities of TIFF permit layers to be saved in a file. Each layer can have a different color value for any specific pixel. Each layer can be considered a separate set of pixels, so any given location in an image can have one pixel on each layer. Although that results in a four-layer image having four different pixels in a single location, in the end the pixel has only one visible/printable pixel when output. The specific color is the result of the interaction among the colors on the various layers. However, if the pixel on the top layer is opaque, the color on that layer is the color of the pixel, regardless of pixel colors on the lower layers (see Figure 17.1).

Figure 17.1
Consider a single pixel in an image with four layers. If the layers are all at 100% opacity, the top color is visible (left). If the layers have partial transparency, a combination of the layers' colors is visible (right).

Unsure about the concept of layers? See "Plotting the X,Y" in the NAPP Help Desk section at the end of this chapter.

Transparency Versus Blending

Two ways that colors can interact are *transparency* and *blending*. When the opacity of a layer or painting tool is reduced, the color's impact is reduced uniformly, much like using a tint in a page layout or an illustration program. Also like a tint, transparency is measured in percent. Opacity can be controlled for both layers and painting tools.

Whether applied with a painting tool or on a layer, blending modes allow you to control *how* a color interacts with an existing color on that layer (painting tool blending mode) or on layers below (layer blending mode). The various blending modes use different attributes of the colors being blended to produce an effect. With blending layers, the hue, saturation, and lightness of the base and blend colors can be used, depending on the blending mode selected. When using a blending mode with a painting tool, the existing and new colors are compared to create the result color. Transparency and blending are contrasted in Figure 17.2.

In a discussion of blending modes, the terms *base color*, *blend color*, and *result color* are used. They are, respectively, the color on the lower layer or the original color, the color on the upper layer or added by the painting tool, and the color that results from the interaction.

Remember that layer blending modes work downward only. The lowest layer of an image appears the same, regardless of blending mode. The exception is the Dissolve blending mode, which does have an effect on a layer, even when there's nothing below. Transparency, on the other hand, is apparent even on the lowest layer.

17

Figure 17.2
On the left, the umbrella is on a layer with reduced transparency. On the right, the layer's opacity is set to 100%, but the blending mode has been changed to Hard Light.

17

The Transparency Theory

Although *transparency* is the term we use, it's not exactly correct. Transparent objects, such as window glass, technically are clear, which would make them invisible in Photoshop images. *Translucent*, on the other hand, is also not quite appropriate for our purposes. It implies distortion of the light coming through, as seen in frosted glass.

In Photoshop, you can use the term *transparency* much as it is used in photography, where it refers to the amount of light passing through the film's emulsion. However, rather than measure an object's transparency, you work backward and describe its opacity. An object can be from 100% opaque (solid) to 0% opaque (invisible). In simpler terms, an object's opacity refers to whether (or how much) you can see an object behind it in the image. In this figure, a black-to-transparent gradient is shown against a transparency grid.

The grid's visibility is dependent on the opacity of the gradient at a given point.

Opacity is not the same as color value. The following figure compares transparency with color. Although the results might seem comparable in the image, an object's interaction with other objects can depend on the difference between color and opacity changes.

A black-to-transparent 11-step gradient (top) is contrasted with a comparable black-to-white gradient. Note that the transparency grid is not visible behind the lower gradient.

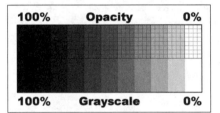

WORKING WITH BLENDING MODES

You can use Photoshop's blending modes while working with painting tools or when applying them to a layer. When applied to a layer, every pixel on the layer is affected. (Each blending mode is explained individually later in this chapter.) Keep in mind, too, that layer blending modes are *live*, meaning they can be changed at any time, as long as the image's layers are intact.

Layer Blending Modes

When a layer's blending mode is changed from Normal to another mode, the relationship between the layer's pixels and those below changes. In Normal mode, each pixel interacts with those below according to the pixel's color and the layer's transparency. If, for example, a group of pixels is filled with a solid color, the layer's blending mode is Normal, and the opacity is set to 100%, the pixels block those below. On the other hand, if the layer is set to most of the other blending modes or the opacity is reduced, the lower pixel is likely to be at least partially visible.

A layer's blending mode can be assigned in the Layers palette or the Layer Style dialog box (see Figure 17.3). The Layer Style dialog box also offers some advanced blending controls. These options, discussed in the sidebar "Layer Style Blending," also calculate the values of pixels on different layers, but are not blending modes.

Blending modes can also be applied to layer sets. By default, the layer set's blending mode is Pass Through. In effect, Pass Through results in the layer set itself having no blending mode; the modes of the layers within the set interact with lower layers as though they were not part of a set. When the layer set's blending mode is changed from Pass Through, two things happen. First, the layers within the set are isolated from the rest of the image, and their blending modes affect only the lower layers within the layer set. Second, the layer set is treated as a single entity for blending, and the layer set's blending mode is used to determine how it interacts with layers below. The difference is shown in Figure 17.4.

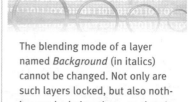

The blending mode of a layer named *Background* (in italics) cannot be changed. Not only are such layers locked, but also nothing can be below them, so there's no reason to change the blending mode from Normal. To move a background layer above another in the Layers palette, first change its name. You'll then be able to change the blending mode, too.

17

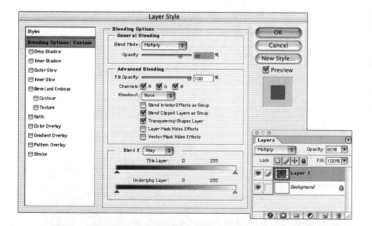

Figure 17.3
The General Blending area of the Layer Style dialog box offers the same options as the top of the Layers palette. Changes made in one are reflected in the other for a layer.

Figure 17.4
On the left, the layer set's blending mode is Pass Through. Each layer interacts with all layers below. On the right, the layer set is assigned the Lighten blending mode, so the layers within the set are composited first, and then Lighten is applied.

When any non-painting tool is active in the Toolbox, you can change the active layer's blending mode with one of the keyboard shortcuts listed in Table 17.1. (If a painting tool is active, the shortcuts change the tool's blending mode.)

Table 17.1   Blending Mode Shortcuts

Mode	Option+Shift (Mac) Alt+Shift (Windows)
Normal	N
Threshold (Bitmap and Index Color)	N
Dissolve	I
Behind (painting tools only)	Q
Clear (painting tools only)	R
Replace (Healing Brush only)	Z
Darken	K
Multiply	M
Color Burn	B
Linear Burn	A
Lighten	G
Screen	S
Color Dodge	D
Linear Dodge	W
Overlay	O
Soft Light	F
Hard Light	H
Vivid Light	V
Linear Light	J
Pin Light	Z
Difference	E
Exclusion	X
Hue	U
Saturation	T
Color	C
Luminosity	Y
Pass Through (layer sets only)	P
Next Blending Mode	Shift+plus key
Previous Blending Mode	Shift+minus key

17

Layer Style Blending

The Layer Style dialog box offers some sophisticated blending capabilities. Used with or instead of the blending modes, the Advanced Blending and Blend If capabilities give you more control over the interaction between layers.

The Fill Opacity slider enables you to change the opacity of a layer's content without changing the opacity of drop shadows, outer glows, or outer bevels. Anything (including effects) within the bounds of the original layer content is reduced in opacity, but effects outside the original pixels remain at the layer's opacity level (see Figure 17.5).

Figure 17.5
The original object, at 100% opacity, is in the middle. On the left, the layer's opacity is reduced to 50%. On the right, the fill opacity is at 50%. Note that the rightmost object's stroke, shadow, and glow are unaffected by the reduction in opacity.

17

Below the Fill Opacity slider are check boxes for the image's color channels. (The boxes match the image's color mode.) Unchecking a box is equivalent to erasing that layer's content from the corresponding color channel.

The Knockout options are a simple way of using one layer to assign transparency to one or more lower layers. The pixels on the top layer, when set to Shallow or Deep Knockout, serve as a digital cookie cutter, chopping through the intervening layers. When set to Shallow, the layer knocks out to the bottom of its layer set or clipping group. Set to Deep, the layer cuts through to the background layer, or to transparency if there is no background layer.

Below the Knockout pop-up menu are five check boxes for changing the way that selected layer effects appear in the document:

- **Blend Interior Effects as Group**—When checked, this option applies the blending mode and opacity to certain layer effects before the layer is blended with underlying layers. The interior layer effects include Inner Glow, Satin, and Overlay.

- **Blend Clipped Layers as Group**—The blend mode of a clipping group's base layer can be applied to all the layers in a group, or each layer's blend mode can appear individually.

- **Transparency Shapes Layer**—If this option is not selected, effects are applied to the entire layer, regardless of transparency. For example, if a layer contains text and the layer effect Pattern Overlay is selected, this option determines where the pattern is applied. When checked, the pattern is restricted to the pixels that make up the type. When unchecked, the entire layer is filled with the pattern.

- **Layer Mask Hides Effects**—Layers to which both effects and layer masks are applied can be treated one of two ways: The mask can clip the content of the layer and then the effects are applied, or the effects can be hidden as part of the layer (see Figure 17.6).

- **Vector Mask Hides Effects**—This is comparable to the preceding option.

Figure 17.6
On the left, the mask (layer or vector) is set to Hide Effects. On the right, the effects are applied after the layer is masked.

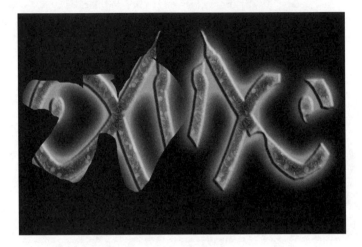

The Blend If sliders enable you to control the interaction of the pixels on the upper and lower layers based on color. Select a channel from the pop-up menu. (Gray represents the composite channel in RGB and CMYK modes, affecting all channels.) Adjust the sliders to determine what pixels should become transparent. The upper slider, This Layer, controls transparency based on the values of the selected layer. Dragging the sliders inward makes the darkest and lightest pixels transparent. Using the (Option) [Alt] key enables you to spilt the slider controls and create a fade.

For example, when the dark slider is split and dragged to the values 245 and 230, the layer is affected like this: Pixels darker than 245 become transparent. Pixels between 245 and 230 gradually fade from transparent to opaque. Pixels lighter than 230 are unaffected and remain opaque.

The lower slider, Underlying Layer, forces visibility of pixels on the lower layer in much the same way. By dragging the sliders, you can determine which pixels will be visible, regardless of the opacity of the upper layer (see Figure 17.7).

Figure 17.7
The original images are shown in the lower center. On the left, the white background was made transparent with the right controller of the This Layer slider. To the right, the wine was also made transparent by switching to the Red channel and using the left controller, too.

Blend Modes for Painting Tools

Unlike the layer blending modes, which affect how pixels on the selected layer interact with those on layers below, the painting tools work on a single layer. By changing a tool's blending mode, you change the way it adds color over an existing color or fill on a layer. With the exception of Dissolve, the blending modes have no effect on color applied to an empty layer.

The painting tools have several blending modes that are not available for layers. The keyboard shortcuts for the painting tools' blending modes are included in Table 17.1, earlier in this chapter. Not all blending modes are available for all painting tools. Table 17.2 shows which modes are available for which tools.

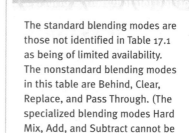

The standard blending modes are those not identified in Table 17.1 as being of limited availability. The nonstandard blending modes in this table are Behind, Clear, Replace, and Pass Through. (The specialized blending modes Hard Mix, Add, and Subtract cannot be selected for tools, and so do not appear in the table.)

Table 17.2 Painting Tools' Blending Modes

Tool	Blending Mode
Brush	(All standard blending modes, plus Behind and Clear)
Pencil	(All standard blending modes, plus Behind and Clear)
Healing Brush	Normal, Replace, Multiply, Screen, Darken, Lighten, Color, Luminosity
Clone Stamp	(All standard blending modes, plus Behind)
Pattern Stamp	(All standard blending modes, plus Behind)
Gradient Tool	(All standard blending modes, plus Behind
Paint Bucket	(All standard blending modes, plus Behind and Clear)
Blur	Normal, Darken, Lighten, Hue, Saturation, Color, Luminosity
Sharpen	Normal, Darken, Lighten, Hue, Saturation, Color, Luminosity
Smudge	Normal, Darken, Lighten, Hue, Saturation, Color, Luminosity

The Shape Tools and Edit Commands

When a shape tool is set to Fill Pixels (see Figure 17.8), blending modes are available. In effect, when creating a filled region on an existing layer, the shape tools work like painting tools—they add colored pixels. The shape tools, when adding pixels, can use all the standard blending modes, plus Behind and Clear.

Figure 17.8
When set to create shape layers or work paths, the shape tools do not use blending modes.

Likewise, the Edit commands Fill and Stroke work like painting tools, and so have blending modes. You can fill and stroke using all the standard blending modes, plus Behind and Clear.

Color Mode Restrictions

Some blending modes, for both layer and painting tools, are not available in all color modes. Obviously those color modes that don't support layers (Bitmap, Indexed Color, Multichannel) don't support layer blending modes. They also can't support some of the painting tools' modes, including Behind and Clear, which rely on layers. Working with images in 16-bit/channel mode also eliminates layers and several blending modes. Here is a summary of blending modes available for various color modes:

- **RGB, CMYK**—All blending modes for both layers and painting tools are available.

- **Grayscale, Duotone**—The blending modes that are dependent on color are not available, including Hue, Saturation, Color, and Luminosity.

- **Bitmap**—No layer modes are available, and painting tools are restricted to Threshold, Dissolve, Darken, and Lighten.

- **Indexed Color**—No layer blending modes are available, and painting tools can be used only in Threshold and Dissolve blending modes.

- **Lab**—All layer and painting tool blending modes are available, except Darken, Color Burn, Lighten, Color Dodge, Difference, and Exclusion.

- **Multichannel**—There are no layer blending modes, and the painting tools do not use Behind, Clear, Hue, Saturation, Color, or Luminosity.

⇨ *What happens when you convert an image to a color mode that doesn't support your blending modes? See "Color Mode Conversion" in the NAPP Help Desk section at the end of this chapter.*

Blending Clipping Groups

By default, the blending mode of the lowermost layer in a clipping group is used to calculate interaction with lower layers in an image. Alternatively, you can restrict that layer's blending mode to the layer itself, allowing all the layers of the clipping group to maintain their own blending modes and, therefore, their original appearance.

To control the blending of a clipping group, open the Layer Style dialog box for the lowest layer of the clipping group. Select or deselect the Blend Clipped Layers as Group check box.

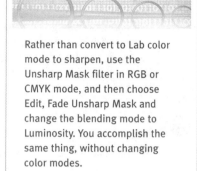

Rather than convert to Lab color mode to sharpen, use the Unsharp Mask filter in RGB or CMYK mode, and then choose Edit, Fade Unsharp Mask and change the blending mode to Luminosity. You accomplish the same thing, without changing color modes.

The Fade Command

Located under the Edit menu, the Fade command can be used to alter the effect of a filter, an adjustment command, a painting tool, or an eraser tool. It is available only immediately after the application of the command or tool. Fade enables you to change the opacity and blending mode of the filter, adjustment, or tool.

BLENDING MODES, ONE BY ONE

Photoshop now offers a total of 30 blending modes. Some, such as Dissolve, are almost always available. Other blending modes are used for one specific purpose, such as Hard Mix for brush textures, Replace for the Healing Brush, and Pass Through for layer sets. The blending modes are presented here generally in the order in which they appear in menus. (Remember that not all blending modes appear in all menus.) Photoshop 7 groups the blending modes according to general effect.

Most of the layer blending modes are shown with a sample image consisting of a background and seven additional layers (see Figure 17.9). For each example, all of the seven additional layers are set to the blending mode under discussion, and in each case the opacity is set to 100%.

Figure 17.9
In this figure, each layer is set to Normal.

17

You will see references to base, blend, and result colors in the User Guide, Help, this book, and elsewhere. For layer blending modes, they are, respectively, the lower color, the upper color, and the color produced when they are combined by using a given blending mode. For painting tools, they are the original color, the added color, and the color that is produced.

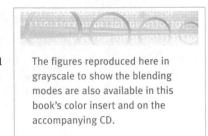

The figures reproduced here in grayscale to show the blending modes are also available in this book's color insert and on the accompanying CD.

Normal

Normal is the default, and the most common, blending mode. The top color supersedes the bottom color. Figure 17.10 shows the sample image, with all layers set to the Normal blending mode.

Figure 17.10
With all layers set to Normal, it is apparent which layer is on top in areas of overlap.

Assuming an opacity of 100%, pixels on layers set to Normal block pixels on layers below. The result color remains the blend color.

Threshold

Threshold, available for Indexed Color and Bitmap modes only, is the "Normal" blending mode for Indexed Color and Bitmap images. These color modes support limited color tables (256 colors for Indexed Color, 2 colors for Bitmap). That limitation prevents such images from using most of Photoshop's blending modes. The result color remains the blend color.

Dissolve

The Dissolve blending mode affects semitransparent pixels, which include pixels applied with a tool or technique with reduced opacity, and edge pixels in anti-aliased artwork. Pixels are replaced randomly in this blending mode. The effect scatters the pixels of the base or blend color (see Figure 17.11).

Figure 17.11
Note that the effect is most evident in the partially transparent areas of the flames and along the anti-aliased edges of the other artwork.

Behind

When working on a layer with transparency, the Behind blending mode allows a painting tool to add the blend color to transparent pixels only, protecting the base color. This blending mode is available only for painting tools. You cannot use Behind on layers with locked transparency.

Clear

Using the Clear blending mode is similar to using the eraser tools: Pixels are changed to transparent. (Clear is used only with the painting tools and is not available for use on background layers or layers with locked transparency.) Unlike the Eraser, which controls the resulting opacity based on the tool's setting, the Clear blending mode makes pixels transparent according to their original opacity. Pixels that were completely opaque become transparent. Pixels that were 75% opaque become 25% opaque. Pixels that were 50% opaque remain 50% opaque.

Darken

The Darken blending mode compares the individual color components of the base and blend colors. It retains the lower value (RGB) or higher percent (CMYK) for each component color. In all cases, the darker value for each component color is retained. If the base pixel has a color value of RGB 25/100/215 and the blend color is 100/200/50, the result color will be 25/100/50. White is ignored on the blend image (see Figure 17.12).

Figure 17.12
Generally, you can expect dark colors on the upper layer to be retained, but dark base colors will have more influence on the result color than lighter base colors.

Multiply

The Multiply blending mode calculates the color values (RGB or CMYK) of both the blend and base colors and multiplies them. Because it is a multiplication calculation, the result color is darker than the original blend color. Figure 17.13 shows the sample image when the upper layers' blending modes are set to Multiply.

Figure 17.13
The Multiply blending mode always results in a darker color, except when the lower color is white (which results in no change). Multiplying with black produces black.

Observe how the flames show prominently through the lighter areas of the dartboard and the flag.

Color Burn

Color Burn simulates the darkroom technique used to darken areas of an image by increasing exposure time. Blending dark colors over a base color results in darkening. Blending with white produces no change in the lower color (see Figure 17.14).

Figure 17.14
Note that the pure white areas of the clouds show through the flames and trophy.

Linear Burn

New in Photoshop 7 is the Linear Burn blending mode. Similar to Color Burn, it results in a generally darker image, except where the base color is white (see Figure 17.15). Color Burn increases contrast, but Linear Burn decreases brightness to produce the result color.

Figure 17.15
In contrast to the Color Burn sample, this image has much less white showing through from the base layer. Rather, the brightness of the overlying images is increased.

Lighten

The Lighten blending mode is the complement to the Darken blending mode. It determines whether the blend or base color is lighter and makes changes accordingly. If the base color is lighter, it is left unchanged. If it is darker, the upper color is blended (see Figure 17.16).

17

Figure 17.16
To the left, the white clouds show through the dark dartboard. Only the highlights of the trophy are visible.

The base and blend colors are compared, with the result color being whichever is lighter.

Screen

Screen is, mathematically, the opposite of Multiply. The inverse of each color value is multiplied. The result color is always lighter. Figure 17.17 shows the result of changing the blending mode of the upper layers to Screen.

Figure 17.17
If the upper color is black when you use Screen as the blend color, the result color is the base color. White, however, always produces white when screening.

Screening red and blue produces magenta; screening red and green yields yellow; and screening blue and green gives you cyan.

Color Dodge

Dodging is a darkroom technique designed to lighten certain areas of a photograph. When you partially block the light before it reaches the paper, the image in that area is neither as dark nor as saturated. The Color Dodge blending mode is typically used with lighter blending colors. Blending with black produces no change (see Figure 17.18).

Figure 17.18
Black in the upper layers becomes transparent and white becomes opaque.

Linear Dodge

As Color Dodge works with contrast, so Linear Dodge works with brightness. It compares the base and blend colors, and then increases the brightness of the base color to produce the result color (see Figure 17.19).

Figure 17.19
Blending with white produces white; blending with black produces no change.

Overlay

Overlay serves as a cross between Multiply and Screen (see Figure 17.20). The base color's values for brightness are retained (highlights and shadows). If the base color is dark, it is multiplied and becomes darker. If it is light, it is screened and becomes lighter. Often a hue shift also occurs.

Desaturated images (in RGB or CMYK mode) can be colorized by adding a layer of solid color set to Overlay. Adding an Overlay layer of gray can intensify highlights or shadows. Grays near neutral gray produce subtle changes.

17

Figure 17.20
Overlay can be comparable to reducing the opacity of the upper layer with extreme highlights and shadows.

Soft Light

Soft Light is a mixture of Color Dodge and Color Burn. If the top color is light, the bottom color is lightened; if dark, the lower color is darkened (see Figure 17.21). The effects of Soft Light are more subtle than many of the other blending modes. Some shifting of hues can be expected.

Figure 17.21
Soft Light can be similar to a less intense version of Overlay blending mode.

Adding areas of light or dark gray to a layer with the Soft Light blending mode selected produces an effect comparable to Dodge and Burn. Unlike several other blending modes, pure black and pure white as blend colors do not produce black and white result colors.

Hard Light

The Soft Light blending mode can be similar to shining a diffused spotlight on the base colors, but Hard Light is much more vivid (see Figure 17.22). When a layer is set to Hard Light, you can paint with dark grays to darken and light grays to lighten.

Figure 17.22
Like many blending modes, using black or white for the blend color leaves it unchanged as the result color.

Blending with shades of gray and Hard Light is effective for adding highlights and shadows to an image. Like some other blending modes, Hard Light acts like Multiply when colors are dark and like Screen with light colors.

Vivid Light

Another of Photoshop 7's new blend modes, Vivid Light produces a result similar to a very saturated version of Overlay (see Figure 17.23).

Figure 17.23
Vivid Light increases or decreases contrast based on the blend color.

Linear Light

A complement to Vivid Light, Linear Light works with brightness rather than contrast (see Figure 17.24). Consider it a combination of Linear Dodge and Linear Burn. If the blend color is light, the brightness of the base color is increased to produce the result color. If the blend color is dark, the base is darkened to generate the result color.

Figure 17.24
In the color version of this figure, you'll see that Linear Light retains the hue of the blend color much more than does Vivid Light.

Pin Light

The fifth of the new layer and painting tool blending modes, Pin Light is similar to both Darken and Lighten. If the blend color is dark, base colors darker than the blend color are retained, and those that are lighter are replaced. If the blend color is light, the lighter base colors are retained and the darker pixels are replaced (see Figure 17.25).

Figure 17.25
Not apparent in the grayscale version of this image are the slight hue shifts that Pin Light can produce.

Add and Subtract

Available only for the Apply Image and Calculations commands (in the Image menu), these blending modes simply add or subtract the component color values for each pixel. They are used only when combining channels.

▷ *For more information about the Add and Subtract blending modes,* **see** *Chapter 15, "Channels: Colors and More," p. 409.*

Difference

Difference can create among the most dramatic of blending changes. The brightness values of the upper and lower colors are compared, and then the color values of the lesser are subtracted from the greater. Because black has a brightness of zero, no change is made. When you're blending with white, expect colors to be inverted. In Figure 17.26, light gray and white areas in the upper layers produce extreme color changes.

Figure 17.26
Even in grayscale, the results of the Difference blending mode are noticeable.

Exclusion

The results of blending with Exclusion are very similar to, but less dramatic than, those of the Difference blending mode. Result colors tend toward grays, with a less contrasting look (see Figure 17.27). Blending with white inverts colors, and black produces no change.

Figure 17.27
Exclusion has a tendency to flatten contrast when working with brightness values approaching 50% in the blend color.

Hue

The Hue blending mode uses the saturation and brightness of the base color and the hue of the blend color. As you can see in Figure 17.28, blending with imperfect blacks and whites can produce speckling.

Figure 17.28
Hue uses a simple substitution to produce the result color, substituting the blend color's hue for that of the base color.

Saturation

In contrast to the Hue blending mode, Saturation uses the hue and brightness from the lower color and the saturation of the upper color. When the upper color is a shade of gray, that neutral saturation overrides the hue. In Figure 17.29, note that using only the saturation of the upper layers produces shadowy silhouettes of the artwork.

Figure 17.29
The flames seem to have disappeared, but they're still there—although the sky behind is already well saturated. The black and white squares of the flag obviously have comparable (and very low) saturation.

For the Saturation blend mode, the result color is a product of the base color's hue and brightness, with the saturation of the blend color. Painting with gray produces no change.

Color

The brightness of the base color is retained in the Color blending mode, and the other two components (hue and saturation) are contributed by the blend color (see Figure 17.30).

Figure 17.30
The flag and trophy areas of this sample image are similar to the preceding figure because of the blend colors' saturation values, but several other areas are dramatically different.

Luminosity

Using the brightness (luminosity) of the blend color and the hue and saturation of the base color, Luminosity is the reverse of the Color blending mode (see Figure 17.31).

Figure 17.31
Using the highlights and shadows of the blend color produces well-defined representations of the artwork on the upper layers.

17

Simplifying: Hue, Saturation, Color, Luminosity

The four blending modes Hue, Saturation, Color, and Luminosity take HSB values from the lower or upper color to create the resulting color. The chart shown in Table 17.3 simplifies the equation for you.

Table 17.3   HSB for Blending Modes

Blending Mode	H	S	B
Hue	Upper	Lower	Lower
Saturation	Lower	Upper	Lower
Color	Upper	Upper	Lower
Luminosity	Lower	Lower	Upper

Pass Through

The Pass Through blending mode is available only for layer sets, and is the default layer set blending mode. This mode results in the layer set itself having no effect on the image's compositing or appearance. Consider Pass Through a neutral mode, allowing the layers to interact both within the layer set and with layers below.

Replace

When working with the Healing Brush (and only the Healing Brush), the Replace blending mode helps ensure that grain and texture near the edges of the brush stroke are preserved.

PHOTOSHOP IN FOCUS

Several of Photoshop's blending modes are best used with painting tools to enhance images. You can create a layer, set the blending mode, and paint with shades of gray to improve shadows, highlights, or both. Other blending modes can create dramatic effects when used with a pair of color images. To see for yourself how blending modes work, try this:

1. Open a photographic image in Photoshop. A suitable picture for this experiment has a number of different colors, many of them bright and well saturated. It should also have definite shadows and highlights.

2. In the Layers palette, click the New Layer button.

3. On that new layer, make a rectangular selection of the lower third (or so) of the image.

4. In the selection, drag a black-to-white linear gradient.

5. Make another rectangular selection, this one across the top third of the image.

6. In the new selection, drag a linear Rainbow gradient.

7. Change through the layer blending modes, seeing how the grayscale and color gradients differ from blending mode to blending mode. Keep track of which are most appropriate for correcting an image's shadows and highlights by painting with gray on a separate layer. (And make note of which blending modes make you say "Cool!" out loud.)

FROM THE NAPP HELP DESK

The National Association of Photoshop Professionals (NAPP) offers e-mail assistance to its members. Here is some advice from the NAPP Help Desk related to issues in this chapter.

Plotting the X,Y

How can there be more than one pixel in the same place?

When the file is saved in a format that doesn't support layers or is sent to a printer, there is, in fact, just a single pixel in each location in the image. However, when working with layers in Photoshop (or TIFF) file format, you can have one pixel for each location on each layer. The location, measured from the upper-left corner as an X,Y coordinate, exists on each layer independently.

Color Mode Conversion

*L*a*b color mode doesn't support Darken, Lighten, or a couple of other blending modes. What if I've used them and have to convert my image to Lab?*

When you use the menu command Image, Mode, Lab Color, you'll be offered an opportunity to flatten your layers. If you do, the appearance will be preserved. If you don't, any layer that uses an unsupported blending mode will be converted to Normal mode. This can have a substantial impact on the overall look of your artwork. Consider, for example, a layer set to Lighten that contains black. In Lighten, the black is transparent; in Normal, it is opaque black.

17

APPLYING PHOTOSHOP'S FILTERS

by Jeff Foster

IN THIS CHAPTER

WHAT DO THE FILTERS DO?

Photoshop filters have several functions, but primarily they
are used to rearrange or modify the pixels on an image or
image layer to blur, sharpen, paint, distort, transform, or tex-
turize. Since the first version of Photoshop, with its dozen or
so built-in filters with minimal functionality and no preview,

Be sure to check out the third-
party demo plug-ins included on
the book's CD-ROM.

there have been several third-party "plug-ins" with varying functions and effects to enhance
Photoshop's creative edge. Adobe has acquired and engineered several of these effects and incorporated them into the base set of plug-in filters that ships with Photoshop 7. You can still purchase several third-party plug-ins from companies such as Extensis, Alien Skin, Procreate, and XAOS Tools, to
name just a few.

These third-party plug-ins provide functionality not available in the built-in filters that ship with
Adobe Photoshop 7. They give you the ability to play "god" by creating an infinite number of original textures, fractals, shapes, lights, and effects. You can do everything from creating fur on a human
to making incredibly accurate color corrections. As cool as these plug-ins are, however, most people
won't need to venture outside Photoshop 7's built-in set of filters.

Instead of just showing you a single image with every filter slapped onto it, the figures in this chapter are designed to give you examples of how to get the best results and options from each filter and
how they might apply to your projects. And some of them are just plain fun!

With these filters, take time to explore the many settings that produce varied results. You'll be
amazed at the difference a higher number or nudge of the slider can make! Experiment with different blending modes and layer opacity settings to get truly unique effects.

➡️ *Wondering about how to adjust a filter's opacity and blending mode? See "Working the Layers" in the
NAPP Help Desk section at the end of this chapter.*

Included under the Filter menu of Photoshop 7 are the Extract, Liquify, and Pattern Maker commands. (If you are a Photoshop 6 user, you'll notice that Adobe has moved these commands from the
Edit menu.) Because they are not really filters, they are not included in this chapter, but you can
learn more about these commands in Chapter 19, "Extract, Liquify, and the Pattern Maker."

FILTER APPLICATIONS

The best way to use a filter on an image is to copy the image layer and apply your filter to the copy.
By doing this, you can experiment with several filters without damaging the original image layer.
Make sure to copy the original image to a new layer with (Command-J) [Ctrl+J], and apply the filter
to the copied layer. For color corrections and blurs, use an adjustment layer to apply the filter to.

The examples in this chapter are scaled to best represent the filter and size for the figures used in
printing this book. Make sure when you apply these filter techniques to your images that you take
into consideration the actual size, scale, and resolution of the image file when applying number values and percentages.

Each image reacts differently to the layer blending modes and the amount of layer opacity you apply to the filtered layer. Experiment with these adjustments until you find a combination that works best for your image—not just the amounts given in the examples.

THE ARTISTIC FILTERS

The Artistic filters are grouped for their creative, artsy feel and painterly effects. Some are subtler than others (and more practical or usable), but all have a usefulness that necessitates being included in this list of examples.

Colored Pencil

The Colored Pencil filter is best used when layering the effect over the original image, allowing some of the details to show through.

In this first example, a dark background is produced by setting the Paper Brightness to 0. Depending on the scale of the original image, adjust the Pencil Width and Stroke Pressure so that you can still make out some of the image's shapes in the preview window.

Set the blending mode of the filtered layer to Screen, and the composite image with the original image beneath it will have a beautiful hand-drawn look (see Figure 18.1).

Figure 18.1
Setting the filtered layer to Screen allows vivid detail in the original image to show through.

18

In the second example, a light background is achieved by setting the Paper Brightness to 50. The layer blending mode is set to Overlay to create the effect of colored markers (see Figure 18.2).

Figure 18.2
Set the Paper Brightness to 50 and the layer blending mode to Overlay to create a colored felt marker effect.

Cutout

The Cutout filter produces a clean posterized effect that simulates an image created with a drawing program, such as Adobe Illustrator. The setting for number of levels divides the image up into a definable color palette. Set the Edge Simplicity and Edge Fidelity to allow the maximum amount of detail to be visible without creating a "speckled" effect.

The filtered image can be printed as a pixel-based image or imported into Adobe Illustrator and auto-traced to produce an accurate and scalable vector-based image (see Figure 18.3).

Figure 18.3
Import the filtered image into Adobe Illustrator and auto-trace to create a vector image.

Dry Brush

When applied correctly, the Dry Brush filter creates a better watercolor effect than the Watercolor filter does.

Adjust the Brush Size and Brush Detail so that the details of the original image still show through in the preview window.

On the filtered layer, set the layer blending mode to Screen over the original image layer (Background). The resulting image is a finely detailed watercolor. Printing this image on watercolor archival paper with your color inkjet produces fabulous results (see Figure 18.4).

Figure 18.4
Print the filtered image on archival watercolor paper for a truly remarkable effect.

Film Grain

Sometimes the warm subtlety of an image on film is lost with the high-contrast harshness and ultra-clarity of a digital camera. The Film Grain filter can add a subtle amount of grainy noise to the image without blowing it out or clouding it up. This effect works best when applied to a copied layer. Be sure to adjust the blending mode to allow the original image to show through.

On the filtered layer, set the layer blending mode to Lighten to allow the film grain noise to softly affect the original image layer below (see Figure 18.5).

Figure 18.5
By blending the filtered layer with the original image, the Film Grain filter produces a softened effect.

Fresco

For a more traditional painterly effect, use the Fresco filter on a floating layer with adjusted blending mode and Opacity settings.

Apply the Fresco filter to the copied layer. Adjust the Brush Size and Brush Detail to match the scale and resolution of your original image. For the best results with this image, I set the layer blending mode to Hard Light and the layer's Opacity to 50%, allowing the background layer to show through and provide more detail (see Figure 18.6).

Neon Glow

Sometimes a filter looks best when the effect is inverted or totally changed by the layer's blending mode. I find that the Neon Glow filter looks best when applied to a copied layer of the original image and inverted over the original.

On the filtered layer, set the layer blending mode to Difference over the original image layer. This setting creates a negative of the image in bright, neon colors—resulting in a more vibrant image than just the filter alone (see Figure 18.7).

Figure 18.6
By blending the filtered layer with the original image, the Fresco filter achieves a painterly effect that shows more details.

Figure 18.7
Setting the layer blending mode of the filtered layer to Difference produces a vibrant neon image of the original.

18

Paint Daubs

The Paint Daubs filter has several Brush Type presets to choose from. The two I prefer are Sparkle and Simple. This is one filter that I don't mind applying directly to the original image at full strength because the results are pleasing.

The Sparkle brush produces a pointillist pattern on the image, giving it a very painterly quality that works great when reproduced in large scale. Be sure to adjust the Brush Size and Sharpness to match your image scale and resolution (see Figure 18.8).

Selecting the Simple brush produces a more blurred effect. Using a larger Brush Size also gives it an acrylic-painting effect (see Figure 18.9).

As with many of the built-in Photoshop Artistic filters, applying them full strength on the original image destroys all the detail in the image. Simply using the Fade option to bring back the original image's detail eliminates too much of the filter's effect, however. The best remedy is to apply the filter to a copied layer of the original image and set the layer blending mode to a desirable effect, or simply adjust the layer's Opacity setting.

Figure 18.8
The Paint Daubs filter with the Sparkle Brush Type produces a pointillist effect.

Figure 18.9
The Paint Daubs filter with the Simple brush produces an acrylic-painting effect.

Palette Knife

Unfortunately, the name of the Palette Knife filter doesn't convey the actual effect that the filter produces. Perhaps some fancy channel operations or underlying embossing might create a more 3D effect of painting with a palette knife, but even the brush strokes and shape don't quite cut it. Nevertheless, you can still achieve a great painted effect with it, by using the layer blending mode on a copied image layer.

Set the layer blending mode to Screen on the filtered layer and position it over the original image layer. The effect should have a definite watercolor look to it—especially in the highlight areas. The edges of the brush strokes appear a bit jagged, as though bleeding onto the paper (see Figure 18.10).

Figure 18.10
The details of the original image still come through the Palette Knife filtered image layer.

Changing the layer blending mode to Vivid Light creates a darker, wetter appearance, as though large color markers or layers of watercolor had been applied to paper (see Figure 18.11).

Figure 18.11
Experiment with different layer blending modes to get varied effects.

Plastic Wrap

The Plastic Wrap filter is fun to play with, but might have limited usability. One practical application is to give objects a wet or glossy appearance. If you adjust the Detail and Highlight Strength sliders while keeping the Smoothness minimal, this image takes on texture and moisture highlights.

If the image has enough depth and detail, you can modify the application of the Plastic Wrap filter to enhance the highlights of fine details, making it look wet (see Figure 18.12).

Figure 18.12
The details of this image are enhanced by the Plastic Wrap filter and given a wet appearance.

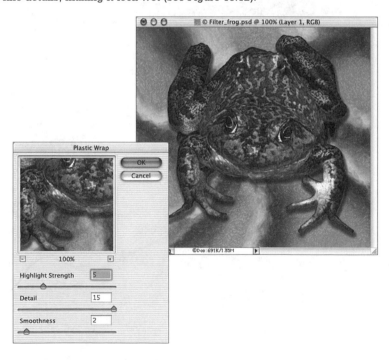

18

Poster Edges

The Poster Edges filter produces an effect similar to the Cutout filter, except that it creates stronger black edges in the details. By keeping the Edge Thickness and Edge Intensity at a minimum, the detail in this image was retained. The filtered image looks as though it were drawn and colored with ink and markers or with watercolor "paint by numbers" (see Figure 18.13).

Figure 18.13
The darker lines look like a Rapidograph drawing that was colored in with markers or water-colors.

Rough Pastels

The effect that the Rough Pastels filter produces is very realistic. This filter can be used full strength on the original image or blended in with a copied layer and layer blending modes.

Select a preset texture or a grayscale image of your choice. By adjusting the Light Dir (direction) setting, the details of the underlying texture are picked up more predominantly. Print this filtered image on a coarse, matte-finish watercolor paper, and you'll have to feel it to see if the pastel smudges (see Figure 18.14)!

Figure 18.14
The Rough Pastels filter does a remarkable job of creating a realistic pastel-drawing look.

Smudge Stick

Take a pastel drawing on fine rag paper and smudge it with a cotton burnisher, and you'll have the effect that the Smudge Stick filter produces. In this sample image, I've blasted the Highlight Area all the way up to maintain a lighter pastel-and-paper appearance. This effect works great on family photos or wildlife images, giving a look of old-fashioned hand-drawn portraits (see Figure 18.15).

Sponge

The Sponge filter tends to blast away all detail in an image when applied directly to the original image. I've gotten the best results when applying the filter to a copied image layer and applying a layer blending mode. The layer's Opacity was then set to 75% and the layer blending mode to Overlay. The resulting image still has photographic qualities in the details, but the colors are richer and the texture of the sponge painting is still predominant (see Figure 18.16).

Figure 18.15
A soft burnished pastel effect is achieved with the Smudge Stick filter.

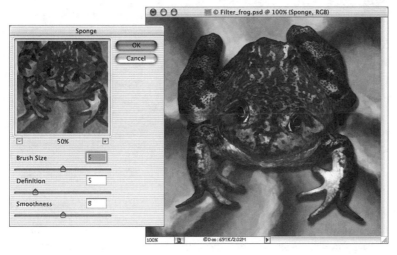

Figure 18.16
The Sponge filter applied to a copied image layer with the layer blending mode set to Overlay.

18

Underpainting

The Underpainting filter is similar to the Texturizer and Rough Pastels filters, in that it applies the image to a textured surface. At full-strength application, even with the Brush Size setting at minimum, the effect is too strong. For best results, apply to a copied image layer and adjust the layer's blending mode.

Applied to a copied image layer with the blending mode set to Lighten, the Underpainting filter affects only midtones and gives a slight painterly effect to the image (see Figure 18.17).

Figure 18.17
The Lighten layer blending mode on the copied image layer produces a more subtle effect with the Underpainting filter.

Watercolor

The Watercolor filter tends to oversaturate and darken images applied at full strength on the original image. In this example, the Shadow Intensity is set to 0 and the Brush Detail is at its highest setting. The dark areas of the image are still too heavy, however, and the Watercolor effect is overstated.

To maintain the look and feel of a detailed watercolor painting, the Opacity of the filtered image layer is set to 50%. You can achieve this same effect by choosing Edit, Fade if the Watercolor filter is applied to the original image (see Figure 18.18).

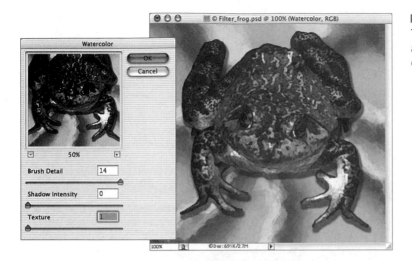

Figure 18.18
The Watercolor filter is applied to a copied image layer for layer effect control.

⇨ *Can't use Fade with your filters? See "Using the Fade Command" in the NAPP Help Desk section at the end of this chapter.*

THE BLUR FILTERS

The preset Blur filters are fine for a few images, but professionals tend to not use them. If you apply the Blur or Blur More filters to an image, the only adjustment options you have are choosing Edit, Fade or applying the filters to a copied image layer and adjusting the layer's Opacity or blending mode.

The Blur filters that give you the most control and functionality are the Gaussian Blur, Motion Blur, and Radial Blur filters. The Smart Blur gives questionable results and creates strange artifacts in the image. In this section, only these filters have examples, as the results of the preset Blur filters are automatic.

Gaussian Blur

Gaussian Blur is the most utilized filter in the Photoshop Filters library. Used for everything from smoothing out a harsh digital image or scan to creating realistic depth of field, the Gaussian Blur filter is the photographer's best friend.

In this first example, the image was taken with a long telephoto lens, which brings the background behind the subject in close and in focus, detracting from the details of the subject itself. To remedy this common problem with outdoor wildlife photography, you can enhance (or imitate) the depth of field by adding Gaussian Blur to the image's background. By painting a Quick Mask around the subject in the background, you can create a selection area for applying the Gaussian Blur filter (see Figure 18.19).

18

Figure 18.19
Paint a Quick Mask around the subject to create a selection area to apply the Gaussian Blur.

Apply the Gaussian Blur filter to the selection on the copied image layer. Depending on the scale and resolution of the image you're working on, set the Pixel Radius to a visually pleasing amount, as shown in the preview window. The resulting image is a bit exaggerated, and blurring the background has darkened the image overall (see Figure 18.20). To remedy this, you should apply a layer blending mode to the filtered image layer.

Figure 18.20
The filtered image is exaggerated and dark.

By setting the layer blending mode to Screen and the Opacity of the filtered layer to 65%, the final effect is a natural depth of field that enhances the image and makes the subject stand out (see Figure 18.21).

18

Figure 18.21
The layer blending mode and Opacity settings were modified to enhance the image's depth of field.

Motion Blur

The Motion Blur filter can add life and excitement to a still image. You can put a parked car in motion or focus on one moving object and make everything else in the image a blur. Professional photographers create this effect by following the moving subject in the camera's viewfinder and tracking it while releasing the shutter.

You can duplicate this technique with the Motion Blur filter by first painting a Quick Mask around the subject you want to isolate (see Figure 18.22).

Figure 18.22
Isolate the subject by using the Quick Mask option.

The Angle and Distance of the Motion Blur filter should be set in the direction that the image's subject is moving (or appears to be moving, if you're setting a stationary object into motion). Set the Distance in pixels according to the scale and resolution of the image you're working on.

The final image has more depth and clarity of the subject as well as the sense of motion (see Figure 18.23).

Figure 18.23
The Motion Blur filter has enhanced the central subject in this image.

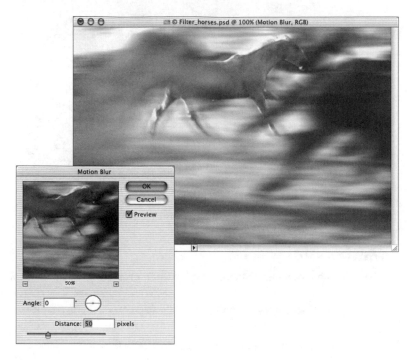

Radial Blur

Similar to Motion Blur, the Radial Blur filter can add motion to an otherwise still world. The trick to using this filter effectively is to constrain the motion in the image to enhance a subject or draw attention to the subject in motion.

Radial Blur has two modes: Spin and Zoom. There is no preview window in this filter, so you have to go through a lot of trial and error while applying Radial Blur. Choosing the Best Quality mode with this filter is always a good idea.

Another way to control the range of motion in which the filter is applied on the image is to use a selection tool or paint a Quick Mask to create a selection area (see Figure 18.24).

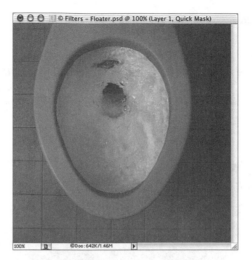

Figure 18.24
The area to apply the Radial Blur to is contained with a Quick Mask.

A helpful feature of the Radial Blur dialog box is that it enables you to center the Spin or Zoom anywhere within your image window by simply clicking on the graph window and dragging inside the box. The amount of the Spin Radial Blur filter depends on the scale and resolution of the source image as well as the amount of blur you need to create motion in your image (see Figure 18.25)

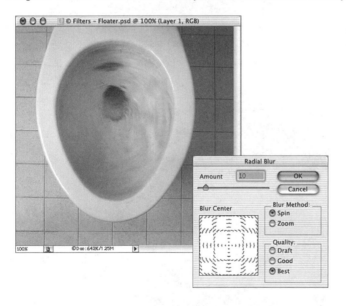

Figure 18.25
The Spin Radial Blur filter adds motion and focus in the image.

The Zoom Radial Blur filter works similarly to the Motion Blur filter, in that it creates motion in a straight angle aimed only at the center of the blur direction. You can move the center around in the graph window when the filter dialog box is open.

A practical application of the Zoom Radial Blur filter is creating highlights, which is achieved through the use of layers and the layer blending mode. This is done in only two steps!

This example shows how easy it is to add realistic rays of light from the sun in this image, using the Zoom Radial Blur filter and a layer blending mode setting (see Figure 18.26).

Figure 18.26
This is the original image to which the light rays will be added—in only two steps!

The Zoom Radial Blur filter enables you to center the zoom's direction by clicking in the graph window and dragging to the area of the image you want to center the zoom on.

The blurred image looks great if you're traveling at warp speed, but the original image details are lost at this point (see Figure 18.27).

Figure 18.27
Hold on—you're traveling at warp speed!

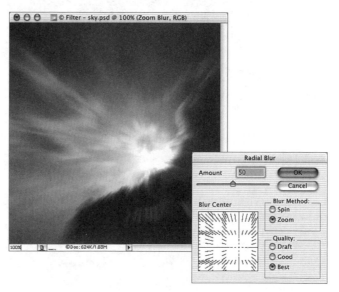

The layer's blending mode is set to Lighten, and voilà! A beautiful burst of light rays appear from the clouds (see Figure 18.28).

Figure 18.28
The final glorious image appears after only two steps.

Smart Blur

Theoretically, the Smart Blur filter should automatically search for areas of an image to apply the blur to, giving you control of the Threshold amount and radius of the blur. Unfortunately, it doesn't always work as designed and creates strange artifacts, pixellation, and posterization in the blur selection.

In this example, the selection was made from a Quick Mask and the Smart Blur filter was applied. Notice the artifacts in the tall grass and weeds directly to the sides of the cheetah. It almost looks as though an Artistic filter has been applied, and strange posterization has shifted the color palette (see Filter 18.29).

Figure 18.29
The Smart Blur filter has caused posterization and artifacts in the mid-range image details.

⇨ *When is the Smart Blur filter appropriate? See "Blurring Smartly" in the NAPP Help Desk section at the end of this chapter.*

THE BRUSH STROKES FILTERS

Similar to the Artistic filters, the Brush Strokes filters have both practical and painterly qualities to their application. Several creative effects can be achieved from almost all the Brush Strokes filters, but I'll be able to cover only a few in this chapter. It's my recommendation that you "joy ride" in these filter dialog boxes and discover all the great effects you can come up with, simply by dragging sliders around and checking the results in the preview window.

Accented Edges

Just by the name of the Accented Edges filter, it's easy to determine what the effect might be on an image. Besides its practical application, you can achieve many artistic and painterly effects by exaggerating the settings. In this example, bumping up Edge Brightness to the maximum setting produces an airbrushed effect and reducing Edge Width to its minimum setting gives you a watercolor effect (see Figure 18.30).

Figure 18.30
Happy accidents happen when you explore the extreme fringe of the Accented Edges filter.

In this example, the intended result was achieved, giving the edges of the bird, branch, and palms a cleaner edge with highlights (see Figure 18.31).

Figure 18.31
The edges of the detailed objects in this image have been highlighted.

Angled Strokes

The Angled Strokes filter can simulate a painted portrait with realistic color and brush strokes. It maintains detail and color integrity when applied to an image.

The final filtered image maintains the original's integrity and color but clearly shows the effects of the angled brush strokes (see Figure 18.32).

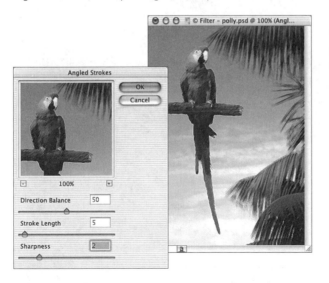

Figure 18.32
The angled brush strokes are clearly seen, with the detail and color integrity intact.

Crosshatch

The Crosshatch filter produces a sketched, colored pencil effect on an angled canvas texture. Details are affected, but the colors remain in the image (see Figure 18.33).

Figure 18.33
Adjust the Strength and Stroke
Length to the desired colored
pencil effect.

Dark Strokes

The Dark Strokes filter does exactly what it says—just watch out for overexaggerated application. In this example, the Black Intensity had to be set to 0 and the White Intensity all the way up to keep the image legible. The effect has some character and artistic qualities to it. The contrast is still strong, but the color balance has shifted considerably (see Figure 18.34).

Figure 18.34
Color balance appears to be
somewhat lost, as does the
image detail.

Ink Outlines

The Ink Outlines filter looks just like a colored pencil and Rapidograph illustration and produces a fun, realistic effect. Like the Dark Strokes filter, the Dark Intensity had to be set to 0 and the Light Intensity all the way up to keep the details of the brush strokes and Ink Outlines visible. Print this image on archival-quality paper, and no one will be the wiser that it was a filter applied to a photograph (see Figure 18.35).

Figure 18.35
The final filtered image has a very realistic colored pencil and ink effect.

Spatter

The Spatter filter actually acts more like a Distort filter when applied to an image. I discovered a nice "wave" pattern created by the filter. Inspired by this effect, I thought it would be nice if our feathered friend could look at his reflection! Simply by inverting the filtered selection, a reflective pool was added to the original image (see Figure 18.36).

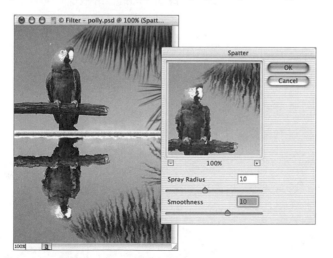

Figure 18.36
Yarrrgh! Whar's me parrot?

Sprayed Strokes

Similar to the Spatter filter, the Sprayed Strokes filter is more like a Distort filter than a brush stroke. You can easily generate another ripple or wave with an angular Stroke Direction setting (see Figure 18.37).

Figure 18.37
A wavelike effect is created by the Sprayed Strokes filter.

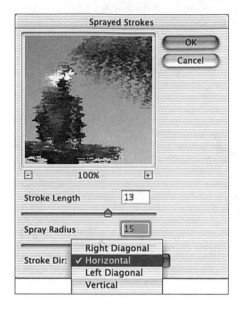

18

Sumi-e

The Sumi-e filter creates a wide, wet brush stroke with a Far Eastern flavor. Depending on your image scale and resolution, adjust the Stroke Width and Pressure.

The effect can be exaggerated if applied too strongly, but it still has realistic brush strokes. Although the details are lost in this image, it still has an artistic charm that would lend itself to being printed on a rough watercolor paper with good results (see Figure 18.38).

Figure 18.38
Realistic brush strokes are visible, although the details of the original image are lost.

THE DISTORT FILTERS

With the exception of the Diffuse Glow filter, all Distort filters rearrange and modify the pixels of an image to create distortion, volume, or a 3D effect. Some of the filters, such as Pinch and Spherize, have a specific and obvious function, and others have several useful applications that aren't immediately obvious.

With the Distort filters, taking time to "joy ride" inside the filter dialog boxes and experiment with the effects of the sliders and options is important. Several of the examples in this section show practical applications of using the Distort filters, which will, I hope, trigger your own ideas for experimenting with them.

Diffuse Glow

The Diffuse Glow filter is the only Distort filter that doesn't distort the image pixels; rather, it adds a diffused white glow around the edges of highlights and whitespace in an image.

In this example, I've used a stock photo image, in which the object has been masked against a white background with no drop shadow. Normally, this image would look harsh all by itself, unless some dimension were added by creating a drop shadow or background texture. In this case, I'd like to create dimension and softness on the object itself, giving the impression that it's been photographed on a backlit light table.

Start by copying the original image to a new layer. Adjust the Clear Amount to reveal the majority of the object, balancing the Glow Amount to encroach on the edges dramatically. Adjust the Graininess to add enough noise so that the image looks more like natural film grain, instead of looking too "Photoshopped."

The filtered layer then has its blending mode set to Screen and Opacity set to 50%. A soft-edged Eraser is then applied to the top edges of the object on the filtered layer. The highlights on the bottom edge of the object are screened, enhancing the bottom-lit glow effect (see Figure 18.39).

Figure 18.39
Set the filtered layer blending mode and Opacity and apply a soft Eraser brush along the top edges of the object, leaving the glow from the bottom.

Displace

The Displace filter stretches the pixels of the original image around the shape of a target grayscale image (called a *displacement map*). With this technique, adding an Emboss layer style on a simple texture has a more dramatic 3D effect.

In this example, first create a displacement map to apply to a sand texture. Make sure the displacement map image is the same scale and resolution as your base texture image, saved as a .psd format file.

Next, you open the base texture image file and create a copy of the original image layer. Because the Horizontal Scale and Vertical Scale are measured in percentages instead of pixels, a very low setting generates a significant displacement in the image. Then select the grayscale displacement map image from your hard drive (see Figure 18.40).

Figure 18.40
It takes only a small percentage of displacement scale to create a large effect.

After the displacement is applied, an outline of shifted pixels appear on the base texture image. Not only do the edge pixels shift, but the entire inner region shifts as a whole, as though the displacement is actually raised up out of the surface (see Figure 18.41).

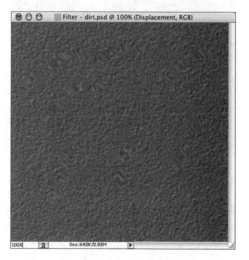

Figure 18.41
Notice how the Displace filter has shifted the pixels to the shape of the displacement map.

To enhance the displacement effect, you can apply an Emboss layer style in the shape of the displacement. Copy and paste the displacement map image into a new channel as an alpha channel. Make a selection from this alpha channel, copy and paste the selection from the Displace filtered layer to a new layer, and apply the Bevel and Emboss layer style. Adjust to fit the scale and resolution of the displaced edges (see Figure 18.42).

18

Figure 18.42
Apply the Bevel and Emboss layer style to a copied shape layer of the displaced image.

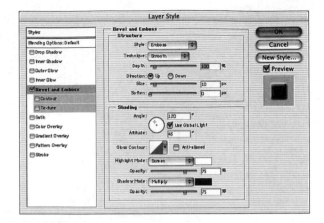

The end result has a much more dramatic 3D effect than just embossing or displacement alone (see Figure 18.43).

Figure 18.43
The 3D effect is enhanced by applying both the Displace filter and the Bevel and Emboss layer style.

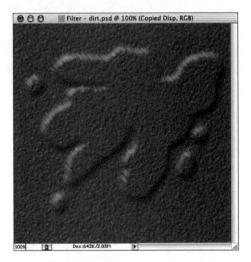

Glass

There isn't much that's practical about this filter, but it's definitely fun! For producing distorted glass effects from a shower door to glass blocks, the Glass filter does an incredible job of doing just that. You can even import your own grayscale texture (displacement map).

18

For this example, I'm just applying the Frosted glass texture (looks like a shower door) to the iguana image used earlier in this chapter. Adjust the Distortion and Smoothness to get the effect you want, and adjust the Scaling to your image's resolution.

With the Glass filter applied to the image, you can almost anticipate movement from the creature behind the "glass." Would you want to wake up in the morning to see this image in your shower (see Figure 18.44)?

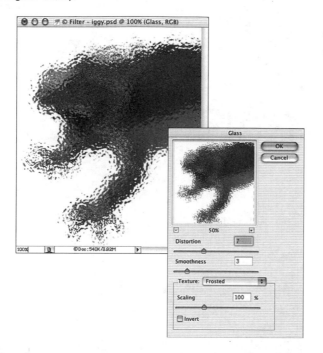

Figure 18.44
Would you want to shower with this?

Ocean Ripple

Besides applying a Distort filter to an image merely to see what cool effects it produces, there are some practical applications for some of them. The Ocean Ripple filter is commonly used to create textures and backgrounds from little or no data.

In this example, I started with a simple sandy dirt texture and applied a very small amount of the Ocean Ripple filter to it. After the filter is applied, the image is adjusted with the Levels adjustment (Image, Adjustments, Levels), which creates a photorealistic stone sidewalk texture (see Figure 18.45).

Figure 18.45
The filtered texture is adjusted with Levels to create a realistic stone texture.

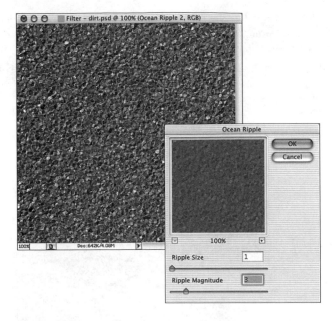

The Ocean Ripple filter is reapplied, and the Ripple Size and Magnitude are increased to create a burled wood texture. This knotted wood texture can be tiled and redistorted several times to keep creating new textures (see Figure 18.46).

Figure 18.46
The burled wood texture created with the Ocean Ripple filter.

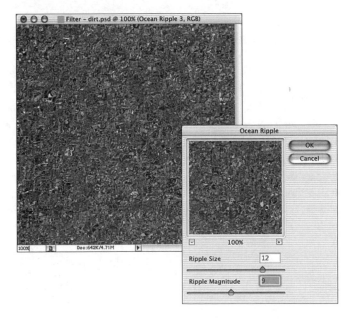

Pinch

The Pinch filter does two things—Pinch In and Pinch Out—but it does them accurately and more evenly than using the Liquify command by itself. Unlike the Spherize filter, it distorts the pixels from the outside edges of a selection, not just a circular shape. It even conforms to a feathered edge selection (see Figure 18.47).

Figure 18.47
A selection is made to apply the Pinch filter to.

To make the Pinch filter distort convexly instead of concavely, drag the slider to the left (negative numbers). The graph window as well as the preview window shows you how the mesh is distorted.

Even the water level was distorted in this example. It looks like that fish is making waves (see Figure 18.48)!

Figure 18.48
Who wants to see a wet, uh... cat?

18

Polar Coordinates

Other than making wacky, crazy distortions of images, you'll be hard-pressed to find a real use for the Polar Coordinates filter. In some cases, it has been used to straighten out mirrored cylindrical images for creating 360-degree panographic photography (such as QTVR). Theoretically, it takes the rectangular coordinates (left and right) and pulls them up together at the top (see Figure 18.49).

Figure 18.49
Polar Coordinates applied to the selection.

Conversely, using the Polar to Rectangular option on the same selection reverses the distortion in a nearly lossless manner (see Figure 18.50).

Figure 18.50
Applying the Polar to Rectangular option reverses the effect.

Ripple

The Ripple filter simulates ripples on a pond, applying a great wavy distortion to any image selection.

I've applied it to the fishbowl selection from the previous example to create the rippling water effect. It looks as though the cat's moving the table and jiggling the water in the fishbowl (see Figure 18.51).

Figure 18.51
Is the fishbowl really jiggling on the table?

Shear

Any image or image selection can be warped in the vertical axis with the Shear filter. In this example, a practical application of the Shear filter is to warp an object's shadow layer so that it seems to add depth to the image.

Starting with a copied layer of the floating object, with a feathered edge and filled with black, the layer is placed beneath the floating object layer and the layer's Opacity is set at 50%.

The Shear filter is applied to the shadow layer and confined to the center of the object outline. The image is updated in the preview window (see Figure 18.52).

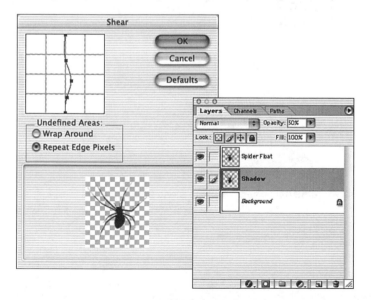

Figure 18.52
The Shear filter is applied to the shadow layer.

The final composite, with the white background, shadow layer, and floating object layer, has more depth and dimension than a flat drop shadow would provide (see Figure 18.53).

Figure 18.53
The image now has more depth and dimension than a flat drop shadow from a layer style would provide.

Spherize

18

Spherize is similar to the Pinch filter, except this mesh warps more at the edges than in the center of the image or selection—as though it were being projected onto a sphere (convex or concave). The first example is exaggerated in the fully convex sphere mode (see Figure 18.54).

Figure 18.54
From a normal spider to a tarantula in one click!

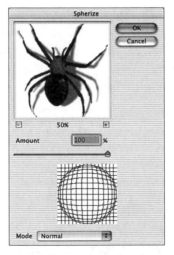

The next example is exaggerated in the fully concave sphere mode (see Figure 18.55).

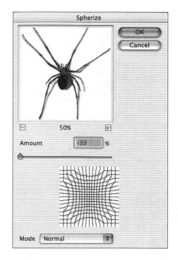

Figure 18.55
And now, a daddy longlegs.

Twirl

Although the Twirl filter is not the most practical Distort filter in the bunch, it definitely does a good job at that one thing—twirling. Depending on whether you're in the northern hemisphere or south of the equator, choose the direction you want to swish, twirl, and twist.

I had fun with this example. (SPCA note: The fish was already floating in the bowl after applying several Distort filters to it.) I made a duplicate layer of the original image layer and used the Clone Stamp tool over the hole in the center of the bowl. A selection area inside the bowl was made by using a Quick Mask (see Figure 18.56).

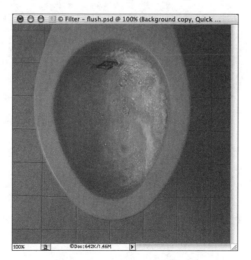

Figure 18.56
A Quick Mask was made on a copied image layer.

The Twirl filter is applied to the selection only—clockwise because we're north of the equator. Using a soft Eraser brush, the center of the twirl effect is removed to reveal the hole and a few bubbles on the original image layer (see Figure 18.57).

Figure 18.57
A soft Eraser is applied to the center of the filtered layer to open the gate to goldfish heaven.

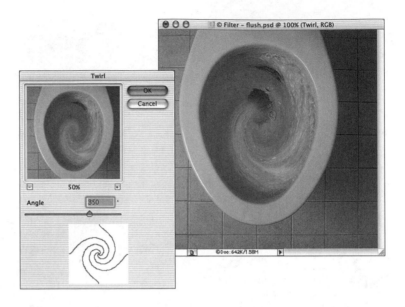

Wave

The Wave filter is similar to the Ripple filter, but with a much more sophisticated Wavelength Generator. It can be applied to create more random waves and ripples in selections than the Ripple filter does. It also makes a good random distortion filter, simply by clicking on the Randomize button and applying what you see in the preview window (see Figure 18.58).

Figure 18.58
The Wave filter has a complex set of Wavelength Generator controls.

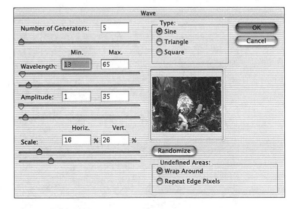

The Wave filter produces a much more natural and organic wave distortion pattern to images (see Figure 18.59).

ZigZag

Used most commonly for droplet ripples (and probably the most overused Distort filter), the ZigZag filter creates three different style effects—Pond Ripples, Around Center, and Out From Center (see Figure 18.60).

Figure 18.59
A natural, organic wave distortion is applied to an underwater scene.

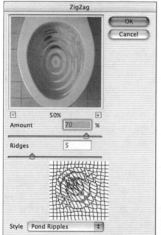

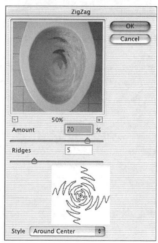

Figure 18.60
The ZigZag filters—Pond Ripples, Around Center, and Out From Center.

18

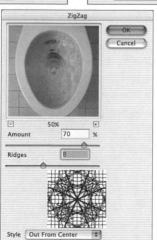

Figure 18.61 shows a different completed image.

Figure 18.61
It's never too late to say goodbye.

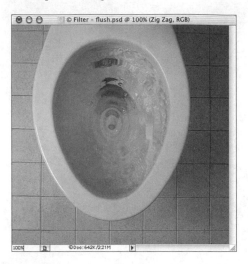

THE NOISE FILTERS

Noise is a random scattering of pixels that can fix problem areas of a digital image, reduce the effects of banding gradients, or add a natural effect of film grain. A good digital imagist or retoucher knows how to effectively use noise to match the new pixels to the original's film grain.

The use of the Noise filters is a somewhat subjective procedure that changes from image to image. Some Noise filters actually remove artifacts from an image or reduce noise. I've chosen a few practical applications of the use of these filters in the following examples.

Add Noise

Add Noise enables you to create noise in an image or a selection by applying random pixels in a Uniform or Gaussian distribution. It is used when you need to add a film grain or texture to a smooth or gradient area. The noise helps break up banding and add texture to an otherwise flat image.

One of the biggest problems digital artists have is *banding*. Banding is caused by the "stair steps" of gradient blends as they fade from one color to the other (or solid color to transparency). If you have a gradient with 216 steps from black to transparent over a large area, you might have a banding of 216 steps visible in that blend. The Add Noise filter, applied sparingly, can break up these steps and create a more natural blending.

Figure 18.62 is an example of a banded blend from 100% black to transparent over a white background.

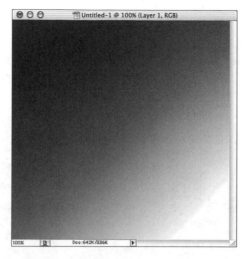

Figure 18.62
A sample of a banding problem in a gradient blend.

A very small amount of noise added to the gradient—approximately 3% to 5% Gaussian Noise—knocks down the banding that can cause real problems, especially in printed materials.

The random noise has broken up the banding and created some texture to the gradient. If this gradient is used in printing, the line screen of the final printed image would eliminate the noise pixels (see Figure 18.63). If the gradient is used in a screen mode, some of the noise pixels could be visible at 100% scale.

18

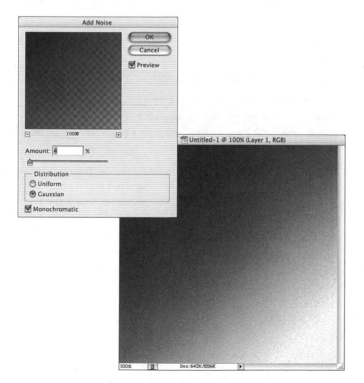

Figure 18.63
The banding is diminished by the random noise applied to the gradient.

Despeckle

The Despeckle filter blurs the noise in an image, except the pixels at the edges of objects in an image. This filter reduces the noise but retains most of the detail. There are no adjustments with the Despeckle filter, so you have to use the Edit, Fade command to back out of the effect gradually (see Figure 18.64).

Figure 18.64
The Despeckle filter reduces the amount of noise in an image but still retains the edge detail.

Before   After

Dust & Scratches

The Dust & Scratches filter searches out dissimilar pixels in an image and blurs them. Because a lot of film and prints are stored improperly, and flatbed scanners might not be totally free of dust, you may find that you need to use this filter quite often.

The sample image I'm using has simulated scratches and dust on it to re-create a worst-case scenario (see Figure 18.65). If you ever have a negative or slide that looks this bad, you might want to consider using the Healing Brush at a high resolution.

Because of the extent to which the Dust & Scratches filter must be applied to repair these deep scratches, it also blurs all the detail in the image. To remedy this, I applied it to a copied layer of the original image. Start with the Threshold all the way to the left at 0 levels and move the Radius slider up in pixels until the scratches disappear. Then increase the Threshold to regain some detail, but not the scratches.

Using soft-edged Eraser brushes, start removing material from the filtered layer in the detail areas, revealing the details of the image below. Take great care not to eliminate any areas that have been repaired by the Dust & Scratches filter (see Figure 18.66).

Figure 18.65
I hope you never have a slide or negative that looks this bad!

Figure 18.66
Use the Eraser brushes to remove the blurred filter layer around the details of the image without revealing the repaired scratched areas.

Median

Somewhat similar in function to the Despeckle filter, the Median filter equalizes surrounding pixels based on brightness. Although possibly better than just cranking up the Gaussian Blur filter, there are better filters than Median for removing too much noise in an image and still retaining fine details (see Figure 18.67).

Figure 18.67
The Median filter blurs an image too much, even at its mildest setting.

THE PIXELATE FILTERS

The Pixelate filters generate their effects by grouping pixels together in various patterns, defined by their brightness or color values. They are similar in some ways to other creative filter groups, in that you can achieve artistic and painterly effects with direct application or in combination with layer blending modes.

Color Halftone

This effect simulates large screen color separations used in silkscreen printing or newsprint. The Color Halftone filter works best on images that will be printed *really* large, such as wall murals or outdoor signage.

In this example, I used a CMYK image at 300dpi so that you can see the scale of the effect (see Figure 18.68).

I set Max. Radius to the lowest setting of 4 pixels (the highest setting is 127 pixels) and left the Screen Angles at their default amounts.

⇨ *For more information about screen angles and printing, see Chapter 28, "Halftones, Screen Frequency, and Separations," p. 825.*

Notice how the dots create a small flower-like pattern. This is called a "rosette pattern," and it's what happens when the screen angles of the different colors intersect (see Figure 18.69).

The Color Halftone filter works in Grayscale, RGB, and CMYK modes. The Screen Angles for Grayscale appear in Channel 1; RGB, in Channels 1, 2, and 3; and CMYK, in all four channels.

Figure 18.68
A higher resolution CMYK image was chosen for scale reference.

Figure 18.69
The effect of the Color Halftone filter is exaggerated in scale compared to an actual color separation for print.

18

Because this filter is used primarily for an effect, not to actually create color separation screens, it exaggerates the scale of what actually happens when a color separation is made for normal printing purposes.

Crystallize

The Crystallize filter breaks the image down into polygonal shapes that simulate a stained-glass window without the leading between the panels. Increase or decrease the Cell Size of the Crystallize filter according to the scale and resolution of your image and the desired effect. The final effect looks like a tissue paper montage or a broken tile mosaic (see Figure 18.70).

Figure 18.70
Birds of a feather flock where?

Facet

The Facet filter automatically converts the image into groups of pixels that resemble an acrylic painting or a painted wood carving (see Figure 18.71).

Figure 18.71
The Facet filter creates an acrylic painting.

Fragment

The Fragment filter makes duplicate copies of the image selection and offsets them, giving you an effect that will make you think you've had too much to drink or give you motion sickness (see Figure 18.72).

Figure 18.72
Do not use this filter while driving!

Mezzotint

Mezzotint is a process that converts the image into random dots of 100% saturated color or black and white. This filter enables you to select dot size and style as well as lines and strokes (see Figure 18.73).

Figure 18.73
Mezzotint with Medium Dots selected.

Select Lines or Strokes to create unique hand-drawn image effects (see Figure 18.74).

Figure 18.74
The Mezzotint filter with Lines or Strokes.

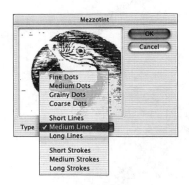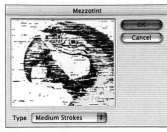

Mosaic

The Mosaic filter does basically the same thing as reducing an image's resolution by using the Nearest Neighbor resampling method. The colored cells are created and grouped based on the generalized sampling of the surrounding colors (see Figure 18.75).

Figure 18.75
The Mosaic filter creates general color blocks from your image selection.

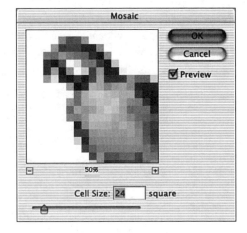

Pointillize

The Pointillize filter turns your image into a pointillist painting against your currently selected background color. The Cell Size is adjustable in the dialog box, with an updated preview window.

Adjust the Cell Size to create the effect in the scale and resolution of your image (see Figure 18.76).

Figure 18.76
Select a contrasting background color to make the image stand out.

THE RENDER FILTERS

The Render filters are a collection of special-effects renderers that create 3D objects, lens flares, lighting effects, and more. Like "mini-applications" by themselves, most create images or effects by starting with a blank page and creating textured fills and images.

3D Transform

Create 3D geometric shapes and objects with this simple filter application. Make new solid objects or wrap image selections around a 3D object, and then change the object's rotation and view angle.

To get started with this filter, first get used to the tools. Create some objects and try all the shapes, rotation tools, and view angles (see Figure 18.77).

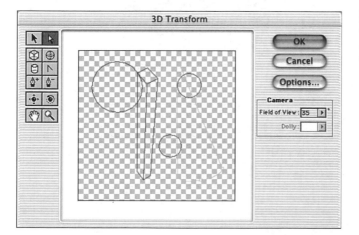

Figure 18.77
Create some objects in a blank document to get used to the tools.

The preview window updates the angle and lighting when you rotate the objects. The final rendered objects will be a bit smoother after they're rendered, but there's no going back to rerender or move objects again. When you click OK, that's it. You'll have to start all over with another set of objects (see Figure 18.78).

Figure 18.78
The rendered objects are rendered only once.

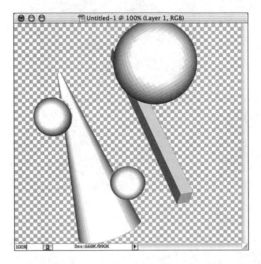

To wrap an image around an object, start by opening an image file and selecting the 3D Transform filter. Select a shape tool, and modify and position it over the part of the image you want rendered on the shape (see Figure 18.79).

Figure 18.79
Position the selected shape over the part of the image you want rendered on the object.

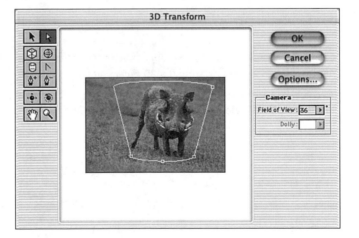

The image renders only on the object's facing surface, so rotation exposes solid shapes on the sides and back surfaces (see Figure 18.80).

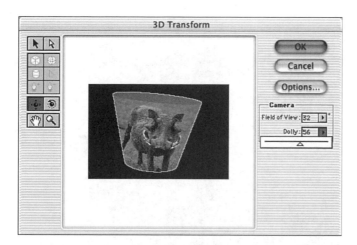

Figure 18.80
The object will render only on the shape's facing side.

Paint the remaining sides, or add text to your shape and add a Drop Shadow layer style for a realistic 3D rendering (see Figure 18.81).

Figure 18.81
Take home a bucket today.

18

Clouds

Yes, this filter creates clouds. Your image's resolution determines how large or small the clouds will be. The clouds are always based on your currently selected foreground and background colors (see Figure 18.82).

Apply the Clouds filter on a new layer over an image and set the layer blending mode to Screen or Lighten to create a smoke effect over the bottom layer image.

Figure 18.82
Create clouds from your currently selected foreground and background colors.

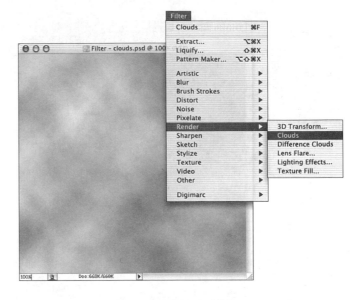

Difference Clouds

Create cool and eerie effects with the Difference Clouds filter. Start with your currently selected foreground and background color, and keep reapplying the filter with (Command-F)[Ctrl+F]. With each application of the filter, the colors shift to the opposite color spectrum and unique original patterns will appear (see Figure 18.83).

Figure 18.83
Difference Clouds reapplied over the same pattern will create unique patterns.

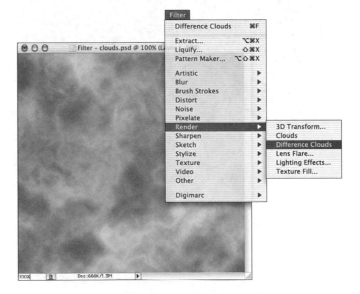

Keep repeating this process to create vivid and wild textures (see Figure 18.84).

Figure 18.84
Imagine if this image were
printed in color!

Lens Flare

The Lens Flare filter creates a starburst light source and simulated refractions, similar to what's caused by light entering a camera lens. Position the Flare Center and then adjust the Brightness and Lens Type.

Whether it's applied in a landscape or an image with an artificial light source, the Lens Flare effect is quite photorealistic when applied in a natural setting (see Figure 18.85).

18

Figure 18.85
Hey, where're my sunglasses?

Lighting Effects

When nature or the photo studio fails to provide the perfect lighting in an image, the Lighting Effects filter will save the day! You can select from several presets, or create and modify lighting to meet your needs. Several light sources, light types, intensity, reflectivity, and much more are adjustable in this progressive filter (see Figure 18.86).

Figure 18.86
The lights are fully adjustable, scalable, and positionable with every option and property imaginable.

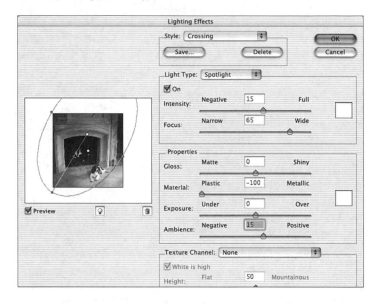

For best results, apply the filter to a copied layer of the original image layer and adjust the layer blending mode to Lighten. In addition, this image had the Opacity set to 50% so that the lighting matched the original more closely (see Figure 18.87).

Figure 18.87
Picture-perfect lighting, even after the photo was taken!

Texture Fill

Texture Fill is a simple filter that fills a selection or image with a grayscale image file. It works well as a template for making a selection by filling a new channel as an alpha channel. Apply the Texture Fill filter to a background layer and add dimension and scale to a composite image (see Figure 18.88).

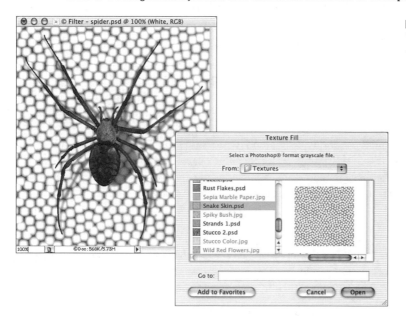

Figure 18.88
Texture and dimension are added to a plain background texture.

To take this one step further, the Texture Fill filter is used as an alpha channel and a Bevel layer style is applied, creating a truly 3D effect with the composite image (see Figure 18.89).

Figure 18.89
Creepy spider eggs created with the Texture Fill and Bevel layer style.

18

THE SHARPEN FILTERS

The Sharpen filters work with the contrast of adjacent pixels to create a "focus" in a blurred or soft image. Although a truly blurry photo might not be totally remedied by these filters, the majority of images softened by scanning or resizing can be helped tremendously.

Sharpen and Sharpen More

Sharpen and Sharpen More are preset, automatic-sharpening filters. They sharpen by a premeasured amount and do not have any controls. It is suggested that Unsharp Mask be used in most cases.

Sharpen Edges

Like the Sharpen and Sharpen More filters, the Sharpen Edges filter is a preconfigured automatic filter. What makes it different is that the filter looks for the edge contrast of objects in an image and sharpens highlights. This filter has limited results on most images tested, even after repeated applications. Unsharp Mask performs with better results and measurable control.

Unsharp Mask

Unsharp Mask gives measured results and offers a preview window of any part of the image being sharpened. It affects not only adjacent pixels, but also object edges and highlights. The Unsharp Mask filter has controls for the amount of sharpening as well as settings for Radius in pixels and Threshold in levels of contrast.

Highlights and detail can be enhanced dramatically in images softened by resizing or scanning, but care must be taken not to oversharpen an image and destroy data. Oversharpening causes harsh edges and blown-out highlights (see Figure 18.90).

Figure 18.90
The Unsharp Mask filter dramatically enhances details in an image.

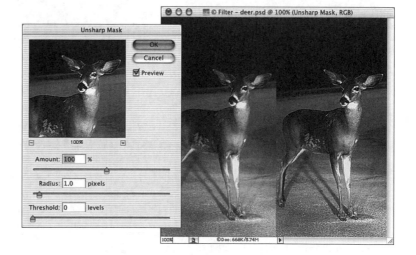

THE SKETCH FILTERS

The Sketch filters create artistic textures, 3D effects, and simulation. Some filters have painterly qualities, pushing pixels across textured canvases and more. These filters might require some layer blending mode options to enhance the effect for practical uses.

Bas Relief

Using the light and dark areas of an image, you can achieve a 3D effect with the current selection of foreground and background colors. In this example, the default color palette is selected. The Bas Relief filter is applied on a copied layer of the original image. The image's Detail setting can be adjusted and the effect smoothed out. The simulated light direction can be selected as well.

The filtered layer is set to the Overlay layer blending mode and the Opacity is set to 50% to create a 3D effect of embossing on the original image (see Figure 18.91).

Figure 18.91
A 3D embossed effect is achieved by setting the filtered layer's blending mode and Opacity.

Chalk & Charcoal

Based on an image's highlights and shadows, diagonal lines are "drawn" with the foreground color in simulated charcoal and the background color as chalk, creating a sketchy appearance.

If the Chalk & Charcoal filter is applied on a copied layer of the original image and the layer blending mode is set to Screen, the original image below looks as though it were illustrated in colored chalk and charcoal. This is a great treatment for creating portraits from ordinary photos when printed on rough archival stock (see Figure 18.92).

Figure 18.92
A great method for creating realistic pastel portraits.

18

Charcoal

The Charcoal filter is similar to the Chalk & Charcoal filter, but much looser in its sketching and drawing angles. It creates an interesting charcoal drawing on its own, with many adjustment controls to achieve the best possible image effect.

In this example, the Charcoal filter is applied on a copied layer of the original image, and the layer blending mode is set to Screen. The Opacity is set to 65% over the original image, giving it a colored-charcoal illustration look (see Figure 18.93).

Chrome

The Chrome filter simulates a reflective smooth chrome or polished metallic surface. Theoretically, an image's highlights and shadows control the polished surfaces and reflections, but my experience has been that it's more of a random procedure. On finely detailed images, you achieve the best results when the Detail and Smoothness adjustments are set to their maximum values.

When the Chrome filter is applied to an object on a floating layer with transparency and composited with background, shadows, and environmental reflections (such as the Clouds filter), a realistic chrome effect is achieved (see Figure 18.94).

Figure 18.93
With blending mode settings applied to the filtered layer over the original image, a detailed colored sketch effect appears.

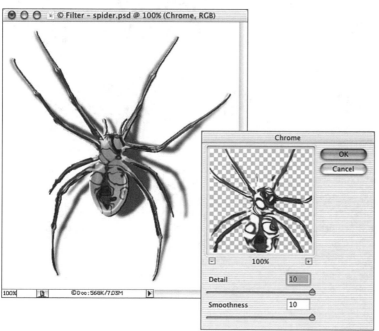

Figure 18.94
Adding environment maps with the Layer Mask and blending modes and a custom layer style for a 3D gloss effect makes the chrome spider jump off the page.

Conté Crayon

The Conté Crayon filter is very definable and has several adjustable controls to create a rough-textured illustration effect, but still retain detail information. Using the default color palette for foreground and background colors is suggested, as they give you the best results.

The preview window is updated instantly with adjustments to the effect's balance in Foreground and Background levels as well as the texture's Scaling and Relief settings. You can choose textures from the defaults or any grayscale image and select from eight angles for the Light Direction.

To create a colored illustration with the Conté Crayon filter, it was applied to a copied image layer, the layer blending mode was set to Overlay, and the Opacity was set to 50% (see Figure 18.95).

Figure 18.95
The filter applied to a copied image layer, with the Overlay blending mode selected above the original image layer.

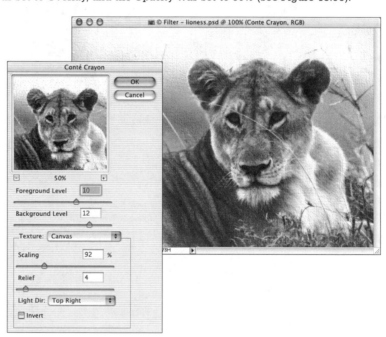

Graphic Pen

The Graphic Pen faithfully reproduces a stroke-sketched ink drawing with a quill or Rapidograph pen. Using an image's contrast, diagonal, vertical, or horizontal lines are "drawn" with the ink from the currently selected foreground color on the paper from the background color. This effect looks great printed on watercolor paper with a fine rag finish. It's hard to tell it's not the real thing (see Figure 18.96)!

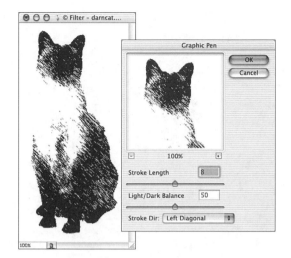

Figure 18.96
Print the illustration on a good
rag-finish paper for a realistic
inked illustration.

Halftone Pattern

Similar to the Color Halftone filter, the Halftone Pattern filter creates exaggerated screen dots, lines, and concentric circles. They are based on the old-fashioned halftone screens used in manual stat cameras, only much bolder on low-resolution images (see Figure 18.97).

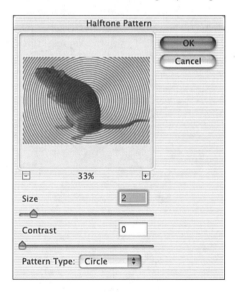

Figure 18.97
The Halftone Pattern filter creates
an exaggerated screen pattern.

Note Paper

The Note Paper filter makes a cool handmade paper effect, with an image's simplified dark areas appearing to be embossed into the paper. Print this filtered image on watercolor paper or rough card stock for a personalized art card (see Figure 18.98).

Figure 18.98
This effect looks great printed on
rough card stock or watercolor
paper.

Photocopy

18

Remember copying that same old photocopy image that's been passed around the office a thousand times? With the Photocopy filter, you can turn any perfectly good photo into a blasted-out and nearly reversed photocopy without making a single trip to the copier. Print this image out on the cheapest paper you have—even better if your cartridge is running low on ink (see Figure 18.99)!

Figure 18.99
Imagine doing this to the boss's
Christmas party photo!

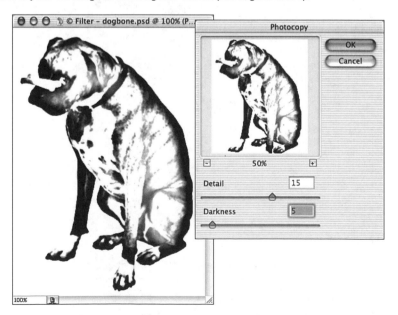

Plaster

Don't let the name fool you. The Plaster filter looks absolutely nothing like plaster. What it does do is take an image's dark areas, raise them in a smooth beveled effect, and apply a gradient across the light areas with a directional light source (see Figure 18.100).

Figure 18.100
This effect can be done better with layer styles.

Reticulation

The Reticulation filter creates a fine stippling pattern that looks like an illustration done with a pen tip. The filter is supposed to look like aged film emulsion that has expanded and shrunk. By adjusting the Density setting and the balance in Foreground Level and Background Level, you can make sure the detail doesn't get lost in the effect.

For a colorized effect, apply the filter to a copied image layer of the original, and set the Opacity to 50% with the layer blending mode set to Overlay (see Figure 18.101).

Figure 18.101
The colorized Reticulation effect looks like a colored ink pointillist illustration.

Stamp

18

A useful tool for creating solid silhouettes from images, the Stamp filter can actually be used to convert an image, logo, or object into a rubber stamp template. Make sure your image has enough contrast from the background or is stripped against white to eliminate any noise in the final image (see Figure 18.102).

Figure 18.102
A clean rubber stamp image can be created from virtually any image, object, or logo.

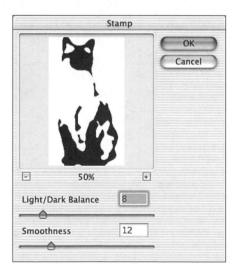

Creating Custom Shapes with the Stamp Filter

Custom shapes can easily be made from the Stamp filter images. Select the new Stamp image by choosing Select, Color Range, and then select Make Work Path from the Paths palette menu.

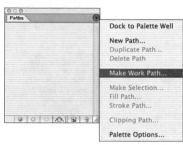

Make a selection of the Stamp image and create a path from the selection.

After a new path is made, select Edit, Define Custom Shape and name the new shape.

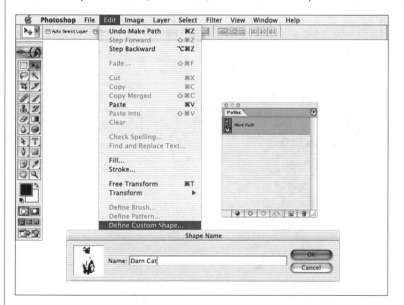

Create a new custom shape from the selected path.

Select your new shape from the Custom Shape palette.

Choose a new shape from the Custom Shape palette.

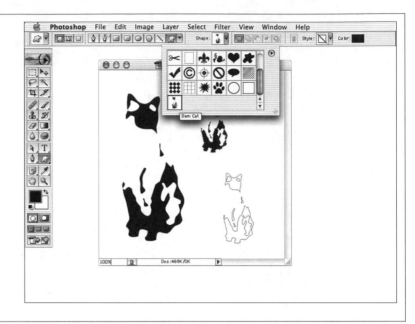

Torn Edges

Similar to the Stamp filter, the Torn Edges filter creates a silhouette from the image contrast. It resembles the edges of torn paper and fills the silhouette with the currently selected foreground color. Adjustments to the Contrast, Smoothness, and Image Balance combine to make a nice effect (see Figure 18.103).

Figure 18.103
The Torn Edges filter creates a silhouette with edges that resemble torn paper.

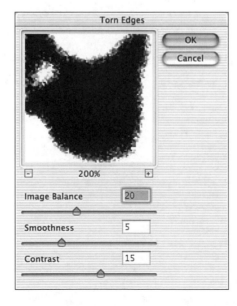

Depending on how the Contrast and Image Balance adjustments are made, you will get varied results in the silhouette's outline (see Figure 18.104).

Figure 18.104
Several levels of Contrast and Image Balance create different results.

Water Paper

The Water Paper filter creates an effect of watercolor on porous paper, resembling paint bleeding into adjoining colors. Variable adjustments for Fiber Length, Brightness, and Contrast can be made in the filter's dialog box. The effect is fairly accurate and looks good printed on watercolor paper (see Figure 18.105).

Figure 18.105
Makes good placemats for Chinese restaurants, too.

18

THE STYLIZE FILTERS

The Stylize filters, like most of the artistic filters in Photoshop, use the contrast and edges of objects in an image to push and transform pixels. Most of the Stylize filters affect the edges, and the effects range from Diffuse to Wind.

Diffuse

The Diffuse filter creates some remarkable effects for a simple action. Choosing modes other than Normal gives you more than just a blurred image (see Figure 18.106).

Figure 18.106
From blurry to fuzzy to smooth, this filter creates some great effects.

 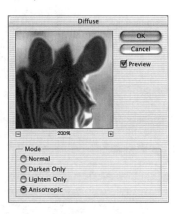

The Anisotropic mode affects the image's contrast edge details the most, creating a soft, eerie effect that looks natural and digital at the same time (see Figure 18.107).

Figure 18.107
The Diffuse filter's Anisotropic mode affects the contrast edges in details.

Emboss

The Emboss filter works by finding the edges of objects in an image, extracting the detailed color information, and overlapping positive/negative images at an offset (see Figure 18.108).

 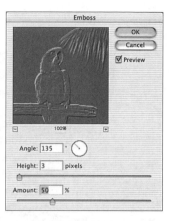

Figure 18.108
Notice the extreme offset on the left to see how the filter is structured.

Because the fill color is gray, some modification or layer blending modes are necessary to emboss a color image. In this case, the Emboss filter was applied to a copied image layer of the original. Then Brightness and Contrast were increased (Image, Adjustments, Brightness & Contrast) and the filtered layer blending mode was set to Overlay. The result is an embossing effect with all the image's color retained (see Figure 18.109).

Figure 18.109
By adjusting the filtered layer and setting the blending mode to Overlay, the image appears embossed without color loss.

18

Extrude

The Extrude filter creates extruded blocks or pyramids from the center of the image, shifting the pixels toward the height in random or fixed levels. Smaller pixel blocks create a finer grid pattern.

This example was applied to a copied image layer and the blending mode was set to Screen over the original image layer. The effect is that of zooming pixels from the center of the image (see Figure 18.110).

Figure 18.110
The zooming effect is achieved by applying a Screen blending mode to the filtered image layer.

Find Edges

18

The Find Edges filter looks for the details and contrast edges in an image and draws dark differential lines around them against a white background. It creates a marblelike texture and unusually bright colors (see Figure 18.111).

Figure 18.111
The Find Edges filter creates lines and squiggles from details in the image.

The effect is applied to a copied image layer and set to the Overlay blending mode over the original image. The effect shows up as lines drawn on the surface and enhances the image's details (see Figure 18.112).

Figure 18.112
Applied through the Overlay
blending mode, the Find Edges
filter looks like lines drawn with
colored pencil.

Glowing Edges

The Glowing Edges filter creates a neonlike glow around the contrast edges and details of an image against a black background. An alternative to just making neon glowing objects is applying the Glowing Edges filter to a copied image layer and setting the blending mode to Overlay. Adjust the Opacity to 50%, and the original image takes on a sketched appearance (see Figure 18.113).

18

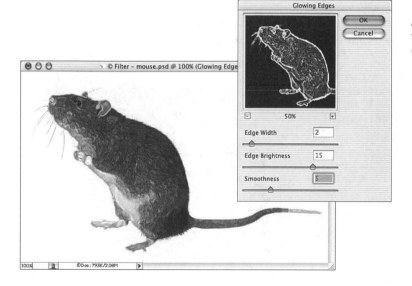

Figure 18.113
A sketched appearance appears
through the filtered layer's
Overlay blending mode.

Solarize

The Solarize filter combines negative and positive images. The image might need to be adjusted with Levels (Image, Adjustments, Levels) to bring out the color and brightness values, as the filter tends to make images a bit dark and muddy (see Figure 18.114).

Figure 18.114
The Solarize filter creates an interesting effect that needs a little color correction.

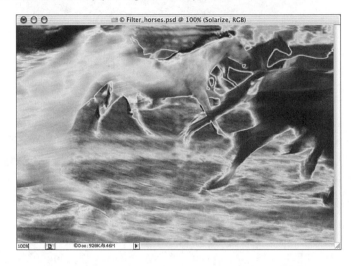

Tiles

The Tiles filter breaks up the image into rows of offset tiles, determined by the number of rows and the Maximum Offset values. To give the tiles a 3D effect over the original image, apply the Tiles filter to a copied image layer, select the open area (foreground or background color), and delete it from the layer (see Figure 18.115).

Figure 18.115
Apply the Tiles filter to a copied image layer and delete the open space.

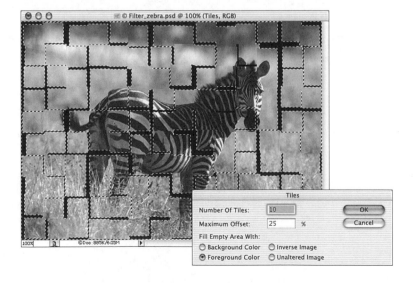

To take the look a step further, apply a Bevel layer style and add a drop shadow. The tiles will seem to float above the surface of the original image layer (see Figure 18.116).

Figure 18.116
The tiles look as though they're floating, with a little Bevel layer style application.

Trace Contour

Similar to the Glowing Edges filter, the Trace Contour filter follows an image's contrast edges and details. The adjustment allows you to select along the luminosity threshold to select which part of the edge transitions you want to trace (see Figure 18.117).

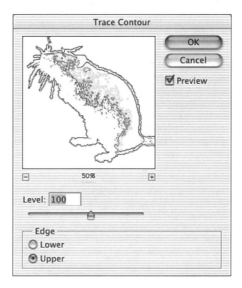

Figure 18.117
Trace Contour follows the edges along a contrast edge.

18

Wind

The Wind filter creates horizontal lines randomly across the image, simulating wind or motion. Select from Wind, Blast, or Stagger, and choose From the Left or From the Right for the wind direction (see Figure 18.118).

Figure 18.118
Break like the wind.

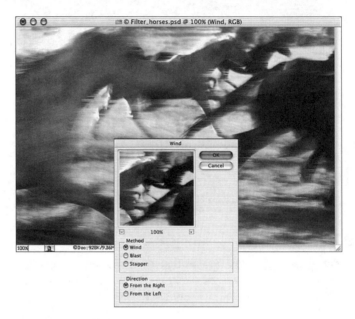

THE TEXTURE FILTERS

The Texture filters add simulated texture and depth to the surfaces of images, often adding an organic appearance that the image appears to be painted on.

Craquelure

The Craquelure filter creates cracked 3D relief in an image's surface that looks like dried mud or aged stone. You can make adjustments to the Crack Spacing and Crack Depth settings and view them in the preview window.

Adjust the spacing and depth of the Craquelure filter to match the image's scale and resolution. Take care in its application, as too much depth obstructs the image's details (see Figure 18.119).

Grain

With several types of film grain to apply with the Grain filter, you can convey a sense of aging or motion. Similar to Noise filters, you can adjust the Intensity and Contrast settings with each selection (see Figure 18.120).

Figure 18.119
The image takes on an effect of airbrushing on an old wall.

Figure 18.120
Select from various Grain textures and adjust Intensity and Contrast.

Mosaic Tiles

Mosaic Tiles is similar to the Craquelure filter but with more grid spacing in the cracks. Adjust Tile Size and Grout Width, and adjust the depth of the effect with the Lighten Grout slider (see Figure 18.121).

Figure 18.121
Tiles can be adjusted by size and grout width.

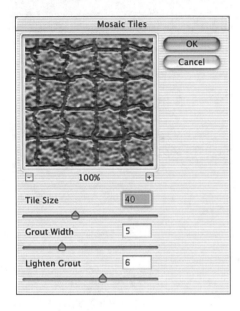

Patchwork

The Patchwork filter simulates cloth needlework by dividing the image up into 3D mosaics; you can adjust the Square Size and Relief sliders to change the tiling.

Although the filter does a good job on most images, it's hard to line up text to be handled legibly by the filter (see Figure 18.122).

Figure 18.122
Grandma would be proud.

Stained Glass

The Stained Glass filter breaks up an image into cells with a leading or Border Thickness adjustment. These borders are based on the current foreground color. The Light Intensity setting brightens highlight areas to simulate a backlit source (see Figure 18.123).

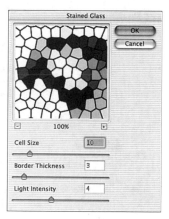

Figure 18.123
Not much in detail, but an interesting transformation.

The effect looks more like a broken tile mosaic than stained glass, but it's an interesting effect nonetheless (see Figure 18.124).

Figure 18.124
The effect is more two-dimensional than you would expect.

Texturizer

A simple and effective texture relief filter, Texturizer includes Scaling, Relief, and Light Direction adjustability. You can select from preset textures or choose your own grayscale image for the texture. The textures are applied in an organic and believable fashion, with the lighting and details matching the surface imperfections created by the filter (see Figure 18.125).

Figure 18.125
Fully adjustable and selectable texture files make this filter great for adding depth and substance to an image.

THE VIDEO AND OTHER FILTERS

The Video filters relate to broadcast video production and screen captures from videotape. On NTSC video, there is a range of colors that are generally safe to prevent bleeding and oversaturation from one frame to the next. In addition, when screen captures are made from standard video (not DV), there are even/odd video fields from one frame to the next, and interlacing occurs, which can show horizontal lines through an image or make it seem as though two frames are visible on the same image. Choosing the De-Interlace filter removes either the even or odd fields from the image to clear it up.

The Other filters are a grab bag of filters that Adobe must not have known how to categorize. You can create strange effects with the Custom filter or choose the Offset filter to make seamless tiled images.

Custom

The Custom filter enables you to create your own effects filters and save them for later use. Experiment with adding pixel brightness values around the series of pixels represented in the boxes. You can enter values from –999 to +999.

In this example, I simply entered a –1 value for the top-left sides of the default values and balanced that with +1 values on the bottom-right sides. These settings created a simulated embossing with a foil-like brightness to the sample image (see Figure 18.126).

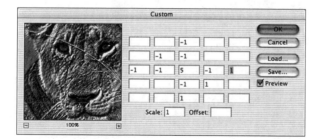

Figure 18.126
Building a custom filter, with an updated preview window.

This Custom filter can be saved and loaded later for application on other images, and you can e-mail and trade Custom filters with other Photoshop users. Experiment with random numbers, and see what you come up with. Making up your own filters can be fun (see Figure 18.127)!

Figure 18.127
Look, Ma—I made my own
Photoshop filter!

High Pass

The High Pass filter creates a gray fill over most of the image, except where edges are detected. The Edge Radius is adjustable, creating a glow around objects in the image (see Figure 18.128).

Figure 18.128
Adjusting the Edge Radius in pixels creates a glow around objects.

18

Minimum and Maximum

The Minimum and Maximum filters re-create the effect of choking and spreading a mask or bleed. They work best on higher resolution images that are being prepared for print or silkscreen. The Minimum filter decreases the white pixel radius while increasing the black pixel radius. The Maximum filter does just the opposite.

Although exaggerated in these examples, you can create some interesting effects by blowing out the normal boundaries of the filter's intended purpose (see Figure 18.129).

Figure 18.129
Exaggerating the Radius setting on low-resolution images creates interesting results.

Offset

The Offset filter shifts the image's pixels off the screen in horizontal or vertical directions. You can select the background color to move in behind the shift, choose the edge pixels to repeat in, or have the entire image wrap around.

The filter can be used to move an image layer across the screen mathematically for an animation sequence and to create a loop or seamless tile pattern for a background (see the "Photoshop in Focus" section).

PHOTOSHOP IN FOCUS

You can use the Offset filter on an image to create seamless tiles by wrapping edge pixels around x and y coordinates. Select a small image and apply the Offset filter, set to approximately half the height and width of the image's pixel dimensions (see Figure 18.130).

Figure 18.130
Set the Horizontal and Vertical pixel dimensions at approximately half of the image dimensions.

 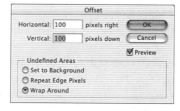

Use the Clone Stamp, Healing Brush, or Motion Blur filter to soften the tile's harsh edges. Use caution so that you do not work out of bounds, or you might create a harsh line that you'll need to repair later (see Figure 18.131).

Figure 18.131
Repair the seams with the
Healing Brush or Clone Stamp.

Apply the Offset filter again, making sure the subject or center of your image is in the middle (see Figure 18.132).

Figure 18.132
Apply the Offset filter and center
the subject.

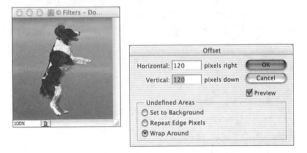

When you're pleased with the tiled image and effects, select Edit, Define Pattern to add it to the library (see Figure 18.133).

Figure 18.133
Save the tile as a pattern in the library.

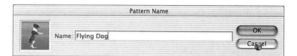

Test the seamless pattern in a larger image by filling it with the saved pattern from the library (see Figure 18.134).

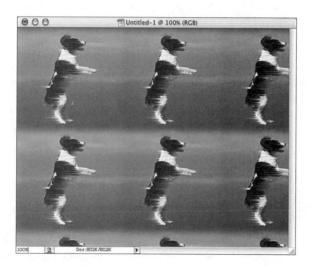

Figure 18.134
See Spot fly.

18

FROM THE NAPP HELP DESK

The National Association of Photoshop Professionals (NAPP) offers e-mail assistance to its members. Here is some advice from the NAPP Help Desk related to issues in this chapter.

Working the Layers

You mention adjusting the opacity of filters and experimenting with their blending modes. I don't see those options in the dialog boxes. How do I do it?

You can change the opacity and blending mode of the layer on which you applied the filter. In some cases, you might want to duplicate the layer, apply the filter to the top layer, and then work with opacity and blending modes. That enables you to alter the filter's effect on a variable basis. At 100% opacity and Normal blending mode, only the upper layer is visible—the filter is applied at the settings you selected in the dialog box. When you reduce the opacity, you are, in effect, reducing the filter's impact by allowing the original layer to show through. You can also work with opacity and blending modes through the Fade command (see next section).

Using the Fade Command

How come the Fade command is always grayed out for me?

Immediately after applying a filter (or using an adjustment command), the Edit menu offers Fade (followed by the name of the filter or adjustment). This command opens a dialog box in which you can reduce the filter's opacity (lessening its effect) and adjust the blending mode used for the filter. Remember that the Fade command is available *only* immediately after applying the filter or adjustment. You cannot use any tool or command between the filter and Fade, not even Save As.

Blurring Smartly

Is there ever a good time to use Smart Blur, or is it just a waste of disk space?

Smart Blur is very appropriate for use with images containing broad areas of similar color. It is not good for images with lots of fine detail that needs to be preserved. Understanding how the filter works can help you understand when to use it. In Normal mode, Smart Blur looks for areas of similar color and blends within those areas. It does *not* blur areas of high contrast. It attempts to maintain edges (the areas of high contrast) and smooth the broad areas of similar color. In Edge Only mode, Smart Blur created a white-on-black sketch of the image, following the edges. Overlay Edge maintains the original image and applies the Edge Only mode on top of it.

The Radius slider determines how much blurring is applied to the areas selected. The Threshold slider determines which areas will be selected. The higher the Threshold, the greater the contrast must be for an "edge" to be defined. Generally speaking, always apply Smart Blur in High Quality mode.

EXTRACT, LIQUIFY, AND THE PATTERN MAKER

by Jeff Foster

IN THIS CHAPTER

USING THE EXTRACT COMMAND

Masking subjects or objects out from a background is easier than having to shoot them in front of a blue or green screen. You can take virtually any photograph with a contrasting subject and background and "lift" the subject off the image by using the Extract command. Obviously, trying to use this method to mask out a white bunny in a snow bank will give you inadequate results—as will a poor-quality scan or compression-damaged JPEG file.

Whether you're creating intricate composite images or just making a simple logo, the Extract command speeds up your masking process. You'll be amazed at how fast and accurate the process is—especially on images you thought were impossible to get a clean mask from.

If you're familiar with the location of the Liquify and Extract commands in Photoshop 6, you're probably wondering where they went. Adobe has moved them under the Filter menu. You will also find the new Pattern Maker command in this location.

Working with the Extract Command

The Extract command window is quite simple and straightforward. See Figure 19.1 for the callouts of the various tools.

Figure 19.1
The various tools of the Extract command window.

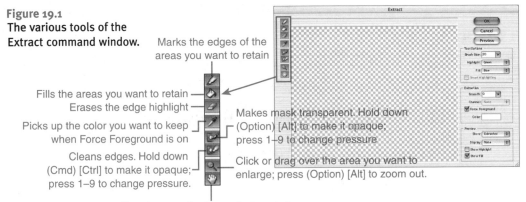

Marks the edges of the areas you want to retain

Fills the areas you want to retain

Erases the edge highlight

Picks up the color you want to keep when Force Foreground is on

Cleans edges. Hold down (Cmd) [Ctrl] to make it opaque; press 1–9 to change pressure.

Makes mask transparent. Hold down (Option) [Alt] to make it opaque; press 1–9 to change pressure

Click or drag over the area you want to enlarge; press (Option) [Alt] to zoom out.

Drag to move the image in the window

To outline your subject, select the Edge Highlighter tool and set Brush Size to a setting just large enough to overlap the edges of your subject, as shown in Figure 19.2. The brush size will vary depending on the resolution of your image. I find that selecting the Smart Highlighting check box produces more accurate results and allows me to work faster.

After you've outlined your subject with the Edge Highlighter tool, click on the Fill tool and click inside the area you want masked—or the areas of the image you want to retain (see Figure 19.3).

Edge Highlighter tool

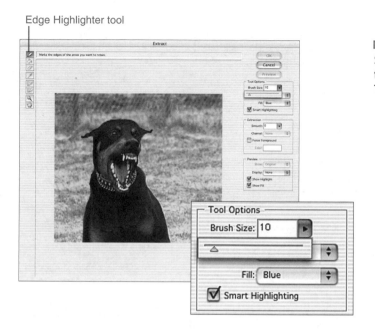

Figure 19.2
Set the brush size and color for the Edge Highlighter tool in the Tool Options section.

Fill tool

Figure 19.3
Highlight the edges of your subject with the Edge Highlighter tool, and use the Fill tool on the areas of the mask you want to retain.

19

If your subject has fine details or fuzzy, transparent edges, you might want to adjust the Smooth slider in the Extraction section. You can also select the Force Foreground check box in the Extraction section to force the foreground color to match the subject's primary color or use the Channel pop-up menu to load an existing alpha channel as a starting point.

The default colors for Edge Highlight and Fill are green and blue (true colors from the RGB palette), but you can change them as needed to contrast with your image and background—especially if you're working with a green screen or blue screen image and your subject has intricate edge details.

Previewing the Mask

Select Extracted from the Show pop-up menu in the Preview section to preview the extracted subject, and then inspect the edges carefully. You can also view the original image, or show the highlight or fill areas by selecting the check boxes in the Preview section (see Figure 19.4).

Figure 19.4
Preview and inspect the edges of the extracted mask to see where you might need some additional cleanup.

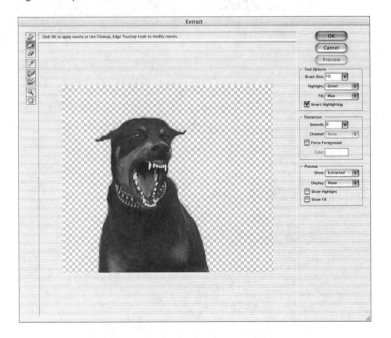

Using the Zoom tool, see if any sections of the extraction mask need cleanup. Use the Edge Touchup and Cleanup tools to repair "holes" or eroded edges in your mask. Figure 19.5 shows the result of the extracted image in a final composition.

Want to know how to make the Extract command non-destructive? See "Extracting to a Mask" in the NAPP Help Desk section at the end of this chapter.

Figure 19.5
The completed masked subject, used for the logo of my blues band.

USING THE LIQUIFY COMMAND

The Liquify command can squish, move, smudge, twirl, and bubble to distort your image in wacky ways that can render it unrecognizable. This section explores some of these techniques and shows you the effects the different features and tools have on an image. These examples are quite exaggerated for demonstration purposes.

You can have a lot of fun distorting people's faces and creating caricatures with the Liquify command, but even that gets old after a while. There are, however, a lot of practical applications for Liquify, to enhance your images without making them look like a reflection in a funhouse mirror.

Working with the Liquify Command

After you select the Liquify command from the Filter menu, a full-screen dialog box opens with your image or image selection in the display window, as shown in Figure 19.6. The default setting has the Mesh grid turned off. You can choose to have the Mesh grid turned on or off while you're working with the Liquify command.

Originally referred to as a "Warp Mesh," the Mesh grid works by actually moving the grid of pixels around as though they were attached to a mesh net. Think of drawing an image or writing your name on a balloon, and then blowing it up (see Figure 19.7).

Just like any other Photoshop filter, the Liquify command works only on the layer and/or the selection of the image you're applying it to. If you have a large, high-resolution image and want to apply Liquify only to a detail, use a selection tool and select a small portion to work on.

19

Figure 19.6
The Liquify dialog box is seen here with the Mesh grid visible. Similar to the Extract command, the Liquify tools are on the left and the available options are organized on the right.

Figure 19.7
The pixels in your image move with the direction of the Mesh grid—whether visible or not.

To visualize how the Liquify mesh works with the image, apply some of the effects tools to the image with Mesh grid turned on, and then hide the image in the View Options section, as shown in Figure 19.8. Notice how the mesh distortions move around with each other, but they never cross over each other. Choosing to make the Mesh grid visible is helpful to see how much distortion you have applied to the image in any one session.

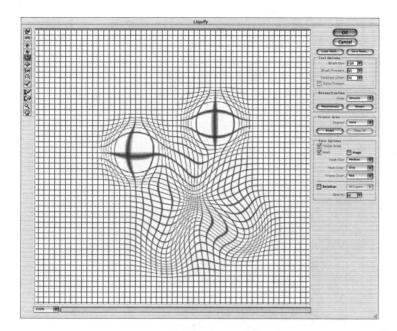

Figure 19.8
With the image hidden, you can see the effects of the Liquify command—and just how much you are distorting those pixels!

Understanding the Liquify Tools

Unlike a standard Photoshop Distort filter plug-in, the Liquify command works almost like a separate application. The tools on the toolbar even have their own set of keyboard shortcuts (see Figure 19.9). Adobe has been kind enough to include Tool Tips for each tool and feature as well.

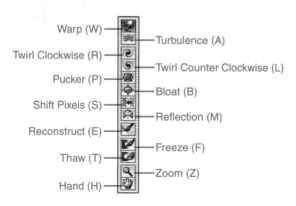

Figure 19.9
The Liquify tools have their own set of shortcuts.

19

The Liquify tools are fairly logical, and with a little "joy riding" around with them, their purposes will be evident. I've provided some exaggerated samples on the same image so that you can determine the differences between the tools' effects. In addition, I'll cover the appropriate Tool Options section on the right side of the Liquify dialog box as it applies to the tools.

The Warp Tool

The Warp tool moves pixels with a brush, adjustable in the Tool Options section of the Liquify dialog box. You can adjust for Brush Size, Pressure (including a check box for a stylus), and Turbulent Jitter (see Figure 19.10). This effect works great for creating caricatures, raising eyebrows, elongating a jaw, and much more.

Figure 19.10
The Warp tool moves pixels with an adjustable brush stroke.

The Turbulence Tool

The Turbulence tool creates a wavy distortion over the image (see Figure 19.11) and is adjusted in the Tool Options section as well. Use this effect for an underwater scene or a dream sequence.

The Twirl Clockwise and Counter Clockwise Tools

These tools are virtually self-explanatory by their names. Both the Twirl Clockwise and Twirl Counter Clockwise tools' brushes are adjustable in the Tool Options section of the Liquify window. The effect of this tool is to make the image look as though it was made of taffy being twisted (see Figure 19.12).

19

Figure 19.11
The Turbulence tool really makes a wave.

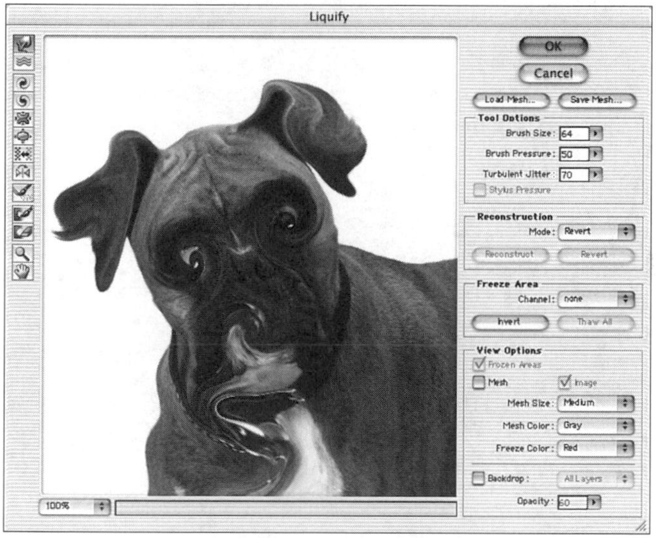

Figure 19.12
The Twirl Clockwise and Twirl Counter Clockwise tools add a new twist to your images.

The Pucker and Bloat Tools

The Pucker and Bloat tools result in the "balloon" effect I mentioned earlier. As with most of the Liquify tools, the brushes are adjustable in the Tool Options section.

The Pucker tool pinches in the image, as though it's being deflated (see Figure 19.13). The Bloat tool bulges out the image, producing an inflated or a blistered effect. This effect has lots of fun and practical uses—especially on buggy-eyed relatives.

Figure 19.13
The Pucker and Bloat tools work like an inflating and deflating balloon on your image.

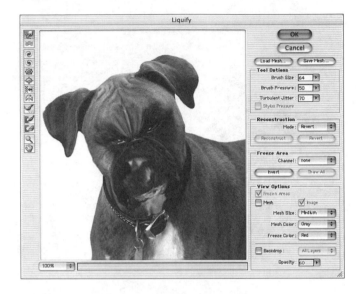

The Shift Pixels Tool

The Shift Pixels tool moves the image pixels perpendicular to the direction of the stroke. Click-drag to move pixels to the left and (Option-drag) [Alt+drag] to move them to the right. Think of it as though it were a polarized magnet (see Figure 19.14).

Figure 19.14
The Shift Pixels tool is just plain wacky fun.

19

The Reflection Tool

The Reflection tool creates a 180° reflection of the adjacent pixels outside the brush. It takes a bit of experimentation to understand where the image starts and stops inside the brush, but you can get some interesting effects with it (see Figure 19.15). As with the other distortion brushes, it is adjustable in the Tool Options section of the Liquify dialog box. You can use this tool to create intricate paisley patterns from images or original artwork on your favorite politician.

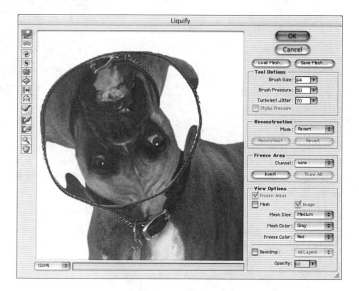

Figure 19.15
The Reflection tool turns your subject on its head.

The Reconstruct Tool

The Reconstruct tool works like an "undo brush" of sorts and is adjustable using the Tool Options section and the Mode pop-up menu in the Reconstruction section. The reconstruction affects only the areas where the brush is applied. If you've gotten carried away with distorting your image, you can apply the Reconstruct tool to as much of the image as you want—in the amount of pressure and the brush size you select for the tool.

The Freeze and Thaw Tools

The Freeze and Thaw tools enable you to lock down portions of the image so that they remain anchored and unaffected by applying effects to the image. Freeze keeps the selection from moving, and Thaw allows it to move. The tools are adjustable in the Tool Options section as well as the Freeze Area section, where you can select an alpha channel to "freeze" a specific shape.

More important, you can freeze an area that you've already distorted, so it won't move when you apply another effect tool around it. This is where the real control of the Liquify command comes in.

In Figure 19.16, the image on the left shows the area that has been frozen over the dog's muzzle. The image on the right shows several distortions without affecting the dog's muzzle.

19

Figure 19.16
The Freeze and Thaw tools give you total control of the distortion effects on your image.

The Zoom and Hand Tools

As you might expect, the Zoom tool, as shown in Figure 19.17, zooms in and out of the image so that you can work in detail (a big plus over Liquify in version 6.0). Both tools work the same as in the standard Photoshop Toolbox. In addition, the Hand tool allows you to move the zoomed-in image around inside the dialog box's preview window.

Figure 19.17
New to the Photoshop 7.0 Liquify dialog box, the Zoom tool lets you work on the details.

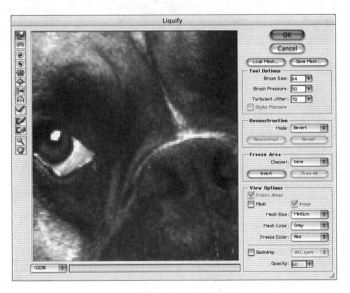

⇨ *Want to use Liquify as a controllable motion blur? See "Adding Some Jitter" in the NAPP Help Desk section at the end of this chapter.*

Animating with the Liquify Command

Animation is achieved by creating a sequential series of events or "frames" in a range of motion over a specified period of time, creating the illusion of movement. In other words, think of stop-motion photography, in which an object is moved a little bit and a frame of film is taken.

The procedure is repeated several times, and when the frames are played back in sequence, the objects appear to move (think "Gumby" or "Wallace and Gromit"). Of course, this process takes forever to do traditionally, but creating quick effects over a few frames in Photoshop layers is quick and easy.

Animation Basics

Before tackling an animation project, you must consider a few rules. Knowing how to fool the eye with a minimum amount of motion (and effort) saves you hours and prevents you from pulling your hair out! Ultimately, you need to rely on trial and error until you figure out the timing of your animation.

To gain a sense of how many frames per second (fps) you need for smooth motion graphics, let's look at a few examples. Broadcast video runs at approximately 30fps (29.97fps, to be precise). Motion picture film runs at 24fps (and there's lots of complicated math that figures out how to convert the 24fps into 29.97fps for home video, but we won't go there). Cartoon animation is usually around 12–15fps, and stop-motion animation can go down to 8fps (think "Gumby"). Of course, the higher the fps, the smoother the motion, but not always necessarily. Most QuickTime movies compressed to run on a CD-ROM are running at 15fps without much noticeable loss of quality. Streaming Web movies are usually noticeably slower, but acceptable because of the delivery of the media streamed over the Web.

It helps to know what type of movie you're creating before you start your animation, as well as its application. If you need to match existing video or animation footage, you have to first determine the speed (fps) and resolution (pixel dimensions) of the existing footage file. You also need to know whether you're creating only a GIF animation or streaming video for the Web—in those cases, obviously you put fewer frames into your animation.

Creating a Simple Animation with the Liquify Command

Start simple, until you get the hang of the animation process and the timing of creating smooth frame transitions. For each frame of animation, you create a duplicate of the preceding layer (or "frame").

The original image frame (or Background layer) is Frame 01 of the animation. This layer is duplicated once, and the Liquify effects are applied to this new layer (see Figure 19.18).

Apply the Liquify tools in small increments, increasing the movement a little more on each frame. To achieve a smooth animation sequence, it's important to keep track of how much you are moving the pixels in each frame. Turning on the Mesh grid might make this process easier for you.

In this example, I'm applying three different actions to the image: raising the eyebrows, making the eyes bigger, and elongating the tongue. I'm using the Warp and Bloat tools to create these distortions (see Figure 19.19). Because the example is a smooth animation that will be about 60 seconds long, very small steps will be made between frames. In this figure, the dog's tongue is extended slightly from the original.

If you are relying on the Mesh grid distortions from each frame, know that Liquify resets the mesh each time you save and exit from the command's dialog box.

Figure 19.18
Create a duplicate layer or "frame" to begin applying the Liquify effects.

Figure 19.19
Apply the Liquify tools in small increments to achieve a smooth animation sequence.

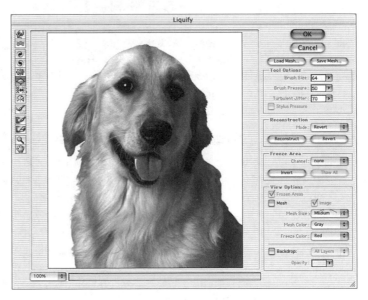

19

Continue duplicating the previous layer and applying the Liquify effects in small increments until you've reached the final frame of the animation (see Figure 19.20). In some cases, as in this example with a still image, you can create the first 50% of the animation, and then duplicate the frames and reverse their order.

For each frame of animation, you can save individual frames in a folder, or select the Jump To ImageReady option and export the animation from layers to create your movie or animated GIF files. To save the individual layers as frames in Photoshop, simply make each layer visible one frame at a time, select Save As a JPEG File, and name (or number) them sequentially for easy importing into your animation or video-editing application (see Figure 19.21). This method flattens each frame automatically as you save it.

Figure 19.20
Duplicate each preceding layer and apply the effects in small increments.

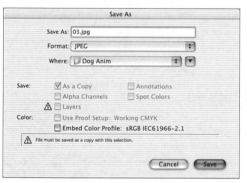

Figure 19.21
Use Save As to create sequential frame files from each layer.

19

PATTERN MAKER FUNDAMENTALS

If you're in a hurry to make a tiled background pattern or simple texture and don't want to take time to create one with a traditional method (using the Offset filter and Clone Stamping the seams), you'll probably find the Pattern Maker useful. Don't expect it to create tiles in a logical sense from the source image, as you would with a traditional Offset filter method. The Pattern Maker has a mind of its own at times. Its features are shown in Figure 19.22.

Tool selection to create a marquee selection, zoom, or move image inside the preview window

Tile Generation section enables you to modify the sample size and offset

Figure 19.22
The Pattern Maker dialog box is simple and easy to navigate and understand.

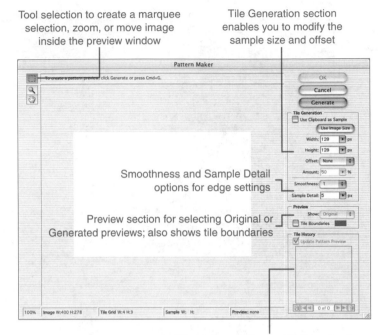

Smoothness and Sample Detail options for edge settings

Preview section for selecting Original or Generated previews; also shows tile boundaries

Tile History section and Pattern Preview box—thumb through preview samples and save patterns in the Custom Pattern Library

Working with the Pattern Maker Command

After opening the Pattern Maker with a source image, use the Marquee tool to make a selection of the area you want to preview as a tiled image, as shown in Figure 19.23.

Figure 19.23
Use the Marquee tool in Pattern Maker to select an area for previewing a tiling sample.

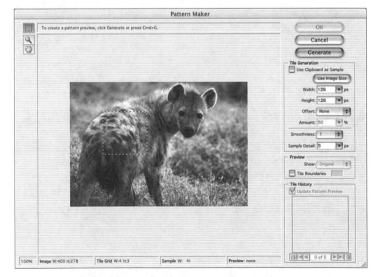

Click the Generate button to get a tile preview in the Pattern Preview box (in the Tile History section) and a sample of the tiled pattern in the Pattern Maker window. To see the original image again, select Original from the Show pop-up menu in the Preview section (see Figure 19.24).

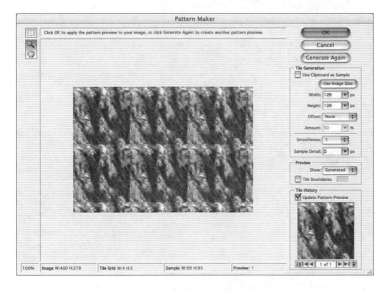

Figure 19.24
Preview the tile image in the Pattern Preview box.

You can make as many selections as you want on the same source image to create several tile patterns. To return to the source image to make another selection, select Original Image from the Show pop-up menu in the Preview section. You can view the edges of the tiles more easily by selecting the Tile Boundaries check box (see Figure 19.25).

Figure 19.25
Select from different areas of your source image to get different tile patterns.

Fine-Tuning the Pattern

You can make a few adjustments in the Tile Generation section that change the way the pattern is generated. Use the Smoothness option to soften the edges of the tile and help make it look more seamless—although it's still quite random in appearance. The Sample Detail setting measures the pixels from the edge of the selection, similar to feathering the edge of a selection (see Figure 19.26).

Figure 19.26
Adjust the Smoothness and
Sample Detail amounts to create
a more seamless tile pattern.

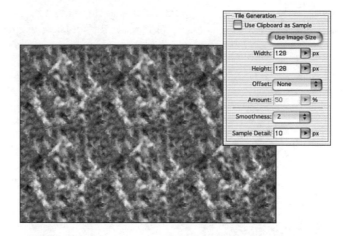

Adjusting the Horizontal and Vertical Offsets has varied effects (see Figure 19.27), but it's not quite as accurate as using the Offset filter and cleaning up the edges by hand.

Figure 19.27
The Vertical and Horizontal
Offsets have a limited effect on
the pattern tiling.

Horizontal Offset

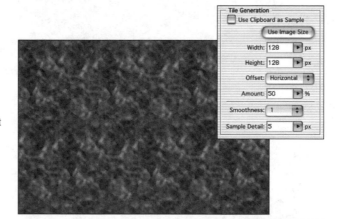

Vertical Offset

19

Saving and Using a Custom Pattern

The Tile History section enables you to scroll through all your tile attempts with that session on the source image. You can save the patterns to the Pattern Preset Library by clicking on the floppy disk icon or dump the unwanted previews with the trash can icon (see Figure 19.28). All your unsaved patterns disappear when you close the Pattern Maker.

To use your new tile pattern, open the Fill dialog box. From the Use pop-up menu, choose Pattern as the fill contents, and then select your Custom Pattern from the pop-up menu (see Figure 19.29).

If you click the OK button, your image will be turned into the current pattern. However, if you save the pattern to the Pattern Preset Library and then cancel out of the Pattern Maker, your image is untouched, but you'll still have the pattern available via the Fill command.

Figure 19.28
Save or dump your preview patterns in the Tile History section.

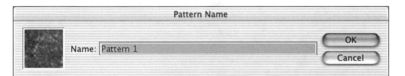

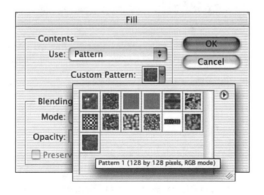

Figure 19.29
Use your newly created pattern by choosing from the Custom Pattern selections in the Fill dialog box.

19

⇨ *Seamless patterns are often the ticket—and you can create them easily in Photoshop 7. See "Seamless Tile Patterns" in the NAPP Help Desk section at the end of this chapter.*

PHOTOSHOP IN FOCUS

Putting the Frames in Motion

To test the animation frame sequence, use the QuickTime Player (registered Pro version), and choose File, Open Image Sequence from the menu. Select the first frame in the sequence, and QuickTime automatically picks the rest for you (see Figure 19.30). QuickTime asks what frame rate you want to set the frame timing to—if you don't know, just choose the default 15fps.

Figure 19.30
Open an image sequence in QuickTime Player to test your animation for speed and smoothness.

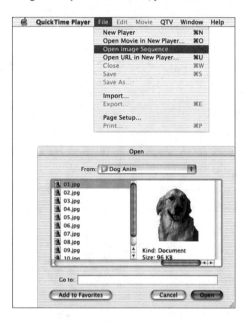

Looping the playback gives you a chance to study how your frames are interacting with each other, as shown in Figure 19.31. If you see that you need to add a frame or fix something in a frame, find the corresponding image sequence file and discard it. Open your Photoshop master production file (with the frame layers), and re-create the corresponding layer to correct the problem (or add another layer where necessary).

Saving and Retrieving Saved Mesh Grids

When you're using the Liquify command for sequential frames and need to control the precise amount of distortion from one frame to the next, you can choose to save your distortion Mesh grid and retrieve it later for subsequent frames.

The Save Mesh feature is great for similar images that you want to apply the same Liquify distortion to. If you turn on the Mesh grid in the View Options section, it's easier to see where on the image the distortions are applied (see Figure 19.32).

Figure 19.31
Playback of the animation sequence loop helps you determine whether your timing and smoothness quality are correct.

Figure 19.32
Turn on the Mesh grid in the View Options section.

19

To view the Mesh grid without the distorted image, deselect the Image check box in the View Options section, and only the Mesh grid will be visible (see Figure 19.33).

Figure 19.33
View the Mesh grid without the distorted image in the Liquify dialog box.

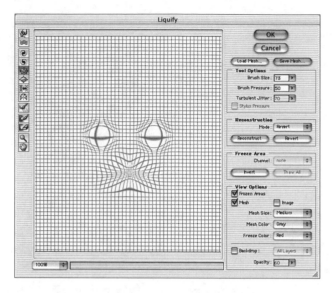

Click the Save Mesh button, and the Save As dialog box opens, asking where to save the Mesh (.msh) file (see Figure 19.34).

Figure 19.34
The Mesh grid can be saved as an .msh file on your hard drive.

Open a similar image, at the same size and resolution as the original, and click the Load Mesh button (see Figure 19.35).

Figure 19.35
Click the Load Mesh button to open the saved Mesh grid file.

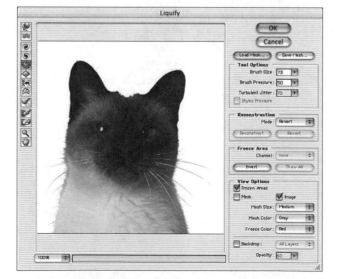

The saved mesh is then applied to the current image. If the mesh is out of alignment with the new image, cancel the Liquify command and reselect an area of the image that the distortion will be applied to in alignment (see Figure 19.36).

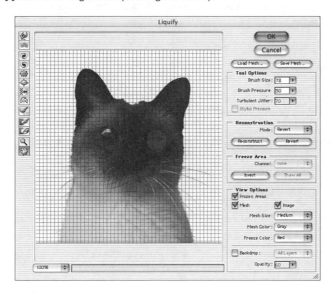

Figure 19.36
When the Mesh grid is loaded into the new image, the original distortions are applied to the image.

FROM THE NAPP HELP DESK

The National Association of Photoshop Professionals (NAPP) offers e-mail assistance to its members. Here is some advice from the NAPP Help Desk related to issues in this chapter.

Extracting to a Mask

I've been trained since Day One to preserve pixels whenever possible. I use adjustment layers, I hide copies of my type layers before rasterizing, all those things. The Extract command, therefore, bothers me—it throws away pixels!

Indeed, Extract is "destructive" and deletes pixels. Here's a way to make Extract nondestructive:

1. Make a copy of the background layer of the image.

2. Hide the copy by clicking the eyeball to the left of the layer in the Layers palette.

3. Apply Extract to the original background layer.

4. After extracting, use the Magic Wand to select the transparent area.

5. Use the Select, Save Selection menu command to create a mask of the extracted area.

6. Delete the extracted layer—you don't need it anymore.

7. Working on the copy of the original layer, use the Select, Load Selection menu command and select your mask.

8. Use the Layer, Add Layer Mask, Hide Selection menu command. You've now hidden the background instead of deleting it.

Adding Some Jitter

Is there some way to make the Liquify command create a movement effect?

Sure! It takes a little planning, but thanks to the History palette, you can always back up and try again.

1. Open a copy of the image in Photoshop.

2. Open Liquify, using the Filter, Liquify menu command.

3. Make a small change to the area of the image that you want to adjust—don't make the change too radical at first.

4. Click the Save Mesh button and give the mesh a name and location that are easy to recall. Click OK.

5. Immediately use the Edit, Fade Liquify menu command. Enter 50% for the Opacity setting, and click OK.

6. Go back to Liquify, click the Load Mesh button, and then click OK.

7. Return to Fade Liquify, and again reduce Opacity to 50%.

8. Repeat as necessary to get the amount of "jitter" that's appropriate for the image.

You can record opening Liquify and applying Fade Liquify in an Action, but you'll have to load the mesh and click OK in Liquify manually.

Seamless Tile Patterns

I want to make a seamless tile of an object, but I want to retain the integrity of the object's shape and details. How do I do this and still retain the image qualities?

The best way to do this is crop your source image to the area you want to tile, and select Filter, Other, Offset. If you divide the dimensions of the source image in half (roughly—both vertically and horizontally) and select Wrap Around, you will get an image with all the outside surfaces turned "inside out." The outer edges will then seamlessly tile.

Next, you need to use the Clone Stamp tool or the Healing Brush to fix the harsh lines that appear down the middle of your tile image. When you have a smooth-looking tile image pattern, select Save As Pattern and test it out. You'll be pleasantly surprised at how easy it is, and you will have control of how the image tiles.

IMAGE COMPOSITION, RETOUCHING, AND COMPOSITING

IN THIS PART

IMAGE CROPPING, RESIZING, AND SHARPENING

IN THIS CHAPTER

A FEW NOTES ON IMAGE COMPOSITION

When working with stock photography, you try to find the most appropriate picture for your project. When taking original photos for a project, there are a few ideas you can keep in mind that will make your work easier.

Planning the Project

At some point, every project has a layout. In some cases, the layout isn't finalized until the project is actually finished, but it's a better practice to work with a final concept in mind. If you work in an advertising agency, you're probably used to working from a sketch or preliminary design, a plan that's been approved by the client. If you are an artist, you might create as you go along, letting the image form itself as you work. The plan could be as simple as a quick scribble on a piece of paper (see Figure 20.1).

Figure 20.1
Although not fancy, even a simple sketch lets you know the general size and location of the subject in the final work.

You can save a lot of image correction and composition work in Photoshop if you take photos that are designed to fill a specific area of the final project. Having a properly composed original can also protect image quality by eliminating the need to resize the picture.

Arranging the Subject

When shooting the image, or when selecting stock art, consider the overall layout. In Figure 20.1, the subject of the layout is off center. Instead of shooting the image with the dog in the middle of the frame and then cropping, you can shoot the image with the dog in the proper position. Compare the images in Figure 20.2.

Because the image on the right requires less cropping, it retains more of the original pixel data when resampled to print resolution. (This might not be a factor, depending on your camera's capability, and is not an issue with properly focused film cameras.) In this situation, the purpose-made photo is appropriate (see Figure 20.3).

Figure 20.2
Either of these images might be appropriate for the idea sketched out earlier. The photo on the right, however, is shot for the concept.

Figure 20.3
Many stock photo and royalty-free suppliers can custom-shoot to your requirements.

CROPPING TO IMPROVE COMPOSITION

Whether recomposing for artistic reasons or changing the picture because of space limitations, you must sometimes crop an image. Cropping deletes (or in some cases, hides) part of an image. Photoshop offers a number of ways to crop, including commands and tools.

Cropping Versus Resampling

Cropping an image differs from *resampling* (resizing by changing the number of pixels portraying the same image) in a couple of important ways. Cropping typically maintains the image resolution and alters the picture by discarding some of the image data. Resampling typically maintains the image's visual content but changes the number of pixels presenting it. Figure 20.4 shows the difference.

Figure 20.4
The original image is shown at the top. On the left, the image has been resampled (resized, downsampled) to a specific size. On the right, the image has been cropped to the identical size.

The image on the left in Figure 20.4 has the same content as the original, but uses a smaller number of pixels to portray the image. (Note that the top image is shown at 66.67% zoom, and both of the lower images are at 100% zoom.) The process of resampling, or in this case *downsampling* because the new image is smaller, has robbed the painting of its texture.

➡ *For detailed information about resampling, **see** "Resizing Canvases and Images," **p. 628**, later in this chapter.*

The image on the right in Figure 20.4 is exactly the same size as that on the left but contains less of the original image. Cropping has deleted areas of the original. However, the section of the painting that remains uses exactly the same pixels as the corresponding area of the original, so there is no loss of quality.

You can think of cropping as changing the canvas size and resampling as changing the image size. The nondigital extension of the example shown in Figure 20.4 would be this: To crop the image, retaining only a portion of the original without changing that portion, the artist could use scissors or a knife to cut the original canvas down to size. To resize the image, maintaining the entire image portrayed in the original, the artist would paint the picture again, this time on a smaller canvas.

20

The Crop Command

The Image, Crop menu command has no dialog box and no options. It changes the canvas size based on an active selection. The selection need not be rectangular, and it can be feathered. The selection shown in Figure 20.5 on the left crops to the image shown on the right.

Figure 20.5
The Crop command always produces a rectangular canvas, cut to the nearest edge of the active selection.

When preparing a selection for the Crop command, the Rectangular Marquee tools offers a couple of important features. Using the Fixed Size option enables you to crop an image to an exact size, using any unit of measure:

1. Select the Rectangular Marquee tool in the Toolbox.

2. Choose Fixed Size for Style in the Options Bar.

3. Enter the desired width and height in the numeric fields in the Options Bar. You can use any of Photoshop's units of measure—follow the number with "px" for pixel, "in" for inches, "cm" for centimeters, and so on (excluding the quotation marks).

4. Click once in the image window with the Rectangular Marquee tool. A selection of the specified size will appear to the lower right of the cursor.

5. Position the cursor inside the selection border and drag to move it. You must have a selection tool active to reposition a selection marquee.

6. Use the Image, Crop menu command to complete the crop.

The Rectangular Marquee tool also has an option that enables you to make a selection based on a height-width ratio rather than a specified size:

1. Select the Rectangular Marquee tool in the Options Bar.

2. Choose Fixed Aspect Ratio from the Style pop-up menu in the Options Bar.

20

3. Instead of an exact size, you enter a relationship between width and height, without any unit of measure. For example, you can enter 8 for Width and 10 for Height to prepare for a 8×10 print. Or you can enter 468 for Width and 60 for Height if you're making a standard-sized Web banner ad.

4. Drag the tool in the image window. The selection border will maintain the exact height-width ratio designated in the Options Bar. Remember that you can reposition the selection border while still dragging by holding down the spacebar. When you release the spacebar, you can continue to drag the selection in its new position. Also keep in mind that the (Option) [Alt] key enables you to drag a marquee from the center.

5. After you release the mouse button, you can reposition the selection border by positioning the cursor inside the selection and dragging.

6. Use the menu command Image, Crop to make the crop.

7. In the Image Size dialog box, select the Resample check box, and enter your target width or height and desired resolution. Click OK.

When working with the Rectangular Marquee tool using Style: Normal, you can refer to the Info palette for the size of the current selection. The W and H fields give you the reading in the document's unit of measure (see Figure 20.6).

Figure 20.6
The box indicates the area of the Info palette where selection size is visible. In this example, the Rectangular Marquee tool is set to Fixed Size in the Options Bar, and the cursor is ready to reposition the selection border.

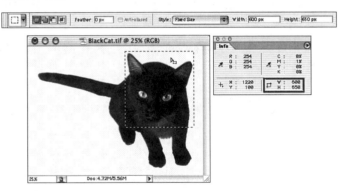

The Crop Tool

The Crop tool works on a basic principle: You position a marquee so that it includes the area you want to keep, accept the change, and anything outside the marquee is eliminated from the image. The image's pixel dimensions are reduced to those of the marquee. The tool has several options that make it more flexible. Like several other Photoshop tools, the Crop tool's Options Bar has different configurations when you select the tool and when you're actually using it.

Initial Crop Tool Options

When you select the Crop tool in the Toolbox or press the keyboard shortcut C, the Options Bar changes to the configuration shown in Figure 20.7.

Before you drag a crop marquee (also known as a crop bounding box), the Options Bar offers you the opportunity to determine one or more characteristics of the resulting image:

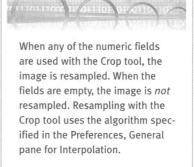

When any of the numeric fields are used with the Crop tool, the image is resampled. When the fields are empty, the image is *not* resampled. Resampling with the Crop tool uses the algorithm specified in the Preferences, General pane for Interpolation.

- The three numeric fields in the Options Bar govern not the size of the crop marquee, but the size of the resulting image. You can specify one, two, or all three variables. If only width or height is specified, the marquee is not constrained and you can drag any rectangular crop marquee. If both width and height are specified, the aspect ratio of the crop is constrained—the rectangular bounding box maintains its shape, regardless of how you drag.

- The resolution of the resulting image can be specified in pixels per inch or pixels per centimeter.

- Clicking the Front Image button automatically inputs the dimensions of the frontmost image open in Photoshop. If you have two images that should match in size and resolution (to composite or collage, for example), this option can automatically set the specs that you need. Bring the image with the desired specs to the front, select the Crop tool, and click the Front Image button. You can then bring the target document to the front and use the Crop tool. The resulting document will match the first document in both pixel dimensions and resolution.

- The Clear button empties the numeric fields in the Options Bar and enables you to use the Crop tool without constraints. The resulting image maintains the original image's resolution and is of the pixel dimensions of the bounding box you drag.

➪ *To learn about Photoshop's three resampling algorithms, **see** "The Three Interpolation Options," **p. 633,** later in this chapter.*

Refining a Crop Marquee

You can drag the Crop tool in any direction. Holding down the Shift key while dragging constrains the width-height ratio to a square. After you've dragged the Crop tool, a crop marquee or bounding box is visible (see Figure 20.8). By default, the area outside the bounding box is *shielded*, shown with a colored overlay. (This option is discussed in the following section.) The bounding box has eight handles, one in each corner and one in the middle of each side.

20

Figure 20.8
The area within the bounding box or crop marquee is retained; the pixels outside are discarded by default.

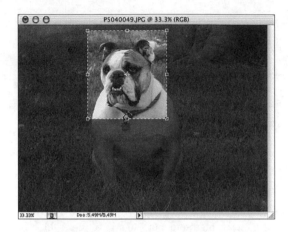

You can resize and reposition the crop marquee in a variety of ways:

■ Position the cursor on any handle and drag to resize the bounding box. When on a side handle, the cursor changes to a vertical or horizontal two-headed arrow. On a corner handle, the cursor becomes a diagonal two-headed arrow.

■ Hold down the Shift key while dragging a corner handle to maintain the original width-height ratio.

■ Hold down the (Option) [Alt] key while dragging to resize from the center.

■ The Shift and (Option) [Alt] keys can be used together.

■ Position the cursor inside the bounding box and drag to move the crop area without resizing it.

■ Position the cursor just outside the bounding box to rotate. (Rotating a crop is discussed in the section "Crop Rotation" later in this chapter.) When positioned to rotate, the cursor shows as a curved two-headed arrow. The Shift key snaps the rotation to increments of 15°. Images in Bitmap mode cannot be rotated with the Crop tool.

■ Reposition the crosshair to change the point around which the bounding box is rotated and from which it is scaled. The *target*, as it is sometimes known, is located in the center of the bounding box by default. It can be dragged to any point in the image window, inside or outside the bounding box.

■ When resizing or rotating the bounding box brings an edge or a handle within 8 pixels of the image's edge, the handle snaps to that edge. You can override this behavior with the Ctrl key. Keep in mind that if the bounding box is rotated, only the handle being dragged will snap—if another handle goes slightly past the edge of the bounding box, you'll have no warning.

■ If resizing or rotating extends the bounding box beyond the edge of the image window, when the crop is executed one of three things happens, depending on the content of the image:

  ■ If the image is flattened (contains only a single layer named *Background*), the area beyond the image window is filled with the background color.

- If the image is not flattened, the area beyond the image window is filled with transparent pixels.

- If the image contains hidden pixels, pixels that exist in that area beyond the image window's edge, the pixels will be visible.

- The Escape key cancels a crop. The (Return) [Enter] key executes the crop.

When the bounding box has been rotated at least 10°, you can *skew* it to produce special effects by (Option-dragging) [Alt+dragging] a corner handle (see Figure 20.9). After skewing, the bounding box can be rotated and resized again. A skewed bounding box still produces a rectangular crop.

Figure 20.9
The skewed bounding box is shown in the large image window. The smaller image shows the result of the skewed crop.

Active Crop Marquee Options

When a bounding box is active in the image window, the Crop tool's options change in the Options Bar (see Figure 20.10).

Figure 20.10
The secondary options are not available until the Crop tool has been dragged in the image window.

20

These are the additional Crop tool options:

- **Cropped Area: Delete/Hide**—The option of hiding rather than deleting the cropped area is not available when the image consists of a background layer only. Adding an empty layer to a flattened image activates this option. When hidden, the cropped area remains part of the image. The Move tool can be used to reposition a layer to change what area is "cropped." Remember that any hidden pixels are lost when the image is flattened, and until the image is flattened, the crop does not reduce the file size.

- **Shield**—This option masks the part of the image to be deleted.

- **Color**—By default, Photoshop uses gray to shield parts of an image to be cropped. Click on the swatch to change the shield color. Remember, too, that the color is not dependent on the image's color mode—any RGB color is available, even when working with an image in Grayscale or Bitmap mode.

- **Opacity**—By default, Photoshop shields at 75% opacity. Use the slider or type in the numeric field to change the opacity. Click on the word "Opacity" in the Options Bar to automatically select the content of the field. You then simply type the new value and press (Return) [Enter].

- **Perspective**—The Perspective option allows you to adjust the cropping marquee to correct perspective errors. This option is essentially an extension of the capability to rotate the crop marquee to correct the horizontal/vertical axes. It is designed to work primarily with architectural photography and is discussed later in this chapter in the section "Perspective Crop."

When you use the Hide option, cropping does not reduce the file size—the cropped pixels remain part of the image. The menu command Image, Reveal All expands the image window to show all hidden pixels. Hidden image data is maintained in Photoshop (.psd) and TIFF file formats.

⇨ *Want to get rid of hidden pixels, but don' t want to flatten the image? See "Trimming the Fat" in the NAPP Help Desk section at the end of this chapter.*

Crop Rotation

You can rotate an active crop marquee to realign the image to the image window. This method is especially useful for images that were scanned at an angle and photographs taken with a hand-held camera. Rotating results in resampling—the image must be re-created—and therefore introduces some softness to the appearance.

⇨ *Sharpening to remove the out-of-focus look that can be introduced by resampling is discussed later in this chapter. See "The Science of Sharpening," p. 634.*

Rotating with the Crop tool can be as simple as dragging a bounding box, moving the cursor outside it, and dragging. However, there are a few basic techniques that can make your rotation more precise:

- Keep the Info palette open, especially if you need a precise rotation. The A: field in the upper-right corner of the Info palette shows the angle of rotation while you work.

- Drag the Measure tool along a straight edge in the image to find the precise angle of rotation.

- The farther the cursor from the bounding box, the greater your control of rotation.

A common method of minimizing moiré patterns when scanning printed images is to place the original on the scanner at a 15° angle. Afterward, rotate the image in Photoshop with the Transform command or when cropping.

Generally speaking, if the image contains even one line that should be horizontal or vertical, you can get a precise rotation by using these simple steps:

1. Drag a crop marquee. Align one corner with the end of a vertical or horizontal line (see Figure 20.11, top left).

2. Drag the point-of-rotation target crosshairs from the center of the bounding box to that corner (Figure 20.11, top right).

3. Rotate the bounding box until one edge aligns with the edge in the image (Figure 20.11, bottom left).

4. Drag the side handles of the bounding box to finish framing the crop (Figure 20.11, bottom right).

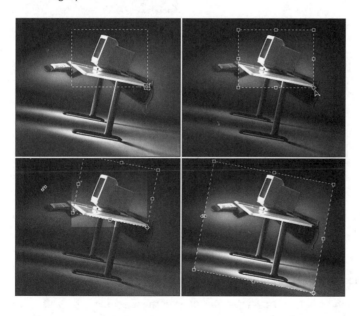

Figure 20.11
The four steps shown ensure a precisely rotated crop.

⇨ *Unable to get an exact rotation for your crop? See "Rotate, Then Crop" in the NAPP Help Desk section at the end of this chapter.*

Perspective Crop

The Crop tool can be used to correct *keystoning* and off-angle images. Keystoning is the perspective distortion that comes from photographing a tall object or shooting upward or downward.

20

When there's an active crop marquee in the image window, you can select the Perspective check box. This setting allows the corners of the marquee to be repositioned (see Figure 20.12). When the crop is executed, the corners of the bounding box are pulled or pushed to again form a rectangle, and the image is re-created to match.

Figure 20.12
Each of the corner points can be dragged to a new position. The goal is to make the four sides of the bounding box align with the four edges of the subject. The result of this crop is shown in the inset.

If you attempt to crop to a perspective that couldn't exist in nature, Photoshop refuses to execute it. The warning message shown in Figure 20.13 appears.

Figure 20.13
If you click Don't Crop, the crop marquee is dismissed and you start over. Clicking Cancel, on the other hand, returns you to the image with the existing bounding box so that you can adjust it and try again.

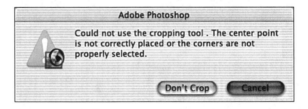

You can avoid this message by ensuring that your bounding box edges align with the actual vertical and horizontal lines of the subject. Here's how to do it:

1. Drag a crop marquee anywhere in the image (see Figure 20.14, Frame A).

2. In the Options Bar, select the Perspective check box (Figure 20.14, Frame B).

3. Position the corners of the bounding box so that the sides of the marquee align with any part of the image that should be rectangular (Figure 20.14, Frame C). The four selected edges need not be the outer edges of the subject. The bounding box will not be rectangular.

4. Zoom in to fine-tune your alignment (Figure 20.14, Frame D). Although you can't switch to the Zoom tool while cropping, you can use the keyboard shortcuts (Command-plus) [Ctrl+plus] and (Command-minus) [Ctrl+minus] to zoom and use the spacebar to reposition the image in the window with the Hand tool. You might find it easier to work with Shield turned off.

5. Drag the side handles (not the corner handles) of the bounding box outward to encompass the entire area to be cropped (Figure 20.14, Frame E). Using the side handles ensures that the relationship among the corners is maintained.

6. Drag the crosshair symbol to the position that you estimate should be the center of the corrected image (Figure 20.14, Frame F). If you place it in a position that could not represent the center of the cropped image in nature, an error message is generated.

7. Use the (Return) [Enter] key or the check mark button in the Options Bar to execute the crop.

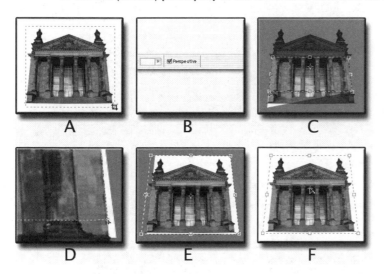

Figure 20.14
Aligning the bounding box edges.

The perspective crop feature can be used for more than just keystone correction in architectural photography. In Figure 20.15, a photograph of a mirror was taken off-center to avoid showing a reflection of the photographer, and then corrected with a perspective crop.

Figure 20.15
The perspective crop bounding box was aligned by using corresponding points on the frame rather than the mirror itself.

20

If you compare the left and right inner edges of the frame in Figure 20.15, you'll see a slight discrepancy that perspective cropping cannot remove. To the left, the inner edge of the frame is visible, but it is not visible on the right (see Figure 20.16).

Figure 20.16
The ovals identify the areas of concern.

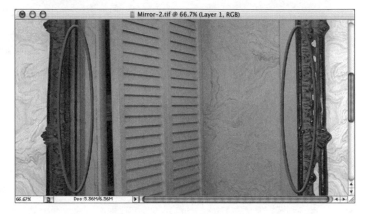

An even more dramatic example of this phenomenon is shown in Figure 20.17. The inner edge of the left side of the arch is visible in the original photo, but the inner part of the right side is not. After cropping, the face of the structure is perfectly aligned to the "camera," but it's apparent that the image is unnatural.

Figure 20.17
Because the left side of the inner arch is visible, it appears that the passageway runs at an angle under the arch, rather than straight through.

Perspective crop is suitable for two-dimensional images and cannot correct for depth presented in a third dimension. You'll find this problem when correcting photos that were taken at an angle. In some cases, such as the arch shown here, the problem is significant enough to make the image unacceptable. In other cases, the problem might be minor enough to overlook or correctable through cloning.

Enlarging a Canvas with the Crop Tool

The Crop tool can also be used to enlarge an image, much like the Canvas Size command. Zoom out and enlarge the image window so that empty gray shows around the actual image. Drag the Crop tool, and then drag one or more of the side or corner handles of the bounding box beyond the existing image (see Figure 20.18).

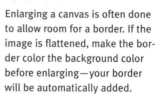

Enlarging a canvas is often done to allow room for a border. If the image is flattened, make the border color the background color before enlarging—your border will be automatically added.

Figure 20.18
Use (Return) [Enter] to execute the canvas enlargement. If the image contains a background layer, the background color is added. If not, transparent pixels are added.

The Trim Command

The Trim command, like the Crop command, is found under the Image menu. It can be considered a "selective crop" command. It removes pixels from an image and reduces the image size based on color. It is especially useful for scans that include a bit of surrounding black or white.

The Trim dialog box (see Figure 20.19) offers the choice of trimming transparent pixels or pixels based on whatever color is found in the image's upper-left or lower-right corner. You can also protect one or more edges by unchecking the boxes in the dialog box before clicking OK. The pixels—and canvas—are deleted only to the extent that the image remains rectangular.

If the Trim command isn't getting everything you want it to remove, try using the Magic Wand and deleting first to create a uniform area to trim. Consider using Trim before any technique that relies on a histogram, too. Removing those excess pixels gives you a more accurate read of the image.

20

Figure 20.19
The color in the corner need not be black or white, but Trim removes only pixels that exactly match the color found.

RESIZING CANVASES AND IMAGES

The Image menu contains a pair of commands that change an image's size. The Canvas Size command works like the Crop tool in its normal mode, deleting (or adding) an image area without changing the image that remains. Image Size resamples the image, maintaining the image appearance as much as possible while increasing or decreasing the number of pixels used to portray the image.

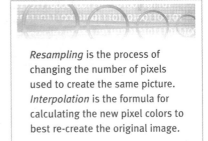

Resampling is the process of changing the number of pixels used to create the same picture. *Interpolation* is the formula for calculating the new pixel colors to best re-create the original image.

Image, Canvas Size

The Canvas Size command can enlarge or reduce the actual image area of a file. Blank pixels can be added or parts of the image can be deleted. Whether enlarging or reducing the canvas, the part of the original image that remains is untouched—it has exactly the same pixels it had before. The Canvas Size dialog box gives you precise control over the amount of canvas added or subtracted, but limited control over *where* it is added or subtracted (see Figure 20.20).

The upper section of the dialog box, Current Size, tells you the starting point. The lower set of numbers, including the new file size, are updated as you make changes. If you change the unit of measure, Photoshop automatically calculates an equivalent value. For example, if the Width unit of measure shown in Figure 20.20 is changed to pixels, the dialog box changes the value from 110 to 1515 (110% of the original 1377-pixel width).

20

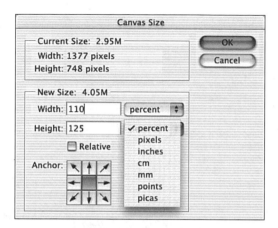

Figure 20.20
The Width and Height pop-up menus offer the same units of measure. Using 100% results in no change to the image's size.

The Relative check box is a relief to the math-weary Photoshop user. Instead of being forced to do addition or multiplication to determine the desired size of the canvas, you can now select the check box and enter the amount you want to add (or subtract). For example, if you wanted to add a 25-pixel border around the image in Figure 20.20, you could select Relative, set the unit of measure to Pixels, and enter 50 for both the Width and Height fields.

The 3×3 grid to the right of the word "Anchor" in the dialog box is referred to as the *proxy*. Click a box to show where you want the original artwork in relation to the new canvas size. If you leave the proxy in the middle, the default, the new pixels are split top/bottom and left/right; half of the new width goes to either side, and half of the new height goes to the top and half to the bottom. If you select the upper-left box of the proxy, all the new pixels are added to the right and the bottom. The proxy shows with arrows where the new canvas will be added.

When you enter a value for width or height that is *smaller* than the original, a message appears onscreen, warning that your image will lose some pixels (see Figure 20.21). Where the canvas is chopped is determined by the proxy—the proxy's arrows indicate parts of the image to be deleted.

Figure 20.21
Clicking the Proceed button crops your image. Cancel returns you to the Canvas Size dialog box.

Image, Image Size

The Image Size command does one or both of two things: It can be used to change the image's *resolution*, which tells the printing device how large or small to make each pixel. It can also change the number of pixels used to create the image, known as resampling. The Image Size dialog box is shown in Figure 20.22. The lower dialog box is set to change the resolution without resampling the image. The upper part of the dialog box is grayed out, indicating that no change will be made to the actual pixel content of the image.

Figure 20.22
If the image will be resampled, the pixel dimensions change, and the new file size is reflected at the top of the dialog box.

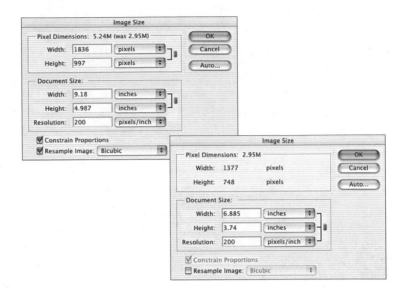

When the Resample check box is not selected, you change only the print information for the image. Whether for commercial offset printing or inkjet output, resolution determines the size of the image on the printed page and the fineness of the printed image's detail. Resolution has no effect on the image's appearance onscreen. Web graphics, for example, occupy a particular amount of space in a Web browser's window based strictly on pixel dimensions—resolution is insignificant for Web graphics.

⇨ For a full discussion of resolution, **see** "Image Resolution," **p. 167**, in Chapter 6, "Pixels, Vectors, and Resolution."

When the Resample check box *is* selected, Photoshop changes the number of pixels used to create the image. The artwork is maintained (to the greatest degree possible), but the number of pixels with which it's portrayed changes. (Resolution and print dimensions can be changed at the same time.) Consider resampling as the process of re-creating the image with more or fewer pixels.

Two Types of Resampling

When resampling with Image Size, you make the image either larger (increase the number of pixels) or smaller (decrease the number of pixels). Certain other operations in Photoshop also resample, such as cropping to a specified size or resolution. Rotating or scaling a selection or image also resamples but maintains the exact number of pixels in the image. The pixels are recalculated to re-create the image with the new size or rotated appearance.

Increasing the number of pixels in an image is called *upsampling*. Reducing the number of pixels in an image is *downsampling*. Figure 20.23 shows a comparison. The top image is the original. The middle image was downsampled to 75% of the original size. The bottom image was upsampled to 125% of the original size.

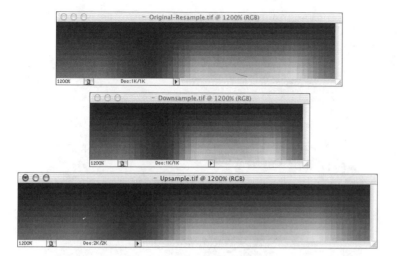

Figure 20.23
All three images are zoomed to 1200% so that the individual pixels are visible. The same basic gradient pattern is maintained, but the three images use different numbers of pixels to do so.

To get a feel for how Photoshop resamples, take a look at Figure 20.24. The original image in the center consists of exactly 8 pixels, 4 black and 4 white. For each of the resampled copies, Photoshop has determined what pixels to add or subtract to best maintain the image's appearance.

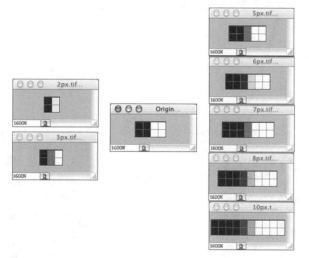

Figure 20.24
To simplify the demonstration, only the width of each sample image was changed. The resampling method was Bicubic.

To the left, two copies have been downsampled. On top, Photoshop had no tough calculation—a pair of black and a pair of white pixels were deleted. On the bottom, the resampling process introduced an intermediate color, a compromise between the two abutting colors.

To the right of the original, the copies were upsampled. In each case, one or two columns of intermediary pixels were added. At the top, you can see that a single column of gray pixels has been added between the black and white pixels. Immediately below that sample, the 6-pixel-wide sample has two columns of gray pixels—one dark gray, one light gray. When a copy was upsampled to 7 pixels wide, Photoshop added a column of gray in the middle *in addition to* a column of black to the left and a column of white to the right. Both of the upsampled copies at the lower right had two gray columns to create a transition between black and white.

When Photoshop has a slightly more complex image, it must calculate the relationships among all the surrounding pixels to determine the new color value for each pixel. Figure 20.25 shows how more and more intermediately colored pixels must be introduced as the same image is upsampled several times.

Figure 20.25
The original image is on the left. It was copied and upsampled, then the copy was duplicated and upsampled, and yet again to create the largest version.

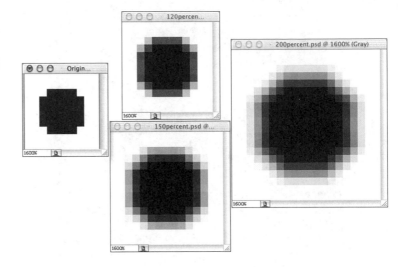

When working with photographic images, Photoshop follows the same basic procedure outlined here. The color values of neighboring pixels are compared and an intermediary color is used. As you can see in Figure 20.26, downsampling, throwing away image data, can have a negative effect on image detail. Upsampling, on the other hand, can introduce softness, an out-of-focus look to an image.

Figure 20.26
The original image (left) was downsampled to 50% width and height (center) and upsampled to 150% width and height (right).

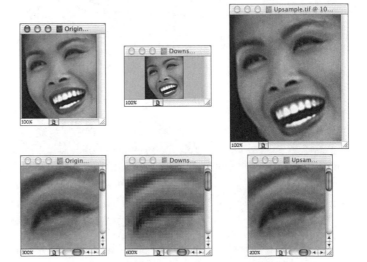

Generally speaking, when preparing images for print, it's better to scan at a higher resolution than necessary and downsample rather than scan at a lower resolution and upsample. When you must upsample, consider using a sharpening filter afterward. (Sharpening is discussed later in this chapter.) Your best bet, however, is to calculate the size you'll need and scan to that size whenever possible.

➡️ *The easiest way to determine how to scan to size? See "Pixel Size, Please" in the NAPP Help Desk section at the end of this chapter.*

The Three Interpolation Options

The Image Size dialog box and Photoshop's General Preferences offer a choice of three types of resampling. The selection made in the Preferences is used for scaling and rotating selections and images. Each time you open the Image Size dialog box, you can choose the method of interpolation:

- **Bicubic**—A comparison is made of all surrounding pixels and a compromise value is assigned.

- **Bilinear**—A comparison is made of the immediately adjoining pixels and a compromise value is assigned.

- **Nearest Neighbor**—The color of one adjoining pixel is duplicated.

The Bicubic interpolation method is the most appropriate for photographic and other continuous tone images. Nearest Neighbor, however, is often the best choice for line art and artwork that contains areas of solid color with distinct edges. Figure 20.27 shows a comparison of Nearest Neighbor and Bicubic for a piece of artwork that consists of solid colors.

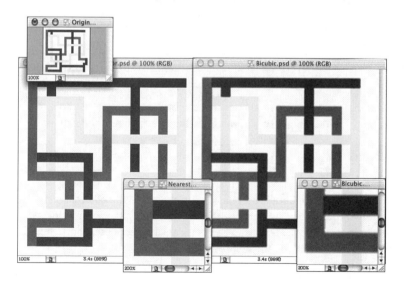

Figure 20.27
At the top left, the original. To the left, a copy was scaled to 400% using Nearest Neighbor. To the right, another copy was scaled to 400% using Bicubic interpolation. The insets are zoomed to show the detail.

20

Resampling Speed

Photoshop labels the resampling interpolation methods according to both quality and speed. Bicubic certainly does a better job with continuous tone images (although it's not appropriate for all artwork), and Nearest Neighbor is certainly faster. How much faster? That depends, of course, on your computer and the file itself. If you work with huge files (25MB or larger) on an older computer, you will see a large speed differential. However, as always, you'll have to balance speed and quality issues.

For comparison, a 32MB file with multiple layers and blending modes was resampled on two different machines. The first computer is a PowerBook G3/400 with 320MB RAM. The other is an Apple G4, dual 800MHz processors, 1.5GB RAM. Neither of these computers can be considered over the hill, and both are appropriate for general Photoshop use. Table 20.1 shows the results.

Table 20.1 Resampling Speed Comparison

Downsampling: 1800×1207 to 600×402		
Interpolation Method	PowerBook G3 (time in seconds)	G4/800MP (time in seconds)
Bicubic	11.6	2.5
Bilinear	8.7	2.3
Nearest Neighbor	0.7	0.4
Upsampling: 1800×1207 to 3600×2414		
Interpolation Method	PowerBook G3 (time in seconds)	G4/800MP (time in seconds)
Bicubic	54.5	9.1
Bilinear	48.7	9.0
Nearest Neighbor	34.1	5.5

Note: All tests were run in Mac OS X. Photoshop was restarted before each test, and no other programs were running. The test file is 32.3MB and consists of five layers.

Obviously, upsampling is far more demanding than downsampling, and Bicubic interpolation requires more calculations than Nearest Neighbor. The dual-processor power is certainly evident in the results.

THE SCIENCE OF SHARPENING

Sharpening is the process of emphasizing the detail of an image. By increasing the contrast along edges and areas of contrast within the image, you can make the picture look "crisper" or more focused. Sharpening is especially important after an image has been upsampled. Photoshop's Filters menu offers four sharpening filters, and you'll find the Sharpen tool in the Toolbox.

How Sharpening Works

The Sharpen tool and the Sharpen and Sharpen More commands increase the contrast between neighboring pixels. They affect every pixel within the image or selection (commands) or under the brush (tool). Figure 20.28 shows the result when Sharpen More is applied to a selection.

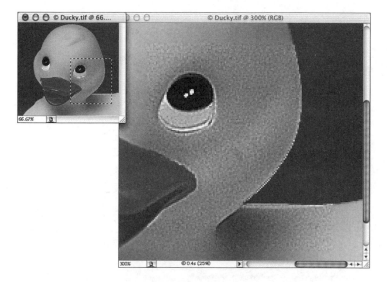

Figure 20.28
The edges of the selection are evident in the zoomed version, even without "marching ants." The Sharpen More filter has increased the contrast among all pixels.

The Sharpen Edges command looks for areas of high contrast to identify edges in an image. The sharpening is applied only along those edges (see Figure 20.29).

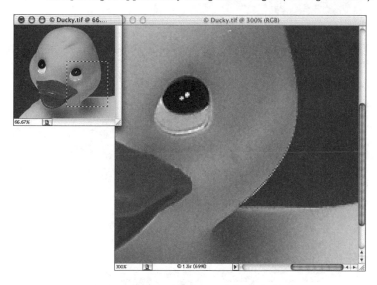

Figure 20.29
In contrast to the Sharpen and Sharpen More filters and the Sharpen tool, Sharpen Edges attempts to apply sharpening only along lines of great contrast.

20

The Unsharp Mask command is far more complicated than the other sharpen commands. It creates a copy of the image or selection, blurs it, and compares it to the original to identify edges. The contrast along those edges is then increased by lightening and darkening the pixels on either side. In a nutshell, Unsharp Mask finds areas of contrast and emphasizes that contrast. Unlike the other three sharpen commands, Unsharp Mask gives you control over its application with a dialog box (see Figure 20.30).

Figure 20.30
Amount is the level of contrast that will be applied. Radius is the width of the area along edges to which the contrast will be applied. Threshold determines how much a pixel must vary from the adjoining pixels to be considered an edge.

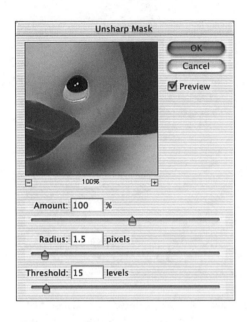

Working with the Unsharp Mask Filter

To increase the amount of contrast along an edge, Unsharp Mask creates a pair of "halos," one on either side of the edge (see Figure 20.31). These light and dark halos, emphasized in the sample image, in effect outline the edges to make them more noticeable.

Figure 20.31
A large amount of sharpening has been applied to emphasize the halos along the edges.

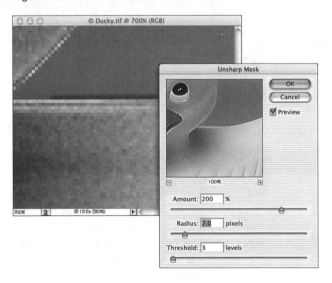

Areas with lots of small detail require special care. In Figure 20.32, oversharpening makes the selected area look garish and unnatural.

Figure 20.32
The Unsharp mask filter is being applied to the right half of the photograph only. The settings are shown in the dialog box.

Instead of reducing the amount of sharpening, an increase in the Threshold setting improves the result (see Figure 20.33).

Figure 20.33
Increasing Threshold for this image applies the sharpening between the leaves and the fruit and between the leaves and the shadows, but does not attempt to sharpen the leaves themselves.

Understanding the three Unsharp Mask sliders is key to knowing how to apply the filter:

- **Amount**—This setting determines the amount of contrast to be added wherever Unsharp Mask finds an edge. Consider it to be the brightness of the halos. The value can range from 1% to 500%. Typically, an Amount of 100% is a good starting point for a low-resolution image, and 150%–200% is more appropriate for high-resolution images.

- **Radius**—Ranging from 0.1 pixel to 250 pixels, the Radius setting determines how wide an area will be affected where Unsharp Mask finds an edge. Think of this setting as the width of the halo. For most images, 1 or 2 pixels is adequate to restore detail.

- **Threshold**—Threshold can range from 0 to 255, just as any other 8-bit value. It determines how much a pixel must vary from the neighboring pixels to be sharpened. Threshold is used to actually find the edges. When 0 is chosen, Unsharp Mask sharpens all pixels in the image. Threshold also helps prevent the filter from introducing noise into areas of relatively uniform color. Typically, a value between 2 and 20 is entered.

Unsharp Mask can introduce color shifts, especially when applied to images in CMYK mode. Here are three techniques for avoiding color shifts near edges:

- Convert the image to Lab mode, apply the Unsharp Mask to the L channel, and then return to RGB or CMYK mode. This technique restricts the effect of the filter to the brightness of each pixel.

- Apply the Unsharp Mask filter normally, and then immediately use the menu command Edit, Fade Unsharp Mask. Switch the blending mode from Normal to Luminosity. (This technique is the same as applying the filter to the L channel in Lab mode, without the need to switch color mode.) You can also reduce the effect of the Unsharp Mask, if necessary, with the Opacity slider.

- When working in CMYK mode, apply the filter to the Black channel only. (It is usually better to sharpen in RGB mode before converting the color mode, but if the image is already in CMYK mode, don't change mode just to sharpen.)

Selective Sharpening

Different areas of an image might require different amounts of sharpening. This is especially true for images that have a detailed subject against a detailed background. Sharpening the foreground to a greater degree can make it much more distinct (see Figure 20.34).

Figure 20.34
The original image (left) can certainly be improved by sharpening. However, using a mask (center) allows the castle to be sharpened separately from the immediate foreground and the very detailed background (right).

The Power Sharpener: nik Sharpener Pro!

An alternative to Unsharp Mask is available from nik multimedia. Available in several configurations for various needs and price ranges, nik Sharpener Pro! produces incredibly sharp images with little effort. Rather than juggle Amount, Radius, and Threshold sliders, you answer a couple of questions about the final destination of the image, and the program does the rest.

The plug-ins are simply dragged to Photoshop's Filters folder. Upon restarting Photoshop, they are available for use. The first step is to tell the plug-in where and how the image will be reproduced by selecting a specific filter from the menu (see Figure 20.35).

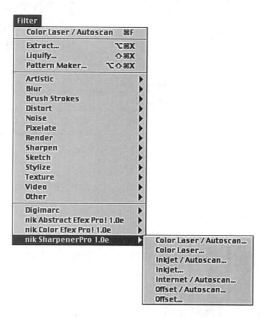

Figure 20.35
Shown are the filters for nik Sharpener Pro! Available filters for Sharpener!, Sharpener Pro! Home Edition, and Sharpener Pro! Inkjet differ.

In the filter's dialog box (see Figure 20.36), you adjust sliders (or click on a numeric value to overtype). Unlike the cryptic Threshold and Radius sliders of Photoshop's Unsharp Mask, nik requires only easily obtainable information about the final output of the image.

Because the sharpening is tailored for the image's ultimate destination, it creates an image that may or may not look better onscreen than the same image after Unsharp Mask. However, because the image is sharpened with the destination in mind, the *final product*, print or Web, is often far superior to the results obtained with Unsharp Mask.

A demo version of nik Sharpener Pro! is available on the CD that accompanies this book. You can review the specifications and capabilities of other versions of nik Sharpener (and check out other nik products) at www.nik-multimedia.com.

20

Figure 20.36
At the bottom of the dialog box is information about the image gathered by the Autoscan feature as the filter loads. It also projects the quality of the final product, based on the selections you've made.

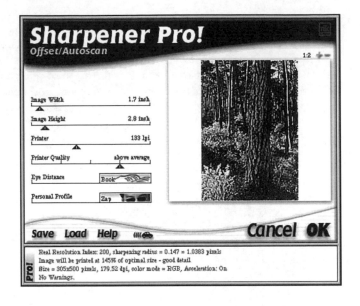

Genuine Fractals

Another third-party product worthy of attention in this discussion is Genuine Fractals. Genuine Fractals, now from LizardTech, enables you to minimize upsampling (and the resulting huge file sizes) when working with large images.

Genuine Fractals enables you to scale an image without loss of quality. It supports RGB, Grayscale, Indexed Color, Duotone, and Multichannel modes. More information is available at www.genuine-fractals.com.

PHOTOSHOP IN FOCUS

The difference between resampling an image and cropping is important. Using the Crop tool in its normal mode doesn't degrade image quality at all—the remaining pixels are the original pixels. Resampling, on the other hand, either creates pixels (upsampling) or throws them away (downsampling).

When you enter any value into the Options Bar while using the Crop tool, you've changed the nature of the procedure. Now you are resampling the image in addition to deleting areas of it. Take a look at Figure 20.37. The crop marquees differ in size, but the Options Bar shows the same values.

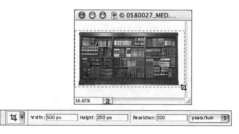

Figure 20.37
These two very different crops will result in images of exactly the same pixel dimensions (and resolution).

Try it yourself:

1. Open an image in Photoshop.

2. Open the History palette and click on the leftmost button, New Document from Current History State. That makes a copy of the image.

3. Select the Crop tool from the Toolbox.

4. In the Options Bar, set the Width to 500 px, the Height to 250 px, and the Resolution to 100 ppi.

5. In the top copy of the image, drag a crop marquee that extends from the upper-left corner of the image window to a point halfway across the top. Don't worry about the height of the bounding box; just make the width one half of the original.

6. Press (Return) [Enter] to execute the crop. Move the resulting document to the side.

7. Make the other copy of the image the active window, and drag a crop marquee that extends from the upper-left corner all the way across the image's entire width.

8. Press (Return) [Enter] to execute the crop. This image, although quite different in appearance, is the same size as the other cropped image.

9. For each image, open Image, Image Size and check the pixel dimensions and the print size. They should be identical.

20

FROM THE NAPP HELP DESK

The National Association of Photoshop Professionals (NAPP) offers e-mail assistance to its members. Here is some advice from the NAPP Help Desk related to issues in this chapter.

Trimming the Fat

My file size is bloated from lots of hidden data. Is there a way to get rid of the excess pixels without flattening my image?

You have a couple of options. You can drag a crop marquee that fills the window and choose Delete rather than Hide. Or you can do it much more easily and precisely with two commands: Select, Select All and Image, Crop. All done!

Rotate, Then Crop

Even using the steps shown, I can't rotate my crop exactly right. Is there anything else I can do?

Try this:

1. From the Toolbox, select the Measure tool. You'll find it under the Eyedropper.

2. Click at one end of a visible line in your image. The edge of a building, a doorjamb, a window ledge, a curb, a distant highway or horizon, even a pencil line you add before scanning will work. Drag the Measure tool along that line. Remember, too, that you can zoom in for precision.

3. Check the Info palette's A: field for the precise angle of the Measure tool's line.

4. Drag a small crop marquee with the Crop tool.

5. Position the cursor far outside the bounding box and drag until the Info palette shows the same rotation recorded for the Measure tool.

6. Drag the side handles of the bounding box to include the area you want in the cropped image, and then press (Return) [Enter].

Alternatively, drag the Measure tool as described, and then use the Image, Rotate Canvas, Arbitrary menu command. The Measure tool's angle will already be input for you, so you need only click OK. Now you can crop the image without worrying about rotating the crop bounding box.

20

Pixel Size, Please

All right, your advice is to scan at the size I need for output. But how do I do that?

The key is calculating the pixel dimensions of the final image and acquiring (scanning) that number of pixels. To scan at your print size, multiply the print dimensions by the print resolution to get the required pixel size. Divide the pixel size by the size of the original in inches. That gives you the required scanning resolution, as shown in this example:

- In your page layout document, the image will occupy a space 3×4 inches, and the line screen frequency for the press that will print the job is 133lpi (lines per inch).

- You know that image resolution should be 1.5 (or 2) times the line screen frequency, so the final image should have a resolution of 200ppi/dpi. (The terms "pixels per inch" and "dots per inch" are often used interchangeably.)

- Therefore, the pixel dimensions of the final image should be 600×800. (That's 3 inches times 200ppi, and 4 inches times 200ppi.)

- The original photo is, let's say, 8×10 inches, but the area of the image that you're going to use in the layout measures only 4.5×6 inches—the rest you either won't scan or will crop out in Photoshop.

- The appropriate scan resolution, therefore, is 133ppi. (That's 600 pixels divided by 4.5 inches, and 800 pixels divided by 6 inches.)

Some scanners make it easy and let you simply type in the print dimensions and resolution. The scan module then calculates the required scan resolution and produces an image of the appropriate pixel dimensions.

20

RETOUCHING AND RESTORATION BASICS

IN THIS CHAPTER

BASIC PHOTO REPAIR

Although Photoshop has hundreds of tools and techniques for applying effects to images and doing all sorts of other fancy things, some of Photoshop's most powerful tools are for prosaic purposes: simply fixing photos. Photo repair can range from something as basic as removing red-eye or dust and scratches to complete restoration of old photos that have become yellowed, creased, or torn over time.

Getting the Red Out

Red-eye is one of the most common problems in flash photography, be it digital or film. Red-eye is caused by light from the camera's flash entering the pupil, bouncing off the retina at the back of the eye, and reflecting back out toward the camera, which gives pets and people that *Village of the Damned*

Many cameras these days, both digital and film, have what is known as a "red-eye reduction" mode. With this feature, the camera emits several brief flashes before releasing the shutter. This causes the subject's pupils to contract, which limits the amount of light that can enter and reflect back out. As the name indicates, this mode doesn't eliminate red-eye completely, but it does reduce it significantly.

look. The effect is red because the blood vessels in the retina are red. (Kinda creepy, huh?) Cats' eyes, by the way, can have a green, alien mutant effect because a layer of guanine makes their eyes especially sensitive to light. (This guanine layer is also what makes cats' eyes shine eerily at night, even without flash photography being involved.)

Although Figure 21.1 is black and white, you can still tell that something is wrong with the eyes—all four of them are suffused with red.

Figure 21.1
In color, these eyes are very red.

To fix this problem, you need to zoom in and, with the Magic Wand tool, select the red pixels (see Figure 21.2).

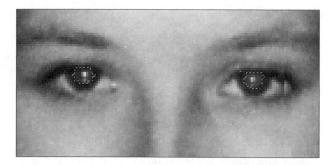

Figure 21.2
To start, select the areas of red in the eye that you want to replace.

Then choose Image, Adjustments, Color Balance, and, making sure Preserve Luminosity is unchecked, adjust the Cyan/Red slider toward Cyan until most of the red is gone. If some remains, you can adjust the Magenta/Green slider toward the Green direction (see Figure 21.3).

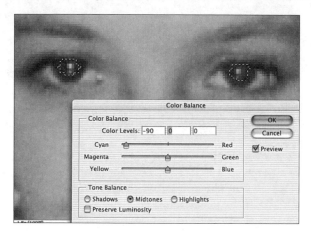

Figure 21.3
With the Color Balance dialog box, you can reduce the red in the selected areas.

The red is gone, and the eyes look more natural. The process isn't perfect, but when viewed at a normal size, it looks good.

It might also be effective to work on each eye individually, but be careful to make sure that both eyes end up with the same color change (if both eyes belong to the same person, that is).

➪ *Some images just need a bit of touch-up on the eyes. Want an alternative technique? See "Red-Eye Reprise" in the NAPP Help Desk section at the end of this chapter.*

Removing Wrinkles

Back before it became fashionable to inject deadly bacteria into our faces to remove "unsightly" signs of aging, removing wrinkles and other facial "defects" was the purview of snake-oil salesmen and programs such as Photoshop—the key difference being that Photoshop actually works.

There are a number of ways of removing not only wrinkles but other dermatological problems, such as cuts, acne, scars, tattoos, and so forth. The new Healing Brush and Patch tool are discussed in the next section, but the old standby is the Clone Stamp tool (also known as the Clone tool and the Rubber Stamp tool).

In Figure 21.4, the subject has some crow's feet around the eyes, which can be easily removed.

Figure 21.4
Crow's feet around the eyes can be eliminated.

The trick is to clone the area immediately above the wrinkle onto the pixels composing the wrinkle. It helps to zoom in pretty close, but not so close that you're unable to see what you're actually doing. With the Clone Stamp tool active, (Option-click) [Alt+click] just above a crease line, and then start painting over the actual crease. A crosshairs cursor tells you where your source pixels are coming from, and the usual Brush cursor shows you where you're painting (see Figure 21.5).

Figure 21.5
By taking the uncreased skin as the source pixels, you can paint over the crease. Ah, if only it were this easy in real life.

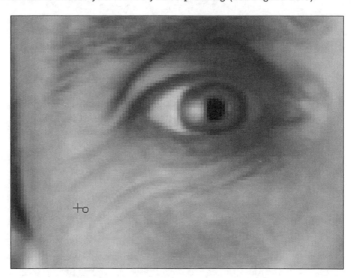

As you can see in Figure 21.6, you can do a decent job of cleaning up skin problems with the Clone Stamp tool.

Figure 21.6
The skin around the left eye (that is, the subject's right eye) has been de-wrinkled.

The trick is to copy the source pixels from as close to the destination as possible; that way, the same skin tone, shadow, lighting, and so forth are retained and the effect looks much more natural.

Nonorganic Problems

The same basic procedure for removing wrinkles can be used to remove other types of image problems, such as creases in scanned images, large globs of dust, and other detritus. You'll look at this in more detail in the "Removing Dust and Scratches" section, but the Clone Stamp tool can also be used to repair these problems. For example, in Figure 21.7, a map was scanned from a fold-out brochure, the result being a prominent crease across the center.

Using the same process as before, use the Clone Stamp tool to paint the pixels just above the crease over the crease itself. You can fix small bits of detail, such as the thin blue lines indicating streams, roads, and so on, affected by the crease by sampling the colors and painting them in with the Pencil tool (see Figure 21.8).

Depending on the level of detail in the image, removing these sorts of problems can be quick or tedious. A crease running right through a photo with lots of detail, for example, might require pixel-by-pixel editing. (This is why photo restoration and retouching can be pricey!)

Figure 21.7
A scanned map has a crease line through the center that can be removed with the Clone Stamp tool.

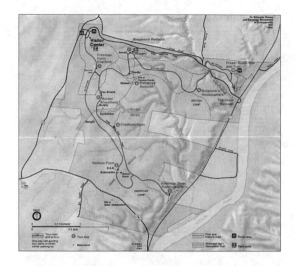

Figure 21.8
The map image has been de-creased.

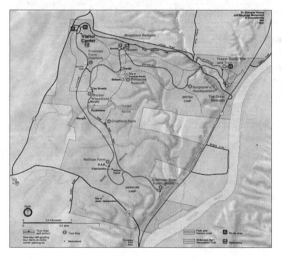

THE HEALING BRUSH AND PATCH TOOL

Two new tools in Photoshop 7 are like the Clone Stamp tool on steroids. The principle is roughly the same—sample pixels from one location and paint them elsewhere—but these tools go about the process a bit more intelligently by matching the lighting, texture, and shading of the copied pixels to the destination pixels. The goal is to have the sampled pixels blend seamlessly into the image.

The Healing Brush

When the Healing Brush is selected, there are, as you would expect, options in the Options Bar (see Figure 21.9).

Figure 21.9
Options for the Healing Brush include the usual Brush options as well as how the sampled pixels get blended and where the pixels come from.

The Brush pop-up menu is where you specify the brush's Diameter, Hardness, Spacing, Angle, and Roundness. You use the Mode pop-up menu to control how the sampled pixels blend with the pixels being replaced:

- **Normal**—In Normal mode, the texture of the sampled pixels is blended with the color and shading of the pixels being replaced. Source pixels are selected in the same way as with the Clone Stamp tool—(Option-click) [Alt+click] where you want the source pixels to come from. It's easy to see what this brush actually does by choosing source pixels that are wildly different from the destination pixels. In Figure 21.10, the source pixels are a patch of grass, and those pixels will be painted onto the front of the white house.

Figure 21.10
In Normal mode, the Healing Brush applies the basic shading and texture of source pixels (the grass, indicated by the selection marquee) to the color of the destination pixels (the front of the house). This brush isn't designed to be used this way, of course—although it certainly can be.

This brush works best when the source and destination pixels are generally the same color. For example, the Healing Brush is an easy way to fix skin problems (like the example you saw earlier). For example, in Figure 21.11, the source pixels from the center of the forehead were painted over the crow's feet around the bottom of the subject's right eye.

21

Figure 21.11
In Normal mode, source pixels sampled from the center of the forehead are blended with the destination pixels below the right eye. The original is shown as an inset.

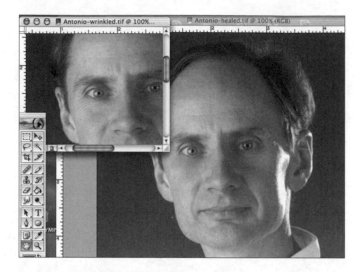

■ **Replace**—In Replace mode, the Healing Brush functions much like the Clone Stamp tool, replacing the destination pixels with the source pixels (see Figure 21.12). Replace protects an image's noise or grain along the edges of the brush stroke.

Figure 21.12
In Replace mode, source pixels sampled from the center of the forehead are painted directly onto the destination pixels with no real blending. This effect might not be desirable, depending on your attitude toward the photo's subject.

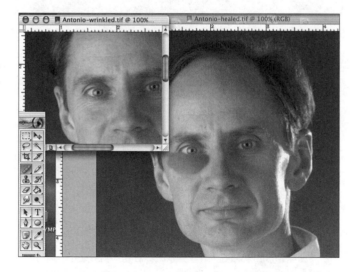

■ **Other Blending Modes**—The Mode pop-up menu also includes the standard Photoshop blending modes Multiply, Screen, Darken, Lighten, Color, and Luminosity.

For detailed information on these standard blending modes, see "Blending Modes, One by One," p. 487, in Chapter 17, "Using Blending Modes."

The Source option for the Healing Brush lets you determine whether you want the source pixels to be sampled from the image or to come from a preset pattern. When the Pattern option is selected, you have access to all your preset patterns, à la the Pattern Stamp tool.

The Aligned option means that when you're painting (or healing, the more appropriate term) and you release the mouse button, you won't lose the current sampling point—where the pixels are coming from. If you start healing again, the pixels will come from where you left off.

If you deselect Aligned, every time you release the mouse button and then start healing again, the pixels will come from the selection point you originally specified. Deselecting Aligned is useful when you have a lot to repair, and you have only a small patch of "intact" pixels to draw from.

The Patch Tool

The Patch tool is akin to the Healing Brush, but instead of being brush based, it's selection based. The principle is this: You select an area to be patched, and then drag it onto the area you want to use as the patch, similar to a skin graft.

In the Options Bar, there are two options: Source and Destination. When Source is selected, you draw a selection marquee around the problem area, and then drag it to the spot you want the replacement pixels to come from (see Figure 21.13).

Figure 21.13
With Source selected in the Options Bar, draw a selection marquee around a problem area (left), and drag it to the spot you want the replacement pixels to come from (center). The pixels are blended, usually seamlessly (right).

When Destination is selected, you draw a selection marquee around the pixels you want to use for the patch, and then drag it onto the flaw (see Figure 21.14).

You can also create and use a pattern to patch a problem area. In that case, after you draw a selection marquee using the Patch tool, click the Use Pattern button in the Options Bar and select a pattern from your presets.

The Patch tool works well when there are large expanses of detail-less pixels to use as the patch. If you include any defects in the patch, they will also be mapped over the problem area, which doesn't really improve the image. Depending on how flawed the image is, you might need to do some prep work with the Clone Stamp tool first to create a spot large enough to use as a patch. (You'll explore the Patch tool in more detail in the "Photo Restoration Techniques" section later in this chapter.)

21

Figure 21.14
With Destination selected in the Options Bar, draw a selection marquee around the pixels you want to use to patch a problem (left), and drag it to the problem area (center). Again, the pixels are blended (right).

REMOVING DUST AND SCRATCHES

One consequence of scanning images is that unless you live or work in one of those clean rooms they use when making microchips or perhaps the completely sterile medical laboratory from *The Andromeda Strain*, you will invariably scan dust along with an image. Even the most meticulous scrubbing of the scanbed (with a non-abrasive cloth, of course) right before scanning doesn't completely get rid of all the filth. Figure 21.15 is an exaggeration—anyone whose scanner bed is this filthy would be better off cleaning it and rescanning—but it illustrates the basic problem.

Figure 21.15
In the dark portions of the image, you can see a lot of dust, filth, and other random detritus.

21

There are several ways of cleaning this image. One, which would be the most laborious, is to use the Clone Stamp tool or any of the other painting tools to paint over each tiny speck. This option would be tedious, however, and is not recommended.

The Dust & Scratches Filter

Fortunately, there is a filter built into Photoshop that can help clean this image. Select Filter, Noise, Dust & Scratches, and you get the dialog box seen in Figure 21.16.

There is a similar filter called Despeckle that you could consider "Dust & Scratches Lite." It removes some of the smaller specks of dust. However, there is no dialog box associated with it; it just goes ahead and despeckles whatever it wants.

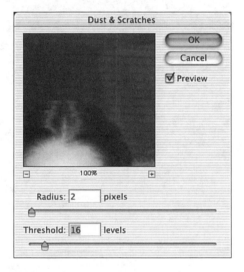

Figure 21.16
The Dust & Scratches filter looks for small, speckly bits of an image and removes them.

Dust & Scratches looks for what it thinks are anomalies in the image—small, speckly highlights amid dark, surrounding pixels. The Radius slider determines how far Photoshop searches for anomalous pixels, and Threshold determines how different the pixel values should be before they are removed. Move the view in the preview window to a particularly gunky portion of the image. Starting with a Radius of 2, move the Radius slider to the right until a significant chunk of the gunk goes away, but before other image distortions start happening (like people's eyes or teeth disappearing). Next, move the Threshold slider to the right until the gunk returns, and then move it back toward the left until most of it is gone. If everything looks okay, click OK.

This filter works well, but there are a couple of caveats. The filter smoothes out differences between adjacent pixels, but sometimes—in fact, remarkably often—differences between adjacent pixels are actual image detail. Even small speckly bits can be image detail. For example, using the Dust & Scratches filter can remove the catchlights from subjects' eyes, which is not really desirable. Other speckly bits of the image can be lost, too, such as specular highlights on watches and jewelry. One way around this problem is to draw selection marquees around the subject's eyes or other image portions you don't want the filter to touch. Then choose the Select, Inverse command, and apply the Dust & Scratches filter. This technique gets rid of the gunk everywhere in the image except the areas you've cordoned off.

21

Touching Up

After using the Dust & Scratches filter, you may find that some larger globs of gunk remain. You can use the techniques you looked at earlier—the Clone Stamp tool, the Healing Brush, and the Patch tool—to touch up additional problems. Sometimes the fix is easy. In Figure 21.17, there is a big piece of dust in the middle of a dark expanse. If you're going to have problems, these are the kinds of problems you *want* to have!

Figure 21.17
A large speck of dust is sitting, exposed, right in the middle of a dark expanse—it's so easy to pick it off.

To remove it, simply select the Clone Stamp tool, (Option-click) [Alt+click] somewhere nearby to select the source pixels, pick a brush size slightly larger than the dust speck, position the cursor over the speck, and click. It's gone.

However, just as the bread always lands butter side down, so, too, do errors and imperfections invariably occur amid busy, complicated parts of images, as in Figure 21.18.

Figure 21.18
Small imperfections amid detailed backgrounds can be more difficult to remove.

21

It's with these types of imperfections that the Healing Brush comes in handy. By selecting source pixels close to the defect, the dust can be healed away (see Figure 21.19).

Figure 21.19
With the Healing Brush, you can easily remove defects amid complex backgrounds.

The process isn't perfect, of course, and it can take some trial and error to make the fixes look natural—after all, it makes no sense if the fix looks worse than the problem! If the background is really busy, small defects might not even be noticeable. Indeed, it may be easier and less time-consuming in the long run to simply clean the scanbed, dust off the photo, and rescan.

USING THE TONING AND FOCUS TOOLS

Many of Photoshop's tools are legacies from the days of traditional photography and darkroom techniques. An unsharp mask, for example, was an actual blurry (that is, unsharp) low-contrast photographic negative made from a transparency. The negative was placed atop the transparency like a mask and used for color correction when making color separations for process-color printing. One happy incidental result was that the unsharp mask enhanced edge detail. Hence, the Unsharp Mask filter in Photoshop is used to enhance edge detail and "sharpen" an image. Many other Photoshop features were originally designed to mimic darkroom techniques and can seem a bit anachronistic or even mysterious to users who have known only digital imaging.

The Toning Tools

Likewise, the "toning tools"—the Dodge and Burn tools—also date from the darkroom ages. The original dodge and burn tools were (and still are) used when an enlarger was making an exposure on a piece of photographic paper. The dodge tool was a disk (usually cardboard) on a wire that was placed between the enlarger and the photographic paper (which explains the Dodge tool's icon in the Toolbox—see Figure 21.20). It blocked the light coming from the enlarger—"dodging it"—and as a result the dodged area would be lighter when the paper was developed. In contrast (so to speak), the original burn tool was either a disk (also cardboard) with a hole in it or the photographer's hand.

Either "tool" allowed light to reach only a specific area on the photographic paper, "burning" those areas. As a result, the burned areas would be darker than non-burned areas. (In Figure 21.20, the Burn tool icon is a hand forming a small circle that allows light to pass through it.)

Figure 21.20
The Dodge and Burn tool icons are derived from their darkroom analogues.

As you can tell from Figure 21.20, there is also a Sponge tool. Yes, that is also a darkroom technique. When a print is being developed, photographers or darkroom technicians might notice that certain areas aren't coming out dark enough, so they can apply full-strength developing solution to a sponge and rub it on the developing image.

The Dodge Tool

The Options Bar for the Dodge tool features the usual Brush pop-up menu. It also lets you specify a Range—the portions of an image you want to adjust, be it Highlights, Midtones, or Shadows. If you want to just lighten the shadows but leave lighter pixels untouched, you'd select Shadows, and so on.

The Exposure slider adjusts how much of an effect the tool has—1% exposure has a minimal effect, and 100% exposure has the maximum effect. For example, in Figure 21.21, the untouched image on the left has a very dark floor. On the right, applying the Dodge tool to the midtones with 50% exposure brings out detail that was lost in the murk.

Figure 21.21
The floor is very dark. With the Dodge tool set to Midtones, some of the detail can be drawn out.

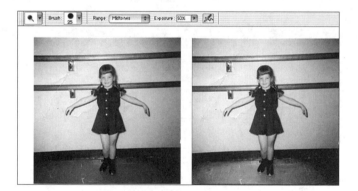

The Burn Tool

The Burn tool has the same options as the Dodge tool but the opposite effect—it darkens the parts of the image on which it is used (see Figure 21.22).

Figure 21.22
On the left, the unretouched image is a bit light, but using the Burn tool on the midtones at 25% exposure brings out some of the detail in the rock (right).

The Dodge and Burn tools can be useful for enhancing small portions of images, bringing out detail, or creating shadows and other effects, but they are best used in small doses. They are also useful in lieu of adjusting, say, Levels or Curves. In some cases, you might want to adjust the Levels for only small portions of an image. The Dodge and Burn tools enable you to finesse small image areas without the adjustment being applied globally.

The Sponge Tool

The Sponge tool is a brush-based version of the Saturation slider in the Image, Adjustments, Hue/Saturation dialog box. Whereas the Saturation slider in the dialog box makes all the colors globally more saturated or "moist," the Sponge tool lets you apply saturation to only specific areas.

You use the Options Bar to select Saturate (all the colors become more vivid and colorful wherever you paint with the Sponge tool) or Desaturate mode (all the colors get grayer and less vivid). See Figure 21.23 for a comparison.

Figure 21.23
Although this is in black-and-white, you can probably get a sense of what is happening. The untouched image is at the top. On the bottom left, the Sponge tool was set to Saturate at 100% flow, and the water and first batch of trees were sponged heavily. On the bottom right, the same area was desaturated.

21

In color (available on the CD for this book), the water in the
bottom-left image in Figure 21.23 is a vibrant bright disco
blue, but the trees look like it is the height of autumn (rather
than early summer, when the photo was actually taken). On
the bottom right, the water and trees look almost like they're
in grayscale.

The Focus Tools

There are two more tools for fine-tuning specific areas of an
image, collectively known as the *focus tools*. As the term
"focus tools" indicates, they are used to selectively blur or
sharpen parts of the image.

To dodge, burn, or sponge only
certain areas and protect others,
you can make or load a selection—using the Select, Color
Range command, the selection
tools, the Quick Mask mode, or
any of the other ways of making
selections. The dodge, burn, or
sponge effect will not be applied
beyond the bounds of the selection marquee.

The Blur tool, like a lot of the tools you have been looking at
in this section, is a brush-based version of a general Photoshop command—in this case, the Blur filter. However, the Blur tool's advantage is that you can control the effect much more precisely than
with the random, shot-in-the-dark Blur filter. Its opposite is the Sharpen tool, which, as you would
expect, sharpens those areas in which it is applied.

The Options Bar for both tools features the standard Brush and Mode (basically, a blending mode)
pop-up menus. The choices for Mode are Normal, Darken, Lighten, Hue, Saturation, Color, and
Luminosity. The Pressure slider controls the extent of the blurring or sharpening effect.

The focus tools are good for enhancing or de-emphasizing small parts of an image. For example,
making a subject stand out from a background is a good use of one or both of these tools. If a background is too "in focus," it can distract from the subject of the image. By applying a slight blur to
the background, you can alter the apparent depth of focus to make the subject more prominent.
Another technique is using the Sharpen tool to emphasize objects such as jewelry or other details of
the image you'd like to draw attention to. This is also another good time to use a selection to mask
out areas of the image you don't want to blur or sharpen.

⇨ *Having trouble controlling the Sharpen tool? See "Dulling the Sharpen" in the NAPP Help Desk section at the end of this chapter.*

WORKING WITH HISTORY

Photoshop's History palette and History Brush work together to help you selectively adjust areas of
an image to a previous state. However, the History Brush is far more than merely a "selective undo"
tool. Instead of simply reversing the most recent procedure, you can revert to any prior stage of the
image's appearance, as long as it's available in the History palette.

Using History to Restore Images

In many respects, Photoshop's history capabilities are merely conveniences. They don't do anything
you can't accomplish otherwise in Photoshop. Consider this procedure for improving a photo of a
face:

1. Duplicate the background layer.

2. Blur the top layer to smooth the skin.

3. Create a layer mask that hides the eyes and lips on the upper layer. That allows the unblurred eyes to show through from the original layer.

4. Merge the two layers.

5. Duplicate the merged layer.

6. Working on the upper layer, use Curves to generally improve the image's tonality.

7. Create a mask that allows the original highlights of the hair to show through from the lower layer.

8. Merge layers.

Compare that workflow to this:

1. Blur the image to smooth the skin.

2. Use the History Brush to paint back the original unblurred eyes and lips.

3. Use Curves to correct the tonality.

4. Restore the hair highlights with the History Brush.

In addition to looking much simpler on paper, the second workflow generally is easier—a few strokes with the History brush is typically simpler than creating complex masks. An example of the result is shown in Figure 21.24.

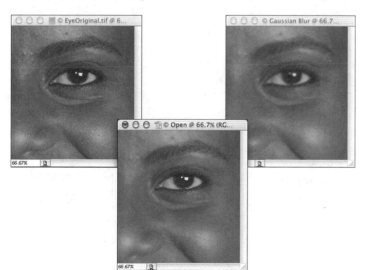

Figure 21.24
The original image (left) has very noticeable skin. After blurring to smooth the skin, the image lacks focus (right). You can use the History Brush to restore the sharpness of an image's focal points (in this case, the eye and eyebrow), as shown in the center image.

21

The History Palette

The History palette records your steps as you work. Unlike the Actions palette, however, the History palette is not a reproducible recording. Rather, it is more comparable to a series of "Undo" commands arranged chronologically, presented visually, and named for convenience (see Figure 21.25).

Figure 21.25
The History palette controls the behavior of the History Brush (and the Art History Brush). Each history state is named after the command or tool used.

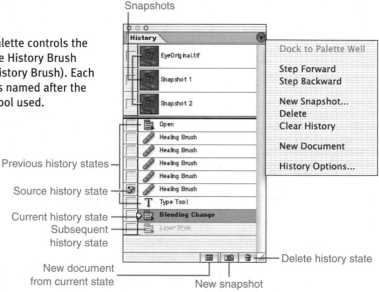

As you work, your steps are added to the bottom of the History palette. You can revert to any state by clicking on it in the palette. The image returns to the appearance and condition at that point in the creation process. Using the commands Undo/Redo and Step Backward/Step Forward is also reflected in the palette. When you click on any previous history state in the History palette, the subsequent states are grayed out, yet can still be selected. The image reverts to the appearance at the time that state was created. You can save a specific state as a *snapshot* in the History palette, which is retained even if the history is cleared or purged to free up memory.

In Figure 21.25, the History palette shows three snapshots and nine history states. The top snapshot was created when the image was opened, which Photoshop does by default. The subsequent snapshots were created manually by clicking the New Snapshot button. When you click on a snapshot, the image reverts to that state and the individual history states in the palette are grayed out, even if the state from which you created the snapshot is visible.

If you click on a snapshot of a previous history state and make any change to the image, the subsequent history states are deleted from the palette.

By default, the History palette saves the 20 most recent history states. You can adjust this number in Photoshop's General Preferences. Increasing the number of history states gives you more flexibility, but also increases Photoshop's memory requirements.

When you click in the left column next to a history state or snapshot, whether that state is active or not in the palette, it becomes the source state for the History Brush and the Art History Brush. Using either tool in the image changes the painted pixels to their appearance when the source state was created.

When you click the leftmost button at the bottom of the History palette, you create a new document from the selected history state. This is not a new view of the file, but a completely new, unsaved document. This method is the simplest way to create a copy of an open document. You can make whatever changes you want to the copy, experiment with filters, try new techniques, and the original file is unaffected. Creating a new document by using the History palette is comparable to using the Save As command to create a copy, except that the copy has not been saved.

Non-Linear History and Other Options

The History palette menu command History Options opens the dialog box shown in Figure 21.26.

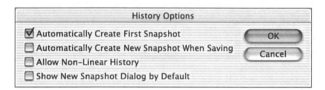

Figure 21.26
The default values for History Options are those shown.

Here are the options:

- **Automatically Create First Snapshot**—When the image is opened, a snapshot is created. This option can save time if you need to revert to the image's original appearance. In addition, the initial appearance of the image is often used as a history state with the History Brush. You might want to deselect this option when using the Batch command. You'll save a bit of time during the automation execution.

- **Automatically Create New Snapshot When Saving**—With this option, every time you save the document, a new snapshot is added to the History palette. If you save regularly, the snapshots can add up quickly and put a strain on the memory.

- **Allow Non-Linear History**—Non-linear history is discussed separately later in this section.

- **Show New Snapshot Dialog by Default**—The New Snapshot dialog box enables you to assign a name to the snapshot and choose to make the snapshot from the full document, a merged version of the document, or just from the current layer. Normally, you'll make the snapshot from the full document, and you can always rename a snapshot by double-clicking the name in the History palette.

Non-linear history is an incredibly powerful option that enables you to delete a history state without affecting the states that follow. Instead of reverting to the previous state when a history state is deleted, the image's current appearance is maintained, except for the deleted state.

21

Keep in mind, however, that deleting a state on which later states rely might actually have no effect on an image. For example, consider these steps:

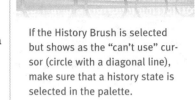

If the History Brush is selected but shows as the "can't use" cursor (circle with a diagonal line), make sure that a history state is selected in the palette.

1. In an image on which you've been working, you create a new layer.

2. You paint on the new layer.

3. You change the new layer's blending mode.

4. You add another new layer and paint on it.

5. You group the layers.

If you then go to the History palette and delete the layer created in step 1, the layer and the pixels on it remain in the image in the last history state.

Alternatively, consider this scenario:

1. You're working on an image and use the Healing Brush to remove a birthmark from the subject's face.

2. You continue with the editing, adjusting color and tonality.

3. The client calls and says "And please leave the birthmark."

In the History palette, you can delete the Healing Brush state in which you removed the birthmark. The rest of the image remains at the last history state.

The History Brush

The History Brush is a painting tool, but rather than paint with color, it paints with pixels from a previous history state. You set the state in the History palette by clicking in the left column next to the state you want to restore. Drag in the image, and the appearance of the area is restored to that of the earlier history state.

Remember that the History Brush's options are the same as those for the Brush tool. You can use any brush from the Brushes palette, any of the standard blending modes (and Behind on layers other than a background layer), variable opacity, flow, and even the Airbrush option.

PHOTO RESTORATION TECHNIQUES

Photo restoration is a skill that takes a great deal of time to master. Much professional photo restoration is still done non-digitally, but Photoshop is making it easier to resurrect old (or even recent) family photos that have not stood the test of time unscathed (like many of those photos' subjects). Over time, images can become discolored, faded, and torn. Not all photos can be saved, but you'd be surprised how many can be.

The first step in photo restoration is to make good-quality scans of the photos. Before scanning, however, decide how big you want the image to be. In other words, what are you going to do with the images? If you want to print them out from an inkjet printer at 100%, you just need to scan at 100%. If you want to make posters or enlargements, scan at or close to the size you'll ultimately want. If you're scanning much larger than 100%, make sure your scanbed is clean, or you'll have a lot of cleanup, in addition to the restoration, to worry about.

➡ *Want a tip on picking scan size and resolution? See "Scanning to Final Size" in the NAPP Help Desk section at the end of this chapter.*

Caution

Photos that have been kept out of the sunlight survive the longest. Light is not good for photographic images, and that includes the bright light of a scanner. Granted, a few scans of an old photo won't do any real damage, but you should keep the number of times you scan an image to the absolute minimum. Therefore, if you're a scanning neophyte, experiment on some "disposable" images before turning to your priceless family heirlooms.

Quick and Easy Repairs

Let's start with an old image that doesn't have too many serious problems, such as the one in Figure 21.27.

Figure 21.27
A photo from 1958 is a little on the blurry side. It has a couple of splotches and a not-too-serious tear in the upper-right corner.

To get rid of the larger blotches, you can use the Healing Brush. For the tear, the Patch tool is in order (see Figure 21.28).

21

Figure 21.28
On the left, with the Patch tool set to Source, draw a selection marquee around the length of the tear and drag the selection a small distance to the left. The new pixels replace the old pixels, and the result is almost seamless (right).

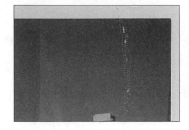

If nothing else major stands out at 100% view, zoom in to 200% and scroll around the image, correcting small spots and splotches as you see them. When everything looks clean, applying the Unsharp Mask filter can help eliminate some of the blurriness.

Finally, the original white border has become gray and stained over the years. It's best to crop the image out of the border and add a new one. Although there are several plug-ins (such as those from Extensis and AutoF/X) for adding all sorts of fancy custom frames and borders, the most basic way to add a simple border around the image is by enlarging the canvas size. To add a simple 70-pixel white border, make sure your background color is set to white, and then choose Image, Canvas Size. Make sure the image is oriented in the exact center of the grid. With the Relative check box selected and Pixels selected as the unit of measure, enter 140 in both the Height and Width fields. Click OK, and you'll have a uniform white border around the image. The final restored image is shown in Figure 21.29.

Figure 21.29
The spots have been removed, the scratch is gone, the blurriness has been removed, and the frame has been replaced.

Less Quick Fixes

Figure 21.30 shows an even older image (1918). It has some more involved problems with general tonality.

Figure 21.30
A much older image is actually sepia colored, has some border problems, and exhibits some fading toward the bottom.

The best way to start is to crop the edges away, which also gets rid of the bent corners. Next, converting to grayscale helps with the basic tonal correction. (You can add a sepia color after the fact, which is covered in the "Coloring and Tinting" section later in the chapter.) Adjusting the Curves and/or Levels helps with overall contrast. The next stage of the process is to go through the image, repairing scratches and other random blemishes with the Clone Stamp and Patch tools as well as the Healing Brush.

As for the fading at the bottom of the image, you could use the Burn tool if you wanted, but using the Sponge tool with a grayscale image heightens the contrast. In Figure 21.31, you can see that judiciously applying the Sponge tool restores some of the contrast.

Figure 21.31
The image on the left exhibits fading at the bottom. Using the Sponge tool in Saturate mode brings out the blacks and enhances the contrast. Applying it judiciously elsewhere improves the overall image tonality.

21

Hopeless Images?

Some images seem beyond rescue, but you'd be surprised what a little work in Photoshop can accomplish. For example, you might think that a washed-out photo (or, conversely, a very dark one) is beyond repair, but it might not be.

Underexposed Images

What about the photo in Figure 21.32? Any hope?

Figure 21.32
Not only has the left side of the image been completely torn, but the image is very faded and washed out.

Yes, there is hope. First, crop off the torn edge. Some additional cropping on the right will improve the composition, too. Second, converting to Grayscale would be a good next step—because it's a black-and-white image, you can eliminate any unwanted color information by converting to Grayscale mode.

Fixing the contrast is easily handled with the Levels dialog box. The histogram suggests that all the pixels might be in roughly the same place (see Figure 21.33).

Figure 21.33
The pixels seem to be concentrated in a narrow zone.

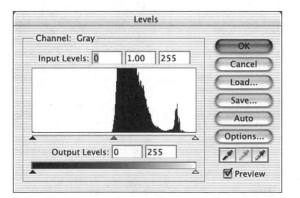

Move the shadow (leftmost) slider toward the mound of pixels, move the highlight (rightmost) slider to the small submound of pixels to the right of the main mound, and then adjust the midtones toward the center of the mound. These adjustments do a fair job of rescuing this image. Some graininess was the result of making adjustments in the Levels dialog box, but applying the Blur filter makes it less harsh.

Zooming in and fixing the usual scratches and specks is the next step. Adding a border by using the Canvas Size dialog box (refer to Figure 21.29) finishes it up. The restored image is in Figure 21.34.

Figure 21.34
The once "hopeless" photo has been cleaned and restored.

Scratches Galore

Remember the dancing girl photo in Figure 21.21? The toning tools were used to bring out detail in the floor. But if you look closely at Figure 21.35, you'll notice a lot more damage.

Figure 21.35
There are cracks, scratches, and a weird stain on the left side of the image.

The first step is to convert to Grayscale (again) to remove discolorations and stains, or at least make them easier to contend with.

For images such as this, the Patch tool is worth the price of the Photoshop upgrade. Each crack was simply selected with the Patch tool, dragged onto an adjacent area, and bam! It's fixed.

As for the missing bit of image on the right, that could probably be cloned in, but you should never forget the role that the Crop tool plays in image restoration! The image can be safely cropped to remove that notch, and an equal amount should be cropped from the left, to maintain image composition.

A more serious problem is revealed by zooming in on the girl's dress (see Figure 21.36).

Before using the Patch tool, it helps to clean up a large area of dust and debris with the Clone Stamp tool or the Healing Brush; otherwise, the Patch tool incorporates the defects into the patch.

The Crop tool can also be used when the subject of the image is slightly off center. Simply crop the image so that the subject is centered.

Figure 21.36
There was a great deal of cracking in the original photograph, which made a mess of this dress.

The Patch tool is of little help here; it simply introduces more defects. The Healing Brush helps, but only after a clear section of dress was cleaned up pixel by pixel, using the Eyedropper and Pencil tools. The Clone Stamp tool made that clean section a little larger, so it could then be used as the source for the Healing Brush. Even at that, it needed to be applied with one hand on the Undo command. The final restored image is in Figure 21.37.

Often, photo restoration is not a quick process. It involves a lot of trial and error, and because all photos—and problems—are different, generalizing about how to fix them is difficult. However, you have seen some common problems and their fixes. As you gain more mastery with Photoshop's tools, you'll likely develop your own custom solutions to these problems.

Figure 21.37
The scratches and cracks are gone, and the contrast has been improved.

COLORIZING AND TINTING TECHNIQUES

In the "Less Quick Fixes" section earlier in this chapter, an old sepia print was converted to grayscale before correcting it. Now you can convert it back to sepia—or whatever color you want.

Simple Colorization

Probably the easiest way to colorize an old image is to convert it back to RGB. Next, choose Image, Adjustments, Hue/Saturation, and select the Colorize check box. Making sure that the Preview check box is selected, drag the sliders, starting with Hue, until you find a tint or color you like (see Figure 21.38).

"Official" sepia is a warm, yellowish brown. The word *sepia* comes from the Latin word—and genus name—for cuttlefish, a relative of the squid that exudes a brown pigment. This brown pigment, also given the name sepia, was originally used as a colorant in artistic drawing in the days before synthetic inks. In Photoshop's Hue/Saturation dialog box, the sepia tone is best simulated by taking the Hue slider down to around 50–40 (38 in the case of Figure 21.38), the Saturation down to around 30–35, and the Lightness down just a tad as needed. There is no set formula, of course; just move the sliders until you like the way it looks.

You don't have to color an old image sepia, however; you can use whatever color or tint suits your fancy.

21

Figure 21.38
A grayscale photo has been colorized and given its sepia tone back.

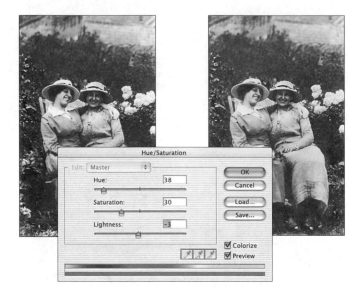

Duotones

As you saw in Chapter 7, "Color Theory and Practice," you can also create duotones, which are especially effective on old photos. To start, make sure your image is in Grayscale mode, and then choose Image, Mode, Duotone. You'll be presented with the Duotone Options dialog box, which is where you set your ink colors. Duotones are most commonly black plus one other color, but you can make them any two colors you like (see Figure 21.39).

Figure 21.39
One of the restored photos has been converted to a duotone of black and a light blue.

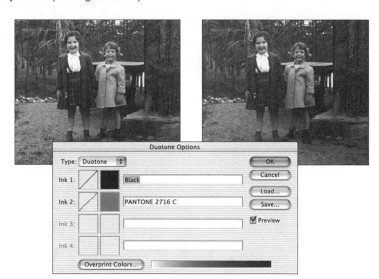

Hand-Tinting

If you want to get fancy, you can hand-tint or hand-paint your images. Depending on your skill, this technique can look simply stylized or as realistic as a colorized movie. To start, make sure your image is in RGB or CMYK mode (depending on the destination of your image). Hand-painting is best handled by painting on a new layer with a reduced Opacity setting. For example, in Figure 21.40, assume you want to colorize the girl on the right by adding flesh tones and giving her a light blue coat, a pink shirt, and pink bows in her blonde hair.

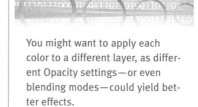

You might want to apply each color to a different layer, as different Opacity settings—or even blending modes—could yield better effects.

Figure 21.40
A black-and-white photo is ripe for colorization.

Create a new layer and set the Opacity slider to 40%. Pick the color you'd like, select the Paintbrush tool, and start painting over the area you'd like to colorize. With the Opacity setting fairly low, you are still retaining texture and shading. If there are large expanses, you can use the selection tools to outline a marquee and then choose Edit, Fill, using the active foreground color. When one color is done, you can pick a new color for other portions of the image, and repeat.

Flesh tones can be especially difficult to add. One way of solving this problem is to use the Eyedropper to sample a specific flesh tone from a color photo and use the sampled color as the starting point when painting. Adjusting the Opacity setting and blending mode can help improve the effect. In Figure 21.40, the clothing, flesh tones, and hair are in different layers, with different Opacity settings.

The tricky part in hand-coloring is deciding what colors to use. Part of that decision can be made based on simple logic: A very dark or black element in an image (such as a coat) is a dark color, such as red, dark green, navy blue, brown, or even black. Light portions are yellows, light blues, light greens, and so on. Pick whatever colors you think look natural—you'll know immediately after you start painting if something looks wrong.

21

PHOTOSHOP IN FOCUS

There are many different tools in Photoshop that can be used to accomplish the same basic goal. Which tool ultimately gets used is up to the user's taste and comfort. To get a sense of how retouching can be done, open a scanned photo you might have with some obvious damage—a tear, a scratch, some dust. Whatever. (Surely you've got one.) Alternatively, if you don't have a scanner or a scanned image, find a photo that has *some* sort of defect. (If you don't have any, we know lots of people who would love to hire you.)

1. In the History palette, click the Create New Document from Current State button twice to make two copies of the opened image.

2. In one copy, find the defect, and, with the Clone Stamp tool selected, pick an appropriate brush size. Select source pixels in close proximity to the defect, and then paint them over the defect to get rid of it.

3. In another copy, use the Healing Brush to do the same thing. Find source pixels that are the same basic color as what you'd like to replace the defect with, and select them as your source pixels. Then paint on the defect. How did that work in comparison to the Clone Stamp tool?

4. In the third copy, use the Patch tool to select the defect, and drag it to some clean pixels. How did *that* work in comparison to the previous use of the Clone Stamp tool and the Healing Brush?

5. Try the preceding steps on different types of image defects—simple globs of dust, scratches, tears, stains, and so forth. As you experiment, you'll quickly get a sense of not only how each tool fares with each type of defect, but also which one you're most comfortable using. After all, the proof is in the final image.

FROM THE NAPP HELP DESK

The National Association of Photoshop Professionals (NAPP) offers e-mail assistance to its members. Here is some advice from the NAPP Help Desk related to issues in this chapter.

Red-Eye Reprise

Is there a simpler red-eye removal technique?

Although the technique presented in this chapter is thorough and does an excellent job, there are other ways to handle the problem. You might find that simply desaturating the area—changing the red to gray—does an excellent job. Use the Sponge tool, set to Desaturate in the Options Bar, and drag little circles in the red area. You can accomplish the same thing by using the Brush tool set to Color as the blending mode.

Dulling the Sharpen

The Sharpen tool always seems to create areas of severe pixellation for me. Is there any way to prevent that?

The pixellation you perceive is a by-product of oversharpening. Sharpening increases the contrast between neighboring pixels. When too much sharpening is applied, the pixels stand out too much from their neighbors. To control the Sharpen tool, simply reduce the Strength setting in the Options Bar to about 25% and spend a little more time with the tool. Several passes at 25% strength sharpen much better than a single pass at 100% strength.

Scanning to Final Size

How do I determine the appropriate scan resolution?

Start from the end. Determine what your final requirements are, calculate the pixel size for those requirements, and scan those pixel dimensions. For example, if the image is destined to fill an area of a Web page measuring 200×200 pixels, scan 200×200 pixels. On the other hand, if you'll be printing the image, you might have to do some math.

Some scanners do the math for you: You input the desired print size and resolution, and the scanner handles the calculations. If your scanner doesn't have that option, here's how to figure the size yourself:

1. Find out the print resolution. For inkjet printers, use 240ppi. For offset presses, use 1.5 or 2 times the line screen frequency, measured in lines per inch (lpi). Your printer can supply that information.

2. Next determine the final print size in inches (or centimeters if that's your preferred unit of measure). Will the image be printed at 8×10 inches from an inkjet? Will it be added to an InDesign layout at 4×6 inches and 266ppi?

3. Multiply the final print dimensions by the target resolution. That gives you the target pixel dimensions.

4. Measure the original image, in inches or centimeters. If you'll be using only part of the original, measure only that area.

5. Divide those dimensions into the target pixel dimensions to find the proper scan resolution.

Say your final image will be 8×10 inches, printed on an inkjet printer at 240ppi. Assume that the original photographic print is 4×6 inches, and you'll be cropping a half inch from each side to reach the 4:5 proportions required by an 8×10 print. The final image must be 1920 pixels by 2400 pixels (8×240=1920; 10×240=2400). Therefore, the scan resolution should be 480ppi (1920÷4 inches=480; 2400÷5 inches=480, too).

ADVANCED COMPOSITING AND COLLAGING IN PHOTOSHOP

IN THIS CHAPTER

COMPOSITING AND COLLAGING: COMMON TECHNIQUES

22

Compositing, roughly defined, is inserting one image or part of an image into another. *Collaging* is combining disparate elements in the same image. Collaging tends to be a bit more artistic than compositing, and collaging in Photoshop is one of the hallmarks of digital art. These techniques are really what Photoshop is known for—and indeed what has made Photoshop something of a household name even among people who have never even used the program. If you've ever read *The Onion* (www.theonion.com) or watched *The Daily Show with Jon Stewart*, you know that Photoshop can often be used to humorous effect. At the same time, the ability to seamlessly integrate different images has also produced some limits on the use of photographs as evidence in court trials—it's too easy to doctor images these days.

There are myriad ways of compositing images in Photoshop, but here are some common ones:

- Drawing tools

- The Clone Stamp tool

- Selections and paths

Compositing Using the Drawing Tools

Depending on your ultimate goal, compositing can be as detailed or as basic as you want it to be. At its most basic level, you can use the drawing tools—such as the pen tools or the Rectangle and Ellipse shape tools—to add shapes to a blank canvas. Figure 22.1, intended to represent the sun over the ocean, was made using just three shapes—two rectangles (each a different shade of blue) and a circle (yellow).

Figure 22.1
A quickie collage composed of two rectangles and a circle, intended to represent the sun over the ocean.

Obviously, this collage is not going to impress anyone that readily, but you could add blurs and feathering to make the shapes a bit more diffuse and add some visual interest, as in Figure 22.2.

Figure 22.2
Applying, say, a Gaussian Blur filter to the shapes makes them look a bit less "pasted on."

This is the digital equivalent of the "colored crepe paper pasted onto a large sheet of paper" collaging technique that probably ended up on your refrigerator when you were five. Depending on your artistic ability, however, you can achieve some spectacular results by using the drawing and shape tools.

The Clone Stamp Tool

The Clone Stamp tool is often used to alter images. As you can see in Figure 22.3, it can be used to take part of an image and copy it—or "clone" it—elsewhere. In this case, the Number 5 horse is suddenly winning!

Figure 22.3
With the Clone Stamp tool, horse Number 5 was "cloned" into the lead (the original is shown as an inset). To further manipulate this image, you could "clone out" the original horse Number 5, causing distress (or joy, as the case may be) to racetrack bettors.

The Clone Stamp tool is very simple to use. When it is selected, you (Option-click) [Alt+click] to select the point from which you're going to be moving pixels. Then you select a brush size from the Brush field in the Options Bar and start painting over the destination pixels.

When compositing with the Clone Stamp tool, there are a few caveats to bear in mind, which are illustrated in Figure 22.4.

Figure 22.4
Common Clone Stamp tool compositing errors include not getting all the image cloned (resulting in a jockey who appears to be "losing his head") and inadvertently cloning bits of the original background.

Problems caused by compositing with the Clone Stamp tool can include the following:

- Including too much (or any) of the original background

- Missing portions of the image, resulting in a sort of "transporter malfunction" look

- Creating errors of perspective

 *Wondering about the difference between aligned and non-aligned cloning? See "Standardizing the Source" in the NAPP Help Desk section at the end of this chapter.*

You'll look at errors of perspective later in this chapter in the "Common Compositing Errors" section.

Compositing Using Paths and Selections

The Clone Stamp tool is fine for some compositing applications, but another, more precise, way is to use paths and selections.

As you saw in Chapter 10, "Making Selections and Creating Masks," you can create a selection around any portion of an image in a variety of ways. In Figure 22.5, the Magnetic Lasso tool was used to quickly make a selection around the balloon. By holding down the Shift key, you can then use the Magnetic Lasso tool to add areas not included in the original selection (such as the bottom-right tip of the basket).

After selecting the part of the image you want to duplicate, you can switch to the Move tool. If you want to move just the selection, click and drag on it. If you do, though, you'll be left with a white space where the image had been. However, if you hold down (Option) [Alt] while dragging with the Move tool, you'll duplicate the selection as you drag (see Figure 22.6).

For even more precise control over the selection, you can go to the Paths palette and select Make Work Path from the Paths palette menu. Using the Pen and Direct Selection tools, you can then edit the anchor points composing the path. When you're done, simply select Make Selection from the Paths palette menu.

Figure 22.5
The Magnetic Lasso tool (or any selection tool, for that matter) can be used to make a selection around part of an image.

Figure 22.6
Holding down the (Option) [Alt] key while dragging with the Move tool duplicates the selection.

You can then choose Edit, Transform, Scale to scale the duplicated image down and create an adjacent balloon (see Figure 22.7).

If you wanted, you could add even more balloons. You could even change the color, map different patterns onto the copies, and so on.

All the composites in this section were made using only one layer. In the next section, you'll look at what can be done by using different layers.

Figure 22.7
Scaling the duplicated selection down with the Transform command creates an additional balloon.

COMPOSITING WITH LAYERS

One of the drawbacks to using the single-layer select-copy-move technique is that after the duplicated copy is deselected, it's part of the background image. If you try to move it, you'll be left with white (or whatever background color you have specified) pixels in its place. Therefore, copying selections for compositing into new layers has a number of advantages. First, pixels on a separate layer can be moved around after the fact, as long as the image is not flattened. Second, all the myriad layer styles, blending modes, and other layer effects can be applied. Third, different filters can be used on each layer independently.

Copying Selections to New Layers

In its most basic form, creating a new layer from a selection is as simple as creating the selection, selecting the Edit, Copy menu command, clicking the New Layer button at the bottom of the Layers palette (or using the menu command Layer, New Layer), and then using the Edit, Paste menu command. This process can be done as many times as necessary, and, as you know from working with layers in general, each layer can be treated differently. You can also duplicate a layer by dragging it to the New Layer button. For example, in Figure 22.8, a selection was copied to a new layer, and that layer was duplicated multiple times. Each layer was then scaled and repositioned to create the illusion of a sky thick with balloons.

➡️ *If you select Edit, Paste Into when pasting a selection into a new layer, the layer will include a layer mask. For a discussion of layer masks, **see** "Layer Masks, Vector Masks, and Clipping Groups," **p. 267**, Chapter 10, "Making Selections and Creating Masks."*

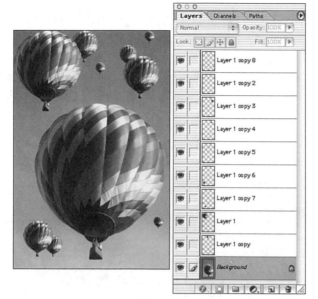

Figure 22.8
The selection from the background layer was copied to a new layer, and eight duplicate layers were made. The balloon on each layer was resized and repositioned.

Applying Layer Styles

As you would expect, you can also apply layer styles to images composited into new layers (see Figure 22.9).

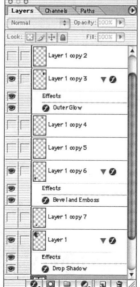

Figure 22.9
You can add a drop shadow (top left), an outer glow (top right), or an emboss (bottom left), among other effects, to selections copied into new layers.

Additionally, you can noodle with blending modes to achieve some interesting layer interactions.

22

MOVING ARTWORK FROM IMAGE TO IMAGE

Although being able to duplicate image elements from the same image can be useful, the real power (and, let's face it, the real fun) of Photoshop is adding elements of other images. Two terms are generally used when discussing moving image data from one document to another. *Source* refers to the file (or area) from which you're copying pixels. *Destination* refers to the file (or area) to which the pixels are being copied. For example, a source image might be an object or a person, and the destination image is perhaps a background or environment. In Figure 22.10, the source image is the cannon, and the destination image is the horse-racing track.

Figure 22.10
The source image was plopped into the middle of the destination image.

Admittedly, the composite does look a little unnatural (and a lot of compositing does), but you'll look at some of the typical pitfalls in "Common Compositing Errors" later in this chapter.

The Clone Stamp Tool Revisited

One of the easiest ways to get images from one file to another is via your old friend the Clone Stamp tool. One cool feature of this tool is that you can set the source pixels in one image and then paint those pixels into another image.

For example, in Figure 22.11, the Clone Stamp tool's source point—(Option-click) [Alt+click]—was set in the Mt. Rushmore image. Then the pixels were painted into the Monument Valley image to make it appear as though the famous faces were carved into an Arizona butte. Although this image looks okay in black and white, in color it still needs some work, as Mount Rushmore is gray and the Arizona buttes are reddish-orange. Playing with the blending modes, Opacity slider, and/or the Replace Color command can produce a more or less seamless integration of the two images.

Figure 22.11
Simply cloning a portion of the Mt. Rushmore image onto a big butte gives the illusion of there being a southwestern version of the national monument.

When copying pixels, keep in mind that there might be a size differential between the source and destination images. So before starting, be sure to check the respective Image Size dialog boxes to make sure you are not copying an 8×10-inch image into a 2×3-inch image—or vice versa. One quick way of gauging the relative sizes is to check each image's zoom percentages. If both image windows onscreen are the same size, but one says 100% while the other says 25%, you're going to run into trouble when you start compositing. Yes, you can resize after the fact, but one way of saving some tweaking later is to measure the spot in the destination image where you want the source image to go. Then resize the source image appropriately. Resolution is an issue, too. A 72dpi image causes the same problem when you try to copy it into a 300dpi image.

⇨ *Want more info on determining whether two images match size-wise? See "Inches Versus Pixels" in the NAPP Help Desk section at the end of this chapter.*

Caution

When using the Clone Stamp tool to copy pixels from one image to another, both the source and destination images need to be in the same color mode, or Photoshop gives you an error message.

You don't need to be extremely exact. As long as you're in the ballpark size-wise, you can copy pixels willy-nilly. As long as you have cloned those pixels to a new layer, you can then simply use Edit, Transform, Scale to resize appropriately.

Copying Selections Between Files

As you've probably surmised by now, there are two basic steps to compositing: grabbing/copying pixels and cleaning up. Let's look at the process in some detail.

Some folks are never happy with their yards. With Photoshop, though, landscaping is a snap. In Figure 22.12, the image on the right is a big, relatively empty expanse of lawn. Wouldn't a stream and a small wooden bridge look lovely there? The image on the left is just what the ambitious homeowner is looking for.

Figure 22.12
The stream (left) would look fetching in the front yard of the house (right).

Because both images—which are digital camera shots—are the exact same pixel dimensions, the stream image needs to be reduced in size slightly so that it fits in the yard. Both images are 6×4.5 inches (at 266dpi), so reducing the stream image by half is a good start. Some tweaking with the Transform command will be needed, but cutting the image down to about 3×2.2 inches is a start.

The next step is to draw a rough selection marquee around the portion that is to be dragged onto the other image (see Figure 22.13).

Figure 22.13
The selection marquee doesn't have to be exact but should be generally within the ballpark.

Next, with the Move tool active, the selection is dragged into the destination image. It will automatically be copied onto a new layer (see Figure 22.14).

Figure 22.14
The dragged selection has been assigned its own layer in the destination image.

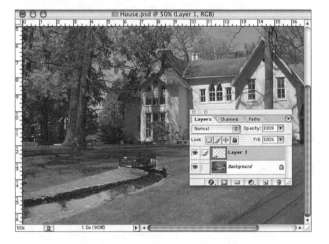

With the new layer active, the size of the stream can be tweaked by using the Transform command—in this case, it looks like it could stand being a tad larger.

The first thing you probably notice (even in the black-and-white reproduction) is that the grass doesn't match. The new grass is lighter than the old grass, but you can fix that with the Eraser tool. Making sure the top layer is active in the Layers palette, select the Eraser tool, make sure its mode is set to Brush, and pick a brush small enough to maneuver into small areas, yet not so small that the process takes forever. Then start erasing the bright green grass of the added image to let the original pixels below become visible. The stream has a solid edge, so it's easy to get close to it (see Figure 22.15).

If you can't get an exact size match, it's better to make the source image larger rather than smaller than required to avoid pixellation when resizing. However, you can usually get away with a small size increase without losing a discernible amount of image quality.

Figure 22.15
By erasing the top layer's pixels, you can restore the original detail, color, and shadows, making the stream look more seamlessly composited.

One more bit of detail is the bridge. The background from the original stream image is still visible though the slats of the bridge. Using the same basic process (and a smaller brush), you can erase the pixels between the slats, revealing the original pixels of the house image. Depending on the amount of detail in the image, this process can be quick or tedious.

Figure 22.16 shows the more or less finished image.

There is still some unnaturalness about the image, of course. For one thing, the stream ends at the bridge, which is odd, although moving the source image up a bit could have made that much less noticeable. Also, the reflection in the water includes trees that don't exist where the stream has been put. Granted, it's impossible to say that there *aren't* trees in those positions now, but it shows the small details that you need to pay attention to when compositing.

Instead of the Eraser tool, you could use the Clone Stamp tool to copy pixels from the bottom layer to the top layer.

There is a better way of solving this problem, which is covered in the next section, "Compositing Using Paths Revisited."

22

Figure 22.16
The stream has now been fully composited and cleaned up.

Compositing Using Paths Revisited

One of the keys to effective compositing is isolating the image to be composited from the background. As has been explored elsewhere in this book, there are many ways of accomplishing that. For simple objects with uncomplicated backgrounds, such as a dark object on a uniformly white background, the process is easy. Simply select the white background with the Magic Wand tool, choose the Select, Invert menu command, and you're done. You have selected the object without any of the background.

Complex backgrounds can cause problems, however, especially those that are close in color to the object you're trying to isolate. Adding to the complexity are objects that have gaps, such as the wooden bridge that was just composited. The Eraser tool was used to "poke holes" through the composited image, but a more effective way of solving the same problem is to draw a complex path in the source image, and then convert that path to a selection. The following example explores this technique.

Remember the cannon-on-the-racetrack image in Figure 22.10? You might have noticed that one of its major compositing problems was the wheels. Each of the sections between the spokes needed to be "poked" through (see Figure 22.17).

Figure 22.17
The original cannon image not only needs to be isolated from a complex background, but also needs to have the areas between the wheel spokes poked through.

To isolate the cannon, a complex path is created that includes the outline of the cannon as well as the spokes (see Figure 22.18).

Figure 22.18
Paths effectively isolate the cannon from a complex background. When creating individual subpaths, such as around the spokes on the wheels, make sure you get all of them, or you'll run into compositing errors.

22

When you're ready to composite, select all the path fragments with the Path Selection tool.

Choosing Make Selection from the Paths palette menu converts all the path segments into a selection. When the selected portion is dragged to the destination image, all the parts that should be poked through are.

This example illustrates that when compositing, it pays to plan the final image before acquiring the source images. Compositing two random images (the cannon and the horse track images, for example) doesn't always work as well as when images are specifically photographed for compositing purposes. That may not be possible, of course, and even with planning, there's still no guarantee that the two images will match up. However, advance planning can go a long way toward helping create better-looking, more realistic composites.

Rather than laboriously Shift+select each path segment individually, you can simply click and drag over the entire image, which selects all the path segments.

As you might have noticed in Figure 22.18, a small portion of the wheels was obscured by a plank of wood, which makes the path around the wheels less round. After compositing, the Clone Stamp tool was used to "reconstruct" the missing wheel portions.

Interstitial Compositing

If you want to get fancy, you can composite objects between objects in the same image—called *interstitial compositing*, for lack of a better term—à la Figure 22.19.

Figure 22.19
In this image, the horses and riders from a racetrack photo were composited into a shot of a suburban street.

To produce a composite like this one, you would follow these basic steps. In the shot of the street, first select the hedges. Draw a selection marquee around just the strip of hedge behind which the horses would be riding (see Figure 22.20).

Figure 22.20
Selecting a narrow band of the hedges makes it easier to select only what you need to select.

Next, using Select, Color Range, select the asphalt of the road with the Eyedropper tool and increase the fuzziness until the asphalt color intermingled in the hedges is selected as well. Then use the Select, Inverse menu command to select just the greens and browns of the hedges. Copy the selection, and then select the menu command Layer, New, Layer Via Copy to line up the copied selection with the original.

Meanwhile, in the horse photo, draw a path around the horses and riders, and make a selection from it (see Figure 22.21).

Figure 22.21
The horses and riders were selected by drawing a path around them and then choosing Make Selection.

Then drag the selected horses into the street image, which will assign them to a new layer. Repeat the process with the second group of horses—draw a path around the horses and riders, convert the path to a selection, and drag the selection into the street image. Position the horse layers in the Layers palette between the layer containing the hedges and the background so that they appear to be walking down the street and are visible through the gaps in the shrubbery. Finally, add shadows to heighten realism, making sure to orient them to match the shadows already in the background image. (For more on shadows, see the "Light and Shadows" section later in this chapter.)

COMMON COMPOSITING ERRORS

Although combining images can be extremely effective and can easily fool the eye, it is not uncommon to miss details that detract from the realism of a composited image. In other words, it just doesn't "look right." Sometimes it's obvious, and a viewer can immediately say, "Hey, that looks fake because the shadow is going in the wrong direction," but other times the error is harder to pinpoint, although it's easy to tell that *something* is wrong. It can be like those "What's Wrong with This Picture?" puzzles in *Highlights* magazine.

Some common compositing problems include the following:

- Bad source image isolation/cloning
- Light and shadow
- Perspective and position
- Depth of focus

Bad Source Image Isolation

One of the most common, yet obvious, compositing problems involves incomplete or sloppy image isolation. This error can be patently obvious, as in Figure 22.22, where a quick lasso-based path was scribbled around the fountain and the sloppy selection dragged into a destination image.

Figure 22.22
An exaggerated example of sloppy source image isolation.

Sometimes it's more subtle, although still egregious, as in Figure 22.23. The source image edges have been cleaned up a bit, but the composite still has that "paper cutout" look.

This problem also manifests itself as a white fringe around a source image that at one point had a white background. To solve this problem, taking the time to use a more detailed source image selection method can pay off. For example, using Select, Color Range to specify a color and a level of fuzziness can help capture similarly colored pixels that compose edge detail.

Figure 22.23
The composite is cleaner, but the lack of edge detail still makes this composite look sloppy.

➡ *For more tips and tricks on effective image selecting, **see** "Selection Commands," **p. 255**, in Chapter 10, "Making Selections and Creating Masks."*

Finessing edge detail can also be done after the fact by zooming in and using the Eraser tool to remove the background pixel-by-pixel. Naturally, this method can be laborious. You can also try the Layer, Matting, Defringe command.

Another example of bad image isolation is shown in Figure 22.24. In this case, not all the individual interspoke spaces were selected before the image was dragged to the destination image.

This example is, again, pretty egregious, but sometimes these errors can be subtle, so it pays to pay close attention to the images you're compositing.

There is also a good Photoshop plug-in called KnockOut (now at version 2) from Procreate (Corel's graphics software "imprint") that aims to help create selections and masks from intricately detailed edges, such as hair and fur. As with Photoshop's built-in selection tools, however, you're still at the mercy of the degree of contrast between the pixels you're trying to isolate and the background you're trying to remove.

A related issue, but par for the course when compositing, is a sharp edge around the source image that can work to make the composite look like a Monty Python animation. If your composite is looking too obviously pasted on, try feathering the edge of the source image. Occasional use of the Smudge tool can also help buff some harsh edges.

Figure 22.24
The original cannon background is still visible between some of the spokes.

Sweating the Small Stuff

As you've seen throughout this chapter, effective compositing can be a simple process (the balloon image—distinct foreground object, uniformly colored background) or a complicated, arduous process (the cannon image—drawing all those paths). Remember that you don't always have to be precise, however. Not every composited pixel needs to be seamlessly integrated.

Take the horses 'n' hedges image you looked at earlier in this chapter. Was every single twig and branch accounted for and selected? No. If you looked closely at that image—in color and at high resolution—you'd probably notice all sorts of flaws, but this book is black and white and the image is reproduced small, so there was no need to "sweat the small stuff." That's the basic determinant of how much attention to detail you need to pay: Deadlines being what they are, you might not have the luxury of spending hours methodically selecting every branch of a hedge—or whatever intricate detail you're working with. If you're compositing images that will be reproduced at high resolution or a large size (say, a magazine cover), you'll need to be extraordinarily precise, however.

Light and Shadows

Another common mistake in compositing is integrating two images that have different lighting. For example, in Figure 22.25, a clear blue sky in the early afternoon was taken out and ominous clouds inserted. This is perfectly acceptable, but the shadows on the ground and the lighting on the fountain suggest that it is actually a sunny day.

Figure 22.25
Although this image could well be meteorologically possible, especially in the Northeast, the lighting on the fountain and the grass doesn't jibe with the sky.

Another problem involves shadows. In Figure 22.26, a shadow was added in an attempt to achieve realism. The layer with the horses was duplicated, the horses selected and filled with black, and then a Gaussian Blur filter was applied. The Edit, Transform, Skew command made it look a bit more "shadowy." However, in this case the shadow works against realism because it is falling in the opposite direction as all the other shadows.

Fortunately, this problem can be easily fixed by selecting Edit, Transform, Flip Vertical and then Edit, Transform, Skew to more closely approximate the other shadows (see Figure 22.27).

Figure 22.26
Unless this planet has two suns, these shadows conflict with each other.

Figure 22.27
Edit, Transform, Skew can be used to make the added shadows more closely approximate the ones that are already there.

Another problem you may notice is that the added horse and jockeys were photographed under different lighting conditions than the street. To fix that, make the horse layer active, draw a selection marquee around the horses, and adjust the levels, curves, brightness, contrast, and so on until the lighting looks right. There are no hard and fast rules—basically, you're just eyeballing it until you think it looks good.

Perspective

It's usually obvious when the perspectives of a source and destination image clash. For example, in Figure 22.28, the attempt at compositing shrubbery into the image of a shrubless house is less than successful, as the shrubbery is oriented more or less horizontally, and the yard is at an angle.

You can easily fix this problem with the Edit, Transform, Rotate command (see Figure 22.29).

Caution

It may not always be possible to solve clashing perspective issues with rotating. Yes, in some cases, using Transform, Distort or Skew might help, but remember, when you rotate or distort, you aren't adding any information. Often, to get an image into the proper perspective, you need to see part of the scene or object that just isn't visible. Refer to Figure 20.17 (see Chapter 20, "Image Cropping, Resizing, and Sharpening") for an example. Yes, the perspective of the arch is correct, but the archway beneath now seems to run at an angle.

Figure 22.28
The composited shrubs are oriented at a different angle than the yard where they are meant to go.

Figure 22.29
Rotating the shrubs helps restore some of the clashing perspective. Aligning the edge of the transform bounding box with the street helps ensure that everything stays aligned accurately. However, notice that the left shrub is blocking the driveway—and appears to be growing out of the pavement!

Depth of Focus

Another common problem with compositing is combining images that have different levels of focus. For example, the destination image is slightly blurred, and the source image is razor sharp. One way of solving this problem is to use the Blur or Sharpen commands on the source image to more closely approximate the focus of the destination image (or vice versa).

Details and Basic Physics

The upshot of all compositing is naturalness, and small details can make or break an image. For example, in Figure 22.30, a piece of meat is being used as a type of removable storage media. It was accomplished by taking a royalty-free image of a roast beef, isolating one of the slices, rotating it, and overlaying it on top of a press release photo of a CD-R drive, so it appears as though it's being inserted into the drive. However, notice one flaw: Although at least half an inch of meat is inserted in the drive, the plastic door where the disc caddy gets inserted is still fully closed.

Figure 22.30
A nice composite spoiled by at least one flaw—the drive door is still closed.

Remember, as a fictional starship engineer once said: "You canna change the laws of physics." As you've seen, Photoshop lets you do just that—so you need to be on your guard.

COLLAGING

Perhaps the opposite of "natural" compositing is collaging—the combination of objects and images. Collages can be collections of mementos and souvenirs or the "artistic" combination of elements, such as leaves, flowers, shapes, and photographs. Although most of this chapter has concentrated on compositing images to make the end result look as realistic as possible, realism is less of a concern in collaging. Basically, you're trying to make it look artistic.

Simple collages can contain only one layer. Indeed, all the collaging may have already been done on, say, the scanner bed—you arrange a group of objects on your scanner and then scan it. If you're adept at making prescan adjustments, you might not even need to do any postscan tweaking. You can just save it and/or print it, if desired.

Complex collages can use as many layers as Photoshop can support and the full arsenal of your Photoshop skills—blending modes, layer styles, layer interactions, filters, as well as just about every other aspect of image control and manipulation. A relatively simple collage is seen in Figure 22.31.

Several brochures and newsletters were scanned and the appropriate sections cropped out. Each separate piece was then dragged into a new layer over a map background. Edit, Free Transform was used to rotate and resize the individual pieces, and drop shadows were added as layer styles.

The ability to easily composite and collage different images together in programs such as Photoshop has spawned much of the whole digital art movement.

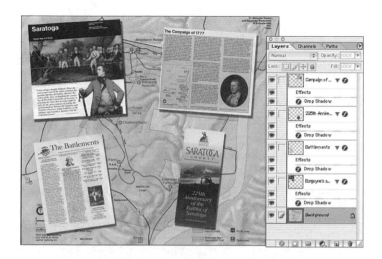

Figure 22.31
A simple collage was created out of several scans and layering them over a background image. Drop shadows were added with layer styles.

22

Is It Art Yet?

In the 1990s, the advent of inexpensive flatbed scanners, good-quality digital cameras, desktop computers powerful enough to work with large image files, and large-format printing created a new art movement. Called "digital art," presumably to differentiate it from nondigital art, the movement began in several small niches around the country. One of the first major proponents was musician Graham Nash, whose Manhattan Beach, California printmaking studio, Nash Editions, was a pilgrimage site for many early digital artists. Digital art was pooh-poohed by the more traditional art cognoscenti (but then, even photography was derided as an artistic medium when it was invented), but thankfully it has become more recognized as a legitimate form of expression—as if there can be an illegitimate form of expression.

Computer and graphics publications began holding digital art contests, sponsored by hardware and software vendors, and there is no shortage of lectures, seminars, tutorials, classrooms, and exhibitions. Three digital art pioneers—Dorothy Simpson Krause, Bonny Lhotka, and Karin Schminke—founded the Digital Atelier, "a printmaking studio for the 21st century," and tour the world demonstrating their techniques and exhibiting their often breathtaking work. They have experimented with all sorts of combinations of traditional and digital techniques—from printing on clothing and canvas to "digital frescoes" to lenticular imaging (images that change depending on the angle they're viewed at). Check them out at www.digitalatelier.com.

PHOTOSHOP IN FOCUS

Try your hand at compositing. Find two images—one that has a person or an object, such as a car, in it (call it the source image), and another one that is a background, such as a yard, a street, a national park, or the surface of the moon (call it the destination image). You're going to place the subject of the source image into the destination image.

1. In the source image, use the Pen tool to draw a detailed path around the edges of the subject you want to isolate.

2. Zoom in and finesse the path, adding or deleting anchor points as needed so that it conforms closely to the outline of the subject you're trying to isolate.

3. When the path is to your liking, open the Paths palette and choose Make Selection from the Paths palette menu. (If you want, you can also save the path by using the New Path command.)

4. Then drag the selection onto the destination image. How does it look? If the source image is too big, make sure its layer is active, and choose Edit, Transform, Scale. Position the pointer over a corner handle and drag toward the center of the image. Be sure to hold down the Shift key as you drag to maintain the proper aspect ratio. When the size is correct, double-click inside the bounding box to apply the transformation.

5. If the source image is too small, repeat step 4 but drag the corner handle outward to scale the new image up. Is the result a large pixellated blob? Or is it still usable?

6. Check for other compositing problems. Are any source image isolation errors, such as stray pixels from the original background, included in the selection? If so, select the Eraser tool, pick an appropriate brush size (one that has a diffuse edge works better than one with a hard edge), and gently start removing the stray pixels.

7. If the composited elements have edges that are too distinct, select the source image, choose the Select, Feather command, and feather the edges by a few pixels.

Try this procedure using different selection techniques. For example, use Select, Color Range to isolate the subject in the source image. Alternatively, switch to the Clone Stamp tool and try painting the subject of the source image into the destination.

FROM THE NAPP HELP DESK

National Association of Photoshop Professionals

The National Association of Photoshop Professionals (NAPP) offers e-mail assistance to its members. Here is some advice from the NAPP Help Desk related to issues in this chapter.

Standardizing the Source

In the Options Bar, the Clone Stamp tool offers a check box labeled "Aligned." What's the difference between aligned and non-aligned cloning?

The difference is where the Clone Stamp tool finds the source pixels on the second and subsequent drags. You (Option-click) [Alt+click] to set the source point, and then drag the Clone Stamp tool. When you start dragging again, either the source point maintains its distance and direction as originally set (aligned), or the source returns to the original spot (non-aligned).

22

Inches Versus Pixels

I'm a bit confused about how you figure out whether two images are the same size. What's the deal with resolution and zoom and all that?

To simplify, always look at an image's pixel dimensions. Image, Image Size shows you both the pixel dimensions and the print size (in inches or centimeters) of an image. Remember that images are created of pixels, not inches. Regardless of print dimensions and resolution, when compositing images, you're working with pixels and pixels alone. And when compositing images, think not only of the image size, but also of the pixel size of the selection you're moving. If you're adding a person from one image to another, make sure that the original is the appropriate *pixel size* to fit in the destination image.

PHOTOSHOP, IMAGEREADY, AND THE WEB

IN THIS PART

PHOTOSHOP, IMAGEREADY, AND WEB DESIGN

by Jeff Foster

IN THIS CHAPTER

23

WEB PAGE DESIGN BASICS

Good Web page design is subjective to the person visiting your site. What one person might like and appreciate, such as nice graphics, animations, or Flash, can drive another person away, and some people might find a sterile information-only site unprofessional. We will not be showing you how to create a great Web site, but will help guide you to ask the right questions of your client and yourself so that you can discover the qualities you need to express in your site's design. Later on in this chapter, you'll learn how to create some basic design elements to enhance your Web site designs.

Several applications are available to help you create a Web page, but they won't necessarily help you create a good design. No application can automatically do that for you, but it does take a good application to help you create your site's design content. Understanding what your viewers want and expect to see is the start to a good design. Keeping them there and enticing them to continue clicking through the site depend on clean navigation, layout, and design.

⇨ *When creating a Web site, you use separate programs for separate jobs. Where do Photoshop and ImageReady fall? See "Using the Proper Tool" in the NAPP Help Desk section at the end of this chapter.*

Web page design has evolved several times in its very short history. In the beginning, there wasn't any design—just pages full of text and content. When the Internet started to catch on, designers and artists jumped in and tried to outdo each other with beautiful designs that were fun to look at and explore, but had little information to offer and took forever to download. Adjustments were made for download times and businesses were encouraged to provide "just the facts," and the seesaw effect between design and function have played a role in Web site construction ever since.

An interesting Web site for going back in history (well, all the way back to 1996, anyway) includes about 100 terabytes of archived "snapshots" in time on the Internet. It's called the Wayback Machine (www.archive.org; see Figure 23.1) and is hosted by the Internet Archive in San Francisco, a non-profit organization. You can see the progression of almost any site published since 1996, although it can be a bit embarrassing. It's hard to look at sites you thought were so cool, but by today's standards are really bad!

There's no shame in creating a beautifully designed Web site that's easy to navigate and gives visitors instant access to the information they came to see. Small pieces of graphic elements and animations or rollovers can be included to keep viewers' interest without interfering with the site's purpose and navigation.

For great design tips and guidance or a chance to get a full-blown education on Web design, visit Lynda Weinman's site (www.lynda.com; see Figure 23.2). Lynda is a professional designer, trainer, and author of several technical and Web design books and training programs, and a fellow speaker at NAPP's Photoshop World Conferences.

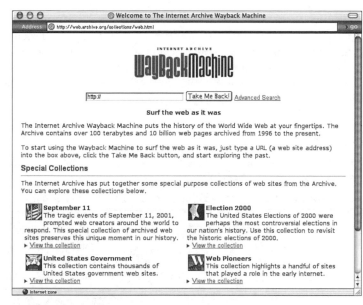

Figure 23.1
Get a blast from the past at the Wayback Machine and see how Web design has changed over the years.

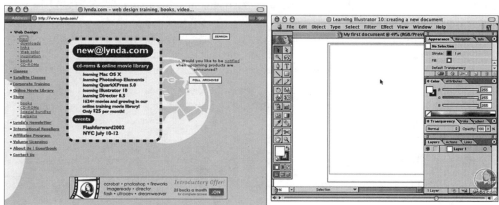

Figure 23.2
Get useful tips and tricks or study in an online design course at Lynda.com.

Know Your Audience

Making your site look "cool" is the last thing you need to worry about. Don't even think about your Web site's design until you fully understand who your audience is and why they should care about your site. You won't be able to reach them with your opening page design or subsequent pages until you know why they will be visiting your site in the first place.

I approach Web site design as I always have any form of production: I start with the desired end results and work backward. After you've established the end results, you can target your design, layout, and site functionality. At this point, you'll need to create a *sitemap* (a diagram of the site's pages and links) so that you know how to approach the overall look and feel of your site. Knowing what the structure of the site will be, including navigation, subdirectories, links, databases, or special functionality, helps you decide how to lay out your site.

What Will Bring Visitors to Your Site?

We've all learned that the "build it and they will come" approach to building a Web-based business didn't work, despite sock puppet mascots and free home delivery.

In addition to any advertising or marketing you have for your site, you need to spend some time "under the hood" of your HTML and research the most effective meta tags (keywords and descriptions) to insert in your HTML header information. Take your time selecting the keywords, and carefully submit your site to the top 10 search engines. Read their submission guidelines, and try to incorporate them into your meta tags. Don't bother with services that offer to submit your site to thousands of search engines for just a few dollars. They are simply a waste of time and money and will only bring you more unsolicited e-mail. Be careful with your choices, especially if you are submitting for a commercial site. Yahoo! now charges a $300 annual listing fee for all commercial sites. It used to charge about $99 to "speed things up," with no guarantee that your site would be listed in *any* category (but it usually was). Personal and noncommercial sites are still free to submit, but might take a long time to get categorized. Most of the top search sites now use intelligent "robot" technology that goes out and searches for site pages that match keywords and descriptions.

Strategic alliances with partner sites or affiliates give you banner click-throughs and links, which can be swapped (by hosting banner ads or click-throughs on each other's sites), or you can often purchase ad space on affiliate sites.

What Will Keep Them There?

Determining what keeps visitors at your site is how you measure the success of your layout and design. If you have effectively planned, designed, and built your site, visitors will spend more time navigating through the site, instead of leaving and looking elsewhere.

Most service providers that host your Web site can provide a system to track the traffic on your site. You can see who is visiting each page and how many click-throughs you are getting for each page on your site. From this information, you can measure how long typical visitors stay interested in your site and what their click-through habits are. Could they be missing the most important information you are providing at your site because it is poorly designed? Is your site laid out so that navigation is sensible and easy to follow?

If you have a shallow site with much of the information only a couple of clicks away, visitors tend to stick around longer to find the information they've come to your Web site for. This type of layout is preferred unless you have a huge Web site that requires many levels and layers of navigation. Remember, the fewer clicks to get where you need to go, the better.

Here's where you need to stop and spend a little time at Vincent Flanders' Web Pages That Suck (www.webpagesthatsuck.com; see Figure 23.3). Vincent offers advice on how to avoid making mistakes in Web site design by pointing out poorly designed pages. He also discusses common mistakes that good designers often make on even the highest profile Web sites, such as "Mystery Meat Navigation"—those irritating hidden rollovers and menu items that aren't labeled, so you have to hunt for them.

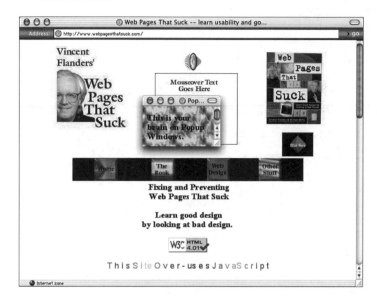

Figure 23.3
Vincent Flanders's site teaches good Web page design through examples of poor design habits.

A few mistakes to avoid when designing your site:

- Confusing or "hidden" navigation

- Animation overkill or Flash abuse

- TMI (Too Much Information) on the opening page

- Missing page titles or Alt tags on rollovers

- Forcing the visitor to download weird plug-ins

- Tons of multicolored HTML text

- Huge graphics or animations on the home page

- Busy backgrounds or annoying tiles

- Cursor-chasing DHTML or JavaScript text

- Being vague in the message or purpose of your site

- Outdated schedules, dates, or information

- Automatic pop-up windows and ads

- MIDI music on your page

A few items to remember when designing your site:

- Get to the point.

- Use clean, easy-to-follow navigation.

- Make tasteful choices with animation or Flash.

- Keep your site visually interesting.

- Make sure to give each page a title.

- Add Alt tags to images wherever possible.

- Keep home pages lean and quick to load.

- Update your site regularly—keep up to date.

- Keep advertising, links, and banners to a minimum.

- Keep frames and window sizes below 800×600.

- Don't *ever* put MIDI music on a page!

- Spell check and proof everything on every page.

What Is Your Web Site's Call to Action?

Are you selling a product or service on your site? Are you requesting visitors to fill out a question-naire or an online form? Are you creating a *portal* site that links to other sites or groups of sites? How are you getting visitors to follow through with that purchase, form, or click-through?

If your site is too cluttered and busy or too "deep"—meaning they have to go on a safari to find the information they need and have several click-throughs—chances are they will give up and leave. It's fine to have a deep site for reference materials or catalogs of content, but avoiding visitors' frustra-tion is all the more reason to organize the site before you start to build it. You want visitors to get to what they're looking for as fast as possible. Regardless of connection speed, people don't have the patience to wait around or go hunting for information. They'll leave without finding what they came for, or they might see only a small representation of what your site is trying to say and miss critical information for making a decision.

If you must include a large catalog of items or content, offer visitors a site search engine to help clean up the design from the outset. It's better to go a bit deep than to bombard the visitor with a ton of decisions upfront.

Unless you're planning on competing with the likes of eBay, Yahoo!, or Amazon.com, don't try to make your site look like theirs by cramming every item on your site on the first page. Information overload or TMI (Too Much Information) scares away visitors before they have a chance to take action at your site.

Why Will They Come Back or Even Refer Others to Your Site?

Are your visitors requesting more information? Are they telling you how helpful or enjoyable your site has been? They might not tell you directly, but you will know if they make a purchase or click through. Better yet, your Web site traffic picks up because visitors are creating a "buzz" about your site. Your effectiveness can be measured in volume and click-throughs on each portion of your site. If a particular section isn't critical and isn't getting visitor click-throughs, prune it! If it serves no purpose other than to provide redundant information or is unnecessary to the site overall, it's just dead weight and only adds to clutter and confusion on your site.

It doesn't hurt to entice your visitors to fill out an evaluation or a short questionnaire and reward them for taking the time to do so. People will be honest with you; even if you are rewarding them, they aren't afraid to tell you the truth about their experiences at your site. Listen to them and don't hesitate to make alterations quickly.

CREATING SEAMLESS BACKGROUND IMAGES

There are several ways to create background textures and tiles for your Web page, using a source image or some simple pixels precisely painted to create a seamless vertical tile. Although there are Photoshop plug-ins to create seamless tiled images to form a background pattern, many plug-ins create patterns that are too busy to be used as a simple texture. You might want to create the illusion of a smooth solid sidebar running down your page, which you can do with only a few tileable pixels. Seamless tiled textures and patterns don't need to be used as the entire background, however. You can choose to fill just a panel or sidebar with a tiled image texture, such as bricks, rocks, wood, or metal, to create volume without forcing the visitor to download a huge image file.

If you want to create a quick but undistinguishable seamless tile from a source image, simply use the Pattern Maker as shown in the following section.

To learn more about the Pattern Maker, **see** "Pattern Maker Fundamentals," **p. 601**, in Chapter 19, "Extract, Liquify, and the Pattern Maker."

Create a Seamless Tile from a Photographic Image

Start with a simple photo of a group of objects, such as stones, a brick wall, cloth and paper textures, beans, candy, pasta, whatever. You can create a small repeating image with an organic seamless tiling effect, as though you are looking at a huge brick wall or into a large barrel of coffee beans. You can also take an image that wouldn't easily be tiled, but through cut and paste and the Clone Stamp tool, you can create a larger tile.

In this first example, I wanted an organic object tiling effect using the coffee beans image shown in Figure 23.4, a stock photo image from PhotoSpin (www.photospin.com). You can also find this image in the PhotoSpin folder on the CD-ROM, if you want to follow along with this exercise.

Figure 23.4
Select an organic object group image, such as coffee beans.

Apply the Offset filter by choosing Filter, Other, Offset, and select Horizontal and Vertical offsets that are approximately one half of the total pixel dimension. In this example, the original image was 300×300 pixels, so the offset is adjusted to 150×150 (see Figure 23.5). Make sure the Wrap Around radio button and Preview check box are selected so that you can see where the dividing lines are located. These lines need to be edited out with the Clone Stamp tool.

Figure 23.5
Using the Offset filter enables you to see the image edges inside out.

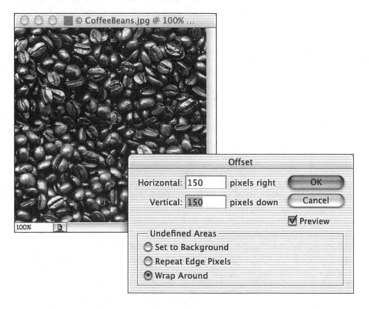

Select the Clone Stamp tool and a hard-edged brush just large enough to copy portions of the grouped objects (in this case, the coffee beans). The objective is to carefully clone over the dividing lines that cross in the middle of the image, as shown in Figure 23.6. Be careful not to clone outside the image or near the edge to avoid creating another hard line when the image tiles.

Figure 23.6
Use the Clone Stamp tool to copy the grouped objects over the dividing lines in the center of the image.

After you are satisfied with the cloned objects, select the Offset filter again to view the tile in its original format, and check for any errors you might have inadvertently created with the Clone Stamp tool around the edges. If your image tile is completed, select Edit, Define Pattern to save the finished tile (see Figure 23.7).

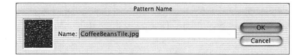

Figure 23.7
Save the finished tile in the Preset Library.

Test the seamlessness of your new tile image in a larger file—at least 300% larger than your tile. Use the Edit, Fill command, and select your new tile in the Custom Pattern pop-menu, as shown in Figure 23.8.

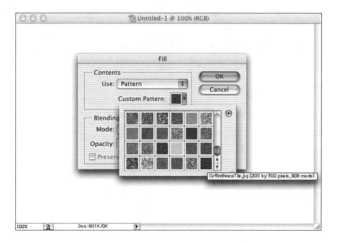

Figure 23.8
Select your new tile image in the Custom Pattern pop-up menu.

After you've filled the new file with the pattern you created, take note of any areas that don't look quite right. The end result should be a tiled image that looks like one larger image without repeating patterns (see Figure 23.9).

Figure 23.9
Fill a larger file with the new tile pattern to see how the edges blend.

Create Small Seamless Tiles That Look Huge

You can create backgrounds composed of tiny tile strips that blend vertically or horizontally to create an illusion that they are huge graphic image files. These tiles (or "micro tiles") are usually made up of a single row of horizontally placed pixels and are much longer than you need for the width of your Web site.

This example is a long sidebar with a beveled edge and drop shadow. Start with a new file 1 pixel high and about 1200 pixels wide. Turn on the rulers and set a guide about 2 inches in from the left side. Zoom in on the left side of the image (see Figure 23.10).

Figure 23.10
Create a 1-pixel-high file and zoom in as far as possible.

Create a new layer, and use a 3-pixel hard-edged brush to paint in the area from the left up to the 2-inch guide. Select a new layer style for the top layer and add a drop shadow. Position the drop shadow angle to 180 degrees, leaving the other options at their default values. Next, select the Bevel and Emboss style and leave the lighting options at the default settings and angles by selecting the Use Global Light check box (see Figure 23.11).

Save the pattern by selecting Edit, Define Pattern and give it a name for the Preset Manager Pattern Library (see Figure 23.12).

To test the tile pattern, create a new file approximately 400 pixels high and the width of your tile. Use the Edit, Fill command, and select your new tile in the Custom Pattern pop-up menu, as shown in Figure 23.13.

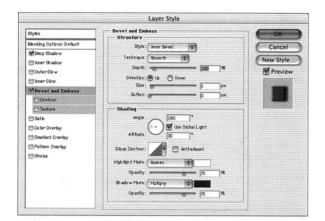

Figure 23.11
Add layer style effects to create a drop shadow and embossing on the sidebar.

Figure 23.12
While zoomed in, it's hard to see what the effect might look like when it's tiled and viewed at 100%.

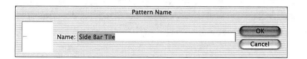

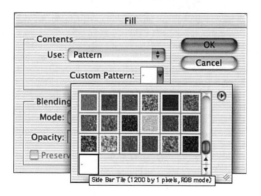

Figure 23.13
Select the saved tile pattern from the Preset Manager Pattern Library.

To use this image as a background in a Web page, use Save for Web to create a GIF file. Although your final saved tile pattern is only 1 pixel by 1200 pixels and should be less than 10KB, it appears to be a smooth large graphic file when tiled in the background (see Figure 23.14). Because the file is so small, the background has a chance to fully load before any of the foreground images, so the Web page visitor will see it integrate seamlessly with your site design.

➡️ *Unsure about the theory of tiled backgrounds? See "Auto Replication" in the NAPP Help Desk section at the end of this chapter.*

23

Figure 23.14
The tiled image file is smooth and
seamless and looks much larger
than only 1 pixel high.

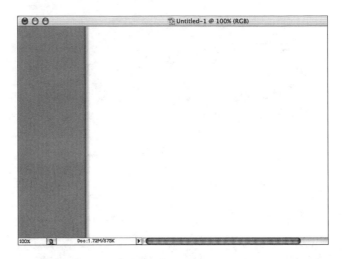

IMAGE MAPS

Image maps are invisible areas defined to overlay an image on a Web page so that you can assign links or rollovers. This is made possible without having to chop up images into small pieces and place them inside a table. In addition, you can select odd-shaped polygons or ovals as definable rollover areas. The only drawbacks are the lack of interactivity during a rollover action and the requirement that the image beneath the map be a GIF.

Open an image file in ImageReady and select an image map tool from the Toolbox (see Figure 23.15). For this example, I'm using the Polygon Image Map tool.

Figure 23.15
Select an image map tool from
the ImageReady Toolbox to begin
creating an image map.

Click and draw a polygon (or a rectangle or ellipse) around an area of the image you want to define as a *hot spot*—the area that will be active when rolled over. Add the URL, Target, and Alt tags in the appropriate fields for the defined map (see Figure 23.16).

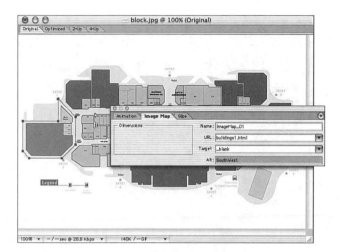

Figure 23.16
Define the rollover areas with the image map tool and enter text for the map's name and tags.

You can fine-tune the outlines by using the Image Map Select tool, shown in Figure 23.17. Take care that none of the defined regions overlap, which causes conflicts in the Web browser.

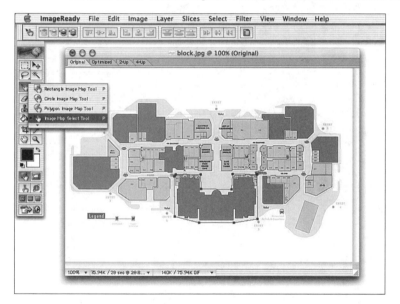

Figure 23.17
Use the Image Map Select tool to make adjustments to the defined regions of the image map.

Preview the image map in your preferred browser from inside ImageReady. You will be able to roll over and click on any of the defined map regions (if the URL links are active). You will also be able to see the HTML that is generated to create the map (see Figure 23.18).

To customize the image map's code and functionality, you can make changes in the Output Settings dialog box. Choose File, Output Settings, Image Maps to open it. The settings determine how your image map functions, whether from the server or client side. The default setting is what you should use in most cases (see Figure 23.19).

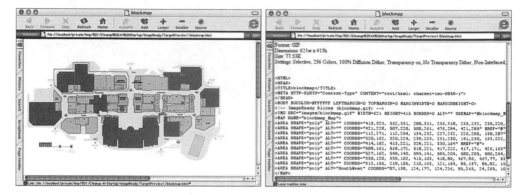

Figure 23.18
Preview the image map in a Web browser to see how all the defined map areas function and to preview the HTML code.

Figure 23.19
Customize the image map's functionality by using the Output Settings dialog box.

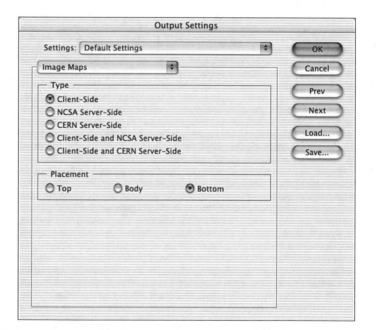

ADDING ROLLOVERS AND ANIMATIONS TO THE PAGE

The basic rollover has only two stages: *normal* and *over*. This has been the standard in human interface design studies in the past decade, with the addition of the third stage, or *click down*, which gives immediate feedback to the user, confirming that the action or command has been accepted.

Simply put, an *animated rollover* is an area of a Web page that contains a hot spot with a JavaScript action attached to it. This hot spot reacts to a mouse cursor moving over the area, which causes an action or a reaction, such as a text pop-up, a rollover replacement graphic, or an animation playing.

Normally, these hot spots are actually cells in a table, with the rollover scripts applied to individual cells. (A *table* is defined in the Web page's HTML and includes two or more distinct and adjacent areas of the page. Tables are often used to ensure the placement of elements on a page and are automatically generated in Photoshop and ImageReady for sliced images.) The mouse rolls over a cell, which triggers the JavaScript code to quickly replace the graphic in that cell (or any other cell on the page). The code can even replace graphics when the mouse button is depressed or released, in addition to invoking an action command, such as opening another window or jumping to another page.

Imagine a typical rollover "button" that looks like it has a matte plastic surface in its dormant state; when the mouse rolls over it, it turns shiny, and the letters on it light up. Depress the button and the graphic changes to a "pressed down" state, which pops back up when the mouse is depressed, as the example shows in Figure 23.20. This process happens so quickly that the visitor sees only the animation sequence of the actions and experiences what might happen in the real world when pressing a button on a machine (well, except for the "finger detection" mode, that is!).

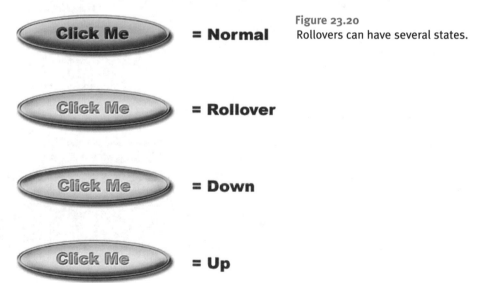

Figure 23.20
Rollovers can have several states.

ImageReady has features that make it quick and easy to create interactive JavaScript rollovers, although true HTML "code warriors" scoff at the amount of code it spits out in doing so. For the examples in this chapter, just the default ImageReady code will be created to simplify the examples.

▷ To learn about the settings and preferences used for HTML when saving files, **see** Chapter 24, "Save for Web and Image Optimization," **p. 725**. For help cleaning up the HTML that ImageReady creates, **see** "Managing Your HTML," **p. 783**, in Chapter 25, "ImageReady Basics."

Creating Basic Rollovers

Creating a basic rollover is quite simple in ImageReady. You create the normal and over states of the rollover buttons, text, or graphics first on layers in Photoshop (see Figure 23.21).

Figure 23.21
The different rollover states are created on layers in Photoshop and turned on as required.

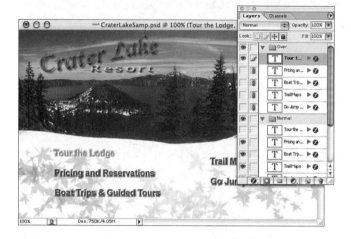

⇨ *Not comfortable with the concept of rollovers? See "Rollover Theory" in the NAPP Help Desk section at the end of this chapter.*

Jump to ImageReady and use the Slice tool to create boxes around the areas that will have a rollover (see Figure 23.22). These areas will actually be cells in a table that have JavaScript code assigned to swap the images in the appropriate cells.

Figure 23.22
Create cells in a table by using the Slice tool where the rollovers are positioned.

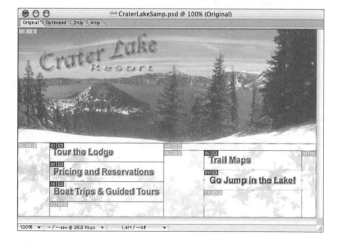

Locate your rollover slices in the Rollovers palette in ImageReady and select New Rollover State from the palette menu. This command creates a rollover state just beneath the slice in the Rollovers palette (see Figure 23.23). Change the action of the rollover state with the palette menu or a contextual menu.

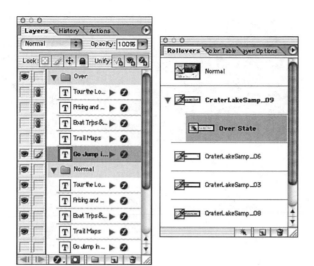

Figure 23.23
Add a rollover state in ImageReady and select the rollover action from the palette menu or a contextual menu.

Make the appropriate layers visible on the rollover state (for the basic rollover, you change only the visible graphic elements in the selected slice). In addition to changing the selected slice name, you can add the link URL and target tag in the Slice palette (see Figure 23.24).

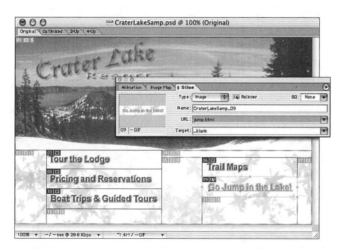

Figure 23.24
Set the rollover state, name, and URL in the Slice palette.

After you've assigned all the active slice rollover states, you can preview the rollovers and make adjustments or reassign rollover states. Click the Preview button in the toolbar, and the guides and slice lines disappear so that you can actively roll over the links (see Figure 23.25).

23

Figure 23.25
Click the Preview button in the
toolbar to test the rollovers without leaving ImageReady.

Adding Animation to your Page

Creating animations (animated GIFs) in ImageReady is easy, but be prepared to cut up a file if you
plan to create the animation with the whole page. Even if you create the animation within the
boundaries of a slice, the whole page is saved as one big animated GIF file.

➡️ *For more information about ImageReady and animations, **see** Chapter 25, "ImageReady Basics,"
p. 763.*

A simple animation can be created with a single floating layer moving about the screen. The animation I created for this Web site design composition shows a car rushing in with a blur and coming to
a stop, and then taking off again in a loop. I used a severely motion-blurred image layer for the quick
motion, a slightly blurred image layer for coming to a stop and taking off, and a clear image layer for
when the car is stopped. The layer in motion is made visible, and the other layers are hidden (see
Figure 23.26).

Figure 23.26
The first frame of animation
shows up when you jump from
Photoshop to ImageReady.

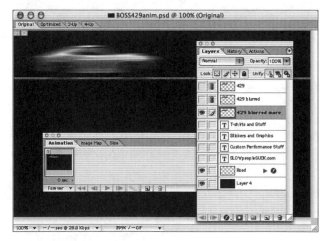

Move the layer in motion to the starting position of the animation sequence. This becomes frame 1 of your animation. If you will be moving the layer linearly, create a new frame in the Animation palette menu and position the layer at the end point of motion (see Figure 23.27).

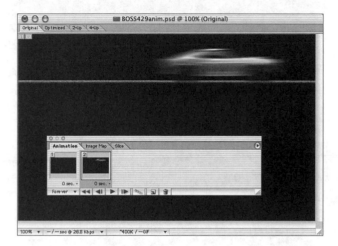

Figure 23.27
Prepare a linear animation by setting the first and last frame positions.

Select both frames in the Animation palette and choose Tween from the palette menu. Set the number of frames to add between the first and last frames, and ImageReady automatically calculates each frame's movement and opacity (see Figure 23.28).

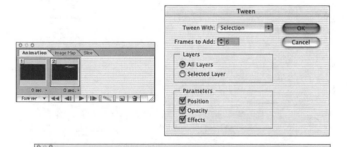

Figure 23.28
Select the Tween command to add frames between the first and last frames of an animation.

To preview your animation, you can simply click the Play button in the Animation palette, which has a very slow playback but at least shows you the animation path. To get a more accurate example of the animation's timing, it's best to click the Preview in Default Browser button on the toolbar. The animation shows up in the browser window (see Figure 23.29).

If you prefer to create a slice around the animation and save only the slice (or cell) with the animation in it, select the slice and choose File, Save Optimized As. Choose the Selected Slices option to save only the animated GIF image (see Figure 23.30). In the Format pop-up menu, you can choose only the image, if you prefer, or include the HTML code.

Figure 23.29
Preview your animation in the default Web browser window.

Figure 23.30
Save only the slice containing the animation or include the HTML code for the page and table.

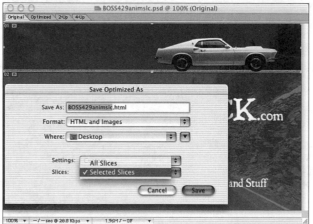

PHOTOSHOP IN FOCUS

HTML, the basic language of the Internet, is actually nothing more than text. The Web browser reads the text, interprets it, and displays the content graphically in the browser window.

It's certainly possible to be a great Web designer without writing a single line of HTML yourself, using such tools as ImageReady and GoLive to create Web pages. However, if you've never worked directly with HTML, it doesn't hurt to take a little peek.

1. Open ImageReady and start a new document. It need not be large—say, 100×100 pixels—and should have a white background.

2. Use the Paintbrush tool with a 13-pixel hard-edged brush to draw a single vertical black line in the middle of the image.

3. Click the New Layer button at the bottom of the Layers palette.

4. Use the same brush to draw a horizontal black line across the middle of the image.

5. Using the technique described earlier in this chapter, create a simple rollover. For the Normal state, have only the background layer visible. For the Over state, show both layers.

6. Use the File, Preview In menu command. Select Internet Explorer if available. If not, preview in any available browser. You'll see that this simple graphic is, in and of itself, a complete stand-alone Web page.

7. If the source code, the HTML, is not visible in the window, use the browser's View, Source menu command (or the comparable command for your browser).

8. HTML uses *tags* to identify the beginning and end of specific sections of the code. Locate <HTML>, which indicates the beginning of the information for the Web browser.

9. Scroll down and find the tag </HTML>. The addition of the slash indicates the end of the section.

10. Find <HEAD> and </HEAD>. They are the beginning and end tags for the Web page header, sort of the administrative information that's included.

11. Identify the actual "meat" of this one-graphic Web page by finding <BODY> and </BODY>. If you're not at all familiar with HTML, this is a little different. Quite a few pieces of information can be included directly in the <BODY> tag. (Look for <BODY rather than <BODY>.)

12. Look at the information within the <BODY> tag. The image's background color (BGCOLOR) is white. The hexadecimal equivalent is FFFFFF. The image is not offset from the Web page, so margins are set to zero.

13. Close the browser window. Close (without saving) the ImageReady file. You've now seen HTML, a Web page at its most basic form!

FROM THE NAPP HELP DESK

National Association of Photoshop Professionals

The National Association of Photoshop Professionals (NAPP) offers e-mail assistance to its members. Here is some advice from the NAPP Help Desk related to issues in this chapter.

Using the Proper Tool

Can I create a professional Web site using just Photoshop and ImageReady?

If you know HTML and are willing to do some hand-coding (writing the HTML yourself rather than having it written automatically), you can even create a Web site in Windows Notepad or the Mac TextEdit. However, Photoshop and ImageReady are designed and intended to create Web *graphics*, not Web *sites*. Certainly you can produce some rudimentary pages without trouble, even using such sophisticated elements as rollovers and animated GIFs. And Photoshop's Web Photo Gallery produces full-blown sites, complete with frames.

However, you're much better off creating Web sites by using a Web development tool, such as Adobe GoLive or Dreamweaver from Macromedia. Both programs have loyal fans, and both offer the tools you need to do the job correctly. Which one to choose? That probably should depend on your other tools. If you use Photoshop, ImageReady, and LiveMotion to create the majority of your Web graphics, you'll probably love the interoperability offered by GoLive. On the other hand, Dreamweaver's integration with its sister program Flash is also very strong.

➪ *For information on creating Web graphics that go beyond ImageReady's capabilities,* ***see*** *Appendix C, "Photoshop with LiveMotion and Flash,"* **p. 923.**

Auto Replication

How does the Web browser use a tiny little file to fill a background?

The HTML, the code that describes the Web page, lets the Web browser know to repeat the graphic image as many times as possible to completely fill the background. When an image is identified as the background, whether of a page, box, or table, the browser treats it as a repeating element.

Rollover Theory

Although I've been using Photoshop for years, I'm new to this Web graphic thing. What actually is a "rollover" and how does it work?

A *rollover* is a graphic image on a Web page that changes its appearance, depending on the location or action of the viewer's cursor. It can change when the cursor is positioned over the image, and can change again when the mouse is clicked or the mouse button released.

In ImageReady, rollovers are created from layers in the image. You put each element that has to change on a separate layer, and then show and hide the layers to change the image's appearance.

SAVE FOR WEB AND IMAGE OPTIMIZATION

IN THIS CHAPTER

GRAPHICS ON THE WEB: OVERVIEW

The World Wide Web has evolved into a visual environment. This graphic-rich environment, however, does have a number of limitations. Because the Web is presented in Hypertext Markup Language (HTML) and related computer languages, graphics must conform to certain rules. Chief among them is the restriction on which file formats can be used. A Web browser will not, for example, display a PSD or TIFF file.

Photoshop and ImageReady are state-of-the-art Web graphic production tools. You can use them to develop a wide range of Web-compatible graphics, from simple logos to rollover buttons to animations.

Remember that Photoshop and ImageReady are designed to create *graphics*, not to produce Web pages. Although it is certainly possible to produce rudimentary Web pages using only Photoshop and ImageReady, they are *not* Web development tools. Use Adobe GoLive or Macromedia Dreamweaver instead.

File Optimization and Compression

Optimization is the process of minimizing file size while protecting image quality. Smaller files download from the Web server to the visitor's computer faster, so they display onscreen quicker. The more quickly the image displays, the less disruption for the site's visitor. The balance between file size and image quality is not an exact science—there is no specific formula for optimization.

Files optimized for Web display are stripped of nonessential data. Image previews and custom icons, for example, are not saved with the file. Such data is not visible over the Web and serves to increase file size.

JPEG files use a *lossy* compression scheme. Image data is discarded to reduce file size and is re-created to display the image. The more data that is thrown away, the smaller the file size. However, the more information that must be re-created, the more likely it is that the image quality will be degraded. When a JPEG image is opened onscreen (or printed), the pixels that were deleted during compression must be restored. Because the exact color of the missing pixels is not recorded, the JPEG process estimates their color, based on surrounding pixels. The more pixels that must be re-created, the fewer original pixels available from which to estimate.

GIF and PNG (both 8-bit and 24-bit) use *lossless* compression—no data is discarded. GIF and PNG-8 file size can be further minimized by reducing the actual number of colors recorded in the file. PNG-24 has no such option.

The Role of the Web Browser

Web pages typically consist of both text and images, wrapped up in HTML so that the page can be displayed on the viewer's computer. You use a Web browser to translate that HTML and re-create the page on your screen. The HTML file contains the page's text and tells the browser where to find the images on the Web server. The two major Web browsers are Microsoft Internet Explorer and Netscape Navigator. They, and most of the lesser-used browsers, can interpret HTML and similar languages natively and can use plug-ins for additional capabilities (such as Scalable Vector Graphics). Without the Web browser, the page can't be downloaded and displayed.

(However, numerous programs, including some word processors, can efficiently display a Web page if it's been downloaded and saved to your hard drive.)

When designing and producing your Web graphics in Photoshop and ImageReady, you must take into account the capabilities of the Web browsers that your visitors are most likely to use. If your visitors or at least your target audience is likely to be using up-to-date versions of major Web browsers, you can save your graphics in a wider variety of file formats. If it's important that visitors with older browsers not be excluded from the full impact of your graphics, you should restrict yourself to JPEG and GIF.

Remember, too, that cellular telephones and personal digital assistants (PDAs) can access the Internet. PDAs typically use wireless connections and have limited color capability. Cell phones are usually limited to 1-bit color—they can display only black and white (or black and gray or green). If your target audience will be accessing your site with cell phones or PDAs, plan accordingly.

HTML and Images

Web graphics can be *sliced*—divided into subsections—and with ImageReady you can create special effects associated with the image. The image can change appearance depending on the mouse's location or behavior, and you can even create animations that play in the Web browser window.

These special attributes and behaviors require HTML code associated with the image. The HTML tells the Web browser how to handle the file and when or why to change the image's appearance. HTML can be generated for sliced images in ImageReady or Photoshop, but only ImageReady can create rollovers and animations. (The component images can be generated in Photoshop, but the special attributes must be developed in ImageReady.)

Saving HTML with Images

If the image has rollovers, is an animation, includes a special background color or background image, or will be used as a tiled background on a Web page, you must save both the image and the associated HTML. With this saving option, HTML code is generated and an .html file is saved along with a folder named (by default) Images.

To incorporate the artwork into an existing Web page, you typically must copy and paste the HTML into the appropriate section of the Web page's HTML document. The Images folder must be saved (and uploaded) with the HTML and other Web page graphics.

Color: 8-bit and 24-bit

Most modern Web browsers (and HTML) support black and white (Bitmap), Grayscale, Indexed Color, and RGB modes. CMYK images cannot be displayed in a Web browser. Indexed color and grayscale images contain a maximum of 256 different colors or shades of gray. RGB images can have millions of subtly different colors in a single image.

> When working with Adobe GoLive, you can simply add a rollover as a "component" by using Adobe's SmartObjects technology. GoLive generates the HTML automatically.

Because less color information per pixel is required in Indexed Color mode, an image of the same pixel dimensions is typically smaller and displays more quickly in a Web browser because it downloads faster.

⇨ *For a discussion of color depth, **see** "Photoshop in Focus," p. 197, in Chapter 7, "Color Theory and Practice."*

Indexed Color mode is appropriate for Web graphics that have few colors or large areas of solid color and for any image smaller than 256 pixels. RGB mode is better suited to capture and present the fine gradations of color typically found in photographs.

> Remember that, with the exception of SVG, all graphics are displayed in a Web browser window at 100% zoom—pixel for pixel—onscreen. Always preview your graphics at 100% zoom.

Resolution Versus Pixel Size

Web browsers ignore any resolution information recorded in an image. (The exception is Scalable Vector Graphics, which require a plug-in for the Web browser and cannot be created in Photoshop or ImageReady.) Images are displayed onscreen strictly according to their pixel dimensions, not their print dimensions. Consider resolution to be an instruction to the printer about how to reproduce the image on paper, not an instruction to the browser about how to reproduce the image onscreen. As you can see in Figure 24.1, graphics of the same pixel dimensions occupy the same amount of Web page, regardless of resolution.

Figure 24.1
The two images are shown in separate Internet Explorer windows.

 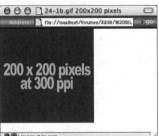

Transparency on the Web

Every graphic you create in Photoshop and ImageReady is rectangular. If you want the image to appear to be another shape, you must make parts of the rectangle transparent. The pixels will still be there; they'll just be invisible. If you want the image to fade to the background or appear with a translucent shadow, you need partially transparent pixels. When each pixel is either completely opaque or completely transparent, the transparency is said to be *hard-edged*. Images that have partially opaque pixels are said to have *variable transparency*.

The key to transparency in Web graphics is understanding the capabilities—and limitations—of the Web-compatible file formats:

- **GIF**—You can create images with hard-edged transparency and save them as GIF. The file format does not support variable transparency.

- **JPEG**—JPEG does not support transparency.

- **PNG-8**—Hard-edged transparency is handled automatically in PNG-8—simply create the image on a transparent background and save it as PNG-8. Variable transparency is simulated in PNG-8 with dithering.

- **PNG-24**—Both hard-edged and variable transparency are supported natively by PNG-24.

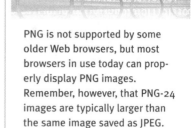

PNG is not supported by some older Web browsers, but most browsers in use today can properly display PNG images. Remember, however, that PNG-24 images are typically larger than the same image saved as JPEG.

In Figure 24.2, an image using both hard-edged and variable transparency is shown in the four major Web-related image formats.

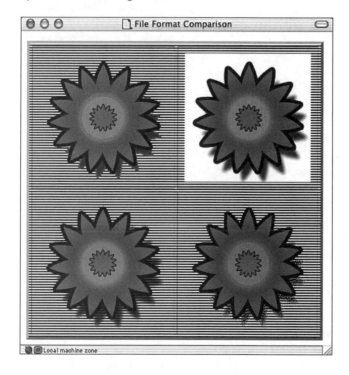

Figure 24.2
Clockwise from upper left, the images are GIF, JPEG, PNG-8, and PNG-24.

⟳ *Need to optimize as JPEG, but want transparency, too? See "Transparent JPEGs" in the NAPP Help Desk section at the end of this chapter.*

Text for Web

Text appears in a Web page one of two ways: as text, embedded in the page's HTML, or as part of an image. Generally speaking, large amounts of type are typically incorporated into the page as HTML; images that contain type often include buttons and banners.

Type displayed in a Web browser window is displayed as pixels, whether HTML or in an image. Because the type is displayed at 100% onscreen, small type is often blurry or jagged. You can use Photoshop's anti-aliasing to smooth the curves of type you incorporate into an image. Fonts with strong, even strokes reproduce more cleanly with pixels than do cursive or ornamental fonts.

➪ *Want more information on type for the Web? See "Letters by Pixel" in the NAPP Help Desk section at the end of this chapter.*

When possible, use sans serif fonts for Web graphics—their straight, even strokes reproduce more clearly in a Web browser.

Save for Web is, in some respects, a separate program within Photoshop. It even creates its own preferences. For the Mac, look for Adobe Save for Web 3.0 Prefs in the same folder as Photoshop's preferences file. In Windows, Save for Web's preferences are written to the Registry.

PHOTOSHOP'S SAVE FOR WEB

Web graphics can be created directly from Photoshop, using the Save for Web feature. You can optimize images as GIF, JPEG, PNG-8, PNG-24, and WBMP. Using Save for Web gives you far more control over the optimization process than you have creating JPEG images with the Save As command or exporting to GIF89a in earlier versions of Photoshop.

➪ *What do you need to do to prepare an image before opening Save for Web? See "Pre-Optimization" in the NAPP Help Desk section at the end of this chapter.*

Photoshop 7's Save for Web dialog box (see Figure 24.3) is resizable—you can drag the lower-right corner to increase the size of the preview area. Because this is a dialog box rather than a window, there is no "maximize" box to click.

The Window Tabs

The four tabs in the upper-left corner of the Save for Web dialog box determine the content of the preview area. You can show the original image alone, a single image that is updated to show you current optimization settings, or you can compare images. When you select 2-Up, a pair of images are visible in the preview area. By default, the original image and an optimized image are shown, although you can change the original to any optimization settings. When you choose 4-Up, you can see the original and three different optimization possibilities for comparison or see four different sets of optimization options.

Window tabs   Preview menu   Saved sets pop-up menu

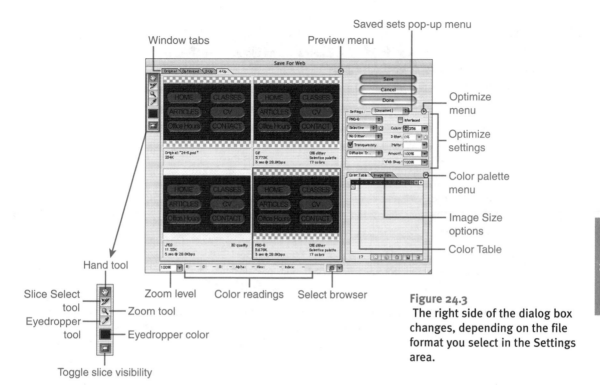

Optimize
menu

Optimize
settings

Color palette
menu

Image Size
options

Color Table

Hand tool

Slice Select
tool

Zoom level   Color readings   Select browser

Zoom tool

Eyedropper
tool

Eyedropper color

Toggle slice visibility

Figure 24.3
The right side of the dialog box changes, depending on the file format you select in the Settings area.

In both the 2-Up and 4-Up variations, you activate a pane by clicking on it. That variation's settings will be shown and can then be changed. Figure 24.3 shows the 4-Up view. When the image is wide and short, the window automatically reconfigures, as shown in Figure 24.4.

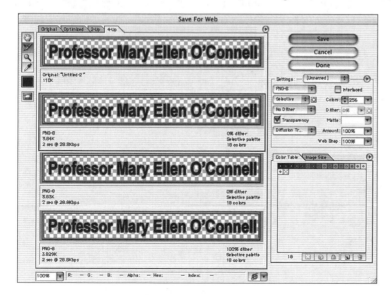

Figure 24.4
The active image is outlined in black, and its settings are visible to the right.

The Tools

To the left of the preview area, you have four tools available. In 2-Up and 4-Up views, the tools can be used only in the active pane. They function similarly to the comparable tools in Photoshop:

Although Save for Web offers preset zoom magnifications from 12.5% to 1600%, you can use the Zoom tool to zoom out as far as 1%. Remember, however, that you should always make your final evaluation of Web graphics at 100% zoom—that's how they'll be seen in a Web browser.

■ **Hand tool**—When the entire image doesn't fit in the window, click and drag with the Hand tool to reposition it. You can temporarily activate the Hand tool by holding down the Spacebar.

■ **Slice Select tool**—When the image has multiple slices, you can use the Slice Select tool to choose a slice to optimize. Different slices can have different optimization settings.

■ **Zoom tool**—Click or drag to zoom in, and (Option-click) [Alt+click] to zoom out. You can also change the magnification by using the pop-up menu to the lower left in the dialog box or with the contextual menu.

■ **Eyedropper tool**—The Eyedropper is used to select a color. You can select colors only in the active pane. If the optimization settings selected are GIF or PNG-8, the color you click on will be selected in the Color Table. For 24-bit images (JPEG and PNG-24), the color is shown only in the swatch below the Eyedropper tool on the left.

Below the tools is the color swatch, which shows the color most recently selected with the Eyedropper. (When you open Save for Web, the last selected color is still visible, even if it's not present in the current image.)

The button below the color swatch toggles slice visibility on and off. Clicking on the Slice Select tool automatically shows slices, too.

Settings and the Settings Menu

The heart of the Save for Web dialog box is the area to the right, where optimization options are selected. When in 2-Up or 4-Up mode, click on a pane or a slice, and then change the options. You can select from a menu of predefined optimization settings, or you can select a file format and choose custom settings (see Figure 24.5).

Figure 24.5
The various fields and sliders available vary from file format to file format. The Settings menu is shown to the right.

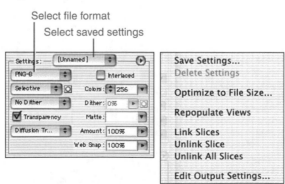

Select file format
Select saved settings

Each of the five file formats has its own options for Settings. **See** *"File Format Optimization Settings," p. 739, later in this chapter.*

You can choose custom optimization settings and save them, using the Save Settings command from the Settings menu. As long as they are saved in the Optimization Settings folder, they will appear in the Settings pop-up menu. Saved settings can also be removed from the pop-up menu by using the Delete Settings command. The file in the Optimized Settings folder is not deleted until you quit Photoshop.

The Optimize to File Size command opens the dialog box shown in Figure 24.6. You select a target file size, and Save for Web generates the most appropriate settings *for that pane*—the other panes in 2-Up and 4-Up are not affected. After you click OK, you can then further adjust the optimization settings, if desired.

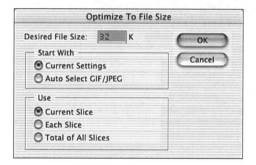

Figure 24.6
You can generate settings to optimize a single slice or an entire image to the specified size.

The Repopulate Views menu command is available only in 4-Up view. It generates a pair of new optimization settings based on the selected pane. The new options use the same file format but different options for comparison. If you've selected the Original pane and changed it to show an optimization configuration, Repopulate Views restores it to Original and replaces the other three panes with their original content.

You can select multiple slices in an image by Shift-clicking with the Slice Select tool. When more than one slice is active, you can link and unlink them with the commands in the Settings menu. Linking slices enables you to optimize them at the same time.

Perhaps the most important of the Settings menu commands is Edit Output Settings. You use this command to specify how Save for Web creates HTML, names slices, generates an image or a background, and more.

For specific information about output settings, **see** *"Editing Output Settings," p. 749, later in this chapter.*

The Color Table

The Color Table palette shows the individual colors of an 8-bit image. You can edit, delete, and shift each color. The color table is used only with GIF and PNG-8 images. You cannot directly manipulate the individual colors of images in 24-bit color.

Even in Save for Web, you can view the Slice Options dialog box. Simply double-click a slice with the Slice Select tool to change the slice's name, URL, target, message, or other options.

⇨ *For specific information about manipulating the colors of an 8-bit image,* **see** *"Working with the Color Table," p. 745, later in this chapter.*

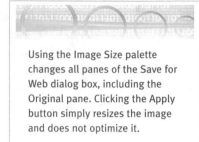

Using the Image Size palette changes all panes of the Save for Web dialog box, including the Original pane. Clicking the Apply button simply resizes the image and does not optimize it.

The Image Size Tab

Docked with the Color Table palette in Save for Web, Image Size enables you to change the size of the image directly in the dialog box (see Figure 24.7).

Figure 24.7
The Image Size palette has options comparable to those found in the Image Size dialog box (opened with the command Image, Image Size), with the exception of resolution (which isn't required for raster Web graphics).

You can specify an exact pixel dimension or a percentage. Selecting the Constrain Proportions check box automatically maintains an image's width/height ratio (as does sizing by percent). The Bicubic option in the Quality pop-up menu should be used with photographic or other continuous tone images. Nearest Neighbor is often more appropriate for interface elements and other Web graphics that have large areas of solid color or distinct edges.

The Preview Menu

Save for Web's Preview menu (see Figure 24.8), accessed through the triangle at the top right of the preview panes, determines how the image will appear in the active preview pane.

Browser Dither simulates how the image will appear on a monitor set to 8-bit color. Hide Auto Slices doesn't hide the content of the slices, just the slice lines and numbers for automatically generated slices. Each pane's color simulation can be set individually, using any of the next four options. The colors selected affect the preview in Save for Web, not the saved image. The Size/Download Time options determine what numbers will be displayed in the lower-left corner of each preview pane.

The Done, Reset, and Remember Buttons

Clicking the Done button makes a record of the current optimization settings (or the settings for the current pane in 4-Up view) and closes the dialog box. The settings are saved in the Save for Web preferences, rather than with the image file. The next time you open Save for Web with the same or a different image, the settings you recorded are used.

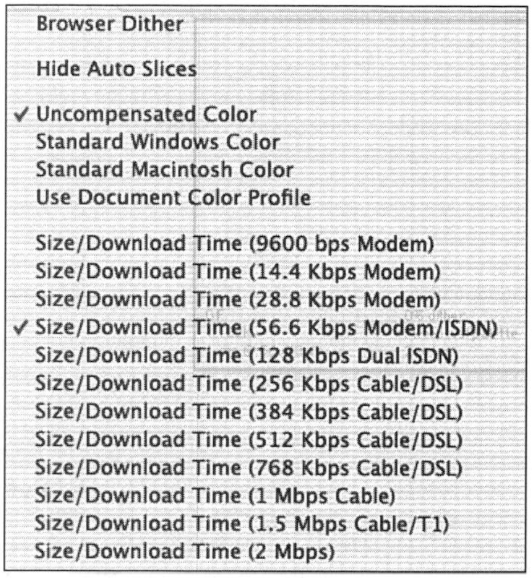

Browser Dither

Hide Auto Slices

✓ Uncompensated Color
Standard Windows Color
Standard Macintosh Color
Use Document Color Profile

Size/Download Time (9600 bps Modem)
Size/Download Time (14.4 Kbps Modem)
Size/Download Time (28.8 Kbps Modem)
✓ Size/Download Time (56.6 Kbps Modem/ISDN)
Size/Download Time (128 Kbps Dual ISDN)
Size/Download Time (256 Kbps Cable/DSL)
Size/Download Time (384 Kbps Cable/DSL)
Size/Download Time (512 Kbps Cable/DSL)
Size/Download Time (768 Kbps Cable/DSL)
Size/Download Time (1 Mbps Cable)
Size/Download Time (1.5 Mbps Cable/T1)
Size/Download Time (2 Mbps)

Figure 24.8
The Browser Dither option is not available for preview panes set to Original.

When you hold down (Option) [Alt], the Done button changes to Remember. Remember stores the current settings for that pane without closing the dialog box.

Although Save for Web doesn't support Undo, you can revert to the settings you had for the active pane or slice when the dialog box was opened (or when you last used Remember). Click in the pane or select the slice, and then hold down the (Option) [Alt] key. The Cancel button changes to Reset.

Using Channels and Layer Data to Optimize

You can use alpha channels or vector layers to govern the application of a number of options when optimizing images. Type and shape layers, or alpha channels you create in Photoshop, can form the basis for where certain settings are applied in an image. The options that can be regulated vary from file format to file format:

- **GIF**—You can use alpha channels and vector layers to regulate the application of dither, lossiness, and color reduction for GIF files.

- **JPEG**—JPEG files can use alpha channels and vector layers to control what level of compression is applied in different areas of an image.

- **PNG-8**—Dither and color reduction can be controlled with alpha channels and vector layers in PNG-8 files.

- **PNG-24**—PNG-24 cannot take advantage of alpha channels or vector layers in optimization.

- **WBMP**—What parts of an image are dithered can be controlled with an alpha channel or vector layer information when preparing images for WMBP format.

Using layer data or an alpha channel with Save for Web enables you to maintain quality in key areas of an image while sacrificing quality in other areas to reduce file size. For example, if you have a photograph of a statue in a park to prepare as a JPEG for the Web, you can use an alpha channel to maintain high quality for the statue and compress the background at a lower quality level.

24

To use layer data or an alpha channel in Save for Web, you click the mask button to the right of the appropriate field in Settings (see Figure 24.9, left). You select a check box for the type of layer data to use, or you can select the alpha channel from the Channel pop-up menu, which lists all available alpha channels.

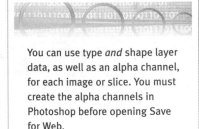

You can use type *and* shape layer data, as well as an alpha channel, for each image or slice. You must create the alpha channels in Photoshop before opening Save for Web.

An alpha channel enables you to set minimum and maximum values for the application of some options. For dithering, lossiness, and JPEG quality, you set a minimum and maximum value by using the slider in the dialog box (see Figure 24.9, bottom right). To use an alpha channel with a color reduction algorithm, you simply choose the alpha channel (see Figure 24.9, top right).

Figure 24.9
The dither, lossiness, and JPEG quality options have identical dialog boxes.

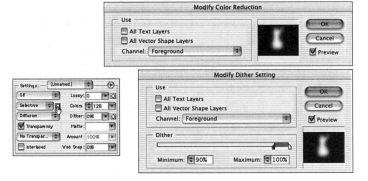

The minimum and maximum values are applied according to the location of black and white in the alpha channel, with intermediate values applied according to grays in the channel.

You can use a separate alpha channel for each setting in GIF and PNG-8, but only one channel can be used for each setting. The exception is, of course, when optimizing slices individually—you can use a different set of channels with each slice. The alpha channels are used during the application of the Save for Web settings, but not retained with the image.

OPTIMIZING IN IMAGEREADY

The basic tools for preparing images for optimization in ImageReady are the image window, the Optimize palette, the Color Table palette, and the Output Settings dialog box (see Figure 24.10). The optimized image is saved with the File, Save Optimized As command.

The Image Window

The image window has four configurations (see Figure 24.11), which you select by using the tabs at the top of the window. If you want to compare different optimization configurations head-to-head, use 4-Up. If you need to conserve screen space, one of the other tabs might better suit your needs.

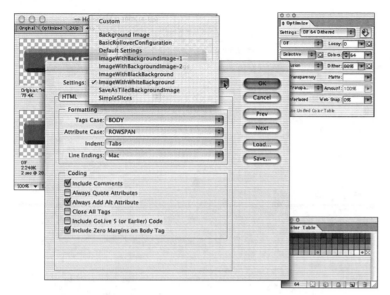

Figure 24.10
The image window (left), the Optimize palette (upper right), and the Color Table (lower right) are shown behind the Output Settings dialog box.

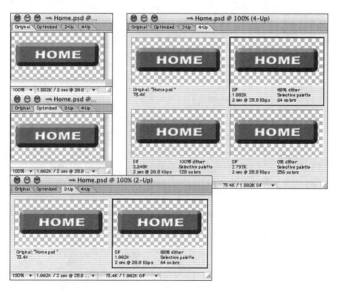

Figure 24.11
The Original and Optimized views show only one version of the image. The 2-Up configuration enables you to compare an optimized version with the original (or a version optimized differently).

The Optimize Palette

The Optimize palette fills the role of the Settings area of the Save for Web dialog box. The content of the palette varies, depending on the file format selected. Clicking the two-headed arrow in the palette's tab shows and hides portions of the palette. Click multiple times to rotate through the configurations (shown in Figure 24.12).

Figure 24.12
The various configurations for each file format are shown. The palette can also show only the tab itself, regardless of the file format.

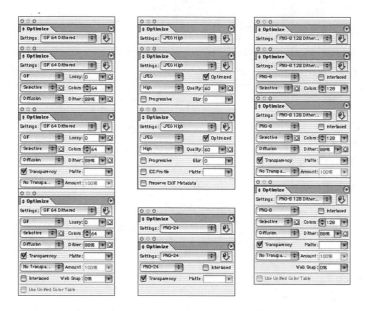

⇨ *For specific details of each format's options, **see** "File Format Optimization Settings," **p. 739**, later in this chapter.*

The Color Table Palette

The Color Table palette is used only with GIF and PNG-8 files. It is empty when working with JPEG and PNG-24 files and shows only the uneditable black and white swatches for WBMP files.

The Color Table palette can display swatches in two sizes (see Figure 24.13). If you edit colors, the large swatches might be handier—you'll be able to see the difference between the original and edited colors much better.

Figure 24.13
Change the palette's configuration by using the palette menu.

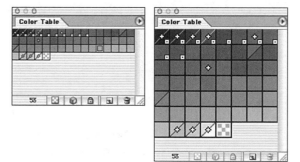

⇨ *Complete information on the Color Table palette and optimizing 8-bit images is presented later in this chapter. **See** "Working with the Color Table," **p. 745**.*

FILE FORMAT OPTIMIZATION SETTINGS

Each of the five available file formats has its own options in the Settings area of Save for Web and in ImageReady's Optimize palette. There is considerable overlap between GIF and PNG-8, so they are discussed together.

> The optimization options are nearly identical in Save for Web and ImageReady. The primary difference is the ImageReady Optimize palette's Create Droplet button. Format-specific differences are discussed in the appropriate sections.

GIF and PNG-8

As you can see in Figure 24.14, the GIF and PNG-8 options in Save for Web are nearly identical. The appropriate options are visible when you select GIF or PNG-8 as the file format from the pop-up menu or when you choose a saved set of GIF or PNG-8 settings in Save for Web or ImageReady.

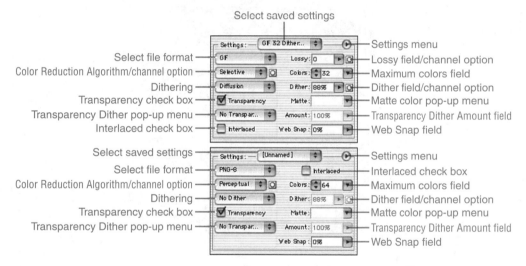

Figure 24.14
The only differences between GIF and PNG-8 in the Settings area of Save for Web are the location of the Interlaced check box and the lack of a Lossy field for PNG-8. In ImageReady, the Use Unified Color Table check box is added to the bottom of the Optimize palette.

Color Reduction Algorithm

The color reduction algorithm determines which colors are retained when you reduce the color table. It is discussed at length in the section "Reducing Colors with Algorithms."

⇨ *To learn more about using vector layers and channels with the Color Reduction Algorithm, Lossy, and Dither fields,* **see** *"Using Channels and Layer Data to Optimize," p. 735, earlier in this chapter.*

You can use dithering to further reduce the number of colors in the color table. When optimizing an image, reduce the number of colors to the point where the image is starting to degrade, and then select Diffusion from the Dithering pop-up menu and adjust the slider to regain image quality.

Dithering

Dithering is, in its most basic form, intermixing two colors to simulate a third color. In Figure 24.15, a sample gradient is visible above the Save for Web preview panes. (In color, the gradient runs from blue to red.) In the preview panes, different dithering options are displayed.

Figure 24.15
Top left: Diffusion dither, 50%.
Top right: Diffusion dither, 88%.
Bottom left: Noise dither. Bottom right: Pattern dither. Only diffusion dither has a variable amount.

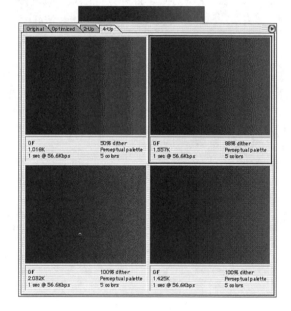

When viewed at 100% in a Web browser, the dithering results in a smoother transition between colors than an undithered image.

Transparency

When a GIF or PNG-8 image is on a transparent background, you can maintain the transparency by selecting the Transparency check box in Save for Web and ImageReady. When it's not selected, the transparent areas of the image are filled with the matte color. If the Matte pop-up menu is set to None, white is used. The Transparency check box must be active when you map colors to transparency using the color table.

Transparency Dither

The Transparency Dither option softens the transition from colors to transparency. It works similarly to the standard Dither option (discussed in the section "Dithering"), but instead of blending colors, it blends from color to transparent.

Like Dithering, you're offered the choice of Diffusion, Pattern, and Noise for Transparency Dither. In addition, when using Diffusion, you can choose the amount by using the slider to the right in the Settings area.

If your image should have distinct edges, as for many interface items, set the pop-up menu to No Transparency Dither to prevent softening of the edges.

Interlacing

Interlaced GIF and PNG-8 images appear in the Web browser as they download. Although it *seems* that the image is loading faster, interlacing doesn't actually speed up the process. Rather, the viewer gets feedback while your page loads. Interlacing is recommended for images over a few KB in size.

24

Lossy Compression (GIF Only)

The standard implementation of the GIF file format uses only lossless compression. However, when using Save for Web and ImageReady, you can further reduce file size by using the Lossy slider. The more information that is discarded, the smaller the file size. However, image quality can suffer. Complex images, such as photographs, can exhibit speckling or blockiness at higher lossiness settings. Lossy compression is less effective at reducing file sizes of plain images that contain large areas of solid color.

Maximum Number of Colors

The Colors field governs how many individual colors the image will contain, up to the 8-bit maximum of 256. You can use the pop-up menu, click the arrows, or type a number in the field. Increasing the maximum number of colors does not add new color to an image that starts with fewer than 256 colors. When you select a lower number, Save for Web and ImageReady use the selected algorithm to decide which colors to eliminate.

Matte

When you deselect Transparency, the matte color is used to fill transparent areas of the image. It can be used to blend the image with a solid-color Web page background. The options are None (no matte), Eyedropper Color (the color most recently selected with Save for Web's Eyedropper tool), White, Black, and Other (which opens the Color Picker). ImageReady doesn't offer the Eyedropper color option, but does display a palette of the 216 Web-safe colors from which you can select.

If your image has a transparent background and feathering or anti-aliasing, selecting your Web page's background color in Matte can prevent or reduce any "halo" around your image.

Web Snap

Increasing the value in the Web Snap field forces colors to the nearest Web-safe color. The higher the value, the more colors are shifted. The percent refers to the tolerance used for changing colors. The higher the Web Snap tolerance, the more change in color that's allowed. Lower tolerances result in only colors closer to their Web-safe counterparts being changed.

Use Unified Color Table (ImageReady Only)

ImageReady's Optimize palette includes the Use Unified Color Table check box, which enables you to standardize the colors used in all rollover states of an image. Selecting this option prevents unwanted color changes in an image's various rollover states. Unifying the color table is available only for GIF and PNG-8 images.

JPEG

When the file format is set to JPEG in Save for Web or ImageReady, the Settings area changes to the configuration shown in Figure 24.16.

Figure 24.16
The options available remain the same—although their values change, regardless of the level of JPEG compression. ImageReady's Optimize palette also offers a check box that enables you to include a JPEG image's EXIF meta-data.

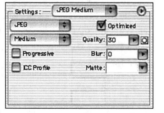

You can select a preconfigured set of JPEG compression options from the pop-up menu at the top of the Settings area, or you can create custom settings. With JPEG selected as the file format, you have the following options:

- **Quality Level**—The pop-up menu directly below the file format pop-up menu offers Low, Medium (shown in Figure 24.16), High, and Maximum. The pop-up menu and the Quality slider are linked—a change to one updates the other. When you select from the pop-up menu, the Quality slider is adjusted to these values: Low—10, Medium—30, High—60, and Maximum—80.

- **Progressive**—When the Progressive check box is selected, the JPEG image appears in the Web browser window in stages. Each stage clarifies the image until the final image is displayed. This display option can result in a slight delay in download, but the viewer gets feedback as the image loads, giving the impression of faster loading.

- **ICC Profile**—You can include an ICC color profile with the image. Some Web browsers can adjust the image's appearance according to an embedded profile, but at the expense of increased file size—and therefore a slightly slower download speed. Browsers that do not support ICC profiles display the image as uncorrected.

- **Optimized**—Optimizing a JPEG file can result in a slightly smaller file size. However, some older Web browsers cannot display optimized JPEGs.

- **Quality Slider**—You can select precise levels of compression by using the Quality slider or by entering a value into the Quality field. The Quality setting is tied to the Quality Level pop-up menu: Quality settings of 0–29 are Low, 30–59 are Medium, 60–79 are High, and 80–100 are Maximum. The Quality Level setting is automatically updated as you change the slider.

> Until an image is saved from Photoshop or otherwise has a color profile embedded, ImageReady won't offer the ICC Profile option.

- **Blur**—Applying a slight blur to an image can substantially reduce file size when compressing as JPEG. The trade-off is, of course, a degradation of image sharpness.

- **Matte**—The color you choose in the Matte pop-up menu determines how the JPEG file handles transparency. Because the JPEG format doesn't support transparency, any pixel in the original that has reduced opacity must be filled with color. The matte color is used for any pixel that is 100% transparent, and is blended with the existing color in any pixel with partial transparency.

In ImageReady, the Optimize palette offers the option of preserving any EXIF data in the image. EXIF data, typically generated by a digital camera, can include information about how and when the image was created and print resolution.

PNG-24

Unlike the JPEG file format, PNG-24 supports transparency. However, you can also choose to use a matte color in lieu of transparency. As you can see in Figure 24.17, when the Transparency check box is selected, the Matte pop-up menu is grayed out. To select a matte color, uncheck Transparency.

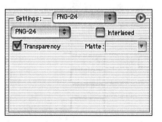

Figure 24.17
Matte choices are None, Eyedropper Color, White, Black, and Other, which opens the Color Picker. ImageReady offers a palette of Web-safe colors rather than the Eyedropper color.

In addition to a choice between transparency and matte, PNG-24 offers interlacing, which is comparable to the JPEG Progressive option and GIF interlacing—the image begins to appear in the Web browser more quickly.

WBMP

The WBMP file format is intended for the creation of tiny black-and-white image files that transfer speedily to wireless Internet devices, including Web-surfing cellular phones. Because the images are 1-bit color, file size is minimized. As you can see in Figure 24.18, the color table contains only white and black.

Figure 24.18
Save for Web and ImageReady offer the same WBMP options.

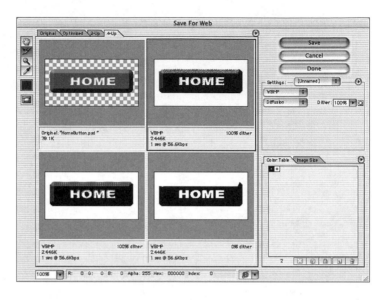

You can use an alpha channel, type layers, or shape layers to control the application of dithering. Click the button to the right of the Dither field. WBMP can use diffusion (from 0%–100%), pattern, or noise dithering. The type of dithering can play a large role in the appearance of sliced images. In Figure 24.19, a three-slice image uses different dithering techniques to produce a couple of different looks.

Figure 24.19
The original has black type on a neutral gray (hex: 999999) background.

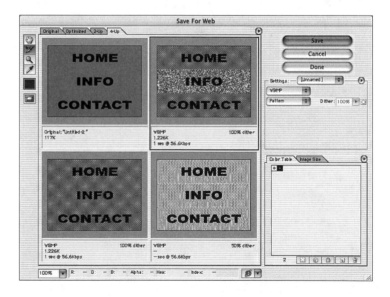

The upper-right sample alternates pattern and noise dithering to better identify the individual buttons. Pattern dithering (lower left) does a good job of hiding the slice seams. Diffusion dithering (lower right) creates irregular patterns and can show the borders between slices.

WORKING WITH THE COLOR TABLE

Images in Indexed Color mode use a *color table* to record the colors used in the file. Because such images use 8-bit color, there can be a maximum of 256 distinct colors in a file. The content of the color table is initially determined by the existing colors in the image (or selected slice) and the Colors field in the Settings area of Save for Web (see Figure 24.20) or ImageReady's Optimize palette.

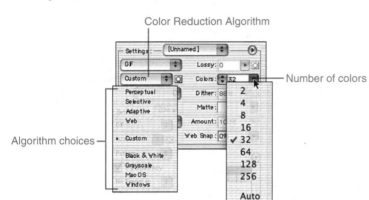

Color Reduction Algorithm

Number of colors

Algorithm choices

Figure 24.20
In addition to using the pop-up menu, you can change the number of colors by using the up and down arrows or typing a value directly in the field.

Reducing Colors with Algorithms

When you reduce the number of colors in an 8-bit image, Photoshop makes decisions in accordance with your choice of color reduction algorithm. You have several options:

- **Perceptual**—Colors are viewed differently by the human eye. Some colors appear more prominent than others. Perceptual color reduction favors the colors that you see with greater sensitivity.

- **Selective**—Like the Perceptual algorithm, Selective favors the colors for which the human eye is more sensitive. However, it also considers the image itself. Areas of broad color are prioritized, and Web colors are retained over similar non-Web colors. The image's overall appearance is best maintained by using Selective, which is the default setting.

- **Adaptive**—The Adaptive color reduction procedure evaluates the image and gives preference to the range of color that appears most in the image. For example, color reduction of a picture of a banana preserves most of the yellows at the expense of other colors in the image.

- **Web**—The colors in the image are converted to Web-safe colors, those 216 colors common to both the Windows and Macintosh system palettes.

- **Custom**—When an image's color table is created by using the Custom option, the colors are "locked in." Further editing of the image won't change the color table. If, for example, you create a custom color table that does not include RGB 255/0/0 (hexidecimal value FF0000) and then attempt to paint with that shade of red, the nearest color already present in the color table is substituted.

- **Black & White**—The color table is reduced to only black and white and consists of only those two colors. The color table is locked after the conversion.

- **Grayscale**—The color table is reduced to grayscale and is then locked.

- **Mac OS**—Only the 256 colors of the Macintosh system palette are used.

- **Windows**—Only the 256 colors of the Windows system palette are used.

Remember that the color table represents either the colors in the selected pane of Save for Web or those of the selected slice in that pane. Each slice can be optimized separately.

⇨ *To learn more about 8-bit color,* **see** *"Indexed Color," p. 186, in Chapter 7, "Color Theory and Practice."*

Editing the Color Table

You can also manipulate the colors of the color table individually. In Save for Web, you open the color table (see Figure 24.21) by clicking the palette's tab in the lower-right section of the dialog box. In ImageReady, use the Color Table palette. In 2-Up and 4-Up configurations, either application reflects the currently selected pane. If the image is 24-bit color (JPEG or PNG-24), the color table is empty.

You can select a color in the table by clicking on it with the Eyedropper in the active pane of the Save for Web dialog box or ImageReady's image window. You can also hold down the Shift key and click on multiple colors. In addition, hold down Shift and *drag* in the active pane to select multiple colors quickly! Deselect all colors by clicking the empty space at the bottom of the color table.

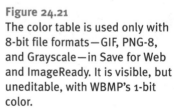

Figure 24.21
The color table is used only with 8-bit file formats—GIF, PNG-8, and Grayscale—in Save for Web and ImageReady. It is visible, but uneditable, with WBMP's 1-bit color.

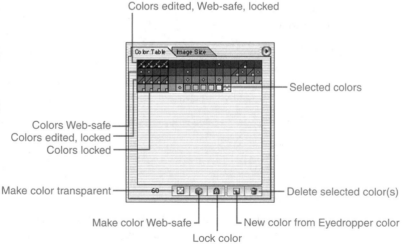

You can double-click any color in the color table or Color Table palette to open the Color Picker and change the color. Every occurrence of the color in the image is automatically updated. Edited colors appear in the color table with a diagonal line, dividing the swatch into the original color (upper left) and the edited color (lower right).

You can also select a color by clicking once and then using the buttons at the bottom of the color table or the Color Table palette. Making the color transparent or Web-safe changes that color throughout the image. Web-safe colors appear in the table with a diamond in the center of the swatch. Colors you convert to transparency or make Web-safe are divided diagonally, with the original color to the upper left.

Locking a color prevents it from being deleted if you decrease the number of colors in the image and also prevents a color shift during a color reduction. Locked colors appear in the table with a small box in the lower-right corner of the swatch.

In Save for Web, clicking the New Color button at the bottom of the color table adds a swatch, using whatever color was most recently selected with the Eyedropper tool. You can click anywhere in the active pane to select a color with the Eyedropper. This enables you to select a color that was dropped in a color reduction or to add a color from the original.

When you select and delete a color from the color table, it is replaced in the image with the nearest remaining color. Save for Web and ImageReady attempt to retain the image's appearance as much as possible.

> ## Caution
>
> After a color is manually deleted from the color table, it is gone. Increasing the number of colors in the image by using the Colors field is no longer possible. In addition, remember that Save for Web has no Undo—however, you can use the Reset button by holding down (Option) [Alt].

The Color Table Menu

The menu for Save for Web's color table (see Figure 24.22) contains several handy commands. ImageReady's Optimize palette menu mirrors those commands and adds commands to view the palette's colors as large or small swatches.

Figure 24.22
You won't find a menu if you open an 8-bit image's color table using Photoshop's Image, Mode, Color Table command.

Many of the commands in the color table menu are self-explanatory, but some deserve further attention:

- **Rebuild Color Table (ImageReady Only)**—When the image has been edited in a way that adds one or more colors, you can regenerate the Color Table with the Rebuild Color Table command or by selecting an optimization pane in the Optimize dialog box.

- **Map/Unmap Selected Colors to/from Transparency**—Whether you use the menu command or the button at the bottom of the color table, mapping a color to transparency makes that color transparent in the image. This change is "live" and can be reversed by using this menu command again, restoring the color to its original areas in the image. Colors that have been mapped to transparency appear at the end of the table when sorted by Hue or Luminance (see Figure 24.23). The color swatch is divided diagonally, showing the original color to the upper left.

- **Unmap All Transparent Colors**—Instead of just selected colors, all colors that have been mapped to transparency can be unmapped at once.

- **Shift/Unshift Selected Colors to/from Web Palette**—Shifting colors to the Web-safe palette, like mapping to transparency, can be reversed, whether you use the command or the button. The swatches appear in the color table with a diagonal line, showing the original color to the upper left and the Web-safe color to the lower right.

- **Unshift All Colors**—This command returns all colors that have been made Web-safe to their original colors, whether selected or not. It does not affect colors that were originally Web-safe.

- **Unsorted**—Colors are shown in the color table in the original sorting order. Look for reverse order, from highest to lowest, using the hexadecimal value.

- **Sort By Hue**—Using the hue value of the color's HSB value, colors are sorted from 0° to 360°. Neutral colors are placed with the reds at 0°.

- **Sort By Luminance**—Colors in the table are sorted according to the brightness value in the HSB value.

- **Sort By Popularity**—Colors are sorted according to the number of pixels of that color in the image or slice. The most common colors appear at the top of the Color Table.

- **Load Color Table/Save Color Table**—Useful for creating uniformity among a group of images or slices, you can create color tables that use specific groups of colors. Loading the color table converts the image (or slice) to that set of colors.

> **Caution**
>
> Keep in mind that colors mapped to transparency and shifted to the Web-safe palette are permanently converted when you save the image. You cannot use the Unmap or Unshift commands after you've saved the file and reopened it.

Figure 24.23
All colors mapped to transparency are moved to the end of the table when sorted by Hue or Luminance. Their position is unaffected by mapping when the table is sorted by Popularity.

EDITING OUTPUT SETTINGS

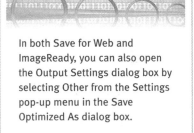

The bottommost command in Save for Web's Settings menu enables you to change how Save for Web handles slices, HTML, the filename, and any background image associated with the file. In ImageReady, use the File, Output Settings command.

In both Save for Web and ImageReady, you can also open the Output Settings dialog box by selecting Other from the Settings pop-up menu in the Save Optimized As dialog box.

Unless an image has been sliced, normally you save only the image itself from Photoshop's Save for Web. Generating an HTML Web page for a single image is possible, but unless the image will be posted as a standalone Web page, there's no need to create the HTML in Save for Web. In ImageReady, you need to save HTML with any artwork that has been sliced, has rollovers, or is an animation.

The Output Settings dialog box has four panes (see Figure 24.24). In addition, you can select from any available saved setting configurations from the pop-up menu at the top of the dialog box.

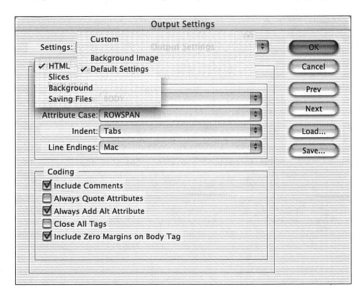

Figure 24.24
These two pop-up menus normally cannot be opened at the same time. They are shown together here for explanatory reasons.

HTML Options

The HTML pane of the Output Settings dialog box governs how HTML will be written (see Figure 24.25).

Figure 24.25
These options determine the formatting of the HTML file generated by Save for Web.

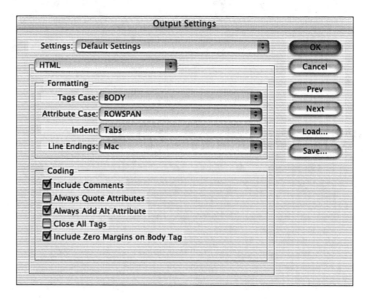

Save for Web offers these HTML options:

- **Tags Case**—The HTML tags can be created in all uppercase, upper- and lowercase, or all lowercase. Web browsers can read tags in any style—this option is primarily for your convenience. If you'll be editing or reviewing the HTML, you might prefer to have the tags stand out by putting them in uppercase.

- **Attribute Case**—Attributes can also be recorded in all uppercase, upper- and lowercase, or all lowercase. Again, it makes no difference to the Web browser.

- **Indent**—You can format the HTML to indent using tabs or a specified number of spaces. If you'll be editing the HTML in a word processing program, either is appropriate. However, some text editors don't recognize tabs, so specifying a number of spaces better preserves the indenting.

- **Line Endings**—Macintosh uses carriage returns at the end of lines, Unix uses line feeds, and Windows uses both. If you know what platform will be hosting your Web site, choose that platform from the pop-up menu. Generally speaking, however, there is no need for concern.

- **Include Comments**—Explanatory comments can be added to the HTML. Comments do not appear in the Web page, but are used by Web design programs and can be used by ImageReady when updating HTML.

- **Always Quote Attributes**—Strict compliance with HTML standards requires that tag attributes be enclosed in quotation marks. The earliest Web browsers also require the quotes. However, you should leave this option unchecked to allow Save for Web to include quotes only when necessary.

- **Always Add Alt Attribute**—Images are identified in HTML by the `<IMG>` tag. When a browser can't display the image, it looks for the ALT attribute and displays any text entered there, along with a symbol indicating that the image wasn't found (see Figure 24.26). Without the ALT attribute, nothing is displayed. Save for Web includes the ALT attribute and quotation marks; you open the HTML file in a Web design program, word processor, or text editor to add a message within the quotes. If you don't add any message, just the symbol is displayed. ALT attributes maintain links, even if the image is missing. Be aware that ALT attributes are required for compliance with U.S. government accessibility standards.

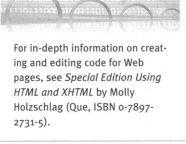

For in-depth information on creating and editing code for Web pages, see *Special Edition Using HTML and XHTML* by Molly Holzschlag (Que, ISBN 0-7897-2731-5).

- **Close All Tags**—If the HTML will be incorporated into an XHTML page, you should select this check box. It ensures that all tags in the HTML have closing tags to match.

- **Include GoLive 5 (or Earlier) Code**—Available only in ImageReady, this option prepares the HTML for maximum compatibility with early versions of Adobe GoLive. It is not required for GoLive 6 or later. The check box is not available in Save for Web because it pertains only to rollovers and animations.

- **Include Zero Margins on Body Tag**—Margins are used by the Web browser much as they are used in a word processing document to offset the document. When you include the margins, you can later simply change the zeros to your desired margin by editing the HTML document (see Figure 24.26).

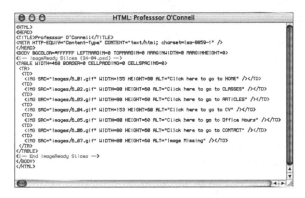

Figure 24.26
The source HTML is shown in an Internet Explorer window. You can open the HTML document in a word processor or text editor to change the margin information and add ALT messages.

Slice Options

Slice options (see Figure 24.27) are necessary only when working with a sliced image. They determine how the slice-related information is recorded in the HTML file. To open this pane, you can select Slices from the dialog box's pop-up menu or click the Next button in the HTML pane. In ImageReady, you can select Slices directly from the File, Output Settings submenu.

Figure 24.27
These options do not pertain to unsliced images.

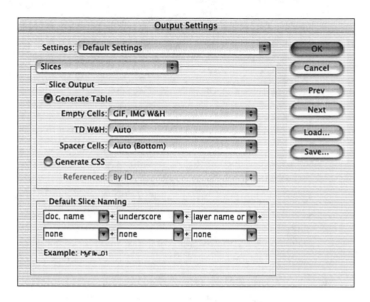

Save for Web and ImageReady offer these options for slice-related HTML:

- **Generate Table**—When you save a sliced image in Photoshop or ImageReady, you are actually creating a separate image from each slice—the slices are saved as individual files. The Web browser requires HTML to tell it how to arrange those slices back into a cohesive whole, the original image. The browser uses the HTML to reassemble the jigsaw puzzle. You can generate an HTML table within which the slices are placed, using these options:

  - **Empty Cells**—Empty cells, used to ensure correct table spacing, can be recorded as single-pixel GIF images, with their width and height (W&H) recorded with the <IMG> (image) tag or the <TD> (table data) tag. The NoWrap option creates a nonstandard attribute and records W&H in the table data tag.

  - **TD W&H**—You can choose to include the width and height for all table data, never include the width and height, or let Save for Web determine when it is necessary. The Auto option is recommended.

  - **Spacer Cells**—A row or column of empty cells can be generated to ensure that a table displays properly in the Web browser window. Spacer cells are particularly important when slice boundaries don't align. Save for Web can generate the extra cells automatically, always, or never, and you can also choose to have the spacer cells only at the bottom of the table. Auto generation is recommended.

- **Generate CSS**—Instead of producing tables to hold slices, Save for Web can create cascading style sheets (CSS). The slices can be identified by a unique ID, in the <DIV> tag as an inline style, or by class.

- **Default Slice Naming**—Save for Web offers six fields for choosing names for slices. You choose the name options from pop-up menus for each field. A generic sample name is generated based on your choices and is displayed below the six fields. The available options are shown in Figure 24.28.

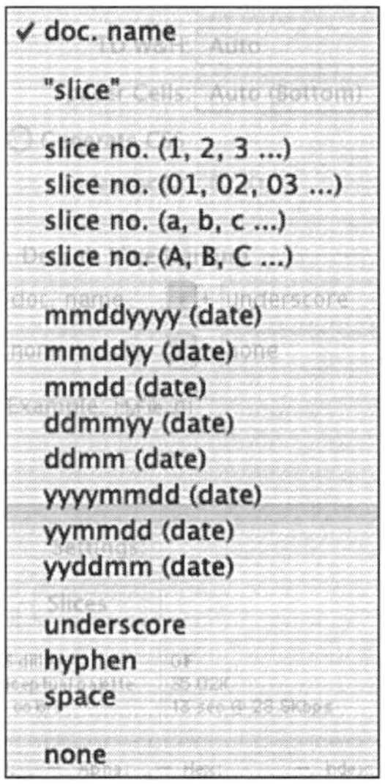

✓ doc. name

"slice"

slice no. (1, 2, 3 ...)
slice no. (01, 02, 03 ...)
slice no. (a, b, c ...)
slice no. (A, B, C ...)

mmddyyyy (date)
mmddyy (date)
mmdd (date)
ddmmyy (date)
ddmm (date)
yyyymmdd (date)
yymmdd (date)
yyddmm (date)

underscore
hyphen
space

Figure 24.28
The slice names must be unique, so you must include at least one variable that changes from slice to slice.

Image Maps (ImageReady Only)

When working with images that contain image maps, ImageReady offers several ways to encode link information. Client-side image maps use the visitor's Web browser to interpret the links. When you opt to use server-side links, the link information is generated as a separate .map file, instead of being embedded in the HTML. The browser must query the server before navigating a server-side image map link.

Caution

You must use client-side links if the image contains slices in addition to image maps. ImageReady cannot generate server-side links for sliced images.

Client-side links are generally much faster for the browser to open. However, server-side links can be updated separately from the Web page's HTML file.

When creating server-side links, you can generate code that complies with the NCSA or CERN standard and can elect to include client-side links within the image's HTML as well.

When you generate client-side links, the Placement buttons at the bottom of the Image Maps pane are available (see Figure 24.29). They determine where in the HTML the image map declaration is placed. The information can appear at the beginning or end of the BODY section of the HTML (Top and Bottom options, respectively), or it can be placed directly above the appropriate <IMG SCR> tag (the Body option). The difference is insignificant for the Web browser, but you might have a preference if you edit HTML.

Figure 24.29
The Placement buttons refer only to image map information generated for an image's HTML. The buttons are grayed out if you generate only server-side image maps.

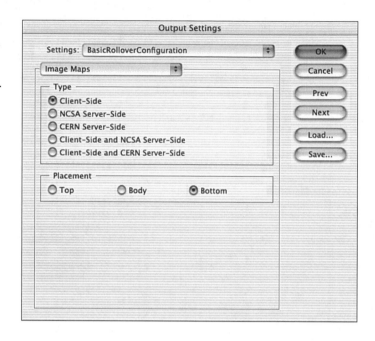

24

Background Options

Using the Background pane of the Output Settings dialog box (see Figure 24.30), you can opt to save the file as an image or to create a background image to be tiled behind a Web page. When saving as a background, you can also select a color to appear behind the image, filling areas that would otherwise be transparent in GIF and PNG images.

Figure 24.30
The Background Image option is not available when you choose Background in the View Document As section of the dialog box.

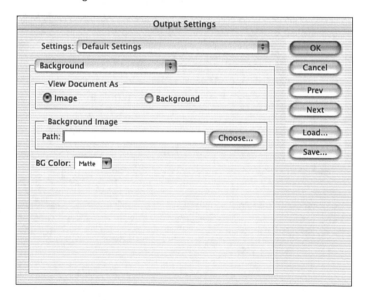

Choosing Image in the View Document As section saves the image regularly. If you choose Image with a background image or color, you must also choose HTML and Images in the Save Optimized As dialog box. (It opens after you click Save in Save for Web.) To see the image displayed with the tiled background image or the selected background color, you then open the HTML file, not the optimized GIF, JPEG, or PNG file.

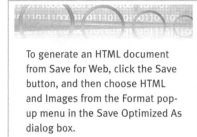

To generate an HTML document from Save for Web, click the Save button, and then choose HTML and Images from the Format pop-up menu in the Save Optimized As dialog box.

When you save an image as a background, you must also generate an HTML document that tells the Web browser to tile the saved image throughout the Web page. See Figure 24.31 for a comparison of saving as an image (left) and as a background (right).

Figure 24.31
To tile the image in the Web page, open the HTML document. If you save only the image or choose to open the image rather than the HTML document, only a single instance appears in the browser window.

File Saving Options

The Saving Files pane of the Output Settings dialog box, shown in Figure 24.32, enables you to specify how slices will be named (when generated) and several additional options.

When an image is sliced, each slice is saved as a separate image. Save for Web automatically generates a separate file for each slice, using filenames that follow the guidelines you choose in the File Naming section of the dialog box.

If your image will be part of a Web page, consider starting the slice names with the "doc. name" option. That makes it easier to find them among a Web site's images.

Each slice name can contain up to nine elements, the last of which must always be the file format extensions. You select the components from a list in each field (see Figure 24.33). You can also enter text into any of the fields, but remember that file extensions *must* be included at the end.

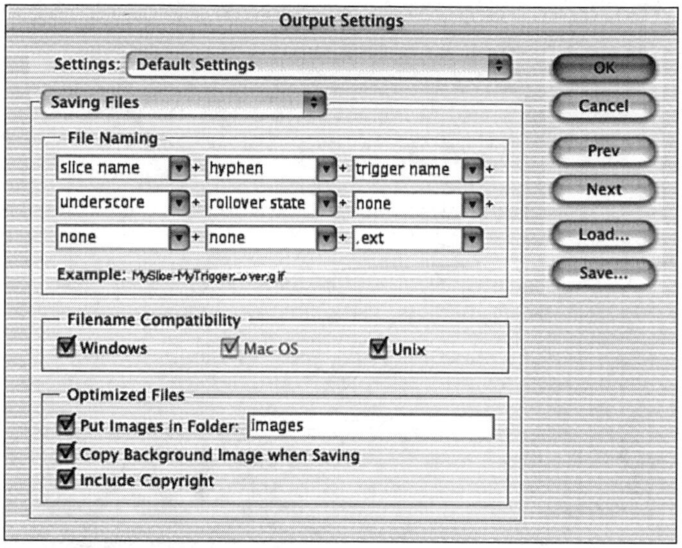

Figure 24.32
The upper parts of the dialog box pertain only to slice naming—the options have no effect on unsliced images.

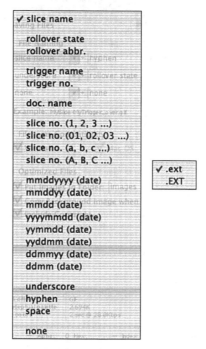

Figure 24.33
The first eight fields use the list on the left. The final field selects a lowercase or an uppercase file extension (as shown on the right).

If you know what type of Web server is hosting the site in which the image will be used, you can uncheck the unnecessary Filename Compatibility options. However, keep in mind that equipment gets upgraded, servers get replaced, and hosting services get changed. Keeping maximum compatibility helps prevent unexpected problems related to server changes.

The Optimized Files section of the dialog box offers three options:

- **Put Images In Folder**—You can select a name for the folder that will hold the images created as slices or backgrounds. The default name, Images, is standard for most Web purposes. The folder is created at the location where you choose to save the file. If a folder with that name already exists, the images are added to it.

- **Copy Background Image When Saving**—When you specify a background image to be tiled behind the image you're saving, the file can be copied to the folder you create. If this option is not selected, you must remember to include the background image separately when adding the image to a Web page or site.

- **Include Copyright**—The copyright information and file title in File Info can be automatically added to each image if you select this option. If no information is available in File Info, nothing is added. To add the information, use the File, File Info menu command. Enter the data in the Copyright Notice and Title fields. The copyright information is added to the file, but not visible in the image.

Saving Custom Setting Configurations

You can save optimization configurations that can be easily accessed in both the Output Settings dialog box and—more important—directly in the Save Optimized As dialog box (see Figure 24.34).

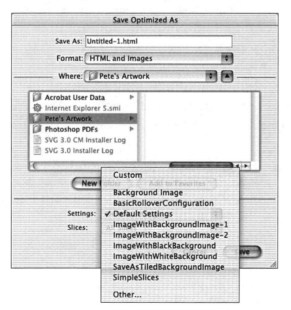

Figure 24.34
Output settings saved in the Presets, Optimized Output Settings folder appear in the pop-up menu for Save for Web. For ImageReady-specific configurations, save the settings to Optimized Output Settings.

Output setting configurations can be saved from the Output Settings dialog box, but not from the Save Optimized As dialog box. In addition, the Output Settings dialog box offers a Load button. It enables you to load setting configurations that are saved in folders other than the Optimized Output Settings folder. The setting configurations should be saved with the .iros file extension.

PHOTOSHOP IN FOCUS

Using an alpha channel in optimization can save precious file size and speed up downloading. Here's how:

1. Open a photograph to be optimized as a JPEG. Because this is a non-destructive process, you can use the original rather than a copy of the image.

2. Create an alpha channel that uses white in areas of your image that should retain the highest quality (typically the subject of the image) and black in less important areas (typically the background). Save the alpha channel as Optimization Mask or a similarly descriptive name.

3. Open the Save for Web dialog box.

4. Select the quality setting that you want for the image's subject (the areas that are white in your mask).

5. Click the mask icon to the right of the Quality field in Save for Web.

6. In the Modify Quality Setting dialog box (shown in Figure 24.35), select your alpha channel from the pop-up menu.

7. Drag the left stop of the slider to the quality setting you want for the background of your image. This is the quality setting used for black areas of the mask. Gray areas of the mask (typically the transition from foreground to background) use quality settings between the minimum and maximum values.

8. Reposition the dialog box as necessary to see the effect of the quality settings on your image. The active preview pane's display is automatically updated, as is the file size information at the bottom of the pane. Remember that you can also adjust the right-hand slider stop, too.

9. When you've reached the perfect balance between image quality and file size, click OK in the Modify Quality Setting dialog box, and then click Save in Save for Web to save the optimized file.

If the image contains type or shape layers, you can select the check boxes to use them for optimization as well. The content of type and shape layers is treated like the white areas in a mask, and surrounding areas are optimized with the Minimum quality setting. Type and shape layers, as well as alpha channels, can be used to modify a variety of optimization settings for GIF and PNG-8 images.

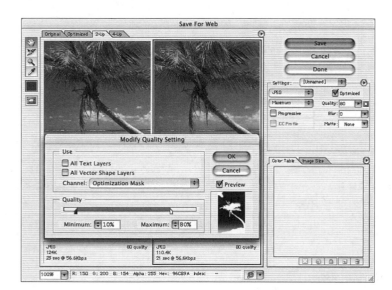

Figure 24.35
In this example, the areas of the image covered by white in the mask are optimized at Quality 80, and black areas of the mask are optimized at Quality 10. The file size savings is about 12%.

FROM THE NAPP HELP DESK

National Association of Photoshop Professionals

The National Association of Photoshop Professionals (NAPP) offers e-mail assistance to its members. Here is some advice from the NAPP Help Desk related to issues in this chapter.

Transparent JPEGs

I want to cut out the foreground of my image and see the Web page's background, but I want to keep it as 24-bit color. Any suggestions?

The first possibility is the PNG-24 file format. Although it produces larger file sizes than JPEG, it natively supports transparency. Remember that some older Web browsers can't display PNG files. That is rarely a problem, however.

Alternatively, you can get the benefits of the JPEG format's smaller file size and wider compatibility by simulating transparency:

1. Make a copy of the image.

2. Merge all layers. If the image is flattened, convert the background layer to a regular layer by renaming it.

3. Make a selection of the area that you want to be "transparent" and delete it. (The area should actually become transparent in the image.)

4. Open Save for Web.

5. Select JPEG as the file format and choose your Quality setting.

6. In the Matte pop-up menu, choose Other.

7. Select the Web page's background color. For best results, the Web page (and the matte color) should use a Web-safe color.

8. Save the image.

This technique is *not* recommended for use with Web pages whose background is a pattern or tiled image. It's difficult to ensure that the pattern will be properly aligned. To get the best possible color match, do not save an ICC profile with the JPEG.

Letters by Pixel

Why does type look so bad on the Web?

Type doesn't *have* to look bad on your Web pages. Keep in mind one simple concept as you design and create, and you'll get excellent quality. In a nutshell, you need only remember that everything on the Web is reproduced with square pixels.

Because Web pages are viewed on a monitor, everything is created from pixels, and every pixel is square. Trying to use square, evenly spaced pixels to show the subtle variations and curves of a script font or an italicized type, for example, can be difficult. And the smaller the type, the fewer pixels can be used for each character. Here are some suggestions:

- Use the largest type size possible. The more pixels you have for each character, the better they will reproduce.

- Sans serif fonts are typically easier to show onscreen. They have uniform stroke sizes throughout the letter and lack the fine details at the end of strokes that often get too fuzzy to see properly.

- Sharp anti-aliasing, new to Photoshop 7, is designed for use with type. It's especially effective for smaller font sizes.

➪ *For more information about how pixels are used to reproduce artwork onscreen, **see** Chapter 6, "Pixels, Vectors, and Resolution," **p. 155**.*

Pre-Optimization

What do I need to do get an image ready for Save for Web? What color mode? What resolution? What else?

Actually, you don't have to do anything—Save for Web automatically converts CMYK to RGB and 16-bit to 8-bit. Layers are flattened, type is rasterized, and blending modes are applied. Save for Web handles all the conversions necessary for the selected file format.

Remember, too, that there's no resolution on the Web. All raster images are displayed according to their pixel dimensions. You don't even need to use Image Size to adjust those dimensions, either. Instead, leave your original as is, and use the Image Size tab in Save for Web to resize the image. You can use the same resampling algorithms as in Image Size, so there's no worry about additional image degradation.

ImageReady, on the other hand, requires 8-bit RGB images. Use the Image, Mode command if necessary before jumping to ImageReady.

24

IMAGEREADY BASICS

by Jeff Foster

IN THIS CHAPTER

NEW TOOLS, PALETTES, AND FEATURES OVERVIEW

Some of the new features in ImageReady 7 are mirrored in Photoshop 7, such as Web Optimization and Transparency, but the most significant change is the addition of the Rollovers palette. With the exception of optimization for Mac OS X and Windows XP, much of ImageReady's interface and layout remains unchanged from the previous version 3, making the transition to the upgrade easy for the experienced user (see Figure 25.1).

Although ImageReady 7 is included with Photoshop 7, Photoshop 6 included ImageReady 3. Skipping 4, 5, and 6 in the numbering scheme simply brought the version numbers for Photoshop and ImageReady into synch.

Figure 25.1
The menus and palettes in ImageReady 7 are quite similar to the previous version.

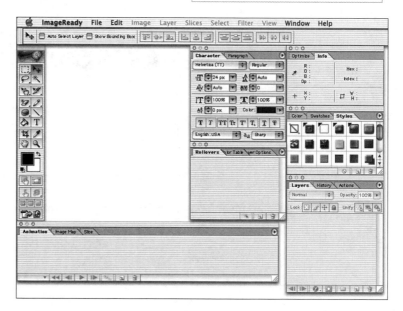

This section outlines a few of the new features in ImageReady with a quick introduction to each. The features are covered in more detail later in this chapter.

The New Rollovers Palette

The new Rollovers palette's functionality is much improved over the previous rollover bar. With the procedural stacking of rollovers, similar to the way layers stack in the Layers palette, it's easy to keep your slices, image maps, animations, and rollover components organized (see Figure 25.2).

Transparency Options

There are many more Transparency options in ImageReady 7, including improved handling of GIF and PNG transparency. This simple procedure is managed by clicking the Transparency check box in the Optimize palette, with a floating image layer and no background layer visible (see Figure 25.3).

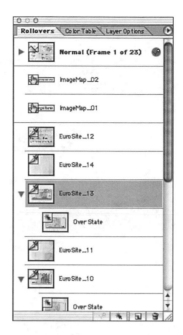

Figure 25.2
The Rollovers palette helps you organize all your interactive functions at a glance.

Figure 25.3
Simply click the Transparency check box in the Optimize palette to achieve excellent edge control of GIF and PNG files.

25

Dithering in Transparent GIFs

Drop shadows and partially transparent areas are no longer a problem in your GIF files, with the new dithering transparency options. Dithering options include Diffusion, Pattern, and Noise. The effect isn't true transparency, but a dissolve effect with opaque pixels in varying patterns (see Figure 25.4).

Figure 25.4
Although you can adjust the amount of diffusion with the Amount slider, the dithering effect looks best applied at 100%.

When a GIF file is floated over a background image or texture, the transparent dithering effect blends in nicely, without any hard edges or tell-tale light pixels (see Figure 25.5).

Figure 25.5
Notice how the edges of the shadow blend in with the background texture to give the illusion of transparency and fading.

25

➡ *Want real drop shadows on the Web? See "Transparency and File Formats" in the NAPP Help Desk section at the end of this chapter.*

Creating WBMP Graphics

Another new feature is the ability to create WBMP files for wireless devices and PDA screens. This is a great effect that screens, dithers, and posterizes your image into opaque black and white pixels (see Figure 25.6).

Changing the amount of dithering you apply to the WBMP image produces more detail in your image, resembling 1960s screened clip art (see Figure 25.7).

If you're dealing with multiple versions of a design in which text is constantly changing or being replaced, the new Data Driven Graphics feature will be a godsend! Create design templates for Web banners, letterheads, personalized business cards, and more, and then create databases or tap into existing ones to select and replace key elements in your design. Select Variables from the Layers palette menu (see Figure 25.8).

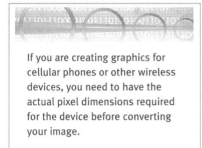

If you are creating graphics for cellular phones or other wireless devices, you need to have the actual pixel dimensions required for the device before converting your image.

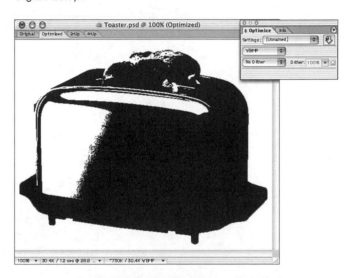

Figure 25.6
The non-dithered WBMP selection can also create great clip art images.

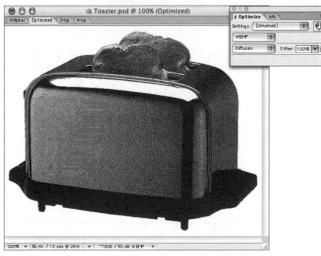

Figure 25.7
Adjust the amount of dithering in a WBMP optimized image to get more detail and shading in the image.

25

Figure 25.8
Use the Variables command to
select an existing or a new database for frequently changed elements.

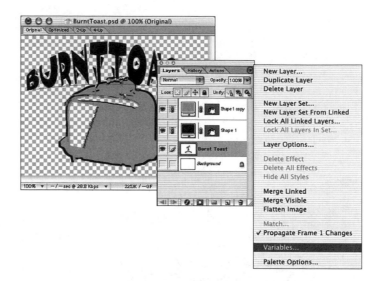

Create a new data set, and enter the text you want to replace or load a variable from an existing
database file (see Figure 25.9).

Figure 25.9
You can load data from an existing database file or enter new
text in a new variable field.

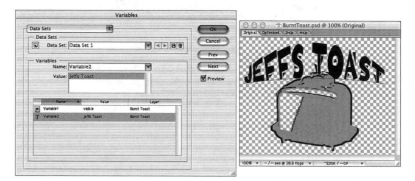

COMPARISON AND INTEGRATION WITH PHOTOSHOP FEATURES

Many of the features new to Photoshop aren't carried over into ImageReady. Not that you would
necessarily want to use all these features in ImageReady, but it can be frustrating when jumping
back and forth between the two applications to reach for a tool or command that isn't there.

Here's a brief list of the major new Photoshop features not readily available in ImageReady:

- File Browser
- Healing Brush and Patch tool

- Saved Workspaces

- Auto Color command

- Enhanced paint brushes

- Pattern Maker

- Spell Checker

- Picture Package

But don't despair—you can still use all these features in your project by simply clicking on the Jump To Photoshop button at the bottom of ImageReady's Toolbox and apply them there before returning to ImageReady.

In addition, it's important to know that some features and effects that are available to both applications don't necessarily work the same way. The following sections help point out some of the major differences, so you'll be aware before jumping into a project and wasting valuable design time in sheer frustration.

Differences Between Photoshop and ImageReady Features

One of the most surprising differences is the optimization of vector shapes and type into GIF format. ImageReady almost completely ignores any attempt at anti-aliasing the edges, even when the full 256-color palette is applied (see Figure 25.10).

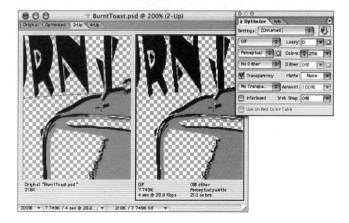

Figure 25.10
The edges of vector shapes and type are rough and jagged when optimized for GIF file format in ImageReady.

When using Save For Web in Photoshop 7.0, optimizing vector graphics and type produces much smoother results. Choosing the Optimize To File Size menu item enables you to create a very small file but still have clean edges and transparency (see Figure 25.11).

Figure 25.11
Photoshop's Save For Web option results in smoother optimization for GIFs created from vector graphics or type.

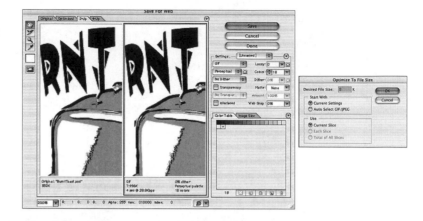

The Photoshop 7 Save For Web dialog box has all the necessary tools for zooming, moving the image, and selecting slices and an eyedropper for selecting matte colors (see Figure 12.12).

Figure 25.12
You will find all of Photoshop's image optimization tools in a couple of palettes in ImageReady.

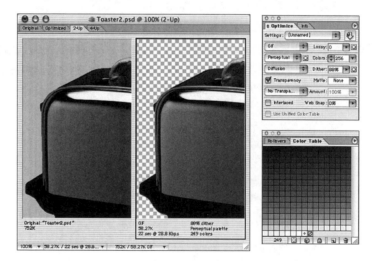

The ImageReady Optimize palette contains all the same image optimization controls, combined with the Color Table palette, to select transparency and matting (see Figure 25.13). Because there is no open dialog box, the ImageReady Toolbox can be used for the same functions of zooming, moving the image, selecting slices, and sampling colors (with the Eyedropper tool).

Another feature to be aware of is ImageReady's Layer Options palette. In Photoshop, a separate dialog box opens when you want to make changes to an existing layer style or create a new one (see Figure 25.14).

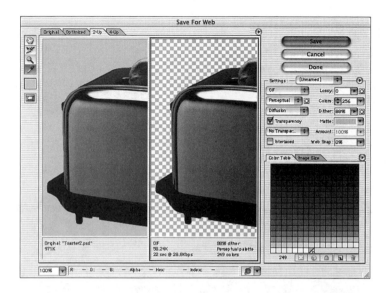

Figure 25.13
ImageReady has all the same optimization features and tools as Photoshop, but you have to look for them in different palettes.

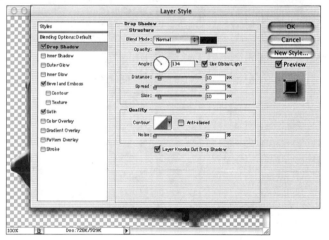

Figure 25.14
In Photoshop's Layer Style dialog box, you can edit all the styles in one big window.

25

In ImageReady, however, the Layer Options palette changes as you select different effects, although you can modify most of the controls and variables as you would in Photoshop (see Figure 25.15).

The two applications have different available layer styles as well and are drawn from different style libraries, as shown in Figure 25.16.

In ImageReady's Window menu, the Layer Options palette is referred to as Layer Options/Style, which gives you an indication of its purpose. Remember that this palette is used to create or adjust styles, and ImageReady's Styles palette holds predefined styles, as does the comparable palette in Photoshop.

Figure 25.15
ImageReady has most of the same controls as Photoshop, but they are in separate palettes that appear when the effect is selected, and they don't cover the entire image.

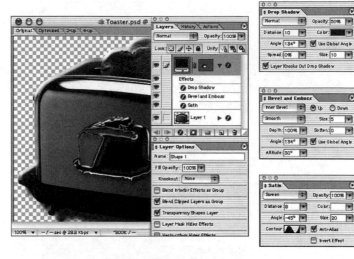

Figure 25.16
In these two palettes (ImageReady on the left, Photoshop on the right), the same style sets were chosen: Default, Buttons, and Text Effects.

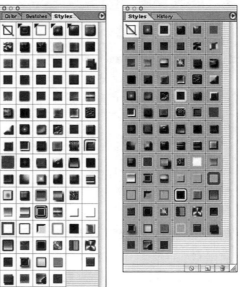

Managing Styles Between Photoshop and ImageReady

Layer styles can be transferred between the two applications by simply applying one to a layer and clicking Jump To Photoshop (or ImageReady). The layer style can then be saved in the Styles palette.

If you want to save layer styles in the library, open the Preset Manager in Photoshop and save just the selected styles as a new style set. Be sure to save them inside the Styles folder within Photoshop's Presets folder (see Figure 25.17).

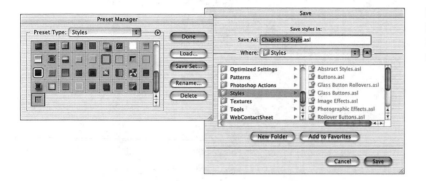

Figure 25.17
Save the selected layer styles in Photoshop's Preset Manager in the Styles folder.

In ImageReady, choose Append Style from the Styles palette menu, and select the previously saved style from Photoshop's library (see Figure 25.18). This method works for other Photoshop styles as well, if you prefer not to use ImageReady's presets.

Figure 25.18
Select Append Style from the palette menu to add the saved style.

You can now select the appended styles from the Styles palette in ImageReady (see Figure 25.19).

Figure 25.19
The new layer style appears in the Styles palette at the bottom of the palette list.

THE ANIMATION PALETTE

If you are upgrading from ImageReady 3, the Animation palette will be familiar because it has remained virtually unchanged. It is very easy to use and understand—and a great way to learn how to create frame-by-frame animation. Review Figure 25.20 to familiarize yourself with the Animation palette and its features.

Figure 25.20
The Animation palette hasn't changed from version 3.0, which is a good thing.

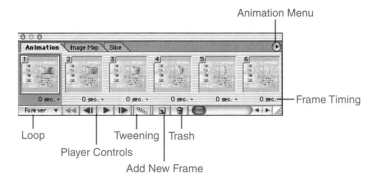

Do you understand the file format limitations on animation? See "Saving Animation" in the NAPP Help Desk section at the end of this chapter.

Each frame's playback timing is controlled from the timing selector under the frame's thumbnail (see Figure 25.21). You can select preset amounts or enter your own.

The Animation palette menu enables you to add, copy or delete frames, tween between two keyframes, optimize the animation, and more. Several of these items can be selected from the Animation palette itself or from the palette's menu.

When animating a sequence, you can use the player controls to preview the loop, modify the timing, or adjust frames. Use the player controls to play, stop, fast-forward, rewind, and go to the beginning or end (see Figure 25.22).

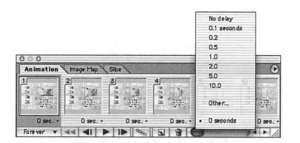

Figure 25.21
Click on the timing selector to set a frame's timing.

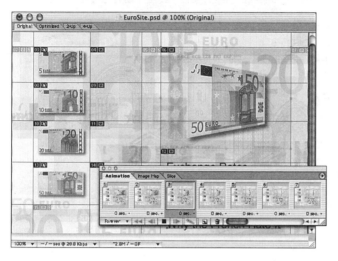

Figure 25.22
Click on the play button to preview the animation in progress or the stop button to stop the animation.

The Tween feature enables you to create smooth fades, effects, and layer movement easily by creating a beginning frame and an ending frame. Select the beginning and end frames in the Animation palette and click the Tween button. This opens the Tween dialog box, where you can select how many frames to create and determine how they will function (see Figure 25.23).

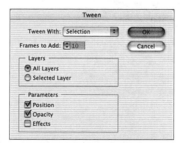

Figure 25.23
Use the Tween feature to create smooth moves and fades.

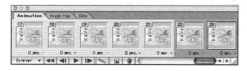

To sort and rearrange frames within the Animation palette, click and drag them to a new position (see Figure 25.24). You can duplicate frames by selecting a frame and clicking the Add New Frame button, or delete them by clicking the Trash icon.

Figure 25.24
Click-drag frames in the Animation palette to rearrange them or to duplicate a frame and reposition it.

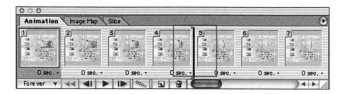

If you are creating animations (animated GIFs) for the Web, take advantage of ImageReady's image optimization feature. It prevents redundant pixels from repeating in each frame and creates a smaller file that plays back more smoothly. Select Optimize Animation from the Animation palette menu (see Figure 25.25).

Figure 25.25
With optimization, animated GIFs are smaller and run smoother.

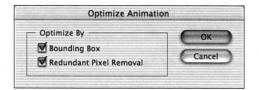

Open the Animation Palette Options dialog box from the palette menu to select the frame thumbnail size (see Figure 25.26). Changing the thumbnail size allows you to either see more frames in the palette or see more detail in each frame thumbnail.

Figure 25.26
Select a smaller frame thumbnail size to gain more screen real estate.

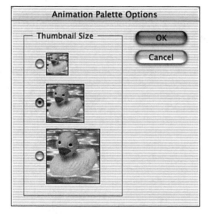

THE ROLLOVERS PALETTE

The Rollovers palette has evolved since ImageReady 3 and enables you to organize several functions from one palette. In addition to rollovers, you can view animation sequences, image maps, and slices (see Figure 25.27).

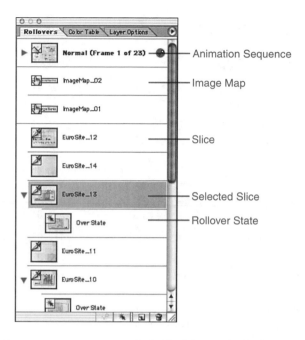

Figure 25.27
The Rollovers palette helps you organize all your interactive functions at a glance.

Animation sequences appear as individual frames in the Animation palette, and you can view and organize the frames in this palette. Through the Rollovers palette menu, you can duplicate, delete, or add frames, or you can delete the entire animation. You can click-drag the frames to rearrange them in this palette, and updates appear in the Animation palette as well (see Figure 25.28).

Figure 25.28
Animation frames can be sorted and reordered in the Animation or Rollovers palette.

You can select and organize image maps in the Rollovers palette and duplicate or delete them through the palette menu. When you double-click on an image map in the Rollovers palette, the Image Map palette comes to the foreground and can be edited (see Figure 25.29).

Figure 25.29
Manage image maps in the Rollovers palette.

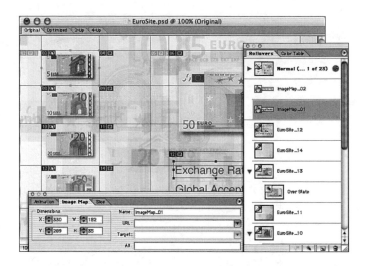

The Rollovers palette organizes items from top to bottom, which is why the first item listed is named Normal. This is the state that a Web page is in when no rollovers are active, and it is where the animation resides under this state in the palette. When a new rollover state is created, it is placed next in the palette's sequence under the slice it is associated with (see Figure 25.30).

Figure 25.30
Rollover states are added in the Rollovers palette directly under their associated slice.

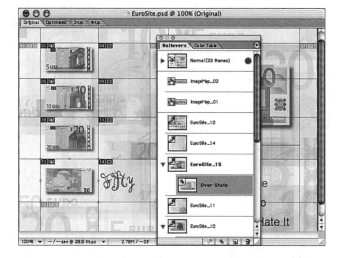

THE DIFFERENCES BETWEEN SAVE FOR WEB AND SAVE OPTIMIZED AS

Save for Web (Photoshop) and Save Optimized As (ImageReady) have very different functions and purposes. Save for Web enables you to select file type, optimization, compression, and transparency features, but it does not allow you to save animations, rollovers, or complete HTML code and multiple file organization.

Save for Web

You use the Save for Web dialog box to save an entire file or one selected image slice as a file suitable for importing into a Web page or viewing in a Web browser (see Figure 25.31).

Figure 25.31
The Save for Web dialog box is used for basic Web graphics generation.

➥ *For more details on how Save for Web works in Photoshop, **see** Chapter 24, "Save for Web and Image Optimization," **p. 725**.*

Save Optimized As

The Save Optimized As feature in ImageReady enables you to not only generate Web-friendly graphic and image files, but also actually create a complete Web site. After you have created the slices and assigned rollovers and animations with links, you can save the optimized images and HTML code with specified configurations, all organized in a folder and ready to upload to your server.

Starting with just a basic image sliced up with two rollovers, I've selected this example to illustrate the options available with Save Optimized As (see Figure 25.32).

Before selecting File, Save Optimized As, you need to open the Output Settings dialog box from the File menu. The default settings in the Output Settings dialog box open with basic HTML settings (covered in more detail later in this chapter in "Managing Your HTML") as well as generic options for table generation and slice (cell) naming conventions (see Figure 25.33).

25

Figure 25.32
Prepare your file with the slices and rollovers, complete with names and links assigned.

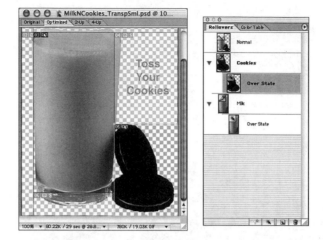

Figure 25.33
The default settings for table and slice options are adequate for simple Web page design.

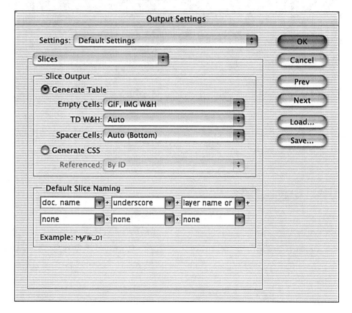

Image maps can be defined as client side in the default settings, and in most cases, you'll want to accept that setting. Click the Next button to view the output setting for the background, where you can select a tiled image file that repeats, a single image, or a solid color (see Figure 25.34).

Filenaming and organization are handled through the Saving Files pane in the Output Settings dialog box. The optimized file directory and filename compatibility settings are located in this pane as well (see Figure 25.35).

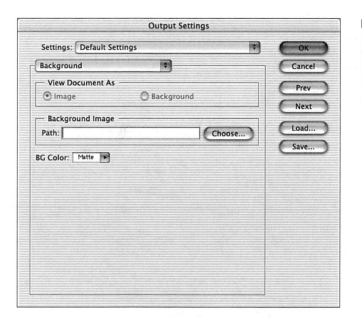

Figure 25.34
For transparent images in the file, you can choose a background image, a tile, or a solid color to be created or linked in the HTML code.

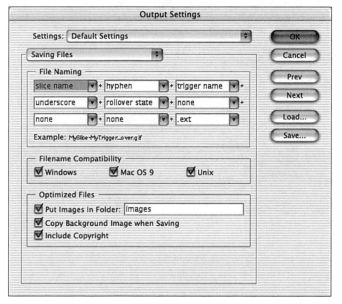

Figure 25.35
The default optimized filenaming and directory settings make it easy to organize the Web page components.

25

The default naming convention in the Output Settings dialog box is fairly lengthy, but tips on optimizing the HTML are in the following section, "Managing Your HTML."

After you have defined the output settings, use the Save Optimized As dialog box to select whether you want to save the HTML, images, or both (see Figure 25.36).

Figure 25.36
Select the Save Optimized As option after the output settings are defined.

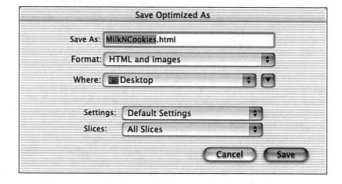

With the default settings selected for this example, an HTML file was generated as well as a folder with all the image files named and organized within it (see Figure 25.37).

Figure 25.37
An HTML file is created with a folder containing the graphic elements.

25

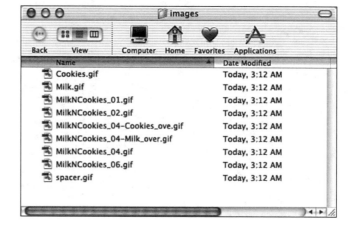

By opening the saved HTML document in a Web browser, you can see how the design example works with rollovers, transparency, and text (see Figure 25.38).

Figure 25.38
Test the HTML file in a Web browser to make sure all rollovers and image files are complete.

MANAGING YOUR HTML

Most people prefer to use an HTML editor, such as Adobe GoLive, Macromedia Dreamweaver, or BBEdit, to create their HTML code. There are ways to effectively incorporate the tables and images created in ImageReady into external HTML editors that can utilize the tables to import the images and add rollover coding.

The default HTML settings in the Output Settings dialog box include basic code to provide enough information for an intermediate code editor to modify as needed (see Figure 25.39).

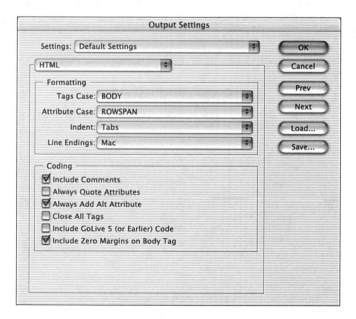

Figure 25.39
The default HTML settings in the Output Settings dialog box are a good start.

When you open the sample file in a Web browser and view the source code, it's easy to see that copyright information and tags from the original image carry through to the page title. In this case, an image from PhotoSpin.com was used, as noted in the code (see Figure 25.40). This title can be edited in an HTML editor, or if you are using an original image without embedded copyright or watermark information, you can add your own title and copyright information in the File Info dialog box.

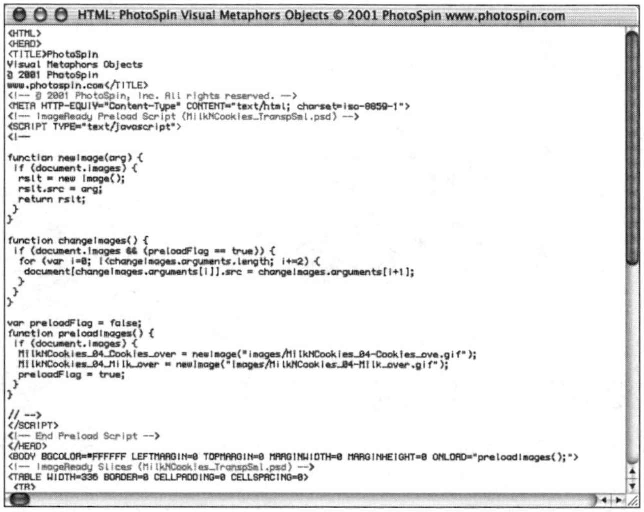

```
HTML: PhotoSpin Visual Metaphors Objects © 2001 PhotoSpin www.photospin.com
<HTML>
<HEAD>
<TITLE>PhotoSpin
Visual Metaphors Objects
© 2001 PhotoSpin
www.photospin.com</TITLE>
<!-- © 2001 PhotoSpin, Inc. All rights reserved. -->
<META HTTP-EQUIV="Content-Type" CONTENT="text/html; charset=iso-8859-1">
<!-- ImageReady Preload Script (MilkNCookies_TranspSml.psd) -->
<SCRIPT TYPE="text/javascript">
<!--

function newImage(arg) {
 if (document.images) {
  rslt = new Image();
  rslt.src = arg;
  return rslt;
 }
}

function changeImages() {
 if (document.images && (preloadFlag == true)) {
  for (var i=0; i<changeImages.arguments.length; i+=2) {
   document[changeImages.arguments[i]].src = changeImages.arguments[i+1];
  }
 }
}

var preloadFlag = false;
function preloadImages() {
 if (document.images) {
  MilkNCookies_04_Cookies_over = newImage("images/MilkNCookies_04-Cookies_ove.gif");
  MilkNCookies_04_Milk_over = newImage("images/MilkNCookies_04-Milk_over.gif");
  preloadFlag = true;
 }
}

// -->
</SCRIPT>
<!-- End Preload Script -->
</HEAD>
<BODY BGCOLOR=#FFFFFF LEFTMARGIN=0 TOPMARGIN=0 MARGINWIDTH=0 MARGINHEIGHT=0 ONLOAD="preloadImages();">
<!-- ImageReady Slices (MilkNCookies_TranspSml.psd) -->
<TABLE WIDTH=336 BORDER=0 CELLPADDING=0 CELLSPACING=0>
 <TR>
```

Figure 25.40
The example's source code shows embedded title and copyright information from the original source photo, which can be edited in an HTML editor.

By examining the source code, you might notice the preloaded JavaScript text code, which differs from most HTML editors but remains quite simple.

The commented text points out the beginning and ending of each section, which helps better organize the code within the HTML document. Looking further down the page in the source code, notice the table with images and rollovers (see Figure 25.41).

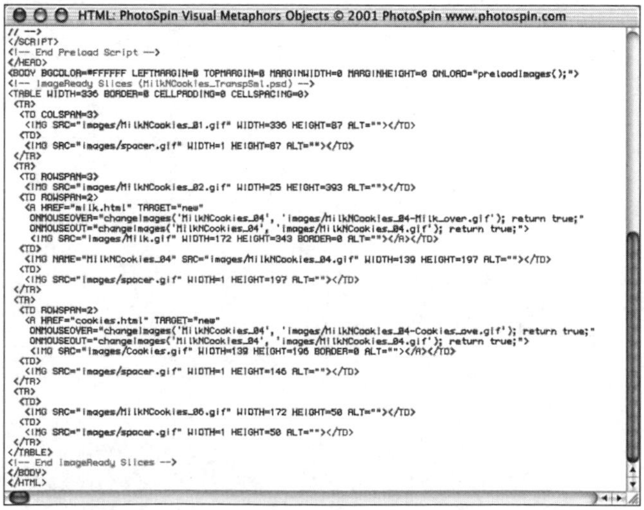

```
HTML: PhotoSpin Visual Metaphors Objects © 2001 PhotoSpin www.photospin.com
// -->
</SCRIPT>
<!-- End Preload Script -->
</HEAD>
<BODY BGCOLOR=#FFFFFF LEFTMARGIN=0 TOPMARGIN=0 MARGINWIDTH=0 MARGINHEIGHT=0 ONLOAD="preloadImages();">
<!-- ImageReady Slices (MilkNCookies_TranspSml.psd) -->
<TABLE WIDTH=336 BORDER=0 CELLPADDING=0 CELLSPACING=0>
 <TR>
  <TD COLSPAN=3>
   <IMG SRC="images/MilkNCookies_01.gif" WIDTH=336 HEIGHT=87 ALT=""></TD>
  <TD>
   <IMG SRC="images/spacer.gif" WIDTH=1 HEIGHT=87 ALT=""></TD>
 </TR>
 <TR>
  <TD ROWSPAN=3>
   <IMG SRC="images/MilkNCookies_02.gif" WIDTH=25 HEIGHT=393 ALT=""></TD>
  <TD ROWSPAN=2>
   <A HREF="milk.html" TARGET="new"
    ONMOUSEOVER="changeImages('MilkNCookies_04', 'images/MilkNCookies_04-Milk_over.gif'); return true;"
    ONMOUSEOUT="changeImages('MilkNCookies_04', 'images/MilkNCookies_04.gif'); return true;">
     <IMG SRC="images/Milk.gif" WIDTH=172 HEIGHT=343 BORDER=0 ALT=""></A></TD>
  <TD>
   <IMG NAME="MilkNCookies_04" SRC="images/MilkNCookies_04.gif" WIDTH=139 HEIGHT=197 ALT=""></TD>
  <TD>
   <IMG SRC="images/spacer.gif" WIDTH=1 HEIGHT=197 ALT=""></TD>
 </TR>
 <TR>
  <TD ROWSPAN=2>
   <A HREF="cookies.html" TARGET="new"
    ONMOUSEOVER="changeImages('MilkNCookies_04', 'images/MilkNCookies_04-Cookies_ove.gif'); return true;"
    ONMOUSEOUT="changeImages('MilkNCookies_04', 'images/MilkNCookies_04.gif'); return true;">
     <IMG SRC="images/Cookies.gif" WIDTH=139 HEIGHT=196 BORDER=0 ALT=""></A></TD>
  <TD>
   <IMG SRC="images/spacer.gif" WIDTH=1 HEIGHT=146 ALT=""></TD>
 </TR>
 <TR>
  <TD>
   <IMG SRC="images/MilkNCookies_06.gif" WIDTH=172 HEIGHT=50 ALT=""></TD>
  <TD>
   <IMG SRC="images/spacer.gif" WIDTH=1 HEIGHT=50 ALT=""></TD>
 </TR>
</TABLE>
<!-- End ImageReady Slices -->
</BODY>
</HTML>
```

Figure 25.41
The cell spacing and image sizes for each slice can be traced in the page's source code.

Cleaning Up Slices

When you create only a few slices in ImageReady and let the application create all the auto slices for you, you end up with a larger HTML file because more code is generated to accommodate the auto slices. You can eliminate the need for auto slices by creating actual slices instead and choosing to align or distribute the slices to take up any unused space (see Figure 25.42). This method can also eliminate the need for extra auto-generated spacer.gif files in your images folder as well as extraneous "empty" cells in your HTML file.

Figure 25.42
Creating actual slices manually instead of letting ImageReady generate auto slices yields a leaner, smaller HTML file.

If you choose to do all your coding in an HTML editor and want to export only the images (and perhaps the HTML table dimensions), select all the slices, choose Save Optimized As, and then select Images Only in the Format pop-up menu (see Figure 25.43). If you want to save just the table element that holds the images, select the HTML Only format.

Figure 25.43
Export just the images from the selected slices or include the HTML table to place the images into the HTML editor.

Cleaning Up the Code with an HTML Editor

One problem that Internet Explorer has had in the past couple of years is revealing the edges of a cell containing a rollover/click-down graphic element. This problem happens when you click on a rollover graphic and the edges of the cell appear as a box outline, thus ruining the overall effect of large graphic designs with rollover spots (see Figure 25.44).

Figure 25.44
A problem inherent with Internet Explorer—clicking on a rollover or link produces a box outline.

To correct this problem, you need to open the HTML file you created in ImageReady in a text editor or an HTML editor that enables you to edit the source code. Locate the exact line of code that contains the affected link or rollover cell, starting with this line:

```
<A HREF="http://your.link.here"
```

Then add this string:

```
onFocus="if(this.blur)this.blur()">
```

This line redirects the focus of the linked cell so that Internet Explorer won't try to draw an outline around it.

If you have to work on the source code of your Web designs much or, better yet, if you pass your work on to a colleague or customer, make sure to clean up the code as much as possible so that it is clear and easy to follow. This cleanup includes naming conventions for the slices, titles, and rollovers in your design document.

By simply renaming the slices in a logical, shortened manner, locating the different items in the Rollovers palette will be much easier (see Figure 25.45)

When you make these simple changes in your naming, you will notice a big difference in the source code of the HTML (see Figure 25.46).

25

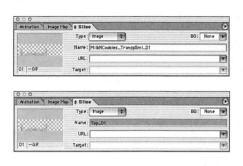

Figure 25.45
Make sure the naming of slices in your ImageReady document is logical and concise.

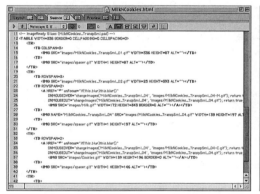

Figure 25.46
Notice how the filenames in lines 15–37 on the right are shorter and easier to locate.

PHOTOSHOP IN FOCUS

ImageReady enables you to tween between frames in three ways or with a combination of the three options. Tweening creates intermediate frames that blend between two existing frames. (Frames of the animation are defined by the content of the visible layers in the image.) Understanding how the three options work enables you to make informed decisions about tweening.

1. In ImageReady, open a new document. Make it 400 pixels wide, 100 pixels tall, and transparent.

2. Select a shade of red from the Swatches palette as the foreground color.

3. Select the Rectangle tool from the Toolbox and drag a small rectangle in the upper-left corner of the document.

4. Select any layer style from the Styles palette.

5. Add a new layer to the document.

6. Change the foreground color to any shade of blue.

7. Select the Ellipse tool and drag a small ellipse in the lower-right corner of the image.

8. Select a different style for this layer.

9. Reduce the layer's Opacity setting to 30% in the Layers palette.

10. In the Layers palette, hide the top layer.

11. In the Animation palette, click the Add New Frame button.

12. In the Layers palette, hide the lower layer and show the upper layer.

13. Select Tween from the Animation palette menu. In the Tween With pop-up menu, select Previous Frame, and select 6 in Frames to Add. Select the All Layers radio button. In the Parameters section, select the Position check box and deselect the Opacity and Effects check boxes. Click OK.

14. Undo.

15. Return to the Animation palette menu and select Tween again. Deselect the Position check box, and select the Opacity check box. Click OK.

16. Undo.

17. Return to the Tween dialog box, deselect Opacity, and select Effects. Click OK.

18. Undo and experiment with the tweening options in combination.

FROM THE NAPP HELP DESK

The National Association of Photoshop Professionals (NAPP) offers e-mail assistance to its members. Here is some advice from the NAPP Help Desk related to issues in this chapter.

Transparency and File Formats

Which formats support which types of transparency on the Web?

The file formats supported by ImageReady, which you select in the Optimize palette, support transparency differently. Here's the bottom line:

- **GIF**—You can create images with hard-edged transparency and save them as GIF. The file format does not support variable transparency. Dithering can be used to simulate variable transparency.

- **JPEG**—JPEG does not support transparency.

- **PNG-8**—Hard-edged transparency is handled automatically in PNG-8—simply create the image on a transparent background and save it as PNG-8. Variable transparency is simulated in PNG-8 with dithering.

- **PNG-24**—Both hard-edged and variable transparency are supported natively by PNG-24.

- **WBMP**—Transparency is not supported in WBMP.

Saving Animation

I want to create an animation using photos, and I understand that GIF isn't the best format for continuous tone images. How do I create an animated JPEG?

JPEG doesn't support animation. Of the file formats you can save from ImageReady, only GIF supports the frames required to create an animation. (However, you can create animations in GIF, SWF, and even SVG formats from Adobe Illustrator.)

25

PRINT AND PREPRESS

IN THIS PART

THE PRINTING PROCESS:
A PRIMER

IN THIS CHAPTER

PROCESS PRINTING

Photoshop is the most commonly used tool for preparing photographic images for print. Whether reproduced in a newspaper, in a magazine, on a billboard, or on the side of a bus, photos most likely passed through Photoshop. (In contrast, non-photographic, vector-based illustrations are typically produced using Illustrator or a similar program.) Properly preparing images in Photoshop for process printing requires some knowledge of resolution and color, and a general understanding of the printing process. (If, on the other hand, you print only to the color printer on your desk, see the sidebar "Photoshop and Inkjet Printers" later in this chapter).

Who Needs to Know What

Commercial printing is a combination of art and science. Generally, just four inks are used to create the entire range of colors needed to reproduce photographic images. Additional colors, called *spot colors*, can be added, but the bulk of the work is done with just four inks. Knowing how and where to put the ink to correctly re-create an image requires a substantial level of expertise. General knowledge of the principles of printing must be supplemented with specific knowledge of the individual printing presses and the particular inks and paper being used for the job, and sometimes even weather conditions.

In contrast, the press operator probably has no need to understand the symbolism in a particular ad campaign or the meaningfulness of a cover shot. The reasons for selecting a specific spot color for a logo might not matter to him or her.

As a professional, however, the press operator likely understands that a specific color *was* chosen, that an ad campaign *does* use symbolism, that a cover shot *is* meaningful, and that proper reproduction on paper is important for these images to fulfill their purposes.

Perhaps the most important guideline when preparing artwork for process printing is the simplest: Talk with your printer or service bureau. In most cases, you are not expected to know (or even understand) the specific tolerances of a huge piece of machinery in another company's building. The people who work directly with that machinery do, theoretically, know its capabilities and foibles and can compensate for them as necessary.

⇨ *What if your printer won't talk with you or can't answer your questions? See "More Than Just Ink-Slingers?" in the NAPP Help Desk section at the end of this chapter.*

Caution

This chapter deals primarily with techniques and procedures for commercial process and spot color printing. Process printing uses CMYK inks applied by huge mechanical printing presses.

The guidelines and background material in this chapter do not pertain to most inkjet printers. Most inkjets also use CMYK inks, but they use software to convert from RGB colors to the CMYK gamut (with the exception of high-end proofers and fine art printers). Generally, you should not prepare CMYK output for inkjet printers; rather, you should send only RGB data.

For the remainder of this chapter, the terms *printing* and *printer* are used to refer to the commercial printing process, using process and spot inks, unless otherwise noted.

26

Photoshop and Inkjet Printers

Both commercial printing presses and home/office inkjet printers use ink on paper to reproduce your artwork. In many cases, they use the same colors of ink, but that's where the similarities end.

On the technical side, huge industrial presses use a series of evenly spaced dots of varying sizes to reproduce color. Stochastic printers, such as most inkjets, use dots of the same size, spaced irregularly, to reproduce an image. That results in differing resolution needs. (Most inkjet printers achieve maximum print quality at resolutions of 240 pixels per inch, ppi. Images prepared for commercial printing should be at a resolution 1.5 to 2 times the line screen frequency of the press.)

Commercial printing usually involves producing large numbers of identical documents, and inkjets are more commonly used to print one or several copies of a single image.

Preparing an image for process printing means converting it to the CMYK color mode. Although you may see those inks under the hood of your own printer, inkjets require RGB images (with some exceptions). Remember that the vast majority of inkjet printers are sold to individuals and businesses who don't have access to software that supports CMYK. Even Photoshop Elements and Photoshop LE have no support for the professional printing color mode. Inkjets are prepared to print from programs such as Excel, Word, PowerPoint, Internet Explorer, and iPhoto and directly from digital cameras. The software that transfers information from the program to the printer *expects* RGB data. If you send a CMYK image to print, the colors are converted *again*, and are likely to become muddy and dark.

In summary, if you send images to an inkjet printer, keep them in RGB color mode and set your resolution to 240 ppi. A couple of tests with slightly higher and lower resolution will tell you what's optimal for your printer. Remember that images with too high a resolution can cause printing problems for inkjets.

The Role of Page Layout Programs

Images prepared in Photoshop for commercial printing are almost never sent directly to press. Instead, they are placed in a page layout or illustration program to be combined with text and/or additional artwork. The document in which an image is placed could be one page long or hundreds of pages. (Each image in this book was prepared in whole or in part in Photoshop and integrated into the book by the fine production staff at Que.)

The page layout or illustration program is more than just a carrier for a Photoshop image. Rather, the artwork created or edited in Photoshop is merely an element of the page. It can stand alone on the printed page, but it is merely an element, nonetheless. When it's printed, there are likely other elements on the paper, including registration marks, color bars, and crop marks (see Figure 26.1).

It's important to remember the role of the document in which the Photoshop image is placed. The Photoshop image's dimensions, resolution, color mode, and even file format depend on the destination document.

➪ *To learn about the specific techniques and requirements for integrating Photoshop images into page layout documents, **see** Appendix B, "Photoshop with InDesign, QuarkXPress, and Other Page Layout Programs," **p. 905**.*

26

Figure 26.1
Shown is the black ink color separation for a document that contains an image from Photoshop.

TERMS AND CONCEPTS

If you are or will be preparing artwork for commercial reproduction, you can benefit from understanding the fundamentals of the process. Clarifying some basic terminology and taking a closer look at some key aspects of printing will set the groundwork for a discussion of preparing projects for print.

The vocabulary presented in this section is not Photoshop-specific. Rather, it includes terms related to the commercial printing process, whether directly applicable to Photoshop or applicable to a page layout or illustration program.

- **Bleed**—In many cases, the paper is larger than the print area. To ensure that the ink extends all the way to the area that will be cut from the larger paper, a bleed is used. Without the bleed, a tiny error in trimming the paper can result in an unwanted white line in places where the design should go to the edge. The bleed extends the ink past the crop marks.

- **Choke**—In trapping, the process of extending the surrounding light color onto an enclosed dark color is called choking. (See also *spread* and *trapping*.)

- **CMYK**—Cyan (C), magenta (M), yellow (Y), and black (K) are the four *process colors* used in commercial printing. Artwork being prepared for color printing must be in this color mode. RGB illustrations and images cannot be separated for printing. (See also *process colors* and *spot colors*.)

For an in-depth look at color and the color modes, **see** Chapter 7, "Color Theory and Practice," **p. 173.**

- **Color stitching**—Color stitching is the undesirable visibility of the transition from vector to raster artwork in an image. It occurs when a printer handles the two types of artwork differently.

■ **Contract proof**—The final approval of a piece of work before printing the final separations and printing plates is called the contract proof. After the client or other approving authority approves the contract proof, the job should roll. The contract proof is the standard against which the final production project is measured. It is critical that the proofs be prepared properly and using the correct technique. Digital proofs should not be used for a job that will eventually be printed from film-based plates. Likewise, creating a laminate proof for a digital output job opens the door to inaccuracy. Final approval of the contract proof is normally in writing, and the contract proof is used to ensure accurate color during the press check. (See also *press check.*)

■ **Duotone**—When only two colors are used to create an image, it can be considered a duotone. Photoshop can also produce images using two colors of ink as CMYK images (with two empty channels) or as Multichannel color mode documents. (See also *tritone.*)

■ **Flatness**—Vector curves are not actually printed as curves when you are creating separations and printing on a press. Rather, the PostScript imagesetter creates a series of straight lines that represent the curve. Flatness is the measure of how many segments are used to represent a given curve. The smaller the number, the shorter the segments used to print curves and, there-fore, the more accurate the curve (see Figure 26.2).

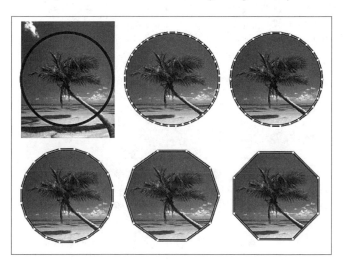

Figure 26.2
As you can see with these "circular" clipping paths, the greater the number of segments, the smoother the curve.

26

Keep in mind that trying to print too many short segments makes a file too complex and can lead to printing errors. Flatness is a function of the imagesetter's resolution divided by the document's output resolution. In Photoshop, the Clipping Path dialog box contains a field for flatness (see Figure 26.3). Leave this field completely empty unless instructed to enter a value by your service bureau or print shop.

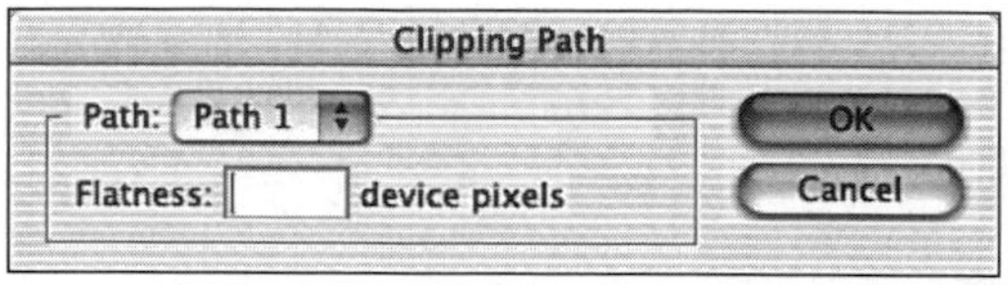

Figure 26.3
Values for flatness can range from 0.2 to 100. The smaller the value, the shorter the path segment — and the more complex and difficult the path is to output.

> **Clipping Path**
>
> Path: [Path 1 ⬍]   OK
>
> Flatness: [   ] device pixels   Cancel

- **Flexography**—This type of printing process uses flexible printing plates and different inks from offset printing. (See the sidebar "Flexographic Printing" later in this chapter.)

- **Frequency modulation (FM) printing**—See *stochastic printing*.

- **Gradient**—Smooth and gradual changes in color, called gradients, are sometimes hard to reproduce in print. Because the printing presses are limited to 256 different amounts of each of the four inks, transitions from one color to another might not be as smooth in print as onscreen. The appearance of a gradient on the printed page is limited by the number of color variations that can physically be printed.

- **Halftone**—One of the keys to producing photographic and other continuous tone images on a printing press is halftoning. The press doesn't produce continuous tone images; rather, it simulates them with a series of dots. The halftone dots are spaced equidistantly in a grid. Each square in the grid, called a cell, can be occupied by only one dot. Typically, the distance from the center of one dot to the center of the next is uniform throughout the grid. The illusion of color variation is created with changes in the size of those dots. Figure 26.4 shows halftone dots spaced in an imaginary grid. The dashed lines represent the line screen frequency.

Figure 26.4
Halftone dots are always equidistant in an imaginary grid. The grid spacing is a function of line screen frequency, and the size of the dot determines how much ink is placed.

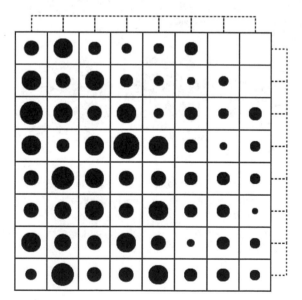

With a grayscale image, the areas with large dots would appear darker than areas with smaller dots. In the case of color, the ink density for that color would be increased where the dots are larger. The size of the dot in relation to the size of the cell (or grid square) is described as tint or screen. The combination of cyan, magenta, yellow, and black dots produces the appearance of the various colors in the CMYK gamut. (See also *line screen frequency* and *tint*.)

- **Knockout**—When two or more areas of solid color overlap in an illustration, one of two things can happen. First, the colors can interact, producing another, different color. If, on the other hand, the overlapping color completely blocks the lower, it is said to "knock out" the lower color, creating a knockout. This is primarily a factor with vector artwork and does not apply to continuous tone images and raster images. (See also *overprint*.)

- **Limitcheck error**—PostScript printers can return limitcheck errors when overwhelmed by data. Specifically, overly long paths can require more memory than is available in the printer. Photoshop can generate overly long paths with extremely complex clipping paths and shape layers. Using a PostScript 3 printer with large amounts of memory can eliminate limitcheck errors.

- **Line screen frequency**—The resolution of commercial printers is measured in lines per inch (lpi). The line screen frequency determines the spacing and size of the dots printed by the imagesetter and used to create the printing plates. The higher the value, the closer the lines and smaller the dots. Small dots and close lines produce a finer image. Line screen frequencies must be matched to the printer producing the separations. Using a line screen frequency that's too high for a lower-resolution imagesetter can seriously degrade the quality of the separations. The PPD for the particular imagesetter usually offers appropriate settings. Refer back to Figure 26.4, which shows halftoning and line screening. The dashed lines in the figure indicate the distance between rows and columns of dots. The number of rows or columns per inch is the line screen. (See also *halftone* and *PPD*.)

- **Lpi**—This abbreviation stands for lines per inch, a measure of line screen frequency. (See also *line screen frequency*.)

- **Misregistration**—As paper is pulled through the multiple units required to place the different colors of inks, slight irregularities in alignment might occur. When the inks are not placed in exact relationship to each other, the press is said to be misregistered. The effect on a four-color image can range from virtually unnoticeable to devastating (see Figure 26.5). The term *out of register* is also used. (See also *registration*.)

26

Figure 26.5
On the left, the original. In the center, one color is slightly out of register. On the right, the same image when the misregistration is more severe.

- **Offset printing**—The majority of printing done worldwide is offset printing. When you think of the production of books, brochures, magazines, and business cards, you're thinking of offset printing.

- **Opacity**—See *transparency*.

- **Out of register**—See *misregistration*.

- **Overprint**—When two colors overlap in artwork, it can result in an overprint or a knockout. Overprinting puts the upper color over the lower, and with translucent inks, that allows them to interact and create a third color. When an upper color knocks out a lower color, the lower color is not printed underneath the overlapping area. (See also *knockout*.)

- **PPD**—PPD stands for PostScript Printer Description. This file, when loaded, supplies all the variables for your PostScript printer or imagesetter. In Windows, PPDs are stored in the System folder. With Macintosh OS 9, you can find them in the Extensions folder within the System folder, in a folder called Printer Descriptions. Mac OS X stores PPDs in the Printers folder within the Library folder.

- **Press check**—The last chance to ensure that colors, knockouts, trapping, and overprinting are correct, the press check uses pages printed at the beginning of the production press run. The printing presses are actually in motion to produce these samples. The press check should be compared only to the contract proof and should be used only for checking color output. It is too late to correct typographical errors or change the appearance of the artwork. If one ink is printing too lightly or darkly, the press operator can usually adjust its flow to compensate. (See also *contract proof*.)

- **Process colors**—The process colors are cyan, magenta, yellow, and black (CMYK). They are the four standard colors on which four-color printing is based. (See also *CMYK* and *spot colors*.)

- **Proof**—Both a noun and a verb, a proof is a sample used to verify the work and is also the process of checking that sample. A proof can be prepared at any step in the creation or production process and in various ways. Proofing is almost always done for client or project lead approval before production. When properly calibrated monitors are used with the appropriate printer profiles, proofing can be done onscreen; this procedure is called *soft proofing*. Hard proofing is usually considered more reliable.

■ **Registration**—Registration is the alignment of printing plates to ensure that colors are placed exactly in relationship to each other. Misregistration is the slight misalignment of the colors on the page. This problem can be the result of shifting the printing plates, stretching the paper, or various other conditions. The term *out of register* is also used. (See also *misregistration*.)

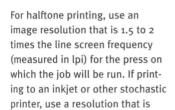

For halftone printing, use an image resolution that is 1.5 to 2 times the line screen frequency (measured in lpi) for the press on which the job will be run. If printing to an inkjet or other stochastic printer, use a resolution that is one-third the printer's resolution.

■ **Resolution**—Resolution refers to the number of pixels per unit of measure for an image. Typically, resolution is recorded in either pixels per inch (ppi) or pixels per centimeter. The image itself simply has pixels. In printing, resolution describes how tightly those pixels should be packed on the paper, which also determines the size of each pixel.

■ **Screening**—See *halftone*.

■ **Separations**—Color separations are the images from which printing plates are usually made. Each separation represents the distribution of one color of ink on the page. Separations are grayscale images, with a maximum of 256 levels of color for their ink. Some printing operations bypass separations by creating printing plates directly from computer files, a process called "direct to plate."

■ **Soft proofing**—See *proof*.

■ **Spot colors**—Sometimes printed work needs to have an exact color match, or a color that's required cannot be reproduced using the four standard inks. Some artwork is overprinted with a protective or glossy varnish. Occasionally, a metallic or neon color must be added to artwork. In all these cases, you use spot colors, which are predefined, premixed inks that produce predictable results in typical circumstances. They usually require an additional run through a printing press, which can add to the cost of a print job. They are output on a different color separation to produce a separate printing plate. (See also *CMYK*, *process colors*, and *separations*; for more information, see Chapter 7.)

■ **Spread**—In trapping, the process of extending a light color into the surrounding dark color is called spreading. (See also *choke* and *trapping*.)

■ **Stochastic printing**—Dots of ink in stochastic printing are all the same size, and an image is created by varying the placement of the dots. (This is in contrast to halftone printing, in which the dots are regularly spaced but vary in size.) It is also called *frequency modulation printing*. Inkjet printers can be considered stochastic printers. (See also *halftone*.)

■ **Tiling**—Sometimes an image or illustration is larger than the pages on which it is to be printed. When that is the case, the image must be divided into rectangles the size of the selected paper. The various parts of the image are printed as separate pages of the document, which can later be pieced together.

26

■ **Tint**—The size of a halftone dot in relation to the halftone cell determines the darkness or density of an ink in a given area. The diameter of the halftone dot in relation to the halftone cell's height or width is measured in percent to give the tint or screen. For example, a 50% tint (or 50% screen) consists of halftone dots that are one-half the size of their cells. (Refer to Figure 24.4 and see also *halftone*.)

■ **Transparency**—Any object or image in an image that does not obscure everything below it is said to be transparent. Although the word *transparent* actually connotes *clear*, it is used in Photoshop to denote various levels of opacity, measured in percent. However, the opacity level, as controlled in the Layers palette, is not the only factor involved in opacity. An object, a group, or a layer's blending mode can also affect transparency.

➪ *To learn about blending modes and opacity,* **see** *Chapter 17, "Using Blending Modes,"* **p. 477.**

■ **Trapping**—Trapping is the process of preparing adjacent colors to ensure that no unwanted whitespace appears between them. Because of a variety of factors, miniscule variations can occur during a print run. As a result, the presses can be slightly misregistered. That tiny gap between the point where one ink ends and the next begins is often very visible. Trapping increases the distribution of a lighter colored ink under a darker ink to ensure that no white area shows through. (See also *choke, knockout, misregistration, overprint,* and *spread*.)

➪ *You've heard about trapping, but you don't know if you should be doing it. See "Avoiding the Trap" in the NAPP Help Desk section at the end of this chapter.*

■ **Tritone**—A tritone is an image that can be reproduced using only three colors of ink. (See also *duotone*.)

THE BASICS OF PRINTING

Regarding commercial printing, the most important piece of advice I can give you is to simply talk with your printer. Just as a race car driver trusts his mechanic to prepare a multimillion-dollar machine to perform at peak efficiency, so should you trust your printer to run his or her machinery at maximum efficiency. Communication is the key. A mechanic might have to tell a driver, "It will pull a little to the outside on Curve 3." So might a printer need to tell a client "With this paper, under these conditions, we'll have to increase the trap by a point."

Commercial printing presses are vastly expensive machines, made up of more individual parts than you can count, some standing two stories tall and costing more than the race car mentioned earlier. The people who run and maintain these monsters should be skilled professionals who know and understand their particular machinery as no other can. On the other end of the project, however, is the client or designer or account executive or artist. This individual has a concept in mind, however fuzzy at the beginning, and wants to achieve that image on paper. Someone must create the digital file that conveys the message; someone must take that series of computerized ideas and turn it from magnetic zeros and ones to ink on paper. One or more individuals can become involved in the process in between.

When your artwork is printed, it is re-created on paper (or another medium) using inks (or dyes). The artwork itself is actually an electronic recording of what you've created. The image exists in the computer or on the disk as a series of zeros and ones. Those zeros and ones (binary data) represent the pixels and colors and effects that you see on the monitor. Going from binary data to ink on paper can be a complicated process. Fortunately, most of the process is transparent to you most of the time—most steps can proceed without your direct control.

You'll discover many variations in offset printing today, including print-on-demand, direct-to-plate, PDF workflow, automated form printing, high-fidelity color, and other options, such as flexographic printing (see the sidebar "Flexographic Printing" later in this chapter). This discussion, however, focuses on the most common types of commercial printing. The artwork can be placed in a page layout program, or the final preparation can take place in an illustration program, such as Illustrator. Typically, in either case, the artwork needs to end up on printing plates, which the presses use to actually place ink on paper.

Proofs

The only way to really see how a print job will come off the press is to run it through the press. Doing so is, however, prohibitively expensive until every aspect of the job is checked. When the plates are on the presses and the paper starts to feed, it's too late to find a mistake.

Proofs are an intermediary stage created before the printing plates are made. Proofs can be actual color separation film (see the next section), bluelines (which are less expensive than film), or laminates to show color. Laminates use the actual film to produce a sample of how the project will print. If problems are found, corrections are made. If separations or film have been made, they are replaced by corrected versions. (These corrections, of course, can be expensive.)

Among the most expensive options is *wet proofing*, in which a small press is used to print the proofs, using plates made from the color separations. This procedure is usually reserved for the most color-sensitive, high-volume projects. Wet proofs can be run on the same paper that will be used for the print run.

Digital proofing uses high-end color laser or special inkjet printers to create proofs. Typically, such proofers (from Kodak, Iris, and Imation) are calibrated to a specific printing press. They replicate, as closely as possible, the press's halftone dots, dot gain compensation, screen angle, and other press-specific conditions. The paper selected for the actual printing can be used.

Soft proofing relies on calibrated color monitors to show onscreen what the final project will look like. The monitor *must* be properly calibrated if color decisions are to be made. If, on the other hand, the job will be run using only colors selected from a swatch book, even an uncalibrated monitor can suffice. The colors onscreen might not be accurate, but using spot colors or color swatches ensures that the printed materials will be accurate. PDF files can be sent to a client or approving authority for soft proofing, if that individual has access to a properly calibrated monitor or understands the limitations of soft proofing.

If problems are found when you are soft proofing or working with digital proofs, making corrections is far less expensive than if color separations have been prepared.

26

Color Separations

In traditional offset printing, your artwork isn't sent from the computer directly to the printing press. Rather, the presses use printing plates made from *color separations*. The *seps* (one for each of the inks being used) are grayscale representations of parts of your image. Each separation covers the whole illustration but indicates only those areas where its particular ink will be placed. If an image is to be printed in grayscale, one separation is required. Standard four-color (CMYK) printing requires four separations, and more seps can be added for additional colors. (See "Process Versus Spot Colors" later in this chapter.) Sometimes you might also print a *duotone* or *tritone*. Duotones use two colors of ink (most often, black and one spot color); tritones use three inks.

Figure 26.6 shows a comparison of the four CMYK separations with the single image from which they were produced.

Figure 26.6
Each of the outer images shows one color channel to indicate what information would appear on that color separation.

The original image, shown in the middle, is the composite. It is made up of all four colors. Keep in mind how the cyan, magenta, yellow, and black interact to produce color. Looking at the separations, you can determine several things about the original, even though it is shown here in grayscale:

- The body of the letters appears dark on the magenta and yellow separations, but is not present at all on the cyan and black plates. This tells you that the fill for the text will be printed with just magenta and yellow inks; therefore, it is red.

- The text outline appears on all four separations; therefore, it will be black.

- Just a little of the cellphone's body appears on the black separation, indicating that the phone is actually dark gray rather than black.

- The gravel at the bottom of the bowl is very dark on the cyan separation, but also appears on the magenta and yellow seps. Expect it to be royal blue.

■ The tangle to the left and lower right of the telephone is likely wires rather than weeds. Various strands look different on each separation—they are bright yellow, red, blue, and green.

➡ *For more information on these topics, **see** the section "Color Issues" later in this chapter and Chapter 7, "Color Theory and Practice," p. 173.*

The separations are sometimes produced as negatives, reversing the black and white areas. They are printed on *imagesetters* (see the following section). Whether positive or negative, separations are used to create the actual printing plates. The step that creates color separations is skipped when you are working "direct to plate."

Remember that separations are grayscale representations. Because grayscale is 8-bit (eight bits of computer data are available to record the shade of gray), theoretically, each ink can have 256 levels of variation. That would produce almost 4.3 *billion* possible colors ($256\times256\times256\times256$). In reality, printing presses can produce only thousands of variations of color with the four process color inks.

Imagesetters

Separations are printed on paper or film from very high-resolution laser printers called *imagesetters*. Whereas the typical office laser printer has a resolution of 600 dots per inch (dpi), imagesetters print at 1,200, 2,400, or 3,600dpi. Most imagesetters are PostScript printers, using PostScript Level 2 or 3.

The paper or film on which the imagesetter prints is then used to produce the actual printing plates. The term *direct to plate* means that the output device actually produces plates rather than film, and so is called a "platesetter."

Printing Plates

The plates are *burned* from the color separations. A light-sensitive material is used, and the miniscule dots of the color separation protect areas of the plate when exposed to light. After the plates are burned, the areas that were protected remain capable of transferring ink to paper.

During production, the printing press rolls the plate against inked rollers and then presses it against the paper. The plate picks up ink (where it wasn't burned) from the rollers and deposits it on the paper. The machinery and processes are vastly more sophisticated, but the theory is similar to what you may have used in elementary school art classes. As a youngster, you might have applied ink to wooden blocks with patterns cut into them. The area that isn't cut away stands out from the rest, receives the ink, and makes contact with paper, leaving the ink behind. This is also the same as the process of being fingerprinted: The police officer rolls the suspect's fingertips on the ink pad. The fingertips are then rolled onto the card. Only the raised ridges of the fingertips transfer ink, leaving behind their distinctive patterns.

Each ink color requires a separate run through a printing unit. The job may use the standard four colors (CMYK), additional spot colors might be added, or the job can be run as a one-, two-, or three-color product.

26

Flexographic Printing

Flexographic printing plates are created from a soft, flexible material. They are wrapped around a roller for printing. Designing for flexography requires that the slight distortion of the design on the plate be taken into account. In addition, the soft plates can result in higher dot gain. Flexographic (or *flexo*) printing, traditionally used for packaging, has been around since the late nineteenth century. At that time, melted rubber was poured into plaster molds to create the plates. The production process took a giant step forward with the introduction, some 50 years later, of metal rollers with tiny etched cells to ink the plates. These little ink holes allowed more precise control over the amount of ink applied to the plate and, therefore, transferred to the paper or other material. Flexography has several advantages:

- It can be used with a wide variety of materials. Unlike traditional offset inks, which require a porous surface such as paper, flexo inks can be used on polymer films and other nonporous materials.

- Many flexo inks are opaque, allowing them to be used on dark materials.

- Flexo presses come in widths up to twice that of most offset presses, up to 10 feet wide. They can also have cylinders of various diameters, used to alter the size or repeat length of a pattern.

Recent improvements in flexo technology have resulted in plates and presses that have the same level of detail as traditional 133lpi screens.

The details of preparing artwork for flexographic printing are best discussed directly with your printer. The printer might prefer that you allow the printer's in-house team to do any necessary conversion, and you are probably well advised to let experienced people handle that aspect of the work.

COLOR ISSUES

Four-color process printing requires artwork in the CMYK color mode. Although work can be created in RGB, it must eventually be converted to CMYK for printing. In addition to the process colors, you can incorporate spot colors into your work and even reduce the number of colors below four for artistic or budgetary reasons.

CMYK Versus RGB Color

As discussed in Chapter 7, the two primary color modes in Photoshop are CMYK and RGB. RGB (red, green, blue) is used by light-generating hardware, such as monitors and projectors. It is the color mode of the World Wide Web because the Web is monitor based. CMYK (cyan, magenta, yellow, black) is the color mode of professional printing, which uses inks of the four colors to reproduce images.

Each color mode has its own *gamut*, or range of colors, that can be reproduced. RGB has an inherently larger gamut, which might need to be constricted when converting to CMYK. The colors that can be reproduced using CMYK inks can vary, too, depending on the inks and paper on which they are applied. Subtle variations in color can also be produced by the printer itself. Printers capable of finer line screens can do a better job of portraying delicate transitions between colors.

CMYK colors are defined by their percentages of the four colors. Photoshop offers CMYK mode in the Color palette and Color Picker (see Figure 26.7).

In Figure 26.7, note that the Color Picker does not have radio buttons next to the CMYK fields. The buttons next to the HSB, RGB, and Lab fields allow the Color Picker to use each of those components as the basis for color definition. CMYK component colors are not available for this purpose.

When an RGB color cannot be reproduced using standard CMYK inks, it is said to be *out of gamut*. Out-of-gamut colors should be corrected (brought into gamut) to protect the image's color fidelity. (See "Viewing and Correcting Colors" later in this chapter.)

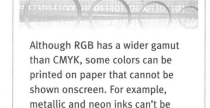

Although RGB has a wider gamut than CMYK, some colors can be printed on paper that cannot be shown onscreen. For example, metallic and neon inks can't be accurately reproduced in RGB.

Figure 26.7
In both the Color palette and Color Picker, you can define CMYK colors numerically.

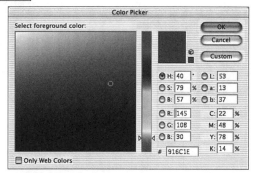

Process Versus Spot Colors

Although the four process inks (cyan, magenta, yellow, and black) can reproduce only some of the visible spectrum, they can be supplemented with *spot colors*. Unlike RGB or CMYK colors, spot colors are not calculated; rather, they are selected. Choosing from a collection of predesignated values, you can identify the appropriate color for your needs. In Photoshop, you can load collections of spot colors, called *swatch libraries* or *books*, into the Swatches palette by using the palette's menu (see Figure 26.8).

Photoshop's Color Picker can also be used to select spot colors. Open the Color Picker and click on the Custom button (below the Cancel button) to open the Custom color picker (see Figure 26.9).

26

Figure 26.8
Photoshop ships with and installs by default a number of spot color libraries.

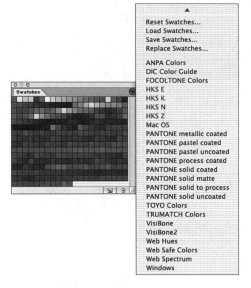

Figure 26.9
The same swatch libraries (or books) are available in the Custom color picker and the Swatches palette menu.

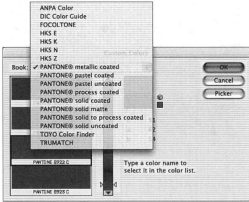

Samples of each color printed in books or ink charts showing swatches are typically used to select the appropriate color. Using a printed swatchbook is always better than trusting the appearance of a spot color on a monitor. Also, keep in mind the naming conventions of the swatches. PANTONE 105 CVU and PANTONE 105 CVC are actually the same color—PANTONE 105 CV. The U (uncoated) and C (coated) at the end of the names simply indicate an attempt to simulate onscreen the difference between uncoated and coated paper.

The term *spot color* can refer to two very different types of color. Some spot colors, such as Pantone Process Coated (one of the swatch libraries available in Photoshop), are actually process (CMYK) colors. They are standardized to ensure that the color requested is the color delivered. For example, PANTONE 269-2 CVS is the same as a CMYK blend of 80/0/70/35.

In addition, the term *spot color* can refer to colors that cannot be reproduced by using blends of the cyan, magenta, yellow, and black inks. Pantone solid colors are an example. Metallic and neon colors are also available. These colors are printed separately from the CMYK inks.

Ensure that the spot colors you apply in the Photoshop image can be used on the printing press that will run the job. Check with your printer about how the job will be printed before using spot colors. Of primary importance is the type of paper that will be used. Uncoated paper and coated paper might require different inks. In addition, spot colors used with blends or gradients may need special attention to print properly.

Spot colors that require a separate printing plate (and a separate run through the press) can increase your printing costs substantially. Using a spot color in place of one of the process colors, creating duotones or tritones, and converting the spot color(s) to process colors are ways to keep costs in check.

Viewing and Correcting Colors

Because the range of color in CMYK is limited and because not all of Photoshop's filters are available in that color mode, design and creation are often done in RGB mode and the artwork later converted for print. The difference in gamut, however, allows you to design in RGB with colors that can't be printed in CMYK. Photoshop warns you if you select an RGB color that cannot be reproduced with CMYK inks. In Figure 26.10, you can see the gamut warning for both the Color palette and Color Picker. It is a small triangle with an exclamation point.

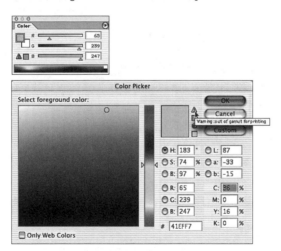

Figure 26.10
The cursor indicates the gamut warning in the Color Picker. The icon is the same in the Color palette.

Clicking the swatch that appears next to the gamut warning triangle in the Color palette or below the triangle in the Color Picker converts the color to the nearest CMYK equivalent. Photoshop automatically converts all colors to their nearest CMYK equivalents when a document is converted from RGB to CMYK mode.

Photoshop also enables you to soft proof your work. By choosing View, Proof Colors, you can check how your project is expected to print. Soft proofing is not usually considered an acceptable substitute for hard proofs, discussed earlier in this chapter. Soft proofing is feasible only when the monitor has been properly calibrated and an appropriate profile for the specific printer is available.

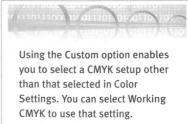

Using the Custom option enables you to select a CMYK setup other than that selected in Color Settings. You can select Working CMYK to use that setting.

The View, Proof Setup, Custom command enables you to select a color profile for the printer. You then use the View, Proof Colors command to toggle the preview on and off. The Custom option opens the Proof Setup dialog box, shown in Figure 26.11.

Figure 26.11
Changes made in this dialog box do not change the selections in the Color Settings dialog box.

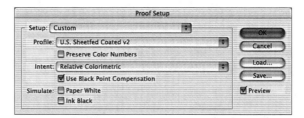

Selecting the appropriate color profile is critical if Proof Setup is to give you an accurate representation of the image. Your printer may be able to supply you with a profile for the particular press and inks that will be used on your project.

The Preserve Color Numbers option shows you what your artwork would look like if it were just thrown on the press "as is." This setting simulates printing the color values without compensating for the profile space. Normally, you should leave this option unchecked.

The Intent pop-up menu gives you the same four options that you can find in the Advanced section of the Color Settings dialog box:

- **Perceptual**—This option preserves the relationships among colors. The range of colors can be changed, but the visual differences among them are maintained. Color values can also change. Perceptual is not suitable for images in which certain colors, such as logos, must be a specific color.

- **Saturation**—The Saturation option is not acceptable for print in many circumstances. It attempts to make colors more vivid and is designed for use with presentation graphics.

- **Relative Colorimetric**—This option, the default, strives to preserve all colors that fall inside the target gamut, maintaining their color accuracy. Colors that are outside the target gamut are mapped as closely as possible but might overlap with other colors. The extreme highlight of the image (white) is mapped to white in the destination space. If the artwork is within the CMYK gamut, you need to consider only the differences among output devices. These differences are usually minor.

- **Absolute Colorimetric**— Like the Relative Colorimetric option, this one tries to preserve colors that are within the target gamut. However, it does not take the image's white point into account.

Simulate Paper White, when selected, compensates for the medium defined in the profile (if any). Simulate Black Ink simulates onscreen the dynamic range of the selected profile.

SERVICE BUREAUS, PRINT BROKERS, AND PRINTERS

A graphic artist must do several things to prepare artwork for commercial printing. Some of the other steps, however, may be best left to others. In some cases, one individual serves as designer, artist, and prepress specialist. Understanding who is responsible for what steps, and communicating about those steps, is often the key to successfully completing a project.

Service Bureaus

It would be lovely if you had a huge budget and an office equipped with the latest and greatest machinery, ready and waiting for any project that comes along. Unfortunately, the reality is that budgets are usually tight, or at least realistic. Spending tens of thousands of dollars for a piece of equipment that you might use only a few times a year is not efficient. Hiring out that particular piece of work a couple of times a year is usually far more practical.

Service bureaus have evolved to fill that niche. The typical service bureau offers drum scanners that can produce the highest quality digital images, imagesetters that can produce the films from which printing plates are made, calibrated color proofing equipment, and various other hardware and services. Finding (and maintaining a good working relationship with) a good service bureau allows a small operation or an independent to offer all the services of a major production house. Within those major production houses, maintaining good relationships between departments is often critical to mission accomplishment. For contractors and independents, most service bureau costs can be built into a bid, an estimate, or a contract. In-house project estimators should also build in such expenses.

In the offset printing workflow, service bureaus can be used for initial scans, color corrections, color proofs, and separations or film. Most service bureaus can handle Windows as well as Macintosh files and can work with files generated by all major graphics and publishing programs. However, asking which file formats, program versions, and platforms are acceptable before you enter into a working relationship with a service bureau is always a good idea.

26

Print Brokers

Print brokers are middlemen, outside vendors who coordinate a print job for you. Some print brokers are sales representatives, with a working knowledge of the business and a stable of clients. Other print brokers may be experts in the field, with extensive experience and endless contacts. In either case, they are expected to serve as your representative to and with the printer.

Your communication with print brokers, as with anyone involved with a project, is important. Print brokers need to understand clearly what you (or the client or boss) expect before finding and contracting with a printer. The specific areas of discussion could include color fidelity, image clarity, paper quality, and finishing. If you're using a broker, you'll also want to clearly delineate areas of responsibility. Perhaps you need the broker to price out the job and determine the best printer for the contract. On the other hand, you might need a broker who is able to handle the job from the time it's completed on your computer to the time it's sent to the distribution channel.

Printers

Some printers have all the capabilities of service bureaus, and some contract out everything except putting ink on paper. The key to a good printer is twofold: fulfilling your requirements at a good price and communicating with you.

After you've received or conceived the project, determine whether any special inks or papers will be involved. If so, one of your first calls should be to the printer. Find out what requirements (and limitations) could have an impact on your creative or production process. You should also know, if you'll be transferring projects digitally, what file formats and program versions the printer can use.

Sometimes you need different printers for different types of jobs, too. One printer may produce superior color fidelity but be too expensive for a two-color insert. Another printer might be able to offer faster turnaround for emergency jobs. Having working relationships with several printers can make it possible to save money or, sometimes more important, time.

FROM THE NAPP HELP DESK

National Association of Photoshop Professionals

The National Association of Photoshop Professionals (NAPP) offers e-mail assistance to its members. Here is some advice from the NAPP Help Desk related to issues in this chapter.

More Than Just Ink-Slingers?

I called my print shop to ask which CMYK profile I should be using in my Color Settings. All they could say was "I dunno." What should I do?

Is accurate color reproduction something you don't care about at all? Is it the only print shop in town? Are you or your wife related by blood to the owner of the print shop? If the answer to *these* three questions is "No," perhaps a few phone calls are in order.

On the other hand, if you never prepare color-critical work, if the price is right, and if delivery meets the deadline, you might not have a problem. Consider your needs. It could be that having the perfect CMYK profile for that shop's Heidelberg press isn't necessary. If the results are good, whether through precise coordination of digital data or by "Kentucky windage," there's no reason to change.

Remember, too, that you can establish working relationships with different shops for different jobs. You can also use service bureaus or print brokers when necessary.

Avoiding the Trap

I hear a lot about trapping, but don't see anything about it in Photoshop. How—or should—I be trapping my images?

Photoshop is primarily an image editor, and most Photoshop work involves raster images. Trapping is typically reserved for vector artwork, in which large areas of solid color abut. You don't need to trap most Photoshop images. Service bureaus and printers often have dedicated workstations with specialized software to do trapping. Trapping can be extremely time-consuming and, therefore, very expensive. Typically, the workstations and trapping software are run by experienced professionals.

> **Caution**
>
> Although an understanding of trapping can be beneficial, leaving the actual procedure to specialists is usually best. Improper trapping can produce severe output problems. Before attempting to trap an image, speak with your printer or service bureau.

To trap properly, if the occasion does arise, expand the lighter color so that it overlaps with the darker color. Expanding the lighter color minimizes distortion of the image. The darker color's shape remains the same, resulting in less apparent change of the image. There are two basic types of trapping. A *spread* occurs when the lighter color sits on a darker background, and the area of lighter color is expanded. A *choke* occurs when the darker color sits on a lighter background, and the lighter color is extended onto the darker.

26

GRAYSCALE, LINE ART, AND VECTORS

by Richard Romano

IN THIS CHAPTER

HOW GRAYSCALE DIFFERS FROM COLOR

How does grayscale differ from color? Well, the most obvious way is that color images are, well, in color, and grayscale image are, for all intents and purposes, in black and white.

Okay, that's a cheeky answer, but grayscale images have their own set of issues and considerations when it comes to printing them. It's easy to give short shrift to grayscale; everyone is so hung up on color, and as reproduction processes continue to allow high-quality color to be reproduced, grayscale becomes the "forgotten mode." But anyone who has ever looked through a book of, say, Ansel Adams photographs knows that black-and-white is in no way inferior to color.

Depending on the images you're working with and how high-quality you need them to be, converting color images to grayscale can be as easy as just selecting Image, Mode, Grayscale in Photoshop. Depending on the image and what you intend to do with it, that's probably all you need to do. If you're working with higher-quality images, however, you'll want to have more control over the conversion process.

Want a quick refresher on converting from color to Grayscale? See "Moving to a Single Channel" in the NAPP Help Desk section at the end of this chapter.

Bit Depth

Grayscale images are often defined in terms of their bit depth, or how many bits per pixel the image has. Grayscale images usually have 8 bits per pixel, for a total of 256 shades of gray. Therefore, each pixel in a grayscale image is somewhere between a level of 0 (black) and 255 (white)(see Figure 27.1).

*For a reminder on bit depth and pixels in grayscale images, **see** Chapter 4, "Getting Pixels into Photoshop," **p. 97**.*

Figure 27.1
A grayscale image contains 256 individual shades of gray.

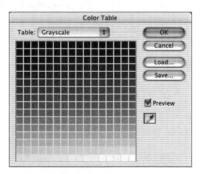

That's the standard bit depth for grayscale images, although higher grayscale bit depths are occasionally found—such as 16-bit, which works out to more than 16,000 shades of gray. Bear in mind, however, that 256 levels is toward the upper limit of what the human eye can discern. Another issue is that not all imaging programs and raster image processors can handle more than 8-bit grayscale images.

27

When you convert to Grayscale mode, Photoshop converts the pixels based on their original luminosity values. However, as you may recall from Chapter 4, this is not the best way to produce a high-quality grayscale image. You can often get better results by using the Channel Mixer to hand-craft a grayscale image out of an RGB image. Basically, you adjust the tonal ranges of each of the three color channels to arrive at an optimal grayscale image. In other words, you take the best of each channel to create the grayscale.

⇨ *For information on using Channel Mixer,* ***see*** *"Advanced Channel Manipulation,"* ***p. 425***, *in Chapter 15, "Channels: Color and More."*

PRINTING GRAYSCALE IMAGES

Like most images ultimately destined for a printing press, grayscale images created in Photoshop will likely be imported into a page layout application, such as InDesign, QuarkXPress, or PageMaker. Just as it is important for color images to be in CMYK mode, it is also important for black-and-white images to be in Grayscale mode. If RGB images are incorporated into a black-and-white page layout from which film will be made, you'll have all sorts of output problems, ranging from three pieces of film to one piece of film with empty spaces where your images should be.

It might seem odd to talk about color management in the context of grayscale images, but it's really not that big of a stretch. After all, the whole point of color management is to make the entire imaging process—from working with images in Photoshop to printing—consistent and predictable. So just as it is important to be able to accurately reproduce color images, so, too, is it important to be able to accurately reproduce black-and-white images. It's more common that you think you see a lovely grayscale image on your monitor, only to get a printed version back that contains little more than an indistinct black blob. It gets especially hairy when you're trying to reproduce certain shades of gray in a specific way—for example, the Ansel Adams book mentioned earlier.

Ink Coverage

As you just read previously, grayscale images can be represented and specified in terms of their bit depths—8-bit grayscale is the standard way of defining a grayscale image, but gray values can also be specified in other ways. In other words, you can choose which 256 shades of gray are actually used. This is accomplished via the Color Settings dialog box, which is under the Photoshop menu in Mac OS X and under the Edit menu in Windows. This is where you can set the working color space for grayscale images (see Figure 27.2).

In Macintosh, the default mode is Gray Gamma 1.8, and in Windows, it is Gray Gamma 2.2. Basically, the working color space refers to the attempt to display a grayscale image based on the monitor's gamma setting.

27

Figure 27.2
In Photoshop's Color Settings dialog box, you can define the working color space of grayscale images.

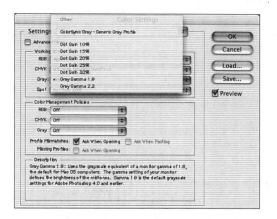

When creating grayscale images for print, often you need to compensate for *dot gain*. When a continuous-tone image such as a photograph is printed on an offset printing press, it needs to be converted to a pattern of dots, as printing presses can't print continuous tones. In other words, presses can't print shades of gray, only black or white. When an image is divided into small dots, the varying size of the dots provides the illusion of continuous tones. When this happens during the printing process, however, the problem is that the dots tend to expand. This can happen for a variety of reasons, from slight distortions during platemaking or, more commonly, by the ink being absorbed by the paper and spreading slightly.

For more information on dot gain, **see** *"Setting Screen Frequency and Angles,"* **p. 832,** *in Chapter 28, "Halftones, Screen Frequency, and Separations."*

If you've ever used plain paper in an inkjet printer, you've seen the basic issue here. The paper slurps up the highly fluid ink and the individual printer pixels spread, blurring whatever it was you printed. Because the same thing can happen (to a lesser degree) during printing, the result can be images that print more murkily than you had intended.

Using the Color Settings dialog box, you can have Photoshop attempt to compensate for dot gain by defining the grayscale in terms of percent dot gain—from 10% to 30% (see Figure 27.3). (The higher the percentage, the greater the dot gain.)

The amount of dot gain varies according to the type of press and the type of paper you'll be printing on. Uncoated papers, such as newsprint, exhibit higher degrees of dot gain than a coated paper, such as might be used for a product brochure or even a magazine. Check with your printer to see what he or she tends to experience with regard to dot gain.

By compensating for the effects of dot gain during the image-editing stage, you can attempt to eliminate any unpleasant surprises when you get your prints. Getting high-quality proofs also helps avoid being unpleasantly surprised, but even they aren't always a good predictor of dot gain.

Caution

Checking with your printer before leaping into attempts to correct for problems that could arise during printing is always a good idea. The printer might already compensate for dot gain when he or she makes film or plates. So if you've compensated for it as well, you'll end up with images that look *lighter* than you had intended.

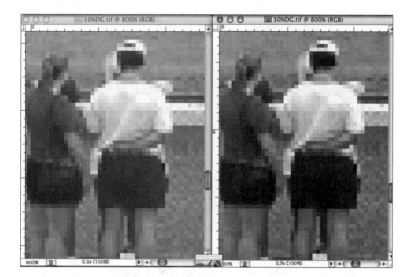

Figure 27.3
Depending on the working color space you have defined for grayscale images, Photoshop adjusts the gray values when you convert to Grayscale mode. You can detect subtle differences between 10% dot gain (left), for example, and 30% dot gain (right.)

PRINTING LINE ART

Bitmap mode, or basically 1-bit images, are typically *line art*—in other words, drawn with lines. Line art is better handled as a vector image created in a program such as Illustrator and saved in EPS format. That way, the lines and shapes that compose the image will print at the resolution of the output device.

➡ *For a detailed look at Photoshop's Bitmap mode,* **see** *"Photoshop's Other Color Modes," **p. 173**, in Chapter 7, "Color Theory and Practice."*

However, it's not always possible to create line art in Illustrator. For example, line art scanned from another source rather than drawn from scratch may have to remain as a raster image, which is where Bitmap mode comes into play.

As you know, to convert an image to Bitmap mode, it first needs to be converted to Grayscale mode (if, indeed, it began as a color image). Why might you want to convert a grayscale image to Bitmap mode? See Figure 27.4 for an example of when this method can be useful.

Sometimes, when scanning simple line art, it needs to be scanned dark (or have the levels, curves, or brightness/contrast adjusted) to get a solid line, but that has the effect of darkening the background, which might not be desirable. By converting to Bitmap mode, you can convert the background to white (see Figure 27.5).

Unless you choose to dither the image when converting to Bitmap mode, you don't have a choice about the grayscale level the program uses as the cutoff between black and white—the only option is 50%. If you use the Threshold command first with the Preview check box selected, however, you can choose your own cutoff point as you convert the image to all black-and-white tones. Then you can use the Bitmap command to switch to the right color mode without making any change to the black-and-white tones you just created.

27

Figure 27.4
This signature has been scanned very dark to get a solid line, yet now it has a grayish background.

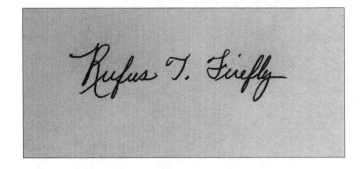

Figure 27.5
Converting a grayscale line art image to Bitmap mode helps clean up the background.

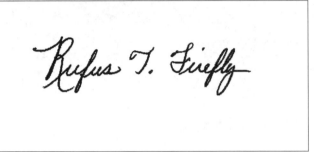

Depending on the image, you might need to use the Eraser tool to remove any random detritus or artifacts. You could then convert it back to Grayscale (if you wanted to add other color elements or layers, for example), or save it as a Bitmap mode image and import it into a page layout program.

There is one advantage to Bitmap mode: The white areas remain transparent. That means if a Bitmap mode image is imported into a page layout program that supports transparency (such as Adobe InDesign), you can overlay the line art image on top of text or other imported graphics (see Figure 27.6). Another potential advantage to Bitmap mode is that files are much smaller than the same image at the same resolution in Grayscale. However, remember that Bitmap images typically require a much higher resolution.

⇨ *Bitmap and Grayscale modes have different resolution requirements. See "Pixels for Printing" in the NAPP Help Desk section at the end of this chapter.*

27

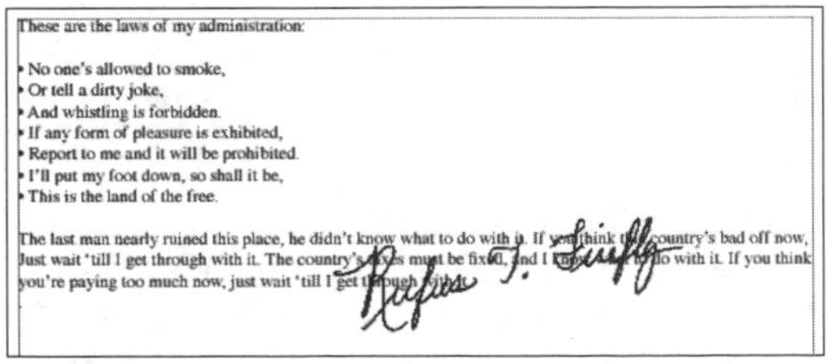

Figure 27.6
Images in Bitmap mode retain transparency in the white areas, allowing you to overlay line art on top of other page elements in a program such as InDesign.

Custom Halftone Screens and Bitmap Mode Images

You can also convert a grayscale image to a bitmap image to apply a halftone screen. That's not as farfetched as it sounds. After all, when continuous-tone images are converted to halftones, they're essentially being converted to Bitmap mode images. In other words, in a halftone, there are no continuous tones or shades of gray; there is only black or white, a dot or no dot.

To convert a grayscale image to a simulated halftone image, you select Image, Mode, Bitmap. Select your target output resolution (typically a function of the line screen at which the job will be printed—which you'll look at in more detail in Chapter 28), and then select Halftone Screen from the Output pop-up menu.

Selecting Halftone Screen in the Bitmap dialog box opens the Halftone Screen dialog box, as seen in Figure 27.7.

You'll look at this setting in more detail in Chapter 28, but basically the *halftone screen frequency* refers to how many halftone dots are in a linear inch. The greater the screen frequency, the finer the dots, and the less detectable they are.

The *screen angle* refers to the angle at which the dots are oriented with respect to the horizontal. Halftone dots are most visible to the eye when aligned with either the horizontal (0 degrees) or the vertical (90 degrees). Therefore, the angle farthest from either axis is 45 degrees, where the dots are the least perceptible.

You can also specify a dot shape other than round; you can use diamonds, ellipses, lines, squares, or crosses. Different shapes add different effects and help relieve some halftone problems, such as dot gain and/or a tendency for dots to "plug up"—or clump together—in the shadow areas.

Figure 27.8 shows a grayscale image and its Bitmap mode/halftone screen equivalent.

Caution

The halftone screen applied when converting to Bitmap mode, as you would expect, becomes part of the actual image. (In general halftoning, the screen is added during the output stage and the original image is left unscreened.) If an image with a "built in" halftone screen were then processed on a halftone printer or screened by an output provider, the two screens would combine to produce an unpleasant interference pattern called moiré. (We'll talk more about moiré in Chapter 28.) So add such a pattern to an image only if you know it won't be screened again.

If you are incorporating your images into a page layout program or are sending everything off to a service bureau or printer for output, there is little reason you would want to set up halftone screens yourself—most folks designing images for print don't usually worry about this and let their service provider handle it. However, if you *are* a service provider and you need to work with custom screens, here is how you would do it.

Figure 27.7
The Halftone Screen dialog box is where you set your halftone screen frequency, screen angle, and dot shape.

Figure 27.8
The original grayscale image (left) has been converted to a Bitmap mode image with a halftone screen (right), giving it a sort of "shot through a screen door" look.

VECTOR GRAPHICS AND PRINTING

If your Photoshop image includes vector data—such as shapes, type, and so on—you can choose to print the file using that vector data, rather than rasterizing the entire image. Why would you want to do this? Vector data prints at the resolution of the actual printer or other output device, regardless of the resolution of the Photoshop file. Raster data, on the other hand, is at the behest of the file's resolution as set in Photoshop's Image Size dialog box.

> *For a discussion of raster versus vector data, **see** "The Two Types of Computer Graphics," **p. 156**, in Chapter 6, "Pixels, Vectors, and Resolution."*

What happens when you print using vector data is that Photoshop sends each vector layer as a separate image, which are all then printed on top of each other. The vector-based images print at the resolution of the output device, and the raster-based images print at the resolution specified in the file.

> *Unsure what constitutes "vector"? See "Path-Based Artwork" in the NAPP Help Desk section at the end of this chapter.*

Preserving Vector Data in a File

You can preserve vector data in EPS and DCS formats as well as in Photoshop's native format, PDF, and the advanced version of TIFF. To do this, save the unflattened file in one of these formats (you'll be told that you can save it only as a copy, of course). In the EPS Options dialog box, make sure that Include Vector Data is checked, and then click Save (see Figure 27.9).

Caution

Files saved with the Include Vector Data option have their vector data available only to other applications, such as Illustrator, InDesign, QuarkXPress, and so on. If the file is reopened in Photoshop, it will be completely rasterized.

Figure 27.9
Saving an EPS (or DCS) image with vector data intact lets other applications take advantage of the resolution-independent nature of vector images.

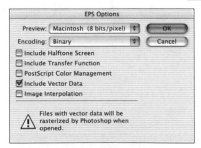

Printing Vector Data

To print this vector data, select File, Print with Preview (formerly File, Print Options in pre-7.0 versions of Photoshop). Select the Show More Options check box, and make sure the Include Vector Data check box is selected (see Figure 27.10).

Remember, however, that printing or otherwise outputting files as a prelude to printing is not always done directly from Photoshop, but from a page layout program such as InDesign or QuarkXPress. Therefore, the best strategy is to save an image with vector data as an EPS file and import into a page layout. As long as vector data exists in the EPS file, when the page layout is output, it will avail itself of that vector data.

> If the Include Vector Data check box is grayed out, you probably have a non-PostScript printer selected. You can send vector data only to a PostScript printer (or to a PDF file).

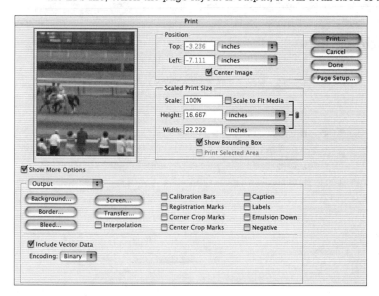

Figure 27.10
Making sure the Include Vector Data check box is enabled in the Print (with Preview) dialog box will send vector data to a PostScript printer.

PHOTOSHOP IN FOCUS

Sometimes just *part* of an image needs to be output as grayscale. When working with a CMYK image, that sometimes means making sure the selected areas of the image output only on the black separation. If they appear on all printing plates, you get *rich black*, a black supplemented with the CMY inks. To keep something in the black channel only, try this:

1. In the Layers palette, make sure the proper layer is active. If the image cannot be flattened, perform the following steps on the appropriate layers individually.

2. Make a selection of the area that needs to be grayscale. It's usually a good idea to feather the selection slightly when possible.

3. Switch to the Channels palette and make the Cyan channel active. Cut.

4. Click on the Black channel to make it active and then paste.

5. Cut from the Magenta channel and paste to the Black channel.

6. Cut from the Yellow channel and paste to the Black channel.

7. If necessary, keep the Black channel active and use Levels or Curves to adjust the selection.

Alternatively, make the selection and use the Channel Mixer. Make the selection, and then use the Image, Adjustments, Channel Mixer command. Select the Monochrome check box, adjust the sliders if desired, and then click OK. The selection is automatically cut from the CMY channels and pasted into the K channel.

FROM THE NAPP HELP DESK

The National Association of Photoshop Professionals (NAPP) offers e-mail assistance to its members. Here is some advice from the NAPP Help Desk related to issues in this chapter.

Moving to a Single Channel

I know it's all in Chapter 15, but can I get a summary of the color-grayscale conversion process?

Sure! You can simply use Image, Mode, Grayscale. You can precede that with the Image, Adjustments, Desaturate command, which often produces a better tonal range. To maintain precise control of the conversion, use the Image, Adjustments, Channel Mixer command. Select the Monochrome check box, and use the sliders to balance the content of the output channel. Afterward, use Image, Mode, Grayscale.

Pixels for Printing

What is a good resolution for Bitmap mode images?

Line art saved in Bitmap mode is not typically screened during output. Instead of converting it to a series of halftone dots, the artwork is output as is. There are no shades of gray to soften edges and curves, so images in Bitmap mode appear as a series of short jagged lines unless they are high resolution. Typically, line art is prepared at 1200dpi for print. By the way, a 1200dpi Bitmap mode image is often larger than a 300dpi Grayscale image of the same print dimensions.

Path-Based Artwork

What is "vector" artwork and how does it differ from the usual stuff?

Rather than a series of pixels, vector artwork consists of *paths* that are filled with color or have color applied as strokes. (The subject is discussed fully in Chapter 6.) In Photoshop, type, shape layers, and layer vector masks are vector based.

HALFTONES, SCREEN FREQUENCY, AND SEPARATIONS

by Richard Romano

IN THIS CHAPTER

HALFTONES AND GRAYSCALE

In Chapter 26, "The Printing Process: A Primer," you got a brief overview of offset printing in general. In this chapter, you'll delve into the process in more detail. Specifically, you will look at the *halftone* and its place in printing.

Why Halftones?

As you saw in Chapter 26, halftones exist because an offset press cannot print continuous tones; in other words, it can't print shades of gray. There is only ink or no ink; you can't vary the amount of ink at any given point. (It's kind of a "binary" process, if you think about it.) That's fine if you're printing only text: black type, white paper, what more do you need? When you want to print photographic images, which are nothing *but* continuous tones, things can get a bit trickier, however.

Take a simple black rectangle, as shown in Figure 28.1.

Figure 28.1
A basic filled shape, such as a black rectangle, is easy to print.

There is no variation of color throughout it, so it can be printed as one solid image. (Such areas of printed documents are, in fact, referred to as *solids*.) Bam! You're done. However, something like Figure 28.2 is a bit more complicated.

Figure 28.2
Printing a photograph, which is comprised of continuous tones, is a trickier proposition.

Happily, the problem was solved more than a hundred years ago with the advent of halftone photography. (It was a descendent of an earlier process for producing *mezzotints*—a term that means, in Italian, "halftone.") In the 1890s, the first lined screen appeared. It was a sheet of glass with grid lines on it. When a continuous-tone image was photographed through it, it was broken up into a series of dots.

All Dot Cons

What you ultimately end up with is a photographic image broken up into a series of equally spaced, very small dots of varying size. Let's think about simple black-and-white images—printing black ink on white paper. The size of the dots is a function of the density of a particular portion of an image. For example, in *highlights* (the lightest portions of an image), the dots are very small or even nonexistent; these areas often appear as white. In *shadows* (the darkest portions of an image), the dots are very large indeed and appear dark gray to black. In *midtones* (portions of an image between highlights and shadows—sort of the middle ground between shadow and substance, as Rod Serling might put it), the dots are larger than highlight dots but smaller than shadow dots, and to the naked eye appear grayish (see Figure 28.3).

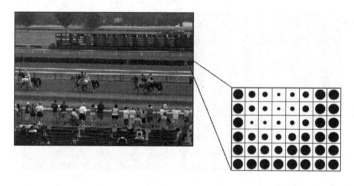

Figure 28.3
A continuous-tone image is turned into a halftone by breaking up the image into a series of evenly spaced dots of varying size.

Each dot is the same color, and it is the variations in size that trick the eye into seeing continuous tones. In other words, printed photographs are an optical illusion. Because this book was printed on a printing press, just look closely at the photograph in Figure 28.3, and you should see a dot pattern.

⇨ *Halftone images are all around us. See "Looking for Dots" in the NAPP Help Desk section at the end of this chapter.*

To further enhance the illusion, black-and-white halftones are made with the screen at a 45-degree angle because the dots are not as detectable as they'd be if they were horizontal or vertical.

The Silent Screen

Halftone screens are measured in *lines per inch* (*lpi*). This number also equals the number of halftone dots in a linear inch. (This measurement is also referred to as "screen frequency" and "line screen." The graphic arts field is notorious for having more than one term that describes the same thing.) So a halftone screen having 133 lines per inch is referred to as a 133-line screen, and it will produce halftones having 133 dots per inch.

28

Halftone screens can range from as low as 60lpi to up to more than 600lpi. Not surprisingly, the higher the screen frequency, the less perceptible the dots and the "better" the image. There are different screens for different purposes. The choice of line screen is largely a function of the printing press that will be used. Just as desktop printers vary in quality, so, too, do printing presses. (The paper and the plates also play roles.) Not all printing presses have the ability to print high screen frequencies. A 60lpi–100lpi screen is typical for newspaper presses. Screens in the 133lpi–150lpi range are common in magazine and commercial printing. For ultra-high-quality printing, 150lpi and up are used. (For those playing along at home, the high end of the screen frequency range is typically reproducible only on a "waterless" offset press, a type of printing press that uses special plates and inks that preclude the need to use a fountain solution.)

➡️ *Want a close look at how line screen frequency affects image quality? See "Line Screen Comparison" in the NAPP Help Desk section at the end of this chapter.*

Electronic Dot Generation

The halftone production process described previously is largely obsolete. The glass screens were the first to go, replaced by film-based "contact screens." Then digital imaging replaced the contact screens. Halftone dots are now produced digitally via a process called *electronic dot generation* (*EDG*). Here's where things get fun. As you know, digital output devices—be they desktop inkjet and laser printers or high-resolution imagesetters and platesetters—print an image as a series of very small pixels. Inkjet printers tend to be in the 600dpi–1440dpi range, and imagesetters tend to be in the 2000+dpi range, so the pixels are very small. Indeed, they're much smaller than halftone dots. For these devices to print halftones, they need to build halftone dots out of pixels. There are a variety of ways to do this, but suffice it to say that device pixels are grouped into halftone *cells* that simulate traditional photographically obtained halftone dots (see Figure 28.4).

Where is EDG done? Typically, in a *raster image processor* (*RIP*), which is a hardware and/or software device that processes PostScript code and converts a graphic file into the array of pixels specific to the output device. Say what?

Caution

By the way, this measure of halftone dots per inch should not be confused with the measure of resolution we have been talking about throughout this book. We're not up to the digital world yet in this discussion.

Inkjet printers don't use halftone dots to create images. Rather than evenly spaced rows containing dots of various sizes, *stochastic* printers use only one tiny size of dots and place them irregularly to create the image. For more information on this type of printing, see the sidebar "What's the Frequency, Kenneth?," later in this chapter.

Not all laser printers are PostScript devices. Because PostScript is licensed from Adobe on a per-device basis (at a rather hefty fee), less expensive laser printers often "emulate" PostScript.

You can send a file directly from Photoshop to a RIP, but it's more common to import a Photoshop graphic into a page layout application, such as InDesign, first.

Okay, think of it like this. When you send a QuarkXPress or InDesign page to a PostScript-based laser printer, the application is converting all the page elements into PostScript code. There is a RIP in the laser printer (built-in RIPs in laser printers are usually referred to as "PostScript interpreters") that takes the PostScript code and converts it into a raster image that corresponds exactly to how the device puts pixels on paper. It's the same basic process when you output a Quark file to an imagesetter, but instead of the magic elves inside the printer doing the RIPing (yes, it's a verb, too), a separate device called a RIP does it.

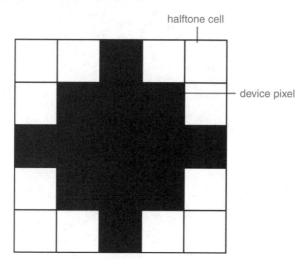

halftone cell

device pixel

Figure 28.4
An output device's pixels are grouped into matrices of various dimensions to form halftone cells that approximate photographically obtained halftone dots.

SEPARATIONS FOR OFFSET PRINTING

The preceding discussion is concerned strictly with black-and-white images. Color images create a whole new set of issues.

A Separate Piece

Process color printing, as you recall, uses four colors—cyan, magenta, yellow, and black. When a color image is to be printed, it first must be separated into four pieces: the cyan portion, the magenta portion, the yellow portion, and the black portion. So you need four halftones. But here's the rub: You'll recall that black-and-white halftones orient the screen at a 45-degree angle. When you have four halftones, each color has to be at a different angle; otherwise, the dot patterns interfere with each other and create an unpleasant optical effect called a moiré (pronounced MWAH-ray) pattern. (The term comes from a type of woven fabric that has a "watery" design.) Unfortunately, it's easy to create a moiré pattern; keeping each screen more than 30 degrees from the others keeps moiré at bay, but 30×4 = 120 degrees, and technically there are only 90 degrees to work with. Over the years, however, printers have found a set of angles for each color that works (see Figure 28.5).

Sometimes these values are expressed relative to the vertical: Yellow would be 90 degrees; magenta, 75 degrees; black, 45 degrees; and cyan, 105 degrees. The four are still the same distance from each other.

28

Figure 28.5
The four process colors are oriented so that the dots are at varying angles so as to eliminate moiré patterns.

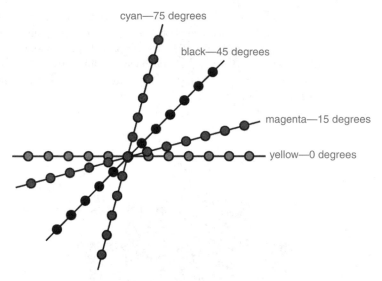

cyan—75 degrees

black—45 degrees

magenta—15 degrees

yellow—0 degrees

A variation of as little as 0.01 degree can cause moiré, so varying the screen angles is not recommended.

Off on a Tangent

When you get into electronic dot generation, things get tricky. As you have seen, on digital output devices halftone dots are actually composed of smaller device pixels, which are grouped into cells. The RIP has to calculate the angle at which to set the cells, but this isn't simply a case of rotating a physical screen. It's a function of the device's resolution and internal "bit map"—the places it can actually put pixels. So the algorithms used by RIPs to determine these angles calculate the tangent (which you might recall from trigonometry is the ratio of the opposite and adjacent sides) of the standard screen angles. At 45 and 0 degrees, this is no problem. However, the tangents of 15 and 75 degrees are irrational numbers—in other words, they repeat endlessly, like *pi* (3.143159 and so on into infinity). So the "digital screens" can't be placed exactly where they need to be. Different screening algorithms take different approaches to this problem. In most cases, they vary the number of pixels in a cell so that they can come close. It's a complicated process, but it works.

Spot colors are also considered color separations; as you'll see in the discussion of spot colors (see "Adding Colors via the Channels Palette"), you produce a separate piece of film and/or plate for each defined spot color. You don't need to worry about screen angles for spot colors; because spot colors are not overprinted the way that process colors are, there is no chance of the dot patterns interfering.

What's the Frequency, Kenneth?

Stochastic screening, a somewhat newish method of producing halftone dots, has been gaining in popularity. Traditional halftoning is based on dots that are evenly spaced but vary in size. In stochastic screening, all the dots are the same size, but they're placed where they're needed. So shadow areas would have thick clusters of dots, highlights would have sparsely spaced dots, and so on. As a result, stochastic screening is also called *frequency modulated (FM) screening*, and traditional halftoning is thus referred to as *amplitude modulated (AM) screening*. The dots in stochastic screening are tiny (about 15–20 microns in diameter). (There are two "orders" of stochastic screening, including one that does vary the size of the dots, but we'll not go there.) This figure shows an example of frequency modulated screening and amplitude modulated screening.

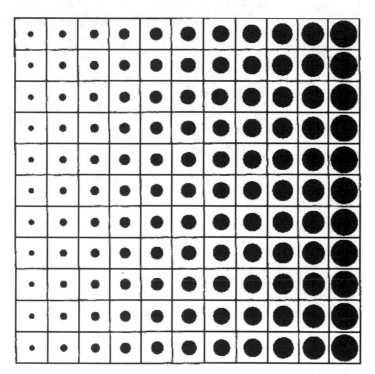

In contrast to traditional AM screening (top), in which the halftone dots are equally spaced but of varying size, FM screening uses dots that are equally sized but vary in their spacing.

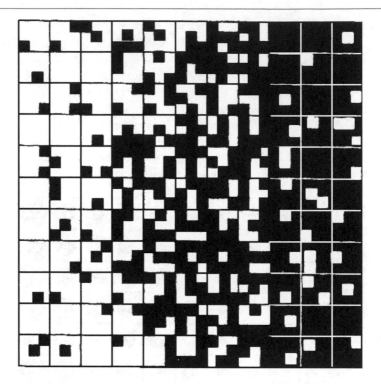

The advantages of stochastic screening include the elimination of moiré and much better approximation of continuous tones. Digital images that use stochastic screening also don't need to have as high a resolution as AM screening requires, so file sizes can be kept small.

The disadvantages include the inability of many presses to handle the small dots, and creating films and plates for stochastic screening were processes fraught with difficulty in the past. However, the increased prevalence of computer-to-plate imaging systems (which image the plates directly from digital data using a laser) has cleared up many of these performance problems, and there are many who think that stochastic may finally be "ready for prime time."

SETTING SCREEN FREQUENCY AND ANGLES

The first step in setting a screen frequency is to talk with your printer (the person who runs the press, not your desktop printer; you shouldn't talk to your office equipment). Because the line screen is determined by the printing press, and therefore the printer, it is pointless to "take a guess."

Setting Screen Information in Photoshop

By default, Photoshop leaves all screen frequency, angle, shape, and similar settings up to the output device/provider. To change this default and enter your own customized settings, go to File, Print with Preview. (Photoshop 6 used the File, Print Options command.) At the bottom of the Print dialog box is a Show More Options check box. Select it, and the bottom of the dialog box unfurls to reveal more output options.

The Screen button, when clicked, opens the Halftone Screens dialog box (see Figure 28.6).

Use Printer's Default Screens is enabled by default, which leaves the burden of screening to the output device/provider. To activate the rest of this dialog box, deselect this option.

You use the Ink pop-up menu to select each of the four process inks so that you can configure settings for them.

Caution

Manually inputting screen settings should be done only on the advice of your service bureau or print shop.

If the image is in grayscale mode, the Ink pop-up menu does not exist.

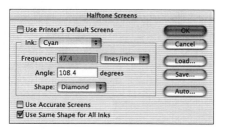

Figure 28.6
The Halftone Screens dialog box is where you change the screen settings.

At that point, you can enter a screen frequency and an angle for each ink. For example, if your printer is using a 150-line screen, you would enter 150 for all four inks. You can also determine whether you want the Frequency setting of 150 to be lines per inch or lines per centimeter. Photoshop doesn't recalculate if you change the measurement unit, so make sure it's correct!

Halftone dots, especially in the digital world, can be all sorts of different shapes (see Figure 28.7).

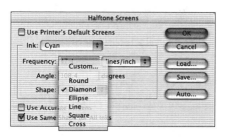

Figure 28.7
In Photoshop, you can vary the shape of the halftone dots.

28

Shapes other than round can help solve some printing problems; elliptical dots, for example, can bring some relief from *dot gain*, the physical expansion of halftone dots when they're printed, especially on highly absorbent substrates (the ink spreads and the dots start to run into each other). (By the way, *substrates* is just a fancy-schmancy term for what you print on—usually, it refers to paper.) Other dot shapes can alleviate other printing problems, such as moiré.

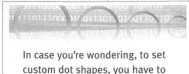

In case you're wondering, to set custom dot shapes, you have to do it by entering PostScript commands in the Custom dialog box.

Customized dot shapes can also add special effects to images, and depending on the RIP, you can create whatever shape you want—bowties, trefoils, even the silhouette of Whistler's mother, if you are so inclined. Needless to say, change the dot shape only if you're sure you know what you're doing.

You can even have differently shaped dots for different inks. If you'd like Photoshop to automatically ensure that the same shape is used throughout, make sure the Use Same Shape for All Inks check box is selected.

If you click the Auto button, you can have Photoshop calculate the best screen frequency and angles (see Figure 28.8).

Figure 28.8
If you tell Photoshop the resolution of the output device and the screen frequency you intend to use, Photoshop can calculate what it thinks are the best frequencies and angles for each ink.

If you create a set of screen settings and want to be able to use them again or hand them off to another user, you can save them by clicking the Save button. To use a previously saved set of screen settings, click the Load button and navigate to the desired file. Halftone screen settings are saved to a file with the .ahs file extension.

Finally, Accurate Screens is an Adobe halftoning system used in Adobe PostScript Level 2 (and higher) RIPs, particularly those using an Emerald controller. If you are outputting to such a device, selecting Use Accurate Screens allows the Accurate Screens software to plug in the correct angles and frequencies specific to the device it's running on. If you are not outputting to such a device, this command will be ignored whether it is selected or not.

Image Resolution and Screen Frequency

Most Photoshop users will probably never have to go through the process described in the previous section. Given how badly you can mess up your images by inserting incorrect screen angles, it's something that's best left to a professional (unless you are a professional, of course).

For the most part, though, screen frequency is an issue only when determining how much image resolution you need. For example, whatever application is doing the screening needs to have enough pixels available to weave them into halftone cells. There are no hard and fast rules here; it's generally held that your image resolution should be 1.5–2 times the screen frequency your printer intends to use. So, for example, if you know your job will be printed using a 133-line screen, your image resolution should be in the 200dpi–266dpi range. If your printer is using a 90-line screen, you can get away with an image resolution of 135dpi–180dpi. If your printer is using a 200-line screen, however, you'll need to be in the neighborhood of 300dpi–400dpi.

Again, these are not hard and fast rules, and depending on whom you ask about resolution versus screen frequency, you'll likely get different responses. These are just rules of thumb, and some people have bigger thumbs than others.

The rule of 1.5-to-2 times the lines screen frequency does not apply to stochastic printers, which have no line screen. Rather, use an image resolution of one-third the printer resolution. For most inkjets, an image resolution of 240 dpi is optimal.

By the way, the term "HiFi Color" was coined by printing industry expert and all-around color guru Don Carli. It's a registered trademark of Mills Davis, a graphic arts consultancy.

HIFI COLOR SEPARATIONS

We know what you're thinking—HiFi color separations? What does my stereo system have to do with color separations? The closest it ever comes is the cover of Pink Floyd's *Dark Side of the Moon*.

What Is HiFi Printing?

The short answer is that it is any type of printing (for our purposes here, offset printing) that uses more than the usual four process color inks. One common iteration that has been around for a long time basically involves adding a fifth or sixth color—what are called "bump plates." These additional colors are usually specially mixed colors, maybe even metallic inks or varnishes, that add effects or make a specific design element stand out. Packaging, for example, often uses special colors, as do many magazines (at least on the cover). Greeting cards also use a variety of fancy inks.

Another answer is that it is a suite of tools, software, and inks for printing with five-, six-, seven-, even eight-color inksets. There are two main approaches to HiFi printing: adding additional plates of C, M, Y, and/or K, or adding additional colors, such as orange, green, red, blue, brown, and so forth. Regardless of how it is actually done, the whole purpose of HiFi printing is to increase the color gamut.

Although many solutions have floated through the industry over the years, probably the most recognized commercial HiFi printing system is Pantone's Hexachrome. Hexachrome uses a six-color inkset comprising modified CMYK inks and adding fluorescent orange and green (hence it's often referred to as CMYK+OG).

Going Big

Large-format printers are output devices that can print larger than 13×19 inches, and usually in excess of 35, 45, even 55 inches wide. They are, more often than not, inkjet printers and can often be considered "HiFi" color devices, as they print with more than the typical CMYK inks. Some use 6 colors (Epson printers, for example, add light cyan and light magenta to boost the color gamut), some use 8, and ColorSpan models even went to as many as 12 colors. With these devices, you don't need to worry unduly about how many separations you've got, as they print much like your average desktop inkjet printer (except that they're huge).

However, for those who want true HiFi color on a large-format device, Pantone's Hexachrome system is available for many models. Check with your service bureau, or visit www.pantone.com for information on how to work with it.

HiFi Printing and Photoshop

The first step in working with HiFi color in Photoshop is to make sure you have found a printer who can actually print it! Many presses can handle up to six colors; check with the printer to see exactly what your options are. Those additional colors might not be Hexachrome or even process colors, but may be spot colors or special inks, such as metallics—in other words, the old "bump plate" approach.

You can find lists of print shops that have four+-color capabilities by checking the ads in your phone book, in trade publications, or in the *Graphic Arts Blue Book*, the premier resource for finding graphic arts vendors, suppliers, and printers. For more information, visit www.gabb.com.

Adding Colors via the Channels Palette

For an image in CMYK mode, four plates are generated when the file is output. To print additional colors, additional separations are needed. This is accomplished by adding channels.

As a simple example, say you were working on a postcard and wanted to print a line of type using a metallic color. The first step is to select the part of the image you want to make a separate channel. After the selection is loaded, go to the Channels palette menu and select New Spot Channel (see Figure 28.9).

Figure 28.9
With the portion of the image you want to make a spot color selected, choose the New Spot Channel command from the Channels palette menu.

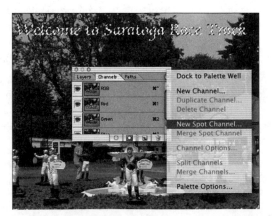

⇨ *Not sure when to use spot colors? See "Adding Color, Adding Cost" in the NAPP Help Desk section at the end of this chapter.*

The New Spot Channel dialog box will appear, as seen in Figure 28.10.

Figure 28.10
The New Spot Channel dialog box is where you select your color.

If you click on the color swatch next to the word *Color*, you'll bring up the usual Photoshop Color Picker. When choosing spot colors, it is customary to pick one from a swatchbook, be it a Pantone, Trumatch, or some other industry-standard book. If you click on the Custom button in the Color Picker, you'll access the Custom Colors dialog box—this is where you can browse through swatchbooks and pick a color you like (see Figure 28.11).

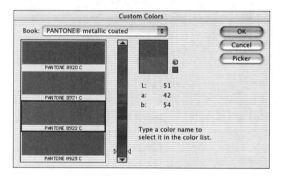

Figure 28.11
Photoshop's Custom Colors dialog box is where you browse through swatchbooks and pick a color.

There are many swatchbooks to choose from—a litany of Pantones (metallic coated, pastel coated/uncoated, process coated, solid coated/uncoated, solid matte, solid to process), Toyo, Focoltone, ANPA, and more.

Assume for this example that you've spoken to your printer, and he or she can indeed run metallic colors. Select Pantone Metallic Coated from the Book pop-up menu. Next, click on one of the color stripes in the narrow vertical bar in the center of the dialog box to select the basic hue, and then click the up or down arrow to scroll through the swatches. When you select a swatch, if your dialog boxes are positioned strategically, you can see the new color applied to the selection (see Figure 28.12).

If you click OK, you'll be taken back to the New Spot Channel dialog box (or if you click Picker, you'll be sent back to the Color Picker).

By the way, when selecting and specifying colors for print, you're better off using a printed swatchbook to see what the colors *really* look like when printed, rather than relying on the onscreen approximations.

"Coated" and "uncoated" refer to coated or uncoated paper. Inks can have different color characteristics on different types of paper.

28

Figure 28.12
No, it's not gray. The selected color is actually gold.

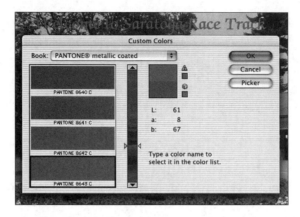

The name of the custom color specified in the swatchbook appears in the Name text box, and it's best not to change it. Because you'll be using that exact name (and/or number, such as "Pantone 8643 C") to specify the additional ink to your printer, it makes sense to keep it. (Other applications, such as InDesign, might need the correct name, too.)

The Solidity text box refers to the onscreen simulation of how the new ink interacts with the colors beneath it. A setting of 100% means that the color will completely obscure the ink beneath it, like a metallic ink. A setting of 0% would make it completely transparent, like a varnish. This setting has no effect on how the image will be printed, just how it is previewed onscreen.

If you click OK, the new channel will appear in your Channels palette (see Figure 28.13).

To preserve spot channels, the image then needs to be saved in DCS format, which preserves spot channel information. (PDF will do the trick, too.)

If the image is then imported into a page layout program, such as InDesign, the spot channel goes with it. When you output the file, you can see in InDesign's print dialog box that five plates will be made (see Figure 28.14).

A *varnish* is a transparent glossy coating applied to a printed sheet. You've surely seen book covers, for example, that were glossy only in certain areas. That's called a *spot varnish*, and it is printed in the same way as a spot color. In other words, a separate plate is made containing the varnish "separation"—the part of the image that is to be varnished. Such a separation would also be prepared in Photoshop the same way you would prepare a spot color separation. To avoid confusion, you can name the plate "Varnish" and simulate its effect with a light gray color and a low solidity setting. Remember to tell your printer that you're using a varnish plate!

Figure 28.13
The new channel appears at the bottom of your Channels palette.

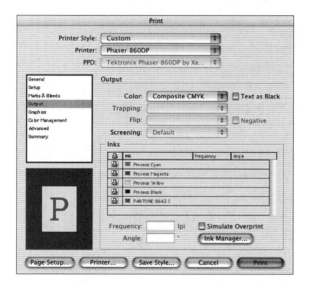

Figure 28.14
The Print dialog box as seen in InDesign. If this file were sent to a service bureau or printer, five color separations would be made.

Other HiFi Color Options

Formal and proprietary HiFi color systems, such as Pantone's Hexachrome and others, are not built in to Photoshop natively. They manage the color separations via special plug-ins to Photoshop. For example, Pantone's HexWare (part of the Pantone ColorSuite) works with Photoshop to make the six-color separations and apply color profiles so that a Hexachrome-certified printer (and they need to be) can print it accurately. These profiles are also used in the proofing process, and special Hexachrome proofing inks need to be used to proof Hexachrome separations.

By the way, if you have an alpha channel in your image, you can convert it to a spot channel by double-clicking on the channel in the Channels palette and selecting Spot Color from the Channel Options dialog box.

28

Proofing HiFi Color

As you can imagine, working with metallics or other specialty inks raises one crucial issue: How do you proof them? Most desktop or even professional proofing devices don't use metallic inks. If your printer offers metallic-ink printing, color profiles are probably built in to the proofing system that can be used to simulate metallic inks (or whatever specialty ink you might be using).

The upshot is that whenever you are working with colors beyond CMYK, make sure you talk with your printer beforehand.

PHOTOSHOP IN FOCUS

To get a firsthand look at how halftone dots work together, follow these steps:

1. In Photoshop, use the File, New command. Create a new CMYK document, 800×600 pixels, filled with white, resolution 72 ppi.

2. Select the Gradient tool from the Toolbox.

3. In the Options Bar, open the Gradient palette by clicking on the arrow to the right of the gradient sample. Select the Spectrum gradient.

4. Drag a linear gradient to fill the new document with color.

5. Filter, Pixelate, Color Halftone opens the Color Halftone dialog box. Click the Default button, then the OK button.

6. Use the Navigator palette to zoom to 400%. Use the Hand tool to drag the image around, looking at the pattern of dots.

7. In the Channels palette, click on the Cyan channel to make it the only active (and visible) channel. Drag around with the Hand tool to see the size of the dots in various areas.

8. Inspect the other channels, one at a time.

9. When finished, close the document without saving it.

FROM THE NAPP HELP DESK

The National Association of Photoshop Professionals (NAPP) offers e-mail assistance to its members. Here are some questions from the NAPP Help Desk related to issues in this chapter.

Looking for Dots

I'd like to see more examples of how photographs are reproduced using dots of various sizes. Where can I look?

Start with any image in this book. And don't forget the color images in the center section. Also, take a gander at magazines and newspapers you have around the house and office. Really, most any printed material you find uses halftone dots to reproduce the images.

Line Screen Comparison

How does line screen frequency affect the image quality?

The line screen frequency is measured in lines per inch (lpi). That "inch" is not a square inch, but rather a linear inch, from top to bottom of the page. The more lines in an inch, the smaller the dots and the closer together the lines of dots. The smaller the dots, the finer the detail of the image.

Grab a magnifying glass and compare the dots in a glossy coffeetable book's images to those in a magazine and pictures in a newspaper. That will give you a good indication of how things vary based on line screen frequency.

Adding Color, Adding Cost

Can I use spot colors in any design, or are there restrictions?

The primary restriction is budget. Each color you add results in an additional pass through a printing press. That extra pass consumes time, ink, and usually results in a setup charge, too. Make sure you (or your client) is willing to spend the extra money before adding spot colors.

Conversely, using one or two spot colors can actually *save* money. Instead of printing in CMYK, consider using black and just a single spot color—only two passes through the presses.

POWER PHOTOSHOP

IN THIS PART

ACTIONS AND AUTOMATION

IN THIS CHAPTER

29

ACTIONS EXPLAINED

Photoshop offers an extremely powerful, yet underused, feature for improving your efficiency. It's likely that there are numerous tasks you perform regularly in Photoshop. Automating those tasks with Actions not only saves time; it ensures precision by applying the same steps every time.

Actions are simply prerecorded steps in Photoshop. You play an Action to repeat those steps on one or more images. Photoshop 7 ships with dozens of Actions, and others are available at minimal cost or free on the Web. The true power of Actions, however, is in recording your own Actions to automate your own tasks.

Virtually anything you can do in Photoshop, an Action can do for you. Some Actions are completely automated and can be run while you're away from the computer; other Actions require you to enter specific values for certain procedures. Photoshop also enables you to specify whether to use the values originally recorded with an Action or to pause the Action for you to input new values.

You create, store, organize, and play back Actions by using the Actions palette. You can create *droplets*, which are mini-applications that run Actions when one or more files are dragged onto them. Droplets are available for both Photoshop and ImageReady. You can even run Actions on multiple files sequentially as a *batch*. Batch processing of a folder of files can include subfolders.

How Actions Work

An Action consists of a series of steps in Photoshop. They are the same steps you normally would use to accomplish the same thing manually. For example, if you want to prepare an image for a page layout program, you might need to change the resolution, sharpen, and change the color mode to CMYK. These are the three steps you take:

1. Image, Image Size

2. Filter, Sharpen, Unsharp Mask

3. Image, Mode, CMYK Color

When this process is recorded as an Action, the same three steps are taken.

Actions can record the same settings as those applied when the Action was recorded, or they can pause so that you can input different settings. Commands and paths can be inserted. Painting tools, which require dragging the cursor in the image, cannot be recorded, however.

The Actions Palette

You use the Actions palette to record, play, and manage Actions. The palette contains three columns and a series of buttons across the bottom. Figure 29.1 shows the first Action of the Default Actions set, installed in the Actions palette when you installed Photoshop 7.

Remember that painting tools can be applied along paths, and that paths can be inserted into Actions. You can insert a path and apply a painting tool (or other brush-related tool) along that path.

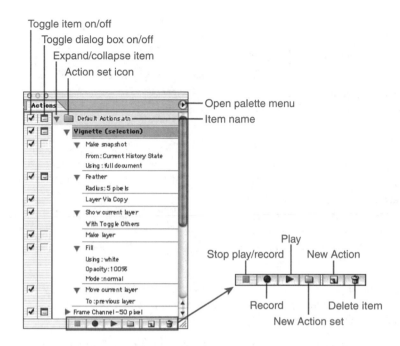

Figure 29.1
Click the triangles next to Action sets, Actions, and the individual steps of the Action to expand them, as shown here.

The On/Off Column

You use the first column to toggle items on and off. When a check mark does not appear to the left of an Action set, none of the Actions in the set are available. When the check mark is black, all Actions and each step of each Action are checked. A red arrow indicates that some, but not all, of the Actions or steps are checked. A black check mark next to an Action shows that all of its steps will run when the Action is played. A red check mark lets you know that at least one step will be skipped. The individual steps of an Action either show a black check mark (the step will play) or are blank (the step will be skipped). Use this column primarily to select which steps of an Action to execute when the Action is played. The check marks next to the Actions and Action sets are there to warn you of steps that have been turned off.

The Modal Control Column

The second column shows an icon of a dialog box, an empty box, or nothing next to each step, Action, and set. These are the *modal* indicators. An icon or an empty box shows that the step (or one or more steps within an Action or set) has user-definable parameters: a dialog box. The Action can play with the options used when the step was recorded (empty), or it can stop at the step and wait for you to change the dialog box and click OK (icon).

Like the first column, the second column is color-coded. A black icon indicates that every step that has a dialog box is set to open its dialog box and wait for input. A red icon shows that one or more steps will play with the prerecorded values. An empty box tells you that *all* steps will play with pre-recorded values. If there is no icon and no empty box, none of the steps within the Action (or set) are modal.

The Palette Body

Examine the third column of the Actions palette shown in Figure 29.1:

- The top line is the Action set to which the Action belongs. Default Actions.atn is identifiable as a set by the folder icon. You can click the downward-pointing triangle to hide the contents of the set.

- The second line, indented slightly, is selected and therefore highlighted. It is the Action named "Vignette (selection)." Selection is part of the name (assigned by the person who prepared the Action) to indicate that a selection must be made before running the Action. Clicking the triangle to the left of the name hides or shows the Action's steps.

> Check the color of the arrows and modal icons before playing an Action. They tell you whether the Action will play as originally recorded, with all steps set to run with the original parameters. If an arrow is red, one or more steps will be skipped. If a modal icon is red or black, one or more dialog boxes will open while the Action is playing.

- Below the name are the steps of the Action, indented slightly from the Action name. They are the actual commands that are executed when you run the Action. Some can be expanded and collapsed with triangles; some steps require a single line in the palette.

- The last item visible in the Actions palette is another Action, named "Frame Channel-50 pixel." Note that it is aligned with the Action "Vignette (selection)," showing that it is also a member of the Default Actions set.

The Actions Palette Buttons

Use the six buttons across the bottom of the Actions palette to create, record, play, and delete Actions. All these capabilities are duplicated by commands in the Actions palette menu.

- The leftmost button's icon is a simple square. This symbol has been used for "stop" buttons on tape recorders, VCRs, CD players, and other electronic devices for decades. When an Action is being recorded or played, click this icon to stop it.

- The Record button is also a replica of that used on various devices for a generation. Click the button to record or re-record a step in the selected Action.

- The Play button, which should also look familiar, plays the selected Action on the active document. The Action will execute according to the check marks in the first two columns next to each step.

- Create new sets of Actions by using the button with the folder icon. Actions can be moved from set to set by dragging them within the Actions palette.

- When you click the New Action button, a dialog box opens in which you can name the new Action and assign it to a function key for quick and easy play. Duplicate an Action set, an Action, or a step by dragging it to the button.

- Action sets, Actions, and individual steps can be deleted by using the button with the trash icon. You can select multiple items by Shift-clicking or (Command-clicking) [Ctrl+clicking] on them in the palette, and then delete them by clicking the button. Alternatively, you can drag items to the button to delete them.

The Actions Palette Menu

The palette's menu contains a variety of commands for creating, using, and managing Actions. Commands specific to recording and playing Actions are discussed in the appropriate sections of this chapter.

Several of the palette's menu commands can be considered "palette maintenance" commands. You can use the menu to remove all Action sets and Actions (Clear All Actions), return the palette to its default content (Reset Actions), add Action sets or Actions to the palette (Load Actions), exchange the current content for a different set of Actions(Replace Actions), and save a set of Actions so that it can be reloaded at a later time (Save Actions).

Button Mode

The Actions palette can also be displayed in Button Mode (see Figure 29.2). In this configuration, you play an Action by clicking on it. Note that the palette shows no buttons for recording Actions—this mode is for playing Actions only. In fact, when in Button Mode, the Actions palette menu commands related to creating, recording, and even playing are grayed out.

Recording actions and creating Action sets in the palette doesn't preserve them. To ensure that you won't accidentally delete your custom Actions by resetting the palette, use the Save Actions command.

Before switching to Button Mode, you can rearrange actions by dragging them up and down in the Actions palette.

Caution

When you play an Action by clicking it in Button Mode, it plays as last configured. Steps that are unchecked do not play, and modal controls are shown or not shown as last set. Button Mode gives no indication if one or more steps of an Action will not play.

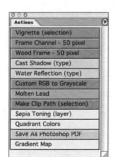

Figure 29.2
Depending on the size and shape of the palette, Button Mode can display Actions in one column or multiple columns.

Actions are sorted in the palette according to their order, not by assigned color. (An Actions color can be assigned when recorded or through the palette's menu command Action Options.) Actions sets are ignored in Button Mode.

29

➡ *If you're running in Button Mode and the Actions are misbehaving, see "Double-Check" in the NAPP Help Desk section at the end of this chapter.*

WORKING WITH ACTIONS

An Action can be played on a selection, an image, or even a folder filled with images (using the Batch command). The Action can run while you're away from the computer—even at home, fast asleep—or you can sit at the keyboard and make changes to how the Action is applied to each image.

Running an Action

In a nutshell, you select the Action in the Actions palette and click on the Play button at the bottom of the palette. Some Actions require that a selection be made first to identify a part of the image with which to work. Other Actions may require that a type layer be available or that an image meet minimum or maximum size requirements. Color mode can also be a factor, especially when an Action applies a filter or uses an Adjustment command.

The Actions palette menu includes the Playback Options command. You can choose from three "speeds" at which the Action can run:

- **Accelerated**—This is the "normal" speed. The Action runs as fast as it can, moving through each step in sequence. It stops for modal dialog boxes and preprogrammed stops.

- **Step by Step**—After each step executes, the screen is completely redrawn, and then the Action continues. This option is somewhat slower, but does give you the opportunity to stop the Action if something drastically unexpected appears.

- **Pause For**—You can have the Action play back in steps, pausing for a specified period, between 1 and 60 seconds, before executing the following step. The screen is updated after each step.

If an audio annotation has been recorded with the Action, you have the option of pausing until the message is completed or continuing with the Action while you listen.

An icon in the column immediately to the left of a step's name in the Actions palette indicates that it is modal, and a dialog box will open. Photoshop waits until you click OK before continuing with the Action. If you click Cancel, the Action stops at that step and waits for you to again click the Play button.

To play a single step of an Action, select that step in the palette and (Command-click) [Ctrl+click] the Play button. Alternatively, you can press (Command) [Ctrl] and double-click the step in the palette.

Because Actions typically execute a number of steps, taking a snapshot in the History palette beforehand is a great idea. Should the Action not produce the expected results, you've got a one-click Undo.

Loading Actions

The Actions palette menu's bottom section shows a list of all Action sets in the Photoshop Actions folder. By default, Photoshop 7 installs several sets of Actions. You can add your own sets to the list by placing them in the folder. You'll find the Photoshop Actions folder inside the Presets folder, within the Adobe Photoshop 7.0 folder.

Remember that you risk losing your custom Actions until you use the Save Actions command. If Photoshop needs to be reinstalled, or if you use the Clear Actions or Reset Actions commands, unsaved Action sets are lost.

Sets of Actions not located in the Photoshop Actions folder can be loaded into the palette by using the palette's menu command Load Actions. In the dialog box, navigate to the Actions, select them, and click Load. They will appear at the bottom of the Actions palette, ready to be played.

The palette menu also offers the commands Clear All Actions (which empties the palette), Reset Actions (which restores the palette to its default content), Replace Actions (which clears the current content and adds the selected set), and Save Actions (which saves the selected Actions set).

Batching It

A folder full of files can have the same Action applied to it with one command. Using the command File, Automate, Batch opens the Batch dialog box shown in Figure 29.3.

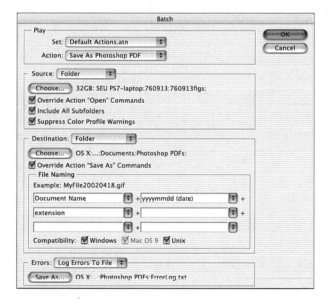

Figure 29.3
The Batch command applies the selected Action to all files in the folder that Photoshop can open. Some Actions, however, might not be appropriate for all files.

You select a number of settings in the Batch dialog box:

- The set that is currently selected in the Actions palette appears; however, you can select another from the Set pop-up menu. If no selection is current in the Actions palette, the first set in the palette is shown.

- The Action is the one currently selected. If no Action is currently selected, the first Action in the selected set is shown. Any other Action in that set can be selected from the pop-up menu.

- The Batch command needs to know which files are to be modified. You can make the selection by using the Choose button in the Source section. In the dialog box, navigate to and select the folder containing the images you want to modify.

- The Override Action "Open" Commands option ignores any commands within the Action that call for opening a file. When a folder is selected, the files inside are automatically opened by Batch.

- If the source folder includes subfolders, the Include All Subfolders option enables you to decide whether to include their contents.

- Suppress Color Profile Warnings is especially useful if you'll be away from your computer when the Action is run. If your color management policies are set to notify you of profile mismatches, this option prevents those warnings from stopping the Batch command. When this option is not selected, any warning stays onscreen (and no work will get done) until you click OK. If your color management policies are *not* set to warn you of mismatches, this option is unnecessary. (The policies are set in the Color Settings dialog box.)

- The Destination pop-up menu offers three choices. None leaves the altered files open in Photoshop. Save and Close replaces the original files with the modified versions. Folder (refer to Figure 29.3) enables you to choose a location for the modified files. This way, you can avoid overwriting the originals.

- When you select Folder as the Destination option, you can choose to override any Save As commands that have been written into the Action. This option ensures that the file is saved to the folder specified in Batch, rather than that specified in the Action.

- The six File Naming fields can be used in combination to create unique names for files when Folder is selected as the destination. The document's original name, a one- to four-digit serial number, a serial letter, the date (in a variety of formats), and the file extension are all possibilities. The document name and extension can be in uppercase or lowercase letters, and the document name can have initial uppercase letters for each word.

Caution

Be aware that *all* Open commands are overridden by the Override Action "Open" Commands option. If an Action requires that a second file be opened to complete its task, that command, too, is ignored. As an example, consider an Action designed to open one file, open a second file, select all and copy from the second file, return to the first, and then paste. If the Override Open option is selected, this Action will fail because it cannot open the second file.

Aliases (Macintosh) or shortcuts (Windows) to other folders are considered subfolders by Batch. You can use them to process multiple folders with a single Batch command.

Caution

If an Action contains a Save As command and it is run on a folder as a Batch command, each file is saved with the name and location specified in the Action—each file overwrites the preceding file. When the Batch command is done, you'll have only one file.

You can also enter text into one or more fields for inclusion in the new files' names. Remember, however, that at least one of the fields must change from file to file, so you must include the original document name or a serial number or letter.

- The Compatibility options ensure that the filename will be acceptable on the selected platform(s). If the original filename includes spaces or forbidden characters (characters not allowed in filenames in the OS), they are deleted or replaced with dashes or underscores. Long filenames may be truncated for Mac OS 9 compatibility. Neither Mac OS 9 or OS X allows the colon (:) in filenames, and neither OS is case sensitive (uppercase and lowercase letters are seen as the same letter).

  Windows filenames can be up to 256 characters long, and they are not case sensitive. Several characters cannot be used in filenames: forward and back slashes, colons, asterisks, question marks, quotation marks, left and right angle brackets, and vertical slashes. In order, these characters are as follows:

  / \ : * ? " < > |

  Unix filenames can be 256 characters long, cannot use the slash character (/), and are case sensitive.

- Error messages can be handled in one of two ways. Photoshop can halt the Batch processing until you've given it the okay to continue after an error, or you can create a text file with the details. If you choose the latter approach, you must select a name and location for the log file before you start the batch.

⮕ *Do you have an Action that stops partway through for no apparent reason? See "Unscheduled Halt" in the NAPP Help Desk section at the end of this chapter.*

Using Batch to Change File Formats

The Batch command saves files in their original format, whether the Destination field is set to Save and Close or to Folder. To automate a change of file format, you must include three steps:

- When recording the Action, include a Save As command followed by a Close (Don't Save) command.

- In the Actions palette, check to make sure that the modal column is not checked next to the Save As command or the Close command.

- In the Batch dialog box, choose Folder in the Destination pop-up menu, and select the Override Action "Save As" Commands check box.

Depending on the file format selected for the Save As command, you might need to flatten the file and delete alpha or spot channels. Record these steps in the Action before the Save As command.

The end result will be copies of the original images in the file format specified in the Action. The original files will be unchanged.

29

Actions as Droplets

Consider a *droplet* to be an Action packaged in an application. Instead of opening a document in Photoshop to play an Action on it, you drag the file to the droplet's icon. The Action is executed automatically. If Photoshop is not running, it is started so that the Action can run.

Actions are converted to droplets by using Photoshop's menu command File, Automate, Create Droplet. The Create Droplet dialog box is shown in Figure 29.4.

Use the Save Droplet In section of the dialog box to name the droplet and choose a location. Select the Action from which the droplet will be created in the Play section. If the Action needs to open another file to execute a step—for example, to copy from one image to another—do not override Open commands. You also have the option of including any subfolders when a droplet is played on a folder. If you'll be running the droplet while away from your computer, make sure to suppress color warnings—otherwise, you might return to find a warning showing onscreen and no files processed.

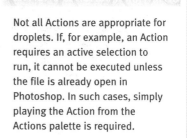

Not all Actions are appropriate for droplets. If, for example, an Action requires an active selection to run, it cannot be executed unless the file is already open in Photoshop. In such cases, simply playing the Action from the Actions palette is required.

If a droplet is created with the option to include subfolders, it plays its Action on all files in the folder and its subfolders. You can also include aliases or shortcuts to other folders.

Figure 29.4
The Destination section of the dialog box looks familiar to anyone who uses the Batch command or the File Browser's Batch Rename command.

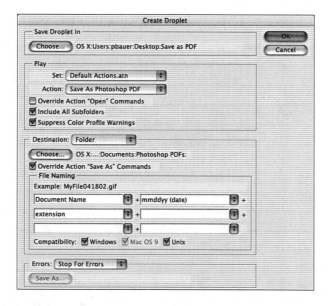

What Photoshop does with the files processed by the droplet is determined in the Destination section of the dialog box. You can elect to leave the files open (None), save the changes and close each file (Save and Close), or save the files to a new location (Folder). When Folder is selected, you have access to the options shown in Figure 29.4.

You can also create droplets in ImageReady. Such droplets automatically run the Action and apply any recorded optimization settings to any files dragged onto them. Folders of images can also be optimized by dragging them onto a droplet.

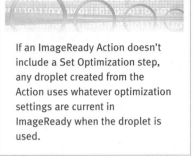

If an ImageReady Action doesn't include a Set Optimization step, any droplet created from the Action uses whatever optimization settings are current in ImageReady when the droplet is used.

Creating a droplet from ImageReady can be as simple as dragging the Action from ImageReady's Actions palette to the desktop. Alternatively, you can choose the Actions palette menu command Create Droplet. The only options are location and name.

You can also create ImageReady droplets directly from the Optimization palette. Instead of executing an Action, such droplets only apply optimization settings. Set the optimization parameters, and either drag the Optimization palette's Droplet icon to the desktop or click the icon to open the dialog box shown in Figure 29.5.

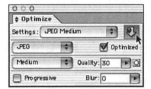

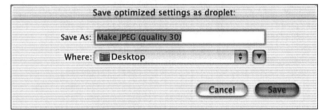

Figure 29.5
ImageReady suggests an appropriate name for the droplet based on the settings selected. You can, of course, choose a different name and specify a location.

CUSTOM ACTIONS

The true power of Actions comes through when you record them yourself. Because your custom Actions are tailored to your needs and your work, they are best suited to improving your productivity.

Recording a New Action

An Action must belong to a set. Actions are not allowed to float free in the Actions palette. You can assign an Action to an existing set by clicking on the set in the Actions palette. Alternatively, you can create a new set by using the Create New Set button at the bottom of the Actions palette or the New Set command from the palette's menu. Both open the New Set dialog box (see Figure 29.6), in which you can give the set a name.

Clicking the New Action button (or using the New Action command from the palette menu) opens the dialog box shown in Figure 29.7.

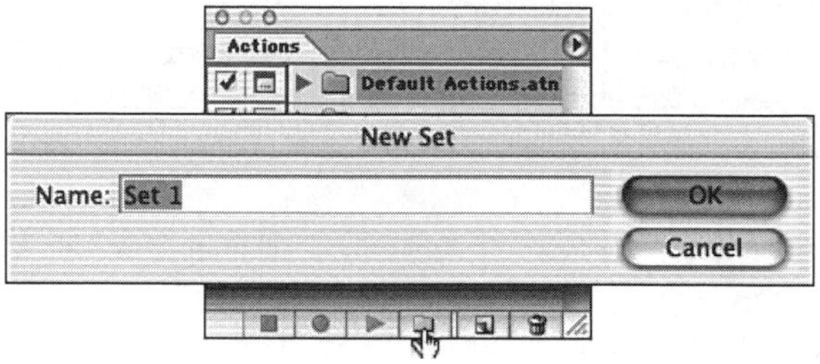

29

Figure 29.6
The only option available for Action sets is the name, which can also be changed by double-clicking it in the Actions palette.

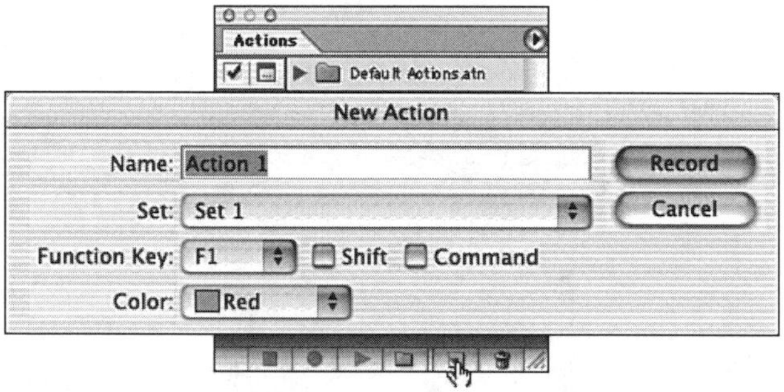

Figure 29.7
You can change your mind and assign the Action to a different set right in the dialog box.

In addition to giving the new Action a name, you can assign it to a function key, with or without modifier keys. Pressing the assigned key combination executes the Action, even if the palette is hidden. Any color assigned to the Action is used only in Button Mode.

After you click the Record button, virtually every move you make in Photoshop becomes part of the Action. You can pause the recording at any time by clicking the Stop button or using the Stop Recording command from the palette menu. To continue, click the Record button. The Record button gives a visual indicator when an Action is actually being created.

The New Action and New Set commands are not grayed out while recording an Action. You can, in fact, create new sets and Actions while recording an Action. You can even work in the Actions palette, deleting Actions and sets, while recording. These activities are not recorded as steps in the current Action.

The actual steps that can be recorded in an Action fall into several categories: recordable commands and tools, nonrecordable commands and tools, inserted paths, and stops. In addition, you can decide whether a command will use the settings with which it was recorded or pause while you enter new settings (modal commands).

After you've gone through all the steps you want in the Action, simply click the Stop button at the bottom of the palette or use the Stop Recording menu command. It is usually a good idea, especially with more complicated Actions, to make another copy of the original file and test the Action.

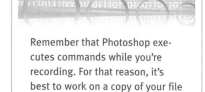

Remember that Photoshop executes commands while you're recording. For that reason, it's best to work on a copy of your file when recording an Action.

What Can and Can't Be Recorded

Generally speaking, any tool that relies on cursor movement cannot be recorded in an Action, including the Move tool and the painting, toning, healing, and eraser tools. The Zoom and Hand tools cannot be recorded, nor can the pen tools. You can, however, record options for many tools, including brushes.

Photoshop's other tools are recordable, as are these palettes: Actions, Channels, Color, History, Layers, Paths, Styles, and Swatches.

Opening dialog boxes for frequently used commands that have no shortcut, such as Image Size, can be recorded in an Action. Record the Action using Insert Menu Command and assign an F-key. Press the key, the dialog box opens—instant shortcut!

Recording Menu Commands

Most menu commands can be recorded in an Action. There are, however, two ways to do so. If, while recording, you select a menu command, enter values in any dialog box, and click OK, the Action is recorded with *those* values. You can record the Action without assigning any value (and without changing the current image while recording). From the palette's menu, choose Insert Menu Item. With the dialog box open (see Figure 29.8), move the cursor to select the desired command. After selecting the command, click OK to close the dialog box.

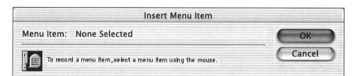

Figure 29.8
This dialog box remains open while you mouse to the command that you want to record in the Action.

When the Action is played back, nonmodal commands are executed immediately. If the command is modal, it doesn't execute until you approve the values in the dialog box by clicking OK. Remember that you cannot disable the modal control for an inserted command—when you play the Action, the dialog box *will* open and wait for you to click OK, whether you're sitting at your computer or not.

Inserting Paths

Although the Pen tool cannot be recorded, the shape tools can, and you can save a custom shape to be added in an Action. You can also insert paths into an Action. The path must already be available in the Paths palette while recording the Action. Select the path in the Paths palette, and then choose Insert Path from the Actions palette menu. When the Action is played back, the path is added as a work path. If you need to retain the path in the image, make sure to also record a Save Path command from the Paths palette menu.

In Figure 29.9, you can see how the Action records a rather simple path.

Caution

Be aware that adding complex paths (whether a custom shape or a work path) to an Action can tax the memory assigned to Photoshop.

Figure 29.9
Only the first six anchor points (corner or smooth) are listed when a path is recorded in an Action, although all points are recorded. Coordinates for anchor points and direction points for smooth anchor points are specified from the upper-left corner of the image.

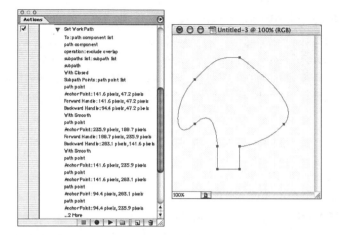

Inserting a Pause for Playback

When an Action is played back, you can force it to stop and display a message. Use the Actions palette menu command Insert Stop at any point in the recording process. You type a message to be displayed in the Message window of the Record Stop dialog box (see Figure 29.10).

Figure 29.10
The message can be up to 255 characters (and spaces) long.

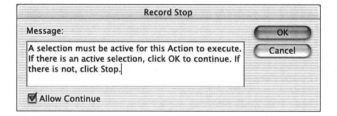

The Allow Continue option determines what buttons will be available in the message box when the Action is played. When Allow Continue is selected, the box contains two buttons: Stop and Continue (see Figure 29.11). When the option is not selected, only one button is available.

Figure 29.11
The best Stops are recorded with explicit instructions.

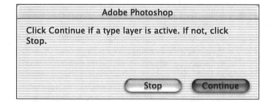

Does the Action seem to run right past your Stop? See "Stop Sign" in the NAPP Help Desk section at the end of this chapter.

Editing an Existing Action

You can perform seven basic types of editing on an existing Action:

You can drag a step from one Action to another. In fact, you can (Option) [Alt] drag to *copy* a step from one Action to another. *And* you can Shift-click to select multiple steps to copy, move, or delete.

- **Delete a step**—Select the step in the Actions palette and either drag it to the trash icon or click the icon.

- **Re-record a step**—Double-click on the step, perform the task as you want it, and then click Stop.

- **Add a step**—Click the step in the Action immediately above where you want the new step(s), and then click the Record button. When you've finished adding to the Action, click the Stop button.

- **Rearrange the order of steps**—Drag a step from one spot in the Action to another.

- **Duplicate a step**—(Option) [Alt] drag a step from one location to another in the Action, drag a step to the New Action button, or use the Actions palette menu command Duplicate.

- **Turn a step off (or on)**—Click in the left column of the Actions palette next to the step. When the check mark is visible, the step runs when the Action is played. If there is no check mark, that step is skipped when the Action is played.

- **Change the modal setting**—The second column of the Actions palette determines whether the dialog box for a modal command or tool shows when the Action is played. If the icon is visible next to a step, the Action stops at that step, shows the dialog box, and waits for you to change options and click OK. If there is an empty box in the column, the Action plays using the values recorded in the step. If the icon is grayed out, the step was added with the command Insert Menu Command, and the dialog box will always show. If there is neither an icon nor an empty box in that column, the step is nonmodal.

Sources of Actions

In addition to the Default Actions set loaded in the Actions palette, six other Photoshop-standard Action sets are immediately available. You can load any of them by selecting the set from the bottom of the Actions palette menu. The new Actions are added to the bottom of the palette.

Actions are also available, commercially and free, from a wide variety of sources on the Internet. ActionFX (www.actionfx.com) is an excellent source of useful, practical, and fun Actions. You'll find a sample of that Web site's Actions on the CD that accompanies this book.

You can also save Action sets and exchange them with other Photoshop users. Make sure that you attach the .atn extension to the filename when saving. To save Actions, follow these steps:

1. Select the Action set in the Actions palette. Remember that only Action sets, not individual Actions or steps, can be saved. To save a single Action, create a new set, (Option) [Alt] drag the Action into the set to copy it, and then save the new set.

2. With the set selected, choose Save Actions from the Actions palette menu. If the command is grayed out, it's likely that an Action or a step, rather than an Action set, is selected in the palette.

3. In the Save dialog box, select a name and location for the saved Action set. Include the .atn file extension in the filename.

PHOTOSHOP'S AUTOMATE COMMANDS

Save your custom and third-party Actions in a folder outside the Photoshop folder. In the event that you must reinstall the program, you won't lose them. You can place copies of the Action sets in the Photoshop Actions folder of the Presets folder to have them appear in the Actions palette menu.

The commands found in the File, Automate submenu don't do anything that you can't do manually in Photoshop. They simply do it faster and more efficiently (although sometimes not as flexibly as you might like).

Batch and Create Droplet

The Batch command is used to run an Action on a folder of images. Instead of opening each image individually and running the Action, you use the Batch command to streamline the process.

The Batch command is explained in depth earlier in this chapter. **See** *"Batching It," p. 851.*

Droplets are mini-applications that open Photoshop and run an Action. You activate a droplet by dragging a file or folder onto it.

There's more information on droplets earlier in this chapter. **See** *"Actions as Droplets," p. 854.*

Conditional Mode Change

This command is designed to be recorded in an Action to prevent error messages while using the Batch command. When an Action changes a color mode or contains a step that can be run only in certain color modes, Conditional Mode Change should be included. If, for example, you record an Action that relies on a specific channel and apply it to a folder of images that are not of the same color mode, an error message appears when the color channel isn't found (see Figure 29.12).

By using the Conditional Mode Change command, all images processed by the Action will be changed to the appropriate color mode. You select the color mode to which you want to convert the images, and you designate which color modes to convert *from* (see Figure 29.13).

Caution

Converting from Bitmap to a color mode requires that Conditional Mode Change first convert the image to Grayscale, and then to color. The conversion to Grayscale is modal and requires that you be at the computer to click OK, even if the modal icon is not visible next to the step in the Actions palette.

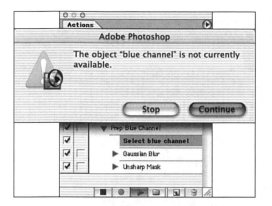

Figure 29.12
The Action requires the presence of a channel named Blue, but the image is CMYK. An error message stops the Batch process.

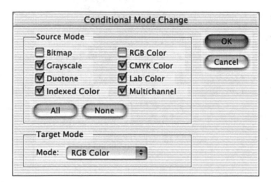

Figure 29.13
If this command had been recorded in the Action before the step shown in Figure 29.12, the image would have been converted to RGB mode and the Batch would not have aborted.

Contact Sheet II

You can create pages of thumbnail images with captions by using Contact Sheet II. Use the dialog box shown in Figure 29.14 to select the source folder of images, describe the page on which the thumbnails will be placed, specify the layout, and add captions from the filenames, if desired.

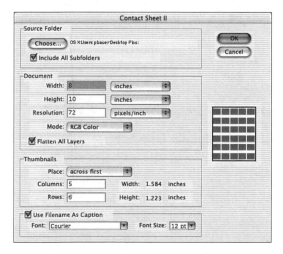

Figure 29.14
Remember that the document size should be the printable area of your page, not the paper size.

29

If you select the Include All Subfolders check box, you can place aliases of or shortcuts to additional folders in the designated source folder.

Contact Sheet II dynamically resizes the thumbnail dimensions to allow adequate space for captions, if that option is selected. As you increase the font size, the thumbnail size shrinks.

This command generates as many documents as needed to include all images in the designated folder and subfolders. The pages are not saved, nor are they automatically printed. However, Contact Sheet II can be recorded in an Action that saves and closes each page of thumbnails.

Because Contact Sheet II must open each image, you can speed things up a bit by setting the number of History states very low (in the General preferences) and electing not to create an initial snapshot (in the History palette options).

Fit Image

The Fit Image command can be recorded in an Action or applied to a single open image. It resizes the image to the smaller of the dimensions specified in the dialog box. Either the height or the width is matched, constraining the proportions of the image to avoid distortion. Think of Fit Image as ensuring that the file to which it is applied will be *no larger* than the dimensions specified, but either width or height can be smaller. The image is resampled using the interpolation method specified in the General preferences.

Multi-Page PDF to PSD

Photoshop's Open command can handle only one PDF page at a time. The Multi-Page PDF to PSD command automatically creates a series of .psd files from a multipage PDF document. In the dialog box (see Figure 29.15), you select the original document, determine which pages to translate, select the resolution and color mode for the resulting Photoshop files, and select a destination folder.

Figure 29.15
Use the Base Name field to create the filename for the resulting Photoshop files. A four-digit sequential number is added to the base name for each .psd file.

Convert Multi-Page PDF to PSD	
Source PDF	
Choose...	OK
OS X: DOWNLOADS:Al10_Features.pdf	Cancel
Page Range	
● All ○ From: 1 To: 1	
Output Options	
Resolution: 72 pixels/inch	
Mode: Grayscale ☑ Anti-aliased	
Destination	
Base Name: Al10_Features	
Choose...	
OS X:Users:pbauer:Desktop PDFs:	
☑ Suppress Warnings	

Picture Package

Picture Package is much improved in Photoshop 7, and quite a bit more customizable. Use this command to place multiple images on a single sheet for printing. You can add multiple copies of a single image or copies of various images from a folder. The dialog box (see Figure 29.16) gives you the choice of three paper sizes: 8×10, 10×16, and 11×17 inches. The resulting document can be of any resolution, and the color mode can be RGB, CMYK, Grayscale, or Lab. The document can also be flattened if desired.

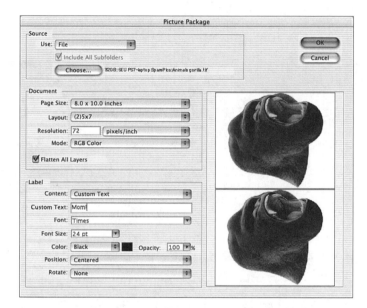

Figure 29.16
Picture Package now enables you to use different images on a single page. Click on each preview image in the dialog box to select a file for that spot.

Picture Package now offers the option of adding text or a caption to the images. You can enter custom text, use the filename, or have Photoshop access the File Info for the copyright, caption, credits, or title data saved with the image.

Web Photo Gallery

Although Photoshop is an image-editing program, it does offer support for the Web. The primary examples are, of course, ImageReady and Save for Web. Both of these are also graphic creation tools. Photoshop does offer one feature aimed at creating Web *pages*. Web Photo Gallery can create an entire Web site, ready for posting to your host server. Keep in mind, however, that this is a very basic capability, and you won't be creating any award-winning e-commerce sites with Web Photo Gallery.

Aimed at assisting photographers and digital artists to post examples of their work on the Web, Web Photo Gallery takes folders filled with images and creates Web pages in which they are displayed. A simple dialog box gives you a number of variations, but limited control, over the final product (see Figure 29.17).

Figure 29.17
One dialog box is all Photoshop requires to build a Web site to display your artwork.

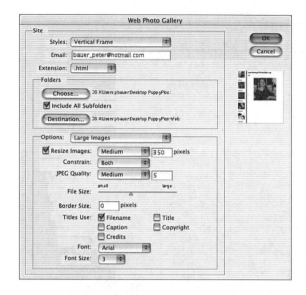

The Site section of the dialog box offers 11 different styles for the Web pages. As you change your selection, the preview to the right is updated to reflect the new look. You can include an e-mail address for the pages, and elect whether to use the file extension .htm or .html for the generated pages. (Some Web servers require a three-character extension—check with your Web hosting service for information about its policy.) One sample layout is pictured in Figure 29.18.

Figure 29.18
Shown is the Vertical Frame style, using options for banner information, custom colors, and security. The Thumbnails size is small and the Large Images size is medium.

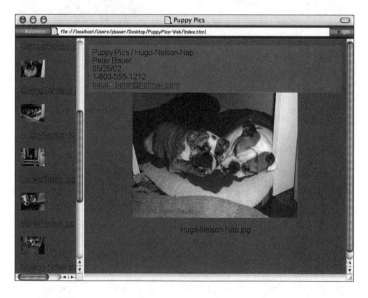

Select both the source and destination folders in the Folders section of the dialog box. The destination folder cannot be within the source folder.

The Options section of the dialog box consists of five separate panes used to customize your Web pages (see Figure 29.19).

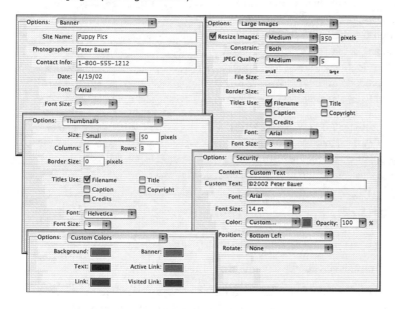

Figure 29.19
Navigate among the panes with the Options pop-up menu.

Here's what options are available in each pane:

- **Banner**—The site name, your name and contact information (one line only), and the date appear in various places, depending on the page style selected in the Site section. Your font choices are limited to Arial, Courier New, Helvetica, and Times New Roman. The font size (1–7) refers to HTML relative size rather than point size.

- **Large Images**—If you select the Resize Images check box, you can choose among Small (250 pixels wide), Medium (350 pixels), or Large (450 pixels), or you can choose a custom size. Constraining both height and width prevents distortion of the image, but you can elect to constrain only one dimension. The images will be optimized as JPEGs to the quality you specify. You can select a border size from 0 (no border) to 99 pixels. The image title, if any, can be the filename or any of several items from the File Info fields, and you have the same font options as you have for the banner. You add File Info through the File menu for each image individually.

- **Thumbnails**—Thumbnails are clickable links to the full-size images. They can be Small (50 pixels wide), Medium (75 pixels), Large (100 pixels), or a custom size. For the Table and Simple layouts, you can choose the number of rows and columns. You have the same border and titling options that you have for the large images.

- **Custom Colors**—Custom colors are used with the Simple, Vertical Frame, and Horizontal Frame styles. You use the Color Picker to assign colors.

■ **Security**—The term "security" in this situation refers to pasting some information on the images to reduce the chance that your artwork will be stolen. You can add custom text or information recorded with the file in File Info. The text, in your choice of five fonts (Times is available, in addition to the four fonts mentioned for Banner), size, and color, can be positioned in the middle of the image or in any corner, and can also be rotated.

Web Photo Gallery is no substitute for Adobe GoLive, but it can quickly and easily produce serviceable Web sites for displaying photos or other artwork. If you're handy with HTML, the code can be customized to suit your individual needs.

> **Caution**
>
> The fancier styles built into Web Photo Gallery create *huge* Web pages. The pages need to be scrolled even on monitors set to 1024×768 pixel resolution. Before investing time in creating a Web site with a lot of pictures, run some tests with a folder containing four or five images, just to make sure that you'll like what you get.

PHOTOSHOP IN FOCUS

To see how all the parts of this chapter come together, try this:

1. Create a folder called Source and add copies of eight of your favorite images.

2. Record an Action (name it Create Tiffs) that resizes an image to a maximum height or width of 500 pixels (use Fit Image rather than Image, Image Size), sharpens (Filter, Sharpen, Sharpen), and saves the file as a TIFF file in a folder named Originals.

3. Run the Action Create Tiffs as a Batch on the Source folder. Create a folder named Destination in which to save the files.

4. Use Contact Sheet II to create a single page with thumbnails of your TIFF images.

5. Use Picture Package to create a single page of eight 2.5×3.5 images, one for each of your TIFFs.

6. Use Web Photo Gallery to create a Web site, in your choice of layout, to show off your images.

⇨ *If you ended up with copies of the files in both Originals and Destination, or if you couldn't get the Batch command to properly save the TIFFs at all, **see** "Using Batch to Change File Formats," p. 853.*

FROM THE NAPP HELP DESK

The National Association of Photoshop Professionals (NAPP) offers e-mail assistance to its members. Here is some advice from the NAPP Help Desk related to issues in this chapter.

Double-Check

I've organized and color-coded all my Actions, and I'm using Button Mode to make things easier to find, but I seem to have messed up some of my Actions. They're not giving me the results I used to get.

Step out of Button Mode for a moment and check the Actions that are giving you trouble. The most common source of this problem is steps being skipped. When you're in Standard Mode, you can easily see whether all steps have the check mark next to them. In Button Mode, you have no such reminder; each Action plays according to the steps selected when you entered Button Mode.

Unscheduled Halt

I have an Action that stops in the middle, but no message appears. I have to click the Play button again to make it continue.

Expand the Action in the Actions palette and look for a Stop at the point where the Action halts. Now look in the second column. An icon must be visible in the Modal Control column for the Stop's warning box to appear.

Stop Sign

My Actions go right past my Stop messages sometimes, just not showing them at all. What can I do to fix this problem?

Open the Actions palette, click the triangle next to the specific Action to expand it in the palette, and take a look at the first column. If you don't see a check mark, the step is skipped.

JAVASCRIPT, APPLESCRIPT, AND SCRIPTING WITH VISUAL BASIC

IN THIS CHAPTER

30

SCRIPTING SUPPORT FOR PHOTOSHOP

New to Photoshop is scripting support. Just as Actions control Photoshop by playing a series of recorded tasks, so too can scripting languages. However, scripting languages can do things that Photoshop's Actions cannot. For example, Visual Basic (Windows) and AppleScript (Macintosh) can *call* or *invoke* another program (make it active and issue commands), working with it along with Photoshop. In addition, scripts can contain conditional logic, unlike Actions, and can make decisions based on the document's current state.

This chapter is not intended to teach programming languages nor script writing. Instead, it is aimed at introducing you to the combination of scripting languages and Photoshop. If you're familiar with scripting (in any of the three languages supported by Photoshop), you'll learn how to integrate those skills with Photoshop. If you're not familiar with scripting, this chapter perhaps will show you a powerful new capability that you might want to learn.

What Is Scripting?

Scripting, like Actions, is a series of recorded commands used to have Photoshop perform a task or a series of tasks. A script is instructions played back to control the program. Unlike Actions, scripts can also control the operating system (in some respects) and other scripting-aware programs. Adobe InDesign 2.0 and Illustrator 10, for example, can be scripted as well. A script could open Illustrator, create artwork, move that artwork to a Photoshop document, apply filters or layer styles, prepare the Photoshop file for print, place it in an InDesign document, and then add elements to the page layout document and prepare it for print.

You might already be using JavaScript without even knowing it. Created any rollovers in ImageReady recently? Although ImageReady did the scripting for you, you created JavaScripts.

You might consider scripting to be of value only for production environments. However, that's not the case. Any procedure you do more than once is a candidate for scripting. More advanced scripts can be written to handle extremely complex creative tasks as well. If you use Actions at all, you're a candidate for scripting.

One of the big differences between Actions and scripting is how they go about controlling the program. Actions use Photoshop's interface. They open dialog boxes, and use existing values or wait for you to add new numbers. Scripts, on the other hand, don't need to use the interface. In addition to making them far faster than Actions, this enables scripts to use external data, make decisions based on existing data or conditions, and apply Boolean logic as they execute.

Scripting is more powerful and more complicated than Photoshop's Actions because it is actually *programming*. Visual Basic is the programming language used to produce much of the available Windows software. AppleScript can also be used to create applications. You can think of writing a script as writing a mini program.

Executing existing scripts is no more difficult than playing an Action. However, writing a script requires knowledge of one or two of the scripting languages supported by Photoshop. You can use AppleScript (Macintosh), Visual Basic (Windows), and JavaScript (both) with Photoshop.

How Scripts Work in Photoshop

The first step in scripting Photoshop is to download the Scripting Support plug-in from Adobe.com. The plug-ins are platform specific, so ensure that you get either the Macintosh or the Windows version. You'll find them both at

www.adobe.com/support/downloads/

The download includes the Scripting plug-in, sample scripts, documentation, and one support plug-in. If you are an experienced scripter, you'll find the Photoshop-specific information you need in the Photoshop 7.0 Scripting Guide and the accompanying JavaScript documentation. If you're new to scripting, the Photoshop 7.0 Scripting Guide has some background information and enough detail to get you started.

After the scripting plug-in is installed, you can execute JavaScripts from within Photoshop through the File, Automate, Scripts command. The Scripts dialog box lists all JavaScripts in the Presets folder inside the Photoshop folder, and you can navigate to other locations on your computer by using the Browse button (see Figure 30.1).

> **Caution**
>
> The Photoshop 7 Scripting plug-in is *not* compatible with PhotoScripter from Main Event software. PhotoScripter must be removed before working with the Photoshop 7 Scripting plug-in.

> **Caution**
>
> Photoshop droplets created in Photoshop 6 do not work properly with the Scripting Support plug-in installed. Photoshop 7 droplets, however, do work. If you rely on both scripting and droplets, re-create legacy droplets in Photoshop 7.

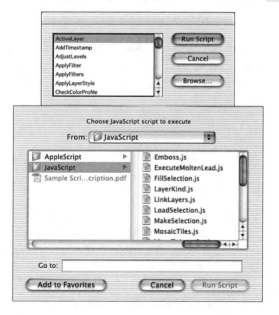

Figure 30.1
The Browse button, directly below Cancel in the Scripts dialog box, enables you to run JavaScripts from outside sources.

You run AppleScripts from the Script Editor, installed by default with the Mac OS. You can double-click an existing script to open the Script Editor, or you can open the program and use the menu command File, Open Script. Clicking the Run button executes the script as written (see Figure 30.2).

Figure 30.2
Script Editor is installed by
default with the Mac OS in the
AppleScript folder. OS X places
the folder in the Applications
folder; OS 9 puts it in Apple
Extras, inside the Applications
folder.

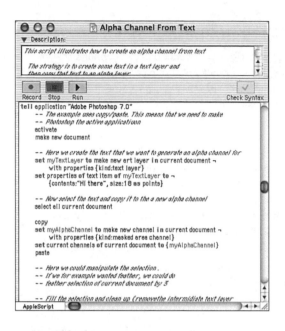

Windows can run Visual Basic scripts from the Windows Scripting Host (included with most versions of Windows). You can edit scripts with Visual Basic Editor or Microsoft Script Editor (see Figure 30.3). The Visual Basic application has a more extensive interface and capabilities.

Figure 30.3
The Microsoft Script Editor is
available in Microsoft Word,
under the Tools, Macros menu.

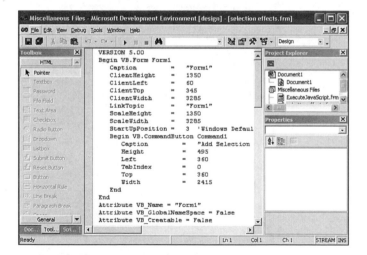

JavaScript, AppleScript, Visual Basic: Which One?

JavaScript is cross-platform—meaning the same script will perform identically on both Windows and Macintosh versions of Photoshop 7. However, a JavaScript must be run from within Photoshop and cannot call another program. AppleScript and Visual Basic are more powerful, can be run from outside Photoshop, and can run multiple programs. However, they are both platform specific—an AppleScript cannot be used in Windows, and Visual Basic cannot run on a Macintosh.

Keep in mind that both AppleScripts and Visual Basic scripts can execute a JavaScript, but JavaScripts can't call the others.

The Action Manager and ScriptingListener

The Action Manager enables you to record non-scriptable functions in a script. Third-party plug-ins, filters, and certain non-scriptable capabilities (such as the Emboss filter) can be added to a script. The ScriptingListener plug-in is downloaded with the Photoshop Scripting Support plug-in, but not installed by default. You'll find ScriptingListener in the Utilities folder after you've downloaded and expanded the Scripting Support package. To use it, move it to Photoshop's Plug-Ins folders, and place it in the Scripting folder.

> **Caution**
>
> Install ScriptingListener *only* when you're actually using it to create scripts. Photoshop might run more slowly with the plug-in installed, and it generates a file on your hard drive that is otherwise not required.

When installed, ScriptingListener records most of what you do in Photoshop as JavaScript code in a file at the root level of your hard drive. For Windows, it also creates VBScript code in a separate file. (AppleScripts call the JavaScript.)

SCRIPTING SUPPORT IN PHOTOSHOP

Generally speaking, Photoshop offers the same type of support for AppleScript and Visual Basic. Most of the program is scriptable, and scripts can call Photoshop while working with another scriptable program. JavaScript support is more limited because these scripts cannot access Photoshop's capabilities from outside the program.

JavaScript Support

JavaScripts are run from within Photoshop and cannot directly call other programs. You use the menu command File, Automate, Scripts to access the available JavaScripts. To have a custom or third-party JavaScript appear in the dialog box, move it to the Scripts folder inside the Presets folder.

The Scripts dialog box is more powerful than it may seem at first glance. In addition to running JavaScripts, you can use it to debug your script. Hold down the (Option) [Alt] key and the Run Script button changes to Debug Script (see Figure 30.4).

The documentation downloaded with the Scripting Support plug-in includes a JavaScript terminology PDF as well as a file and folder object reference.

> **Caution**
>
> Before executing an AppleScript or a Visual Basic script, make sure that the Type tool isn't selected in Photoshop and that there are no open dialog boxes. Either situation causes a script runtime error.

☞ *Don't see the Scripts command? Then see "Preparing for Scripting" in the NAPP Help Desk section at the end of this chapter.*

Figure 30.4
The JavaScript Debugger, shown behind the Scripts dialog box, is not fancy, but certainly functional.

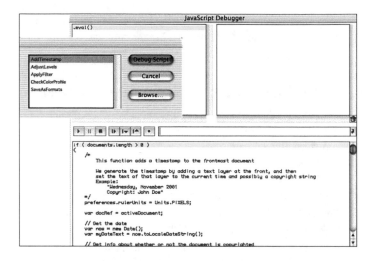

30

AppleScript Support

The Photoshop 7.0 Scripting Guide, downloaded in PDF format with the Scripting Support plug-in, provides all the information an experienced AppleScripter needs to create scripts for Photoshop.

There is one important point to note when working with Apple's Script Editor: It cannot display the entire list of open and save formats when you view the Photoshop dictionary. Table 30.1 has the full list.

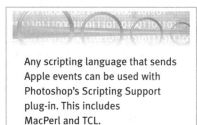

Any scripting language that sends Apple events can be used with Photoshop's Scripting Support plug-in. This includes MacPerl and TCL.

Table 30.1 AppleScript Open and Save File Formats

Command	Formats
Open	Acrobat TouchUp Image, Alias PIX, BMP, CompuServe GIF, EPS, EPS PICT Preview, EPS TIFF Preview, Electric Image, Filmstrip, JPEG, PCX, PDF, PICT file, PICT resource, PNG, PhotoCD, Photoshop DCS 1.0, Photoshop DCS 2.0, Photoshop EPS, Photoshop format, Photoshop PDF, Pixar, Portable Bitmap, Raw, SGI RGB, Scitex CT, SoftImage, TIFF, Targa, Wavefront RLA, Wireless Bitmap
Save	Alias PIX, BMP, CompuServe GIF, Electric Image, JPEG, PCX, PICT file, PICT resource, PNG, Photoshop DCS 1.0, Photoshop DCS 2.0, Photoshop EPS, Photoshop format, Photoshop PDF, Pixar, Portable Bitmap, Raw, SGI RGB, Scitex CT, SoftImage, TIFF, Targa, Wavefront RLA, Wireless Bitmap

➡ *You can't run your AppleScripts from within Photoshop? See "Outside Influence" in the NAPP Help Desk section at the end of this chapter.*

Scripting Support for Windows

The information needed to write scripts in Visual Basic for Photoshop is included in the Photoshop 7.0 Scripting Guide. The PDF version of the document was downloaded with the Scripting Support plug-in.

Any COM-aware language can be used to script Photoshop. VBScript, JScript, Perl, Tcl/Tk, and Python are some examples.

JavaScripts Included with Photoshop 7

Along with the Photoshop 7 Scripting Support plug-in, five sample scripts are installed into the Presets folder, in a folder named Scripts. A couple of the scripts are useful as is, but they can also be customized to meet your individual needs. You can edit JavaScript in a word processor or text-editing program.

Another 23 JavaScripts are available with the Scripting Support plug-in, including the following:

ActiveLayer	ExecuteMoltenLead	NewDocument
ApplyFilters	FillSelection	OpenDocument
ApplyLayerStyle	LayerKind	RotateLayer
CompareColors	LinkLayers	RulerUnit
ConvertColors	LoadSelection	SelectionStroke
CopyAndPaste	MakeSelection	SetChannels
CropAndRotate	MosaicTiles	WorkingWithText
Emboss	MoveToLayerSet	

Consider these scripts as frameworks from which you can build your own scripts. Using the samples as examples, or editing them as necessary, you can easily create JavaScripts to perform a variety of tasks. Remember, too, that JavaScripts can be run from within an AppleScript or Visual Basic script.

☞ *Don't see the sample scripts? Check "Loading the Scripts" in the NAPP Help Desk section at the end of this chapter.*

AppleScripts Included with Photoshop 7

No AppleScripts are included with Photoshop 7.0. However, 18 scripts are downloaded with the Scripting Support plug-in. Like the JavaScripts in the package, these are samples that can be adapted for your particular needs:

Alpha Channel from Text	Layer Style
Apply Text Style	Make Selection
Batch Convert	Make Warp Text
Convert Colors	New Document
Create New Text Item	Run JavaScript
Crop	Save As TIFF
Crop and Rotate Art Layers	Trim
Get Document By Name	Trim Document
Get Text Item Center	Unit Types

30

The script Run JavaScript enables you to access the JavaScripts installed with Photoshop and downloaded with the Scripting Support plug-in. It can be included in a custom AppleScript.

Visual Basic Scripts

No Visual Basic scripts are installed with Photoshop 7. However, 19 sample scripts are included with the Scripting Support plug-in:

art layer style	new text art
batch process	open document
clipboard interaction	save formats
create and execute action	selection
duplicate layers	selection effects
execute action	text art
execute javascript	text art center
filters	transform art
get document by name	trim document
history state	

These scripts are best considered examples or frameworks from which you can write your own scripts. Note that the sample scripts include one that enables you to run a JavaScript from within a Visual Basic script as well as a script that can call a Photoshop Action.

PHOTOSHOP IN FOCUS

Native support for scripting in Photoshop is new with version 7.0. However, it's likely that new Web pages devoted to the subject are popping up regularly. You can check the latest:

1. Open your Web browser and head for your favorite search engine. On the Mac, fire up Sherlock.

2. Do a search for the keywords scripting *and* Photoshop.

3. Visit several of the sites to see what they have to offer. Bookmark or add to your Favorites those sites that appear to be of greatest value to you.

4. Visit the following sites:

   - www.javascript.com
   - www.jsworld.com
   - www.javascriptcity.com
   - http://javascript.internet.com/tutorials/
   - www.apple.com/applescript/
   - www.applescriptsourcebook.com
   - www.macscripting.com

- www.scriptweb.com

- http://msdn.microsoft.com/vbasic/

- www.vb-world.net

The Internet is just one source of information on scripting. Especially if you're new to high-level automation, check out these additional resources:

- *Special Edition Using JavaScript*, Paul McFedries

- *JavaScript Goodies*, Joe Burns and Andree Growney

- *Sams Teach Yourself JavaScript in 24 Hours*, Michael Moncur

- *Sams Teach Yourself JavaScript in 21 Days*, Jinjer Simon

- *Visual Basic 6 From Scratch*, Bob Donald and Gabriel Oancea

- *Visual Basic and COM+ Programming by Example*, Peishu Li

- *Platinum Edition Using Visual Basic 6*, Loren Eidahl

FROM THE NAPP HELP DESK

The National Association of Photoshop Professionals (NAPP) offers e-mail assistance to its members. Here is some advice from the NAPP Help Desk related to issues in this chapter.

Preparing for Scripting

I can't find the Scripting command. Do I have to buy something extra?

The Scripting Support plug-in is free, but it doesn't come on your Photoshop CD. You'll have to download and install the plug-in. Visit www.adobe.com/support/downloads to get the plug-in. After it's downloaded, run the installer.

Outside Influence

I can't get my AppleScripts to run in Photoshop. They won't even appear in the Scripts dialog box.

The command File, Automate, Scripts is for use with JavaScripts only. AppleScripts are activated from outside Photoshop. Try double-clicking the script to get it rolling.

Loading the Scripts

I downloaded the Scripting Support plug-in and ran the installer, but I see only five samples in the Scripts dialog box. Where are the others?

You downloaded a folder with the additional sample scripts when you downloaded the Scripting Support plug-in. Use the Browse button in the Scripts dialog box and navigate to where you saved the documentation and other items that came with the plug-in. Alternatively, you can copy or move those files to the Presets folder inside the Photoshop folder. Put them in the Scripts folder, and they'll appear in the list in the Scripts dialog box.

EFFICIENCY TIPS AND TRICKS

SETTING UP AND OPTIMIZING THE WORKSPACE

Customizing Photoshop can improve your efficiency. Learning a few simple techniques can save seconds here and there that add up to precious minutes when a deadline (or the weekend) approaches.

Using the Contextual Menu

Just about everything in Photoshop has a contextual menu that can be accessed with a click. The contextual menu enables you to quickly do such things as select a brush (any of the painting tools), change the unit of measure (Rulers), duplicate a layer (selection tools), even change the thumbnail size in a palette. Make it a habit to right-click (Windows) or Control-click (Macintosh) on everything a few times, just to see what the contextual menu holds.

Exploiting the New Window Command

The Window, Documents, New Window command opens an additional view of the same image. Keep these points in mind:

- You can set each new window to a separate zoom factor.

- You can scroll each window to a separate view. (The Navigator palette reflects the frontmost window.)

- When no longer needed, simply close the extra window(s). As long as one view stays open, the image is open.

- Changes made to the image in one window are reflected in all—the changes are made to the image itself and so to all views of the image.

There are a variety of situations in which multiple windows are an advantage. Here are just a few examples:

- You can open a second view, zoom way in, and set guides precisely without losing your original view.

- You can scroll a second window to get a close-up view of another area of the image.

- While doing color correction, you can set one window to show the color composite and another to show a single channel.

- You can set a separate window to Proof Colors (under the View menu) while you work in RGB in the primary window.

Mac OS X supports multiple-button mice. The right mouse button in OS X accesses the contextual menu. You might also want to get a mouse with a scroll wheel—you can pan and zoom when the window is smaller than the image.

When doing detail work, you can open a second window and set it to 100% zoom to see the overall effect of your work. Always use 100% zoom when applying filters—it's the only accurate view. You also need to proof your Web graphics at 100% zoom (the only way Web browsers show them).

Instant Copies with the History Menu

You can create a copy of an image outside Photoshop (by using Windows Explorer, My Computer, or the Mac OS Finder). You use the Image, Duplicate within Photoshop menu command, or you can create an exact copy of an image with a single click of the Create New Document from Current State button (the leftmost button at the bottom of the History palette, shown in Figure 31.1). The new document is unsaved and, by default, assumes the name of the current history state.

Figure 31.1
Clicking the button opens an exact copy of the document in a new window. The document is a separate file—perfect for experimentation without risking your original.

Neutral Backgrounds Without Full Screen Mode

You can eliminate background distractions and colors that may throw off your perception by using Photoshop's Full Screen Mode. That puts your working image in the middle of a neutral gray background. Unfortunately, this mode eliminates the advantages of a resizable, repositionable window.

Here's a way to have the advantages of an image window while eliminating background distractions:

1. Open a new document. It can be any color mode except Bitmap, any resolution, and filled with white or transparency. The document can be any size. (If you're short on RAM, make it small.)

2. Fill the new image with neutral gray. Choose the 50% gray swatch from the Swatches palette (by default, the rightmost swatch in the upper row), and press (Option-Delete) [Alt+Backspace].

3. Press F once to switch this new gray document to Full Screen Mode with Menu Bars.

4. Zoom in until the image fills the screen. You can use the Zoom tool, the Navigator palette, the View menu, or keyboard shortcuts.

5. Open your work images and get started!

Preset Manager, Saved Workspaces, Tool Presets

Photoshop 7 has some incredibly powerful capabilities built right in. Preset Manager (opened from palette menus or the Edit menu) enables you to set the default content of a variety of palettes (see Figure 31.2).

Workspaces are arrangements of palettes that save which palettes are visible and their locations. You can position each and every palette all at once by using workspaces. Save one for every situation you normally face.

The difference between creating a new window and creating a new document (History palette) boils down to a file versus a window. When you use the New Window command, you've still got only one file in multiple windows. When you use the button in the History palette, you've created a separate (as yet unsaved) file.

Figure 31.2
The Preset Manager can save and
load sets for the palette contents.

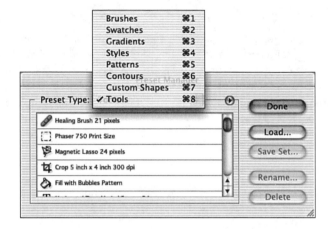

Tool presets are saved sets of options for a particular tool.
You can save each tool with specific settings—if it can be set
in the Options Bar, it can be saved in a tool preset.

⇨ *For a full discussion of tool presets, **see** Chapter 2, "The
Photoshop Interface," p. 43.*

Open the File Browser. Navigate
to a specific folder you use often.
Save the arrangement as a workspace. Voilà—instant bookmark
for the File Browser!

Clearing Away Palettes

Even when working on an extremely large monitor, there are times when palettes are in the way. If
nothing else, they can distort color perception and distract from an image. The Tab key hides all
palettes, and Shift-Tab hides all except the Toolbox and the Options Bar. Press Tab again to show
the palettes. Here are some other tips for clearing your workspace:

- Palette arrangements can be saved as workspaces. You can save a workspace that shows one,
  two, all, or even no palettes.

- Double-click the tab of any palette to minimize (and show) a palette and any palettes docked
  with it.

- Double-click the title bar of a palette window to shrink it to the tab.

- In Mac OS X, there are three dots in the title bar for floating palettes. The left button (red)
  closes the palette; the right button (green) optimizes the palette. The palette shrinks to the size
  that shows the current content, and only the content. The middle button is a dummy—it doesn't
  do anything.

- Shift-click the title bar of a palette floating over your image, and it will jump to the nearest edge
  of the screen. When it jumps, it jumps straight—it ignores the presence of other palettes and
  overlaps them to dock to the edge.

- Don't forget the Palette Well! When the monitor is set to a resolution higher than 800×600 pixels, it appears to the right of the Options Bar. You can drag a palette there, and then click its tab
  to expand it. Click again to collapse the palette back into the well.

■ No matter what you've done with which palettes, you can always rely on the Window, Workspace, Reset Palette Locations menu command to bring you back to the default layout.

Custom Keyboard Shortcuts

Although Photoshop doesn't support customizable keyboard shortcuts, as does Adobe Illustrator, you can still create your own. Using the Actions palette, you can assign Function keys (F-keys) to execute menu commands:

1. In Photoshop, open the Actions palette.

2. Select an existing Actions set or create a new set.

3. Click the New Action button.

4. In the New Action dialog box, give the Action a name (typically the name of the menu command). Assign an F-key, with or without modifiers (see Figure 31.3). Click the Record button.

5. Immediately use the Actions palette menu command Insert Menu Item.

6. With that dialog box open, navigate to the menu command and select it.

7. Close the Insert Menu Command dialog box.

8. Click the Stop button in the Actions palette.

Figure 31.3
The palette menu and the dialog box will not be visible at the same time.

When you press the F-key (or combination), the menu command will execute or its dialog box will open.

Concentrate on a Single Layer

Sometimes it's easier to do precise work when you see only the pixels on a single layer. (Control-click) [right+click] the eyeball icon to the left of the layer on which you're working and select Show/Hide All Other Layers from the contextual menu. Alternatively, you can simply (Option-click) [Alt+click] the eyeball. Repeat the process to show all the layers again. You can also color-code your layers in the Layers palette by using the contextual menu for the visibility column. (Background layers cannot be color-coded.)

> ### Caution
> When assigning F-key combinations, don't overwrite the built-in shortcuts. F5 through F9 (without modifiers) show and hide palettes.

Resetting Dialog Boxes

Most of Photoshop's dialog boxes have a hidden Reset button. If a filter or adjustment gets out of control, you don't need to cancel and reopen the dialog box. Rather, hold down the (Option) [Alt] key and watch Cancel change to Reset. Hold down the key, click the button, and the dialog box reverts to the settings you saw when it opened.

Crop Command to Delete Hidden Pixels

In a variety of circumstances, there can be hidden pixels outside the canvas area of an image. Repositioning a layer brings those pixels back into the picture. That can be great—if you need the pixels. If you're done with them, crop them away and reduce the file size. Use the menu commands Select, All and Image, Crop.

Streamline the Brushes Palette

The Brushes palette can get crowded, especially when you create custom brushes. You can delete unnecessary brushes by (Option-clicking) [Alt+clicking] them in the Brushes palette. Remember that you have to select a brush-using tool and that you must have the Brush Presets pane active to edit the Brushes palette.

Before saving a set of custom brushes, delete all but the custom brushes. It'll make the saved set easier to use when you load it.

Precision Guide Placement

Using Photoshop's Guides is a great way to ensure exact placement and selection. However, your precision depends on *their* precision. If they're not in exactly the correct place, they don't serve you properly. To get perfect placement, use the menu command View, New Guide. The dialog box enables you to input a location to a couple of decimal places (see Figure 31.4).

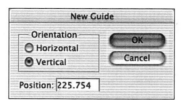

Figure 31.4
The dialog box uses input to three decimal places.

Changing the Color Picker Selection Criteria

The majority of Photoshop users simply use the Color Picker as they find it, but that's not always the best configuration. By default, the Color Picker places the hue component on the vertical slider in the middle and the saturation and brightness in the square to the left. However, clicking the radio buttons to the left of any other color component puts that item on the slider.

Adjusting the selection criteria for the Color Picker is especially useful when you're using Web-safe colors (see Figure 31.5). With the Only Web Colors option selected, click on R, G, or B to form the Color Picker into rectangles of Web-safe color, rather than unusual geometric patterns.

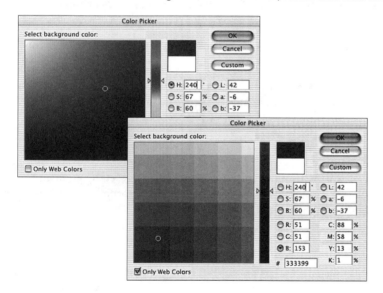

Figure 31.5
You cannot reconfigure the Color Picker with the CMYK component colors.

Previewing Fonts

Photoshop's type engine doesn't include a what-you-see-is-what-you-get (WYSIWYG) font menu. The fonts are all listed in the interface's own font. That doesn't mean you can't preview a typeface. Follow these steps:

1. Set some type. Leave the type layer active in the Layers palette, but switch from the Type tool to the Move tool.

2. In the Character palette, click in the font field, where the current font's name is displayed. The font name will be highlighted.

3. Use the up and down arrow keys to change fonts—the type layer will be automatically updated with the new font. You can also type a letter or two to jump to a specific font.

Keeping Track of Your Steps

Sometimes you need to keep a record of what steps were performed on an image. Other times you might want to make a record of what you did so that you can replicate it in the future. Record your work session as an Action. The Action can even be printed later, complete with the settings you used in each filter:

1. Create a new set, especially if you'll want to print the Action later. You can't print individual Actions, just sets.

2. In the Actions palette, click the New Action button.

3. Give the Action a name and click the Record button.

4. Proceed with your work, doing things as normal, completely ignoring the Action being recorded.

5. When you're finished with your editing, save the file and click the Stop button at the bottom of the Actions palette.

6. To save the Action set as a text file (which you can print at your leisure), hold down (Command-Option) [Ctrl+Alt] and select Save Actions from the Actions palette menu.

SELECTIONS AND MASKS

Making selections and masks is one of the primary skills in Photoshop. They let the program know what part of the image you want to change. Creating accurate, efficient selections and masks can be one of the keys to efficient Photoshop operation.

Selection Tool Versatility

The basic selection tools, the Rectangular and Elliptical Marquee tools, seem pretty straightforward. You drag and make a selection. They've got some tricks, however, that make using them much easier:

- Hold down the (Option) [Alt] key when you start dragging a new selection. This technique creates the selection from the center—very handy for selecting circles and ovals, such as eyes.

- Shift-dragging adds to an existing selection. (Option) [Alt] dragging subtracts from an existing selection. You can skip the modifier keys by using the Options Bar. After you've got an active selection, click on the appropriate button to set the tool to that mode (see Figure 31.6).

- To reposition a selection while dragging, keep the mouse button down and press the spacebar. You can now move the selection where you need it. Release the spacebar and continue dragging the tool to finish the selection.

■ After you've finished creating a selection, you can move it. Make sure that you have a selection tool active (not the Move tool) and drag the "marching ants" marquee anywhere.

Figure 31.6
From the left, the four buttons set the selection tools to make new selections, add to existing selections, subtract from existing selections, or intersect with existing selections.

Transforming Selections

Don't forget about the Select, Transform Selection command. Use this command to alter the shape of an active selection. When a bounding box appears around the selection, you can do the following:

■ Position the cursor just outside the bounding box and drag to rotate the selection.

■ Drag any of the eight handles on the bounding box to resize the selection.

■ Hold down Shift while dragging a corner handle to constrain proportions.

■ Hold down (Option) [Alt] and then drag a side or corner handle to resize from the center.

■ Hold down (Option) [Alt] and Shift to resize from the center while constraining proportions.

■ Hold down (Command) [Ctrl] while dragging a side handle to shear.

■ Hold down (Command) [Ctrl] while dragging a corner handle to skew.

■ Hold down (Command-Option) [Ctrl+Alt] to skew or shear from the center.

■ Hold down (Command-Shift-Option) [Ctrl+Shift+Alt] while dragging a corner handle to change perspective.

■ Use the (Return) [Enter] key to accept a transformation and the Escape key to cancel.

Instantly Select All Pixels on a Layer

You can select a layer's entire content, without selecting completely transparent pixels, by (Command-clicking) [Ctrl+clicking] the layer in the Layers palette. You can also make a selection in the shape of a type layer's content this way, and then use the selection on another layer. (You won't have to rasterize your type; just hide that layer after making a selection.)

Use the (Shift-Command) [Shift+Ctrl] keys and click on a different layer to add those pixels to the selection (the active layer doesn't change). Hold down (Command-Option) [Ctrl+Alt] and click on another layer to deselect areas of overlap. Hold down (Shift-Command-Option) [Shift+Ctrl+Alt) and click on another layer to make a selection of the intersection.

Save Selections

If it took more than a simple click or drag to make a selection, consider saving it as an alpha channel—a mask. You may be *positive* that you'll never need that selection again, but it takes only a few seconds to save the selection and delete the channel at the end of the project.

Make the selection, and then use the Select, Save Selection menu command. If you'll be saving multiple selections, give it a descriptive name. If you need the selection again, use the Select, Load Selection menu command.

Remember, too, that you can save and load selections to documents other than the one that's active. When you save the first selection, create a new file. Save all the subsequent selections to that same file. At the end of the project, simply delete the file.

Eyeing the Info Palette While Selecting

Need a precise selection? Open the Info palette and drag the tool. Using the Info palette with the Rectangular Marquee tool is an excellent way to get an exact selection. This technique lets you skip the hassle of using the Options Bar to create a fixed size—and having to switch back to Normal later.

Hiding the Selection

Many precision jobs require that you be able to see the edges of your selection while working. The selection marquee—the so-called "marching ants"—is sometimes a liability, hiding critical info right at the edge of the selection. (Command-H) [Ctrl+H] hides the marching ants. Use the keyboard shortcut a second time to show the border again.

This shortcut is especially valuable when changing the color of selected type. Because the selection marquee for type reverses the colors, it's hard to see what's going on. Select the type, use the shortcut, and the type appears in its assigned color(s) as you work.

Filtering Masks

Remember that alpha channels are nothing more than grayscale representations. Anything you can do to a grayscale image can be done to an alpha channel. That includes filters, the Adjustment commands, and painting. Applying blur and sharpen filters to masks can fine-tune a selection's edges quickly and easily.

COMMON PHOTOSHOP TASKS

Some situations come up regularly as you work with Photoshop. Here are some tried-and-true techniques for some of the most common jobs.

Removing Red-eye

Red-eye is that unnatural red reflection (green for some animals) that appears when a flash reflects off the back of an eye. There are lots of techniques for removing red-eye. Here's an easy one:

1. Zoom in on one of the eyes.

2. Select the Sponge tool (you'll find it under the Dodge tool).

3. In the Options Bar, set the tool to Desaturate, select a soft-edged brush a little smaller than the size of the pupil, and set the Flow to 50%.

4. Drag small circles over the red area of the eye, releasing and repressing the mouse button as you work.

This technique maintains the reflections on the eye while eliminating the color.

Precision Rotation

Instead of using a Transform, Rotate command and dragging a bounding box, you can get a precise rotation:

1. Select the Measure tool in the Toolbox (you'll find it under the Eyedropper tool).

2. Click and drag a line along anything in the image that should be horizontal or vertical.

3. Use the Image, Rotate Canvas, Arbitrary menu command.

4. Click OK. The appropriate value will already have been entered in the dialog box. If the rotation goes in the wrong direction, select Undo. Now choose the menu command again and switch from CCW to CW or vice versa.

Resampling Algorithms

The majority of the time when you resample an image (change its pixel dimensions), you should use the Bicubic interpolation method. You select it in the Image Size dialog box. When scaling with a Transform command, you typically want to have Bicubic selected in the General pane of the Preferences. However, there are some exceptions. If you're changing the size of line art, artwork that contains blocks of well-defined color, or such images as screenshots, try Nearest Neighbor. Especially when there are vertical and horizontal stripes or blocks of color, Nearest Neighbor does a better job of preserving edges and preventing "fuzziness" from being introduced.

The Image Size, Auto Button

In the Image, Image Size dialog box, you'll find the seldom used Auto button. Next time you're resizing an image for offset printing, don't calculate the resolution versus the line screen frequency; instead, use this button. It opens the dialog box shown in Figure 31.7. You enter the line screen frequency of the press on which the job will be run, select a quality value, and click OK. Photoshop calculates the appropriate resolution and enters it into the Image Size dialog box. You need then only click OK.

Figure 31.7
If you select Draft for the Quality setting, the resolution will always be 72ppi, regardless of the line screen. Good produces a resolution 1.5 times the line screen. Best doubles the line screen to determine the appropriate resolution. You'll typically be best served by Good.

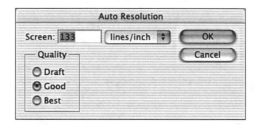

Creating Gradient Masks

When creating a mask, especially in Quick Mask mode, it's common to drag a gradient to create a gradual application of the mask. Remembering that masks are grayscale at heart, it's natural to use a black-to-white gradient. The problem of multiple gradients then comes to a head—each time you drag an additional gradient, it overwrites the existing gradient. To create a gradient that goes in multiple directions, select the black-to-transparent gradient from the Gradient palette. You can then drag multiple gradients, building on rather than replacing the preceding gradients.

Reapplying Filters

Say you need to apply the same filter to several layers, or perhaps you're working in Multichannel mode and need to repeat a filter on each channel. You can write down the settings and work with notes, or you can instantly reapply the filter with the same settings.

Apply the filter, switch layers or channels, and then use the keyboard shortcut (Command-F) [Ctrl+F]. The filter is reapplied with exactly the same settings.

If you want to use the same filter again, but with different settings, press (Command-Options-F) [Ctrl+Alt+F] to open the dialog box.

Creating Glass Type

Translucent type is an excellent way to show copyright information or otherwise identify an image without hiding too much of it. It's extremely simple to create:

1. Set the type in an appropriate font, size, and style. Make sure you use black as the font color.

2. In the Layers palette, change the type layer's blending mode to Screen. The type will disappear.

3. Double-click the type layer in the Layers palette to open the Layer Style dialog box.

4. Select Bevel and Emboss. You can use virtually any settings. The lower the Depth setting, the less obtrusive the type. Click OK, and the type reappears (see Figure 31.8).

Figure 31.8
The appearance of the type depends greatly on the settings you choose in the Bevel and Emboss pane of the Layer Style dialog box.

31

Exact Crops with the Rectangular Marquee Tool

You can crop to an exact size in a variety of ways in Photoshop. To crop to an exact size while maintaining the quality of the original image requires that you avoid resampling. Here's how:

1. Select the Rectangular Marquee tool from the Toolbox.

2. In the Options Bar, set the tools to a fixed size, or you can open the Info palette.

3. If you used a fixed size, click the tool once in the image window and drag to position it. If you're using the Info palette, drag the tool and watch the Info palette dimensions.

4. After the selection marquee is in place, choose the Image, Crop menu command. The image is cropped to the exact dimensions, without resampling.

Partially Undo a Filter or Adjustment

Immediately after applying a filter or an adjustment command, the Edit menu offers the Fade command. You can reduce the intensity of the filter or adjustment, and even change an effect's blending mode. Remember, though, that the Fade command is available *only* immediately after a filter or adjustment command.

Sharpening Luminosity

Using the Fade command is a great way to avoid introducing colored artifacts when sharpening. Immediately after applying the Unsharp Mask command, go to the Edit menu and select Fade Unsharp Mask. In the dialog box, change the blending mode to Luminosity and, if necessary, reduce the opacity of the filter.

Changing the Unsharp Mask's blending mode to Luminosity applies the sharpening only to the image's brightness. This is equivalent to sharpening in Lab color mode—without having to change color modes at all.

31

PHOTOSHOP 7 AND ILLUSTRATOR 10

ILLUSTRATOR AND PHOTOSHOP

A

Adobe Illustrator is primarily a vector illustration program. It does an excellent job of working with raster images, such as those produced by Photoshop, but that is not its primary focus. Photoshop is an image editor, designed to work with raster images. It uses vector type and can simulate vector objects using layer clipping paths, but its *forte* is working with raster images. The two programs are designed to do different jobs, but there is some overlap between their capabilities. Each is the best at its own job, and each is certainly more than merely capable in the crossover areas. (A full exploration of Illustrator 10's capabilities is available in *Special Edition Using Adobe Illustrator 10*, Que Publishing, 2002.)

Between Vector and Raster

Vector file formats record artwork as objects. Each object is described mathematically in relationship to the other objects in the file. Starting point, shape, stroke, fill, and effects are among the data recorded. Because these descriptions are independent of the size of the page, vector art can be scaled to any size and maintain its sharpness and appearance.

Raster images, also known as bitmap images, do not recognize objects. Each file is simply a record of a given number of squares (pixels), each with its particular color. The squares are arranged in rows and columns: a raster. Every raster image is rectangular, although some file formats allow transparency that can make the image's outline appear to be other than rectangular. Transparent pixels actually fill in the remainder of the rectangle. Raster image can use paths, but those paths are not objects.

⇨ *For a more in-depth look at the difference between the two types of artwork,* **see** *Chapter 6, "Pixels, Vectors, and Resolution," p. 155.*

Objects and Layers: Illustrator-Photoshop Common Ground

As you know, Photoshop works with pixels instead of objects. That doesn't mean you can't manipulate parts of a Photoshop file independently in Illustrator. The key is understanding the relationship between Photoshop layers and Illustrator objects.

When creating an image in Photoshop, you have the option of working with multiple layers, just as you do in Illustrator. Each Photoshop layer can be treated as a separate entity in Illustrator. (Note the use of the word *entity*, not *object*.) Illustrator enables you to retain Photoshop layers when embedding a .psd file into an Illustrator document. You can then edit the contents of each layer as an individual raster object. Photoshop's shape layers are embedded as path-based objects or compound shapes.

Caution

When added to an Illustrator file with the Place command, Photoshop (.psd) images must be embedded, not linked, for layers to be maintained.

Remember that Illustrator offers the command Release to Layers (Sequence), which places each object on an individual layer. Exporting as .psd allows Photoshop to then see each object on a separate layer.

Conversely, keep layers in mind when exporting from Illustrator in Photoshop's .psd format. If each object is placed on a separate layer, later you can manipulate them individually in Photoshop.

Web Graphics with Photoshop, ImageReady, and Illustrator

Both Illustrator and Photoshop offer the Save for Web option, but their Web graphic capabilities do differ. Photoshop, for example, offers ImageReady and its range of Web graphic capabilities, such as rollover and animation creation. Illustrator, on the other hand, offers support for SWF (Flash) and SVG (Scalable Vector Graphic) file formats. In addition, Illustrator can create cascading style sheets (CSS) through its Save for Web command.

Because almost all Web browsers in use today are Flash-capable, and because Flash is a vector art program, you might not need to move Illustrator's artwork to ImageReady to create animations. However, you may find it necessary to use ImageReady to create GIF and JPEG rollover buttons. The key concept is, again, placing each object on a separate layer by using the Release to Layers command.

Conversely, moving artwork from Photoshop to Illustrator allows you to take advantage of the latter's still superior type-handling capability, including type on a path, type wrapping, and linked type containers. You might also need to send some raster artwork to be included in an Illustrator single-page layout or even for an SVG image.

Evolving Capabilities

Although the focus of this appendix is using Photoshop 7 with Illustrator 10, most of the information also pertains to Illustrator 9 (and even Photoshop 6). It's important to note that Illustrator 8 and earlier do not support transparency, so interoperability with Photoshop is severely restricted. Likewise, Photoshop 5.5 and earlier do not support vector type or shape layers, so there are some rather substantial limitations there, too.

Overview: Moving Data Between Programs

You can move objects, images, text, and other data between programs in a number of different ways. Copying and pasting, dragging and dropping, and using mutually recognizable file formats are some of the techniques and commands available. Some have advantages over others. You can also insert Illustrator, EPS, and PDF files into a Photoshop document by using Photoshop's Place command, just as you can link or embed Photoshop files into an Illustrator document.

When you copy information from a file in any program, it is recorded in the computer's memory. With both the Macintosh and Windows operating systems, you can refer to this process as *putting something on the Clipboard*. The Clipboard is simply RAM, the computer's memory. Typically, both Mac and Windows use the memory that's available to the operating system, rather than the program's allocated memory, for the Clipboard. (This distinction is of reasonably small significance in most cases.)

The information on the Clipboard can be pasted back into the same program, perhaps on another layer or in a different location, or it can be pasted into another program. There are some limitations on Copy/Paste. As just one example, if you copy text from a word processing program to the Clipboard, Photoshop requires that you have an active type entry before pasting. If a type tool has not been clicked or dragged in an image, the Paste command is not available. (Photoshop does not recognize text as something that can be added to a file unless it is added into a type layer.) The content of the Clipboard can be pasted multiple times, and it remains on the Clipboard (in the computer's memory) until overwritten or the computer is shut down.

Because drag-and-drop bypasses the Clipboard, it doesn't erase any content there. If there's something on the Clipboard that you'll need again, use drag-and-drop in the interim.

The Clipboard can hold only one item at a time. When you use the Copy command (or keyboard shortcut), any information already on the Clipboard is overwritten and lost. Some shareware programs and utilities, however, can increase the number of items that can be copied at any one time by providing additional Clipboards.

Dragging from one window and dropping into another is similar to cutting and pasting. The primary difference is that the operating system's Clipboard is bypassed. Both the source and destination document windows must be visible onscreen to drag and drop. Click on an active selection and hold down the mouse button while dragging the cursor to the destination window. Releasing the mouse button completes the copy. Most of the limitations that apply to copying and pasting are the same with dragging and dropping.

Information can also be transferred between programs by using a mutually compatible file format. Illustrator can open Photoshop documents, but Photoshop can't handle Illustrator files. (An Illustrator file opened by Photoshop is rasterized as a generic PDF file.) If you save an Illustrator file with PDF compatibility, Photoshop can open (and will rasterize) the file as a generic PDF file.

Among the file formats common to both Photoshop and Illustrator are EPS and TIFF for print-oriented documents and GIF, JPEG, and PNG for Web graphics.

MOVING ARTWORK FROM ILLUSTRATOR TO PHOTOSHOP

Illustrator's support for transparency greatly reduced the need to move artwork to Photoshop. Many of the most important filters are available right in Illustrator itself. However, there are still reasons to use both programs (even with the same artwork), not the least of which is ImageReady.

Saving as Illustrator, Opening in Photoshop

At its core, the modern Illustrator file format is the Portable Document Format (PDF). When saved with PDF compatibility and then opened in Photoshop, an Illustrator file is treated as a generic PDF document. When the image is opened in Photoshop, it consists of a single layer that contains all artwork on a transparent background. Once in Photoshop, the file can be edited as a typical raster image.

If the Illustrator file is saved without PDF compatibility, you'll see the same rasterization dialog box, but the file itself appears as an error message (see Figure A.1).

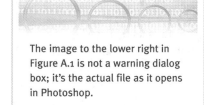

The image to the lower right in Figure A.1 is not a warning dialog box; it's the actual file as it opens in Photoshop.

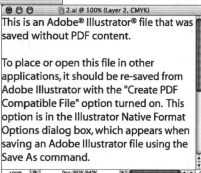

Figure A.1
The Rasterize Generic PDF Format dialog box always appears. However, if the .ai file wasn't saved with PDF compatibility, it opens as the message shown to the lower right.

Exporting from Illustrator in Photoshop Format

Transferring artwork from Illustrator to its sister program using the Photoshop format requires two steps. First, you must export the file, and second, you must open it.

When your artwork is ready, the first step in creating a Photoshop file from Illustrator is to choose the menu command File, Export. In the Export dialog box, specify the Photoshop format (see Figure A.2).

After you've selected a name and location to go with the file format, Illustrator displays the Photoshop Options dialog box (see Figure A.3).

Figure A.2
Photoshop's .psd is just one of many formats that can be exported from Illustrator.

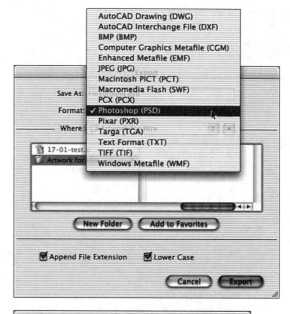

Figure A.3
Options that are not available are grayed out and may or may not show a check mark in the selection box.

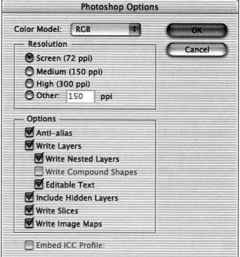

The options in this dialog box are as follows:

- **Color Model**—RGB, CMYK, and Grayscale are offered. You are not restricted to the document's original color mode.

- **Resolution**—Higher resolution is used for print; the Screen option is appropriate for the Web. This choice determines how many pixels the Photoshop image will contain and how big the file will be.

- **Anti-Alias**—Anti-aliasing helps smooth the appearance of curves and text in raster artwork.

- **Write Layers**—If this option is not selected, the Photoshop file will contain a single layer. Although Photoshop 7 can handle a virtually unlimited number of layers, Photoshop 5.5 and earlier are restricted to 99 layers. Three additional layer-related choices are available:

  - **Write Nested Layers**—This option preserves Illustrator's sublayers as Photoshop layer sets.

  - **Write Compound Shapes**—Illustrator's compound shapes, created through the Pathfinder palette, are converted to Photoshop shape layers.

  - **Editable Text**—Checking this box enables you to select and alter the text in Photoshop. If this option is not selected, the text is rasterized.

- **Include Hidden Layers**—This option is available only if the document contains layers with their visibility set to hidden.

- **Write Slices**—If you have designated slices in Illustrator, that data can be included in the Photoshop file. Make sure that slices are visible (View, Show Slices) before exporting the document.

- **Write Image Maps**—Image maps can be saved with a .psd file for use with ImageReady.

- **Embed ICC Profile**—An embedded color profile enables Photoshop to display the image's colors correctly. A profile can be embedded only when one is selected in the Edit, Color Settings dialog box.

Editable Text from Illustrator to Photoshop

Starting with version 6.0, Photoshop has been capable of handling vector type, such as that created in Illustrator. This feature is considered to be among the most important improvements in recent Photoshop upgrades.

If Illustrator text is to remain editable when exported to Photoshop, it cannot share a layer with anything else. That means you cannot export text on a path as editable text (the path causes the layer to be rendered), nor can you export area type (the container also causes rendering). Applying a stroke to text also keeps it from being editable when exported. When two type objects share a layer, they're split into two separate layers automatically.

When an exported .psd file with editable type is opened in Photoshop, you'll be asked to update the type (see Figure A.4). (When sending a file out, remember to include fonts that the recipient might not have.)

If the layer is not updated, it retains its appearance until or unless edited. Editing the type can result in font substitution or other changes in appearance. For that reason, it's a good idea to click the Update button in the dialog box if you might need to edit the type later. Remember, too, that Photoshop offers the command Layer, Type, Update All Text Layers.

Figure A.4

Opening an exported .psd file that contains editable type generates this message in Photoshop.

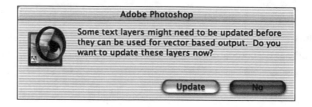

Copy and Paste, Drag and Drop

When you copy a selection in Illustrator to paste into Photoshop, your actions are governed by one of the preferences. Choosing Edit, Preferences, Files & Clipboard opens the dialog box shown in Figure A.5.

Figure A.5

The lower half of the dialog box pertains to copying and pasting.

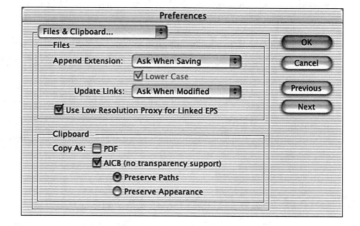

Illustrator copies selections to the Clipboard as PICT files and, if you so choose, PDF or AICB (Adobe Illustrator Clipboard):

- **PICT**—On the Clipboard, this file format is raster only. The selection is converted to pixels and placed in memory. Most programs receive the PICT version of the selection, which is added to the Clipboard automatically. The other options are in addition to the PICT data. When pasting into Photoshop, a new layer is created and the pixels are added to the layer.

- **PDF**—The PDF version, if available, copies a rasterized version of the selected object or objects to the Clipboard. When pasted into Photoshop, the artwork is placed on a new layer and Free Transform becomes active.

- **AICB**—This format is best used with Photoshop. It offers you a choice of giving preference to the integrity of paths over the look of the illustration, or maintaining the appearance of the selection at the possible expense of editable paths.

Whether Preserve Paths or Preserve Appearance is selected in the preferences, how Illustrator copies is less important than how Photoshop pastes. When you have AICB selected, Photoshop offers you a choice of how to handle the data on the Clipboard (see Figure A.6).

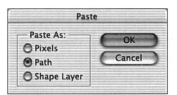

Figure A.6
This dialog box appears when pasting into Photoshop with Illustrator's AICB option.

The results of the paste vary widely, depending on your selection:

- **Pixels**—Photoshop pastes a rasterized version of the artwork and activates Free Transform, just as it does when using Illustrator's PDF Clipboard option.

- **Path**—As you can see in Figure A.7, a single work path is generated, regardless of the complexity of the artwork copied. The path loses any fill or stroke from Illustrator.

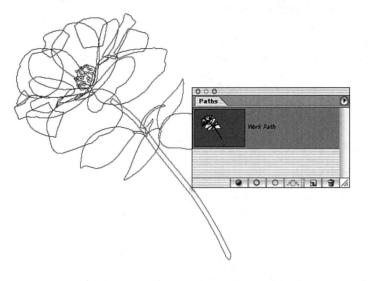

Figure A.7
The Paths palette shows the new path as a work path, which must be renamed to be saved.

- **Shape Layer**—Photoshop creates a new layer, fills it, and creates a clipping path to expose the fill in the shape of the Illustrator object (see Figure A.8). Although not equivalent to a vector object, Photoshop's shape layers can serve many of the same functions.

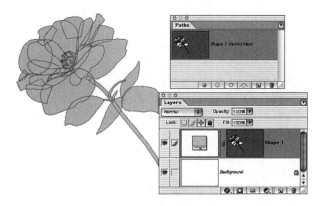

Figure A.8
The path is selected and therefore visible, but it is unstroked.

When using Illustrator's AICB Clipboard option with selections that have a more complex appearance than a simple object, expect to paste as pixels. Pasting as a path, of course, removes all appearance characteristics. Pasting as a shape layer results in a single color.

If you press (Command) [Ctrl] while dragging from Illustrator to Photoshop, paths are created, much like pasting with the Path option selected.

To truly protect the appearance of a selection being copied to Photoshop, rasterize in Illustrator first. After pasting into a Photoshop document, you can return to Illustrator and use the Undo command twice (once for Copy, again for Rasterize).

Alternative File Formats

Illustrator and Photoshop have a number of file formats in common, most of which are raster formats. Exporting an Illustrator file in any such format rasterizes all data and flattens the image as well. Both TIFF and EPS do an excellent job of preserving the appearance of the Illustrator file. PDF also works well with the appearance of the file, but the entire image is rasterized, even if Preserve Illustrator Editing Capabilities is selected in the Adobe PDF Format Options dialog box.

Remember that Photoshop rasterizes vector text in an EPS file upon opening.

MOVING ARTWORK FROM PHOTOSHOP TO ILLUSTRATOR

There was a time that bringing a Photoshop image into Illustrator simply meant using an appropriate file format to get a rectangle full of pixels in place. Occasionally, you might have needed to export paths from Photoshop to Illustrator for purposes of alignment or preparation of a trap.

Things have changed, now that Photoshop supports vector type and shape layers. These capabilities make transferring images between the programs feasible, perhaps even attractive in a variety of situations. Illustrator's capability to maintain Photoshop layers and transparency also adds to the feasibility of moving Photoshop files into Illustrator. Photoshop's opacity masks are converted to layer masks when you open a Photoshop file in Illustrator.

Opening Photoshop Files in Illustrator

When you choose Illustrator's menu command File, Open and select a file, you must decide whether to flatten the file or preserve layers, as shown in Figure A.9.

If you elect to flatten the layers of a Photoshop object, the file opens with one rasterized object on one layer. When you elect to convert each Photoshop layer into an object, Illustrator creates a separate layer for each Photoshop layer, and the contents become a single rasterized object.

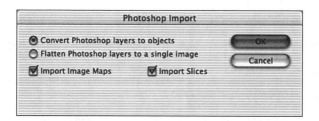

Figure A.9
You can elect to save a variety of features, including slices and image maps.

Copy and Paste, Drag and Drop

Using the Copy and Paste commands enables you to move image data between Photoshop and Illustrator, but transparency is lost. When you switch to Illustrator and use the Paste command, the pixels are pasted as a flattened image and transparency effects are lost. This happens regardless of whether PDF is selected in the Illustrator preferences (Edit, Preferences, Files & Clipboards).

When dragging and dropping between a Photoshop window and an Illustrator window, you also lose transparency features, but you do gain some other capabilities. Dragging from Photoshop to Illustrator, for example, enables you to transfer linked layers as a set. (Copying and pasting requires that you put each layer on the Clipboard and transfer it individually.)

Exporting Paths to Illustrator

Photoshop enables you to transfer paths to Illustrator through an export process. Choosing File, Export, Paths to Illustrator opens the Export Paths dialog box, shown in Figure A.10.

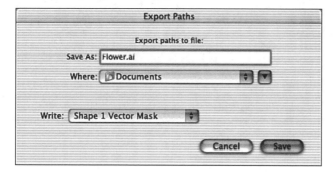

Figure A.10
Notice that there is no file format choice. All paths in the file are listed in the Write pop-up menu.

The file is exported as an Illustrator native file (with the file extension .ai) and can be opened directly in Illustrator. The paths appear in the Layers palette, but are not visible on the artboard unless selected because they are unstroked and unfilled.

Round-Tripping

Sometimes an image must go from Photoshop to Illustrator and then back to Photoshop. (This round-tripping is not as frequent as it was before Photoshop's vector type and shape tools.) Likewise, an Illustrator file might have to go into Photoshop and then back to Illustrator. (This, too, is far less common now that Illustrator has transparency capabilities.)

You can make several choices when preparing to return a file to Photoshop from Illustrator:

- You can export the file back to Photoshop format. If you make this choice, the layers are rasterized.

- You can save the file as an Illustrator document. When you reopen it in Photoshop, it is opened as a generic PDF file, rasterized at the resolution and dimension you select.

- You can save the file as EPS or PDF. The results are identical to those for an Illustrator file.

- You can export the file in any of a variety of raster formats, including TIFF and JPEG. The image is rasterized and saved according to the capabilities of the individual file format. In all cases, a single layer is created, and the file is flattened.

Files going from Illustrator to Photoshop and back to Illustrator follow the same basic pattern established here. Images saved in Illustrator, EPS, or PDF file formats are rasterized and layers are merged. When you export as Photoshop, the files retain their layers, but all objects are rasterized.

PHOTOSHOP WITH INDESIGN, QUARKXPRESS, AND OTHER PAGE LAYOUT PROGRAMS

by Richard Romano

IN THIS APPENDIX

PAGE LAYOUT PROGRAMS

Many imaging pros use Photoshop strictly as part of the "digital darkroom," doing little more than optimizing and editing images that will be distributed electronically or, at best, printed on an inkjet printer. However, for those doing print publishing, Photoshop is just the beginning of the journey. In that case, you need to venture into the world of the *page layout program*.

The page layout program is where all your text and graphics are combined to create the actual page(s) of the document. (In the dim and distant past, these programs were also called "desktop publishing" programs, but "electronic publishing" tends to be the more favored term these days.) The page layout program is (usually) the final step before the document goes to a service bureau or printer.

B

Common Page Layout Programs

There are a number of popular (and unpopular) applications on the market for page layout. They include the following:

- **QuarkXPress**—Known familiarly as "Quark" or "XPress." Since its debut in 1987, it has risen to become the industry standard for page layout. Version 5.0 appeared in early 2002.

- **Adobe InDesign**—If there's one thing you can say about industry standards, it's that there's always someone eager to usurp their position. Case in point: InDesign, which appeared in 1999 and aims to be a "next generation" publishing program. Version 2.0 appeared in early 2002.

- **Adobe PageMaker**—The "grande dame" of page layout, this was the application that started the whole "desktop publishing" movement back in 1985 (it was developed by a company called Aldus; Adobe acquired Aldus in 1994). It lost market share to Quark over the years, and has largely been retooled to appeal to the corporate publishing crowd. Version 7.0 appeared in mid-2001.

- **Adobe FrameMaker**—A layout program that has fans in such publishing niches as technical publishing, given its history of support for long documents as well as sophisticated SGML and XML capabilities. Version 7.0 was released in mid-2002.

- **Deneba Canvas**—A multi-purpose program, Canvas 8 includes page layout, image editing, illustration, and Web design in a single package. While it has its fans, Canvas is generally considered to be not as powerful as a suite of Adobe products.

- **Corel Ventura**—Ventura was developed in the late 1980s by Xerox and at the time was called Ventura Publisher. It was the seminal program for doing page layout on the PC. Corel acquired it in the mid-1990s and the current version is 10.

- **Microsoft Publisher**—Not to be left out of any niche, Microsoft developed Publisher as part of the Office suite. It is targeted toward corporate publishers and others who are used to the Office way of doing things, but need a tool that is more adept at page layout finessing than Word.

- **Microsoft Word**—Say what? Microsoft Word? For page layout? Sure. It is often used for page layout.

De Facto the Matter

For professional publishing, the top two (well, two-and-a-half) applications are QuarkXPress and InDesign. PageMaker still has a very high install base, but Adobe is trying to get professional publishers to switch to InDesign. The reasons those two (or two-and-a-half) are the de facto standards for desktop publishing are that they have feature sets that enable designers to be as creative as they want to be and, at the same time, they are the most supported applications among printers and service bureaus. InDesign, being the new kid on the block, has taken a while to catch on among everyday service bureaus, but large publication printers and publishers are starting to switch over to it.

Photoshop and Page Layout Applications

Dealing with Photoshop images in a page layout application can be as simple or as complicated as it needs to be. At its most basic, the process involves little more than importing a TIFF file, positioning it on the page, and forgetting about it. At its most complicated, there are things like clipping paths, runarounds, alpha channels, and color issues to contend with.

What follows isn't intended to be a thorough look at page layout programs. There are many fine books that detail all the nuances of those applications. Rather, this appendix concentrates on specific issues involving importing, working with, and exporting Photoshop-created images.

Despite the wide variety of applications for doing page layout, this discussion focuses on two—Adobe InDesign and QuarkXPress. The goal of this appendix is not to cover every feature of these applications, but rather to raise some general issues that tend to arise regardless of the actual program. Just about everything mentioned in the following sections is done in similar ways in other programs.

IMPORTING IMAGES INTO PAGE LAYOUTS

When images are imported into a page layout program, they are usually "linked," which means that the image file remains external to the page layout file, and all that's piped in is a preview. Also imported are instructions that let the program keep track of where linked files are. Basically, the layout file says to itself, "Self, the image named 'Image 1.tiff' is on the hard drive in a folder named 'Project,' and then in a subfolder named 'Images.' If someone moves them, there's gonna be trouble!" (Page layout programs are big on attitude.) So if an image file is moved, the page layout program won't be able to find it and you'll usually get an error message of some kind.

Some page layout programs give you the option of embedding the entire image file in the page layout document itself. Depending on the image, and how many there are, embedding can cause page layout files to swell to immense proportions, which can cause all sorts of performance issues and slowdowns.

> ## Caution
>
> When you send your document to a service bureau or printer, you need to be careful to make sure you send the image files, too; otherwise, only the low-res screen previews will be output. Gathering linked files is referred to as "collecting for output" and can be done manually or by using the automated "collect" features of either InDesign or QuarkXPress, or of a third-party program, such as Markzware's FlightCheck.

Getting Images into InDesign

InDesign lets you import a wide variety of image file types, including Adobe Illustrator (.ai), Photoshop (.psd), Windows bitmap (.bmp), Desktop Color Separations (.dcs), Encapsulated PostScript (.eps), CompuServe GIF (.gif), JPEG (.jpeg), PICT (.pict), Windows Metafile Format (.wmf), PCX (.pcx), PDF (.pdf), Portable Network Graphics (.png), Scitex Continuous Tone (.sct), and TIFF (.tiff).

B

Just My [File] Type

Although InDesign—and other page layout programs—let you import a seemingly infinite variety of image file types, you might not want to avail yourself of this ability. For example, it might be nice to import a Photoshop file with layers intact, and you can even do this in QuarkXPress via an XTension (plug-in), but it might not output properly—if at all—when you send the file to your service provider or printer. The rule of thumb for Quark is to stick with TIFFs for raster images and EPSs for vector images. InDesign handles .psd files natively.

That said, it's unnecessarily limiting to stick with low-rent standard formats. One thing you can do is work with the Photoshop-native files until you're ready to output, and then just relink to a flattened TIFF when you're done.

The easiest way to get an image into InDesign is to simply drag an image from the desktop or another folder right into an open InDesign document. Bam! You're done.

Alternatively, there is the Place command, which is under the File menu or is accessed with the keyboard shortcut (Command-D)[Ctrl+D]. You use the Place dialog box to navigate to and select an image. The Place command is also used to get text files, and most of the options at the bottom of the Place dialog box are specific to text files (such as Convert Quotes, which converts "unsmart" quote marks to the smart variety).

By default, Show Import Options is unchecked, but if you select it and then click Choose, you get a set of import options that, although they are primarily concerned with clipping paths and color management, vary according to the file type you are importing. Figure B.1 shows the options for a basic TIFF file.

For most file types, the Image Import Options dialog box has two panes: Image Settings and Color Settings. For most bitmap file formats, Image Settings deals with any clipping paths that might be saved with the image.

> **Caution**
>
> We have no idea how often this situation will crop up, if ever, but if you import a native Photoshop file containing unrasterized type, and have failed to select the Use Smart Quotes option in Photoshop, InDesign's Convert Quotes import filter does not correct any unsmart quotes.

Figure B.1
The Image Import Options for a TIFF file are pretty much relegated to clipping paths.

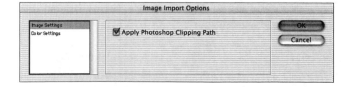

↪ *For a detailed look at clipping paths, **see** Chapter 10, "Making Selections and Creating Masks," **p. xxx**.*

When importing EPS files, InDesign's Image Import Options dialog box has the options shown in Figure B.2.

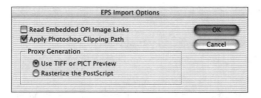

Figure B.2
The Image Import Options for an EPS file let you, once again, import clipping paths and specify how you want the application to generate the preview image.

In the EPS Import Options dialog box, you can determine whether you want to read any embedded OPI links (if you're using an Open Prepress Interface–based workflow) and apply any clipping paths. (You'll see how you can use Photoshop clipping paths in InDesign shortly.)

Because PostScript can't actually be displayed onscreen, applications like InDesign need to use a proxy image, as many users find it helpful to see what is actually in the EPS file. If a TIFF or PICT preview file is associated with the EPS, you can elect to have it piped in as the proxy. If there is no preview, a rasterized bitmap version of the EPS is generated. Alternatively, you can choose to have InDesign rasterize the PostScript and ignore the preview. This option produces a higher-quality screen display (often useful when you need to accurately see small details in an image) but tends to be slower.

The other file format with import options that vary from the norm is PNG. PNG images add a third pane to the Image Import Options dialog box, cleverly called PNG Settings (see Figure B.3). In this pane, you can decide whether you want to use the transparency information contained in the original image. If you want to apply any gamma correction (such as tweaking the midtone values to match the image gamma to the device you plan to print to), you can do so.

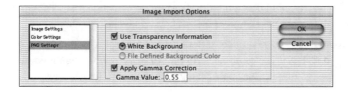

Figure B.3
The PNG Settings of the Image Import Options dialog box enable you to use the transparency information specified in the original file as well as apply any gamma correction to the image.

You might be wondering why InDesign even *has* PNG settings—after all, isn't the program designed for print publications, and isn't PNG a Web format? That's a very good question. Actually, Adobe has been positioning InDesign as a tool for publishing simultaneously to several different types of media—print, Web, and even wireless. As a result, InDesign can also export pages as HTML.

Importing Images in QuarkXPress

QuarkXPress can also import a variety of image file formats, such as DCS 2.0, EPS, GIF, JPEG, PICT, PNG, TIFF, and WMF. It can also import Photo CD and PCX files as well as TIFFs with LZW compression, but only via XTensions.

What some Quark power users know is that you can also drag an image file from the desktop or a folder right onto a QuarkXPress page. It's not a native feature but is available via a free XTension from Extensis called QX-Drag&Drop (available at www.creativepro.com).

"Plug-ins" for QuarkXPress are called XTensions.

Otherwise with Quark, the process is this: Draw a picture box, then select File, Get Picture—or use the shortcut (Command-E)[Ctrl+E]—and navigate to the correct file (see Figure B.4).

B

Figure B.4
In QuarkXPress, the Get Picture dialog box tells you all about the image you're about to import.

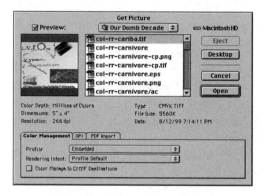

At the bottom of the dialog box, you can choose to color-manage the image by selecting a profile and deciding on your rendering intent. We'll return to this in the section on color management later in this appendix.

New in QuarkXPress 5.0 is the ability to import a grayscale TIFF as black-and-white line art (Photoshop's Bitmap mode). You can also go the other way, and import black-and-white line art as a grayscale image. For the former, hold down (Command)[Ctrl] while clicking the Open button in the Get Picture dialog box. For the latter, hold down (Option)[Alt] while clicking Open. To import a color TIFF as a grayscale image, hold down the (Command)[Ctrl] key while clicking Open.

Each pixel's individual RGB or CMYK value is used to determine the level of gray. This is good for quickie color-to-gray conversions, but if you're doing high-end grayscale work, you'll want to convert to grayscale in Photoshop, as explained in Chapter 4, "Getting Pixels into Photoshop."

Looking at Images in InDesign

When working with images—especially high-resolution images—in a page layout program, you often need to walk the fine line between being able to clearly see what an image is and being able to scroll around a document without it taking a small eternity. As a result, you can adjust the display performance in InDesign, either globally (in the Preferences) or locally using the contextual menu (Ctrl-click)[Right+click].

These are the three options:

- **Optimized Display**—This option replaces all images with gray boxes. You can scroll pretty quickly, but, well, all your images are gray boxes.

- **Typical Display**—This option, which is the default, creates a low-resolution preview image. You can see most of the image, but it's pixellated, and you can't often see small detail.

- **High Quality Display**—This option creates a whoppingly high-res preview image that lets you see as much image detail as there is but makes scrolling take a long time. Depending on the image and your system, scroll times could be measured on a geological scale.

Figure B.5 shows the differences among these three options.

Figure B.5
Left to right: The three display settings—Optimized, Typical, and High Quality—let you see varying amounts of image detail.

Moderately low-res settings work best, but sometimes you need to be able to see image detail if you want to, say, write a caption. Without this ability, you often need to open the actual image in Photoshop, which is a pain in the middle of a production environment.

Looking at Images in QuarkXPress

In contrast to InDesign, Quark gives you little control over the resolution of the screen preview. By default, a 72dpi version is imported, although holding down the Shift key while clicking Open in the Get Picture dialog box imports a 36dpi proxy. One invaluable XTension called Enhance Preview XT is from Koyosha Graphics of America (KGA, www.koyosha.com). It creates high-resolution screen previews of imported pictures in Quark, and those high-res previews can be toggled on or off.

Managing Linked Images in InDesign

Finally, in InDesign, imported images are managed via a Links palette (see Figure B.6).

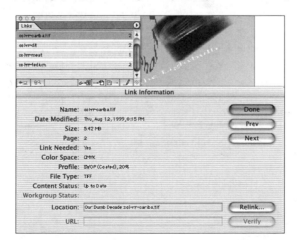

Figure B.6
The Links palette in InDesign enables you to manage all your linked images—and it tells you when a file has moved from its original location. The Link Information command brings up a detailed list of specifications about the image.

The Links palette tells you what files (text and graphics) have been imported, what page they're on, and whether they're missing or have been edited. This last piece of information is necessary, as the edits can affect the placement of the image on the page (if it has changed size, for example).

Managing Linked Images in QuarkXPress

Like InDesign, QuarkXPress also gives you the ability to see linked images (see Figure B.7).

Figure B.7
You can use the Picture Usage dialog box in QuarkXPress to ensure that your links are intact and have not been edited. It also gives you some basic information about the image.

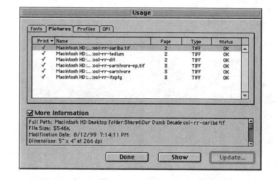

Under Utilities, Usage, you can click on the Pictures tab to get file size and format information about imported images, whether they are still linked and if they have been edited.

ADDING EFFECTS TO IMAGES IN LAYOUT PROGRAMS

Although most effects are best added to images in Photoshop, there are many things you can do with images in page layout programs. You can add borders and stylized frames as well as drop shadows.

Drop Shadows

InDesign 2.0 has a great drop shadow feature built in, and there is a terrific Quark XTension called ShadowCaster from A Lowly Apprentice Productions that enables you to easily add all sorts of customized drop shadows. Figure B.8 shows how the Drop Shadow feature works in InDesign.

The options in the Mode pop-up menu refer to how the shadow interacts with images or page elements that may be beneath it. It can be any of the blending modes you're familiar with in Photoshop (Multiply, Screen, Overlay, and so forth). You can also set the opacity and specify how much the shadow is offset from the original. The Blur amount, not surprisingly, refers to how solid or "gaseous" the shadow is. Finally, you can make the shadow any color you like, based on a preset color swatch or mixed on-the-fly.

⇨ For more information, **see** Chapter 17, "Using Blending Modes," **p. xxx.**

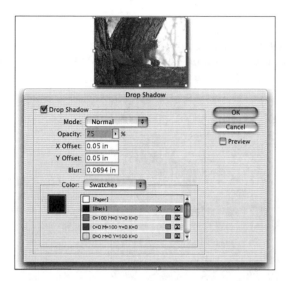

Figure B.8
In InDesign 2.0, a built-in Drop Shadow command enables you to easily and quickly add a customized drop shadow to imported graphics.

Feathering

InDesign 2.0 also gives you the ability to "feather" images—that is, to make the edges soft by fading them to transparency (see Figure B.9).

Figure B.9
Feathering an image in InDesign fades the edges away into transparency.

It's pretty easy to feather an image's edges—just enter a feather width (that is, how much of the edge you want to feather), and select whether you want the corners Diffused, Sharp, or Rounded. Click OK, and you're done. The live preview lets you see what's happening, so you don't get any unpleasant surprises.

Drop shadows and feathering are but two effects you can use on imported images in InDesign, and we mention them here to lead up to a discussion of what is one of the most highly touted new features of InDesign 2.0: working with transparency.

Transparency

With Photoshop you can create and export transparent images. How does this affect your ability to work with images in InDesign? Look at Figure B.10. A regular ol' TIFF was saved in Photoshop and placed in a sidebar-type text box in InDesign.

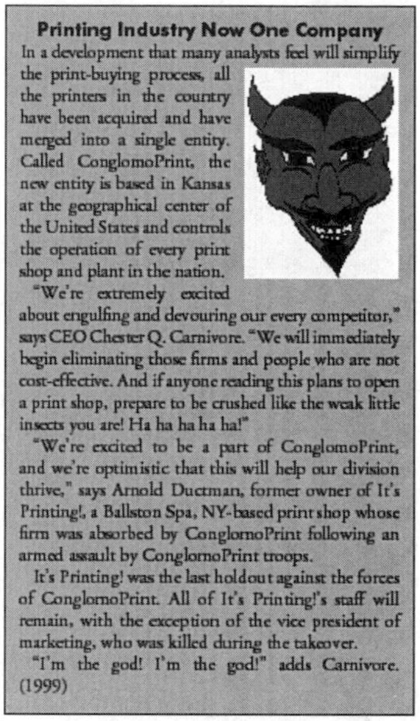

Figure B.10
An untransparent (that is, opaque) image imported into an InDesign page and placed over a colored background looks inelegant.

Printing Industry Now One Company

In a development that many analysts feel will simplify the print-buying process, all the printers in the country have been acquired and have merged into a single entity. Called ConglomoPrint, the new entity is based in Kansas at the geographical center of the United States and controls the operation of every print shop and plant in the nation.

"We're extremely excited about engulfing and devouring our every competitor," says CEO Chester Q. Carnivore. "We will immediately begin eliminating those firms and people who are not cost-effective. And if anyone reading this plans to open a print shop, prepare to be crushed like the weak little insects you are! Ha ha ha ha ha!"

"We're excited to be a part of ConglomoPrint, and we're optimistic that this will help our division thrive," says Arnold Ductman, former owner of It's Printing!, a Ballston Spa, NY-based print shop whose firm was absorbed by ConglomoPrint following an armed assault by ConglomoPrint troops.

It's Printing! was the last holdout against the forces of ConglomoPrint. All of It's Printing!'s staff will remain, with the exception of the vice president of marketing, who was killed during the takeover.

"I'm the god! I'm the god!" adds Carnivore. (1999)

Kind of icky, right? But if you instead save the image using the Export Transparent Image feature in Photoshop, you can eliminate the white background, as seen in Figure B.11.

Figure B.11
By exporting the image with transparency, the white background is eliminated, and the layout looks a lot better.

Printing Industry Now One Company

In a development that many analysts feel will simplify the print-buying process, all the printers in the country have been acquired and have merged into a single entity. Called ConglomoPrint, the new entity is based in Kansas at the geographical center of the United States and controls the operation of every print shop and plant in the nation.

"We're extremely excited about engulfing and devouring our every competitor," says CEO Chester Q. Carnivore. "We will immediately begin eliminating those firms and people who are not cost-effective. And if anyone reading this plans to open a print shop, prepare to be crushed like the weak little insects you are! Ha ha ha ha ha!"

"We're excited to be a part of ConglomoPrint, and we're optimistic that this will help our division thrive," says Arnold Ductman, former owner of It's Printing!, a Ballston Spa, NY-based print shop whose firm was absorbed by ConglomoPrint following an armed assault by ConglomoPrint troops.

It's Printing! was the last holdout against the forces of ConglomoPrint. All of It's Printing!'s staff will remain, with the exception of the vice president of marketing, who was killed during the takeover.

"I'm the god! I'm the god!" adds Carnivore. (1999)

Now doesn't that look a whole lot better? By the way, as you may recall from Chapter 10, this transparency effect is accomplished by means of a clipping path. You'll look specifically at clipping paths and how else they can be used in page layout programs in a moment.

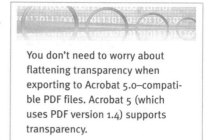

You don't need to worry about flattening transparency when exporting to Acrobat 5.0–compatible PDF files. Acrobat 5 (which uses PDF version 1.4) supports transparency.

There are a few caveats when working with transparency in InDesign, the most important of which is that when pages are output—be it to PDF, film, plates, and so on—the transparency needs to be "flattened." This is somewhat analogous to flattening layers in Photoshop, the exception being that InDesign does it automatically; there's no "flatten transparency" command. All the transparency in InDesign is the result of page elements being stacked on top of each other and the program allowing those bottom elements to peek through. When you print it, however, everything needs to be on the same plane.

The transparency flattening issue isn't a big deal when working with the kinds of pages you have been looking at here. The issue gets hairy in more complex layouts when type, vector art, raster art, and all sorts of other page elements are stacked on top of each other, which can make color blending and graphic interaction somewhat unpredictable, especially when going out to film or digital printing. Transparency isn't a universally supported feature yet, so if you are doing a lot of complex transparency work, be sure to consult with your service bureau/printer before you end up producing pages that won't output properly.

Working with Clipping Paths in InDesign

You saw earlier that the Image Import Options dialog box is used to determine whether you want to import any clipping path an image might have. Why would you want to import one? Not only can clipping paths be used to remove backgrounds from objects, but they can also let you do interesting text wraps. Not that you need a clipping path for a text wrap. For example, when you put an image in the middle of a block of text, you can set text to wrap around its bounding box, as shown in Figure B.12.

Figure B.12
An image can be combined with text and have the text wrap around it. The amount that the text is offset from the image can be precisely controlled.

Rectangular images can be kind of boring, however. If you have a clipping path around a contoured image, you can have the page layout program use that path as the basis of the text wrap. Figure B.13 shows InDesign's implementation of this method.

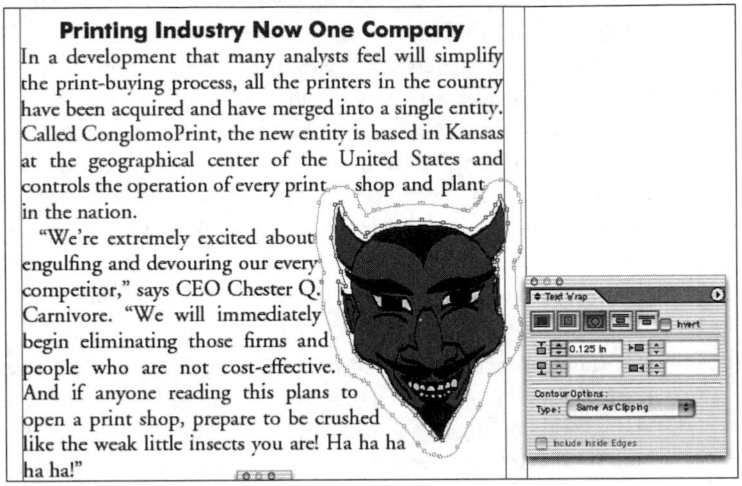

Figure B.13
In InDesign, an image's clipping path can be used as the basis of a text wrap. Again, the offset amount can be precisely controlled.

Printing Industry Now One Company

In a development that many analysts feel will simplify the print-buying process, all the printers in the country have been acquired and have merged into a single entity. Called ConglomoPrint, the new entity is based in Kansas at the geographical center of the United States and controls the operation of every print shop and plant in the nation.

"We're extremely excited about engulfing and devouring our every competitor," says CEO Chester Q. Carnivore. "We will immediately begin eliminating those firms and people who are not cost-effective. And if anyone reading this plans to open a print shop, prepare to be crushed like the weak little insects you are! Ha ha ha ha ha!"

In InDesign's Text Wrap palette, it's a simple case of selecting Same as Clipping from the Type pop-up menu under Contour Options.

Working with Clipping Paths in QuarkXPress

In QuarkXPress, the process is generally the same (although "text wrap" is called "runaround"). In the Runaround tab of the Modify dialog box, you can have XPress apply the runaround to an embedded clipping path (see Figure B.14).

Both QuarkXPress and InDesign can create a clipping path on-the-fly; in InDesign, the command to do this is called Detect Edges. If you're using this method to try to remove an object from a background, it can be kind of hit or miss, depending on the background. The Detect Edges feature works okay when you're trying to get a clipping path for text-wrap purposes, but for removing-objects-from-background purposes, you're better off generating a clipping path in Photoshop. Alternatively, both InDesign and QuarkXPress also have Pen tools that allow you to draw your own clipping paths on images in the layout.

Figure B.14
In QuarkXPress, the Runaround tab is used to apply the runaround to the clipping path.

SYNCHRONIZING COLOR MANAGEMENT

It has been said that color management is like the weather: Everyone talks about it, but no one ever does anything about it.

Color management is a vast, unwieldy topic, and a lengthy discussion of it is beyond the scope of this appendix. As far as Photoshop is concerned, it has been dealt with at length in Chapter 9, "Photoshop Color Management."

If you thought just trying to color-manage images between Photoshop and an inkjet printer was a pain, just try adding more links in the image chain, such as page layout programs, raster image processors (RIPs), and printing presses.

We won't have this become a treatise on color management, but we can at least run through a look at how you can keep everything reasonably color-managed by enabling color management between Photoshop and a page layout program and by embedding profiles.

Photoshop Settings

The first step is to enable color management in Photoshop, à la Chapter 9. After that's done, you then synchronize color management among applications.

As you saw in Chapter 9, you turn on Photoshop's color management in the Color Settings dialog box, assigning the working color spaces that you want to use. So, for example, you can use the options shown in Figure B.15.

After you have opened and edited a file, when you save it, you'll be prompted to save it with an embedded color profile, which corresponds to the one you had instructed Photoshop to use. If your image is in RGB mode, you'll embed the RGB profile; if your image is in CMYK, you'll embed the CMYK profile.

Figure B.15
A set of customized color management settings in Photoshop.

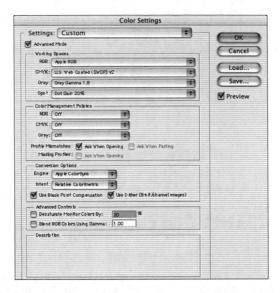

Back in InDesign or QuarkXPress, you turn on color management, assigning the same profiles you assigned in Photoshop. In InDesign, you also make sure the Show Import Options check box is selected in the Place dialog box, and you get the Color Settings pane of Image Import Options, as seen in Figure B.16.

Figure B.16
The Color Settings pane of the Image Import Options dialog box is where you decide how you want to color-manage imported images.

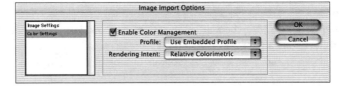

You can choose whether you even want to enable color management for the imported image, but if you do, you can decide which profile you want to use, be it the one you embedded in Photoshop or any of the other profiles available on your system. You also set the Rendering Intent, which indicates how you want InDesign to translate the colors to the target color space.

The import options are much the same for QuarkXPress (see Figure B.17).

Figure B.17
With Quark CMS (Color Management System) enabled, the Get Picture dialog box offers a set of options for dealing with embedded profiles and rendering intents.

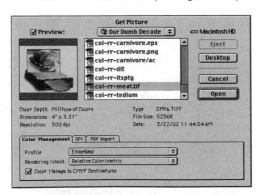

Does this approach to color management solve all the problems of managing color? Of course it does! And if you believe that, we have a lovely bridge to sell you.

There is no such thing as a perfect solution to color management, be it simple interapplication management like the previous discussion or third-party solutions that can involve pricey hardware and software packages.

The previous workflow—about which you can get a lot more information in books specifically written about InDesign, QuarkXPress, or whatever page layout application you are using—is a good start, however. Basically, color management is as nasty as you wanna be.

If your color management just doesn't seem to work for you, you may have a conflict. You can often resolve the conflict by *not* embedding a profile in the Photoshop Save As dialog box, and using only Quark's color management system.

B

How Color Management Is Managed

TrendWatch Graphic Arts, a division of Reed Business Information (formerly Cahners), is one of the foremost providers of extensive survey data on the graphic arts markets. It has been tracking printers' and creatives' approach to color management (among myriad other things) over the years, and, in a recent special report titled "Color Management: Another Gray Area," it identifies three basic approaches to color print and Web design and production:

Critical color refers to jobs for clients in which the color has to be accurate within a tolerance of something like 1 angstrom—you know, *Architectural Digest* or high, print ad–type quality.

Good enough (or "pleasing") color refers to jobs in which as long as nothing is freakish or disturbing colorwise, it's good enough.

The only color I can print refers to the fact that more and more people are printing to desktop color devices. This approach is gaining popularity in, say, corporate publishing; rather than run over to Kinko's or the local quick print shop, they'll just pump out copies on a desktop color laser or even inkjet printer. In this case, color management is mostly moot. In other words, Microsoft Excel pie chart colors are not "memory" colors, for example. (If they are, someone needs a vacation.)

TrendWatch Graphic Arts has been tracking a decline in critical color jobs and a rise in simple good-enough color jobs. Why? A lot of it has to do with the fact that as turnaround times get faster and faster (in other words, we're quickly becoming a 24/7 society, and if you do the division [$24 \div 7$], you get 3.42857—not quite as irrational as *pi*, but close!), speed tends to trump quality. In other words, people still have standards. They're low, but they're standards.

Part of the reason also has to do with what we have seen in this chapter: Built-in color "management"—not only in software like Photoshop or Quark, but also in hardware such as scanners, digital cameras, printers, and so forth—is getting better. In other words, it's becoming easier to get good, reasonably consistent color right out of the box. So standards are dropping and inherent quality is rising, and the point at which they meet defines the standard for "color management."

TIPS FOR PREPARING PHOTOSHOP FILES FOR PAGE LAYOUT

Here are some tips, tricks, and general rules of thumb to bear in mind when creating files in Photoshop that are destined for a page layout program:

- Resize images in Photoshop rather than in the layout file—in other words, InDesign or Quark lets you make images larger or smaller than their print size as set in Photoshop. However, doing so means extra work for whatever RIP is outputting the file. Granted, the situation is not as dire these days as it used to be, and you'd probably be hard-pressed to find anyone who pays a great deal of attention to this. Still, if you are preparing a document with 100 imported images, and in Photoshop they're all 5×7 inches, and you're reducing them all in Quark to 2×3 inches, you might want to consider making them smaller in Photoshop.

- Use only standard file formats. The rule of thumb in print publishing is TIFFs for raster art, EPSs for vector art. Although page layout applications can import myriad formats, not all output services or printers can process them. Even JPEGs are not usually recommended for print output. If you want to import native, unflattened Photoshop files into a layout to try different design ideas, go right ahead. When you're ready to send out your file, however, your best bet is to relink to a flattened TIFF or EPS file.

- Do all image editing in Photoshop. Some layout programs (like the new QuarkXPress 5.0) give you the ability to do some minor image-editing work—for example, adjust contrast—right in the page layout. Although that's nice, you'll still get higher-quality results if you optimize everything in Photoshop beforehand. (Also, if you need to use the image in another layout, you won't have to recorrect it.)

- Make sure your images are in the correct color space—in other words, RGB for the Web, CMYK for print. There's nothing worse than getting The Call from your service provider telling you that he or she can't make color separations because your files are in the wrong color space. (It's even worse—and way more expensive—to get film back and find out that not all the images separated properly.)

- If you are working only with spot colors in your page layout, make sure you are not using CMYK images. By the same token, if you are working only with CMYK, make sure there are no spot colors defined in your document, or you'll have more color separation negatives than you can use.

- Make sure you have enough resolution to keep the image from pixellating. This is why the Links and Picture Usage palettes and dialog boxes give you all this information, so there is no doubt about whether you'll have enough data to produce a decent image. (In other words, if you create a 50KB GIF for the Web, don't expect to be able to print it larger than about a half inch by a half inch.)

- Preflight your files before sending them out. *Preflighting* involves using software tools to double-check that all images are at the correct resolution, all color spaces are correct, and so forth.

InDesign has a built-in preflighting feature, and third-party programs, such as the pioneering FlightCheck from Markzware Software, are also extremely powerful and compatible with a wide variety of application file types. FlightCheck can run extensive preflight checks on InDesign, QuarkXPress, PageMaker, Illustrator, Photoshop, Acrobat, and even Word files.

- Talk to your printer or service provider if you are using some new features, such as transparency. Also, if you are using InDesign, double-check whether your service provider can accept InDesign files at all. In some quarters, the program has been slow to catch on, and some folks find they have to export files as PDFs to get them output. Not that that's too much of a problem (PDF is probably the way all of this is going to go in the future, anyway), but it does add an extra step.

B

PHOTOSHOP WITH LIVEMOTION AND FLASH

IN THIS APPENDIX

LIVEMOTION AND FLASH: ANIMATION AND MORE

Adobe LiveMotion and Macromedia Flash create Web-based animations and other interactive media. They have capabilities to produce far more than just animated Web pages. You can create interactive learning programs, even QuickTime movies.

The terms *raster* and *bitmap*, in this context, both refer to images created from pixels. Throughout this appendix, *raster* is used to avoid confusion with the Bitmap mode, which uses only black and white pixels to reproduce an image.

Adding Raster Images to Projects

When developing so-called *rich media* (files with interactivity or animation), you may need to integrate images from Photoshop. Although both Flash and LiveMotion are vector-based programs, you can easily add photographs or other raster images. You might also want to use a raster image as a texture or fill for a vector object in Flash or LiveMotion. In addition, you can add animated GIF files from ImageReady to LiveMotion and Flash projects.

⇨ *For information about the differences between vector and raster images, **see** Chapter 6, "Pixels, Vectors, and Resolution," p. 155.*

Exporting Images as Raster Images

Interaction between Photoshop and LiveMotion or Flash can go in the opposite direction, too. You might find that you need to send an image from an interactive file to Photoshop, perhaps for related products, advertising, a thumbnail in a composite, or as a link for a Web page. Both Flash and LiveMotion can produce image files that you can open in Photoshop.

IMPORTING RASTER IMAGES INTO LIVEMOTION

LiveMotion uses the File, Place command to add raster images to a *composition*, a LiveMotion project. You can place a variety of file formats, including EPS, GIF, JPEG, PDF, PNG, BMP, PICT, and Photoshop's native PSD files. Animated GIFs created in ImageReady can also be added to compositions.

Placing Photoshop Files into LiveMotion

When placing a Photoshop file, the image's appearance is maintained, including layer effects and transparency (see Figure C.1).

When you place a layered Photoshop file, you have the option of converting each layer to a separate object. Use LiveMotion's command Object, Convert Into, Objects or the command Object, Convert Into, Group of Objects. Each Photoshop layer becomes a separate raster object in the composition (see Figure C.2).

LiveMotion renders raster images at the size used in the composition. However, it retains the image as placed—if you place a 2MB file to use at 50×50 pixels, the .liv file retains all 2MB. To minimize file size, resize raster images in Photoshop to the size required in LiveMotion before placing.

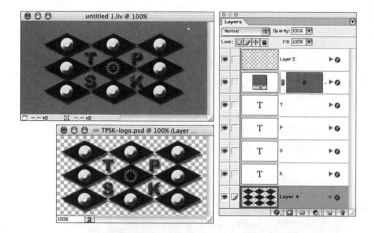

Figure C.1
The LiveMotion file (top) includes the Photoshop file shown below. The Photoshop Layers palette shows the various layers in the placed .psd file.

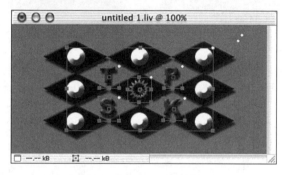

Figure C.2
The individual objects can be manipulated individually as separate raster images.

Editing Files Placed in LiveMotion

Raster images placed into a LiveMotion composition can be edited in Photoshop and updated automatically:

1. Select the placed image in LiveMotion.

2. Use the menu command Edit, Edit Original.

3. The image will be opened in Photoshop (assuming Photoshop is available on the computer).

4. Edit the image as necessary.

5. Save the image in Photoshop and close. It will automatically be updated in LiveMotion.

> **Caution**
>
> If the image's layers have been converted into objects, do not change the number or relative position of the layers. If you do add, subtract, or rearrange layers in Photoshop, the image will not update properly in LiveMotion. If you must change the layers, delete the original image from LiveMotion and use the Place command to add the edited version.

When you use the Edit Original command, you're not actually editing the original image file. Rather, you're editing a *copy* of the file that's been embedded into the LiveMotion composition. After you've edited, saved, and closed the file, return to LiveMotion and the updated version appears. If you then return to Photoshop, the Open Recent Document list is not updated to show that you edited the image, and if you open the *actual* original, it is unchanged.

You can edit the following raster file formats in Photoshop using LiveMotion's Edit Original command: BMP, GIF, EPS, JPEG, PDF, PNG, PICT, and Photoshop's PSD format. LiveMotion can also import these file formats as textures.

IMPORTING RASTER IMAGES INTO FLASH

Macromedia Flash can work with a variety of file formats, including BMP, GIF and Animated GIF, JPEG, PICT, PNG, TIFF, and Photoshop's PSD format. QuickTime 4 or later is required for several formats. When QuickTime is required, Flash lets you know (see Figure C.3).

Figure C.3
When you click Yes, QuickTime adds the raster image to the Flash document without any additional dialog boxes.

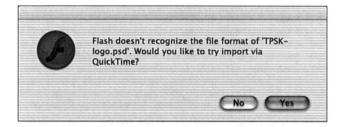

The raster image is added as a library item and appears in the Flash document. If an item of the same name already exists or was imported earlier, Flash asks if you want to replace the previous artwork (see Figure C.4).

Figure C.4
Electing not to replace the existing library item cancels the Import operation. Replacing deletes the existing object.

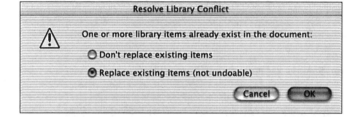

Using Flash to Create Vectors from Raster Images

Flash has the capability of creating vector artwork from pixels. It looks for areas of similar color and creates objects. The Modify, Trace Bitmap command opens the dialog box shown in Figure C.5.

Figure C.5
You can specify how closely colors must match, the minimum size of an object, and with what precision the vectors will be created.

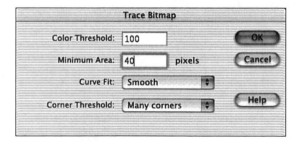

Depending on the content of the image to be traced, you can direct Flash to create corners or to attempt to smooth curves. Figure C.6 shows one example of bitmap tracing. Each of the areas of solid color becomes a separate, ungrouped vector object.

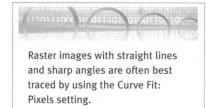

Raster images with straight lines and sharp angles are often best traced by using the Curve Fit: Pixels setting.

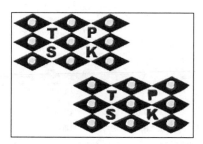

Figure C.6
A copy of the raster object is shown in the upper left. The vector objects to the lower right were created using the settings shown in Figure C.5.

Editing Imported Raster Images in Flash

When you *break apart* a raster image in Flash, the pixels are separated into discrete areas. You can then alter the pixels with Flash's painting and drawing tools. Areas of the raster image can be selected with Flash's Magic Wand and Lasso tools. (To access the Magic Wand, select the Lasso tool.) The Modify, Break Apart command actually reduces the raster image to its pixels and gives you some limited editing capability. After you break apart a raster image, you can also select pixels with the Eyedropper tool to use as a fill for other objects.

EXPORTING RASTER IMAGES

A single frame of an animation can be saved as a raster image file from LiveMotion or Flash. This frame can be used to create collateral materials, such as advertising or packaging, or as the basis for a link on a Web page.

Exporting from LiveMotion

You use LiveMotion's Export palette (see Figure C.7) to choose a file format and options (when available). Open the Export palette by using the keyboard shortcut (Command-Option-Shift-E) [Ctrl+Alt+Shift+E] or the Window, Export or File, Export Settings commands. Hide the palette by clicking the Close button at the top or by choosing Window, Export Settings. The File, Export command then creates and saves the file.

Figure C.7
Shown are the palette configurations for the file formats supported by Photoshop. LiveMotion also exports SWF (Flash) and QuickTime file formats and can export AutoLayouts and Live Tabs.

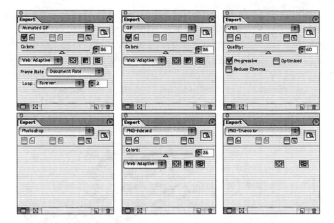

As you can see in Figure C.7, the options differ for the various file formats. The Photoshop format exports a flattened version of the file. All the raster formats offer the Trim option, which crops the exported file to the pixel data. The Web-related formats (all raster formats except Photoshop) can also export the file's HTML data.

> **Caution**
>
> When running Flash under Mac OS 9.1 or 9.2, you must increase the program's memory allocation. At least 37MB of RAM must be available to export images or sequences.

Exporting from Flash

You can use the menu command File, Export Image to create a raster image from a frame of a Flash movie. You can also use the Export Movie command to create a series of raster image files from the movie's frames. Exporting a series of frames is called creating a *sequence*. You can export to EPS, GIF, JPEG, PICT, or PNG formats.

INDEX

Advanced Technology
Attachment (ATA), 73

Advanced TIFFs, 82

aged stone effect, 576

Agfa | Monotype Web site, 303

.ahs file extension, 834

AICB file format, 900

Airbrush, 32, 46, 312, 315, 342

algorithms
adaptive, 745
black and white, 746
color reduction, 739-742,
745-746
custom, 745
grayscale, 746
Mac OS, 746
perceptual, 745
resampling, 889
selective, 745
Web, 745
Windows, 746

aligned cloning, 698

Aligned option (Healing
Brush), 653

alignment
linked layers, 406
paragraphs, 298
printing, 799-801

All Tools configuration (Tool
Presets Picker), 55

alliances (Web pages), 706

allocations (memory), 90-92

alpha channels, 262, 414-415
converting to spot channels,
420
creating, 262-263
editing, 414
file formats, 266
grayscale, 265
masks, storing, 245
modifying, 263-264
renaming, 420
Save for Web dialog box,
735-736
viewing image behind, 264

alpha channels, 266

AM (Amplitude Modulated)
screening, 831

Amount slider, 637

amplitude modulated screening, 831

anatomy
Channels palette, 416-417
gradients, 318-319
paths, 352-353

anchor points
adding, 165, 360
converting, 360
corner, 356
deleting, 165, 251, 360
paths, 158, 352-354
selecting, 361
smooth corner, creating, 374
work paths, 283

angle gradient tool, 320

angle jitter (brushes), 336

Angled Strokes filter, 525

angles
brushes, 313
Motion Blur, 519
screen, 821

Animation palette, 721
frames, 62
hiding, 62
ImageReady, 774
viewing, 62

animations, 598
basics, 599
creating, 599-600
frame sequences, 606
GIFs, 130
mesh grids, 606, 608
pxr files, 141
rollovers, 717
saving, 789
Web pages, 720-721

Anisotropic mode (Diffuse
filter), 570

ANPA colors, 182

Anti-Alias Crisp command,
285

Anti-Alias None command,
285

Anti-Alias Sharp command,
285

Anti-Alias Smooth command,
285

Anti-Alias Strong command,
285

anti-aliasing, 899
raster images, 161
selections, 248
text, 294
type, 285-288

apostrophes ('), 36

appearance
brush strokes, 336-337
histograms, 439
interface, 48
color depth, 52
differing operating sys-
tems, 48-49
menus, 49
Options Bar, 50
screen resolution, 51
Toolbox, 50-51
masks, 414
Options Bar, 50
Toolbox, 50-51

Apple
Color Picker, 214-216
iPhoto, 102
Script Editor, 874

AppleScripts, 40
included, 875-876
running, 871
support, 874
troubleshooting, 877

applications. *See* programs

Apply Image command, 427

applying
color, 174
filters, 504, 890
images, 427
layer styles, 683
textures, 172

archives, 125

Batch Rename command, 16, 22

beeps, 79

Behind blending mode, 489

Berthold Web site, 303

Bezier curves, 158, 350

bicubic interpolation, 78, 633

bilinear interpolation, 78, 633

binary, 132

binary data, 803

bit depth
 color, 197
 flatbed scanners, 106
 grayscale images, 816-817

bitmaps, 129, 174. *See also* raster images
 blending mode restrictions, 486
 color mode, 183-185, 412
 grayscale image conversions, 819-820
 resolution, 824
 wireless, 146

black and white algorithms, 746

black and white points, 445-446

black point compensation, 236

black-and-white images, 829-830

black-and-white photos, 673

bleed, 796

blending
 colors, 479
 layers, 40
 RGB, 236

Blending Mode
 layers, 381

Blending Mode dialog box, 386

blending modes, 478, 487
 Add, 496
 add/subtract, 427
 base color, 479

Behind, 489
blend color, 479
brushes, 314
Clear, 489
clipping groups, 487
Color, 479, 499
Color Burn, 490
Color Dodge, 492
color mode restrictions, 486
Darken, 489, 491
Difference, 497
Dissolve, 488
Exclusion, 497
fading, 487
filters, 586
Hard Light, 494
Healing Brush, 652
HSB, 500
Hue, 497
interior effects, 483
keyboard shortcuts, 482
layer, 487
layer masks, 484
layer sets, 390
layer style, 483-484
layers, 384, 480-482
 assigning, 481
 clipped, 483
 Lighten, 387
 Luminosity, 388
 Multiply, 387
 Normal, 387
 Screen, 388
 sets, 481
 setting, 386
Lighten, 491
Linear Burn, 35, 491
Linear Dodge, 35, 493
Linear Light, 35, 495
Luminosity, 499-500
Multiply, 490
new, 34-35
Normal, 488
Overlay, 493
painting tools, 485
Pass Through, 500
pencil tool, 314
Pin Light, 496
pixels, 478
Replace, 500

result color, 479
Saturation, 498
Screen, 492
shape tool, 486
Soft Lights, 494
Subtract, 496
Threshold, 488
transparency, 479, 483
Vivid Light, 35, 495

Blending Options pane, 40

Bloat tool, 595

Blur filters, 517
 Gaussian Blur, 517-518
 Motion Blur, 519-520
 Radial Blur, 520-522
 Smart Blur, 523

Blur tool, 660

bluriness (photos), 666

blurring
 automatically, 523
 JPEGs, 743
 noise, 544

BMP Advanced Modes dialog box, 129

.bmp files. *See* bitmaps

body (Actions palette), 848

books, 212

Border command, 256

borders, 247, 256

bounding boxes. *See* crop marquees

brightness, 196, 441-442
 color adjustments, 457-461
 Lightness slider, 459

Brightness slider, 442

Brightness/Contrast dialog box, 441

brokers (print), 811

browsers
 backgrounds, 724
 File, 14-15
 Batch Rename command, 16, 22
 Clear Ranking command, 22

How can we make this index more useful? Email us at indexes@quepublishing.com

F

F-key assignments, 884

Facet filter, 548

Fade command, 586

fading
blending modes, 487
brushes, 334
patterns, 29

fair use (copyright), 117

falloff, 460

families (font), 290, 303
adding, 304-307
creating, 304
deleting, 304-307
managing, 307
sources, 303-304
Web sites, 303

feathering
images, 913
selections, 248
viewing, 266

File Browser, 14-15
Batch Rename, 16
commands
Batch Rename, 22
Clear Ranking, 22
Refresh Desktop, 23
Reveal Location, 23
deleting
images, 22
selections, 20
Details view, 17
EXIF data, 41
Expanded view, 16
folders, 22
layout, 16-17
menu, 18, 20
opening, 45
opening files, 21
panes, 16-18
ranks, 19
renaming files, 21
rotating images, 20, 23
switching between views,
19
thumbnails, 17, 23
tree, 17
views, 20

File Browser command, 45

file data pane, 18

file formats
GIFs, 729
JPEG, 729
PNG-24, 729
PNG-8, 729
transparency support,
788-789
Web graphics, 739
GIFs, 739-742
JPEGs, 742-743
PNG-24, 743
PNG-8, 739-742
WBMP, 743-744
WMBP, 735

File Handling pane, 123

File menu
changes from Photoshop 6,
44
commands
Automate, Scripts, 871
Manage Workflow, 44
Open Script, 871
Print Options, 44

filenames
asterisks, 222
component assignments, 16
pound signs, 222

files
Adobe Photoshop 7.0 Prefs,
77
.ahs extension, 834
archives, 125
.atn extension, 860
bitmap, 129
bmp, 129
compatibility, 82
compression, 125, 726
DCS 1.0, 144-145
DCS 2.0, 145-146
editing, 925-926
EPS, 131-132
color management, 132
color mode support, 131
encoding, 132
halftone screens, 132
importing into InDesign,
909

low-resolution images,
upsampling, 132
transfer functions, 132
viewing, 131
exporting, 122, 123
extensions, 82
Flash, 895
formats, 120
accepted, 148
actions, 853
AICB, 900
alpha channels, 266
AppleScript, 874
assigning, 120-122
associating, 151
capabilities, 127-128
cross-platform, 124
digital cameras, 100
duotones, 194
EXIF, 41
Illustrator, 896
Illustrator alternative,
902
page layout program
acceptible, 147
page layout programs,
920
PDF, 900
Photoshop 2, 129
PICT, 900
plug-ins, 146
psd, 120
Raw, 141-142
SVG, 895
SWF, 895
Targa, 143
TIFF, 122, 143-144
vector type support, 275
GIF. See GIFs
Illustrator
exporting, 897-899
opening, 896-897
image types, 908
JPEG, 133
naming
illegal characters, 853
UNIX, 853
Windows, 853
opening
File Browser, 21
Illustrator, 902

How can we make this index more useful? Email us at indexes@quepublishing.com

How can we make this index more useful? Email us at indexes@quepublishing.com

WHAT'S ON THE DISC

The companion CD-ROM contains many useful third party tools and utilities plus the samples from the book.

WINDOWS 95/98/ME/NT/2000/XP INSTALLATION INSTRUCTIONS

1. Insert the CD-ROM disc into your CD-ROM drive.

2. From the Windows desktop, double-click on the My Computer icon.

3. Double-click on the icon representing your CD-ROM drive.

4. Double-click on the icon titled START.EXE to run the installation program.

If Windows 95 is installed on your computer, and you have the AutoPlay feature enabled, the START.EXE program starts automatically whenever you insert the disc into your CD-ROM drive.

WINDOWS NT INSTALLATION INSTRUCTIONS

1. Insert the CD-ROM disc into your CD-ROM drive.

2. From File Manager or Program Manager, choose Run from the File menu.

3. Type `<drive>\START.EXE` and press Enter, where `<drive>` corresponds to the drive letter of your CD-ROM. For example, if your CD-ROM is drive D:, type `D:\START.EXE` and press Enter.

MACINTOSH INSTALLATION INSTRUCTIONS

1. Insert the CD-ROM disc into your CD-ROM drive.

2. When an icon for the CD appears on your desktop, open the disc by double-clicking on its icon.

3. Double-click on the icon named Guide to the CD-ROM, and follow the directions that appear.

Technical Support from Que Publishing

We can't help you with Windows or Macintosh problems or software from third parties, but we can assist you if a problem arises with the CD-ROM itself.